I0214275

הַשַּׁבָּת בַּאֲשֶׁר קוֹמַם יֵשׁוּעַ הַמָּשִׁיחַ מִן־הַמֵּתִים

The Sabbath Yeshua the Messiah rose from the dead

REVISED AND UPDATED EDITION

When it Happened

According to The Original Texts

The Sabbath Yeshua the Messiah rose from the dead

Fourth Edition: 2021.

www.torahtimes.org

Cover: 100 Mega-parsec string of galaxies baffles cosmologists unable to find enough time for them to form according to their assumptions. **Spine:** GISP2 ice core from 1827 meters depth dated insanely old. **Edge:** Petrified wood, typically assumed to be millions of years old.

When and how long did it take for the ice sheet to build up? How long does it take wood to petrify? Which theory of gravity actually agrees with the Scripture? The physical creation reveals the truth about the Almighty, but mankind chooses to believe the evolutionists' cosmological lie. Today's astrophysicist was yesterday's Babylonian astrologer.

So also, the Scripture reveals the truth about when and how long important events took. But religious mankind likewise chooses to believe the religious lie. Today's religious clerics and priests are not so much different than their secular counterparts. They, too, give no heed to what the Almighty revealed in Scripture. Neither did their ancient counterparts, called the priests of Ba'al.

Table Of Contents

Preface

If we are Christians* then we are privileged to follow the Messiah of Israel and to name Him as Almighty Creator and Saviour. I call him Yeshua, for that is his given and proper Hebrew name, and acknowledge him as YHWH in human form. (Heresy hunters will therefore be disappointed.) It is alright if your pronunciation of Yeshua's name is somewhat inaccurate, and alright if we do not know how to say the name he shares with His Father perfectly, which is the name above all names. That is not the issue of this book. Perfection is not required for salvation. But if we are true Christians, does that mean we have all the truth? Does it mean that Yeshua always works with us with a smile on his face, and never a tear in one eye for what we lack? I think not. The Holy Spirit has condescended to dwell with and work with Christians of all ages during the exile of Israel, no matter how ignorant they may be. I am still learning more of the truth, also.

The age of exile is the age of ignorance, the age when the children of Nineveh did not know their right hand from their left. Like Jonah, I will now rise up and tell you a story of redemption, a story of three days and three nights. This is one truth that I do know. This is the sign I have been taught, and the sign that should be given to all Israel. I will tell this story anew to Christians, who like Joseph, have taken on the languages and cultures of foreign nations, yet who still remember the Almighty of Abraham, Isaac, and Jacob. I will try to tell the story in Christian terms so that Christians can understand. I will merely point out that the misbehaviour and ignorance of most Christians makes my fellow Israelites who follow Yeshua so ill that they do not even want to identify with the name Christian anymore, and substitute the term Messianic. That is what it used to mean to be a Christian in the days of Peter and John. If one were a Christian, then what was really meant is that you were a Messianic follower of Israel's Messiah. The thing that makes us so ill at ease with most Christianity is that it hardly resembles the Messianic (Christian) Faith taught by Yeshua's first Jewish followers, or by Yeshua himself. The reader will have to understand why I use the word "Christian" to refer to a majority of the professed followers of Messiah, concerning some

* See *The Good News of Messiah*, pg. 347 for a fuller explanation of this term and its origin. Some terms can be neither rejected for their original historical sense, nor identified with in their subsequent corruption by the body politic. It is therefore best to retire the term as much as possible and communicate the truth with other terms.

point on which I disagree with them. This does not mean I reject the term when it describes what I do agree on.

The realization that the professed Christian faith of many is fraudulent and really faith in human tradition can make one very ill of heart. I really do not know how many lies the Father can or will tolerate placed next to the golden truth of Messiah Yeshua. I think His tolerance is higher when it is just a question of ignorance, and lower when it is not. I leave it up to the Holy Spirit to show you personally what you should change and at what rate you should change it. That is how we continue to walk in the ways of the Almighty. But such change as needs to happen, cannot happen without knowledge. One must first discover the truth before making any changes. This book aims to reveal that truth.

Therefore, we must ask some hard questions. The questions are hard because their answers may not be addressed with objectivity, but with an emotionally programmed reaction. The reader must overcome this, and I pray they do so with the help of the Ruakh (Spirit), so that you can discover the truth in order to follow Yeshua as a good and faithful servant that puts a smile on His face.

Why do Christians hold their main worship services on Sunday? It is because they want to memorialize the resurrection of Yeshua on Sunday. Remembering His resurrection is commendable and all important, but the way we remember things best, is to have the correct facts about what we want to remember. We are not correctly remembering if we get the story half wrong. As we shall see, Messiah's resurrection has nothing to do with Sunday. We also want to remember his death, and what it means. This is good. But to remember it rightly means we must learn that it has nothing to do with Friday.

The Scripture says nothing about observing Sunday. It says to observe the Sabbath. The basic issue is that most saying they are Christians do not want to keep the Instruction* of the Almighty. They want to keep their own tradition even if it requires a made up excuse. When faced with the fact that heaven and earth have not passed away, and therefore, all things cannot be fulfilled, so the Torah must remain valid, many do not want to discuss it anymore. Yet, in their resolution to turn off the discussion they have left quite a flaw in their thinking.

* i.e. the Torah or Law.

Ignoring the question does not do away with the future fulfillment of YHWH's Law.

We who observe the Sabbath sign between us and the Almighty of Israel, must also know the truth and check our assumptions. When did Yeshua rise from the dead? Is the common Christian reasoning also a lie? This book will demonstrate that Messiah rose on the Sabbath at the edge of dawn for the seventh day and not on Sunday morning as Christians commonly claim. It will show that Messiah was three days and three nights in the gave, and not two nights, as Christians commonly believe.

Christians will consider this an extraordinary claim requiring extraordinary proof. Extraordinary proof will be provided in this book because most are extraordinarily deceived. The proof will involve many details and amazing facts that most have never heard of, which are true, and can be verified. To uncover the truth we must first uncover layers and layers of deception. If the reader endures to the end, then he or she will come away not only convinced, but truly amazed at the degree to which most Christians have been deceived.

So, if the resurrection of Messiah was on the Sabbath, then why do the traditions not remember it? Why does everyone think it was on Sunday? If every Christian believes the resurrection was on Sunday, then it must be so? If all the Christian writers of history believed the same, then that makes it true? Is it so possible for the mass of Christians to forget the original day?

Weigh carefully the following prophecies in answer:

> Yãhweh has caused to be forgotten the appointed feast and Sabbath in Zion. (Lam 2:6).
>
> I will also put an end to all her gaiety, her feasts, her new moons, her Sabbaths, and all her festal assemblies. And I will destroy her vines and fig trees, of which she said, 'These are my wages which my lovers have given me.' And I will make them a forest, and the beasts of the field will devour them. And I will visit* upon her the days of the Ba'als when she used to offer sacrifices to them and adorn herself with her earrings and jewelry, and follow her lovers, so that she forgot me," declares

* or, "I will have attended upon her." The false gods replaced the true form of worship with their own corruptions and caused the Almighty to be dishonored through neglect of the true appointed times. Therefore it is necessary for Israel to receive the new made heart in order that she may serve Yahweh faithfully.

Yãhweh. (Hosea 2:11-13)[1].

The Reformed Church calls itself *Israel*, and so if it is the house of Israel, then it also comes under the curse of the house of Israel. As the house of Israel, it has forgotten the seventh day, forgotten the Sabbath and feasts of YHWH and has put the days of Ba'al in its place—Christmas, Easter, Sunday Pentecost, and the weekly Sunday in their place.[2] They even learned to call Sunday the Sabbath for many centuries, and many even believed it to be the seventh day of creation. A review of English Church history will show that Sunday was habitially called the Sabbath by Christians. History will show that in disputes with those who kept the 'Jewish' Sabbath, that it was claimed that Sunday could be the seventh day of creation, or that no one could possibly know when the real seventh day was.[3] Does this situation describe the words of the prophet? Surely it does. Surely Christians should look into their hearts and find out what motivated their fathers to forget the original Sabbath of creation.

But not all was forgotten, and all will not remain forgotten. For YHWH has a controversy with the sinners in Zion, and he will separate the wheat from the chaff, and the chaff he will burn up, but the wheat will be gathered into the kingdom:

> Afterward the sons of Israel will return and seek Yãhweh their Almĩghty and David their king; and they will come trem-

---

[1] The book of Hosea is addressed mainly to the northern kingdom of Israel, and the prophecy relates to the northern kingdom's time of dispersion among the nations.

[2] This is the real meaning of "replacement theology." Some Jews who believe in Yeshua still wish to exclude the believing nations from the house of Israel. They accuse the non-Jews who assert their complete union with Israel through Messiah of "replacement theology." What they are exploiting is past persecution of Jews by Christians, by associating it with the truth that true Christians have joined Israel. The desire to affirm union with Israel is not replacement theology. Substituting pagan or traditional days for the appointed times of Scripture, however, is replacement theology, and the reason why Jews were persecuted by Christians in the first place. For those Christians did not want to be reminded of their lawlessness by Jewish neighbors.

[3] To this day continental Europe numbers Sunday as the seventh day of the week. Some scholars produced long chronological works to try to show that Sunday was the original seventh day.

bling to Yãhweh and to his goodness in the last days. (Hosea 3:5).

The "goodness" that the Scripture promises, will be the restoration of the kingdom of Israel. The sons of Israel will come trembling; perhaps it will be a sudden event, and their eyes will be opened, and they will know that they do not deserve the blessings. The bishops of the Church said that the tribe of Judah would never return to Israel, and then it happened. And they still say the kingdom will not be established there, but it will happen just the same, and they themselves will be left behind observing their "days of Ba'al." It does seem that the word "Bishop" has evolved backward from its innocent Greek meaning of "overseer" to one resembling Babylonian priests or Philistine priests with their fish hats.

The Sunday worship service is one of those "days of Ba'al" which Hosea mentioned: אֶת־יְמֵי הַבְּעָלִים. It is falsely justified by the belief that Messiah rose on that day. Yet even that is a poor excuse for ignoring the Sabbath commandment. But even this excuse has been doubted or disbelieved during every age of Church history. Wherever one can look in detail, there is always a remnant that knows Messiah died on the fourth day of the week and rose on the Sabbath.

Many are the seventh day Sabbath observers who have believed the resurrection was on the Sabbath, and a significant number of these have known it was at the end of night before daybreak. But Catholicism has overcome their public voice and rendered them powerless so that their voices are not heard. Their writings are suppressed, rewritten, or reinterpreted. History is whitewashed. This is the curse of the exile prophesied for the house of Israel.

One of those dissenting voices told the truth 255 years ago, but had to publish anonymously in A.D. 1756: [4] I have located a font, and

[4] **THE CONTEST** BETWEEN **SEBASTIAN**, *a Spaniſh Frier*, AND THE FOUR EVANGELISTS, Whether the BODY of **JESUS CHRIST** Aroſe from the DEAD upon the *Jewiſh Sabbath*, or *Roman Sunday*, OR, THE **DEVIL'S DISPUTE** About the BODY of *MOSES* Fairly ſtated and determined. By a MEMBER of the CHURCH of *England*. Printed for the AUTHOR, at the *Angel* Inn in *St. Giles's*, *London* M.DCC.LVI. The text is 20 pages archived in BIBLIOTHECA BODLEIANA. While the author's criticisms of Sebastian's Latin translation of the resurrection passages are justified, his association of

Note: out of habit the author assumes a sunset to sunset calendar day. See * marks. The usage is post biblical were so marked. But he makes it plain the third day is from dawn to dawn at the end.

have reproduced the original text nearly as it appeared then. Notice that the letter "ſ" is really an "s", /e/ =/e/, /ct/ = /ct/.

From the ſeveral Evangeliſts it appears plain to me, that our Lord aroſe from the Dead upon the Jewiſh Sabbath, *very early*, before*the Day was light; I ſay, before*the Day was light. No Fact ſurely was ever plainer than that of our Lord's Reſurrection upon one of the Sabbath*Days. And here it is to be noted, and the whole Myſtery ſeems to lie here. Our Lord Jeſus Chriſt ſuffered upon the Day of Preparation of the Paſſover, not the Day before the ordinary *Jewiſh* Sabbath. And it is worth our Obſervation, that upon whatever Day of the Week, the firſt Day of unleavened Bread happeneth to fall, it was always an holy Convocation, a Day of Reſt or Sabboth, and no ſervile Work was to be done thereon. And that this Sabbath fell in the Middle of the Week, or before the ordinary Sabbath, . . . And thus *St. Mark's* words are very eaſy to be underſtood . . . Verſe the firſt he tells us, When the Sabbath was paſt, Mary Magdalen, and Mary the Mother of James and Salome, had bought ſweet Spices, that they might come and anoint him. And again Verſe 9. Riſing in the Morning, the firſt of the*Sabbath Days[5], he appeared firſt to Mary Magdalen. One Evangeliſt tells us, the Sabbath Day was paſt; and afterwards, they came upon the Sabbath Day and find him riſen, and were told ſo by a Viſion of Angels. By another they reſted the Sabbath, according to the Commandment[6], and then came, as all agree, upon the

*The author uses a post Temple definition of the day.

Sebastian Castellio with the Jesuits is not. The author's error is understandable though, because John Calvin is responsible for slandering the reformer thus, and our author only seems to repeat it. I have therefore left out calumnious criticisms of Sebastian. Sebastian was a lover of religious freedom and was slandered by Calvin because he dared rebuke Calvin for burning Michael Servetus.

[5] The text says, "first Sabbath day" (πρώτῃ σαββάτου) in the singular. The author makes no major chronological mistakes or serious misinterpretations of the texts, but he does have some minor errors that he would not have known how to correct in 1756. Mark 16:9, which should have been omitted.

[6] Luke 23:56, but Codex Bezae omits the words "And they rested according to the commandment." There is a commandment to rest on the annual

Sabbath early in the Morning, *viz.* the * Day of his Reſurrection.

*The author uses a post Temple calendar day.

It is almoſt certain that our Lord ſuffered Death upon the *Wedneſday*, which is alſo moſt agreeable to his own Prediction, and the Prophecies that went before of him, or what may be called Signs and Repreſentations of his Death and Reſurrection; And our Saviour himſelf gives the Prophet *Jonas* as a Sign, and tells us, as Jonas lay three Days and three Nights in the Whale's Belly, ſo alſo ſhall the Son of Man lie three Days and three Nights in the Heart of the Earth. The prophet *Hoſea* vi. 2. expreſſes himſelf ſomewhat obſcurely, After two Days will he revive us, and in the third day will he raiſe us up[7].

I am ſure it muſt weaken the Evidence of our Lord's Reſurrection, and ſeveral Paſſages of Scripture ſeem altogether irreconcileable, to ſuppoſe he roſe ſooner than his own Prophecy mention: For thus ſaith the Scripture, it behoved him to ſuffer and to riſe again the third Day, or more expreſs, after three days to riſe again.[8]

But if we ſuppoſe that our Lord ſuffered on the *Wedneſday, which was the Day of Preparation*, this Day being nailed to the Croſs, may be called the firſt Day, and *Wedneſday* Night the firſt Night; *Thurſday* the Sabbath of Reſt, or *ante Sabbatum*[9], and all that Night makes two Days and two Nights; *Friday* and *Friday* Night compleats the

---

Sabbath, which was quoted above by the author, from Lev. 23:7.

[7] A 24 hour, daybreak to daybreak, calendar day is being used by Hosea, with which this author agrees. Thus, "on the third day" means a twenty-four hour calendar day from daybreak to daybreak—a day and a night.

[8] Mark 8:31. "After three days" takes "day" literally as 12 hours, i.e. after three 12 hour days. Thus the resurrection in the third night is after the third day. "On the third day" takes "day" as 24 hours from daybreak to daybreak, and this is the explanation of Hosea 6:2 also.

[9] *Ante Sabbatum.* Meaning, "the Sabbath before" or the "before-Sabbath."

three Days and the three Nights; and *Saturday* Morning, the firft Morning of the *Jewifh* Sabbath[10], came the Women.

Our author explains it according to the following diagram, such that the three days are Wednesday Day, Thursday Day, and Friday Day, and the three nights are Wednesday-Thu Night, Thursday-Fri Night, and Friday-Sat Night. This is to reckon the day from daybreak to daybreak:

Figure 1: Three Days And Three Nights

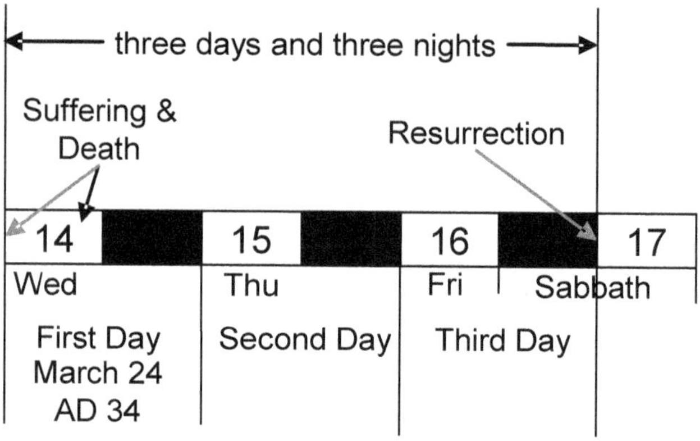

And they came the firft Morning of the Sabbath very early, not the firft day of the Week, as *Sebaftian* and our *Englifh* Tranflators render thofe feveral Texts of Scripture.

Observe the first day is a day and a night, and the second day a day and a night, and the third day a day and a night. Thus day precedes the night, and the calendar day is a day and a night, or 24 hours. The remarkable thing is that this unknown author had it all exactly right.

I have included this old author in the preface to show that the views expressed in this book are not unique, nor did they originate with me. However, I can say that I constructed the same chronology

[10] Our author is compelled to call the Sabbath the *Jewish* Sabbath because Christians were in the habit of calling Sunday the Sabbath. Only by calling it the *Jewish* Sabbath or *Saturday* can he make clear that the seventh day is meant, as even then Sunday Christians would dispute Sunday to be the seventh day, or say that no one knows.

of Yeshua's passion as this author without any help from him. For it is only recently that his writing was discovered shoved away in an old library and forgotten for several hundred years. I came to the same views by studying the Scripture and reconstructing the chronology, simply by using a little logic and reason. But it is always nice to know that someone else was able to read Scripture and to use reason also. It is granted that one needs to know Greek or Latin to figure it out. Our author writes:

> **I appeal to all Mankind, both Friends and Enemies; and let every Gentleman, let every School-Boy, that can conſtrue a plain Sentence of Greek or Latin, declare their Opinion upon it.**

And we shall see that the Hebrew sources also support the Resurrection Sabbath of Messiah Yeshua.

Addendum to Preface

Satan hates Yahweh and his Law, because he wants to be first and the Law puts Yahweh first in the greatest commandment (Deut. 6:4-5). The Sabbath honors Yahweh as the Creator, and therefore Satan wishes men to dishonor what honors Yahweh. The other appointed times honor the redemptive acts of the Almighty. So Satan wants to dishonor these also including the place of his worship in Jerusalem.

Satan also hates the fact that Yahweh intends to judge him, but has offered a ransom for mankind. But Satan wishes mankind to join him in condemnation. The Almighty requires repentance from men as the condition of forgiveness. So Satan's greatest lie about God concerns these two things, repentance and forgiveness.

Satan has created a charicature of God, a Mr. Hyde god and as Dr. Jekyll god. In Stevenson's story, "*Strange Case of Dr Jekyll and Mr Hyde*", Mr. Hyde is the evil alter ego of Dr. Jekyll. Mr. Hyde is the harsh, overbearing, and judgmental god of the OT, who demands perfection for salvation, who yoked his people with the burden of the Sabbath, and the curse of circumcision. When his people could not abide these things, Satan's Mr. Hyde god turns into Dr. Jeykll in the NT, a wise and understanding Father, who really requires no repenteance, just a mere "believe" only. But this Dr. Jeykll god is really Satan's Mr. Hyde. Dr. Jeykll is secretely unforgiving because he requires to be paid off and compensated for his services.

And he quickly reverts to Mr. Hyde in the fine print of the new contract. Dr. Jeykll must announce forgiveness to his clients lest they avoid him, and some volunteer to repent and take forgiveness at face value, realizing that Messiah's death demonstrates just what the Almighty is forgiving. But when it comes to explaining how forgiveness occurs it is Mr. Hyde's theory.

This dispute over the resurrection day is not just a matter of difference in time. It is the watershed of "change" that leads Christians to slander Yahweh as Mr. Hyde, like an inferior god, and then look to Dr. Jekyll afterward as better, who it turns out is really Dr. Hyde all along.

Dr. Jekyll's forgiveness is based on the notion that his clients owe a debt to Mr. Hyde that can be paid for in a currency called righteousness, the problem being that the sinners do not have enough real righteousness to please Dr. Hyde. So Dr. Jekyll says he will graciously allow his client to put on his most expensive clothes with the aura of his righteousness, so that when Mr. Hyde appears, he will see a righteous robe on the client and therefore presume there is no fault to blame on the client. Mr. Hyde then will acquit the client without any of the "harsh demands" for repentance.

Is compensation really made for sin here? Not at all, because the damages of sin have not been reversed. The injustices done to others have not been made whole again. A creditor getting paid off is not forgiveness. The creditor gets everything back again. In the Parable, the servant is forgiven his debt, and no collection is made from anyone! Presenting a false righteousness may fool a human judge, but it does not fool Yahweh, who declared that he would not acquit the guilty when forgiving sin. Nay he really forgives, and to make it an acquittal makes a mockery of forgiveness. So we see that the imputed righteousness theory of justification really is Mr. Hyde's pseudo-forgiveness. Imputed righteousness is really Satan's legal counsel to Christians on how to get an acquittal from his Mr. Hyde caricature of Yahweh. It is legally pleading the case by works rather than asking for forgiveness.

My point then is that the dispute over the resurrection day is all about change. It is about the misrepresentation of Yahweh by the Devil (aka

(Continued on page 488)

Introduction

I will now describe in brief the true chronology of Messiah's death and resurrection. Yeshua died on a Wednesday afternoon, at about 3 pm, and was raised on the Sabbath, just before the dawn. Most people call the Sabbath "Saturday"[11]:

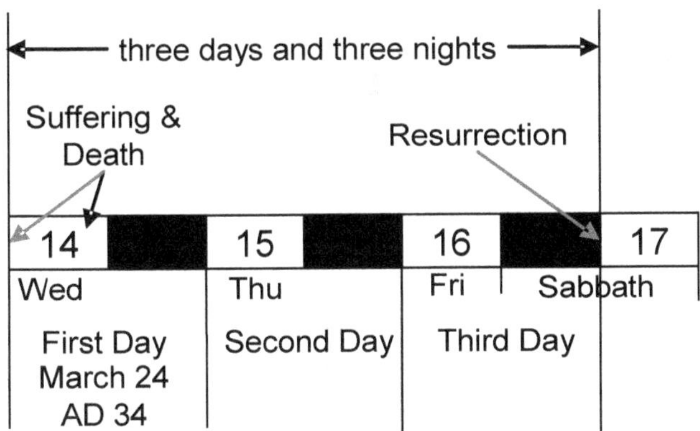

His sufferings began at dawn on Wednesday and continued on the cross till he died. So, the whole period starting from his sufferings until his resurrection was 72 hours—three days and three nights (Mat. 12:40). This book explains the Wednesday crucifixion and corrects some errors in other recent versions of it by placing the resurrection at dawn on the Sabbath. The visit of the women is on the same day, called "the first of the Sabbaths," which is the first after Passover, instead of "the first day of the week," which is a corrupt translation forced on the faithful by the traditions of the Church of Rome, and by the destruction or mistranslation of any books that would make them wiser. Such is the curse of exile and YHWH's judgment on Israel. And in this subject is demonstrated how deep the pit the sheep have slid into, and how complete the destruction of knowledge.

This is the basic model used in this book, and I will add pieces to it, and describe various details. I would like at this point to emphasize that there is a major difference between the chronological solution

---

[11] The day part of Saturday is the seventh day of the week, but the Sabbath begins with sunset on Friday evening, so that a Sabbath is parts of two Roman days, Friday and Saturday.

laid out in this book and the most popular attempts to recover the lost chronology using a Wednesday Crucifixion model. I did say the resurrection was near DAWN ON THE SABBATH[*]. It was not in the afternoon nor was it near sunset, either a little before sunset or a little after it. This difference frees the explanation from all past criticisms leveled by the Sunday Church upon the Wednesday Crucifixion, and I may excuse those who hold to the Wednesday Crucifixion and misplace the resurrection by some 12 hours on the basis that they have but barely escaped from the notorious error of the Friday-Sunday calumny of the Church of Rome, and have yet to learn how deep the rot of prevarication descends.

You, the reader, may be a skeptic, or you may not be. Being skeptical is not a bad thing, unless it is for personally dishonest reasons. Most people are skeptics because they have an inherited set of errant assumptions and false teachings. It is these assumptions that we must examine and deal with. For lack of a better term, I have to call the person who takes a contrary assumption a "skeptic" or "critic." I tried to pick terms that represent opposition without picking terms that demonize the opposition. Most people in the opposition do not deserve to have their personal motives questioned, unless they object past the point of being shown the whole truth by the Holy Spirit. It is sad to say that the critics who attain power in the Sunday Church are all too ready to demonize and slander us as their main tactic, and to bully their flocks into line with unwarranted dogmatisms. A lesser tactic is to belittle the importance of this subject as if it did not matter to salvation or maturity. Nothing could be further from the truth.

Indeed, it is important to know when Messiah rose from the dead, as knowing when reveals further truth on some major subjects: (1) The truthfulness of the Church's traditional position since the second century. (2) Whether the Church should celebrate an Easter resurrection or Resurrection Sabbath. (3) Whether the more faithful observe Sabbath, Sunday, or no day at all. (4) Whether the original Pentecost was Sunday, and whether all other Pentecosts are on a Sunday. These are obvious things of major importance to be affected.

Less obvious, but also very important, are the "spin off" effects of

* If there be a difference of opinion here, it is not the Sabbath, but how far before dawn the resurrection was, as in Jewish reckoning the third night need not be a complete night. What I do hold is that he came out of the tomb just before dawn according to Hosea 6:3, "About earliest dawn is fixed his going forth."

a correct chronology. These include: (5) The correct calculation of the Daniel 9:24-27 prophecy, and for those who know about this, getting it right is very important. (6) When the actual sabbatical and Jubilee years occur. (7) The actual timing of Passover. (8) The manner of calculating the new moon. (9) The time the Jews read the Torah every seven years. (10) The solution to the synoptic problem, and whether the last supper was eaten on Nisan 14 or Nisan 15. None of these things are trivial side issues, for they all relate to fundamental points of loving Messiah by keeping his commandments (John 15:10).

While all of these things relate to hard core chronology and proper observances, getting it right is also important in relation to Yeshua's fulfillments. There are a host of symbolical and typological connections that can be observed only in the framework of a correct chronology. Many people realize that Yeshua died at the same time as the Passover lamb. This alignment was intentionally predetermined by God. However, there is much that will be missed without the rest of the chronological picture. The chronology is the superstructure, and the fulfillment patterns and connections between Yeshua and the institutions of Israel give the spiritual meaning. When the reader finishes this book, he or she will know how and why the modern Church is almost totally impoverished on a host of subjects, and will not cease to be stunned by the difference between Church practice and the truth for a very long time.

Moreover, while on the topic of the importance of this subject, and though the reader does not fully grasp it until the end, the fact is that Torah, divine Law, cannot be correctly observed in its major and main institutions, without correcting the enormous and wicked error of the Church on the timing of our Messiah's death and resurrection. The Passover cannot be correctly observed without this correction. Neither can the feast of Shavuot (Pentecost). Neither can the new moon or the Sabbatical or Jubilee year be properly kept. For all these things are linked into Messiah's Passion, and to run away from the truth of it, is at the same time, to despise the divine Law.

Through this book, I will have to correct quite a number of mistranslations. Such evidence will be presented in every case, that it will be clear that the explanation is correct, or at least that it is possible, and that the greater context makes it certain. I will also explain the necessity of ignoring tradition and relying only on verifiable hard linguistic data from sources contemporary with Messiah, or such linguistic data that survives in authorities that have not been erased, and which leads to a contrary conclusion to the status quo. In other words, when the Church or Synagogue witnesses against itself, then the witness will be considered to have no conflict of interest. However, what the Church or Synagogue says, that could have been in the self interest of the heresies of either side, will be discounted, unless it can be confirmed from Scripture only.

The evidence in this book can only be truly understood or appreciated by combining it all into one whole harmonious picture. Eventually, it is clear that all the texts in the Scriptures go together only one way, which is correct by the strictest mathematical standards and the hardest grammatical rules. When all the pieces are put together, the final picture becomes so certain that it is no longer open to interpretation. Each piece has weaknesses and ambiguities that can be exploited, incorrectly explained, and twisted out of shape on an individual basis. But when all the evidence is put together, this potential disappears completely.

The greatest hurdle for many readers of this book to get over, or for those with whom it is discussed, will be the feeling of how they could be so wrong and so deceived, and how all their leaders and bishops and scholars could be in such error. That is the price that religion pays for ignoring the whole truth for so long. Belief in the correctness of the majority because it is a majority is a worldly principle. Yet time and again it is the argument given when someone does not want to hear the truth. Our leaders could never be so deceived, could they? They are so righteous and religious and studious. Yet this is the way that every person who is a member of a false religion feels. But, if the faithful should be so proud as to think they cannot err, then I will point to the example of Israel, which rebelled and was sentenced to thousands of years of exile, indeed, thousands of years to forget the Sabbath, as prophesied by Jeremiah and Hosea.

And the way Christians feel about other religions (or denominations) is that others are deceived because of insincerity. And because others are not sincere, the excuse is given that because they themselves are sincere, that they must have the whole truth and do not need to examine the evidence that contradicts their position. And so it is explained why false teaching lasts so long—because everyone believes in their own sincerity, and self-righteously, every man does what is right in his own eyes, refusing to check the matter out by prayer and Scripture. Their pride in knowing the "truth" has gotten the better of them. For they think they know the truth because they are sincere. Facts, however, are no respecter of sincerity. And lies, if clever enough, can deceive the most sincere. Having one's false beliefs exposed is the most soul wrenching and emotionally disorienting thing that can happen to a person. I pray for you, dear reader, that you will survive the transition so that you can confidently believe the truth without an overdose of skeptical trauma.

I would not seek to correct Sunday Christians at this time, except that knowledge has increased, as prophesied by Daniel, and if it had not been increased and revealed to me, then I would have had to live with the errors of the past and would not be able to prosecute the argument to its conclusion, as with many in the past who understood but part. Indeed, I would have been able to do no more than publish a short book, leaving many things unexplained, and many loose ends, like the unknown member of the Church of England 255 years ago. And then I would have found some other more profitable mission in the Kingdom of Messiah. However, the evil wrought by the Catholic view and the damage to the good news of Yeshua has also been shown to me, in figures, and in types, and in attacks against the Torah.

With great knowledge comes great sorrow and pain concerning that which was lost, and that which could have been but was not. Yet now I am here to impart this same knowledge to you, the reader, so that you can read and understand. This is not to just understand an opinion or dogma of another, but to know the facts and figures that make up the truth, so that you can know it as clearly as two plus two equals four. I am merely removing the brush out of the way. The path ahead will be clear with anyone who has eyes to see, and whether eyes be opened or not is the work of Yeshua, by the sword of his mouth, which is the word of God, and the Holy Spirit.

I apologize in advance for the length of this book. But it is my intention to cover as many angles as possible and to answer as many objections as possible, while at the same time making this book readable by the majority of adults. I am including many side issues that add to the total picture and secure it beyond doubt. For I intend to strike such a blow that Rome's false doctrine shall never recover from it again. As for those of you who are skeptics, rest assured that my piqued expressions are not for you personally, but for the false teaching foisted on the Church by the emissaries of Satan. And finally, my zeal is for those who will come to fully understand the Torah and good news of Yeshua, and his fulfillment of both, for this knowledge is a great blessing.

My dogmatism on certain points may sound like arrogance to some. Maybe I am a bit arrogant. Well, that is for the Ruakh to correct. As for those who know me and agree on this topic, they will witness that such is not the case. And dogmatism is justified by the severity of the truth. Charges of arrogance are generally made simply because my opposition does not want to agree with the presentation, and they find it expedient to attack the messenger rather than face the message.

The Limits Of Inclusive Counting

And Other Counting Myths

For just as Jonah was three days and three nights in the belly of the sea monster, so shall the Sõn of Man be three days and three nights in the heart of the earth.

This passage from Matthew 12:40 disproves the Good Friday and Easter Sunday tradition, which lacks the three nights. The skeptic will object to my dogmatism, and declare that Jews counted days inclusively. He will also say that part of a day is counted as a whole. He hopes to persuade you (or himself) that "three days and three nights" in Jewish usage, or Hebrew usage, or Semitic usage may mean only three days and "two nights." I will examine this objection and we will see whether my dogmatism that Matthew 12:40 disproves the Friday-Sunday scenario is justified.

Figure 2: Three Days And Two Nights

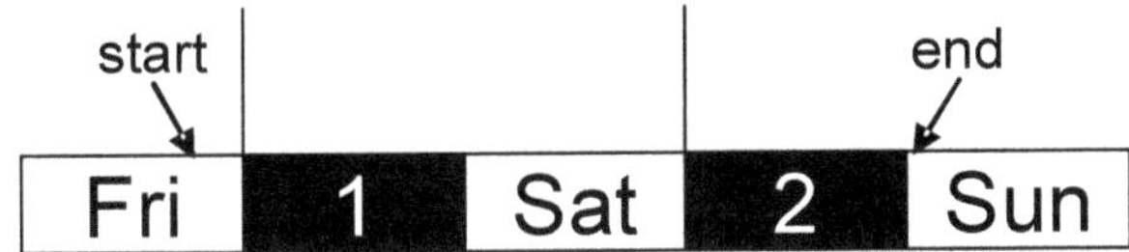

The skeptic tries to quote examples from Scripture and Talmud to try to prove that three days and three nights are less than three parts day and three parts night. Of the many attempts, none actually prove what they aim to prove. They are all failures. If you have to come up against any of these attempts, then there is always a way to show that the time period stated is, in fact, the time period required by the source.

If you persevere and examine the attempts to prove a valid language example of any period of time being less than the stated number of days or nights, then you will soon discover that some skeptics are only trying to be crafty, and that the rest actually don't know that their argument fails to prove their case. Some know full well that their examples prove no such thing as three days and three nights being shorter than three parts day and three parts night.

Jewish, biblical, and Semitic sources do indeed count inclusively. For example, a part day, a day, and a part day, are termed "three days." Using inclusive counting "three days and three nights" can be a part day, a whole night, a whole day, a whole night, a whole day, and a part night. Even so, there is nothing to say in Messiah's case that it is not three whole days and three whole nights. We shall see later in this book that the 72 hour interpretation and inclusive counting are both possible. But it is not Matthew 12:40 that secures 72 hours. Matthew 12:40 only proves three days or parts thereof, and three nights or parts thereof, and allows up to 72 hours. Other evidence will be used to show that it was 72 hours from the beginning of his suffering to his resurrection, and it will also be shown that Matthew 12:40 includes the suffering.

Therefore, if the skeptic responds with the examples aiming to show that three days and three nights is to be shortened to less than three parts night, then you should confidently dismiss the examples as deceptions, or insufficient, or you should think about the examples until you understand their faults. There are some examples that require knowledge of the exact Hebrew or Greek wording to refute. The sad thing is, that we have to undo the damage of mistranslating that those who were entrusted the rule over the Church have committed, in order to be free from their error.

If you are given an argument that seems in English to prove the point, then you should not swallow it. I will give an example of such an argument. The KJV says, "Come again unto me <u>after three days</u>" (2 Chron. 10:5), and then "So Jeroboam and all the people came to Rehoboam <u>on the third day</u> as the king had directed, saying, 'Return to me <u>on the third day</u>'" (2 Chron. 10:12). It seems that 2 Chron. 10:5 says to come "<u>after</u> three days" are passed, i.e. on the fourth day, or in the night after the day part of the third day.[12] But then 2 Chron. 10:12

[12] Using a twenty-four hour calendar day from daybreak to daybreak, "after three days," can mean the night of the third calendar day, and "after" is with respect to the daytime part of the third day, whereas "on the third day" may be with respect to the whole twenty-four hour calendar day from daybreak to daybreak. This explanation works for Yeshua's statements, because the resurrection was in the night after the third day, but still on the third calendar

says it was really "on the third day." Is somehow stating "after three days" a Hebrew direct idiom for "on the third day"?[13] Are these simply two ways of expressing the exact same thing? Not at all! The Hebrew text of 2 Chron. 10:5 says: עוֹד שְׁלֹשֶׁת יָמִים = *while still three days*. Several other translations agree with this. The NAS has "in three days," and the NIV has "in three days." Don't be misled by "after." It is a mistranslation. The Hebrew says "while still" (עוֹד). And the Septuagint says, "ἕως τριῶν ἡμερῶν," "as far as three days."[14]

In some cases, only by knowing more than the skeptic about the original source can you expose his faulty assumption. The key word is the Hebrew word עוֹד. This word never means "after." It means "still."[15] Therefore the example does not prove that "after three days" equals "on the third day."[16]

Here is another inclusive counting argument:

> Go, assemble all the Jews who are found in Susa, and fast for me; do not eat or drink <u>for three days, night or day</u> [שְׁלֹשֶׁת יָמִים לַיְלָה וָיוֹם]. I and my maidens also will fast in

---

day. But it does not work here, because the people were not expected to hold audience with the King at night.

[13] Obviously, the question is assuming the same definition of "day" on both sides of the equivocation, such that the solution is not in two different definitions of "day" but in assuming the equivalency of "after" and "on" as some supposed Semitic manner of speaking.

[14] Like the King James Version, Josephus has "ὁ δὲ μετὰ τρεῖς ἡμέρας (*Ant* 8:214)," "after three days," but this has the MT and LXX against it, as well as most of Josephus' other usages of "μετὰ," which are strictly "after." There are two more exceptions. One concerns Hezekiah (μετὰ τρίτην ἡμέραν, *Ant* 10:27), but also disagrees with the MT and LXX (τῇ ἡμέρᾳ τῇ τρίτῃ, 2 Kings 20:5, 8). The final example concerns Amasa (μεθ' ἡμέρας τρεῖς, *Ant* 7:280), but this disagrees with the MT and LXX (τρεῖς ἡμέρας, 2Sa 20:4). The follow up in Ant 7:281 (τῇ τρίτῃ τῶν ἡμερῶν) is without parallel in the Hebrew or Septuagint. All three of these cases take unjustified liberties with the Scriptural texts. Against these errors are, e.g. *Ant* 3:143 (μετὰ δὲ ἡμέρας ἑπτα), and *War* 3:145 (μετὰ μίαν ἡμέραν), and all other passages in Josephus with "after," that clearly mean "after *n* days" in which *n* is counted exclusive of the starting point.

[15] pg. 267 Holladay. pg 648, vol. II, TWOT. pg 728, "still, yet, again, besides" (BDB).

[16] Both phrases can be used to describe the same event, but only if "day" is understood differently.

the same way. And thus I will go in to the king, which is not according to the law; and if I perish, I perish (Esther 4:16).

Now it came about <u>on the third day</u> [בַּיּוֹם הַשְּׁלִישִׁי] that Esther put on her royal robes and stood in the inner court of the king's palace in front of the king's rooms, and the king was sitting on his royal throne in the throne room, opposite the entrance to the palace (Esther 5:1).

This text does show that Esther saw the king before the third day was completed. For it was "on the third day;" also she said the banquet was "this day." It thus shows that part of a day can be counted as a whole. However, it does not prove that there were less than three parts day or three parts night. We should assume that Esther was giving the orders at night, because she puts the order "night or day." In Persia the civil day was probably from dawn to dawn. Esther is scheduling a fast that will begin sometime in the night. So the matter diagrams this way:

Figure 3: How Esther Counted The Nights And Days

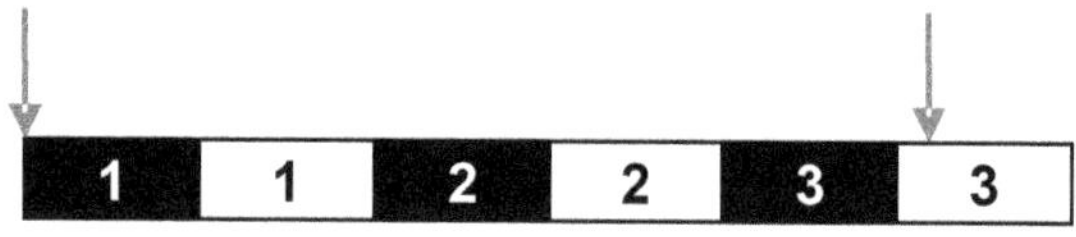

The Queen's language fits the above diagram. She mentions night before day,[17] and it is likely that she went to the king earlier on the third day rather than later, because later the king and his nobles might have had too much wine. Even though Esther did not explicitly mention "three nights," it is clear that three nights fit with no problem. You can also see that there are three parts night and three parts day. So the skeptic that cites this example against Matthew 12:40 is not proving his case against a literal "three nights." Yet, in a great deal of the Sunday Church polemical literature against "three

---

[17] Only if the Queen did not mean to imply that the night did come before the day can we shorten the period to d+n+d+n+d. There are still three parts day here. Yes, there are two parts night, but Esther did not actually say "three nights," so it would not be fair to dismiss her "night or day" ordering, and so shorten the period and proclaim it equivalent to Matthew 12:40.

days and three nights," you will find this very example used, and it reveals the amount of integrity those writers really have.

Other skeptics quote from the Talmud. Rabbi Eliazar Ben Azariah (ca A.D. 100) is reported to say "A day and night are a period [onah] and the part of a period [onah] is as the whole of it" (יום ולילה עונה ומקצת עונה ככולה). This is really nothing but the statement that counting may be inclusive, and the Rabbi is making no claim that parts of days or nights may be deleted entirely from the counting.*

Yet, John Lightfoot writes concerning Matthew 12:40:

> It is not easy to translate the word 'onah' into good Latin: for to some it is the same with the half of a natural day [i.e. either a day or a night, 12 hours]; to some it is all one with 'a whole natural day' [i.e. a night + day, or day + night = 24 hours]. According to the first sense, we may observe, from the words of R. Ishmael, that sometimes four "onoth," or halves of a natural day, may be accounted for three days: and that they, also, are so numbered, that one part or the other of those halves may be accounted for a whole [of the half-day, i.e. a day or night, 12 hours]. Compare the latter sense with the words of our Savior, which are now before us:—"A day and a night (saith the tradition) make an Onah, and a part of an Onah is as the whole." Therefore Christ may truly be said to have been in his grave three Onoth, or "three natural days" (when yet the greatest part of the first day was wanting [lacking], and the night altogether, and the greatest part by far of the third day also), the consent of the schools and dialect of the nation agreeing thereunto. For, "the least part of the Onah concluded the whole." So that according to this idiom, that diminutive [smallest] part of the third day, upon which Christ arose, may be computed for the whole day, and the night following it" (John Lightfoot).[18]

---

* The Rabbis' statements hold true for a calendar day with a dawn or dusk epoch (day and night or night and day) OR a "day" or a "night" with a dawn to dusk or dusk to dawn epoch. A calendar day is only called "a day" in the sense of "a time cycle." If any number of nights are stated (or implied) only variations including the specified number of nights are allowed, since 'day' may be extended to include a night in a calendar day, but when night is also mentioned then strictly only literal nights or days are in view. When night is present 'day' only means dawn to dusk.

[18] Volume XI, Hebrew and Talmudical Exercitations upon the Gospels of St. Matthew and St. Mark, pg. 201-202, Rev. John Lightfoot, D.D. Also Hebraicæ et Talmudicæ, 1823.

Lightfoot's interpretation is faulty. It should be noted that Rabbi Eliazar Ben Azariah (רבי אלעזר בן עזריה) did not mean his statement to be put to such an illogical use. For Lightfoot wants to count a few hours of daylight on Friday afternoon as "a day and a night." When the Rabbi says "a part of a period" he has these situations in mind:

Figure 4: Various Ways to Count an Onah when both Days and Nights are Numbered

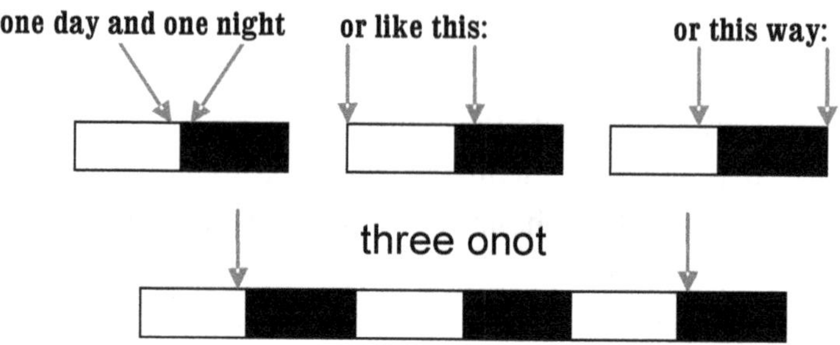

This can be seen by using the Rabbi's definition. Since an "onah" is defined as "a day and a night," an onah must always be some part of a day followed by some part of a night (or the reverse of it). What the whole discussion in the Jerusalem Talmud (9.3)† is about, is what it means to say that a woman is unclean for "three days" after intercourse because the man's seed remains in her.

רבי ישמעאל אומר פעמים שהן ארבע עונות. פעמים שהן ה' פעמים שהן שש ר"ע אומר לעולם הן חמש. אם יצאת מקצת עונה הראשונה משלימין לה מקצת עונה ששית. הא רבי ישמעאל עבד יום עונה ולילה עונה. ר"ע עבד יום עונה ולילה עונה. מה ביניהון עונות שלימות ביניהון. ר' ישמעאל עבד מקצת עונה ככולה. ותני כן על דר' עקיבה לפיכך אם נכנסה מקצת עונה ראשונה משלימין לה מקצת עונה ששית. תני רבי אלעזר בן עזריה אומר יום ולילה עונה ומקצת עונה ככולה. ותני כן על דר' אלעזר בן עזריה פעמים יש שם יום וכל שהוא והיא טהורה. שני ימים וחסר כל שהוא והיא טמאה.

"Rabbi Ishmael says sometimes it [three days] is four onah, sometimes that it is five, sometimes that it is six. Akiba says for ages they are five[19] [onah]. If she has intercourse in part of the

---

[19] i.e. "For ages" (לעולם) he means from long past reckoning. We must remember that the Rabbis are interpreting "three days" and not "three days →

† See also Mishnah Mikvaot 8.3: הַפּוֹלֶטֶת זֶרַע בַּיּוֹם הַשְּׁלִישִׁי, טְהוֹרָה, דִּבְרֵי רַבִּי אֶלְעָזָר בֶּן עֲזַרְיָה. רַבִּי יִשְׁמָעֵאל אוֹמֵר, פְּעָמִים שֶׁהֵם אַרְבַּע עוֹנוֹת, פְּעָמִים שֶׁהֵם חָמֵשׁ, פְּעָמִים שֶׁהֵם שֵׁשׁ. רַבִּי עֲקִיבָא אוֹמֵר, לְעוֹלָם חָמֵשׁ:
See Shabbat 86a:4. But see Lev. 15:18. She is only unclean until evening of whatever day seed is discharged, and it is not likely to be past evening on the day of relations. The Rabbis probably decided to nullify 3rd day discharge on the basis of Exodus 19:15, but only after the first onah of it was complete..

first onah, then her time is complete in part of the sixth onah. Rabbi Ishmael computed a day an onah, and a night an onah. Akiba computed a day an onah, and a night an onah. What is the span of onot of three spans? Ishmael computed part of an onah as the whole of it. And the Tanna'im so affirm on the word of Rabbi Akiba, *that* when she is entered in part of the first onah, *then* make completed for her part of the sixth onah. Tanna Rabbi Eliazar Ben Azariah says: a day and a night are an onah, and part of an onah is as the whole of it.

And the Tanna'im so affirm on the word of Rabbi Eliazar Ben Azariah, "sometimes there is day [at the end] and all of it —that she is clean; [but if the] second day, and is lacking any of it, then she is unclean."

Rabbi Ishmael is not giving a legal ruling. He is just observing how "three days" can be computed. Here is his option, and the others:

Figure 5: Four Onoth with Day First

Figure 6: Five Onoth

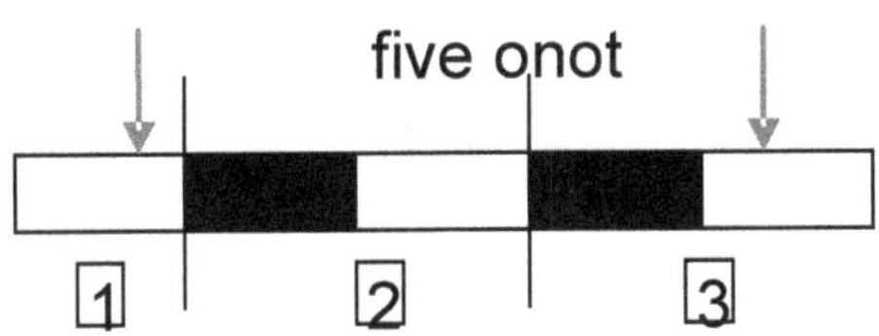

Figure 7: Six Onoth with Day First

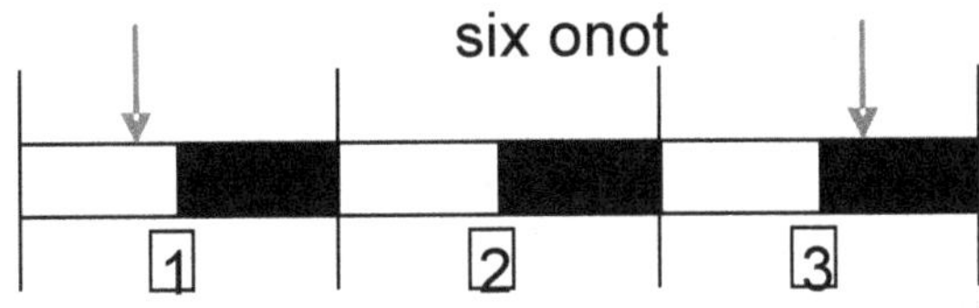

---

and three nights."

After the possibilities are mentioned, the rulings say that if a woman has intercourse then she must count inclusively six onot before she is clean again, like in the last diagram above, or in the one following:

Figure 8: Six Onoth with Night First

Now if we overlay Rabbi Ishmael's 12 hour definition of an onah (day or night) with Rabbi Eliazar Ben Azariah's 24 hour definition of an onah (day and night), then we see how both work with the final ruling:

Figure 9: Overlay of 12 hour Onah with 24 hour Onah

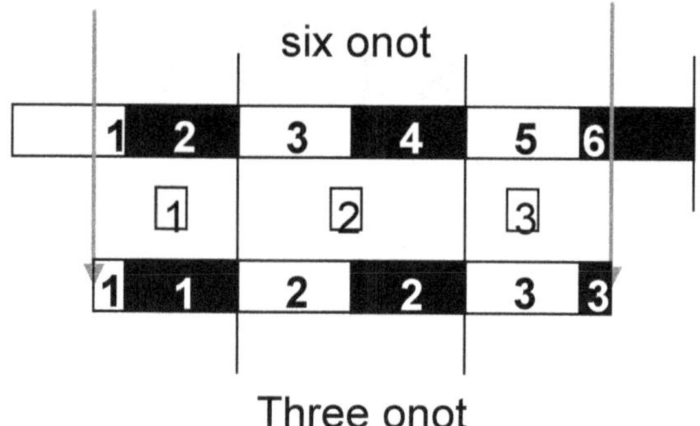

Rabbi Eliazar can say "three days" must be "three onah" (for the woman to become clean again), and because he has defined an onah as "a day and a night" it is clear that 6 onah are meant. The 'part of an onah is as the whole of it' statement is simply so that it is understood that the first day (see above) can be translated into a part day+ whole night, and the third day into a whole day+part night.

There is therefore no demonstrable intention on the Rabbis' part to say that a few hours of day can be expanded to a day and a night, nor is there an example given by the Rabbis showing such.

Lightfoot's application is to apply what the Rabbis said in a new way to a new situation that the Rabbis did not think of.[20] And the Rabbis would most strenuously object to Lightfoot's reasoning to say the period required for a woman to be *clean* can be shortened. If the learned Reverend[21] were to don the rabbinical hat and contribute to the Talmudic debate, then the other Rabbis would be sure to rebuke him for reinterpreting the tradition of three days his way. For the Reverend's function amounts to x + 1 = x, and may be used to reduce any factual number to any other factual number.

There are, of course, many Scripture passages that suggest or prove inclusive counting. However, none of them show that "x days" is less than x parts day, or that "x nights" is less than x parts night. Here is a list of texts that show inclusive counting: Gen. 40:13, 20; 42:17-18; 1 Sam. 30:12-13; 1 Kings 20:29, 22:1-2; Hosea 6:2; Luke 13:32-33; 24:21. However many days or nights are counted, the number of each will always correspond to the actual number of days or nights or parts thereof.

As with 2 Chron. 10:5, this text is also mistranslated:

> At the edge [מִקֵּץ] of seven years each of you shall set free his Hebrew brother, who has been sold to you and has served you six years,[22] you shall send him out free from you; but your forefathers did not obey me, or incline their ear to me.
>
> (Jer. 34:14, my translation)

The usual translations have "end" where I have corrected it to "edge." It would be rather strange for the law to permit only six years of service and then make the servant serve the seventh year also. The Hebrew מִקֵּץ means "edge," "boundary," or "extremity" as well as "end" (cf. William Holladay's Hebrew Lexicon, pg. 321). Likewise, in Deut. 15:1, "At the edge of seven years" (cf. Deut. 31:10). This sense was proved by Eben Ezra (1089-1164 A.D.) disputing with other

[20] Unless of course, we are to suppose that the Rabbis were laying a trap for Christians to fall into. In any case, the Christians fell into it.
[21] "Reverend" sounds remarkably like "Rabbi" and means essentially the same thing—revered, exalted one, great one.
[22] See Exodus 21:2, "six years he shall serve: and in the seventh he shall go free. . ."

Rabbis. Yet, the very mistranslation of Jer. 34:14 is injudiciously cited as proving that there is some mysterious Semitic idiom that mismatches the time stated with the reality.

What about the parallel passages, Luke 9:28 and Matthew 17:1? Luke says "after[23] . . . about eight days" (ὡσεὶ ἡμέραι ὀκτώ) Yeshua went up the mountain, and Matthew says, "after six days" (μεθ' ἡμέρας ἓξ). Yeshua's words in Matthew 16:28 and Luke 9:27 were spoken on the Sabbath. "After eight days" counts exclusively from Friday night to the day part of the next Sabbath. "After six days" on the other hand, is a shorthand phase for saying "on the seventh day," which is the Sabbath, and is borrowed from Exodus 24:16 to connect the transfiguration with Moses meeting YHWH on the mountain on the Sabbath. "After six days" really means "after [the] six days" of the regular working week. An English colloquialism for this would be, "And then after the following workweek." The "six days" are identified with Sunday to Friday, and after those days is the Sabbath.

So there is no contradiction between Luke and Matthew here, and there is no stating of a number of days or nights that is not in fact the stated number of days or nights or parts thereof being referred to.

Figure 10: After Eight or Six Days?

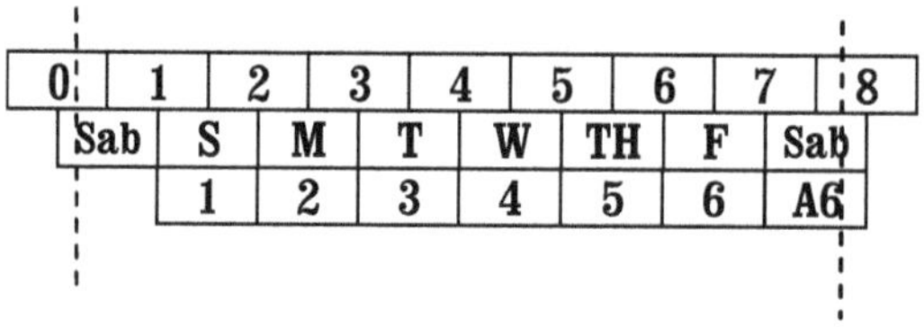

0	1	2	3	4	5	6	7	8
Sab	S	M	T	W	TH	F	Sab	
	1	2	3	4	5	6	A6	

The top row renders Luke's "after eight days", counting calendar days according to daybreak.[24] Thus, Sabbath morning is after one day, and the next Sabbath morning is "after eight days." The bottom row has the same starting point (Friday night), except here "after six days" means the six days of the work week. "A6" is "after [the] six

[23] Luke chooses the word "after" which suggests that Yeshua spoke his words at the beginning of the Sabbath, sometime after sunset Friday. He uses the standard method of saying the same day next week (8 days), but appends the word "about" in case the reader should misunderstand. As soon as dawn comes on the Sabbath, it is "after one day" (using the dawn to dawn Temple day).

[24] The daybreak day is to be explained in coming chapters.

days," which is also on the Sabbath. John 20:26 (μεθ' ἡμέρας ὀκτὼ), "after eight days" has the same explanation as Luke 9:28. The "0th" day is the day of the resurrection, (the "third day" from the crucifixion). The "eighth day" is the next Sabbath. Of course, the normal mode of saying the same day the next week is to say "eight days from today," or "in eight days," or "on the eighth day" and not "after eight days." However, once sunrise to sunrise calendar reckoning of the "third day" is understood from the following chapters, "after eight days" will make sense, as the day part of the Sabbath was reckoned as the first day after the resurrection. The normal sense of "after *n* days" is the $n+1^{th}$ day counting from, or including the starting point.. This is proved in Hosea 6:2, "after two days...in the third day" (μετὰ δύο ἡμέρας ἐν τῇ ἡμέρᾳ τῇ τρίτῃ), מִיֹּמָיִם בַּיּוֹם הַשְּׁלִישִׁי. The same way of saying "the third day" is found in Mark 14:1: μετὰ δύο ἡμέρας, and Mathew 26:2 (μετὰ δύο ἡμέρας).

I have had much experience with skeptics that bring up inclusive counting passages to try to dispense with "three nights." Except for a very few, almost all of them knew before hand that the passages only prove inclusive counting and not that "three nights" can be reduced to two. Most of them will never admit this. They will keep bringing up the passages as if it proves they can get away with Friday-Sunday. This is because to admit the truth is to abandon their position. Therefore, they are reduced to intellectual dishonesty; and setting themselves forth as supporters of the position, they hope that somehow the fault of their argument will escape the notice of their audiences, and that the volume of their words on the subject of inclusive counting will convince their audiences to set aside their judgment in favor of the speaker's erudite authority. However, even the most mathematically challenged can see that their position is a simple case of contradiction to Matthew 12:40.

There is not just one passage with "three days and three nights" (Matthew 12:40) of Messianic significance. Equally important is 1 Samuel 30:12 and the surrounding passage. I will get to it later in this book. Yeshua only mentioned the Jonah passage, but anyone who knows their Messianic prophecy and typology well, and who knows how to detect the hint of Messianic prophecy in the Scripture without being told it is Messianic, will at once see that the Sign of David is equally as potent as the Sign of Jonah.

The Prohetic Third Day Is Counted Inclusively

> Yeshua said, "Thus it is written, that the Mẽssiah should suffer and rise again from the dead the third day; (Luke 24:46).

Paul also explains that the 'third day' is 'according to the Scriptures' (1 Cor. 15:4) meaning many texts, not just one. So, according to the prophetic types Messiah suffered on the 'third day' (Gen 22:4; 40:20) and rose on the 'third day' (Gen. 22:4; 40:20). The third day is "after two days" (Hos. 6:1-3; Mat. 26:2; Mark 14:1), and "within three days" (Gen 40:13; 19). On may wonder how the crucifixion could be on the third day. The Scripture does not just count forward from the crucifixion. It counts backward from the resurrection, and forward from two days before the Passover. Thus the day of the crucifixion is also the 'third day' in the prophetic types. The forward and backward counting only works using the inclusive method.

Therefore, when counting calendar days from the crucifixion one must count inclusively. The day of the crucifixion counts as *day one*. This is only possible with Matthew 12:40 when the calendar day is from daybreak to daybreak, according to the Scriptural day which begins in the morning.

The types call the crucifixion day the 'third day' (Gen. 22:4; 40:20; 1Sam 30:1) as the day when grief is realized, and likewise the 'third day' when life is spared (indicating resurrection). 1Samuel 4:7 and 14:21 tells how to count three days backwards, "for it was not like this yesterday or three days ago": אֶתְמוֹל שִׁלְשׁוֹם. Also Gen 31:2,5: 'as yesterday, or three days ago' כִּתְמוֹל שִׁלְשׁוֹם. And Exodus 4:10, גַּם מִתְּמוֹל גַּם מִשִּׁלְשֹׁם 'also yesterday, also on the third day.' See also Exodus 5:7, 8. Exodus 5:14 'as yesterday, third day, also yesterday, also today.' Also Ex. 21:29.

If there is any doubt here, the LXX gives the meaning, *ὡς ἐχθὲς καὶ τρίτην ἡμέραν* (Gen. 31:2, 5); *ἐχθὲς καὶ τρίτην ἡμέραν* (Exo 5:7), 'as yesterday and the third day.' There are some 25 verses with this idiom. The key point is that in Hebrew the 'day before yesterday' is always identified as the 'third day'; the counting is inclusive. 'Today' is the first day, 'yesterday' is the second, and the 'third day' is the third. The same works for counting forward, 'today and tomorrow' (Exo 19:10) and 'let them be ready for the third day.' Uriah's death sentence is issued on the third day (cf. 2Sam. 11:12-14). Yeshua himself speaks this way, 'today and tomorrow, and the third day' (Luke 13:32) σήμερον καὶ αὔριον καὶ τῇ τρίτῃ.

All of the aforementioned passages with the word שִׁלְשׁוֹם are mistranslated in the English versions. The word is a joining of two Hebrew words, *shelosh* and *yom* to form the contraction *shilshom*. It is always placed as the day before yesterday, thus counting backwards inclusively from 'today.'

Take a look at ***Figure 1: Three Days And Three Nights*** on page 16. The three days are counted forward. Now count them backward from the third day. At the moment of the resurrection, it is 'today', and then Thursday is 'yesterday' and Wednesday is *shilshom. Shelosh Yom!*

Yeshua counts this as, 'today and tomorrow and the next day...for it cannot be that a prophet should perish outside of Jerusalem' (Luke 13:33). For he says, 'and on the third day I will be finished' (Luke 13:32). And he said, 'it is finished' (John 19:30). So whatever events happen 'today' such as Yeshua's dying, then the third day is counted inclusively from then.

Yeshua died on the 4th day of the week. That day must be included in the counting. There are no exceptions in the typology of the third day. None. Thus, for instance, he could not have died on Wednesday and then be raised at any time after dawn on the Sabbath. For that would exceed three calendar days (daybreak to daybreak), or any other way one wants to reckon a day. Yeshua was raised in the night after the third day, which still belongs to the third calendar day. Sometimes Yeshua would say, 'after three days', but what he meant was the night after the third twelve-hour day (Friday, dawn to dusk), which was Friday night.[25] Next to Salvation itself, this teaching is the most important teaching of the entire scriptures. See 1Cor. 15:1-4!

---

[25] This is explained later starting on page 189.

The "*First Day*" Deception

They will say that the resurrection was on the "first day of the week," citing Mat. 28:1; Mark 16:2; Luke 24:1; John 20:1, 19, and possibly Acts 20:7 and 1 Cor. 16:2. This argument is really circular since it is *they* who translated these texts the way they wanted to in the first place. Their deception depends on using one corruption as their authority for teaching another corruption. So they insist on "first day of the week" on their own authority, and ignore the literal text, "first of the Sabbaths" as best they can.

A superficially easy way out of this argument is to accept the skeptic's translation and argue that it only means that the women went to the tomb on Sunday and that the resurrection happened on the preceding day.[26] However, this proposal, put forward by the proponents of the Sabbath afternoon resurrection, is a fatal trap, and is the result of repairing only part of the error in the Church's traditional position. Part of the error is plainly obvious, which is that part having to do with Matthew 12:40. But such is not the only error. It is the only error that is plain to see. The rest has been covered up with lies and mistranslations that are not plain to see. The question is, if the Church is seduced to error on one plainly obvious point, then should we not recheck everything else right back to the foundations? Indeed, we should. And it is not safe to accept only a partial solution, because one might be forced to retreat from it. A re-examination of every translation bearing on the subject is needed, and not just Matthew 12:40 which presents an obvious contradiction to their chronology.

They will parry the afternoon or evening resurrection proposals with Luke 24:21, "to day is the third day since these things were done" (KJV). They will observe that the Emmaus story happened on Sunday. Then they will point out that counting inclusively from Wednesday makes Sunday the 5th day.

The afternoon or evening resurrection advocate may be tempted

---

[26] The Evangelists themselves do not actually say that the resurrection was immediately before the women arrived, but the prophet Hosea does give the time in Hosea 6:3, and this corresponds to when the women sought Him (cf. Hosea 5:15). This will be discussed later. Luke 24:21 also prevents such a delay.

to defend by counting exclusively from Thursday. But this still makes Sunday the 4th day. Skeptics will correctly say that exclusive counting is not possible in this case, and will correct the translation of Luke 24:21 to say "to day is the third day from when[27] these things were done."

There is no way to avoid the above contradiction unless the critic is corrected on both the "first day of the week" mistranslation and the mistake in "to day is the third day from when these things were done." Without correction, the critic can hold Luke 24:21 and the "first day of the week" passages over Matthew 12:40, and would be justified in choosing two passages on his side for Friday-Sunday against one on the other for Wednesday-Sabbath. Where is he wrong, then? His proof texts were mistranslated by like-minded ancestors who wanted Friday-Sunday to be true. Here are the corrections:

> [1]Now on the FIRST[μ] OF THE ŞABBAŧHS[η] Miryam Ha-Magdalit, is herself coming early, darkness still being[ε], to the tomb, [ρ]when she sees the stone having been [γ]getting removed from the tomb (John 20:1, GNM).[28]

> But indeed, even with all this, *a* third *day*, this day, passes by, from when these things happened (Luke 24:21, GNM).

The John passage indicates the resurrection was before Sabbath dawn apparently the first Sabbath in some counting of Sabbaths, which will be explained later. The Luke passage says that on the same day, the third day expired, or 'passes by.'[29]

What is the "third day"? The Sabbath was from sunset Friday to dusk Saturday. But the "third day" was from Friday dawn to Sabbath dawn (which will be proved in the following chapter). The

---

[27] "From when" = "ἀφ' οὗ." An examination of the LXX and other NT usages will show that inclusive counting is always required when these words are used. The Hebrew expressions parallel to the LXX also show this.

[28] And all the passages like it: Mat. 28:1; Mark 16:2, 9; Luke 24:1; John 20:19; Acts 20:7; 1 Cor 16:2.

[29] The literal sense is "[a] third [day], this day, [he] passes" (NA-27th). Without a context the phrase is ambiguous, where 'passes' could be used in the sense of *spend time*, e.g. "[a] third [day], this day, [he] spends," but here it means *passes by, leads off, carries away*, which is adopted in GNM, because in context, the hopeless remark only makes sense if the third day has indeed passed. If the third day was not passed, the immediate objection arises that they have not waited till its end before giving up.

picture looks like this:

Figure 11: Luke 24:21

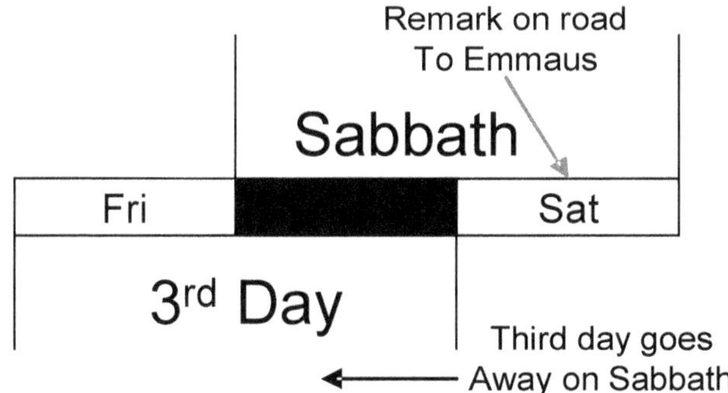

So, for one speaking during the day part of the Sabbath, you will see that, "a third day, this day (on the Sabbath), passes (by)." This explains Luke 24:21. And the skeptics' proof that the crucifixion was not on Wednesday falls to the ground. The text also shows the third day was just ending when the women arrived at the tomb, and that it ended with the third night.

They will object that "the third day" cannot be from daybreak to daybreak, and argue that the three days must be calculated on a sunset to sunset basis "because that is how Jews must reckon a day." They will also claim that the Greek word for "Sabbath" means "week." They will say that the women cannot go to the tomb on the Sabbath without breaking it. Also they will say that Cleopas and his fellow disciple cannot travel to Emmaus on the Sabbath. Finally, they observe that the resurrection is matched by the wave sheaf offering, which they claim was on Sunday that year.

None of these objections are based on truth, but they will all be answered in the following chapters just as clearly as the reinterpretation of Matthew 12:40 was shown to be unjustified. The objections are based on the assumptions and traditions of Judaism and Christianity introduced after Yeshua's death and resurrection. But Judaism, Christianity, history and secular sources have preserved enough of the truth so that we can sort out the truth from the fiction. The actual texts of the Torah and Prophets, and the writings of the Apostles testify against the traditions.

The Road to the First Day of the Week
Historical Summary*

In the DSS, we first meet up with a pious idiom for counting to the Sabbath, "one unto the Sabbath," (ca 100 BC) (אחד בשבת), and in the Good News of the New Made Covenant of Old with "one [day] of the Sabbaths" (after AD 34) These are not equivalent because the genitive case in Greek in the Evangelists does not support the sense "unto." "Day of the Sabbaths" is also the literal idiom for "the Sabbath Day" by itself without "one." All recognize that "one" is used in the sense of "first" according to Hebrew idiom. The DSS scroll usage is explained by counting to the Sabbath, and the Evangelists by counting the seven Sabbaths mentioned in Lev. 23:15.

The Gnostics reinterpreted "first of the Sabbaths" by rejecting the Law and redefining this Sabbath to mean the first of the new Sabbaths of the new age on the eighth day after the abolishment of the old carnal Sabbaths (ca. AD 100 and after). This interpretation has still been floated in recent centuries by some theologians and scholars. When knowledge of Scripture increased this interpretation began to appear contrived, as it surely was. After some generations, Christians with Gnostic parentage, which was most, began to seek for another explanation.

The needed revision was supplied by the Rabbis who brought the DSS pious idiom to notice by adopting it more frequently, and who then introduced the word שבא into Aramaic with the final letter transmuted from שבע. They hoped Christians would confuse שבא with שבתא (Sabbath), when they themselves meant nothing but "one in the seven" (חד בשבועתא) by this innovation. Under the eye of Aquilla of Sinope and the last Tannaim the Synagogue Septuagint was revised at Lev. 23:11-15, 25:8†. Certain Psalm titles also added. Also Targum Onkelos was introduced with the same revision where שבוען was substituted for Sabbaths. Because σαββατων was in the Evangelists, Christians were highly motivated by this prod from the Rabbis to claim that σαββατων meant "week," and they ignorantly did so.

---

* This page was blank in the earlier edition. This material is gone over thoroughly in later chapters.

†Lev. 25:8 in Targum Onkelos: שְׁבַע שְׁמִטִּין דִשְׁנִין. In the LXX: ἑπτὰ ἑβδομάδες ἐτῶν. But the sense of the Hebrew construct (genitive) is, "seven Sabbaths of the years" where "of" means *in* or *from*, i.e. seven Sabbaths *from* the years. In this case the Targum is more correct, "seven shemittin of the years," and 'shemittin' does not mean 'weeks.' A 'Release' is only the seventh year. The Rabbis were highly motivated to remove Christians from any observance of Torah to the point of even passing a death sentence upon the non-Jew who should keep the Sabbath. The Rabbis sought to make obeying the law as odious as possible to Christians while the Church sought to make Messiah as odious as they could observant Jews, because both sides have the same boss leading them down the Road to Hell paved with lies.

The Reckoning of a Day

Jews and Christians have been indoctrinated into the belief that a day in ancient Israel, and the Genesis day, always began with the setting of the light. However, remarkably prominent Jewish and Christian scholars contradict this belief, and they will be cited in this chapter. But first, I wish to show the logic of their position does not rely on their authority to say so. It relies on the plain sense of the Scriptures. The twenty-four hour calendar day, other than Sabbaths, is from daybreak to daybreak.

Most people are incorrectly informed that a Genesis day begins with evening, and then believing this as their paradigm, they proceed to read the text with the words "evening" and "morning" by redefining everything they see in the text to fit the paradigm.[30] For, as usual, the authority of teachers is regarded higher than what they see with their own eyes. But, as we shall see, this tradition is a fatal poison to understanding the Passover chronology,[31] Yeshua's death and resurrection, and many other scriptures. The majority of the Rabbis and the Bishops make Church and Synagogue drink this cup, because their fathers hated the conclusions implied by the truth, or rather the one below who deceived them hates where the truth leads.

Beginning the day at sunset became the norm only sometime after A.D. 70. After the destruction of the Temple, the chief religious reason for the daybreak to daybreak day was taken away. This was the sacrificial system, for which the twenty-four hour day was from first light until its return twenty-four hours later. After the destruction, the Jews no longer had a constant reminder of the daybreak twenty-four hour day via the daily offering, yet they continued to observe Sabbaths, so a sunset day became the norm for everything.

Further, the rabbinic Jews had good reason to begin ignoring the daybreak to daybreak twenty-four hour day after the Temple was destroyed, and to completely supplant it with the sunset day for all purposes, besides Sabbaths, and this was to obscure Yeshua's "three

---

[30] The usual redefinition equates "evening" with "night" and "morning" with day, but that is not what "evening" and "morning" mean.

[31] That is Exodus 12 and Deut. 16.

days and three nights." For this sign to the Jews used the daybreak calendar of the Temple service. Therefore, after A.D. 70 the suppression of the daybreak calendar served to obfuscate the sign of Jonah. Even if they did not think of this reason, unseen enemies caused them to forget about the Temple reckoning of a day.

So, in modern times, the Jewish day always begins with sunset. But, it would be a mistake to impose this view on the Scripture except tangentially to Sabbaths, and a few post-exilic passages in the context of exile. The occasional use of the sunset day comes into Scripture about the time of Esther, alongside the previous use of the daybreak day. From this time both methods were used until A.D. 70, after which the daybreak method fell into disuse. In order to understand historical passages in the Scripture, a historical understanding of how a day was reckoned must be used. It would be an anachronistic fallacy to universally impose a sunset day before A.D. 70.

There are two ways to reckon a twenty-four period of time in Scripture, one starting in the morning at daybreak, and the other starting at sunset. Sabbaths always began with the night before the day, and all other twenty-four hour days began and ended with daybreak. In particular, I will discuss the calendar day governing Temple offerings, which was daybreak to daybreak.

The existence of two ways of reckoning time has an obvious counterpart with the year. There are also two ways of reckoning a year. The natural year that governs the timing of the first month is reckoned from the spring *tequfah* (equinox). On the other hand, the Sabbath years are reckoned as starting in the fall of the year.[32] Think

[32] This is necessarily so, because early planting occurs between the fall and the spring, and harvest between the spring and the fall. This is required due to rain patterns; yet there are those who ignore this basic agricultural fact and attempt to give the seventh year a spring basis, which results in a prohibition of harvesting a legally planted crop and a prohibition of planting a crop that could be legally harvested. For instance, barley is planted before the spring, and then harvested after spring comes. If the Sabbath year begins in spring, then it would not be practical to plant barley in the preceding six months, since it could not be harvested. The Sabbath year itself is 12 or 13 months. As it would end in the spring, the next six months go to waste, since new barley will not be planted until fall. Therefore, the actual cessation of agriculture would be twenty-four months, which is unreasonable. On the other hand, starting the Sabbath year in the fall requires only a twelve month cessation of

of the spring as the daybreak of the year and the fall of the year as the setting of the year. So, there are two kinds of year. Likewise, there are two kinds of 24 hour time periods. The sunset cycle is for the Sabbaths, and the dawn day is for all other purposes. Now, I will show that the Genesis twenty-four hour day began at daybreak:

> Then the Almighty says: "Let there be light;" then there is light. Then the Almighty sees that the light is good; then the Almighty is making the light to be dividing from the darkness. Then the Almighty is calling the light day (and the darkness he calleth night). Then there is setting; then there is daybreak; | Day One. (Gen. 1:3-5).

The traditionalists will fight hard for their sunset day in the creation account, because they falsely believe that everything depends on it. Little do they know that understanding depends on the opposite, and that the sunset dogmatism was put in place to keep them from it.

Notice that in the middle of the text it says, "And the Almighty is calling the light day (and the darkness he calleth night)." The temporal locus (point of view) of this statement is during the day. The first verb phrase with object, "calling the light day," is in the Hebrew imperfect. The imperfect is used to indicate something that is incomplete, or that is still ongoing. Thus, it is used for present, present progressive, and future tense ideas. It is used to narrate sequences.

Every verb in the passage above is imperfect except "calleth" קָרָא before "night." The imperfect verbs are sequential, describing a sequence of events. But the phrase "(and the darkness he calleth night)" is in the perfect. The biblical Hebrew perfect should be thought of as an omni-temporal perfective aspect. The proof that it is not a past tense is its extensive use for future prophecy.* In this case, the reason for the perfect is to make this phrase background information (by way of contrast with the surrounding imperfect), and hence, I have put it in parenthesis.

The skeptic will have no difficulty with the Hebrew perfect indicating a background detail for "and to the darkness he calleth

---

agriculture, or 13 months with an Adar II.

*For example Isa. 9:6 is often translated "a child is born" (present tense), when technically it is a future perfect, "a child will have been born." The translators avoid "has been born" for obvious reasons and avoid "will have been born" because they do not understand the futuristic usage of the perfect. "And he will have called the darkness night" is the technical sense if we wish to avoid using the present tense 'calleth.'

night." This is because if he takes it as part of the sequence, then the order of statements, first day, and then night, contradicts his interpretation of a calendar day. So, he wants to concede that these words are just a gnomic[33] background detail or past tense. And indeed it is. That's why the Hebrew has it in the perfect, in the middle of a string of imperfects. So, in charting the sequence of events as the Hebrew mentions them, we will leave off numbering the parenthetical statement. However, it is worth noting that the order of reporting this detail is suggestive of the order, *day* and then *night*.

The immediate context does apply the label "night" to the primordial darkness ~~from which light was separated~~†, but because "and the darkness he calleth night" is a non-sequential background detail, the term "night" applies to all other nights, even the night that comes between the following "setting" and "daybreak" refrains. From the Genesis perspective, the primordial darkness is not part of any day. The first definition of "day" is the *light* (אוֹר), twelve hours, from dawn to dusk. The second definition of day "one day," (יוֹם אֶחָד) twenty-four hours, comes after the night which falls between "setting" and "daybreak." So, the night included in the second definition of day comes after the twelve-hour day, making twenty-four hours.

This raises a question. Were the primordial waters in vs. 2 made out of nothing in the six days of creation? Exodus 20:11 says, "For six days Yahweh made the heavens and the earth, the sea, and all which is in them." The Hebrew text omits the word "in" before the word "six," which leaves open the possibility that something was not made "in" the six days. The starting point was the "waters," and the word "made" (עָשָׂה) most often means "fashioned" or "constructed." It does not imply "created out of nothing." There is no doubt that Yahweh could create out of nothing in theory, but to impose it on the text is the speculation of philosophers. It is more likely that he started with waters pre-existing before the first day of creation. Also, we may note that the Hebrew word *bara* (בָּרָא) does not mean "created out of nothing," because the word is used in the creation of Adam, where the elements of the earth were mentioned as one of the components used

[33] "Gnomic" in grammar is a timeless truism or observation.

† I have since realized this sentence is incorrect. It says, "Then the Almighty is making a dividing between the light and between the darkness," which is a dividing in time, the day and night cycle. There was no mixture of light/darkness to separate in the primordial darkness. The first dawn was not a pulling of light out of darkness, but the creation of light *de novo*. So the darkness referred to is the night following the day, and not the primordial darkness. This in turn suggests that, "And the darkness he will have called night" refers to the darkness between setting and daybreak following the day.

in the creation of Adam. So when Yahweh *bara*-ed Adam, He started with something.

What this means is that we do not have to include the primordial darkness, and the waters in it, in the first day of creation. It leaves open the possibility that Yahweh created something before the six days, and the creative nature of the Almighty implies that he did create before the six days of this creation. The waters were probably derived from elsewhere, of which we are not told.

I will now re-quote the text. Only this time, each event is going to be numbered, skipping only the parenthetical statement, which is not meant to be taken in sequence. It is background information, which refers to nights in the day and night cycle.

> **1.** Then the Almighty says: "Let there be light;" [1.1]then there is light. [1.2]Then the Almighty sees that the light is good; **2.** then the Almighty is making the light to be dividing from the darkness. **3.** Then the Almighty is calling the light day (and the darkness he calleth night).* **4.** Then there is setting; **5.** then there is daybreak. | Day One. (Gen. 1:3-5).

Now, it is obvious that the placement of the words "Day One" are not sequential.† "Day one" does not come after the preceding sentence in time. It is just a summary of the preceding sequence, and so I have offset it with a line |, and have given it no number. It labels the preceding sequence. It gives it a name, "one day." So it is not numbered. The definition "one day" is really one calendar day, not to be confused with the literal definition of day in the preceding clause.[34] A calendar day is twenty-four hours and includes a night. A literal day is twelve hours and excludes the night. A literal day is dawn to dusk, and a calendar day includes a night. A calendar day is a complete cycle of day and night and brings us back to the start of the cycle.

The statements about the light *being,* and *being* good, need not be given separate numbers, as they happened nearly simultaneously with the calling forth of light. I have numbered 1.1 and 1.2 in the quoted passage, and placed these numbers in superscript, but I will simply

[34] "And the Almighty is calling the light "day," i.e. a literal definition of day from dawn to dusk.

*Or, "And the darkness he will have called night." The perfect is being viewed from the point of view of the indefinite future producing a gnomic sense. English uses the present tense for the same effect. See GNM pg. 391 for further explanation.

† Since writing this, it occurs to me that it may be regarded as sequential if the meaning is *one complete calendar day.* With dawn of the second day, one calendar day was completed. At that point in time, the elapsaed time added to one whole calendar day.

refer to #1.

The following chart, expressing the traditional assumption (that makes the primordial darkness the night of the first twenty-four hour day), shows the numbered events and their assumed order vs. their order in the text:

Figure 12: Genesis Day (Out Of Order)

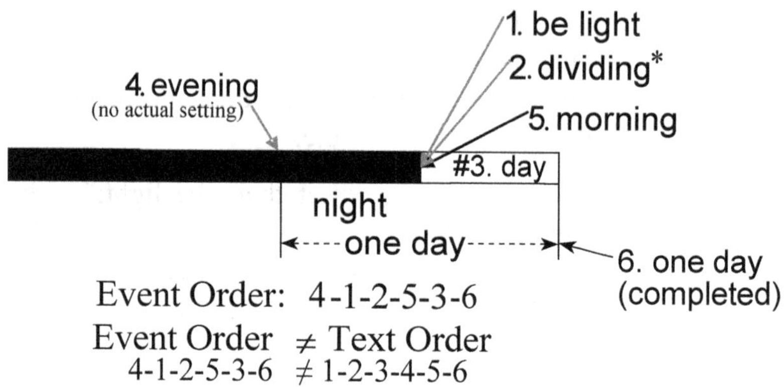

Observe that the assumed event order is almost totally out of order with the order reported in the text. I was generous with the label "evening."[35] The Hebrew word עֶרֶב really means "setting." But there is no light to set where "evening" is placed in the chart. Further, being most generous, the "evening" can only refer to half the night. It certainly does not mean after midnight, yet that appears to be required in the chart. Likewise, translating "morning" and taking it in the English sense of stretching to noon still leaves out half the day. The meaning of בֹּקֶר is "daybreak."[36]

But, the first twenty-four hour calendar day (as Genesis reports it) does not begin with the primordial darkness. Notice in the chart above that "evening" points to a time in the primordial darkness that is

---

[35] And also generous with the order 4-1-2-5-3. It could be worse: 4-1-5-2-3.

[36] BDB, pg. 133, "**morning** (NH id.; from *split, penetrate*, as the dawn . . . 1. *morning* (of point of time, time at which, never during which, Eng. *morning* = forenoon): a. of end of night b. implying the coming of dawn, and even daylight c. of coming of sunrise d. of beginning of day e. and *evening came and then morning* Gn[1.5.8.13.19.23.31], i.e. the day ended with evening, and the night with morning" [so noted: BDB has a daybreak to daybreak calendar day here]. Holladay, pg. 46, "**morning, daybreak**"

* For No. 2 to be in order, it has to be interpreted as separating light from a mixture of light and darkness. This is improper since light was created *de novo*. Properly it refers to division in time of day and night. Or as improper here 'night and day' and would go right after No. 4 where evening is initiated, where it would be out of order.

undefined. The word עֶרֶב *'ereb* means "setting,"[37] but there is no light to set. "Setting" requires a light to set. So we must reject the above chart, because it contradicts the order of the text, and the meaning of the word עֶרֶב.

Also, the traditional view requires the key phrase to be translated past tense, "And there was evening, and there was morning." But the verbs are imperfect.[38] The only way to justify the past tense is with the faulty "converted perfect" theory. This theory says that "waw" + "imperfect," "converts" the tense to "perfect." This theory is another deception, as was pointed out by Robert Young in the preface to his translation.[39] Young translates this key phrase, "and there is an evening, and there is a morning -- day one" (YLT). Now refer to the corrected chart in **Figure 13: Genesis Day (In Order)** below.

Everything comes out in the same order as in the text. The calendar day is labeled "one day" and this goes all the way back to the bringing forth of light. Notice the sequence of events. First the Almighty brings forth light. He sees that it is good. He makes day and night divide into cycles. Then he calls it "day." Then the Hebrew switches to *wə-* + perfect clause and says "and the darkness he

---

[37] Brown, Driver, Briggs, pg. 787, "(sun) **set, evening**." The root is compared to Assyrian, "enter, go in, sunset" and Arabic, "set," and Sabean, "withdraw," Ethiopic, "set." Also BDB, pg. 788, Strong 6150, "become evening; grow dark (?). As a participle substantive "west. . . setting place." A study of contexts will show that this term is always used at a time when light is receding. Gesenius' Lexicon defines the root word to mean "TO SET, as the sun." The KJV translates this word as "night" four times. But every one of these cases is an error (cf. Gen. 49:27; Lev. 6:20; Job 7:4, "and setting is measured, and I am full of tossings until twilight"; Psa. 30:5, "at setting weeping may lodge, but at daybreak joy")

[38] Typically present or future in BH and future in Mod. Hebrew.

[39] See Young's Literal Translation. See also *The Semantics of aspect and modality: evidence from English and biblical Hebrew*, Galia Hatav, 1997. I find the best approach is to mark *wa-* as "then" (sequence), and *wə-* as "and," "when," "now" etc. (coordinate or non-sequential), and the imperfect as the simple or progressive English present. The perfect is treated as a past perfect, present perfect, or future perfect, as the context indicates. The converted perfect idea is a result of a failure to understand the time frame in which the speaker or writer puts himself when using the perfect. The utterance is thought of as spoken at some time in the future and is looking back at events as if they were completed. The converted imperfect is a failure to understand, in the barbaric terms of English grammar, that a story narrative may be conducted in the present tense even though it is in the past. The writer is just writing as if present events where unfolding by relocating his temporal locus in the mind's eye.

calleth[*] night," referring to the nights following the days, that is the darkness between the settings and daybreaks. The *wə-* + perfect clause is non-sequential.

Figure 13: Genesis Day (In Order)

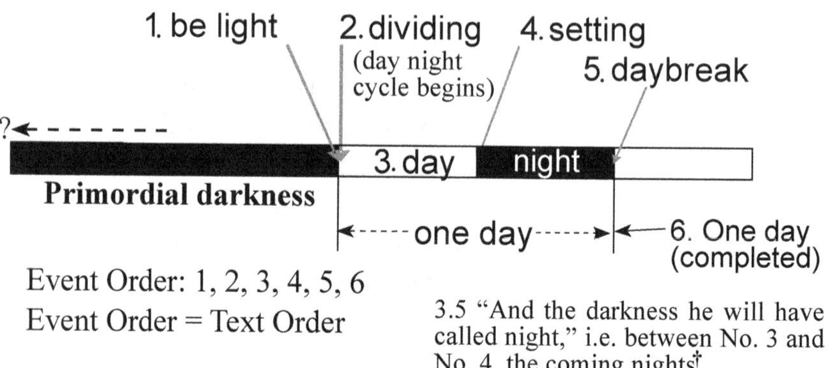

Then the text says, "Then there is setting; then there is daybreak." What comes at the end of the day? Setting (עֶרֶב). What comes after that? Night. And what comes at the end of night? Daybreak/morning. So the sequence is: 1. light is called forth, and 2. a temporal separation starts; 3. light is named day, 4. the light sets, 5. daybreak arrives again. So "one *calendar day*" here goes all the way back to the calling forth of light. The calendar day is from the calling forth of the light till daybreak when the light reappears. This is indicated by placing the whole sequence in one paragraph, and offsetting "| Day One" with a separator line.

The whole of the creation account continues this way. The Almighty creates during the days, "then there is setting, and then there is daybreak. | Day {1, 2, 3, 4, 5, 6}." He does not create during the nights delimited by setting and daybreak.

It should be noticed that the "setting" (עֶרֶב) always comes at the end of each literal day. Night logically follows, and daybreak (בֹּקֶר) ends the night. Then the day tally is given. The day tally thus covers everything from the preceding daybreak to the next daybreak, stating the calendar day at the point in time each calendar day is full.

For each day, the creative acts are placed between the daybreak (בֹּקֶר) and the next setting (עֶרֶב). The preceding day is not tallied

---

*Or "will have called." The Hebrew locates in the indefinite future and makes the assertion true for all previous time. The English locates in the present and makes the assertion true for all presents, and thus all time. English convention would put the narrative in the simple past and then say "(and the darkness he calls night)." † If we were to put the statement, "And the darkness he will have called night" onto the timeline, the statement would be made at no. 3.5 (between 3 and 4), and it would be a future perfect referring to the time between 4 and 5. But the statement is gnomic and refers to any time the Almighty would refer to night, Gen. 1:14; 8:22; Exo. 12:8.

until the next day is ready to start at daybreak (בֹקֶר).

It should also be noticed that since עֶרֶב means "setting," that light must be made *de novo* before there can be "setting." Thus, there is no "setting" somewhere out in the primordial darkness of Genesis vs. 2 that could qualify as a setting עֶרֶב.

What most people read into the text is a total misunderstanding. They are listening to tradition and not to what the Hebrew says. They read "setting" and "daybreak" to mean "nighttime" and "daytime," so they can equate nighttime plus daytime to "one day."[40] But "setting" עֶרֶב never means "night." In Hebrew usage it is only connected to the receding of the light; the maximum extent is from noon[41] to the end of twilight. Likewise the Hebrew word for "daybreak" (בֹקֶר has a maximum extent of the earliest dawn till full light.[42] When interpreted this way, with their maximum times, neither "setting" nor "daybreak" add up to a whole calendar day. These terms, in fact, mark two points in this context: 1. the disappearance of the light at setting, and 2. its reappearance at daybreak.

Genesis One first defines a literal day as "light," which would be from dawn to dusk (vs. 5a), a twelve hour day, and then it extends the definition into an enumerated twenty-four hour calendar day by adding setting and daybreak to the end of it (vs. 5b), resulting in a calendar day from daybreak to daybreak. "Setting" and "daybreak" demarcate the start and end of the following night.

Now that we have examined a small part of the scriptural evidence for a daybreak day, I will mention some famous scholars that have come to the same conclusions, both Jewish and Christian. Rabbi Samuel b. Meir (1080-1160), known as Rashbam,[43] taught a

---

[40] A further part of this misunderstanding is the unparsimonious use of the past tense, "And there *was* evening, and there *was* morning," so that the phrase can be read retroactively. See note 30 on page 43.

[41] In the phrase "between the settings," the first setting begins at noon with the decline of the sun.

[42] The Mishnah clearly tells us that the morning sacrifice was at first light, i.e. when full dawn was certain. This was the beginning of the day for sacrifices, according to the priests. Indeed, the "morning sacrifice" was often completed before sunrise. The definition of "setting" was broader than the definition of "morning." "Setting" included the whole afternoon.

[43] Ibn Ezra's attack in his [Hebrew] (Kerem Hemed V [Prague 1839], 115 ff.)

daybreak day. In modern times, Jacob Z. Lauterbach (Jewish) says the same.[44] Also C. F. Keil and Franz Delitzsch[45] so teach; also Edward J. Young and C.H. Leupold; also Umberto Cassuto;[46] also P.J. Heawood, Solomon Zeitlin[47] (Jewish), R. de Vaux, and Jacob Milgrom (Jewish); also G. Barrois and G. von Rad and H.R. Stroes. This list is a true "who's who" of scholars respected in both Jewish and Christian circles for their linguistic skill. And while there are other scholars who do not see the evidence in the creation account, they nevertheless allow for a daybreak to daybreak day. Once such scholar is Samuele Bacchiocchi, who advanced sunrise reckoning in his book on Yeshua's death and resurrection.

Jacob Milgrom (the JPS Commentary scholar) states:

> Most exegetes posit that Gen 1 proves the reverse, namely, that the day begins with evening (most recently Levinson, 1988: 123). Not so. God creates only during daylight; hence the first thing he creates is light. Each day ends with the refrain, "And there was evening and there was morning, day—." This can only mean that the day was completed at the end of the following night. When morning arrived, God began his creative labors; it was a new day (see Ibn Ezra and Rashbam on Gen 1:5, Hartom and Loewenstamm 1958). That the term *'ereb* "evening" refers to the evening that follows God's creative acts is proved by the refrain of the first day (Gen. 1:5). Obviously, there was no evening preceding the creation of light.[48]

In Genesis 1:14-18, day (or light) is mentioned before night (or

---

was directed not against R. Samuel b. Meir and his interpretation of Gen.1.5, but against those heretical sects who drew practical conclusions from this interpretation and observed the Sabbath from morning to morning. Cf. also Bornstein, op cit., 304.

[44] Rabbinical Essays by Jacob Z. Lauterbach, Hebrew Union College Press, 1951, pg. 446-451.

[45] Author of the famous Delitzsch Hebrew New Testament.

[46] cf *Theological Wordbook of the Old Testament*, Harris, Archer, Walke, vol. II, pg. 694. And Cassuto, *Commentary on Genesis*, Gen. 1:5.

[47] Author of numerous chronological articles in the *Journal of Biblical Literature* and *Jewish Quarterly Review* including one where he places the crucifixion in A.D. 34.

[48] *The Third Day Bible Code*, Kermit Zarley.

darkness) three times: 1. "to separate the day from the night," 2. "govern the day . . . govern the night," 3. "to govern the day and the night." 4. "to separate the light from the darkness." The order 'day' and then 'night,' by parallelism, confirms the order of the twenty-four hour day.

The natural human cycle begins at dawn and ends at night, usually 9 pm for hard working farmers, and later for less strenuous work. The natural time to start a day is in the morning when one wakes up. One day is naturally equated to one waking period.

Also, in the ancient near east, Egypt used a sunrise to sunrise day while in Mesopotamia they used a sunset to sunset day. Israel lived 210 years in Egypt, so it should not be surprising that they understood the calendar day as the Egyptians did. Coming out of Egypt, the common person would have begun the day at daybreak. The Passover legislation shows this to be the case, which we will get into later in this book.

So, we have seen some of the evidence that the day normally began at daybreak, but not Sabbaths, to be further explained shortly, and like the sabbatical year, were exceptional. As the sabbatical year began in the fall, so also the Sabbath begins in the middle of the natural period. The natural period is daybreak to daybreak, and the middle of it is sunset. So also the natural year is spring to spring, and the middle of it is fall, when the Sabbath year begins. The Sabbath is parallel to the concept of the Sabbath year. It is thus set apart and treated specially, different from the natural created cycle from daybreak to daybreak. The daybreak to daybreak day, day and then night, has been proved to be the natural and orderly sequence of the creation account.

There are other indicators that the day begins with daybreak, besides those mentioned already, and which are too minor to be brought up later in this book, and will be mentioned here. In the "night" (הַלַּ֫יְלָה) David's wife says, "tomorrow you are put to death" (1 Sam 19:11) (מָחָר אַתָּה מוּמָת). The word "tomorrow" ('מָ"חָר) means "day after" (יוֹם אַחַר). Evidently, "tomorrow" starts with the daybreak. Even more clear is Saul's encounter with the medium at Endor. He disguises himself and approaches her by night (1) (לָ֫יְלָה

Sam 28:8). Samuel identifies this night as “this day” (הַיּוֹם הַזֶּה) (vs. 18), and then prophesies “tomorrow you...will be with me” (מָחָר) (vs. 19).

THE SABBATH†

The Sabbath is a sign between the God of creation and His people, called Israel. The Sabbath is concrete evidence that Israel serves and worships Yahweh, the Almighty of Abraham, Isaac, and Jacob, and not some other god attempting to pretend to be the Most High. Satan sought godhood, and was cast out of heaven. He also tempts men to seek godhood. Satan is responsible for the false signs that mark his victims, which are the “days of Ba‘al.” He promotes a false sign of Jonah, resulting in solemnizing Sunday, and thus succeeds in separating Christians from the Almighty of Israel. He promotes solemnization of Friday via Islam, and this also separates Muslims from the God of creation. So it is necessary to know exactly when the Sabbath is, so that we may honor the Creator. It is also necessary to know exactly how the Sabbath is reckoned, to properly understand biblical chronology and the festival observances we are to obey.

The reader might be a bit worried, at this point, that I have weakened the basis for the Sabbath starting at sunset. The reader should not be so anxious. I will show that the Sabbath should be sanctified beginning with the setting. I will also show that having the normal day begin with daybreak serves to better define Sabbaths, which begin at sunset. However, there are some exegetes that define the Sabbath to begin in the morning. Jacob Z. Lauterbach and some contemporaries of Eben Ezra were some of these who departed from the usual reckoning of the Sabbath. We need to be aware also of groups that do the same, of which I do not approve. However, we must be very careful in the manner that they are answered, and not overlook the truth just so that we can easily win the argument. The answer depends on realizing the difference in two definitions of “day” and the difference between both of these meanings and the meaning of the word “Sabbath.”

Firstly, note that between Genesis chapter one and two there are

† Other elements of the timing argument are presented on pg. 290. Sometimes it may be best to challenge opponents of the evening to evening Sabbath to show where the Scripture opposes it. Then explain whatever texts they bring up reasonably.

two definitions of day. The first is a twelve hour[49] literal day, from dawn to dusk. The second is a calendar day of twenty-four hours from daybreak to daybreak (dawn to dawn). The twenty-four hour day is mentioned six times in chapter one, and the twelve hour day once, when it is defined.

When we come into Genesis chapter two, the seventh day is referring to a twelve hour day. For without the sequence of "day" and then "setting" and "daybreak," we are left to assume the first definition of "day" from Genesis 1:5a, which is dawn to dusk. The use of the words "seventh day" do not tell us which night to put with the day in order to make a twenty-four hour Sabbath. We cannot use the daybreak to daybreak calendar day from Gen. 1:5b because the text does not use the "setting" and "daybreak" formula in the case of the seventh day.

Finally, we need to note that the word for "Sabbath" is both a verb and a noun. The verb form is used in Genesis two. The verb means "to cease" and the noun means a "ceasing" or "cessation." The word "Sabbath" therefore, does not define any day at all. It only refers to the fact of "ceasing." It is for this reason that a whole year can be called a "Sabbath" or any day of the week can be called "Sabbath," as Yom Kippur, which occurs on the 10th day of the seventh month, is a "Sabbath." Likewise, the annual Passover Sabbath is a "ceasing," which occurs on the 15th of Nisan. Therefore, the word Sabbath does not have to agree, by definition, with a particular day. There is, however, a special association between the Sabbath and the seventh day.

So then we must ask, when did Yahweh cease from his work? When did he stop working? Genesis two says he "rested" from working "on the seventh day" (בַּיּוֹם הַשְּׁבִיעִי). It is clear that this was at least from dawn to dusk, or twelve-hours. The question is, which night goes with it to make a twenty-four hour Sabbath? It is clear from Genesis 1:31 that the night of the sixth twenty-four hour day goes with the seventh day to make the Sabbath.

The sixth day (Gen. 1:31) is indeed from daybreak to daybreak.

[49] I am using 12 hours here in the biblical sense, which is to divide the period between dawn and dusk into 12 parts. In terms of the modern hour of 60 minutes per hour and 60 seconds per minute the day length varies.

The last time marker mentioned is "daybreak" in Gen. 1:31. To understand the Sabbath, we merely have to understand when all the creating was finished. In Gen. 1:31, it says, "And the Almighty saw all that he had made, and behold, it was very good* Then there was setting; then there was daybreak: the sixth day." Notice that all the creating was done before the "setting" point, because he "saw all that he had made," and then it says there was "setting." So, nothing was created after sunset on the sixth day! It is, therefore, implicit that the Sabbath begins with the setting of the sixth day, and will continue to the setting of the seventh day:†

Figure 14: The Sixth Day and the Sabbath

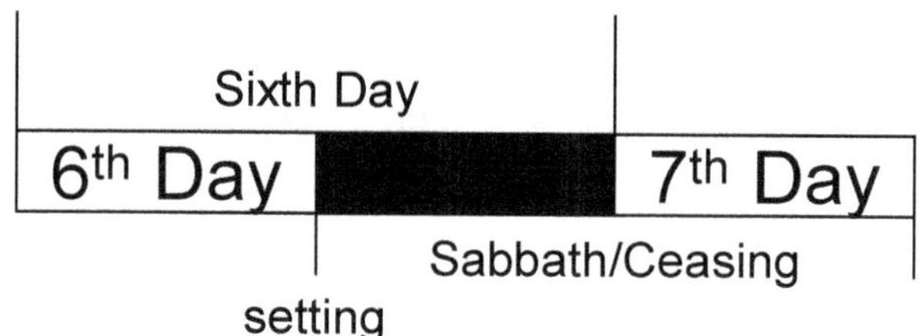

The point of the Sabbath is to remember creation and follow the example of the Creator. Creation was finished at setting on the sixth day. Before this point YHWH saw "all" (אֶת־כָּל) that he made. Nothing more can be made. For then it would not be true that he saw "all" he made. Therefore, he rested in the night following the sixth day, which is before the seventh day. But the text also says he rested "on the seventh day." So the Sabbath "ceasing" corresponds to the seventh day (daylight part). Also, however, the Sabbath "ceasing" corresponds to a twenty-four hour time cycle beginning at sunset.

The annual Sabbath, Yom Kippur, is explained in terms of a daybreak to daybreak day, or, that is, parts of two daybreak to daybreak days:

> A Sabbath of complete cessation it is for you. And you shall humble your souls in the <u>ninth</u> <u>of</u> <u>the</u> <u>month</u>; in the setting, from setting onward to setting you shall keep your Sabbath. (Lev. 23:32).

שַׁבַּת שַׁבָּתוֹן הוּא לָכֶם וְעִנִּיתֶם אֶת־

*very good. This is stated for the seventh and final time at sunset on the 6th day, signaling completion.

† This is not the best argument, because the objection may be made that he always rested at night. It is better to say that every example of Sabbathing which addresses the timing issue does so with the night before. Leaven is to cease at sunset on the Passover Sabbath. The Yom Kippur Sabbath begins with evening on the 9th day. Nehemiah closed the city gates as the sun was going down. The sick were brought to Messiah after sunset. It was still dark on the Resurrection Sabbath. Dawn broke 'into' that Sabbath (cf. Jn 20:1; Mt. 28:1). See also page 194 note.

נַפְשֹׁתֵיכֶם בְּתִשְׁעָה לַחֹדֶשׁ בָּעֶרֶב מֵעֶרֶב
עַד־עֶרֶב תִּשְׁבְּתוּ שַׁבַּתְּכֶם

On the tenth day of this seventh month is the day of atonement; it shall be a holy convocation for you, and you shall humble your souls and present an offering by fire to Yãhweh (Lev. 23:27).

If one understands the normal creation day, then Lev. 23:32 is plainly understood:

Figure 15: Daybreak Day & Reckoning of Yom Kippur

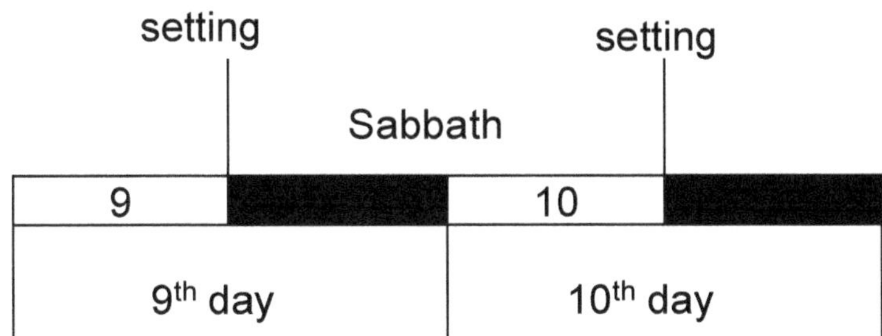

The ninth day is from daybreak to daybreak, and so also the tenth day. Setting on the ninth day to the next setting defines the Yom Kippur Sabbath as a night and a day. In vs. 27, the text says the "tenth day." The only way to reconcile these two texts is to know that the ninth and tenth days are daybreak to daybreak and that the Yom Kippur Sabbath uses parts of both of them. It uses the night part of the ninth day, and the day part of the tenth day. This allows one to "humble the soul of ye on the ninth day," as starting the fast before sunset will render one hungry by bedtime "on the ninth day" or most certainly by daybreak before the tenth day begins. If the night after the ninth day is not included in the ninth day, then one might have to begin the fast sometime before noon in order to be afflicted "on the ninth day." If one is using a sunset day for the underlying definition of the ninth day, then "on the ninth day" naturally leads to the following definition of Yom Kippur, taking the first setting as that at the start of the 9th day, and the second as the end of it:†

† 12 hour only and sunrise Sabbath advocates always argue that Yom Kippur is an "exception" to their rule, but this is an *ad hoc* argument so that they do not have to consider the evidence. Showing the normal day begins at dawn does not make it the rule for Sabbaths anymore than showing the normal year begins around the first month at the spring equinox proves Sabbath years should begin in the spring. The norm against which to declare Yom Kippur an exception is lacking, shown to be inadequate on the pattern of the Sabbath years. We may argue that the agricultural cycle, sowing and reaping makes Sabbath year timing plain, but since Sabbaths were less plain, we may suppose the Almighty decided to define the most important Sabbath of the year explicitly to serve as an example.

Figure 16: Ninth Day Using Sunset Standard

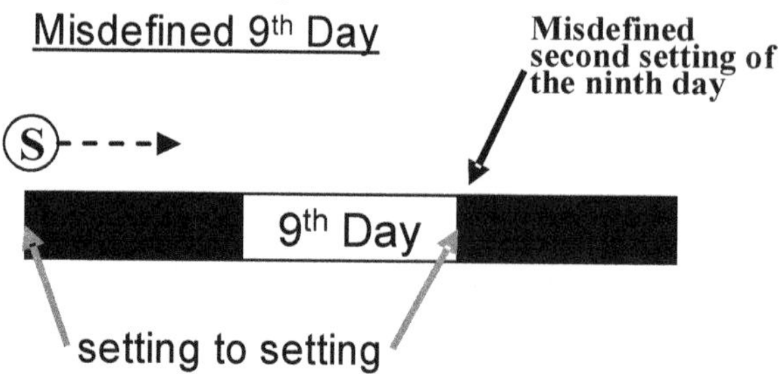

If the ninth day is miss-defined to begin the night before, then the day of atonement will be misplaced by twenty-four hours, since Lev. 23:27 says "on the tenth…ye shall afflict your souls." If the day always begins at sunset, then when the text says "You shall humble your souls on the ninth day of the month;" it is speaking of sunset at point **S** and the time following it (the dotted arrow) is "on the ninth day" (בְּתִשְׁעָה). If one takes sunset at the end of the ninth day, then it would not be true that the humbling would be "on the ninth day" as well as the tenth (vs. 27). The Rabbis, nevertheless, start Yom Kippur at the end of the 9th day, defining it as the 10th, and so have the difficulty that the commandment is not fulfilled for any significant part of the 9th day, unless they start fasting well before sunset. But they know that technically, before sunset does not count, for the commandment says "in the setting, from setting to setting you shall sabbath *the* sabbath of ye" If all the time between these settings is only defined as the 10th day, then they are not humbling their souls on the 9th day. (Jacob Z. Lauterbach shows the Talmudic Rabbis had difficulties here.[50]) The Rabbinic understanding creates a contra-

[50] (ibid) note: [54] The Rabbis of the Talmud who nowhere allude to and probably no longer knew of the earlier mode of reckoning the day felt the difficulty in the phrase: "Ye shall afflict your souls on the ninth day," and when commenting on it they say: "But are we to fast on the ninth day?" (Yoma 81b, R. H. 9a, b). A very sound objection indeed. For if the day had in Bible times been reckoned from evening to evening, as it was in Talmudic times, then the phrase: "In the ninth day of the month at evening" contains a contradiction in terms, for the evening is already part of the tenth day. Besides, the special injunction "from even unto even shall ye keep your Sabbath" would be entirely superfluous, for any other day also extends from evening to evening. The Talmudic explanation that the meaning of the

diction between vs. 27 and vs. 32. If the ninth day can only be counted from sunset to sunset, then the fast could only be on the ninth day, and not on the tenth day. If the natural day started at sunset, then the text would have simply said the tenth day.

The timing of the regular Sabbath, from the setting of the sixth day to the setting of the seventh day, is quite rightly related to the timing of Yom Kippur, even though the latter is an annual Sabbath. The regular Sabbath is called "שַׁבַּת שַׁבָּתוֹן," which is to say, "A cessation of complete ceasing" (Lev. 23:3). And so also Yom Kippur in Lev. 23:32: שַׁבַּת שַׁבָּתוֹן. Both sabbaths are defined to begin at the setting of the previous day.

Now, the fact that the "setting" and "daybreak" refrain is left off of the Sabbath day, and off of the seventh day in the creation account, demonstrates, with the context, that the Sabbath is not defined by the phrase "then there is setting; then there is daybreak," and neither the seventh day. However, this fact is mistreated by the Church to argue that the Sabbath, or seventh day, has no boundaries at all. The Church wishes us to believe that YHWH entered into a perpetual rest on the seventh day. This is called a spiritual rest and is divorced from the concept of physical rest.

This view was inherited from the Gnostic Christians, and its influence is still felt to this day. The Gnostics believed that matter was evil, and that the physical world was not spiritual. They also identified the God of Israel, because He created matter, with a demon they called the *demiurge*. The *demiurge* was related to the number seven, while they related their own god to the number eight. Therefore, the Gnostics rejected any commandment connected with the physical.

The Gnostic views of spirituality and the physical made a huge

---

passage: "Ye shall afflict your souls on the ninth day" is to say he who eats on the ninth day performs a Jewish religious duty and it is accounted to him as if he had fasted both on the ninth and tenth days (ibid., loc. cit.) is, of course, a homiletical subterfuge. The fact is that the Rabbis of the Talmud no longer knew or would not acknowledge that in ancient times there was another mode of reckoning the day, according to which the evening preceding the tenth day still belongs to the ninth day. In the case of the Day of Atonement, the Law especially prescribes that the fast be observed... covering part of the ninth and part of the tenth days."

impact on the more orthodox Gentile Church, which adopted the view of a continuous spiritual Sabbath. Their argument was that God could not really rest, or did not need to rest, and that therefore, the Sabbath, for God, was really an eternal spiritual rest that continued from the seventh day to an eternal eighth day, which, nevertheless, they fixed on Sunday. They also argued for the continuance (or transfer) of the seventh day to the eighth, because God did not create anything more after the seventh day.

The view that YHWH did not have a physical rest on the seventh day is unbiblical, and the view that we should not follow this physical example is also unbiblical. The following passage refutes both the idea that YHWH did not physically rest, and the idea that we should not follow his example in this physical rest:

> And Yahweh spoke to Moses, saying, "But as for you, speak to the sons of Israel, saying, 'You shall surely observe my Sabbaths; for this is a sign between me and you throughout your generations, that you may know that I am Yãhweh who sanctifies you. 'Therefore you are to observe the Sabbath, for it is holy to you. Everyone who profanes it shall surely be put to death; for whoever does any work on it, that person shall be cut off from among his people. 'For six days work may be done, but on the seventh day there is a Sabbath of complete rest, holy to Yãhweh; whoever does any work on the day of the Sabbath shall surely be put to death. 'So the sons of Israel shall observe the Sabbath, to celebrate the Sabbath throughout their generations as an enduring covenant.' "It is a sign between me and the sons of Israel to time immemorial; for in six days Yãhweh made heaven and earth, but on the seventh day he ceased from labor, and was refreshed."

The last words of Exodus 31:17 are "and was refreshed" (וַיִּנָּפַשׁ). The Hebrew means to "take a breath," or in colloquial English, "to take a breather." This proves that YHWH actually rested. Now, one may ask why YHWH needed a rest? The Almighty does not get tired, does he? That is the assumption people make, but it is incorrect.

Getting tired is not part of the fall. Tiring is part of the natural created order. But still, how does YHWH get tired so that he needs a "breather"? Who was it that was "refreshed"? John 1:3 says, "All things were made by him; and without him was not any thing made that was made." So, the one that was refreshed is the same one who walked in the garden with Adam. He is YHWH the son of YHWH. This is Messiah Yeshua before he was born of a woman. Even before He was born of woman he took a physical form that needed rest. He appeared as the "Messenger of YHWH." It was the Son that was "refreshed." "Was refreshed" implies that YHWH was tired, and then he rested, and then was tired no more. Thus it implies that the Sabbath was limited in time. It also implies that the need for rest occurs periodically.

Yeshua is the *Malakh Yahweh* (מַלְאַךְ יַהְוֶה). In Genesis 32:24-30 Jacob wrestled with *Elohim* (אֱלֹהִים), whom he declares that he saw "face to face" (פָּנִים אֶל פָּנִים), and the text calls *Elohim* "a man" (אִישׁ). This does not contradict Num. 23:19, because there it is said that "God is not a man that is made to be a liar" (לֹא אִישׁ אֵל וִיכַזֵּב). The use of the *waw* is explanatory.[51] In common English, "God is not a lying man." That does not keep Yahweh from taking the form of a man, though—so long as he does not exist as a lying man.

In the form of a man, Yahweh got tired and Jacob was winning the wrestling match:

> In the womb he took his brother by the heel, and in his vigor he prevailed with the Almighty (אֱלֹהִים). He wrestled with the Messenger (מַלְאָךְ) and prevailed; He wept and sought His favor. He found Him at Bethel and there he spoke with us, even Yahweh Almighty of the Armies, Yahweh his memorial (Hos. 12:3-5).

So, the one whom Jacob wrestled with was "Yahweh Almighty of Armies" (יַהְוֶה אֱלֹהֵי הַצְּבָאוֹת). Both the Rabbis and the Bishops of the Church introduced false teaching about the *Malakh Yahweh*. The Church denies it* since they do not like to associate the acts of the *Malakh Yahweh* with Yeshua, in particular it would mean that Yeshua

---

[51] Holladay, "5. explanatory: **and indeed**...**namely**," i.e. "God is not a man, namely one that lies . . ." (pg. 84).

* This generally began with Augustine. Before that this denial was confined to the gnostics and Rabbis.

was directly involved in giving the Torah and the commandments. The Church wants to limit this to just "New Testament" commandments. Further, Gnostic theology infected the Church, and the Gnostics hated the God of Israel, and blasphemed him as a *demiurge*. The Rabbis teach falsely, too. They do not want Yahweh to take a physical form, because this would allow Yeshua to be the same Almighty in physical form. But the Torah refutes Church Gnostics and the Rabbis alike. Yahweh took a form, even when creating man, in which he could get tired, and he rested and "was refreshed."

The Sabbath is set apart from setting to setting, just as Yom Kippur is similarly set apart. Yahweh saw "all" that he made before the setting of the sixth day. He was done with it, and the rest began at the setting, and lasted till the setting of the seventh day. There are other indicators that the Sabbath begins with the setting. Nehemiah orders the gates of Jerusalem shut before the Sabbath, "Then it was when the gates of Jerusalem were in shadow (צָלֲלוּ) before the Sabbath (לִפְנֵי הַשַּׁבָּת), then I said, 'then they should shut the doors.'" (Neh. 13:19). So clearly, Nehemiah made commerce impossible in the night before the day part of the Sabbath†, yet the merchants tried to camp outside the gates during the night, hoping the gates would be reopened at daybreak (vs. 20).

The Evangelist Mark also indicates the ending of the Sabbath, "And when evening had come, when the sun set (ὅτε ἔδυ ὁ ἥλιος), they were bringing to him all who were ill and those who were demon-possessed" (Mark 1:32). Since Sabbaths are twenty-four hours, and not twelve, the start would have to be at sunset on Friday night. Also, the annual Sabbath began at sundown (John 19:31; Mark 15:42),‡ which is why it was urgent to get Yeshua off the cross and in the grave before sunset. We also have that the "first of the Sabbaths" is identified as such "while still dark" (John 20:1, πρωΐ σκοτίας ἔτι οὔσης), and "at deep dawn" (Luke 24:1, ὄρθρου βαθέως), and "very early" (Mark 16:2, λίαν πρωΐ),[52] all which are clearly before sunrise,

[52] Mark is supposed to have added "when the sun had risen." Codex Bezae changed this to a present participle, "is rising" to soften the contradiction. Codex Bobiensis omits these words altogether. Eusebius strangely quotes the text as saying, "The sun was still risen," and this does not make any sense whatsoever in light of the other passages. In fact it makes the contradiction worse. Theodore Bezae therefore con-

† This would have been illegal if work was permitted Friday night. Because no law is to be made adding to the Torah. Some city merchants stayed open part of regular nights (cf. John 13:29). It would also be theft of business (cf. Exo. 20:15).

as well as Hosea 6:3, "כְּשַׁחַר נָכוֹן מוֹצָאוֹ";[53] "*at earliest dawn his going forth is fixed.*" Thus, the Sabbath cannot begin with sunrise, but must begin with the setting. While I will cover some of these points again later, the conclusion is that the Sabbath, and the "first of the Sabbaths" had to begin before sunrise on the Sabbath.

In the next section, I return to the subject of the daybreak twenty-four hour day used by the Temple, and will include here a quote by Jacob Milgrom:

> The sacrificial service at the Temple never changed; until the destruction of the Temple in CE 70, the day began in the morning."[54]

One will read in many modern exegetes the notion that the original Sabbath started at sunrise and was later switched to sunset, or that the original year was solar (associated with sunrise) and was later changed to lunar (associated with sunset). Such views either accept or imply a contradiction in the Scriptures as to the legal definitions of the holy days. I teach that there are no contradictions. There are two definitions of the year, the solar from "days to days," which is explained later, and the sacred, that starts with the new moon of the seventh month. There are two twenty-four hour reckonings. The first is natural from daybreak to daybreak, and the other is for the Sabbaths, and is from setting to setting. To imply otherwise is to posit disunity in the Scriptures, and reject *Elohim's Ruakh* in the oversight of His prophets.

---

jectured that the word "not" had dropped out of the text, so that the original reading was "the sun had still not risen" (ουκετι ἀνατείλαντος τοῦ ἡλίου). This solution seems altogether the most probable, and is what is adopted in *The Good News of Messiah*, where the reader will find a more detailed footnote. Clearly, the women arrived at the tomb on the first of the Sabbaths while it was still dark, at deep dawn, and very early, when the sun had not risen, and so clearly the Sabbath is being reckoned from the previous sunset.

[53] The Hebrew word שחר *shakhar* is derived from a root meaning "be black," and is used for the earliest hint of red in the east. It is a black to dark red color that marks the earliest dawn. See Baumgartner. Holladay summarizes, "(reddish)(light before) dawn." Friberg notes that the Greek ὄρθρου βαθέως means "literally *of depth of early morning*, i.e. *at the first streak of dawn, very early.*" Thus, to argue that these time notes are at sunrise or after sunrise is contradictory to the language used.

[54] J. Milgrom, Leviticus 23-27, 1968. Milgrom cites *Mishnah Yoma* 3:1 and *Hullin* 83a. Cited from Kermit Zarley, pg. 73, note 11, *The Third Day Bible Code*. ‡ The Jewish authorities began the Sabbath at sundown. See Josephus, War 4:582. The priests blew a trumpet "in the evening twilight (δείλης)... as giving notice to the people when they were to stop work."

Also "and he was refreshed" (Ex. 31:17) which as I have pointed out, literally means "took a breather," has the same root as is used in Gen. 2:7 in connection to Adam's becoming a living soul (לְנֶפֶשׁ חַיָּה). A standard objection to the Resurrection Sabbath of Yeshua is that "he rested in the grave." This objection has no merit considering Exodus 31:17, since taking the breath of life on the Sabbath is the Scriptural point of refreshment. So Yeshua, as YHWH, literally "took a breath" on the Resurrection Sabbath, and "was refreshed." A state of death does not entail restoration or rejuvenation, and therefore does not qualify as resting on the Shabbat. Yeshua awoke from the third night's sleep at dawn and was refreshed on the Shabbat.

The Temple (Sanctuary) Day

The first part of this chapter proved that the Genesis day was from daybreak to daybreak, and the last section showed that the Sabbath was reckoned from the setting to setting. There are many other evidences for a daybreak to daybreak day, but we will for now skip over those other worthy proofs to move on to the one that counts with respect to Messiah's death and resurrection. There are three sacrifices that correspond to Messiah's death and resurrection. These are 1. The Passover offering of Nisan 14; 2. The Passover offering of Nisan 15; and 3. The wave sheaf offering of Nisan 16.

The law that governs these three offerings, and all other mandatory offerings is:

> Now as for the flesh of the sacrifice of his thanksgiving peace offerings, it shall be eaten in the day of his offering; he shall not leave any of it until [בֹּקֶר] daybreak. (Lev. 7:15).

This applied to the Passover offering that was sacrificed on the 14th of Nisan about 3 p.m. The Scripture says:

> And you shall not leave any of it over until daybreak, but whatever is left of it until daybreak [בֹּקֶר], you shall have burned with fire.[55] (Ex. 12:10).

It also applies to the offering made on the 15th of Nisan:

---

[55] Since the offering was made in the afternoon, and eaten at night, it is clear that the calendar day is daybreak to daybreak.

> For seven days no leaven shall be seen with you in all your territory, and none of the flesh which you sacrifice in the setting of the first day shall remain all night until the daybreak [בֹּקֶר][56]. (Deut. 16:4).

While freewill offerings [נְדָבָה] or a vow offering [נֶדֶר] could be eaten the second day, and none on the third[57], what concerns us with the wave offering is how long the sacrificial portion of it lasted. The Scripture tells us how long the wave offering was allowed to burn on the altar:

> This is the instruction for the whole-ascending *sacrifice*: the whole-ascending [הָעֹלָה] *sacrifice* itself *shall remain* on the hearth on the altar all the night [כָּל־הַלַּיְלָה] until the morning [עַד־הַבֹּקֶר], and the fire on the altar is to be kept burning on it. (Lev. 6:9).

After the wave offering was waved before Yahweh, the Priest took a handful as a sacrificial portion and cast it onto the altar. Along with it was offered a male lamb:

> Now on the day when you wave the sheaf [הָעֹמֶר], you shall offer a male lamb one year old without defect for a whole-ascending [עֹלָה] sacrifice to Yãhweh. (Lev. 23:12).

So the lamb and the handful of the wave offering for Yahweh remained on the altar until the morning. The significance of this for Messiah's resurrection is explained here:

> But the Messenger of Yãhweh said to him, "Why do you ask my name, seeing it is Wonderful?[58]" So Manoah took the kid with the grain offering and offered it on the rock to Yãhweh, and He performed wonders while Manoah and his wife looked on. For it came about when the flame went up from the altar toward heaven, that the Messenger of Yãhweh ascended in the flame of the altar. When Manoah and his wife

---

[56] This offering was made "as enters the sun" (כְּבוֹא הַשֶּׁמֶשׁ) Deut. 16:6, so it too, was made just before sunset and eaten at night.

[57] Lev. 7:16.

[58] "Wonderful": a Messianic title for Yeshua. See Isa. 9:6 [5].

> saw this, they fell on their faces to the ground. Now the Messenger of Yãhweh appeared no more to Manoah or his wife. Then Manoah knew that he was the Messenger of Yãhweh. So Manoah said to his wife, "We shall surely die, for we have seen the Almĩghty." But his wife said to him, "If Yãhweh had desired to kill us, he would not have accepted a whole-ascending [עֹלָה] sacrifice and a grain offering [וּמִנְחָה] from our hands, nor would he have shown us all these things, nor would he have let us hear things like this at this time" (Judges 13:18-23).

We see that Yahweh ascended in the offering. And as long as the ascending offering of the lamb and its grain offering remains on the altar ascending to heaven, then Yahweh may ascend with the offering. Since the Priest removed the ashes of the offering off of the altar at daybreak, then that is the limit of the offering. So also, the Priests had until morning to eat the portion of the offering for the Priests.[59] Of course, they should finish before they went to bed, but there were always priests on duty to burn what remained, and a bit to eat might be left over for their duty shift, but they had to see to it that the uneaten portion was burned before the dawn.[60]

What is important here, is that the sacrifice of the Passover on the day part of the 14th of Nisan is not the end of the sacrificial meal, nor is the sacrifice on the day part of the 15th of Nisan the end of the sacrificial meal, and likewise with the wave offering. The waving of the offering and placing of it on the altar is only the beginning of the offering! These end with the morning, and no one is to eat them after daybreak.

So then, those who time the resurrection with the initial waving of the wave offering are mistaken.[61] The sacrifice is not over until

---

[59] The limit for eating the wave offering was the next daybreak because it was a non-votive peace offering, that is, it was not a voluntary offering. Only freewill offerings could be eaten on the second day (cf. Lev. 7:16).

[60] Later Rabbis set an arbitrary limit of midnight as a fence.

[61] And indeed, by all accounts of the Friday-Sunday error, the resurrection was over and done with before the wave offering would, according to the theory, occur later Sunday morning. Most expositors of that view place it about 9 a.m. Sunday morning.

daybreak, or close to it. Further, for the purposes of eating a sacrificial offering, the "same day" (בְּיוֹם קָרְבָּנוֹ)[62] counts as a day and a night. It is just as we saw with the Genesis day. The offerings are to burn "all the night" (Lev. 6:9).

Rashi (the most famous Jewish commentator) explains:

> "15. וּבְשַׂר זֶבַח תּוֹדַת שְׁלָמָיו — AND THE FLESH OF THE SACRIFICE OF HIS THANKS-GIVING PEACE-OFFERING—There are many inclusions here, לְרַבּוֹת חַטָּאת—to include the sin-offering, וְאָשָׁם—and the guilt-offering, וְאֵיל נָזִיר - and the ram of the *nazir*, וַחֲגִיגַת אַרְבָּעָה עָשָׂר — and the festival-offering of the fourteenth of Nissan, שֶׁיִּהְיוּ נֶאֱכָלִין — that they should be eaten לְיוֹם וָלַיְלָה — **for a day and a night**, **the day of the sacrifice and the night which follows**." (Lev. 7:15, Rashi, Sapirstein Edition, Rabbi Nosson Scherman, Rabbi Meir Zlotowitz, emphasis mine).

Rashi correctly explains here: לְיוֹם וָלַיְלָה "for a day and a night," "the day of the sacrifice and the night which follows."

Since Messiah was the Passover offering, the festive offering, and the wave offering, we are bound to use the same schedule for these offerings as for His death and resurrection! This means that each of the days that Yeshua suffered, died, and was in the grave must follow the sacrificial schedule: from daybreak to daybreak. See **Figure 17: Daybreak Day Temple Offerings**, below.

Yeshua was raised from the dead just* before dawn at the end of the third calendar day, which was the weekly Sabbath. This matches with the final ascending of the remnants of Yahweh's portion of the wave offering, which was put on the altar to burn with a lamb:

> But each in his own order: Mĕssiah, the first fruits, after that those who are Mĕssiah's at his coming. (1 Cor. 15:23).

Paul is showing that the first fruits offering symbolizes Messiah's resurrection. As the final smoke of the first-fruit offerings ascends,

---

[62] Literally, "on the day of offering of it." The word "offering" comes from a root meaning "to bring near" (Lev. 7:15). Thus, the daybreak limit defines "day" as calendar day from "daybreak to daybreak."

* Strictly speaking, 'before dawn' in the third night. He came out of the grave at the crack of dawn (Hos. 6:3).

(See also Gen. 32:24, the struggle with "death" until the going up of the early dawn. Also Joshua 6:15.)

Messiah is raised from the dead.

Figure 17: Daybreak Day Temple Offerings

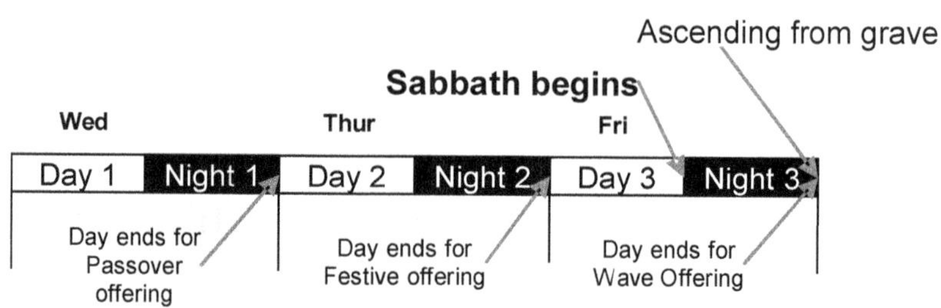

If the resurrection was on Sunday morning, then it was at such an early hour that it would completely miss occurring at the time of the wave offering. For we are told in John that Mary Magdalene mistook Yeshua for the gardener (who was strolling or meditating alone) because it was too dark to see (cf. John 20:1). The daily offering would be next, occurring at dawn*, and then the wave offering would be later. Most seem to think it was about 9 a.m. in the morning. Where then is the touted correspondence between the wave offering and the resurrection in the Sunday chronology?[63] It seems the timings do not coincide at all, and are only closer to the beginning of the offering rather than its finishing.

Or if the resurrection was in the afternoon or at sunset at the end of the Sabbath, then how does this correspond to the wave offering? It cannot, because the wave offering would be over with at sunrise on the Sabbath when calculated correctly on Nisan 16, or it would not have begun according to the incorrect calculations of the Karaites, which would put it on Nisan 18. Thus in the three false theories of the resurrection, Sabbath afternoon, Sabbath sunset, or Sunday morning, no part of the wave sheaf offering corresponds to the resurrection of Yeshua.

The wave offering ended at dawn when the priest removed the ashes off of the altar. Until then, its smoke ascended to the Almighty, and it was at dawn that Yeshua made his final exodus from the grave.

* This appears to be a point in the dawn late enough to be called 'day' when sunrise was just about to happen, after the resurrection, after Messiah's exit from the tomb, and after the women arrived at the tomb, according to Jewish sources.

63 To rescue themselves some try to make the type correspond to Yeshua's ascension to heaven, which might be later, but Paul makes it clear that the type corresponds to the resurrection of Messiah from the grave, and not his presentation in heaven. See GNM, John 20:17 text and notes.

First of the Sabbaths

I have covered the first objection that a day cannot be reckoned from daybreak to daybreak, and have shown that with regard to Temple offerings it is, and also Messiah's offering. Now I will turn to the mistranslation "first day of the week." Here is the corrected version:

> Now on the FIRST OF THE ŞABBAŧHS Miryam Ha-Magdalit, is herself coming early, darkness[64] still being, to the tomb, when she sees the stone having been getting removed from the tomb. (John 20:1, GNM)

Observe first that this phrase "first of the Sabbaths" *mia tōn sabbatōn* [Τῇ...μιᾷ τῶν σαββάτων ,†בְּאַחַת הַשַּׁבָּתוֹת] is the correct translation of the Greek in all four evangelists (Matthew 28:1; Mark 16:2; Luke 24:1; John 20:1, 19) and also in Acts 20:7 and 1 Cor. 16:2. This will be copiously illustrated and proved later in this chapter.* For now I will point out that the Greek grammar expands the phrase to "first *day* of the Sabbaths"[65], and that the ordinary meaning of "day of the Sabbaths" is "Sabbath day." So with the number = "first Sabbath day."

Second, even in Acts 20:7 and 1 Corinthians 16:2 the phrase occurs in a context right after Passover and with Shavuot (Pentecost) mentioned as following in the context. The reason for this is that the

---

[64] It should be noted that the words "while still dark" prevent a resurrection after sunrise, which is required by the Friday-Sunday view.

[65] "μιᾷ τῶν σαββάτων": *[one of-the Sabbaths].* The word "μιᾷ" *[one, first]* is feminine, and suggests to the Greek that the word "day" (also feminine) be supplied. Hence the phrase expands to "μιᾷ [ἡμέρᾳ] τῶν σαββάτων" *[one {day} of-the Sabbaths].* This expansion is exactly like the case of "first [day] of unleavened bread" = "πρώτῃ [ἡμέρᾳ] τῶν ἀζύμων" (Mt. 26:17). Again the word "day" *[ἡμέρᾳ]* is implied by the numeral. The days of unleavened bread are numbered one through seven, each day of unleavened bread coming in a series. The same grammar is evident in Josephus "τῇ δὲ δευτέρᾳ τῶν ἀζύμων ἡμέρᾳ" (Ant. 3:250). The formal inclusion of the word "day" (ἡμέρᾳ) is optional, but it is implied if not included. The sense is "the first day of unleavens," "the second day of unleavens," etc. Likewise the sense of "μιᾷ [ἡμέρᾳ] τῶν σαββάτων" is "first day of the Sabbaths," "second day of the Sabbaths" (δευτέρᾳ [ἡμέρᾳ] τῶν σαββάτων), and so on. The sense is confirmed by the fact that the phrase ἡμέρᾳ τῶν σαββάτων itself always means the "day of the Sabbaths," i.e. Sabbath day.

* There are more recent footnotes and endnotes in the *Good News of Messiah*, particularly an expanded study on pages 435-436 dealing with 'one to the Sabbath' in the Dead Sea Scrolls and the paradigm in Isaiah 66:23. † See page 324.

explanation of "first of the Sabbaths" via Leviticus 23:15 sets it in the context of the first Sabbath between Passover and Shavuot. So it is significant that the phrase is found in no other context in the scripture. To the original audience of Jews and non-Jews the meaning was plainly connected with Lev. 23:15 because the practice of counting Sabbaths after Passover was then current.[66] If "first of the Sabbaths" were an ordinary meaning for the first day of the week, then it begs the question why it is not used in some other context that is not between the Passover and Shavuot.

Third, note that the plural form of the word *sabbatōn* (σαββάτων, שַׁבָּתוֹת) is never insignificant in the New Testament. While the plural is indeed rendered in English translations in a singular sense, this is not how it appears in Greek.* The following story will illustrate, "The upcoming day of elections (the fourth of November), Josiah T. Butler hoped to be elected mayor. The vote was a tie. So the town scheduled a second day of elections the next week." The significance of the plural is that the days in question are used for an election periodically, whenever a new mayor is needed or whenever a runoff is needed. So, too, with "day of the Sabbaths." The seventh day is periodically used for resting. So the plural is really the collection of seventh days.

Fourth, note the inconsistency of rendering the same word "Sabbath" and then "week" in the same context, i.e. Mat. 28:1a and Mat. 28:1b; Mark 16:1 and Mark 16:2; Luke 23:56 and Luke 24:1; John 19:31 and 20:1. The texts are clearly viewing two Sabbaths, an annual Sabbath, Nisan 15, and a weekly Sabbath on Nisan 17 that year. In the Greek text, Hebrew original, or a Latin translation there would not be two different translations of the same word. There would only be "Sabbath" or "Sabbaths." The innovation of "week" is as late as the English translation of John Wycliffe.

Young's Literal Translation should dispel any doubt that "first of the Sabbaths" (Mat 28:1; Mark 16:2, 9; Luke 24:1; John 20:1, 19) is literal. There is no way that this respected Sunday Christian would

---

[66] It is hard to imagine that Yeshua or his fellow Jews did not obey the Torah on this point of counting the Sabbaths. However, as we shall see later, Lev. 23:15-16 was virtually blacked out for the Church starting in the second century.

* See Mark 3:2 in GNM. There may be one exception in Mat. 12:11, but it is still possible for an animal to fall into a pit on the Sabbaths if it happens on more than one Sabbath. More than one kind of Sabbath may be in view also.

have translated this phrase this way if it were not literal, or if the Greek were not compelling. Robert Young was also the author of *Young's Analytical Concordance*.

But this is backed up by J.P. Green, *A Literal Translation of the Bible* (Mat. 28:1; Mark 16:2; Luke 24:1; John 20:1, 19; Acts 20:7) and also J.P. Green's, *The Interlinear Greek-English New Testament* (Mat. 28:1; Mark 16:2; John 20:1, 19; Acts 20:7). Again, J.P. Green had no sympathy for a Sabbath resurrection. It is only his knowledge of Greek that compelled him to so render.

Some early Bibles:

Coverdale[67] Bible:

Mat. 28:1, "Upon the evening of the sabbath holy-day which dawneth the morrow of the first day of the Sabbaths"
Mark 16:2, "And yerly in the morninge upon a day of the Sabbaths"
Mark 16:9, "When Jesus was risen the first daye of the Sabboths"
Luke 24:1, "Upon one daye of the Sabboths very early" ["upon the first": *Cr[anmer]. B[isho]ps.*]
John 20:1, "Upon one daye of the sabboths came Mary" [and "The first daye of the sabboth, *Cr. Bps.*]
John 20:19, "one daye of the sabboths" [and "first daye of the sabboth, *Cr. Bps.*]
Acts 20:7, "One of the sabboth daies" [*Cr. Bps*; "On a saboth daye" *Tyndale*;]
1 Cor 16:1, "In some Saboth daye" (also Tyndale).

Latin:

Mat. 28:1, "Vespere autem sabbati quae lucescit in prima sabbati"
Mark 16:2, "Et valde mane, prima sabbatorum"
Mark 16:9, "Surgens autem mane, prima sabbati, apparuit primo"
Luke 24:1, "Prima autem sabbatorum, valde diluculo venerunt"
John 20:1, "Prima autem sabbatorum Maria Magdalene venit"
John 20:19, "Cum esset ergo sero die illa prima sabbatorum"
Acts 20:7, "In una autem sabbatorum cum convenissemus ad frangendum"
1 Cor. 16:2, "Per primam sabbati unusquisque vestrum apud se ponat"

Jubilee Bible 2000:

Mat 28:1, "as it began to dawn on the first of the sabbaths,"
Mark 16:2, "And very early in the morning the first of the sabbaths,"
Luke 24:1, "Now upon the first of the sabbaths,"
John 20:1, "The first of the sabbaths,"
John 20:19, "being the first of the sabbaths,"
Acts 20:7, "And the first of the sabbaths,"
1 Cor. 16:2, "Each first Sabbath let each one of you set aside...."

[67] The first complete English Bible was that of Miles Coverdale.

Anglo-Saxon, 995 A.D./ Gothic 360 A.D.[68]:

Mat. 28:1, "Soplice dam reste-dæges æfene, se de onlihte on dam forman reste-dæge, com seo Magdalenisce Maria, and seo order Maria... »
Mark 16:2: missing
Mark 16:9: "Da he aras on ærne morgen on rest-dæge. . ."/ "Usstandands pan in maurgin frumin sabbato . . ."
Luke 23:54, "and sæter-dæg onlyhte"
Luke 23:56, "and on sæter-dæg hig gestildon"
Luke 24:1, "On anum reste-dæge. . ."
John 20:1, "Witodlice on anum rest-dæge, seo Magdalenisce Maria com on mergen, aer hit leoht wære, . . ."
John 20:1, "Forsothe in the oon of the saboth, Mary Mawdeleyn cam erly, whanne derknessis weren . . ." (1389 A.D., John Wycliffe)
John 20:19, "on anon dæra reste-daga . . ."
John 20:19, "oon of the sabotis . . ." (1389 A.D., John Wycliffe)

Concordant Literal New Testament[69]:

Mat. 28:1, "At the lighting up into one of the Sabbaths"
Mark 16:2, "And, very early in the morning on one of the Sabbaths"
Mark 16:9, "Now, rising in the morning in the first sabbath"
Luke 24:1, "Now in the early depths of one of the Sabbaths"
John 20:1, "Now, on one of the Sabbaths"
John 20:19, "one of the Sabbaths"
Acts 20:7, "Now on one of the Sabbaths"
1 Cor 16:2, "On one of the Sabbaths"

The Anchor Bible Commentary on *Matthew*, by W.F. Albright and C.S. Mann, for Mat. 28:1 says:

The proliferation of recent studies on the calendar, both sectarian and orthodox, prompts us to add a note of caution here. The Greek phrase which we have translated *the first day of the week* and which is found in all four gospels (*mia sabbatou* or *mia tōn sabbatōn*) is not as obvious an indication of a particular "day" of a "week" as the English suggests. By

[68] *The Gospels Gothic, Anglo-Saxon, Wycliffe and Tyndale Versions*, Joseph Bosworth.
[69] Likewise the *Concordant Greek Text*, and ULTRALITERAL ENGLISH TRANSLATION IN THE SUBLINEAR. This author did not reinterpret Sunday to be the Sabbath. He believed the resurrection was on the Sabbath.

> the time we reach the *Didache* the plural *sabbata* certainly meant "week," and the enumeration of the days certainly makes Sunday the "first day" of the week; cf. *Didache* vi[70]. But the notes of time in our gospels concerning the resurrection, together with the confused chronology of Holy Week, make it hazardous to say with any confidence whether the evangelists wished us to understand Saturday or Sunday at this point (pg. 358).

The above concession comes from some well known scholars and a well known Bible commentary. Later in this book I will quote a number of Sunday Christians arguing that Sunday is the Sabbath on the basis of the phrase. The critics, therefore, will themselves be shown to witness against themselves.

THE SECOND-FIRST SABBATH

When the resurrection is not in view a number of commentaries tell us when the "first of the Sabbaths" occurs. They are commenting on the curious phrase "second first Sabbath"[71] in Luke 6:1. These disclosures are a case of the right hand of Church scholarship not knowing what the left hand is doing, or to put it another way, not realizing that explaining one thing correctly will bring down the whole house of cards in another department.

> What is the meaning of "the second First Sabbath?" A clue to its probable meaning is found in Leviticus 23:15-21, where directions for setting the date of Pentecost are given. Seven Sabbaths were to be counted from the Feast of First-fruits or Passover. Consequently, these came to be known as "First Sabbath," "Second Sabbath" etc., down to the seventh. And according to Julian Morgenstern, former President of Hebrew University, this practice continued in Galilee till the time of Christ or the Common Era. It is still observed by some groups

[70] VIII.1: δευτέρα σαββάτων καὶ πέμπτῃ·. The Didache is a case of an early Catholic document produced sometime between A.D. 135 and 165 (Harnack).
[71] σαββάτῳ δευτεροπρώτῳ.

in Palestine[72] today. Thus, there was an annual date known as "First Sabbath," just after Passover. And Luke, the careful historian, records that this event in the grain fields took place on the "second First Sabbath" of Jesus' ministry. This then pinpoints the occasion of the second Passover and indicates the completion of the first year of His public ministry.[73]

Cheney is exactly right about it being the second First Sabbath of Yeshua's ministry.* His public ministry lasted four years, from Passover of A.D. 30 to the Passover of A.D. 34. In the second year of His ministry, the 15th of Nisan fell Tuesday sunset to Wednesday sunset (March 27-28, *Julian*), and the "first of the Sabbaths" fell on March 30/31.[74] The four year ministry is confirmed in Luke 13:6-9.

Another scholar from 1866 remarks:

> The next interpretation supposes that the *second-first* Sabbath is the first Sabbath after the second day of the Passover; which second day of Passover was the day of the *wave-sheaf.* This day of the wave-sheaf was the ritual beginning of the harvest; previous to which it was unlawful for any Jew to pluck or eat parched corn or green ears. And as the day of the wave-sheaf was the *beginning* of the harvest, so the Pentecost was the great thanksgiving feast of the completed harvest or in-gathering; the *ending* of the harvest. Between the wave-sheaf and the Pentecost were *seven weeks*; that is, as *seven days* are a week of days, so these seven weeks were a *week of weeks*. Of course th[ese] seven weeks included seven Sabbaths. And the first of these Sabbaths being the first after the second day of the Passover, was called the *second-first*

---

[72] i.e. Israel. Before Israel became a state both Jews and non-Jews called themselves Palestinians. Morgenstern lived while the term was still used by Jews. Morgenstern is doubtless referring to the Karaites here whose counting came a week late in 5 out of 7 cases. The Karaites revived the old counting in the 9th century (suppressed since the early second century), but got it wrong, as they interpreted Lev. 23:11 incorrectly.

[73] pg. 230, Appendix IV, *The Life of Christ in Stereo*, Johnston M. Cheney, Ed. by Stanley A. Ellisen, Forward by Earl D. Radmacher, Western Conservative Baptist Seminary.

[74] See Appendix V: Yeshua's Ministry, page 471.

* But his rightness is either a coincidence or a double meaning by Luke in the spirit of the sense in Ezekiel 4 for the 390 years. Cheney appears to overlook the primary sense that it was the second of two first Sabbaths in Passover week.

> Sabbath . . .Although this is the most prevalent interpretation, it is not obvious how the second after the first would naturally be called the *second-first*.[75]

In the first quotation, Cheney explained one way it could be the “second First Sabbath.” And now let us go back to 1837:

> Theophylact §, who is followed by J. Scaliger ||, - Lightfoot ¶, and Whitby, makes the σαββατον δευτεροπωτον to be the first of the seven sabbaths between the passover and pentecost, or the first sabbath after the second day of unleavened bread, from when the fifty days to pentecost were computed; Lev. xxiii. 15, 16 However, though it be not quite free from uncertainty,* it seems to stand as fair in point of probability as any of them.[76]

And how does the Salkinson-Ginsburg Hebrew New Testament render Luke 6:1?

וַיְהִי בְּיוֹם הַשַּׁבָּת אַחֲרֵי תְנוּפַת הָעֹמֶר וַיֵּלֶךְ בִּשְׂדֵה
קָמָה וְתַלְמִידָיו קָטְפוּ מְלִילוֹת וַיִּכְתְּשׁוּן בִּידֵיהֶם וַיֹּאכֵלוּ

> And it was on the day of the Sabbath after being waved the Omer, and he went into the fields of grain, and His disciples plucked from the ears, and they rubbed them in their hands and they ate.

And indeed, the “second First Sabbath,” or simply “First Sabbath” is the first one after the waving of the sheaf, which is also the first Sabbath after the Passover. I will explain Lev. 23:11-16 more thoroughly in a chapter to come, and there will show why the Pharisees are correct, and how to dispense with the Sadducean arguments. For this section the following chart shows the “first of the Sabbaths” in relation to the resurrection:

* These scholars, while getting Luke 6:1 right, seem to contract a case of perfect tunnel vision when it comes to comparing this passage and its implications to the resurrection day passages, and the counting of Sabbaths.

[75] Quoted from page 71, Luke 6:1, *Commentary on the New Testament*, volume 2, edited by Daniel Denison Whedon (1866).

[76] Quoted from page 371-372, *Jewish antiquities: or, A course of lectures on the three first books of Godwin's Moses And Aaron*, David Jennings (1837).

Figure 18: The Annual Sabbath and the First of the Sabbaths

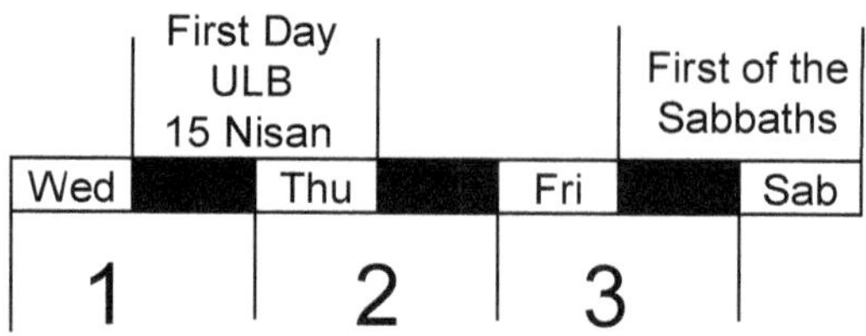

These authorities assume that the counting of the seven Sabbaths begins after the first day of unleavened bread, and not after the weekly Sabbath after Passover. They are thus siding with the Rabbis on when to start counting, but with the Karaites as to the counting of actual Sabbaths. This is correct, but the question is why did they generally get it correct? The reason why is that they did not assume Cheney's solution above, which requires a degree more sophistication, and it is really too much for Luke to assume on his readers. Granted, Cheney is technically correct, perhaps because the Holy Spirit put double sense on the number.[77] Rather, they regarded the first day of unleavened bread itself as the "First first-Sabbath" (cf. Lev. 23:11), and that the counting should commence after it, or they connected the word "second" with Nisan 16. That view which makes the "first first-Sabbath" the feast day is indeed the primary and correct explanation from the Scriptural point of view. The word "second" has reference to two Sabbaths, and not to the second day of the feast.

Therefore, the weekly Sabbath immediately after the first day of the feast should be the "second first Sabbath." It would not make sense to skip over this Sabbath (as the Karaites would), and postpone the "second first Sabbath" a whole week. For then, there would be an unnamed Sabbath.

The only way the Karaites or those who believe Sadducean doctrine could accommodate Luke 6:1 is to name either one of the preceding two Sabbaths the "first first-Sabbath," and both would be unacceptable to them. For the Sadducees' whole doctrine depended on denying that the first day of unleavened bread could be called "the Sabbath." Therefore, they would not call it such, with a number or

[77] Such has happened before with the 390 years of Ezekiel. One series counts the actual number of years of sin, and the other the time from the division of the kingdom to the date of the prophecy.

without. Nor would they allow referring to the weekly Sabbath after the first day of unleavened bread as the "first Sabbath" to have something from which to reckon a "second first Sabbath." For by mere fact of referring to it as the "first" they would be basing their explanation of Luke 6:1 on the validity of the Pharisees' counting!

Figure 19: AD 31, Pharisee and Karaite Counting Compared (Luke 6:1)

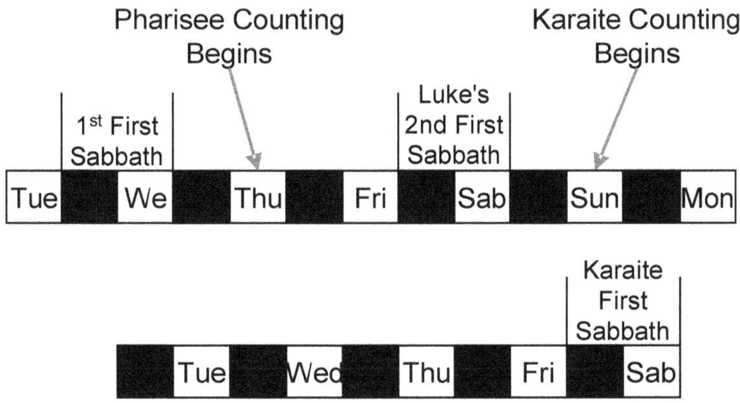

The consensus view that the "second first Sabbath" is the first weekly Sabbath after Passover, then, is correct. A Sadducean explanation would be hopelessly compromised in using the terminology of its opponents and thereby conceding their own doctrine to be incorrect! Furthermore, the "second first-Sabbath" finds Yeshua's disciples eating the new grain. This proves that the sheaf was already waved and that the Sadducean belief is doubly incorrect. See **Figure 19: AD 31, Pharisee and Karaite Counting Compared (Luke 6:1)** above.

> Epiphanius expressly says, 'our Lord's disciples did this, on the sabbath following the first day of unleavened bread,' *Whitby*.[78]

There is little explaining how the words "second first" could come accidentally into manuscripts and at the same time avoid the conclusion that a Pharisaic tradition existed to count Sabbaths. For

[78] *The Comprehensive Commentary on the Holy Bible*, vol 4; Luke 6:1, page. 452; A.D. 1834. Epiphanius ca. 400 A.D., "δευτερον σαββατον μετα το πρωτον" (cf. *Hæres*. i, 30, 51).

even if the word δευτεροπρώτῳ was inserted by some sectarian, it is admitted that said sectarian regarded the Sabbath after Passover as the "first Sabbath." And if this be admitted, then one is hard pressed to account for the tradition if indeed it was not genuine.

What would be gained by doing this when the Luke 6:1 scribe could simply cite the resurrection passages as evidence of the "first of the Sabbaths"? Therefore, such an insertion lacks a logical motive for willful tampering. It must therefore be regarded as genuine.

John Wesley:

> Luke 6:1 The first Sabbath - So the Jews reckoned their Sabbaths, from the passover to pentecost; the first, second, third, and so on, till the seventh Sabbath (after the second day.) This immediately preceded pentecost, which was the fiftieth day after the second day of unleavened bread. Mt. 12:1; Mr 2:23.[79]

It is hard to imagine how John Wesley blundered into stating the matter correctly on his own, rather, he probably repeated the tradition.

> The earliest opinion is that of Epiphanius (*Hæres.* i, 30, 51) followed by Isidore of Pelusium (iii., 110), Suidas (s.v. Σάββατον), Theophylact (*ad loc.*), and cited among later writers by Petavius (i, 61) and Scaliger (*Emend. Temp.* vi 551), viz. that the Sabbath thus indicated was that which immediately succeeded the Paschal festival; for (argue they) the "morrow after the Sabbath" [i.e. the Passover] (מִמָּחֳרַת הַשַּׁבָּת, i.e. ἀπὸ δεύτερος τοῦ Πασχα) is the point from which the law orders the seven weeks to be reckoned till Pentecost. Hence all the weeks and Sabbaths of that interval are designated from this name (ספירת־העומר, αριθμος του δραγματος, *numerus manipuli*, i.e. the number of the omer, or first-fruits presented as a wave-offering). This is the view embraced by most moderns, quoted in detail by Wolf (*Curæ in N.T.* i, 619 sq., where several arbitrary opinions by various authors are likewise enumerated); see also Köcher, (*Analect,* ad loc), Russ (*Harmon. Evangel.* p.

[79] Wesley's Notes.

639 sq.), Marsh (*Notes to Michaelis's Introd.* ii. 61).[80]

Note here that the counting of Sabbaths is regarded as compatible with counting the fifty days from the day after the Passover, which will be fully analyzed and explained later in this book.

What is most interesting is that these writers did not suspect that repeating this tradition or explaining it thus actually threatened their "first day of the week" tradition. It is a case of the right hand not knowing what the left is doing. They did not think to compare this tradition with the resurrection passages. In fact, the two discussions of those pointing out the "first of the Sabbaths" is literal, and the explanations of Luke 6:1, never seem to meet until the 20th century.

Regarding the authenticity of the passage, we have the following testimony to add to the critical Greek text:

> 'I once asked my teacher Gregory of Nazianzus' (the words are Jerome's in a letter to Nepotianus) 'to explain to me the meaning of S. Luke's expression σάββατον δευτεροπρώτον, — literally the "*second-first* sabbath." "I will tell you all about it in church," he replied. 'Eleganter lusit,' says Jerome. In other words Gregory of Nazianzus [A.D. 360] is found to have more understood the word than Jerome did [A.D. 370]. Ambrose of Milan [A.D. 370] attempts to explain the difficult expression, but with indifferent success. Ephiphanius of Cyprus [370] does the same; and so does Isidorus [A.D. 400], called 'Pelusiota' after the place of his residence in Lower Egypt. Ps.-Cæsarius also volunteers remarks on the word. [A.D. 400?] It is further explained in the Paschal Chronicle, and by Chrysostom [A.D. 370] at Antioch. We venture to assume that a word so attested must at least be entitled to *its place in the Gospel*. Such a body of first-rate positive fourth-century evidence coming from every part of ancient Christendom, added to the significant fact that δευτεροπρώτον is found in every codex extant except ℵ B L and half a dozen cursives of suspicious character, ought

[80] Cyclopaedia of Biblical, Theological, and Ecclesiastical Literature, Volume 9. John McClintock, James Strong, 498. "Second-first Sabbath."

surely to be regarded as decisive[81]. That an unintelligible word should have got *omitted* from a few copies, requires no explanation. But it would have been inexplicable indeed, that such a singular expression should have *established itself* universally, if it were actually spurious.[82]

If we suppose that δευτεροπρώτον was added to the MSS by an unauthorized source, then we have to consider that it would not be an ordinary adulteration of the text. The usual addition to the text actually makes sense to the reader who proofs the text and thereby goes undetected. However, a spurious addition that has no explanation would be quickly labeled spurious and crossed out of the offending manuscripts as soon as it was proof-read. Further, no one adds what would be unintelligible to a text on purpose. For it serves no end but to discredit the text copier. It is indeed to be supposed that the word δευτεροπρώτον was questioned by the first readers to be ignorant of its meaning, and that the invariable answer that came back from any scribe was that it was what he found in the exemplar copy.

The word δευτεροπρώτον was deleted from certain texts for two reasons. The first is that its explanation was lost and some scribes thought the text was better without it. The second is that the true explanation of the phrase is pro-Torah, as can be seen from the consensus of the explanations, and for this reason alone scholars would discriminate against the word.

Alfred Edersheim[83] writes:

St. Luke describes the Sabbath of this occurrence as 'the second-first'—an expression so peculiar that it cannot be

---

[81] UBS: omitting δευτεροπρώτον $\mathfrak{P}^{4}$ ℵ B L W f^{1} 33 1241 1365 l^{547} $it^{b,c,l,q,r1}$ $syr^{p,hmg,pal}$ $cop^{sa,bo}$eth Diatessaron^{a,i,n}. UBS: supporting manuscripts: A C D K X Δ Θ Π Ψ (f^{13} 28 1344* δευτερω πρωτω) 565 700 892 1009 1010 1071 1079 1195 1216 1230 1242 (1253 δευτερω πρωτον) 1344^{c} 1546 1646 2148 2174 *Byz* $it^{a,aur,d,f,ff2}$ vg syr^{h} goth arm geo Caesarius-Nazianzus Gregory-Nanzianzus Ambrose Epiphanius Jerome Isidore Paschal Chronicle Theophylact.

[82] The Quarterly Review, Vol. 152, William Gifford, pg. 349, July & October 1881. London.

[83] Well known famous Jewish-Christian expert in Rabbinical literature.

> regarded as an interpolation,[84] but as designedly chosen by the Evangelist to indicate something well understood in Palestine at the time...But we know that the fifty days between the Feast of Passover and that of Pentecost were counted from the presentation of the wave-omer on the Second Paschal Day, at the first, second, third day, &c. after the 'Omer.' Thus the 'second-first' Sabbath might be either 'the first Sabbath after the second day,' which was that of the presentation of the Omer, or else the second Sabbath after this the first day of reckoning, or 'Sephirah,' as it was called (ספירת העמר). To us the first of these dates seems most in accord with the manner in which St. Luke would describe to Gentile readers the Sabbath which was 'the first after the second,' or Sephirath-day.[85]

Edersheim's explanation of the word "second" is faulty here. It is granted that he identifies the "first Sabbath" as that first one after Passover. But he omits the explanation from Lev. 23:11-16, and explains "second" as second day of unleavened bread, which is to say the first Sabbath counted from the second day of unleavened bread. To explain the idiom this way is contrived and unnecessary. It would surely require a longer phrase for intelligibility! The real explanation here is being avoided by Edersheim, and that is that there are two "first Sabbaths," namely 1. the first day of the feast, and 2. the weekly Sabbath following it. Therefore "second first-Sabbath" clarifies which "first Sabbath" is meant when saying "first Sabbath." This was obviously a necessity which the passion narratives meet by first mentioning the annual Sabbath, and then following it with the "first of the Sabbaths," i.e. John 19:31 and 20:1; Luke 23:56 and 24:1; Mark 16:1 and 16:2. Only Matthew uses a different method, "And the later of the Sabbaths, at the dawning on the first of the Sabbaths . . ." which is just as effective in clarifying which one is meant. So in the passion narratives it is not necessary to say "second first of the Sabbaths."

---

[84] Edersheim's note 2, "The great majority of critics are agreed as to its authenticity."

[85] *The Life and Times of Jesus the Messiah*, Vol. 2, pg. 54, Alfred Edersheim.

Edersheim's second option, "second Sabbath after the first day of unleavened bread" wrongly inverts the order of the phrase. It is equally contrived and there is no way one can expect anyone to unambiguously understand such. The key to understanding the passage is the prior knowledge that the first weekly Sabbath after the passover is called the "first of the Sabbaths." This would be clear enough from the resurrection passages and Lev. 23:15, and an accompanying practice of counting seven Sabbaths. Further, the knowledge that the first day of the feast is called "the Sabbath" (cf. Lev. 23:11) is assumed, and this is understood as the "first Sabbath" of the feast. Therefore, the need for the clarification becomes clear. "Second first-Sabbath" clarified which of the two was meant.

HOW THE CHANGE WAS ACCOMPLISHED

Now I will give an historical accounting of how the "first of the Sabbaths" was changed to the "first day of the week," and of the conspiracy of Judaism and Christianity to change it.

אחת השבתות ←

I. The Evangelists translated Hebrew to Greek preserving "first of the Sabbaths" (μιᾷ τῶν σαββάτων).

II. Gnostics forsake the Sabbath and reject Torah.

III. Gnostics introduce Friday-Sunday and symbolic interpretation of a new perpetual Sabbath (calling it the eighth day), and meld it with Mithraism, marking Sunday as their day of worship.

IV. The faithful Jews in Yeshua and converts from the nations continue to understand "first of the Sabbaths" as the first Sabbath after Passover, but are outnumbered by apostate Gnostic Gentiles on one side who refuse to acknowledge the Resurrection Sabbath in favor of Sunday, and unbelieving Rabbinic Jews who realize that it is in their best interests to leave these errors uncorrected and indeed to do what they can to encourage them.

V. Aquila opens the Rabbinic campaign of subversion by altering Lev. 23:11-16 in the LXX and introducing a few Psalm titles† to the same effect; he introduces "week" as the gloss in the text and in the Targum Onkelos.‡ [Rabbi Halaphta popularizes "one to the Sabbath" in Seder Olam. The Rabbis also introduce "one to seven" into Aramaic in such a way as it is possible to confuse "seven" with Sabbath or "week."]*

VI. The proto-Catholic backlash against the Gnostic excess begins; they reintroduce the "Old Testament" and adopt Aquila's translation in the

---

* See GNM, pp. 435-436. The Rabbis were in favor of Christians misunderstanding their idiom and thus departing from Torah observance. The circumstantial evidence suggests they were encouraging it as much as they were denying Messianic texts.

†See page 151 "Psalm Titles." ‡ שבועתא, שבע שבוען

case of Lev. 23:11-16 as the key to interpreting Sabbath as 'week."

VII. The Syriac Gospels are translated with a later Aramaic innovation,* but Greek and Latin continue unaltered, and non-Semitic translations from Greek and Latin keep "first of the Sabbaths" intact. Christians rely on tradition to interpret the text as "first day of the week."

VIII. John Wycliffe is the first to introduce the translation "first day of the week," putting what was heretofore an interpretation of the text into the actual text, ruling out any other interpretation.

IX. William Tyndale introduces the translation "one day *after* the Sabbath" as an attempted explanation of the original. Coverdale rejects Wycliffe and Tyndale's innovation and translates, "first of the Sabbaths" according to the Latin and Greek, preferring to rely on the scholastic understanding "first day of the week," without actually putting it in the text. Sunday is widely regarded as the "Sabbath" on the basis of the resurrection passages and Coverdale does not want to undermine this belief. Meanwhile, the Geneva Bible sides with Wycliffe on the question.

X. The "first day of the week" wins out with the King James translators due to the fact that the Royalist party rejected the strict Sabbatarian view of Sunday.

XI. Whenever the translation "first day of the week" is questioned, invariably by those honoring the seventh day Sabbath, or by chronologists seeing the problem with it, the Rabbinic or Syriac sources are cited as proof of the interpretation.

Now, the Gnostic Christians were faced with the obvious Greek text "first of the Sabbaths." It is plain that their leaders allegorized it for their flocks in diverse ways without respect for the Torah and Prophets, which they rejected as valid revelation. The resurrection day was to be the "first of the new perpetual Sabbath"—on the day of the sun. This fit in with their attraction to Mithraism and the new "light." The Sabbath was made into an eschatological rest on the eighth day, one step beyond the old, a new age of enlightenment by the light that came down from beyond the seventh sphere. It was the first day beyond the seventh, or the eighth day as they liked to call it. Without the biblical text to guide them on "first of the Sabbaths," they were free to play with the phrase as they liked. They certainly took "first [day]" literally, but they were inclined to ignore the rest of the phrase or take it as "first day *after* the Sabbath" if really pressed—an explanation to be picked up later by translators such as Tyndale.

*The pious idiom 'one unto the Sabbath' was a Jewish usage in counting the days of the week dating back to the DSS. Since the NT Greek would not reproduce this, later Jewish sources introduced בחד בשבא into Aramaic such that non-Jews were easily deceived into confusing שבא with שבע or שבת, and as a result supposing that Jews used the word Sabbath to mean 'week.' Usage suggests that to Jews שבא only means 'seven,' but non-Jews supposed it to be a legitimate translation of שבת with the meaning of שבע.

However, the need rarely arose since most did not have access to the manuscripts and their understanding was based on what they heard preached. And the preaching of the Gnostics simply substituted "eighth day" for Sabbath, and equated the eighth day to the first day, leaving the literal sense of the text aside.*

They also rejected the notion of literal rest and interpreted it as their own version of a spiritual "rest." Their reasoning was to read anything into the context that suited their desire to abandon Torah, and to justify it with any symbolism possible. If this sounds much like modern Christianity, this is because modern Christianity absorbed Gnosticism.

The Gnostic practice of allegorizing things out of context was not just applied to the Sabbath. They applied it to everything, remaking a once Torah observant faith into their own idolatrous version. This tendency toward an uncontrolled use of symbolism is not dead. The Gnostic spirit continues. One author from the 19th century expounds on the Gnostic eighth day in the same spirit:

> The phrase, "The first of the Sabbaths," may be readily understood as meaning *the first of the Sabbaths* under the New Covenant order, that order which was fully established by the death and resurrection of the Christ. Indeed, it seems quite impossible for the phrase to have any other meaning.
>
> That Young's translation of the foregoing texts is the exactly correct one, may be seen by consulting the same texts in the Greek as found in Wilson's or Griesbach's *Emphatic Diaglott*, or in any Greek New Testament, for there we find that the Greek word *Sabbaton* is the same as the English word Sabbath, and that it occurs as in the texts quoted from Young's Translation as before shown.[86]

And another:

> At the end of Sabbaths, in the beginning of the first of the

[86] pg. 135-136, *The Christian Sabbath, or Weekly Rest Day*, Columbus Scott, 1891, pub. Reorganized Church Jesus Christ of Latter Day Saints. The Mormons are about as Gnostic as modern Gnosticism gets.

* Gnostic teachers claimed to know the hidden meaning of texts, passing themselves off as having a deep connection to God giving themselves spiritual insight. But in reality they were speculating on the meaning of the texts to gain followers. The novice presumes they "know," but when they are pressed for a *two witness* proof of their speculations one is left staring into an abyss of subjective knowledge based on

(continued next page)

Sabbaths, etc....and we should see that *at the* END *of the seventh-day Sabbaths* (or at the end of the Jewish Sabbath—which was given to the "*children of Israel*" to be a "*sign*" unto *them* "throughout their generations") THERE *would be* the BEGINNING of the LORD JESUS CHRIST'S DAY, or SABBATH. Or in other words, where one series of days *ended*, there another series of days *began*.[87]

Lewis Sperry Chafer:

There is significance in the fact that the Greek word for week is *sabbaton*,[88] which also means Sabbath. Thus in Matthew 28:1, referring to the day of CHRIST's resurrection, we have the possible literal reading: "At the end of the sabbath[89] as it began to dawn on the first day of sabbaths" (Cf Mark 16:2, 9; Luke 24:1; John 20:1, 19; Acts 13:14; 16:13).

At least three expositions of this passage are possible.

1. That there is no significance in the fact that the resurrection day is called Sabbath since it is the same Greek word for week...

2. That the use of the word *sabbaton* in connection with the day of resurrection warrants the use of the phrase, Christian Sabbath, ...

3. That the resurrection morning was the first day of all the days which were to enter into the age of grace, and that age, so far as a Sabbath is concerned, is a period in which the believer has entered into rest. Under this interpretation, the resurrection day was the first day of Sabbaths, which series was to include every succeeding day until the Lord returns.[90]

---

[87] pg. 46. *The First-Day Sabbath: clearly proved*, T.M. Preble, 1867. Preble's 471 page book was meant to dispute the Seventh Day Adventists, particularly J.N. Andrews History of the Sabbath.
[88] The Greek word for week is ἑβδομάδος.
[89] Greek: "On the later of the Sabbaths."
[90] Grace: An Exposition of God's Marvelous Gift, Chafer, pg. 216-117,

presumptuous authority. Their method is no different from divination using oracle bones and the wiser of the shamans who know they are injecting their own ideas. Modern religious movements are not exempt from these unscientific deceptions passed off as "special knowlege" and "special sciences."

And in the Presbyterian Quarterly, by a Sunday Sabbath proponent:

> There are just eight passages where this English phrase, "first day of the week," appears, namely...[Mat. 28:1; Mark 16:2, 9; Luke 24:1; John 20:1, 19; Acts 20:7; 1Cor. 16:2] A careful examination of these passages leads us to wonder how the whole Christian world have consented to such a construction. As to the force of interpretation, all these passages may be regarded as but a *single case*, since the Greek expression, whether found in the New Testament, or cited by the Fathers, with some slight grammatical variations, is substantially the same in all; and its literal English signification is, "On one of the Sabbaths." That we are not presuming, without a precedent, to array our individual opinion, as to this rendering against that of the entire conclave of Christian scholars, let us here observe that no less a man than John Calvin,[91] in his notes on 1 Cor. xvi: 2, gives it this identical construction—"On one of the Sabbaths!"
>
> Where, then, is the authority in any other Greek usage [prior to A.D. 100] for making the phrase mean "first day of the week?" Out of the hundreds of places where this word σάββατον occurs, both in the Scripture Greek, and all other Greek, so far as we can find, there is not one single instance where the word in any its forms has, or can have, the signification of ἑβδομάς. We are aware of the almost universal consent to give the word in these eight or nine passages of the New Testament the meaning of *week*. Scholars seems to have blindly followed one another generation after generation
>
> What then follows? Why, simply that Christ rose on a day which is called in the Scriptures *a Sabbath* ; that on that day he

---

Kregal Classics (1995).

[91] Of course a Presbyterian must exalt Calvin. But the truth is that he subverted the Reformation and was a murderer. Credit for the Reformation goes to the fact that the Scripture was freed from Catholic suppression so that the common man could read it, and not the teachings of John Calvin.

> first met with his disciples; that "eight days after," which is confessedly the idiom for a *week*, . . . If Christ rose on a Sabbath, as we have shown, and on the same day met with his disciples, and then "eight days" after they met again, the second meeting must have been likewise on the Sabbath.[92]

If these arguments are so temping to 19th century writers, and even some 20th century writers[93] when all the popular translations say "first day of the week," we can only imagine how fast the Gnostics would have capitalized on similar symbolical exegesis as the easy way to re-explain, "first of the Sabbaths" and put down the Sabbath of the Scriptures.

The Gnostic majority in the Church in the late first century introduced the interpretation that the "first of the Sabbaths" was the first of the new sabbatisms of the new age, summarized as the eighth day or by reinterpreting the Creation Sabbath as perpetually continuing beyond the seventh day. The Jewish Sabbath was relegated to the old dispensation. The Gnostic interpretation at first was merely a symbolical abuse of the context. It required no grammar tricks or lexical perversions. It just required ignorance of Torah and a tendency to reinterpret or redefine everything in the New Testament according to their secret knowledge of symbolism.

Two approaches would have worked. The "first of the Sabbath" was the first sabbatism of the new age. This was a new age of spiritual rest (a.k.a. enlightenment), symbolized in the eighth day, as one sphere beyond Saturn. This moved them forward one day, and allowed them to exploit the chronological ignorance of the Gentiles. The other interpretation allowed them to go back to the first day, and refer it to the first day of creation of light.

Now there is no doubt that such interpretation is wildly out of

---

[92] "Art. V.—THE SABBATH QUESTION." Rev. Byron Sunderland, D.D, pg. 88-107, THE PRESBYTERIAN QUARTERLY AND PRINCETON REVIEW, 1877, vol. vi. The author defends "one of the Sabbaths," but sadly, like all the others he applies it to Sunday. Yet, we shall see that this testimony is important. For it shows that once anyone begins to be exposed to the evidence the lies begin to crumble.

[93] Among them is numbered the infamous Harold Camping, hero of the failed May 21st, 2011 prediction of the Rapture. Camping gave essentially the same argument for "first of the Sabbaths."

context. But when ignorance is universal, any interpretation can become the norm. It breaks with all precedent and is completely non grammatical and unhistorical. Yet it is the heart and soul of the ubiquitous allegorical interpretation of the first three centuries. Organized Christianity did not conquer the mystical and magical world view of the pagans. Rather the pagans organized the Christians to their world view.[94] The Gnostic movement was the easiest response paganism could make to the irrefutable truth of the Scripture. They did not try to refute it based on context or the principle of Scripture interpreting Scripture. Rather they reduced everything to their own symbolic relativism, and then dismissed the Torah and Prophets entirely as a valid guide to interpretation.[95] Once that is done, it would be simple for them to claim that "first of the Sabbaths" means the first Sabbath of the new age, the eighth day beyond the seventh, or the new spiritual sabbatism *after* the old Sabbath.

However the Jewish faithful in Messiah retained the Torah, and the non-Jews joined to them still looked to them for guidance, though the forces of anti-Semitism were trying to sow division between the non-Jewish believer and the Jewish. When the Torah is consulted, the explanation is made plain in Leviticus 23:15:

> You shall also count for yourselves in the time to come after the ceasing [הַשַּׁבָּת], from the day when you brought in the sheaf of the wave offering; there shall be seven complete Sabbaths [שֶׁבַע שַׁבָּתוֹת תְּמִימֹת].

The day of the "ceasing" or "cessation" is the 15th of Nisan. Just after sunset on this day, the Passover Seder commenced. It was an annual "Sabbath" (John 19:31; Mark 16:1; Luke 23:54, 56a). John calls it the "great Sabbath."[96]

---

[94] This was not without purpose however. God's word, though misinterpreted was being spread among the nations. At some point in time, the Word of God would slowly infuse the nations until they had a more scientific worldview. In the end of days, then, God will remove the deceptions and harvest the crop.

[95] Marcion was chiefly responsible for this.

[96] The meaning of "Great Sabbath" was later redefined by the Roman Catholic Church and Judaism to avoid connecting Torah with Messiah. Judaism chose the Sabbath before Passover to be the "Great Sabbath" and

*This explanation is now superseded by that given in GNM. "I fast twice *with* the Sabbath," where a long footnote explains the genitive of comparison. See note 99 below.

After the 15th of Nisan, or to be more precise, "in the time to come after" it, seven Sabbaths [שֶׁבַע שַׁבָּתוֹת] are counted. They are enumerated in sequence, "first of the Sabbaths," "second of the Sabbaths," and so on until the "seventh of the Sabbaths" is counted.

The Hebrew for "first of the Sabbaths" is: בְּאַחַת הַשַּׁבָּתוֹת†. The skeptic cannot deny that the word σαββάτων from Greek means "sabbaths." Because that is exactly what it means everywhere else except in the eight texts strategically mistranslated starting with Syriac[97] (Mat. 28:1; Mark 16:2, 9; Luke 18:12; Luke 24:1; John 20:1, 19; Acts 20:7; 1 Cor. 16:2). No contemporary source[98] requires the meaning "week" for this Greek word. "Week" has certainly been forced into these texts, but good sense does not require it. They all make perfect sense without it, and indeed better chronological sense.

So then, what do we say about Luke 18:12, lest the critic should urge on us the meaning "week" from it?:

> * I fast twice *on* the Sabbath.[99]

This text is supposed to show that "Sabbath" means "week."[100] But, there was a minority of Judaism that fasted on the Sabbath. These would eat Friday before sunset, and then skip breakfast and the noon meal on Sabbath. They would eat after sunset on the Sabbath. So they are really skipping two meals, but fasting the whole Sabbath. There were probably other Jews who took only the noon meal on

---

the Church made the "Great Sabbath" the day after good Friday, arguing that what makes it "great" is that a feast day fell upon the weekly Sabbath. Both traditions are nonsensical.

[97] The Syriac texts were the first to actually impose the reinterpretation onto the texts. The Syriac translates "one into the Sabbath." These translations originate between the middle of the second century and the beginning of the third.

[98] One will search Josephus, Philo, and other contemporary Greek literature in vain for σάββατον meaning "week."

[99] Greek: νηστεύω δὶς τοῦ σαββάτου. Latin: *ieiuno bis in sabbato*. Hebrew: אֲנִי צָם פַּעֲמַיִם בַּשַּׁבָּת, or better: אֲנִי צָם פַּעֲמַיִם מִשַּׁבָּת = ...twice *more than* the S.

[100] The argument goes that there was a tradition that some Pharisees fasted on Mondays and Thursdays, and that Luke 18:12 must therefore be referring to these fasts. That is of course an unwarranted assumption that depends on assuming the meaning "week" is valid to start with. Linguistic conservatism requires us to make sense of the passage without it if at all possible.

† See page 324.

sabbath, having an early Friday dinner and late Saturday supper. This was a more common piety, and was done to study. Those who fasted "twice" (i.e. skipped all meals) were the ultra-pious and for them it was a mark of self-righteousness.

Figure 20: Fasting Twice On the Sabbath

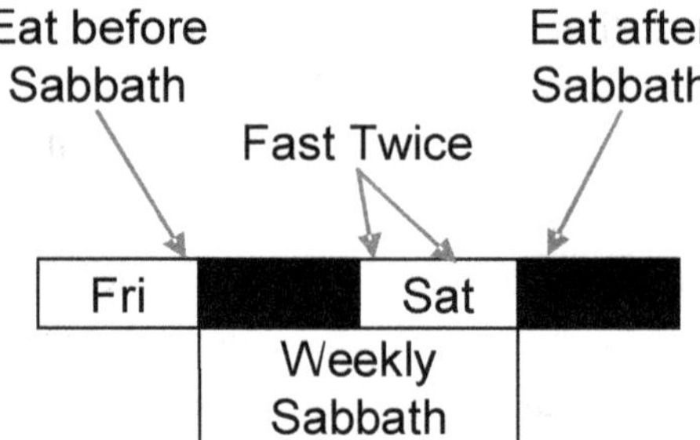

The majority of later Rabbis rejected this ultra piety:

> "It is forbidden," say they, "to fast on the sabbath; but, on the contrary, men are bound to delight themselves with meat and drink. For we must live more delicately on the sabbath than on other days: and he is highly to be commended who provides the most delicious junkets against that day. <u>We must eat thrice on the sabbath</u>, and all men are to be admonished of it. And even the poor themselves who live on alms, <u>let them eat thrice on the sabbath</u>. For he that f<u>easts thrice on the sabbath</u> shall be delivered from the calamities of the Messias, from the judgment of hell, and from the war of God and Magog."[101]

However, other Jews saw it differently and measured their piety by skipping the two meals that could not be scheduled before or after the Sabbath.[102] It should be noted that the language to "feast thrice on the sabbath" is in almost exact opposition to the practice of the ultra-pious minority. Notice that the Rabbis did not just say one must feast on the Sabbath. They specified the number of times. Likewise the

---

[101] Maimonides, Schab. cap. 30, Kimchi, in Isai. cap. lviii. Quoted page 195, *Exercitations upon St. Matthew*, John Lightfoot, Mat. 12:1.

[102] See "Sabbath: To Feast or to Fast?" by Eliezer Segal, University of Calgary, *The Jewish Free Press*, Calgary, October 31, 2002, pp. 10-11. Gilat, Yitzhak D. "On Fasting on the Sabbath," Tarbiz 52, no. 1 (1982): 1-15.

ones who fasted did not just specify that they fasted on Sabbath, but they specified the number of times as a measure of their piety.

The argument that "I fast twice on the Sabbath" must mean "twice a week" is based on the assumption that "twice on the Sabbath" cannot possibly make any sense. But as it can make sense (as shown above), it would be injudicious to urge Luke 18:12 as proof that "sabbath" meant "week" in Yeshua's day.[103] And this is still the case even though GNM favors a better explanation.

> Rabbi Yosé ben Zimra went so far as to declare that Jews who fasted on Shabbat were assured of the cancellation of any negative decrees that had been issued against them by the heavenly court.[102]

It may be charged that it be a matter of speculation if the practice was to refer to fasting as equivalent to "I skip two meals on the Sabbath," however, it may be said that sectarian opinion and the terminology used to express it develop in parallel, and are just as quickly forgotten when the theological mood changes. It is equally uncommon to meet up with "feast thrice the Sabbath" in English as an anti-fasting sentiment. We are much less able to judge the phrase, or those like it, when it be a Greek translation of a Hebrew utterance spoken two thousand years ago. It is further injudicious to build a new lexical sense upon the mere interpretation of a hapax phrase when the same use is nowhere else proved in the same time period.

Certainties in one department lead to useful speculations in others. For when the parameters are established by the overall chronology via the rule of non-contradiction, then speculations which can be neither proved nor disproved are allowed in supporting departments such that there be no contradiction with what is proved.*

THE SEPTUAGINT

> **The princes of Judah were like them that remove the bound: therefore I will pour out my wrath upon them like water.**[104]

---

[103] Lewis Sperry Chafer also allows for this: "The one passage, 'I fast twice in the week' (Luke 18:12) would be difficult under a Sabbath interpretation unless it be taken to mean, 'I fast twice on the sabbath.'" [104] On next page.

* Another possibility is explained in *The Good News of Messiah* footnotes for Luke 18:12, "I fast twice the Sabbath," i.e. on the second day before it (Thursday), and on the second day after it (Monday). Though he feasts on the Sabbath the Pharisee compensates by fasting twice longer on two other days. This sense (cont. next page)

The skeptic will make the argument that because the extant LXX uses ἑβδομάδας to interpret שַׁבָּתוֹת, that the Hebrew word must mean "week" because the Greek word means "week" or "weeks":

Lev. 23:15 ἑπτὰ ἑβδομάδας ὁλοκλήρους [שַׁבָּתוֹת]
Lev. 23:16 τῆς ἐσχάτης ἑβδομάδος [שַׁבָּת]
Lev. 25:8a ἑπτὰ ἑβδομάδες ἐτῶν [שַׁבְּתֹת]
Lev. 25:8b ἑπτὰ ἑβδομάδες ἐτῶν [שַׁבָּתֹת]

These texts are commonly used by skeptics to "prove" that "sabbath" means "week." Rather it proves that someone wanted the word "sabbath" to mean "week" and they also wanted to suppress the plain evidence for the counting of Sabbaths. To understand how this can be so, we have to establish some laws of textual criticism.

Motive 1: It is an established fact that Christian translators have the propensity and desire to mistranslate passages that support the continuing validity of the Torah and to make text critical decisions that favor a lawless Christianity. While independent evidence has caught them out on this practice, it is not always the case. Sometimes we have to correct them in this department based only on the fact that it is possible to read a text in harmony with Torah rather than against. A few examples of textual corruption by the Church are: Acts 15:24, KJV; Acts 21:25 KJV; Rev. 22:14 NAS. And translational corruption: John 1:17, KJV; Rom. 3:21; 10:4; Gal. 3:21.[105] These alterations were deliberate, and not accidental. The Church did conspire to introduce antinomianism into the text.

Motive 2: It is an established fact that the Rabbis have the propensity and desire to corrupt texts and mistranslate texts that originally favored Messianic interpretation applied to Yeshua. If anyone does not believe this then a comparison of KJV messianic

---

[104] Hos. 5:9.

[105] John 1:17: the word *but* in the KJV does not belong. Rom. 3:21: "apart from the law" should be "apart from the norm." Rom. 10:4: "end of the law" should be "end of the norm"; Gal. 3:21: "righteousness" should be "justice," and "law" should be "norm," etc. The reader should see my translation of the New Testament, *The Good News of Messiah.*

---

is based on a genitive of comparison, "I fast twice *more than* the Sabbath," or "I fast double the Sabbath." See LSJ δις ***twice, doubly***. While some Jews fasted on the Sabbath, the Pharisees outdid their piety by fasting twice as long on other days, using the Sabbath as a unit of measurement to make their point. I think this answer more satisfactory than my earlier answers for this text. The Rabbis forbade Sabbath fasting, and Monday's and Thursdays were often kept for private fasting days. See Didache 8.1.

passages with JPS messianic passages will prove the direction of the bias.[106] Furthermore, this bias extends to alterations in the Hebrew text, usually corruptions of a single letter or pointing of vowels. A comparison of messianic passages in the LXX vs. that of the MT text will also show the tendency to oppose messianic prophecy in the MT text in the vowel pointing, the accent marking, and sometimes the consonantal text has been changed. When the mass of evidence is considered on this, it becomes clear again that these changes were deliberate, and not accidental.

The resulting rules would then apply:

Rule 1. Anti-Torah readings should be expected in Church versions, and we should assume they are incorrect, and they should be corrected using the Torah as a resource.

Rule 2. Anti-Messianic readings should be expected in Jewish versions and we should assume they are incorrect, and they should be corrected using Church versions as a resource.

Rule 3. Sometimes the two motives overlap. A text is both anti-Torah and anti-Messianic. Both the Jewish version and the Church version should be assumed incorrect. For sometimes the anti Yeshua Rabbis and the anti Torah Church has a common cause against the messianic faith. In such case, the version that can be translated or corrected most parsimoniously to undo both problems must be deemed correct.

4. Most other corruptions can be attributed to accidents, and textual decisions should be made using the usual rules of textual criticism.

It is clear that the Septuagint translation of Lev. 23:11-15 falls under rule three. The rendering is both anti-Messianic and anti-Torah. The Church wanted the counting of Sabbaths to be obscured so that the key to the resurrection day would be removed along with its implications for Sabbath observance. The Rabbis wanted the counting of Sabbaths obscured because it is the key to figuring the sign of Jonah out, and they are not interested in proof that Yeshua is the Messiah.

---

[106] Gen. 3:15 KJV "his heel" vs. JPS "their heel"; Zech. 12:10 KJV "upon me whom they have pierced" vs. JPS "unto Me because they have thrust him through"; Psa. 22:16 KJV "they pierced my hands and my feet" vs. JPS "like a lion, they are at my hands and my feet."

So we must reverse engineer the damage caused by overlapping motives. First, the teaching of the text to count seven Sabbaths after Passover is against the Church desire to rid themselves of the explanation for the resurrection passages. Therefore, they allowed the LXX to be altered to obscure the counting of the seven Sabbaths. The actual literal text, meaning "first of the Sabbaths" (μιᾷ τῶν σαββάτων) stood unopposed while men still read the bible in Greek or Latin: *Prima autem sabbatorum*. Meanwhile the LXX was unavailable to correct the false Church interpretation that it meant Sunday. The LXX gave way to the Vulgate, which similarly obscured Lev. 23:15: *septem edbomada plenas*. When the English version translated "first day of the week," then Lev. 23:15 was allowed to be corrected by the Hebrew to "seven Sabbaths," since the English was no longer in danger of being explained by the Leviticus passage.

In order to understand the anti-Messianic motive of the Rabbis concerning Lev. 23:15-16 we have to understand the dispute between the Jewish-Nazarene disciples of Yeshua and the evolution of post Temple Judaism as a reaction against Yeshua. Yeshua's emissaries knew when the sabbatical year was and they knew how to explain Daniel 9:24-25. They also knew that the resurrection was on the Sabbath and all the types and symbols of Torah pertaining to his death before the annual Sabbath and resurrection on the first of the Sabbaths. (Readers will have to read this book several times to get all the connections and understand the historical context as it is not possible to tell everything in chronological order and correct it all at the same time.) Only when the correct chronology is clearly explained can it be understood what the Rabbis did and why they were motivated to do it. And only then can we understand that we should not redact the history and theology of the Nazarenes via the Christian appeal to Rabbinic arguments designed to destroy the original faith.

So the Jewish followers of Yeshua had an air tight chronology that aligned Daniel 9:24-27, the biblical types and prophecies, and his death on the fourth day and his resurrection on the Sabbath. Thus began an ever escalating religious war between the Jews who would not support Yeshua and those who did. This is the war by which the Second Jewish Commonwealth was destroyed in two stages, first in

A.D. 70 and then in A.D. 135. The Rabbis first pushed the Jewish faithful out of the synagogue and required them to sojourn with the non-Jewish believers. Then they defined anyone who believed in Yeshua as a Gentile. Then Rabbi Akiba proclaimed Simon Bar Kochba* to be the Messiah, and this led shortly to the destruction of the Second Jewish Commonwealth.

Akiba and his fellow Rabbis took a great interest in any argument that could be used to undermine the Messianic Faith, and for this they stooped to deliberate sabotage focused on the testimony of Yeshua's death and resurrection. They wanted, by all means possible, to get this disconnected from the Torah and the prophets both chronologically and typologically. The main agent for the chronological counter-attack against the Nazarenes was Rabbi Yose Halaphta. The other principle agent was Aquila of Sinope. And here we will focus on Aquila since we are discussing the Septuagint.

It was the aim of the Rabbis to eliminate Yeshua from Judaism. Thus any misunderstanding that would promote a purely Gentile Christianity over the Messianic version was embraced as "right" for Gentiles, and indeed as "right" for the Jewish believers they wanted to get out of the Jewish Faith. To this day, the same propensity exists wherever Rabbinic doctrine infects a Messianic assembly. Torah is for Jews, but Gentiles must worship another way. Modern Messianic Jews have not yet come to terms with the Rabbinic campaign to disunite the non-Jew from the Torah and Yeshua.**

Therefore, whenever the Rabbis dialogued with Christians they nearly always dialogued with the weaker party, which is Gentile Christians, particularly those who had rejected Torah. These Gentile Christians did not fully understand the Torah and indeed were rejecting it as divine revelation at the time of the Bar Coziva revolt and afterward. Their champions were Cerinthus and Marcion, Gnostics, who were later branded heretics. This was during the time when the Friday-Sunday theory was introduced.

The Rabbis would have noticed something however, and this is when the Nazarene Jews explained Daniel 9 and the Passion chronology correctly that some of these Gnostics repented and started following Torah. And they would have noticed that Jews who

* This title was adopted by Simon. His real name was שמעון בר כוסבה, known from the Cave of Letters. The title means "son of the star" and is taken from Numbers 24:17. But as we will see in this book, the Mĕssiah Yĕshua is the dawn star, the morning star, that ascends from the sun. Rev. 7:2, 10:1; Mat. 2:2; Rev. 22:16; 2:28, and Numbers 24:17. But Simon was after called, "son of a lie."

** The Talmud says non-Jews who keep Sabbath are worthy of death. To this day the traditional rabbis consider a non-Jew keeping Sabbath as cultural appropriation, i.e. stealing what belongs only to the Jews.

understood Daniel 9 in conjunction with the Passion Chronology and the biblical types kept joining the Nazarenes. They would have also realized that most non-Jews got their knowledge of Judaism from Rabbinic Judaism. Such is still the case today, but even more so then. And while they could not stop the Nazarenes from believing the truth, they could certainly take it away from their own people and misdirect the Gnostic Christians.

Figure 21: Converging Conspiracies

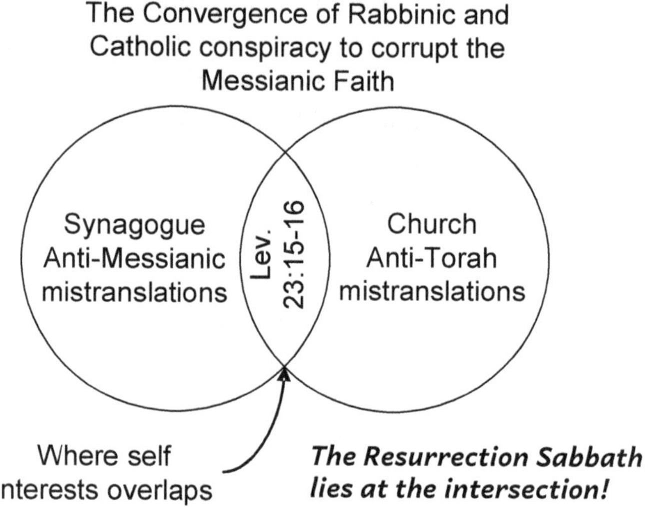

The plan therefore was to obscure the counting of Sabbaths, and eject it from Judaism. They would have to introduce the meaning "week" to Sabbath to do this, and they would have to do it in their Hebrew sources and in the Greek Septuagint used by Jews in the Synagogue. Then the meaning of "first of the sabbaths" would become obscure and the Gentiles would stumble into the trap of explaining "sabbath" to mean "week."

Let us consider the historical situation in order to further answer this criticism. It is well known that the Septuagint has been heavily edited since its beginnings. The Torah and Prophets come before the Evangelists in time, and the Greek version came before too. However, because of later changes introduced into the LXX, the versions we now have are not the original version. The original LXX was modified by three Jewish versions. The first was that of Aquila ca.

A.D. 140, followed by Symmachus and Theodotion. Thus there were four versions. Origin of Alexandria took these along with the Hebrew text and produced the Hexapla. This sixth version by Origin was a critical text combining the four versions and the Hebrew. The combined version was copied and became the basis of the present extant LXX. The original LXX was discarded. Thus, it is no longer clear which parts of the LXX are original and which parts are the result of editing. And most of this editing took place after A.D. 100.

So we must investigate the exceedingly sectarian translation of the LXX on Lev. 23:11-16 and 25:8. The first thing to note is that a literal translation of the Hebrew text into Greek suggests that the original LXX contained the following readings:

Lev 23:11 τῆς πρώτης = τῇ ἐπαύριον τοῦ σαββάτου = in the tomorrow of the Sabbath.

Lev 23:15a ἀπὸ τῆς ἐπαύριον τῶν σαββάτων = τῇ ἐπαύριον τοῦ σαββάτου = in the tomorrow of the Sabbath.

Lev 23:15b ἑβδομάδας = ἡμέρας τῶν σαββάτων = days of the sabbaths.

Lev 23:16 ἕως τῆς ἐσχάτης ἑβδομάδος = ἔτι ἐν τῇ ἐπαύριον τοῦ σαββάτου τοῦ ἑβδόμου = yet in the tomorrow of the seventh Sabbath

Lev 25:8a ἑπτὰ ἑβδομάδες ἐτῶν = ἑπτὰ σάββατα ἐτῶν = seven Sabbaths of years.

Lev 25:8b ἑπτὰ ἑβδομάδες ἐτῶν = ἑπτὰ σάββατα ἐτῶν = seven Sabbaths of years. That is, "seven Sabbaths from [the] years" (ablatival genitive, classical Greek.

The second thing to note is that according to the Passion chronology the Jews apparently did count the first Sabbath after Passover and that this view was written down by followers of Yeshua when they translated the good news into Greek. Apparently all of biblical chronology converges on this one date of the resurrection on the "first of the Sabbaths." Then comes the initial Gnostic rebellion and their reinterpretation of "first of the Sabbaths" to the eighth day, one day beyond the Sabbath, in a new series of Sabbaths of the new age.

One of the things from Judaism these Gnostics would have been sure to adopt is the sectarian position on Pentecost—namely that it always came on a Sunday. They would thus explain the first-fruits type using the Sadducean views, and mark an Easter Sunday and Pentecost Sunday every year. And if this was not enough then they would naturally place the crucifixion on a Friday and the Resurrection on Sunday making that Sunday the 16th of Nisan.[107]

Meanwhile the unbelieving Jews and their Rabbis are considering how to rid the Jewish Community of the followers of Yeshua, and particularly how to undermine the arguments for Yeshua's fulfillment of the times and prophecies of Scripture. These Rabbis are more concerned with Jewish followers of Yeshua and non-Jews adopting Torah observances than they are with the Gnostics. The Gnostics, in their view, are safely Gentiles and no threat to Rabbinical Judaism. The key figures here are one Rabbi Akiba, Rabbi Halaphta, and Aquila of Sinope, who produced a new version of the Septuagint for the exact purpose of disputing messianic prophecies about Yeshua:

> Aquila the translator was also of Pontus, from the famous sea-port Sinope, which had been constituted by Julius Caesar a Roman colony; but he was of Gentile origin. He lived in the reign of Hadrian (A.D. 117-138), and was a connexion of the Emperor. Hadrian employed his relative to superintend the building of Aelia Capitolina on the site of Jerusalem, and while there Aquila was converted to Christianity by Christians who had returned from Pella.[108] Refusing, however to abandon the pagan practice of astrology, he was excommunicated; upon which he shewed his resentment by submitting to circumcision and attaching himself to the teaching of the Jewish Rabbis. The purpose of his translation was to set aside the interpretation of the LXX., in so far as it appeared to support the views of the Christian Church.[109]

Aquila re-translated the LXX from the Hebrew in accord with the

---

[107] I know this is over simplifying. There were many variations of Gnosticism and many different calendar nuances. The period of A.D. 80-150 was very chaotic. So the Gnosticism that I am simplifying things toward is that variety which was tough enough to evolve into the proto-Catholic Church. One can view the chaos of the times as sorting out which heresy would be the most convincing corruption of Scripture.

[108] These returning "Christians" could not be Jews however, since Hadrian banned them from living in Jerusalem. Swete's chronology may be incorrect.

[109] pg. 31, *An Introduction To the Old Testament in Greek*, by Henry Barclay Swete, Cambridge University Press, 1900.

anti-Yeshua views of the Rabbis, making a particular point to dispute Messianic Prophecy. He no doubt had a lot of assistance in this project. His translation became the standard in the Jewish Synagogue where Greek was still spoken in the following centuries until the Synagogue gave up on Greek altogether. Now when it came to Lev. 23:11-15, it is clear that the Gnostic Church would have never have considered a Sadducean explanation of Shavuot from our present LXX, which it did, and still does. Thus, it is equally clear that the LXX was changed from a form that would allow all the views—assuming no other contexts or texts are used to explain it. Further, it is clear that the Jewish followers of Yeshua counted Sabbaths. So it is established that a crime was committed upon the LXX.

This crime had the advantageous side effect of supporting Gnostic Christianity[110] and its Friday-Sunday theory with alleged appeal to the Sunday first-fruits of the Sadducees. It removed the "first of the Sabbaths" from the LXX preventing the Gnostics from returning to the proper explanation, and confirmed their view that Nisan 16 and Sunday must have aligned in the year of the Passion. The door was shut behind them by Aquila, and also shut against the Greek speaking Jews from explaining things correctly. For now they could not show their fellow Jews in the synagogue who used Aquila's translation anything about "first of the Sabbaths."

It was also engineered to spite the Nazarenes, the followers of Yeshua who counted the Sabbaths, but who agreed otherwise with the early Pharisees. These Pharisees, however, now evolved into later Rabbinical Judaism which strategically decided to drop the counting of Sabbaths so near and dear to the Nazarenes. The object was to favor getting Christians out of Judaism without affirming their doctrines.

Next we have motive. Aquila's aim was to destroy Messianic prophecy and as many Messianic connections between the Torah and

---

[110] Gnostic Christianity was at the time of Aquila changing into the proto-Catholic Church. The Old Testament was being reintroduced. Further, it cannot be said that Gnostics never used the Septuagint at all. After all they had to defend some Messianic prophecies, and the one's chosen would be those most agreeable to rapprochement with Mithraism. They would have known the Sadducean position.

the Evangelists as possible. A second aim of Aquila and Akiva was to push the non-Jews and followers of Yeshua as far away from Judaism as possible. It was with these goals in mind that they reformed Judaism. So, for instance, it was made a crime punishable by death for a non-Jew to keep the Sabbath.

Then we have opportunity. Aquila had every opportunity to introduce the translation "weeks" and "week" into Lev. 23:15-16. He also had the opportunity to introduce "first day" into Lev. 23:11. So here is the situation. Aquila and the Rabbis know that the Jewish Christians count the "First of the Sabbaths" as the resurrection day. But they also know that the Gnostic Christians, which are now reforming into the proto-Catholic Church have placed the resurrection on the Sunday. The power of the Jewish faithful in Messiah had up to that point been their success in evangelizing the non-Jew. The key is how to push them apart, and the answer is a stroke that aids the lawlessness of the non-Jew while stripping the Messianic interpretation at the same time.[111]

The Jews have long since given up religious plotting on this scale. Yet, that generation should not be excused from the charge just because they are Jews. It is quite evident that they were plotting against Imperial Rome at the same time, and also against Yeshua. For it was Rabbi Akiba who certified that Simon Bar Kochba was the promised Messiah. They would hinder and subvert in every way possible. A more recent analogy to this is the activity of the Jesuits in promoting the interests of the Church of Rome. Their policy was to infiltrate and subvert whole kingdoms by plotting. The Jesuits are the "scholarly" Roman Catholics, and where they leave off plotting against kings they take up plotting against history to tell it in their way.

The Church teaches a continuous doctrinal and traditional continuity back to the original apostles, yet the switch between a Gnostic majority and a later proto-Catholic majority proves that no such continuity existed. A successful lie is extrapolated into the past,

---

[111] This conspiracy was not wholly made of human self interest. It is certain that it was coordinated by unseen spiritual forces. The critical moments came when their were enough human allies on his side with evil propensities. The deceptions were then inserted into tradition at critical points.

past even the liar who introduced the lie. The lie is an imposition of a false view of previous history. What went before is falsely interpreted. The retelling of history is really a system of lies designed to cover what in reality is a huge black hole of information. Yet there is some information pointing in the right direction. But they simply do not want to hear it.

The translation "week" and "weeks" in Lev. 23:15-16 does just this. 1. It eliminates the hated "first of the Sabbaths" from connection to the resurrection day, 2. It disconnects the text from the Jewish Sabbath by allowing the Gnostic proto-Catholic Church to argue both sides of the Pentecost coin. For all they have to do to accept the "week" innovation is put the resurrection on the 16th of Nisan—on a Sunday. This they did accept. For when the proto-Catholic Church reintroduced the *Old Testament* despised by the Gnostics, Lev. 23:11-16 was carefully neutered so that it could no longer explain "first of the Sabbaths." Again, Aquila had the opportunity, and the Church had the willingness to close their eyes to the original counting of Sabbaths. By promoting this, the Rabbis get a Church disconnected from Jewish institutions, and the Jewish followers of Yeshua get smashed in between the two forces.

Next we have the evidence. Aquila is also the author of Targum Onkelos,[112] which is the standard Aramaic Targum (interpretation) of the Torah and Prophets. This version puts "week" and "weeks" into the Leviticus passages. And we can be assured that if Aquila did it to the Targum, then Aquila did the same to the Septuagint. What happened afterward is that the Church approved of Aquila's translation in Lev. 23:11-16 because it removed from the eyes of the Church the true meaning of the "first of the Sabbaths." And if the Church had a reason for disliking the original reading of the Septuagint, they had even more reason for going along with Aquila. Meanwhile the followers of Yeshua holding to the original are dropped into a black hole and forgotten about as both sides proceed to persecute them while preserving their own heretical and corrupt

[112] Aquila probably did not do the whole Targum, but it was standardized and his name attached. Obviously it is conformed to Aquila's LXX on the passages in question.

traditions.[113] And somewhat inconsistently, the Church still holds to the Sadducean calculation of Pentecost to keep their Sunday interpretation of first-fruits.

Meanwhile Rabbi Halaphta (ca. A.D. 140) is busy composing Seder Olam to try to redefine Daniel 9. As a further way to attack "first of the Sabbaths" he popularizes "one to the Sabbaths" from Hebrew, which is later adopted into the Mishnah and multiplied in the Talmud. The same is repeated in Aramaic and sows a Semitic basis for the Syriac rendering later used to translate the Evangelists.

So in summary, all the Aramaic, Hebrew, and Greek sources for Sabbath meaning "week" have been contrived by enemies of the faith deceived by the powers, and have their origin in the three way battle between 1. the Rabbis, 2. Jewish believers and their non-Jewish associates, and 3. The proto-Catholic Gnostic Church.[114] In short Aquila and the Rabbis plotted in favor of the proto-Catholics to destroy the influence of the Nazarenes. The interpretation of "week" put into Seder Olam, the Mishnah, Aramaic, and the Septuagint was deliberately done to destroy the chronology of Yeshua's fulfillment, which we have seen is so perfect and so precise, that the only possible response that enemies can make is to suppress it by swindling everyone into redefining of the key term.

The change was made in the wake of the second revolt. There was motive to do it. There was opportunity. There is the evidence of the Targum. And there were men to do it, like Aquila, with evil consciences and hatred of Christianity, but more truly hatred of those Jews that believed in Yeshua.

We must above all remember that when the Church cites these sources what they are actually citing. They cite Seder Olam to interpret the resurrection day passages. However, Seder Olam is a work composed especially against Daniel 9, and explicitly to undermine Yeshua's

---

[113] Where the Nazarenes were persecuted their enemies had the backing of the Roman government due to the ban on Torah observance. They were pushed to the fringes of the Empire, and even outside it. But this was the will of the Almighty to spread the good news to the nations, and to take it away from those who already had their chance.

[114] The overall effect of misdirecting the Catholic Church and dialoging with it whist ignoring the Nazarenes made Christianity relatively weak viz. a viz. Judaism. This is exactly what the Rabbis wanted.

fulfillment. We must also remember that those who cite the Septuagint have to reckon with the fact that the trail leads right back to the apostate Aquila whose aim in creating his version of the Septuagint was anti-Messianic. If the Rabbis and Aquila can pervert Messianic Prophecy, then they can certainly pervert anything else in their interests and against the interests of the Jewish faithful in Messiah and their non-Jewish associates who they so hated.

> But like Adam they have transgressed the covenant; there they have dealt treacherously against me.[115]

After the Covenant of Old was gradually brought back into the picture, the mystical and magical world view of Gnosticism began to give way under the influence of the word of God. The Gnostics could not really deliver on their promises of enlightenment, and so little by little some Gentiles returned to the texts, and sought confirmation of their beliefs.

It was at this point that Christian scholars, having learned through the filter of Gnostic interpretation, made an attempt to explain "first of the Sabbaths" by recourse to history, context, and languages, but this miniscule effort only tolerated scientific inquiries that would give a traditional result. And what was thought to be knowledge in the Septuagint and used to interpret "sabbath" as "week" was in fact false information. Therefore, the explanations were merely to satisfy those who asked the historical questions that their Gnostic fathers would not have considered. The weight of tradition overcame any objection that could not expose the error from start to finish.

The Gnostics bequeathed to the Roman Church the notion that *mia tōn sabbatōn* meant Sunday. However, the Gnostic acceptance of extreme symbolism gave way to a more rationalistic approach, and the Church soon learned that the extremes of Gnosticism had no moorings. Thus the Roman Church reintroduced the Covenant of Old as background material, particularly the Septuagint, and promptly fell into the mutual interest traps laid in the Septuagint by Aquila, while the Eastern Church after the Bar Kochba revolt fell into the traps laid in Aramaic sources like Targum Onkelos and the Mishnah.*

---

[115] Hos. 6:7. * The reader should see this in the larger context of the war between the house of Judah and the house of Israel dating back to the 11th century BC. This war never really ended and is now waged via the pen of Church scribes vs. the pens of the Rabbis.

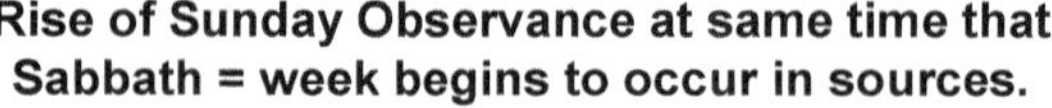

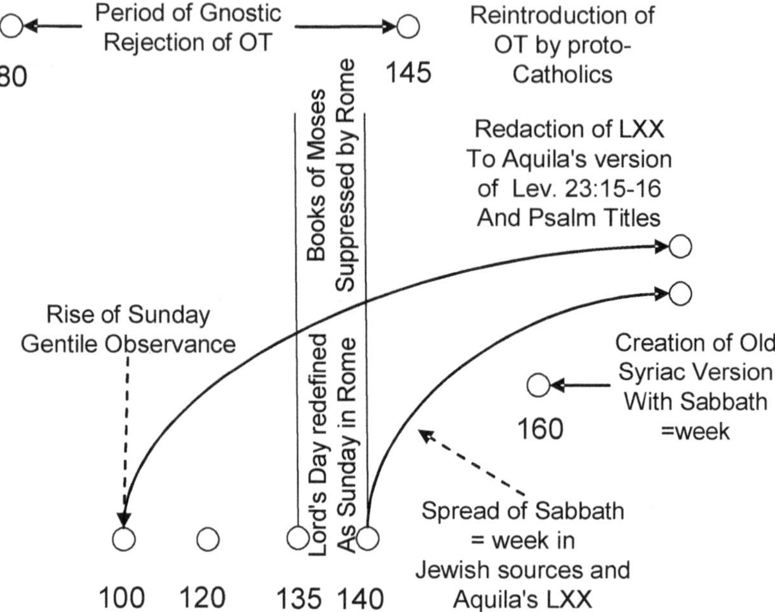

So now in A.D. 180, Theophilus of Antioch writes:

> What by the Hebrews is called *sabbaton* is interpreted *hebdomas* in Greek.[116]

> And He also spoke a parable to them: "A blind man cannot guide a blind man, can he? Will they not both fall into a pit? (Luke 6:39).

Thus the Greek Church began interpreting "sabbath" to mean "week," and the emergent Western Church, speaking Latin, interpreted the Latin word for "sabbath" as "week." The question is how does one tell which interpretation is right, either "sabbath" or "week" in a particular context where both senses make chronological

[116] Ad Autolycum §2, 12. "The Derivation of Sabbath," pg. 187. Robert North, S.J., Biblica, April 1955. Lactantius also, ca. A.D. 300, "Dies sabbati, qui lingua Hebraeorum a numero nomen accepit, unde septenarius numerus legitimus acplenus est" (ibid., North).

sense? The answer is that you erase the information needed to make chronological sense out of the primary sense of the word, and then you introduce tradition to force the other sense into place.

After the fall of the Roman Empire learning declined until the time of the Reformation. At this time, the Church seems to be of three minds on how to explain "prima autem sabbatorum" and "μιᾷ τῶν σαββάτων." Some prefer to equate Sunday with a new Sabbath and continue to translate "one of the Sabbaths." Others continue to fall into the Rabbinic trap* and translate "first day of the week," and others try to take a middle position and translate "one day *after* the Sabbath."

The Rabbinic trap is very tempting to the faithful who want to over identify with Judaism. So we find that scholars who are former Rabbinic Jews, or that Christian scholars who learn Hebrew and Aramaic have the propensity to uncritically overvalue Jewish traditions, and take it for granted that the tradition represents the original state of things. It is not a happy scene to see many recognizing the errors and traps of Catholic tradition only to run into Jewish tradition. But the fact is that the Talmud, Gemara, and Mishnah are just as corrupt as the writings of the Church Fathers.

In both traditions, therefore, it was necessary to suppress as much information as needed to prevent either Jew or Christian from connecting the dots. The evolutionary principle of survival of the fittest has validity here. Only a successful heresy of Judaism against Messiah could succeed in deceiving, and only a successful heresy of Christianity could succeed against the Torah. And to be successful requires sufficient alteration of facts. It is the natural tendency of man to devolve religiously. And this is what happens without divine intervention.

Where the truth is known, it is known because history has been redeemed by divine intervention, (1) Noah, (2) Abraham, (3) Moses (4) Samuel (5) Nehemiah, (6) Ezra, (7) Messiah Yeshua. But after each intervention the weight of sin dragged Israel back down. The continuity of tradition cannot be relied on to recover the truth. Rather the small inconsistencies the tradition was unable to suppress or cover over must be recognized with the help of the Holy Spirit.

*The trap consists in falling into misunderstanding אחד בשבת as חד בשבא, meaning "one in the week (seven)" vs. properly "one unto the Sabbath." This mistake is furthered by Rabbinic translations into other langauges giving the sense as "first in the week," but biblical usage shows that ב means, "unto" as in 'day unto day' (יוֹם בְּיוֹם) or 'month unto month' (חֹדֶשׁ בְּחָדְשׁ) or 'year unto year' (שָׁנָה בְּשָׁנָה). Proof of the matter lies in the fact that 'seventh day of the week' or 'sixth day of the week' do not occur in Rabbinic or Syriac texts, but rather 'eve of Sabbath,' and 'Sabbath.'

On the other hand, not too much tradition was changed. Just enough was changed to get the desired results. For the most successful lie is the lie that integrates the most true facts before telling the lie. But no lie is ever told perfectly. There are always inconsistencies. There are always cracks and loose ends. The liar typically shows some gesture or sign of lying. Let us now return to exploring some of those cracks.

William Tyndale's translations:

> Mat. 28:1, "The saboth daye att even which dauneth the morowe after the saboth Mary magdalene and the other Mary cam to se the sepulcre."
> Mark 16:2, "And yerly in the morning the next daye after the sabboth day they cam vnto the sepulcre when the sun was risen."
> Mark 16:9, "When Jesus was risen the morowe after the sabboth daye"
> Luke 24:1, "On the morowe after the saboth erly in the mornynge they cam vnto the toumbe and brought the odoures whych they had prepared."
> John 20:1, "The morowe after the saboth daye cam Mary magdalene erly when it was yet darcke vnto the sepulcre."
> John 20:19, "The same daye at nyght, which was the morowe after the saboth daye, when the dores were shutt"
> Acts 20:7, "On a saboth daye the disciples cam to gedder forto breake"
> 1 Cor. 16:2, "In some saboth daye let every one off you put a syde at home"

What makes it possible that μιᾷ τῶν σαββάτων means "day *after* the Sabbath" is what is called the ablative genitive common in classical Greek. This genitive is literally, "one [day] *from* the Sabbaths†." The genitive case (an inflection) is translated "from." This classical sense was imported into Byzantine period Ecclesiastical Greek. "[Professor Sophocles regards the genitive (dependent on ἡμέρᾳ) in such examples as those that follow (cf. Mk. xvi. 9 above) as equiv. to μετὰ with accusative, the first day after the sabbath; see his Lex. p. 43 par 6]: Mt. xxviii. 1; Mk. xvi. 2; Lk. xxiv. 1; Jn xx. 1, 19; Acts xx. 7;" [117]

This "after the sabbath" argument was an interpretation of the phrase. However when it is considered that the whole phrase is "one day of the Sabbaths" (μιᾷ ἡμέρᾳ τῶν σαββάτων), and that this breaks down into μιᾷ + ἡμέρᾳ τῶν σαββάτων, and that ἡμέρᾳ τῶν σαββάτων always means *the Sabbath* elsewhere in scripture, it is clear that ἡμέρᾳ
day

[117] pg. 566, *Thayer Greek-English Lexicon of the New Testament.*

† It has since occurred to the writer that a temporal ablative makes less sense with Sabbaths in the plural. It appears to require an annual Sabbath conjoined with a weekly Sabbath in order to work out, or if taken to mean all Sabbaths, then one day from all Sabbaths would mean all Sundays. Hence those who adopt this view promptly ignore the plural.

τῶν σαββάτων never means "day *from* the Sabbaths," but only "day of the sabbaths." Thus the "after the sabbath" translation can only be obtained by ignoring the use of the phrase elsewhere—by isolating the texts, and then arbitrarily imposing a Hellenistic Greek grammatical interpretation.

Every reader of Greek, Latin, and early English versions could still see the meaning "first of the Sabbaths" as a possibility. And if such reader were exposed to the Hebrew Lev. 23:15, the meaning would be explained. For the Scripture was written to be plain and clear. Yet this Hebrew had been overwritten with "weeks" since the days of Aquila, and this used as the re-interpretive key to "first of the Sabbaths" by the Church. But there are a number of holes in the Septuagintal argument, other than the fact that it is a late translational editing of the Septuagint.

If the skeptics accept that the Septuagint proves that "sabbath" means "week," then they must also accept that it proves the count to Shavuot starts from Nisan 16, and that the word "sabbath" means "first day." In Lev. 23:11, the rendering is, "τῇ ἐπαύριον τῆς πρώτης" = "On the morrow of the first day the priest shall raise it up." The rendering "first day" in the Septuagint at Lev. 23:11 aligns with הַשַּׁבָּת ("The Sabbath") in Hebrew. Does this now mean that "the Sabbath" means "first day?" Of course the word *shabbat* does not have that lexical meaning just because the Septuagint rendered it "first day." Therefore, the translation does not prove the word *shabbat* has the lexical meaning *first day*. And likewise in vs. 15, interpreting *shabbatot* as *weeks* does not impart that meaning to the Hebrew. For if the fallacy of equating the Septuagint gloss in vs. 11 with lexical Hebrew meaning is admitted, then the fallacy of equating the interpretation "week" and "weeks" as a lexical meaning of "sabbath" and "sabbaths" must be admitted in vs. 15-16.

Just because the Septuagint glosses the Hebrew word *Shabbat* in vs. 11 with "first day" does not make the one word mean the other. It is only in this one context that the first day of unleavened bread also happens to be called *Sabbath*. This alignment, however, is not a dictionary meaning of the word. Likewise, the alignment of "weeks" and "sabbaths" in vs. 15 is not a dictionary meaning of Sabbath. It is no more than that weeks and sabbaths are counted at the same time, and that each week corresponds to the Sabbath which falls in it.

Lexical meaning is not automatically determined by lining up two translations. This is a huge fallacy. In English we say, "You are pulling my leg." The Russian idiom for the same meaning goes "You are putting spaghetti on my ear."* Should we now say that the Russian word "ear" also means "leg," and then enter "leg" into the Russian Lexicon so that wherever the Russian word "ear" appears we can change it to "leg" if it is convenient?

There is a further fallacy in the equation. The "weeks" are not regular weeks, because the interpretation in vs. 16 has "ἕως τῆς ἐπαύριον τῆς ἐσχάτης ἑβδομάδος" = until the morrow of the last week. If Sabbath meant "week" it would have to be regular. But ἑβδομάδος is not regular.

The true sense of Lev. 23:15-16 is pasted over with the command to count "seven sevens" that is found in Deut. 16:9—שִׁבְעָה שָׁבֻעוֹת (ἑπτὰ ἑβδομάδας). This is to count seven days seven times. And these "sevens" are not regular weeks. The following chart illustrates: [118]

Figure 23: The Irregular Week on the Rabbinic Reckoning

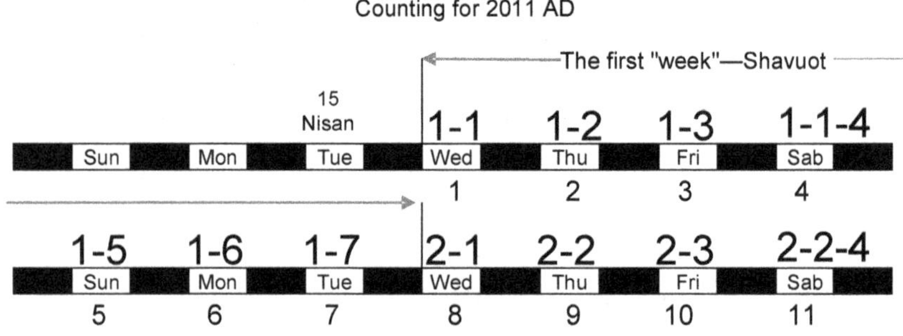

And clearly, counting from after the first day of the feast, these

[118] In each number pair, the first number counts the *seven* (Shavuot/week) that the count is currently on. The second number of the pair counts the current day of that *seven* (Shavuot/week). The triple number on the weekly Sabbath prefixes the pair with the number of the sabbaths. Hence 1-1-4 = first of Sabbaths, first seven, 4th day. The smaller number beneath counts the days to 50.

* вешать лапшу на уши, 'hang noodles on the ears.'

Shavuot are irregular weeks. If ever "Sabbath" meant week, then it should have to be anchored between the weekly Sabbaths, with Sunday as the first of the week, and Sabbath as the seventh day. Yet, here we see that the so called "week" is non-synchronous with a week ending with Sabbath! That is some vague basis to base an appeal for "Sabbath" = "week" on! It also contradicts the other usages in the Mishnah, Seder Olam, and the Syriac Bible, where counting to the Sabbath is normally a regular week. What we may say then is that the attempt to interpret Sabbaths as weeks in the Septuagint is inconsistent. For the very idea of equating sabbath to week suggests a regular week only.

If the Septuagint is really taken seriously then a "week" should begin on any day due to the fact that the text adopts the Pharisees position that the counting of "weeks" starts on Nisan 16 (cf. Lev. 23:11, LXX). Thus, "first day of the week(s)" would be whatever day was Nisan 16. In that case, the LXX could allow the following construction:

Figure 24: Vague Week Supports Sabbath Resurrection

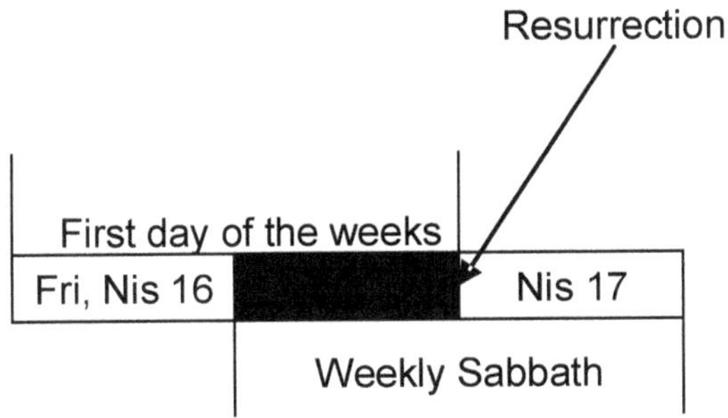

So the Septuagint does not prove that "sabbath" means "week" in any such sense as that the "first day of the week(s)" would mean Sunday. Rather along with the plural σαββάτων in the resurrection passages, it would just prove that it was the "first day of the weeks." One has to assume that Nisan 16 falls on a Sunday to get the "first day of the weeks" to be a Sunday. If the word "sabbaths" were to mean "weeks" on the basis of the Septuagint, then the above chart shows that it really explains nothing about which day of the week "first day of the weeks" would be. And it goes to show that when the facts of a matter are sufficiently obfuscated, then one can prove anything from the facts that remain.

Such an inconsistency (of the irregular week) does not make sense unless the primary purpose of the corruption of the Septuagint is not to explain, but to obscure. For there is no way that sabbath-weeks makes any sense when in six out of seven cases the sabbath-week does not end on the Sabbath. The inconsistency of a sabbath-week starting on Nisan 16 (other than Sunday) would be unacceptable if the "sabbath" meant "week." It would rather support the timing of the Sadducees to keep the week regular. Somewhere around the 9th century the Karaites spotted this inconsistency and began to use it against the Rabbis. But the Rabbis could not go back to the pre-Aquila or pre-Targum Onkelos rendering. The deception was fixed in tradition. However, we can know the truth, because Scripture is written not to obscure, but to be plain and clear. The seven Sabbaths are seven Sabbaths and nothing else. There is no need to go along with the devolution of the texts into an obscure meaning "week" which can begin on any day whatsoever. All that need be done is sweep aside all the post first century LXX, Aramaic, Mishnaic, and Targum interpretations on this question and go by the Hebrew only.*

The difference on Lev. 23:11-16 is most often blamed on the dispute between the Pharisees and Sadducees. They were before the second century B.C. opposed on the question of when to start counting. This difference was one of the causes of the wars between the royalist party (i.e. priestly Hasmonean Kings) and the Separatist party (the Pharisees) among the Jews after Judah Maccabeus defeated Syria (165/164 B.C.). The priestly party were Sadducees. Sadducean corruption was perpetuated due to the birthright inheritance of their offices, their vast riches, and the fact that they could not be voted out, because they were the nobility. But the common people who knew the Scripture opposed them. The result was one of the bloodiest civil wars in Jewish history, which can be compared with the English civil war between Oliver Cromwell and the Scottish Presbyterian Covenanters. The Jewish Civil war was over religion, and the differences between the Sadducees and Pharisees were at the center of it. The Sadducees were defeated and they never recovered, but in their

* Under "interpretations" I am combining two problems, (a) the false interpretation of extant Hebrew texts, and (b) later translations themselves that are false interpretations.

inherited positions were compelled to perform every ritual according to the Pharisees rulings.[119] The exception was that they retained control over the criminal justice system.

Was the Septuagint modified at its inception? And should we attribute it to the dispute between the Sadducees and Pharisees? The answer to this question is no. The definition "week" for Sabbath only comes into the literature starting in the middle of the second century. The proof of this is that the dispute was quite alive on the basis of the Hebrew text alone, and did not need the Septuagint to justify its previous existence. In fact, if the Septuagint were accommodated to the Hebrew, a pre-Aquila Septuagint would translate the text as follows:

> 23:11 καὶ ἀνοίσει τὸ δράγμα ἔναντι κυρίου δεκτὸν ὑμῖν τῇ ἐπαύριον <u>τῇ ἐπαύριον τοῦ σαββάτου</u> ἀνοίσει αὐτὸ ὁ ἱερεύς. 23:15 καὶ ἀριθμήσετε ὑμεῖς <u>τῇ ἐπαύριον τοῦ σαββάτου</u> ἀπὸ τῆς ἡμέρας ἧς ἂν προσενέγκητε τὸ δράγμα τοῦ ἐπιθέματος ἑπτὰ <u>σαββάτων</u> ὁλοκλήρους. 23:16 <u>ἔτι ἐν τῇ ἐπαύριον τοῦ σαββάτου τοῦ ἑβδόμου</u> ἀριθμήσετε πεντηκοστὴν ἡμέραν καὶ προσοίσετε θυσίαν νέαν τῷ κυρίῳ. . . 25:8 καὶ ἐξαριθμήσεις σεαυτῷ ἑπτὰ <u>σαββάτων</u> ἐτῶν ἑπτὰ ἔτη ἑπτάκις καὶ ἔσονταί σοι ἡμερῶν ἑπτὰ <u>σαββάτων</u> <u>τῶν</u> ἐτῶν ἐννέα καὶ τεσσαράκοντα ἔτη

> 23:11 And he shall raise up the sheaf before the Lord acceptable for you; <u>in the tomorrow of the Sabbath</u> the priest shall raise it up. 23:15 And you shall count <u>in the tomorrow of the Sabbath</u>, from the day which you bring the sheaf of the addition, seven <u>Sabbaths</u> complete. 23:16 Still, <u>in the tomorrow of the seventh Sabbath</u> you will count a fiftieth day, and you shall bring a new offering to the Lord 25:8 And you shall count out for yourself seven <u>Sabbaths</u> of *the* years, seven years, seven times, and they will be to you days of seven Sabbaths of the years[120], nine and forty years.

---

[119] Josephus Ant. 18:17, "But they are able to do almost nothing by themselves; for when they become magistrates, as they are unwillingly and by force sometimes obliged to be, they addict themselves to the notions of the Pharisees, because the multitude would not otherwise bear them."

[120] The genitive relation here is that of the *part* of the *whole*. "seven Sabbaths [the part] of years [the whole]," and "seven Sabbaths [part] of the years [the whole]"; This could be translated "seven Sabbaths from the years" or "seven Sabbaths in the years." It is called *partitive genitive*. For examples see 2Chron. 21:17, "smallest of his sons"; Gen. 22:2, "one of the mountains"; Judges 5:29, "wise ones of ladies of her"; "years" represents the whole, which is 49 years.

And the ambiguities in the text would allow the dispute to continue, only this time both sides would be counting Sabbaths, and the dispute would be purely over Lev. 23:11. The "tomorrow of" can mean "hereafter" or the next day. Both sides would admit it.[121]

So the LXX rendering "first day" (23:11), "weeks" (23:15), "week" (23:16), and "weeks" (25:8) is essentially to obscure the counting of Sabbaths and to introduce the meaning of "week" to the word Sabbath. Obviously the attempt to do so left some flaws behind it. But the flaws are not apparent until one looks closely and realizes the fallacy of using an interpretation to establish lexical meaning. But this does not stop the Church from using the excuse provided or the simple from believing it. The second century Rabbis fully knew what this would mean for the New Testament passages. For they knew that "first of the Sabbaths" is a key anchor point of the Nazarene chronology and all that goes with it.

Meanwhile, the Sadducees had lost all leverage by which they could at least keep the text ambiguous. By the time of Aquila, there would be no opposition from them. For all their political power was swept away in A.D. 70 when the Temple was lost.

The Church left their New Testament texts untouched as it was easier and more clever to appeal to the Septuagint and use it as in interpretive tool. The Greek texts continued to read "first of the Sabbaths" (μιᾷ τῶν σαββάτων) and the Latin texts read the same: una sabbatorum. Only with the Septuagint they had an excuse for interpreting the text to mean Sunday. That would be the scholarly excuse for deep questioners. The popular explanations remained the Gnostic one about a new series of spiritual Sabbaths or the eighth day,[122] and the slightly more sensible one "after the Sabbath."

Meanwhile, sometime between the end of the Bar Kochba revolt (A.D. 140) and the final compilation of the Mishnah (A.D. 200), the

---

[121] Discussed and proved at length elsewhere in this book.

[122] The Greeks did not identify a regular week with *ebdomados*. Rather it was any period of seven. It was probably more common to say "eight days," or on the eighth day counting inclusively from the current day. The "first day" equals the eighth day was the Gnostic code for referring to the first day of the week. . . eight days from one period to the next inclusively. They liked it because it fit their symbolism of the heavenly spheres.

word "Sabbath" was expanded in Rabbinic literary usage as a manner of counting days of the week. The earliest usage of this is in 4Q252.‡ This use came into regular use in the Mishnah, and further use in the Talmud, which had the effect giving a back up to the obscure Septuagint translation, and also serving as a way to trap Christians into the first day of the week interpretations. So while Sunday observance arose due to Gnostic apostasy, complicity with Mithraism, and rebellion against the Torah, it was the Rabbis who certified the long term endurance of the myth by repaving the foundations with lies.[123] "But behold, the lying pen of the scribes has made it into a lie" (Jer. 8:8).

It is not lightly that I charge the Jewish side with conspiring to corrupt the Septuagint and to create a corrupt literary tradition in Seder Olam, Mishnah, and Talmud, as well as the Targums to misdirect the Church concerning the "first of the Sabbaths." Nor is it lightly that I charge the Church with starting the Sunday myth and of excusing themselves on the authority of the Rabbis, and of perpetuating their own misunderstanding of Scripture in the writings of the Church Fathers. I must remind the world that the Church charges Synagogue with conspiracy to corrupt the truth, and the Synagogue charges the Church with the same crime. I have already outlined their respective biases, and say that both sides are in the wrong and guilty of conspiracy, and that both their houses are under the divine curse because of it. This curse must be broken to unite Israel.

But the Scriptural chronology leads to no other conclusion than that they did so conspire against both Messiah and Torah so as to corrupt it at those very points fulfilled by Yeshua. Naturally, there are limits to the ability of humans who are opposed to each other to mutually conspire, but the fact that one side conspired against Yeshua, and the other side against His Torah left both sides vulnerable to the

---

[123] Judaism and Christianity were as closely related as Catholics and Protestants in those days. So we can learn a lesson by understanding the activities of the Jesuits. The Jesuits infiltrated Protestant countries and Churches and even stooped to planting false doctrines to divine and conquer, i.e. doctrines that the Church of Rome might not agree with, but which served to divide its opposition. The Jesuits are the classic *agent provocateurs*. We should not assume that Judaism was incapable of such tactics.

‡ i.e. the Dead Sea Scrolls. The problem is not the Hebrew text or its proper interpretation as "one into the Sabbath," but the equivocation thereof that Sabbath should mean "week."

exploitation of Satan and his angels, and it is evident that Yahweh allowed Satan to deceive both houses of Israel because their offenses against Him were so serious.

The first version to mistranslate the Greek μιᾷ τῶν σαββάτων "first of the Sabbaths" was the Syriac New Testament, of which the oldest manuscripts are the old Syriac (ca 250 A.D.) and came soon after the creation of the Mishnah. The Rabbis had introduced the Aramaic variation with a "hybrid" word between "sabbath" and "seven": שַׁבָּא. This word could easily be confused with the word for seven: שֶׁבַע. In this way the Eastern Church was deceived. The Aramaic Peshitta is descended from these early Syriac texts and reached its final form sometime in the 5th century.*

The Gnostic explanation survived in the western Church until the reformation. For this reason they had no trouble with "first of the Sabbaths" and this explains why the phrase remained in Latin. The few Sabbath observing Christians continued to believe the resurrection was on the Sabbath. Gregory of Tours testifies to this in the 6th century:

> **22.** James fasts from the death of the Lord to the resurrection **23.** Now in our belief the resurrection of the Lord was on the first day, and not on the seventh as many deem. [*non septiman sicut multi putant*] **24.** Pilate transmits an account of Christ to Tiberius. The end of Pilate and of Herod. **25.** Peter and Paul are executed at Rome by order of Nero, who later kills himself. **26.** The martyrs, Stephen, James and Mark; burning of Jerusalem by Vespasian; death of John.[124]

---

[124] Gregory of Tours (539-594): *The History of the Franks*, Vol. 2, (trans. By D.M. Dalton), Oxford: Clarendon Press, 1927, pg. 24 (Underlined portion), "23. De die resurrectiones dominicae. Dominicam vero resurrectionem die prima facta credimus, non septimam, sicut multi putant." Some sources seem to quote only, "the resurrection of the Lord was on the first day, and not on the seventh" leaving off the critical words "as many believe" (sicut multi putant). But that begs the question as to why Gregory had to deny it was on the seventh. About this time, Sunday began to be treated as the Sabbath, and indeed, it may have been called the Seventh day as well as the rest day or Sabbath. For this reason ancient testimony is under a cloud of ambiguity in some cases regarding whether the people so mentioned observed the Jewish Sabbath or not.

* The Syriac of the Peshitta is a different dialect from the earlier Galilean Aramaic understood by Yeshua, so much so, that it is quite obvious that the Peshitta is not a copy of some first century Aramaic text. It is rather a translation from Greek into a later phase of Syriac infused with Christian interpretive traditions.

So in the western Church whether one believed the resurrection was on the Sabbath or Sunday depended not on the translations. They all had "first of the Sabbaths." It depended on the interpretation. In the Sunday-Sabbath interpretation Sunday was the new "chief of the Sabbaths" or "first of the Sabbaths" of the new age after the old Sabbaths of the Jewish age. However, should this position be questioned via greater knowledge of the Torah or common sense, then the scholastic opinion came back that the phrase means "one day *from* the Sabbath" or "of the week." Ignoring the plural was justified by the fact that it seemed that a singular Sabbath was referred to in the plural. This was rebutted earlier in this book.

So when we come to William Tyndale, and Miles Coverdale, there are two opinions prevailing. Tyndale represents the scholastic opinion of "one day from the Sabbath" and so translates "after the Sabbath." Coverdale represents the Sunday-Sabbath majority that thinks Sunday is the Sabbath and translates "first of the Sabbaths." But neither of these positions could hold out against the increasing knowledge of the people. There is a third scholastic position that introduced the meaning of "week," and is evidenced by John Wycliffe. However, this opinion was weaker than the other two.

The interesting thing is that the Sunday-Sabbath interpretation prevailed for Acts 20:7 and 1 Cor. 16:2. These texts were not close enough to the resurrection passages to threaten the status quo or otherwise allow people to put the broken cart back together. So they were translated to indicate that days of Christian assembly were called Sabbaths by treating the word "one" as a sort of indefinite article.

Take notice of Coverdale:

Acts 20:7, "One of the sabboth daies" [*Cr[anmer]. B[isho]ps*;]
1 Cor 16:1, "In some Saboth daye."

And Tyndale:

Acts 20:7, "On a saboth daye the disciples cam to gedder forto breake"
1 Cor. 16:2, "In some saboth daye let every one off you put a syde at home"

And Wycliffe[125] (1380).

John 20:1, "And in oo dai of the woke . . ."
John 20:19, "in that dai oon of the sabotis"
Acts 20:7, "first dai of the woke"
1 Cor 16:2, "oo dai of the woke"

Anglo-Saxon 995 A.D.:

Luke 23:54, "and sæter-dæg onlyhte"
Luke 23:56, "and on sæter-dæg hig gestildon"
Luke 24:1, "On anum reste-dæge. . ."

Several conclusions can be drawn here. Among Sunday Christians in Europe, the Christian Sabbath replaced the Jewish Sabbath to the extent that when "Sabbath" is used in the translations, there is no consciousness of it being the Jewish Sabbath. So the translators of the Anglo-Saxon version render the Jewish Sabbath "sæter-dæg" (saturn-day) and the resurrection day "reste-dæge." This allows literal conformity to the original language. However, it is clear that the literal language of the original has undergone Gnostic redefinition. Notice the inconsistency in John Wycliffe between John 20:1 and John 20:19. This is no accident. Wycliffe was doubtless aware of it, and what he is saying is that one is equal to the other. Wycliffe seems to be the first to originate "first day of the week" in English. But neither Tyndale nor Coverdale followed him on this.

But eventually Wycliffe's innovation won the day in English.[126] This is because as the scholars read the bible more and more, and learned more of the opinions of the Jews and read the *Old Testament* more, they became aware of the faultiness of the Gnostic interpretation. The word Sabbath emerged as referring only to the

---

[125] The Wycliffe Bible was not so important or influential as Tyndale and Coverdale. It was hand copied before the invention of the printing press, and the circle of translators were all scholastic academics. The Wycliffe Bible New Testament was first printed in 1731, and the whole in 1850. There were two versions of the Wycliffe Bible.

[126] Continental Europe was another matter, and the tension between Wycliffe and Tyndale and Coverdale seems to be that the latter two spent much time in Continental Europe. There they adopted the notion that the Sunday was the seventh day, and even to this day the Continental Europeans ignorantly number the days of the week from Monday, making Sunday their seventh day.

seventh day. Tyndale tried to fix this with the interpretation, “one day *from* the Sabbath,” which allows for the word Sabbath to be expressed, but keeps the resurrection on Sunday. But this position proved to be untenable because it reminded people of the real Sabbath. Even if the resurrection was miss-dated in terms of the phrase “after the Saboth,” the people were now made aware of when the real Sabbath was. This was not acceptable to the Church. Sunday was the new Sabbath.

Therefore, when the King James version was produced, the scholarly standard has become “first day of the week.” The justification for this was sought in the Mishnaic and Syriac usages, “one day to the Sabbath.” Particularly relied on was the Mishnaic innovation from ca A.D. 200. While there is a similarity between *μιᾷ τῶν σαββάτων*, and בְּאֶחָד בַּשַּׁבָּת (or Aramaic: בחַד בּשַׁבָּא), there is no evidence that the one phrase means the other, or that the one phrase should be used to interpret the other, yet the trap was laid in Hebrew at that time and the reformed Church fell right into it and thus a true Torah based reformation was aborted.

The first implicit claims of equivalence lie with the translation of the Greek into the Syriac, and exactly how this came about is rather obscure. One Catholic scholar, Robert North, S.J., states:

> Through doubtless an ignorant overlooking of the final ‘*ayin* in *šeba’* (seven), early Christian Fathers were led to equate seven (-day week) with Sabbath. [see E. Vogt, *Biblica* 40 (1959) 1008, who disproves that *šabbāt* ever meant week] Still, the best grammarians now admit cases in which ‘*ayin* is in fact transmuted or lost. In the existing Syriac form *šabbā,* the loss of the final *t* is no less anomalous than that of the final ‘*ayin* would be.”[127]

North is absolutely correct that “Sabbath” was conflated with “seven.” This is what happens if one tries to use Deut. 16:9 [שָׁבֻעֹת]

---

[127] *The New Catholic Encyclopedia*, “Sabbath,” © 2003, pg. 458; R. North. [ ] notation original. The 1996 article is substantially the same and carries the Vatican's *imprimatur.* Also remarkable is that R. North’s paper is cited in the third edition of BDAG, “The Derivation of ‘Sabbath’, Biblica 36, ’55, 182-201.”

to determine the Lexical meaning of Lev. 23:15 [שַׁבָּתוֹת]. As far as we know, it was Aquila, the translator of the new synagogue Septuagint that inserted ἑβδομάδας and tried to obscure the counting of sabbaths this way, and at the same time in the Targum. The Church Fathers fell neatly into the trap. That this opinion was known in the East at Antioch is testified by Theophilus of Antioch. He was born in Iraq, so he probably knew Aramaic:

> "What by the Hebrews is called *sabbaton* is interpreted *hebdomas* in Greek."[128] "But the most know not that what among the Hebrews is called 'Sabbath,' is translated into Greek the 'seventh' (ebdomas)."[129]

This Theophilus was the patriarch of Antioch ca. 169-183 A.D.

So we see that the Church was provided with several tools to subvert the "first of the Sabbaths." The first was the Gnostic transference theory. Then there is the ablative "one day *from* the Sabbath" theory based on classical Greek. And most importantly Aquila's corruption of the Septuagint combined with the Rabbinic literature and the hearsay from Jews concerning it.

While the Septuagint and hearsay served to mislead the Church, Judaism maintained "one day to Sabbath" בְּאֶחָד בַּשַּׁבָּת as its own variant, which was reproduced in Aramaic: בְּחַד בְּשַׁבָּא. This found its way into the Babylonian and Palestinian Jewish Academies such that by the time the Eastern Church wanted an Aramaic version for the Syrian Church they were already familiar with the new usage. The dropping of the ת in final version: שַׁבָּא surely must have been an attempt to connect the Aramaic שַׁבְּתָא with the sense of "seven" or "week," since the form שַׁבָּא sounds so close to שֶׁבַע.†

The Talmudic idiom חד בשבא is an Aramaic dialect. So also the rest of the days of the week: [130]

1. בחד בשבא — *on one in the week**
2. בתרי בשבא — *on second in the week**

---

[128] *The Derivation of Sabbath*, pg. 187 (ibid).

[129] Book II, Chap. XII. *Autolycus*.

[130] These usages are found the Jerusalem and Babylonian Talmud. See *Shabbat* 9 (*daf: pz,a, gemara*), 18 (*daf: qkt, b, gemara*), 24 (*daf: qnv,a, gemara*). †One witness is the circumstantial evidence, and the other is Theophilis above.

3. בתלתא בשבא *on third in the week**
4. בארבעא בשבא *on fourth in the week**
5. בחמשא בשבא *on third in the week**
6. במעלי שבתא *on preparation to Sabbath*
7. בשבתא *on the Sabbath*

What should first be observed is that ת is rejected in the forms for days one to five. In a few cases the ת is retained (e.g. *Shabbath 18*), which is explained below. The form שבא does not really originate with *Shabbat.* It derives from the Aramaic word for "seven" שבע only with an א exchanged for ע.[131] This is merely an alternate spelling of the Aramaic for "seven," or "week" which is שבועא. [שבא < שובא < שְׁבַע][132] שבא is a defective spelling of

---

[131] Both these letters are indistinguishable in spoken Hebrew. In written Hebrew they stand as place holders for vowels and serve to identify the root meaning.

[132] The form שובא is Mandaean, and שְׁבַע is biblical Aramaic. See Koehler, *Lexicon In Veteris Testamenti Libros.*

The Mandaic language is the liturgical language of the Mandaean religion; a vernacular form is still spoken by a small community in Iran around Ahvaz. It is a variety of Aramaic, notable for its use of vowel letters (see Mandaic alphabet) and the striking amount of Iranian influence in its grammar and lexicon. Classical Mandaic is a Northwest Semitic language of the Eastern Aramaic sub-family, and is closely related to the language of the Aramaic portions of the Babylonian Talmud, as well as the language of the incantation texts found throughout Mesopotamia. It is also related to Syriac, another member of the Eastern Aramaic sub-family, which is the liturgical language of many Christian denominations throughout the Middle East.

Jewish Babylonian Aramaic is the form of Middle Aramaic employed by Jewish writers in Babylonia between the 4th century and the 11th century CE. It is most commonly identified with the language of the Babylonian Talmud (which was completed in the seventh century) and of post-Talmudic (Geonic) literature, which are the most important cultural products of Babylonian Jewry. The most important epigraphic sources for the dialect are the hundreds of Aramaic magic bowls written in the Jewish script.

The language is closely related to other Eastern Aramaic dialects such as Mandaic and the Eastern Syriac of the Assyrian Church. Its original pronunciation is uncertain, and has to be reconstructed with the help of these kindred dialects and of the reading tradition of the Yemenite Jews. (The vocalized Aramaic texts with which Jews are familiar, from the Bible and the prayer book, are of limited usefulness for this purpose, as they are in a different dialect.)

Talmudic Aramaic bears all the marks of being a specialist language

שׁובא. Therefore, the usage בחד בשׁבא in the Talmud is literally "one in the seven" and not "one in the *Sabbath"

Furthermore, this is proved by the reintroduction of the ת on day six. במעלי שׁבתא means "on preparation of sabbath." Notice that the preposition ב is missing also, because the word שׁבתא really means "Sabbath." Likewise, בשׁבתא means "on Sabbath."

The same rejection of the final *tav* (ܬ) occurs in Chaldee Syriac (ܚܕ ܒܫܒܐ *one in seven* vs. ܫܒܬܐ *Sabbath*) and Ancient Syriac (ܚܰܕ ܒܫܰܒܳܐ vs. ܫܰܒܬܳܐ).[133]

The Targum of the dialect of the Jews of Kurdistan explicitly counts in the same fashion, "one day in the seven," (יומית כושׁיבא) "two in the seven" (יומית תירושׁבא) etc.[134] The lack of the final *tav* in all the usages of counting is the proverbial smoking gun. It shows that the popular spoken dialects rejected the idea of counting days of the week to the Sabbath, and that such

---

of study and legal argumentation, like Law French, rather than a vernacular mother tongue, and continued in use for these purposes long after Arabic had become the language of daily life. It has developed a battery of technical logical terms, such as *tiyuvta* (conclusive refutation) and *teyku* (undecidable moot point), which are still used in Jewish legal writings, including those in other languages, and have influenced modern Hebrew.
.... However, the majority of those who are familiar with it, namely Orthodox Jewish students of Talmud, are given no systematic instruction in the language, and are expected to "sink or swim" in the course of Talmudic studies, with the help of some informal pointers showing similarities and differences with Hebrew. For this reason, insights based on grammar or philology tend to be received with bewilderment in Orthodox Talmudic circles (see Chaim Potok's novels *The Chosen* and *The Promise*).

[133] William Mead Jones says, "Each day proceeds on, and belongs to the Sabbath. This is the meaning in all languages where "into Sabbath" or 'into the Sabbath,' is employed." While this is certainly the meaning the pious users of this idiom ascribed to ב when counting to the Sabbath, Jones clearly was taken in by the Church tradition that *khad bĕ-shabbo* meant "one to Sabbath" rather than "one to week/seven." The missing ת is the clue. We only need to explain the idiom as Jones does when the ת is present. The purpose of the idiom with the Jews was to accent the Sabbath. To suppose they thought *week* when reading it defeats the *raison de être*. As for the Church, they did not want to accent the Sabbath, but only confuse it with the meaning of week. Hence the *tav* was omitted, and the result explained to mean *Sabbath/week*. However, the language clearly shows that *week/seven* is the original meaning of the usage.

[134] William Mead Jones, "Chart of the Week," 1886.

countings were with respect to the word "week" or "seven" and not the Sabbath.[135]

So in concluding this section, it may be noted that the Western Church caught up to the Eastern Church at the time of the Reformation, and thus based its translation of "first day of the week" on the Syriac, Mishnaic, and Talmudic examples. However, the connection between *μιᾷ τῶν σαββάτων* and בְּאֶחָד בַּשַּׁבָּת is assumed on the basis of the Sunday resurrection tradition. There is no compelling reason to associate the resurrection day with this usage.

A literal translation of Tῇ *δὲ μιᾷ τῶν σαββάτων* into Biblical Hebrew would be: †בְּאַחַד הַשַּׁבָּתוֹת or in Biblical Hebrew, avoiding the archaic use of the word 'one' for the sense 'first': בָּרִאשֹׁון הַשַּׁבָּתוֹת. Using late Hebrew: בָּרִאשׁוֹן שֶׁל הַשַּׁבָּתוֹת.

Feminine adjectives may also be used: בְּאַחַת הַשַּׁבָּתוֹת (on the first of the Sabbaths). And this would be put into Greek as: Tῇ *δὲ μιᾷ τῶν σαββάτων*. Alternatively: בְּרֵאשִׁית הַשַּׁבָּתוֹת. Or using late Hebrew: בָּרִאשׁוֹנָה שֶׁל הַשַּׁבָּתוֹת. Or in theory: * בְּרִאשֹׁונַת הַשַּׁבָּתוֹת.

Let us now work forward. One counts seven Sabbaths between Passover and Shavuot every year, and for counting the first Sabbath we may say: בְּאַחַת הַשַּׁבָּתוֹת (on #one of the Sabbaths). Or we may say

---

[135] This is not the place to elaborate, but if there were any Aramaic or Hebrew originals to the gospels, they remain yet undiscovered, or were all destroyed by the Romans or Ecclesiastical Authorities. But "The Latin, Syriac and Coptic versions were unquestionably made directly from the Greek" (NA-27th, pg. 63*, *Novum Testamentum Graece*). The extant Syriac MSS were not copied before the fifth century, and it is clear that the translators used the oral tradition of the "first day of the week" and the chronological misunderstanding to translate "first in the seven" in much the same way that Catholic missionaries translate "first day of the week" today. Any MSS reading "first of the Sabbaths" in a version of Aramaic would have been destroyed by Ecclesiastical authorities on the assumption that it was a heretical production of a small sect of Judaizers and not in line with Church doctrine. Such an artifact would lie too close to the original text for them to tolerate. On the other hand, the same could be tolerated in Latin, e.g. *prima autem sabbatorum*, because it was not Hebrew (or too close to it as Aramaic is) and was already sold to the flock as a Hebrew method of reckoning the week without significant fear that anyone could double check it. Such was not possible in Aramaic. An accurate translation in Aramaic would betray no ability to mean "first day of the week," and would have to be destroyed to be successfully repressed. † See page 324.

say הַשַּׁבָּת הָרִאשׁוֹנָה, but this might be confused with the first day of unleavened bread. The advantage of saying שַׁבָּתוֹת is that it recalls Lev. 23:15 more clearly. Τῇ δὲ μιᾷ τῶν σαββάτων is also equivalent to early Biblical Hebrew: רִאשׁוֹן לַשַּׁבָּתוֹת. It should be noted that the Greek and Hebrew words for 'day' have opposite genders. The Greek word ἡμέρᾳ implied by μιᾷ has a feminine gender, and the Hebrew יוֹם word implied by רִאשׁוֹן has a masculine gender. Likewise with the idiom "the one" for first, the gender of אֶחָד implies יוֹם.

Further Discussion

The Greek itself does not recommend the translation "first day of the week" on any linguistic or grammatical grounds. The argument that the word *day* should be interpolated into the phrase, "first [day] of the Sabbaths" is not persuasive toward "first day of the week" due to the fact that the phrase "day of the Sabbaths" (ἡμέρᾳ τῶν σαββάτων) itself means the Sabbath day. The skeptic only makes their own case worse by insisting on it. The grammar is easily enough explained as a Hebrew idiom. The feminine gender of the Greek word μιᾷ is explained by the corresponding masculine gender of the Hebrew word אֶחָד. In the Hebrew phrase, 'the one' is masculine while 'of the Sabbaths' is feminine. In the Greek, it is opposite, "the one" is feminine, and "of the Sabbaths" is neuter. The Greek grammar is the same as Mat. 26:17: πρώτῃ τῶν ἀζύμων, e.g. "first *day* of unleavens."†

Don't expect the religious skeptic educated in Greek to be honest on these passages. They have too much at stake. I have found non-religious experts in Greek (who study classical literature) much more honest. But the Church will try every trick, deception, and tactic in the book of craftiness to persuade you and their own that the plain sense is not "first of the Sabbaths." If they do, that is because they are often unconverted Catholics in heart who follow Christ in name only.

The phrases usually translated "the first day of the week" are found with trifling variations in the eight different passages. The writer above alluded to translated them one for all: "On one of the Sabbaths."[136] Leaving his translation without

---

[136] "Art. V.—The Sabbath Question." Rev. Byron Sunderland, D.D, pg. 88-107,

* The Greek is more like the feel of, "first one of the Sabbaths," where the adjective "first" is made a substantive "first one" and "one" is understood to be feminine implying a 'day.'

†It should be noted that in Hebrew a gender agreement is not required →

explanatory analysis, he virtually says that this is the true rendering and *intention*, this and nothing else.

The same idea occurred to the writer many years since; but he soon found that it was neither sustained by philology nor by an induction of facts. We reject the version as violating the grammar of the original, and therefore as not a possible rendering of the Greek text so long as any grammatical rendering can be found out. In order to this translation [SIC] the partitive of the co-joined genitive plural must agree with the numeral in gender. Thus "one of the days" is equivalent to "one day of the days." In Greek, *μιᾷ τῶν ἡμερῶν* is equivalent to *ἡμέρᾳ μιᾷ τῶν ἡμερῶν*. Now *μιᾷ* is feminine in gender, and *σάββατον* neuter. Hence the *μίαν*, in Matthew xxviii: 1, cannot govern *σάββατον* as a partitive. But *ἡμέραν* understood governs it by another rule well known to all Greek scholars, it would be necessary to go still further and supply *τῶν ἡμερῶν*, in which case the phrase would read "the first day of the Sabbath days." But so bungling does this course appear, and so foreign to the analogy of Greek grammatical usage, that no critic has ever ventured to suggest it in explaining the phrases under consideration. . .The proper phrase in the original Greek for "one of the Sabbaths" would be *ἓν τῶν σαββάτων*.[137]

And now the Methodist reply of Wilbur Steele to certain Methodists:

But this widely heralded Klondike discovery as to *μίαν σαββάτων* turns out to be only the glitter of fool's gold. It rests upon the profoundest ignoring or ignorance of a law of syntax fundamental to inflected speech, and especially of the usage and influence of the Aramaic tongue which was the vernacular

---

THE PRESBYTERIAN QUARTERLY AND PRINCETON REVIEW, 1877, vol. vi. The author defends "one of the Sabbaths."

[137] "Art. IX.—THE FIRST DAY OF THE WEEK." Rev. John M. Layman, pg. 703-718, THE PRESBYTERIAN QUARTERLY AND PRINCETON REVIEW, 1877, vol. vi. In the same periodical, Layman's answer to Sunderland.

between the elements of a construct relation. For example, in Exo. 23:11, "beast of the field" (חַיַּת הַשָּׂדֶה) features a feminine noun in the construct state before a masculine noun in the absolute state. Number agreement is not required either, e.g. Job 3:6: "days of the year" (יְמֵי שָׁנָה) or Dan. 9:2: "the number of the years" (מִסְפַּר הַשָּׁנִים) or Psa 101:6, "on the faithful ones of the land" (בְּנֶאֶמְנֵי־אֶרֶץ). Thus we could put "one of the Sabbaths" (בְּאַחַד הַשַּׁבָּתוֹת). Compare Gen. 37:20, "one of the pits" (בְּאַחַד הַבֹּרוֹת). See page 325 for further discussion of the Hebrew translation.

of Jesus and his apostles.[138] Must syntax die that the Sabbath may live?[139]

Steele's argument is the state of the art, so we would do well to pay attention to it, and see where he goes wrong. I will agree in [agreed] where possible or [disagree] and explain briefly in a footnote and at length afterward.

Let these affirmations be traversed: "4. No Greek word for 'day' occurs in any of the passages." Made simple for readers of English, that statement lacks candor. [agreed] Said word is there, latent, to a much greater degree than it is in our phrase, "The 25th of the month." Upon being asked, "The 25th of what?" the veriest child instantly replies, "day." [agreed] But stronger yet is the case in hand. The adjectival word μίαν is in the feminine gender, and an immutable law requires adjective modifiers to agree with their nouns in gender. [qualification][140] Σάββατον is of the neuter gender (Mark ii, 27 τὸ σάββατον; iii, 2, τοῖς σάββασιν), and out of the question. [agreed] What feminine Greek word is latent in this phrase, and yet so patent as to reflect upon this adjective number its feminine hue? Plainly the feminine word ἡμέρᾳ "day," as analogously it is found in Mark xiv, 12, πρώτῃ ἡμέρᾳ τῶν ἀζύμων, though latent in Matthew's parallel (xxvi, 17), πρώτῃ τῶν ἀζύμων, "the first day of unleavened bread." [agreed][141] Baldly to aver that "no Greek word for 'day' occurs in any of the passages," is to blind

[138] The apostles' and Yeshua's vernacular was Hebrew, not Aramaic. See my book *Exploding the Aramaic Myth.*

[139] pg. 401-409, "ART. VI.—MUST SYNTAX DIE THAT THE SABBATH MAY LIVE?" Wilbur Fletcher Steele, The Methodist Review, Vol. LXXXI,—Fifth Series, Volume XV., 1899.

[140] There are only "normal" laws in language, not immutable ones. There are plenty of examples of departures from such "laws." However, in this case we will find that we can abide by the norm. I think that Steele states it this way out of his desire for a quick dogmatic closure on the subject. For it threatens the very foundation of Sunday Christianity.

[141] I shall show that Steele is right to cite Mark 14:12 and Mathew 26:17, though he leaves out Luke 22:7 and the parallel with "day of the Sabbaths" goes unnoticed. I will show subsequently that his argument collapses when this is taken into consideration.

the simple English reader to the fact that an inflected language, by its numerous genders and cases, can indicate the presence and force of latent words to an extent undreamed in English. Of Every candid Greek scholar it is properly demanded what feminine Greek word it is which compels the numeral adjective to don its feminine dress. Until a more suitable word is proved we insist that it is ἡμέρᾳ, "day." [qualification][142]

But difficulties thicken fast. Only a tyro would render that phrase as "the first (or one) of the Sabbaths" [disagree][143] Such a rendering could arise only from a construction known as that of "the part and the whole." Amplified it would be "the first [or one] Sabbath [the part] of the Sabbaths [the whole]." [agree] Elsewhere, however, the Holy Ghost has invariable taught that the numeral adjective governing the word for the part must agree in gender with the word for the whole. [disagree]

The disagreement on this part needs to be explained, since Steele's remark is only true of one set of cases, and not the case at hand. In the Septuagint we find in Judith 12:13: *θυγάτηρ μία τῶν υἱῶν Ασσουρ* = *one daughter of the sons of Assyria*. It is to be observed that *θυγάτηρ μία* = *one daughter* is a part of the whole *τῶν υἱῶν* Ασσουρ = *of the sons of Assyria*. The rule thus needs to be modified. When the feminine word *θυγάτηρ* (daughter) is present to agree with the numeral's gender *μία*, then agreement with the accompanying genitive phrase *τῶν υἱῶν* Ασσουρ is no longer required. The "one" is still part of the whole. We can well guess that if the implied word is

---

[142] We shall see that the case for "first day of the Sabbaths" can be made based on Greek alone and that the rule holds fast. However, the Greek text is translating a technical term originally from Hebrew, and here we may expect a Hebrew literalism to disregard the Greek syntax. Examples of such syntax violating Hebraisms abound in the Septuagint. We will find that the case for "first of the Sabbaths," and "one of the Sabbaths" may thus be proved on the force of Hebrew Semiticism. On the other hand the same meaning can be proved on the force of pure Greek without appeal to Semiticism: "one day of the Sabbaths."

[143] Steele would contradict many scholars here who realize that the word "day" is latent, but omit it, as the Greek formally omits it, because its presence does not change the meaning of the text. This will be proved after.

only latent and not actually supplied in the text, that the listener upon mentally supplying the word does not expect the following genitive phrase to agree in gender. We shall see this to be the case with Mat. 26:17; Mark 14:2, and Luke 22:7.

This is all the more seen in Judith 14:18: μία γυνὴ τῶν Εβραίων = *one woman of the Hebrews*. It is not expected that the genitive τῶν Εβραίων phrase agree. And if *woman* should drop out of the text, e.g. μία τῶν Εβραίων then common sense would supply *woman* and not require the genitive phrase to agree. Either way, the one woman is still a part of the whole of the Hebrews. Steele's dictum must be reworded, "Elsewhere, however, the Holy Ghost has invariably taught that the numeral adjective governing the word for the part must agree in gender with the word for the whole, *and if the text shows a disagreement the omitted but latent word must be supplied to go with the numeral, and then the words of the whole do not have to agree.*" With this we can proceed to acknowledge Steele's examples where no word need be supplied:

> This, with masculine nouns of the whole, the form of the numeral governing the latent noun of the part is ever in the masculine also. The following are examples of this rule: Matt. xviii, 28, ἕνα [*masc., σύνδουλον, masc.*] τῶν συνδούλων [*masc.*], "one of his fellow-servants;" Mark xii, 28, εἷς [*m. γραμματεύς, m.*] τῶν γραμματέων [*m.*], "one of the scribes;" Luke xi, 46, ἑνὶ [*m., δάκτυλω, m.*] τῶν δακτύλων [*m.*] ὑμῶν, "one of your fingers." The same holds good with neuter nouns of the whole: Matt. v, 29, "one of thy members;"[144] Matt. vi. 28, "one of these"; Rev. xv. 7, "one of the four beasts." Nor is it otherwise with feminine nouns: Matt. v., 19, "one of these commandments;" Mark xiv, 66, "one of the maids;" Luke v, 12, "one of the cities" [R.V.]; Luke xiii, 10, "one of the synagogues;" and notably, Luke xx, 1, "one of those days."

The above applies to μιᾷ τῶν σαββάτων only insofar as the phrase has to be expanded to: μιᾷ ἡμέρᾳ τῶν σαββάτων. This then satisfies the applicable part of the rule. The part of Steele's rule that does not

[144] I have here omitted Steele's Greek quotations for sake of brevity.

apply is proved by Judith 14:18: μία γυνὴ τῶν Εβραίων = *one woman of the Hebrews*. Here we see that when the latent word IS supplied γυνὴ, *woman*, then the genitive phrase specifying the whole, τῶν Εβραίων, *of the Hebrews*, does not have to agree in gender. The supplied word intercedes. Let us see now how Steele continues to misdirect us from this fact:

> According to this law, had the Holy Ghost seen fit to write either πρῶτον or ἓν τῶν σαββάτων. we could and must have rendered his phrase as "first [or one] of the Sabbaths." Or, were σάββατον feminine in gender, μίαν σαββάτων should be rendered as alleged.

This last point is worthwhile. From the Jewish point of view σαββάτων is a feminine word. And from the Greek point of view the inflection -ων on the end is ambiguous. It is only the usage of σάββατον in other contexts that gives us the neuter. But without any other indication the -ων ending can be feminine. Without denying the neuter usages, could it be that σαββάτων is treated as a feminine word in Greek by some writers, or by some writers in certain places. Thus it would be a word with "two" genders.

The Hebrew word שבת is listed as feminine and masculine in the Hebrew Lexicon (BDB). However, there is every reason to question the suggestion that the word is ever really masculine. First the ת ending is normally feminine. Second, its plural form שבתות is feminine. Further, the cognate Aramaic שבתא is feminine. And in the overwhelming examples of usage there is no problem in regarding שבת as feminine. HALOT lists the 3 exceptions: Isaiah 56:2, 6; 58:13 where the phrase "polluting it" is used, and "it" is masculine in Hebrew. Also in Lev. 23:32, HALOT cites that the Hebrew word "he" is used in reference to the Sabbath. On the other hand Lev. 16:31 uses the word "she" to refer to the Sabbath. Exodus 31:14 likewise uses the word "she" to refer to the Sabbath, and Lev. 25:6 used the "she" form of the verb in connection with it.

Most of the exceptions can be disposed of as rare or possible mistakes. First Isaiah 53:13 may be using the noun ענג and not the verb in which case agreement is not required. For 56:2, 6, the intent of "polluting it" may really be "polluting oneself" in which case the ו would not refer to the Sabbath. In Lev. 23:32, the same phrase is contradicted in 16:31, i.e. הוא vs. היא. It was a common mistake to lengthen a yud too far so that it became a waw.

On the other hand, there is no way to argue with שבתות or the fact that the masculine plural never appears on the ending.

The question then is how σαββατα ended up being a neuter noun in the Greek language. This is explained by the fact that σαββατα is an obvious loan word transliteration of the Aramaic שבתא. The Aramaic word is feminine, but the Greek word looks like a neuter, because words ending in -α are regarded as neuter in Greek. Hence σαββατα is construed in the neuter, i.e. τα σαββατα. Speakers of Judeo-Greek, with even a smattering of Hebrew would know that σαββατων represents a feminine Hebrew word. In the first place the -ων ending is ambiguous and is used for the feminine genitive plural as well as the neuter. In the second place, the sabbath day is regularly stated as ημερα των σαββατων in which example, ημερα is feminine. In the Jewish mind the phrase was not a gender clash because the Hebrew was obviously feminine, and the Greek was flexible or to put it another way, bent to the use. And finally, -ων is merely the translation of the Hebrew feminine plural ending ות-.

At this point we must disabuse the reader of some modern notions. There was no such thing as the study of "grammar" in ancient times such that it mattered to common people. There was no common science of grammar, and no science of linguistics. Popular notions of grammar where innate learned patterns, with little or no formal acknowledgment. Someone would just say, that doesn't sound right, and that was the end of the matter. In Judeo-Greek σαββατων could be regarded as feminine despite the fact that τα σαββατα or του σαββατου were not to be in strict grammar. Even the later words could be regarded as feminine according to *construtio ad sensum*. To illustrate this we merely need to look at a true English neuter, the word "it". "Look at that boat. It is beautiful. Yes, she is." In a certain sense, neuter is the gender of all English nouns (in the sense that English has only one gender: neuter), and gender only enters the picture when someone uses "she" or "he" or a gender marked word like "actor" or "actress". Just because we use a neuter word like "boat" does not mean that it has no recognized gender. Boats are "she" and not "he", and any inanimate object, idea or concept can be an "it" that people have no problem genderizing according to the sense.

There are important reasons why *μια των σαββατων* is constructed according to the sense. If *Σαββατων* were truly a genderless word in the Jewish mind, then we might expect "one of the sabbaths" to be "*εν των σαββατων*" (using the neuter, nom.) but the direct Hebrew feminine, and even the use of *ημερα* in Greek reinforced the feminine idea, not to mention the closely related Aramaic: שבתא. It is also well known that were gender agreement is required is in a direct adjectival relationship, <u>but in the genitive chain or construct chain, it is not</u>, and this is a case of a construct/genitive chain. Also, neuter is not really gender. It is merely a form indicating lack of explicitly grammaticalized gender in either masculine or feminine. In the Hebrew language, everything has gender. There is no grammaticalized neuter. So when the Jews learned Greek, the use of a neuter simply meant that the gender was not being noticed. It did not mean to speakers of Hebrew that the noun had no gender sense. One may consider this ethnocentric, but this is how different languages first related: ethnocentrically.

So from the Hebrew point of view, *μια των σαββατων*, is a normal phrase for "one/first of the Sabbaths" where all parts of the phrase are regarded as feminine. It is really the number *μια* that tells us the *constructio ad sensum*, even though in form *σαββατων* is neuter. Refer to the boat example above.

So now if we return to Steele who would deny that any Semiticism is involved in the case, as is convenient, then the obvious route to solving the gender conflict is simply to interpolate the word phrase this way: *μιᾷ ἡμέρᾳ τῶν σαββάτων*. Now I proceed to refute Steele on Greek grounds alone and by Greek example alone without any appeal to Semiticism.

The correct translation of *μιᾷ τῶν σαββάτων* is “first *day* of the Sabbaths.” I completely agree with the critics that the word “day” is implied by the texts. But that is where the agreement ends. Let us start with a parallel construction whose meaning is agreed on: ἡμέρα τῶν ἀζύμων (Luke 22:7) = *day of unleavens* in reference to the 15th of Nisan. We see here that day is of feminine gender and the following two words neuter plural. So it is clear that the phrase contains a gender clash. The genitive phrase τῶν ἀζύμων is descriptive of what kind of day the text is describing. It need not agree in gender with what is so described.

Now this is exactly like "day of the Sabbaths" ἡμέρᾳ τῶν σαββάτων (Acts 16:13). Again the genitive phrase is descriptive of what kind of day the text speaks of—<u>a sabbaths</u> Day. And again, "day" agrees in neither gender nor number with the head noun ἡμέρᾳ. As a rule the genitive phrase in Greek does not have to agree with the head noun in either number or gender. For example, "Kingdom of the heavens" βασιλεία τῶν οὐρανῶν (Mat. 3:2). The head noun βασιλεία is feminine singular, and the genitive description τῶν οὐρανῶν is masculine plural. Also Mat. 3:10: τὴν ῥίζαν τῶν δένδρων; Mat. 4:15: Γαλιλαία τῶν ἐθνῶν. Luke 22:1: ἡ ἑορτὴ τῶν ἀζύμων. These examples can be multiplied endlessly.

Now let us observe what happens when an attempt is made to enumerate the "day of unleavens." We have that in Mark 14:12: τῇ πρώτῃ ἡμέρᾳ τῶν ἀζύμων. This is exactly like Luke 22:7 except that now the word πρώτῃ has been prefixed. All agree that the meaning may be "first day of the unleavens."[145] Observe that "unleavens" did not change meaning upon addition of πρώτῃ. Whereas before it was "day of the unleavens," and it was not specifically said which one, now it is "first day of the unleavens" and it is known that the first one is meant. Also notice that before addition of the word "first" a precise day is meant, and that after the addition of the word "first" the same precise day is meant. For Mathew means the exact same day as Mark. The addition of the word "first" does not change which day. It only gives more information about that day. So also is the case with "day

[145] For the sake of argument, I am sticking to "first day of the unleavens," which is an accepted a-contextual sense; however the phrase is a Hebraism: "head day of unleavens", "the day ahead of unleavens" or "the day before unleavened bread." Also in Luke 22:7, codex Bezae reads "day of the Passover" which is adopted in this book. The translations in this section are simply to make a grammatical point.

of the sabbaths" vs. "first day of the sabbaths". The grammar is exactly parallel and the word first does not change it from the sabbath. It only gives more information about the day.

In like manner the addition of the same word here: *πρώτῃ ἡμέρᾳ τῶν σαββάτων = *first day of the Sabbaths*, or *Τῇ δὲ μιᾷ ἡμέρᾳ τῶν σαββάτων = *and the one day of the Sabbaths*. The critics all agree that the use of μιᾷ as "one" for "first" is a Hebraism. The usage is seen in Genesis 1:5: ἡμέρα μία = first day. Now while these examples are non extant, the extant example πρώτῃ ἡμέρᾳ τῶν ἀζύμων (Mark 14:12) completely illustrates what would be meant if they were; Τῇ δὲ μιᾷ ἡμέρᾳ τῶν σαββάτων can mean nothing but *and on the first day of the sabbaths*. We will see in a bit that it is irrelevant that the expanded forms above are not seen in usage.

Let us now take the extant form Καὶ τῇ πρώτῃ ἡμέρᾳ τῶν ἀζύμων (Mark 14:12) and observe what happens when the word ἡμέρᾳ drops out. The form is now: Καὶ τῇ πρώτῃ τῶν ἀζύμων = *and the first of unleavens*. And this form is extant in Matthew 26:17 Τῇ δὲ πρώτῃ τῶν ἀζύμων. The meaning is exactly the same, "And on the first of the unleavens." The substitution of δὲ for Καὶ is not relevant. It is only a variant conjunction, and the two represent *waw* in Hebrew. What is observed is that first the addition of the word "first" or "one" does not alter the meaning of the genitive noun phrase either τῶν ἀζύμων or τῶν σαββάτων to some other day. And then second, the omission of the word "day" does not alter the meaning of τῶν ἀζύμων to some other day. It follows that there is no grammatical reason to expect the meaning of τῶν σαββάτων to change on omission of the word "day": Τῇ δὲ μιᾷ τῶν σαββάτων = *the first of the Sabbaths*. This is just as legal as: Τῇ δὲ πρώτῃ τῶν ἀζύμων = *the first of the unleavens*.

The reason that πρώτῃ does not need to alter to a neuter "gender" is the intent of the language to imply ἡμέρᾳ. The numeral thus must agree with ἡμέρᾳ, and by the proof given above is exempt from having to agree with either τῶν ἀζύμων or τῶν σαββάτων as shown above. Likewise, Judith 14:18, μία γυνὴ τῶν Εβραίων, confirms the fact that the nominative noun, whether implied or supplied for μία excuses the following genitive of the whole τῶν Εβραίων from agreement with the numeral.

Steele has appealed to the Holy Ghost as certifying his results, but vainly so using the wrong set of texts to interpret. Rather he should have used Luke 22:7, Mark 14:12 and Matthew 26:27 along with Acts 13:14. He mentions some of these, but ignores their significance. Here then is a summary:

1a. Luke 22:7: ἡμέρα τῶν ἀζύμων day of the unleavens	1b. Acts 13:14: ἡμέρᾳ τῶν σαββάτων day of the sabbaths
2a. Mar. 14:12: πρώτῃ ἡμέρᾳ τῶν ἀζύμων first day of the unleavens (no change of day from 1a)	2b. Non-extant expansion: *μία ἡμέρᾳ τῶν σαββάτων one day of the sabbaths (no change of day from 1b).
3a. Mat 26:17: πρώτῃ τῶν ἀζύμων first of the unleavens (no change of day from 1a)	3b. John 20:1: μία τῶν σαββάτων one of the sabbaths (no change of day from 1b)

Observe that the two sets of phrases are exactly equivalent in every grammatical sense except in the difference between an ordinal number and a cardinal number.[146] Observe also that no change in the genitive phrase is required: "...of the unleavens" is invariant throughout and so "...of the sabbaths" should be invariant throughout. Further, observe that the extant form ἡμέρᾳ τῶν σαββάτων *day of the sabbaths* is the ordinary idiom for the "Sabbath Day." The words all go together. The construct genitive phrase allows an internal number and gender clash. The construct phrase is a substitute for an adjective construction. With regular adjective constructions, number, gender, and definiteness must agree. With the construct substitute for an adjective, no agreement is required. And finally, notice that without or without the word "first", Matthew, Mark, and Luke meant the exact same day. "first" only gives more information about the same day.

---

[146] And this difference is slight. It is admitted on all hands that the Greek word for "one" is used in the ordinal sense after the pattern of the Hebrew in Genesis One, "one day" = "first day." The use of the Greek cardinal, however, does open up the possibility of reading the phrase "a Sabbath" or "some one of the Sabbaths." While this is possible, it gives the same practical result for the chronology as "first of the Sabbaths."

The construct is often used to express adjectival meaning when the adjective form is not available. In the English "Sabbath Day," the word "Sabbath" is used as an adjective. It describes what kind of day it is. But in Hebrew there are no adjective forms for Sabbath, and day is masculine while Sabbath is feminine, so the regular adjective construction cannot be used. A construct phrase is required: יוֹם הַשַּׁבָּת = *day-of*$_m$ *the-sabbath*$_f$. Likewise, in Greek, no separate adjective exists for "sabbath" or "day," so a genitive phrase is required to say what kind of day we are talking about: ἡμέρᾳ$_f$ τῶν$_n$ σαββάτων$_n$. Gender agreement is not required between the head noun and the attributive noun. In such cases, if a numeral is added to count the entity or idea so constructed, the numeral will agree with the head noun. If the head noun is missing, then it can be supplied from the context.

If the phrase is enumerated, then the numeral only needs to agree with the head noun phrase.[147] For example, in 2Sam. 2:1 εἰς μίαν τῶν πόλεων Ιουδα, *to one*$_f$ *of-the*$_f$ *cities*$_f$ *-of Judah*$_m$, the words עָרֵי יְהוּדָה *cities*$_f$*-of Judah*$_m$ are in construct relation. The numeral agrees in gender only with the words "the cities" (fem.), and not "Judah" (masc.): בְּאַחַת עָרֵי יְהוּדָה. Again, only the head noun phrase עָרֵי, τῶν πόλεων agrees with the numeral: אַחַת, μίαν. So when the head noun must be supplied, or is only implicit, then the numeral need only agree with the implicit head noun.

So also 1Sam. 27:5: בְּאַחַת עָרֵי הַשָּׂדֶה, *in-one*$_f$*-of*$_f$ *cities*$_f$*-of the-country*$_m$. Exceptions are possible. In 2Sam. 17:9, the Hebrew has a gender clash: בְּאַחַת הַפְּחָתִים = *in-one*$_f$*-of the-pits*$_m$. And in apparent imitation of the Hebrew אַחַת הַלְּשָׁכוֹת, *one*$_f$*-of the-chambers*$_f$, Jer. 35:2 (LXX 42:2), in the LXX has: μίαν$_f$ τῶν$_m$ αὐλῶν$_m$, *one*$_f$ *of-the*$_m$ *courts*$_m$ (NETS). With a Greek genitive phrase, the head noun can be in any main case: nominative, accusative, dative, or genitive. Only the following genitive noun needs to be genitive. In Hebrew the head noun must be construct form (or so understood) and the following noun can look like any ordinary noun with or without the article.

---

[147] I say *noun phrase* because the definite article may be included with the noun, sharing its number, case, and gender.

Therefore, there is nothing unusual about the case and number combination in the resurrection passages disagreeing with the following attributive. And there is nothing unusual about the numeral enumerating or specifying a particular "one of" something. The only thing that might be slightly unusual is the need to supply the head noun needed to agree with the gender of the numeral. But we have seen in the exactly parallel example of "first *day* of unleavens" that the needed head noun can be supplied without changing the fact that the genitive phrase "of the unleavens" tells *what kind of day* (describes) in the adjectival sense. And in every variation of the phrase, "first of the unleavens," "day of the unleavens," or "first day of the unleavens", the phrase "of the unleavens" describes the kind of day, and this day does not alter to another day upon addition of "first."

So also, "of the Sabbaths" describes what kind of "first *day*" it is.

In Luke 22:7, ἡμέρα τῶν ἀζύμων, *day of the unleavens*, "of the unleavens" describes the kind of day. In Acts 16:13 ἡμέρᾳ τῶν σαββάτων, *day of the Sabbaths*, "of the Sabbaths" describes what kind of day. In Mark 14:12 and Mat. 26:17 the phrase varies, dropping the word day, and adding a numeral. But still "of the unleavens" exactly describes the nature of the day whether it is counted or not, whether the word day is present or not. For this reason, there is absolutely no way a grammatical law can be invented or conjured up against the plain sense of the resurrection passages "one *day* of the Sabbaths" or "first of the Sabbaths."

Now previously, I have removed the siren song of second century idioms in Hebrew, Aramaic, Syriac, and LXX sources for "first day of the week." These were the result of a conspiracy in Rabbinical Judaism against the Nazarenes, a conspiracy just as devilish as the Church's replacement of Sabbath with Sunday. It had to have happened. For there is no other explanation as to why the chronology based on *Scripture alone* adds up against them. Nine passages have been corrupted to refer to Sunday rather than the Sabbath.

> "And nine, nine rings were gifted to the race of men, who, above all else, desire power. But they were, all of them, deceived, for another Ring was made. In the land of Mordor, in

> the fires of Mount Doom, the Dark Lord Sauron forged in secret a master Ring, to control all others. And into this Ring he poured his cruelty, his malice and his will to dominate all life. One Ring to rule them all.[148]

Acts 20:

Sooner or later the skeptic tries to use Acts 20:6-7:

> 5But these had gone on ahead and were waiting for us at Troas. 6And
> we sailed during the days of Unleavened Bread from Philippi. And we came
> to them unto Troas, up to five days, where we used up the seven days[λ].
> 7And on the FIRST OF THE ŞABBAŧHS[ψ], when we [θ]had been getting gath-
> ered together to break bread, Paul kept on talking to them, intending to
> be departing in the morning. And besides he was stretching out the word
> as far as [μ]midnight (*The Good News of Messiah*).

I have supplied a corrected translation above. The skeptic says that they sailed "after the days of unleavened bread," and that they spent seven days at their destination after their arrival, and then the "first of the Sabbaths." They confidently proclaim that it is two weeks after Passover and that it is no longer the first sabbath after Passover.

To answer the skeptic I first point out that if you add up the rest of Paul's travelogue to Jerusalem, then that would put him in Jerusalem after the day of Shavuot (Pentecost), and that such a two week delay is completely inconsistent with his stated desire to reach Jerusalem by the feast date (cf. Acts 20:16).

Now to rid ourselves of these two extra weeks I first render the Greek, "we sailed from Philippi in the middle of the days of unleavened bread" (Acts 20:6). The accusative μετὰ can indeed be rendered "in the middle of."[149] The second step is to make sure the translation, "where we *finally*[150] consumed *the* seven days" is sufficiently literal.

---

[148] Matthew 28:1; Mark 16:2, 9; Luke 24:1; John 20:1, 19; Acts 20:7; 1 Cor. 16:2; Rev. 1:10. Fellowship of the Ring (2001).

[149] See Liddell, Scott, and Jones Greek Lexicon. Meta with the accusative and a verb of motion, i.e. "sailing" regularly has this sense. See "C. WITH ACCUS." This Lexicon is also online. Continued below the line. **

[150] The literal text reads, "where we consumed seven days [ὅπου διετρίψαμεν ἡμέρας ἑπτα]." The italicized words are to prevent a misunderstanding of when Luke begins to count those seven days. Luke assumes the reader knows that those seven days began with the first day of unleavened bread. Friberg

** μετα means "with." The exact sense appears to be governed by word order and the presence of a verb of motion (cf. Thayer). Compare, "we sailed with the days of unleavened bread" and "with three days to rise" (Mark 8:31). "To rise" coming after the preposition, and not logically implying movement from one place to another during the time period, gives the sense of the action happening "with" the time period being completed, thus "after" the third literal day, but "we sailed with" gives the sense of alongside of.

The question is, “What seven days?” And the answer is that they reached the end of the seven days of unleavened bread in Troas. And immediately after the 7th day of the feast came the “first of the sabbaths.”[151] So now the text is harmonious with Paul’s intent to reach Jerusalem, and his travelogue does not contain too many days to allow him to do so.

Figure 25: Chronology of Acts 20:7

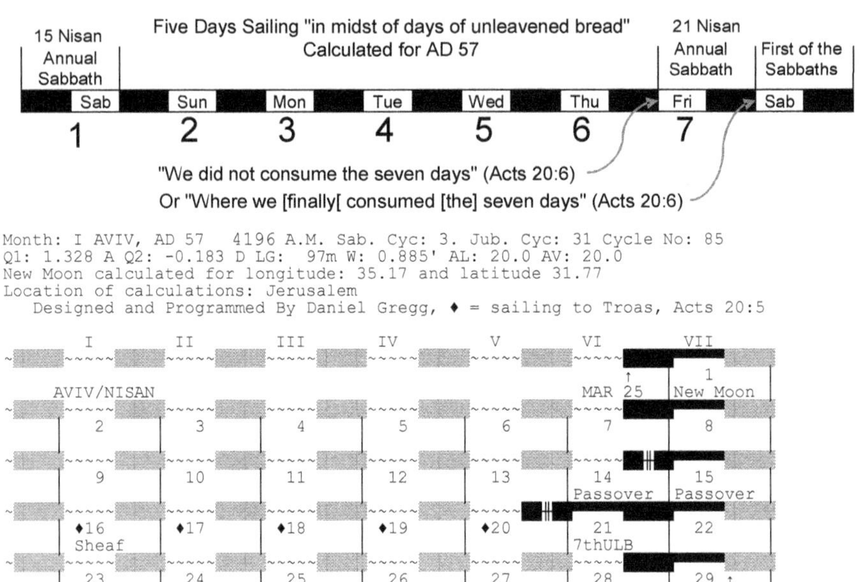

Not all of the skeptics are law rejecting Church defenders or Messiah denying Rabbis. Some of them are sincerely Torah observant, and do trust in Messiah Yeshua, but due to a lack of education come to this subject with erroneous assumptions and

---

(διατρίβω): “rub through, wear away”; Thayer, “consume.” The Majority text and B witness another reading, “We did not consume *the* seven days” (οὐ διετρίψαμεν ἡμέρας ἑπτα) [with accents remarked on οὐ].

[151] (SEE www.torahtimes.org): In THE SCROLL OF BIBLICAL CHRONOLOGY by the author, pg. 56, it is shown that the Passover feast for A.D. 57 calculates out with the 15th of Nisan landing on the Sabbath, and the 21st coming on a Friday. There are five ordinary days between the annual Sabbaths, and the “first of the Sabbaths” after Nisan 15 turns out to be on the 22nd of Nisan. This is astronomically determined. Paul and his companions sailed during the five intermediate days of the feast. (Ebook only as of 2021).

overreactions to the Greek texts. Yet, the truth is that the Greek texts are the best translation available of the Hebrew spoken by Yeshua's disciples. Yeshua may have known Aramaic as well, but the Aramaic Peshitta[152] currently available today was translated from the Greek texts. So the Greek texts remain the most accurate representation of the primary Hebrew sources.

The smartest of Church skeptics tell their people that the Greek *μιᾷ τῶν σαββάτων* translates into a Hebrew idiom for "first day of the week" (בְּאֶחָד בַּשַּׁבָּת).[153] They cite the same idiom in the Talmud and Aramaic: בחַד־בְּשַׁבָּא. This idiom did not come into wide use until after A.D. 140.* And it is indeed an archaeo-conspiracy between the proto-Catholic Church and the Rabbis. The Church decided to use *μιᾷ τῶν σαββάτων* in its ecclesiastical Greek to mean "first day of the week," but the Rabbis meant, "one unto the Sabbath" by אחד בשבת, and both "one in the seven (week)" or "one unto the Sabbath" by חד בשבא. In other words שבא is a word deliberately ambiguous meant to suggest that the Biblical Hebrew word שבת and the Greek σαββατων may have the sense "week."

It was also at this time that Rabbinical Judaism modified its explanation of Shavuot. The Rabbis kept the Scriptural timing for the feast but decided to stop reading Lev. 23:15 as instructions to count "seven sabbaths."[154] How this came about is not hard to imagine. At that time large numbers of Jews were defecting to Christianity. But there were always periods when Christians were defecting to Judaism. When an apostate switches sides, they take with them some of the knowledge they once had, and they are most eager to make sure that knowledge that connects Yeshua with true Torah observance is covered up to smoother their own negative emotions.

So the Rabbis and Bishops of the Church are like the two faced

---

[152] There are some that go so far as to say that Yeshua actually spoke the exact Aramaic words in the Peshitta text. But this is traditional dogmatism of Church of the East. Yeshua would not have used the word *Namusa* (derived from Greek *nomos*) instead of Torah to talk about the Torah in Matthew 5:17-20. Yet the Peshitta text does betrays its Greek source by doing just that.

[153] *Seder Olam*, ca 140 A.D., pg. 67, Heinrich W. Guggenheimer.

[154] This resulted in some inconsistencies in their explanation of the passage that are exploited by the Karaites.

* שבא derives from שבע derives, "seven," being originally an interchange of the ayin for the alef, but it was used in late Jewish literature to also mean "Sabbath." Cf. Targum Y. Exodus 20:10: ויומא שביעאה שבא. See Jastrow, "שׁוּבָא, שַׁבָּא, שַׁב," where it states, "= h. שָׁבוּעַ. week." But this word was confused with Sabbath. In Biblical Hebrew, the DSS usage, and Evangelists the meaning "week" is not confused with the Sabbath. The equivocation to Sabbath was a Rabbinic ploy to mislead Christians. In all earlier texts "seven" and "Sabbath" are two different distinct Hebrew or Aramaic words. While counting to Sabbath existed in the DSS, there is no evidence that "Sabbath" was being used to mean "week" before ca. AD 150.

false god Janus. It is the same false god. The synagogue of Satan is in the Vatican, but it is also the institution of Rabbinical Authority. One side of this false god looks like a Jewish Rabbi, and the other side like a Catholic bishop. This false god is united in its opposition to Yeshua and to the Torah that Yeshua upholds, not only in practice, but in the manner in which he fulfilled the times and seasons.

The way around these false authorities is to learn not to believe their sources because of their conflict of interest. Only true linguistic sources without a clear conflict of interest can be regarded as valid—and I mean contemporary Greek and Hebrew sources from before the destruction of the Temple (A.D. 70). So like the reformers John Wycliffe and William Tyndale, it is necessary to obtain one's Greek and Hebrew from the most unbiased source as possible. That is the principle of the matter.

The reformers had to rely on Rabbinic Jews for their Hebrew and on Byzantine Church scholars of Greek from Constantinople that was destroyed by the Muslims in A.D. 1453. So it is not surprising that they did not detect the error in rendering *μιᾷ τῶν σαββάτων* as "the first day of the week." They did not have the tools to get behind these sources and check them out on an independent basis.

Today we do. The Rabbis and Bishops have been compelled to publish many sources of Greek and Hebrew that were before unavailable. And when something is unavailable, people tend to trust what is: Rabbinic or Church pronouncements.

The key here is to ensure that all the Scriptural sources are taken literally and the mistakes corrected on an independent basis without relying on later sources or authorities which have become corrupt. When this is done the whole chronology of Scripture comes together. When the keystone of knowledge from Yeshua is locked into place, then all the pieces of the temple align themselves exposing the lies of our fathers.

So like the reformers, we must go behind the Church of Rome, and like the few Jews who come out of Judaism, we must realize that when it comes to Yeshua and his fulfillment of Scripture that the Rabbis cannot be trusted.

The Church launched the counter reformation against the

reformers, and they step by step subverted the gains of the reformers. At the start, it was not a counter attack of reason and superior evidence. Rather it was a program of war, assassination, and political subversion, bribery, murder, and religious coercion. No sooner had the Protestants discovered a little truth than they found themselves in a total war for their lives with the Church of Rome. Therefore, there was little time to pursue the depths of deception of the Church. It was a luxury that they had no time for since Rome was insisting on winning the argument with the sword.

When the Protestants finally won some victories, they were all too ready to compromise and seek a middle way of peace with Rome rather than continue to risk further bloody war. This practical peace however resulted in a laziness of mind for digging deeper and exposing all the iniquities of Rome. Along with their zeal for suffering the Protestants slowly lost their zeal for the truth.

So the second reason Rome succeed with this counter attack is that the descendents of the reformers have lost their scientific inquiry and have started trusting conflicted human sources again. When it comes to deception, freedom from it can only come through independent confirmation of a truth, and not through acceptance based on authority of what the other side says.

They are few indeed that can examine an issue while suspending all of the assumptions and emotional attachments to the opinions[155] of their forbearers. I am one of the few with this gift, or a greater measure of it. However I realize that it will take the Spirit of Yahweh to cut the emotional chains of bondage. These emotional shackles are more powerful than any logical argument, and I'd have no hope of anyone overcoming them except for one thing: the Almighty has a plan to redeem Israel and to restore the truth of Messiah and Torah.

So there is a counter reformation going on right now against the

---

[155] I mean those opinions with a clear conflict of interest. If a more logical and scientific position holds together against a traditional position, and the traditional position is a support in the system of lies against Yeshua or Torah, then it must be assigned no weight in determining the truth. We need not become universal skeptics who are people who doubt everything. We need not doubt the fact that Yeshua was a Jew or that the four Evangelists wrote the gospels. We need not become liberal doubters of everything.

people who want to trust in Yeshua and return to Torah. Many cultists and people dressed in the garb of Torah and Messiah have been rushing into the midst of us who are returning to Torah and Messiah. And they are sowing doubt, confusion, and discord, and all kinds of ignorance. They are becoming false shepherds and leaders. Yeshua has a day of reckoning with these false teachers. They are succeeding only because the hunger of Christians for Torah truth is so great that even a spoonful of poisoned food will satisfy.

These people are the disorganized fringe of the synagogue of Satan. They will tell you that they have nothing to do with the Roman Church, and they will tell you that they reject Rabbinical Judaism. I tell you that where they reject the Rabbis, then they accept Rome, and where they reject Rome they accept the Rabbis! This is because though they claim to reject authority, they, in fact, do not know how to discover the truth through prayer, and independent scientific inquiry. They therefore end up rejecting authority and spouting all kinds of other nonsense, and never succeed in escaping from the deeper deceptions of Rome and Rabbis.

There is an explanation for everything, but it must be discovered by prayer and independent confirmation of the truth. If there is a good anti-Messiah/Torah motive for the other side keeping a certain "truth," and an examination of the evidence that is still uncontaminated by that "truth" shows another conclusion, then that so called "truth" is really a lie. You can call this Gregg's dictum. It is really a biblical truth, "Test all things and hold fast to that which is good" (1 Thess. 5:21). And what must be tested first are those items that are used to support either rebellion against Messiah or His Torah. The need for *Gregg's dictum* is a testimony to the depravity of human nature and the power of a sinful tradition.

So then we must put Talmudic, Aramaic Peshitta, and Targum usages on the shelf along with Ecclesiastical Greek. These are conflicted sources. The Aramaic is a mistranslation of Greek sources made at a time when the Church had already rebelled against the Torah. If someone needs to have this proved, then they need only read my book, *Exploding the Aramaic Myth: An Investigation of Aramaic Primacy*.* Further, there is no conflict of interest with the Greek texts.

* Currently out of print, and no ebook currently available as of April 2020.

There are no other texts at the present time that are more original. However, there are differences between Greek manuscripts, and some of these differences are critical, and expose Church corruptions.

I say this because among us are many who needlessly and recklessly attack the Greek records. Yeshua spoke Hebrew, and so did his followers, but some of them knew Greek and that is how his words were recorded for us. They tear down the Greek because they associate it emotionally with the Church, but I will show bit by bit that the original Greek is the best defender of the truth there is, and that it is at the expense of Church falsehood.

So of course to get behind the Church and Synagogue we must dismiss anything they say that is either anti Messiah or anti Torah. If indeed Yeshua rose on the "first of the sabbaths" and this matches Torah so clearly in Lev. 23:15-16, and if indeed Yeshua's death and resurrection so clearly match up the days for sacrificial offerings in the Temple, then the Synagogue of Satan[156] has every reason to leaven their literature with poisons against this truth.

We must seek the truth independently without listening to anything either has put in their writings after the polemical war escalated. The Church cites the Church Fathers as evidence for its positions, and their own translations. The Rabbis cite the Talmud and their own translations. When the Church and Rabbis can use each other for common support of their opposite conclusions, then they cite each other. Everything depends on the motive for the citation.

And Yeshua's death and resurrection is at the very center of all wars and all conflicts. If you do not know this, then you soon will because it exposes the errors of Church and Synagogue on many related points.

<u>*Matthew 28:1:*</u>

28 [1]But *the* [ξ]later of *the* Ȿabbaŧhs, at the dawning for *the* [θ]FIRST [ζ]OF THE ȾABBAŦHS, Miryam Ha-Magdalit and the other Miryam came to look at the grave.

(From: *The Good News of Messiah*)

---

[156] When I use this phrase, I mean the Church (arch-synagogue) and also the leaven of the Rabbis.

In the end of the Sabbath, as it began to dawn toward the first *day* of the week, came Mary Magdalene and the other Mary to see the sepulchre (KJV).

In the evening of the Sabbath, as it was twilight [on] the first day of the week Mary Magdalene and the other Mary came to see the grave (MGI Peshitta NT).

The second clause of the verse says "at the dawning." This is what the Greek means. The words τῇ ἐπιφωσκούσῃ literally mean "at the lighting up" when taken apart. The Greek is a compound word, "lighting-up." ἐπι means "up" or "upon" and φωσκούσῃ means "lighting." The King James Version correctly translates the words, "as it began to dawn." This phrase shows that something is wrong with the words found in the first clause of the verse, "In the end of the Sabbath" (KJV) or "eve of the sabbaths" (YLT, cf. MGI). For the sabbath ended at sunset, which was evening. Thus, the first phrase is in direct conflict with the second. The Sabbath ends with dark, but the text says it was "at the dawning."

Some skeptics will respond by saying that "dawning" was a manner of speaking of the beginning of a day based on the Jewish beginning of the day at sunset. They will use the mistranslation of the first clause to interpret the second. For example the Magiera Peshitta translation above, "twilight."[157] And so they claim that dawning means evening twilight. This excuse adds another assumption to the case at hand, and makes it unclear. It deprives the text of clarity. Others leave us to assume that the "evening of the Sabbath" lasted all night in order to retain the dawning clause. This is hardly acceptable. It is clear from the sentence structure that the first and second clause are time indicators and that one explains the other. Thus they must both refer to the same moment in time.

The way to deal with this is repair the first clause. Matthew says, "the later of the Sabbaths" (Ὀψὲ δὲ σαββάτων). Since there were two Sabbaths that could be called the "first sabbath," Matthew was compelled to point out that it was the second first sabbath.[158] In his

[157] But the Syriac text means "dawning." (See J. Payne-Smith, pg. 327.)
[158] Luke 6:1, "second first sabbath" also refers to the anniversary of the

words it is the "Later of the Sabbaths."

The first day of unleavened bread was the first Sabbath of the feast, but the weekly Sabbath following was the first Sabbath between Passover and Shavuot that was supposed to be counted (cf. Lev. 23:15). The words "later of the sabbaths" point out the "later" of the two Sabbaths. The Greek word phrase corresponds to the Hebrew: וּבְאַחֲרוֹן הַשַּׁבָּתוֹת or וּבְשַׁבָּתוֹן אַחֲרוֹן. The word וְ = δὲ; and אַחֲרוֹן = 'Οψὲ; and שַׁבָּתוֹת = σαββάτων or שַׁבָּתוֹן = σαββάτων.

B-D-F (Blass, Debrunner, Funk) say, "the genitive with ὀψὲ and μετ' ὀλίγον have become associated in meaning with ὕστερον τούτων,[159] πρότερον τούτων" (§164.4, pg. 91).[160] Translation, "the genitive with *later* and a *after a little while* have become associated in meaning with *latter of these*, *earlier of these*." And examination of LSJ, Middle Liddell, Slater, and Autenrieth show that "late" is the basic sense of ὀψὲ. BDAG (3rd edition) states "late" and glosses "later" on one example. LSJ show "later" in the compound word οψιγενης "*later-born*, i.e. *younger*."[161] This linguistic evidence shows that 'Οψὲ δὲ σαββάτων = "And the later of the sabbaths" (literally: "late yet of-sabbaths"). This also makes sense out of the plural "sabbaths" (σαββάτων): "And *the* late of *the* Sabbaths." When two Sabbaths are considered the second one is "late" with respect to the first. See **Figure 26: The Annual Sabbath and Later Sabbath** below.*

Another skeptic will reply that the word means "after." While this may be true, it has not gone without dispute. LSJ append a question mark to that sense, and Thayer's editor writes a paragraph disputing it. In Greek grammars, the sense "after" for this word has earned it the ignominious label "improper preposition," which is to say it does not fit the expected norm. This is because the attested ways of saying "after" in Greek are ὀπίσω τοῦ σαββάτου, or μετὰ with the accusative. The former witness is found in the Septuagint for

---

resurrection.

[159] The significance of B-D-F's remark becomes clearer by looking up ὕστερον in BDAG (3rd edition): "1. pertaining to being subsequent in a series, the second one...2. in the second place, later, then, thereafter." LSJ is more direct, "latter, last...coming after, behind"

[160] *A Greek Grammar of the New Testament and Other Early Christian Literature.*

[161] pg. 1282, Greek-English Lexicon, Liddell & Scott, 1968.

* Certain words appear in several parts of speech. "Late" is one of these words, e.g. 'the late man' (adj. use), 'the man came late' (adv. use), or 'the late [one] of the men' (noun use). It the case of an adj. used as a noun, it is called a 'substantive.' The use in Mt. 28:1 is clearly substantive, 'the late [one] of the Sabbaths....'

Nehemiah 13:19: אַחַר־הַשַּׁבָּת. It would seem that if Matthew meant "after" then clarity would require him to use a recognized phrase. So the skeptical proposal is unparsimonious. The plain sense is "latter of the Sabbaths" so long as we are not blind to seeing it. And this sense is based on the most normative sense of the words and grammar.

Figure 26: The Annual Sabbath and Later Sabbath

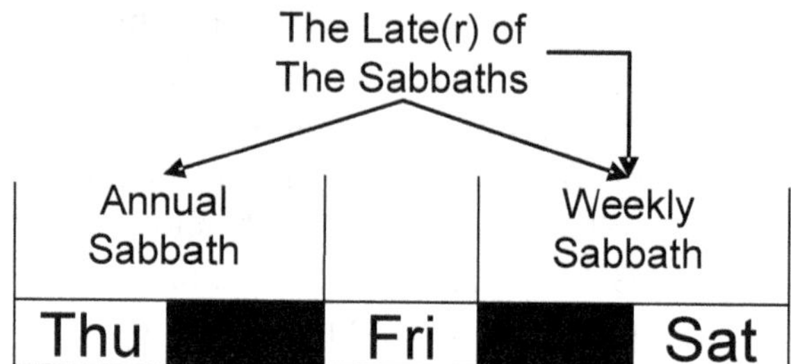

Another thing to point out to the skeptic is that one cannot get to the sense "after" without admitting the sense "later" on the way to their goal of "after." This is because the argument for "after" depends on interpreting the genitive as "later [than]." "Later [than]," "later [from], and "later [of]" are all functions of the genitive case. The first two cannot be asserted without including the third as possible. But it is to be noted that "later [from]" is a function of the classical genitive and is rare in Koine Greek. It is also to be noted that "later [than]" is comparative in Koine Greek and rarer than "late [of]" which would be the norm in Koine Greek. Therefore, "late of Sabbaths" (Ὀψὲ σαββάτων) is the normative sense in Koine Greek. That is pedantically literal. In plain English that is "The latter of the Sabbaths."

So Matthew 28:1 speaks of the "latter of the Sabbaths." This is the weekly sabbath after the Passover Sabbath. It also solves the problem of the King James Version and the Peshitta which say "end of the sabbath" and "evening of the Sabbath" (Magiera) respectively. Since we are speaking of the later Sabbath it is clear that the text is speaking of dawn on the later Sabbath.

The skeptic might point out that Luke 23:54 says, "and the sabbath was dawning" (καὶ σάββατον ἐπέφωσκεν), and that it is talking about sunset, and uses the same word as Mat. 28:1. This gaffe is swept under the rug by almost every translation, “drew on” (KJV), “about to begin” (NAS, NIV), “approaching” (YLT), “beginning” (RSV). The translators therefore recognized that the literal Greek was nonsense to them. For the Greek texts they used say “dawning,” and they felt the need to obscure it. They might feel compelled to resurrect what they buried in Luke 23:54 in order to defend themselves in Matthew 28:1.

They would then justify “end of the sabbath” or “evening of the sabbath” this way by asserting that dawn really means the same thing. The only problem is that Matthew has the women going to the tomb at the time stated in the text. That argument would make the time evening instead of morning, and would contradict the other three Evangelists who state that it was morning using other Greek words. There is a solution to Luke 23:54. The text needs to be rearranged in the style of a literary cliffhanger after the example of Mark 16:8:[162]

> [53]And he took it down and wrapped it in a linen cloth, and laid him
> in a tomb cut into the rock, where no one was ever getting laid. [54a]And
> it was the day of preparation. [54b⸢]Then the Şabbaŧh [ψ]WAS DAWNING.[⸣]

> **24** [54b]And, having followed *him* [λ]throughout *his ministry*, [55]the wom-
> en (who had been been coming with him out of Galil) [δ]saw the
> tomb and how his body was laid, [56]and having returned, they prepared
> spices and perfumes. [56b]And on the one ŞABBAŦH[α] they [ρ]rested,[T] [24.1]but on
> the [θ]FIRST OF THE ŞABBAŦHS,[β] [χ]in [θ]deep dawn, they came upon the tomb,
> bringing the [γ]spices which they had prepared (Luke 23:53-24:1, GNM).

Luke ends the chapter at 23:54b at the point of Messiah’s exit from the grave and the women’s arrival. The day of preparation was the first of three days. The third night passed into the dawning on the Sabbath. And this is where Luke leaves matters hanging. Beginning in the next chapter, Luke backtracks to explain the role of the women followed by the details of the chronology he had skipped over at the end of the pre-

---

[162] The book of Mark ends on a cliffhanger in vs. 8 saying: “[8]And when they went out, they fled from the tomb, because trembling and amazement had been gripping them, and they said nothing to anyone, because they were being in a state of awe (GNM). The Good News of Messiah explains in Appendix V that the shorter ending of Mark is indeed correct, and the translation explains how to make sense out of it.

vious chapter. This only makes sense if Messiah has resurrected in that third night. He comes out of the grave at the earliest dawn to appear alive to the women. This solution allows us to take "dawning" in its normal sense. It just referred to the dawning in which Messiah appeared to the women, and not to a 'dawning' before his burial. Luke skipped ahead at the end of chapter twenty-three to the point in time where he wants to focus the readers attention.

Mark 16:1-2:

16 [1]And when the ŞABBAŧH[ς] was past[τ], Miryam Ha-Magdalit, and Miryam
the mother of Ya'aqov, and Shelomit, [ω]bought spices, that having come,
they might anoint him. [2]And very early on the [η]FIRST OF THE ŞABBAŧHS[χ], they are
coming upon the tomb, ⸢the sun still *not having risen⸣, [3]when they were saying
to themselves, "Who will roll away the stone for us from the door of the tomb?"

The Greek says "very early" (λίαν πρωΐ) here. Also in Luke 24:1 it says "at deep dawn" (ὄρθρου βαθέως) and in John 20:1, "while still dark" (πρωΐ σκοτίας ἔτι). This agrees with the literal and unadulterated sense in Matthew 28:1, "at the dawning" (τῇ ἐπιφωσκούσῃ). The earthquake in Matthew 28:2 (σεισμὸς ἐγένετο μέγας) corresponds to the time of Messiah's exit from the gave.

HOSEA 6:1-3: THE THIRD DAY

Scriptural prophecy also indicates that the resurrection† was to occur about dawn. As one of the "third day" passages, Hosea 6:1-3 is Messianic, and speaks about Messiah, who is here identified as Israel, "us":

> Come, let us return to Yãhweh. For he has torn us, but he will heal us; he has wounded us, but he will bandage us. He will cause us to live after two days; in the third day he will make us to rise, that we may live before his face. So let us know, let us press on to know Yãhweh. His going forth is fixed at earliest dawn; and he will come to us like the rain, like the spring rain watering the earth. (Hosea 6:1-3).

This prophecy is a cryptic multi-layered prophecy. We have to peel back a few layers. First, there is a national and eschatological fulfillment having to do with two days having the sense of 2000 years. Second, the "us" mentioned refers to the great company of holy ones that were resurrected when Yeshua was.‡ Finally, Messiah's

* See note 52, page 62.
† or his *exit* from the grave.
‡ See Mat. 27:52-53.

resurrection itself is hidden in the text under these other two layers.

The text says, "His[163] going forth is fixed at dawn." This may be rendered, "about dawn" or "near dawn." The Hebrew phrase is, " כְּשַׁחַר נָכוֹן מוֹצָאוֹ." The word "שחר" (*shakhar*) means the earliest possible dawn, when the first red streaks appear in the east.[164] The root word means "black," so the idea is a red-black hint of dawn. *Shakhar* is well before sunrise. The preposition "כְּ" gives the sense "at" or "about."

This prophecy also requires us to use the daybreak to daybreak calendar day: "He will cause us to live after two days; in the third day he will make us to rise, that we may live before his face."

The key Hebrew words are "after two days" and "in the third day" (בַּיּוֹם הַשְּׁלִישִׁי). The Hebrew phrase for "after two days" is: מִיֹּמָיִם. The ending a dual plural meaning "two": *ayim*, and it is prefixed with the preposition מִן, with *nun* absorbed into dagesh. The resurrection is stated two ways, 1. after two days, and 2. in the third day. This means that chronologically, "after two days" = "on the third day." The Septuagint confirms "after two days, in the third day" (μετὰ δύο ἡμέρας ἐν τῇ ἡμέρᾳ τῇ τρίτῃ).

It is also evident that it is two days after Yahweh (the Father) has "torn" that he will "heal" and "bind." So the difference is that "in the third day" is counting inclusively, while "after two days" is counting exclusively. There is only one way to justify this with "three days and three nights" (Matthew 12:40), and that is with the daybreak to daybreak calendar day and the resurrection near dawn:

Figure 27: Hosea's Prophecy of the Resurrection

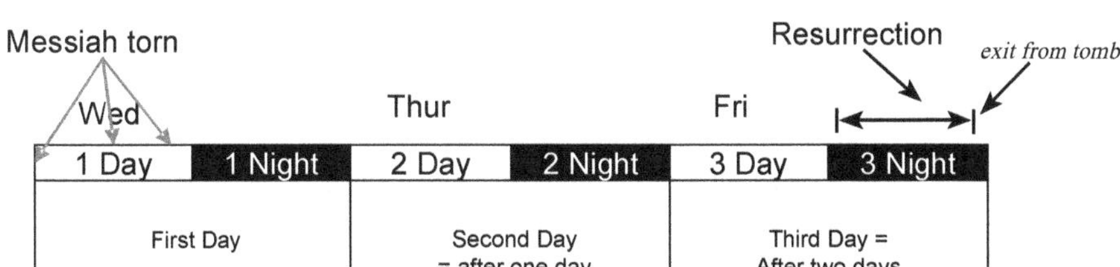

No matter how one tries to calculate "after two days," it cannot be

[163] YHWH's going forth is fixed at dawn. Thus confessing that Messiah is YHWH and that YHWH, the Son, was raised from the dead is taught here.
[164] pg. 962 *Lexicon In Veteris Testamenti Libros*, Koehler/Baumgartner "*the reddish light preceding dawn.*"

stretched out beyond daybreak on the Sabbath. If one tries to start a day at sunset, then after two days will end at sunset on Friday! The "third day" prophecy in Hosea 6:1-3 definitely contradicts the idea that the resurrection was later on the Sabbath than dawn.

Many critics are bound to question if this prophecy is Messianic; let me say that it was always held to be so by all the "Church fathers." Such a unanimous tradition must have its origin in the interpretations of the Apostles. But even without such tradition it would be necessary to regard the passage as Messianic, because certain details come alive. Modern exegetes fail to pay attention to the symbolic and layered hints (remez) in the details toward the prophetic fulfillment.

Hos. 5:14 melds eschatology and Messianic prophecy together, "I, I will tear and go away." The first "I" is the Father; the second "I" is the Son. YHWH was pleased to put him to grief (Isa. 53:10). The idea of "I, I" (אֲנִי אֲנִי) is basically I tear myself. It also refers to the tearing of Israel, and the sending of both of Ephraim and Judah into exile till the regathering in the end of days. "There will be none to deliver." There was none to deliver Yeshua from death. There will be none to deliver Israel from exile. Again the eschatological and the Messianic themes are melded together. "In their distress they will seek me at earliest dawn" (יְשַׁחֲרֻנְנִי vs. 15).[165] This refers to the grieving disciples coming to the tomb Sabbath morning. The Hebrew root is "dawn" the same as Hos. 6:3.

The eschatological aspect of Hosea 6:1 calls for national repentance, which will happen on the third day. A.D. 2012 will mark 2732 years of exile for the kingdom of Israel, which is arguably 732 years into the third day.† Also 2000 years beyond the resurrection of Yeshua could begin the third day. Israel is referred to as "us" half a dozen times in the passage. The way to decode this is that Messiah receives the suffering from our sins to show the cost to God while waiting for our repentance.* The servant Israel/Messiah passages in Isaiah give a similar picture. And of course, there was an "us" that quite literally resurrected "on the third day," mentioned in Matthew 27:53. In Hosea 6:3 is mentioned the "latter rain" (כְּמַלְקוֹשׁ), which is the spring rain. Yeshua's passion matches up with the spring feast of passover. And

† From the exile of the northern kingdom in 720 BC, the 9th year of Hoshea, and the 6th year of Hezekiah.

165 Translations vary from "seek me earnestly" to "seek me early," but the sense of "early" is derived from the original lexical meaning "dawn" (BDB).

* Messiah died "to demonstrate God's justice" (Rom. 3:25), to show what we were being forgiven. Our condemnation is canceled in conjunction with an offering illustrating for us the cost sin takes from the Almighty while he waits to forgive us.

his resurrection was on the first day of the spring harvest offering, the first day of the counting to shavuot.

> [54b]And, having followed *him* [λ]throughout *his ministry*, [55]the women (who
> had been been coming with him out of Galil) [δ]saw the tomb and how his
> body was laid, [56]and having returned, they prepared spices and perfumes.
> [56b]And on the one ŞABBAŧH[α] they [ρ]rested,[T] [24.1]but on the [θ]FIRST OF THE
> ŞABBAŧHS,[β] [χ]in [θ]deep dawn, they came upon the tomb, bringing the [γ]spices
> which they had prepared. (GNM, Luke 23-24)

These two verses go together.† For like Mark 16:1-2, the text is talking about two sabbaths. In fact, all the evangelists talk about the two sabbaths. Mark 16:1 refers to the annual Sabbath that began Wednesday at sunset that year. And Mark 16:2 refers to the following weekly Sabbath. Matthew 28:1 alludes to both sabbaths saying "later of the sabbaths," so we can see that both are comprehended in the plural "sabbaths." John 19:31 mentions the sabbath after the crucifixion and calls it a "high sabbath" or "great sabbath."

So also Luke 23:56-24:1. Both Sabbaths are mentioned. Luke 23:56b references the Passover Sabbath. Now the women did rest on this Sabbath, for which there is a commandment in Lev. 23:7, but I have placed the words‡ in the margin because Bezae omits them. However, on the "first of the sabbaths" they came to the tomb to anoint the body of Yeshua.

An interlocutor will object that Jewish women would never do this on the Sabbath. However, one cannot reinterpret a chronology by human behavior. Chronological statements take precedence. Jews were not supposed to heal on the Sabbath. But I know one who did. Healed men were not supposed to pick up their bed on Sabbath either, yet I know one who did. Warriors are not supposed to eat the bread of the presence in the Temple, but I know a band who did and got excused. This all refers to legitimate behavior.

But pious Jews are also capable of illegitimate behavior. Should I

---

[166] The eschatological types of the third day pertain to the "day of Yahweh," which is one thousand years. Yeshua's resurrection was at the end of the third day, and we see that the nations that repent during this time will be resurrected to life at the end of the thousand years. On the other hand, the beginning of the third day is also marked as a type, and so the resurrection at the beginning of the "day of Yahweh" also matches the type, and this is the beginning of the first-fruits. Matthew 27:53 says the graves were opened at the crucifixion. It is possible that these dead were raised at the time of the wave sheaf, at the start of the third day, which explains Matthew's ordering and also that of Hosea 6:1-3, with Messiah himself coming at the end of the "third day."

† Luke 23:56b & 24:1.

‡ "according to the commandment."

speak of King David ordering that the Ark of the Covenant be carried on a cart? So the objection that the women would not go to the tomb on the Sabbath is of no weight. Nevertheless, the Mishnah made provision for tending the dead on the Sabbath:

> עוֹשִׂין כָּל צָרְכֵי הַמֵּת, סָכִין וּמְדִיחִין אוֹתוֹ, וּבִלְבַד שֶׁלֹּא יָזִיזוּ בוֹ אֵבֶר. שׁוֹמְטִין אֶת הַכַּר מִתַּחְתָּיו וּמַטִּילִין אוֹתוֹ עַל הַחֹל בִּשְׁבִיל שֶׁיַּמְתִּין. קוֹשְׁרִים אֶת הַלֶּחִי, לֹא שֶׁיַּעֲלֶה, אֶלָּא שֶׁלֹּא יוֹסִיף. וְכֵן קוֹרָה שֶׁנִּשְׁבְּרָה, סוֹמְכִין אוֹתָהּ בְּסַפְסָל אוֹ בַּאֲרֻכּוֹת הַמִּטָּה, לֹא שֶׁתַּעֲלֶה, אֶלָּא שֶׁלֹּא תוֹסִיף. אֵין מְעַמְּצִין אֶת הַמֵּת בְּשַׁבָּת, וְלֹא בְחֹל עִם יְצִיאַת נֶפֶשׁ. וְהַמְעַמֵּץ עִם יְצִיאַת נֶפֶשׁ, הֲרֵי זֶה שׁוֹפֵךְ דָּמִים:

> They may make ready [on the Sabbath] all that is needful for the dead, and anoint and wash it, provided that they do not move any member of it. They may draw the mattress away from beneath it and let it lie on the sand that it may be the longer preserved; they may bind up the chin, not in order to raise it but that it may not sink lower. So, too, if a rafter is broken they may support it with a bench or with the side-pieces of a bed that the break may grow no greater, but not in order to prop it up. They may not close a corpse's eyes on the Sabbath; nor may they do so on a weekday at the moment when the soul is departing; and he that closes the eyes [of the dying man] at the moment when the soul is departing, such a one is a shedder of blood. Danby, Mishnah 23:5.

Just how much the Jewish authorities would have permitted the women to do or not to do really is not relevant. The Scripture records that they did it.* The same kind of objection might be raised concerning the two men on the road to Emmaus. Yeshua appeared to them on the Sabbath. Again they had their reasons for leaving. For sure, they did not want to be around Jerusalem to be implicated in a missing body plot or accusation. The reason that interlocutors bring up these sort of objections is that it makes for an easy excuse for not paying attention to the chronology.

Why does Luke 23:56b-24:1 mention the two Sabbaths without the day in between as in Mark 16:1-2? Luke is focusing on how the two Sabbaths were observed. The first they rested on, but the second they used a legal exception to make one last anointing of the body before the tomb became inaccessible. In any case, the day in between was alluded to at the"end"of chapter 23, "and they returned and prepared spices and perfumes" (vs. 56a). They bought the spices after the annual Sabbath (Mark 16:1). Luke simply assumed his reader would know that after they returned that they waited twenty-four

* The reasoning behind the Mishnah ruling has now come to my attention. The dead person was until the third day passed regarded in the same category as an elderly person who was ill and needed taking care of. The work involved was justified on the same principle as someone who needed critical assistance on the Sabbath. Such was the ancient Jewish respect for the dead that laws were passed about who could and could not defile themselves for their sake. Such care reflects genuine hope in the resurrection of the dead.

hours before preparing any spices.

Why did the women visit at the end of the third day? After Yeshua was taken down by Joseph, the disciples most likely had a consultation about who would do what. Joseph himself found space in his new tomb, and quickly wrapped Yeshua in a singular sheet (σινδόνι). The first twenty-four hours, the body would need no further attention. After the annual Sabbath the guards let Nicodemus in to embalm the body, during which he re-wrapped the body with linen strips (ὀθονίοις). The task of anointing the body one last time with sweet spices (ἀρώματα) on the weekly Sabbath was left to the women.

From page 82: **Psalm Titles:**

In the Septuagint (LXX) Psalm 23:1 (MT: 24:1) contains the following superscription lacking in the Hebrew text: "τῆς μιᾶς σαββάτων," (But the only superscription corresponding to a designated day in the canonical Hebrew text is in Psalm 92:1 (LXX 91.1), "εἰς τὴν ἡμέραν τοῦ σαββάτου," "לְיוֹם הַשַּׁבָּת," "A song for the day of the Sabbath." The additional weekday designations were added into the LXX at a later date. In Old Latin, additionally, Psa. 81 has, "*quinta sabbati.*"). There is no doubt that the creator of this title meant it to mean "first [day] of the week." Likewise the meaning "week" was intended with the addition to Psa. 47:1 in the LXX (MT 48:1). It was superscripted with, "δευτέρᾳ σαββάτου," taken to mean "second [day] of the week" in ecclesiastical Greek. And also Psa 93:1 in the LXX (MT 94:1), "τετράδι σαββάτων," "fourth [day] of the week." But in Psalm 92:1 in the LXX (MT 93:1), "εἰς τὴν ἡμέραν τοῦ προσαββάτου," "for the day of the fore-Sabbath," i.e. for the day of preparation is meant, and the word Sabbath is taken literally. While there are Jewish sources relating to designated days for these Psalms, a late Christian editor of the LXX has assumed that Hebrew usage supports his interpretation of the NT "first day of the week" passages. And he has reinterpreted the Hebrew usage according to his assumption so that it matches his interpretation of the NT. But Jewish sources do not support the sense "week." One example is from, *Forms of Prayer according to the Custom of the Spanish and Portuguese Jews,* D.A. De Sola and Isaac Leeser, p. 46, vol. 1. Here the titles occur in Hebrew as: "ביום הראשון, ליום שני, ליום רביעי," and "ליום ששי." In this source there is no evidence of counting with the word שבת. Further back, the earlier source for the inspiration of these titles is the Mishnah (Tamid 7.4) as: בַּיּוֹם הָרִאשׁוֹן, בַּשֵּׁנִי, בַּשְּׁלִישִׁי, בָּרְבִיעִי, בַּחֲמִישִׁי,

בַּשִּׁשִּׁי, בְּשַׁבָּת, viz:

> MISHNA 7:4 The following is a list of each daily psalm that the Levites would recite in the Temple. On the first day ~~of the week~~ they would recite the psalm beginning: “A psalm of David. The earth is the Lord’s and all it contains, the world and all who live in it” (Psalms, chapter 24). On the second ~~day~~ they would recite the psalm beginning: “A song; a psalm of the sons of Korah. Great is the Lord and highly to be praised in the city of God, on His sacred mountain” (Psalms, chapter 48). On the third ~~day~~ they would recite the psalm beginning: “A psalm of Asaph. God stands in the divine assembly; among the judges He delivers judgment” (Psalms, chapter 82). On the fourth ~~day~~ they would recite the psalm beginning: “O Lord God, to Whom vengeance belongs, God to Whom vengeance belongs, shine forth” (Psalms, chapter 94). On the fifth ~~day~~ they would recite the psalm beginning: “For the leader; upon the Gittith, a psalm of Asaph. Sing for joy to God, our strength; shout aloud to the God of Jacob” (Psalms, chapter 81). On the sixth ~~day~~ they would recite the psalm beginning: “The Lord reigns: He is robed in majesty; the Lord is robed, girded with strength” (Psalms, chapter 93). On Shabbat they would recite the psalm beginning: “A psalm, a song for Shabbat day” (Psalms, chapter 92). This is interpreted as a psalm, a song for the future, for the day that will be entirely Shabbat and rest for everlasting life.

The usage in the Mishnah is “on the first day,” “on the second,” “on the third,” “on the fourth,” “on the fifth,” “on the sixth,” “on the Sabbath.” There is no trace of counting to the Sabbath in this Mishnah passage, which is the obvious source for the redactor of the LXX who added the titles. When he added the titles, the LXX redactor introduced his own tradition from ecclessiastical Greek, assuming it was the same as אֶחד בַּשַּׁבָּת or חַד בְּשַׁבָּא. This ecclesiastical usage also shows up in the Didache 8:1, “δευτέρᾳ σαββάτων καὶ πέμπτη...τετράδα καὶ παρασκευήν.” (The early datings of the Didache are all based on negative arguments, i.e. what it does not contain, and therefore are speculative. Even if an early date be assigned, the extant versions are so late in the key texts that there is plenty of room for an editor to alter the text so as to conform to ecclesiastical Greek.)

To be most charitable, the Christian editor of the LXX unwittingly expanded the LXX titles to reflect his interpretation of NT Greek. Or to be not charitable, he planted his interpretation in the LXX so that it could serve as evidence that his interpretation of the NT was correct.* One thing we can be certain of. Satan was in favor of either happening and somehow deceived Christians into altering Scripture. To claim the Psalm titles as evidence is circular reasoning, using tradition to prove tradition, rather than Scripture to test tradition. When an LXX scribe altered the chronology, he wasn’t detected until someone noticed that it made Methuselah die after the deluge. So you see, liars can only change some texts. Other texts beyond their reach expose their lies.

---

* The likely editor was Aquila of Sinope, who redacted the LXX while still a Christian. He was excommunicated on the charge of astrology, and converted to Judaism, where he produced Targum Onkelos.

The Exodus and the Resurrection

In order to understand Yeshua's death and resurrection fully, it is necessary to understand the timing of the original Passover, and the subsequent celebration of it. The main Jewish and Christian translations are in complete error on the critical point of when the Passover lamb was to be sacrificed. The NASB says it was "at twilight;" the KJV: "in the evening;" the JPS: "at dusk;" the TNK "at twilight." These are all incorrect, because they indicate a time after sunset. The *Stone Edition Tanakh* has "afternoon," which is the correct time period, but not as literal as it should be. Here is the corrected translation:

> And you shall keep it till on the fourteenth day of the same month; then the whole assembly of the congregation of Israel is to kill it **between the settings**. (MISB Ex. 12:6).

The following chart shows when this is:

Figure 28: Between the Settings Defined

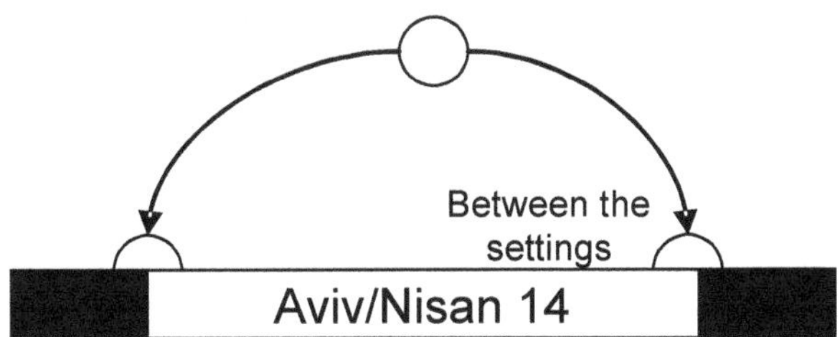

The first setting point is at noon when the sun begins setting (or descending) in the sky. The second setting point is at sunset when the sun finishes setting (or declining) in the visible sky and disappears from view. The Hebrew word *Erev* עֶרֶב means "setting,"[37] and in Exodus 12:6 the compound phrase "בֵּין הָעַרְבָּיִם" means "between the settings." The ending ָיִם is a special plural called "dual" and means "two" of something. The prefix הָ is the definite article and means "the." The word בֵּין means "between." To prove that the time period refers to the time between setting beginning at noon and setting ending at sunset I refer to the exact same phrase in Exodus

30:7-8:

> And Aaron shall burn fragrant incense upon it [the golden altar], daybreak by daybreak—when he trims the lamps, he shall burn incense on it. And when Aaron lights the lamps **between the settings**, he shall burn incense—perpetually before Yahweh throughout your generations.

The lamps were trimmed (cleaned out and prepared) at daybreak at the same time as the morning incense offering. Then they were lit *between the settings*, and at the same time more incense was burned. Since the tabernacle faced east, there was no need to light lamps until afternoon when the sun passed over the top of the tabernacle. The later temple was oriented the same way. Now there were two hours of prayer, and these "hours of prayer" were timed with the morning incense offering and the afternoon incense offering. We are not told in Luke 1:10 which of the two incense offerings Zechariah's lot fell on, though it seems to me that it was the afternoon. Whichever it was, it was the time when "the people were praying outside." As to the second hour of prayer, which was at the same time as the afternoon incense offering, we are told what time it happened in Acts 3:1: "at the ninth hour, the hour of prayer." The ninth hour is counted from sunrise (when the temple day began) , and this would be at 3 p.m. in the afternoon.[167]

This is the normative Rabbinic understanding the phrase, despite the incorrect translation of the JPS. Next, let us look at when the Passover lamb was eaten:

> And they shall eat the flesh that night, roasted with fire, and they shall eat it with unleavened bread and bitter herbs.

[167] Numbers 28:4 says that the second lamb for the continual offering should be "between the settings." Associating the second lamb with 'between the settings' (which is *after* the first lamb at daybreak), yet on the same day, proves that 'between the settings' means late in the day. The time of the continual offering is mentioned in 1Kings 18:36, and is clearly placed in the afternoon. Before the end of the day, Elijah had time to execute the prophets of Ba'al. Ahab had time to have a feast, and Elijah had time to send his servant seven times to the peak of Carmel to see if there was a cloud on the horizon. Then the sky grew black with clouds (not night), and Elijah had time to run from Carmel to the Jezreel Valley (1Ki. 18:46).

(Exodus 12:8).

Further, it says:

> And none of you shall go outside the door of his house until morning. (Exodus 12:22b)

This text makes it clear that the Exodus did not begin until daybreak.[168] In Exodus 12:31 Pharaoh calls "to Moses" לְמֹשֶׁה by night, and not "for Moses." Aaron and Moses obeyed the commandment to remain in the house until morning. Also Pharaoh never saw Moses face again (cf. Ex 10:28-29). So it is clear that Pharaoh communicated to Moses in the darkness of night.

Figure 29: Nisan 14 Defined by Daybreak

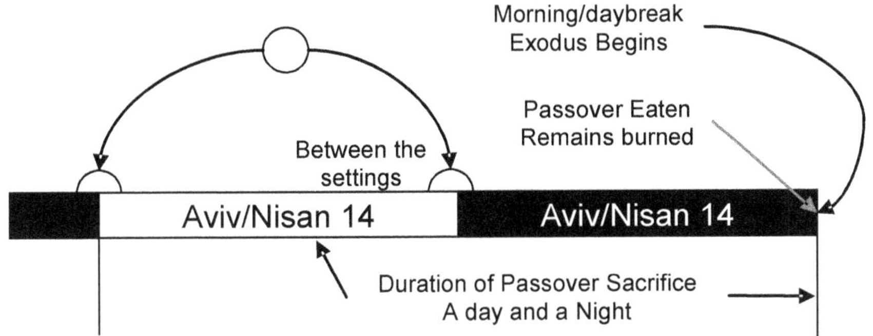

Many have thought that morning here began while it was still totally dark, and that the Exodus commenced that night, but the question is if you were a first-born Israelite what interpretation would you put on "morning"? When did Israel plunder the Egyptian gold and silver if not after daybreak, and when would the Egyptians bury their dead if not after daybreak (cf. Ex. 12:36; Num. 33:3). The Passover in Egypt to save the firstborn and the Exodus are two different events, taking place on two different days. Only the annual Sabbath connects them.

Also observe that when the day is understood as daybreak to daybreak matters are cleared up. The Exodus began on the next day:

---

[168] Exodus 12:17, "for on this very day" speaks of the day part of the first day of unleavened bread, which was part of the annual Sabbath.

And they set out from Rameses in the first month, in the fifteenth day of the first month. In **the day after the Passover** the sons of Israel went out with a high hand before the eyes of all the Egyptians, while the Egyptians were burying all their first-born whom Yãhweh had struck down among them. Yãhweh had also executed judgments on their gods.
Num. 33:3-4

And further, the night they went out of Egypt was the night following the day part of the 15th:

> Observe the month of the Aviv and celebrate the Passover to Yãhweh your Almĩghty, for in the month of Aviv Yãhweh your Almĩghty brought you out of Egypt by night. (Deut. 16:1, MISB).

The text speaks of a second Passover offering to memorialize the Exodus, which will be detailed in a few pages. Here is the chart of the last two texts:

Figure 30: Nisan 15 Defined By Daybreak

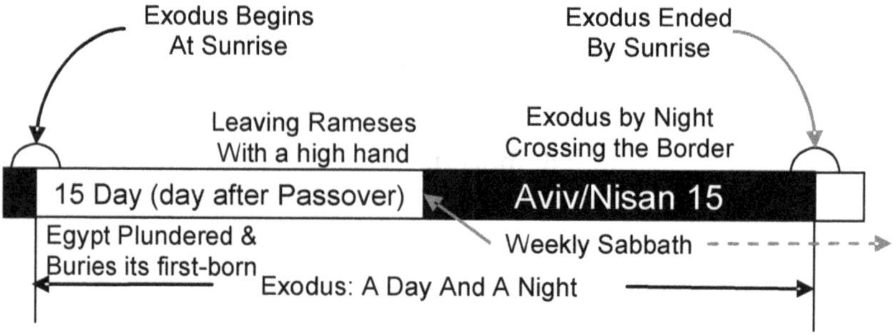

Exodus Begins
At Sunrise
Exodus Ended
By Sunrise
Leaving Rameses
With a high hand
Exodus by Night
Crossing the Border
15 Day (day after Passover)
Aviv/Nisan 15
Egypt Plundered &
Buries its first-born
Weekly Sabbath
Exodus: A Day And A Night

Notice that as they were being delivered from Egypt by night that this night was the beginning of the weekly Sabbath.[169] Thus, the weekly sabbath is a time of redemption and deliverance. In the morning, they camped:

[169] This computation is complex and is shown in my other book, *The Scroll of Biblical Chronology and Ancient Near Eastern History*. It was 1632 BC, 4/11 sunset to 4/12 sunset. See Appendix VI, page 475.

Figure 31: Nisan 16 Defined By Daybreak

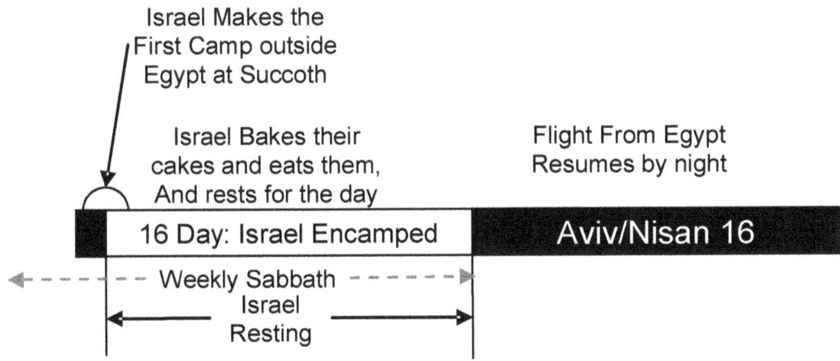

Notice here that they camped and baked their bread on the 16th day of the month. Since they had been on the road for 24 hours it would have been necessary to stop and rest. Also they likely resumed their trek on the next night (cf. Exodus 13:21). The 16th day of the month marks the first day completely out of Egypt. It is therefore the reason why the counting of 50 days begins on the 16th day of the month. The next chart shows the additional offerings added later:

Figure 32: Additional Memorial Offerings

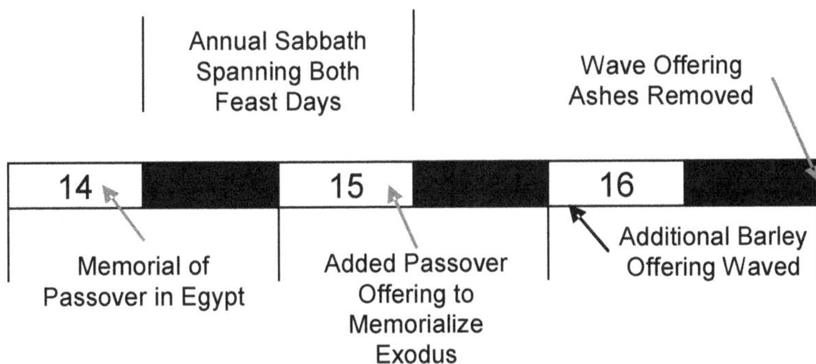

The annual Sabbath was instituted to span both feast days, and to be the first day of unleavened bread. Now I have shown before that all of these offerings were eaten, or burned on the altar with the limit being daybreak. Hence all offerings are for a day and a night (Exodus 12:10; Deut. 16:4; Lev. 6:9; cf. Lev. 7:15).

The annual holy day joined the two feast days into one Sabbath, which is the first day of unleavened bread. On this day Israel makes the leaven to cease (take a Sabbath), hence the day is a Sabbath (literally: cessation, ceasing) from leaven, and also a ceasing from servile labor. This is the 15th of Nisan. Now in the day after the ceasing (rest, cessation, Sabbath) a sheaf of barley is waved. This is linked to Nisan 16 when Israel first camped after the Exodus and baked their dough into unleavened bread. Let us now see how all this lines up in the year of Yeshua's death and resurrection:

Figure 33: Symbolic Connections with Messiah

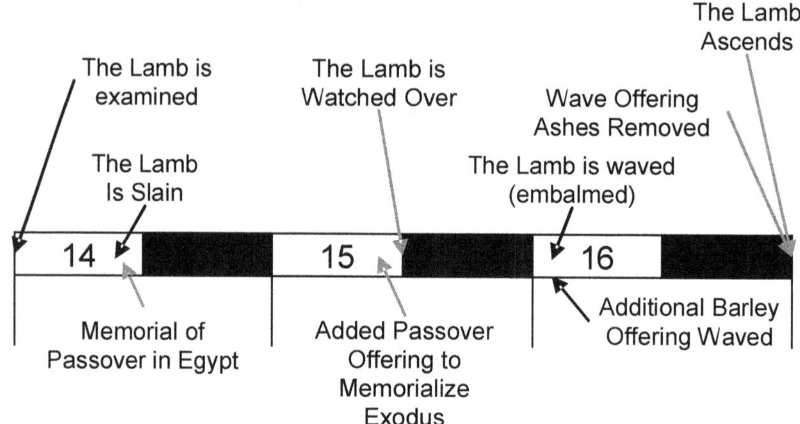

The Passover lamb would go through one last check over on Nisan 14 to make sure there were no flaws rendering it unfit for sacrifice. So Yeshua was examined by the High Priest starting at dawn. Also the tamid offering was being examined at this time. Yeshua is slain at the same time as the Passover lambs, about 3 p.m. in the afternoon.

Now something that I did not mention in describing the Exodus is that in the night (following the 15th), Yahweh kept watch over Israel (Exodus 12:42). This is why Israel is to keep watch that night;* and return to their tents (to sleep) in the morning (Deut. 16:7). So also the watch was set over Yeshua's grave for that night.

There are then six days of unleavened bread left (Deut. 16:8) at dawn on the 16th of Nisan because one was already used up. Then on Nisan 16 the counting of the seven Shavuot (weeks) begins (Deut. 16:9). This is the day of the wave-offering. So also Yeshua is the first-fruits of the resurrection.

---

* The precept that each offering is to be eaten the 'same day,' and the limits of it being 'until the daybreak' establish that the days are being reckoned from dawn to dawn. The offering memorializes the day up to the end of the day (Exodus 12:10; Deut. 16:4; cf. Lev. 7:15). The redemption of the firstborn was the first offering on the 14th. The offering on the 15th was a memorial offering of the Exodus on the 15th, celebrated during the day and into the night following, which is the night he brought them out of Egypt. None was to remain till dawn (Deut. 16:4). After dawn, six days remained (Deut. 16:8). The vigil in Exodus 12:42 relates to going out of Egypt, and not to the redemption of the firstborn in Egypt. Although tradition assumes it, nothing is said about Israel going out before dawn on the 15th (cf. Exodus 12:22), and so the vigil in Exodus 12:42 pertains to the night after the daytime of the 15th, when he actually brought them out (cf. Deut. 16:1).

Shavuot (Pentecost) Timing

What relevance does the timing of Pentecost have to the Resurrection Sabbath? Quite a bit. The types and timing of this feast are linked to the day of the resurrection through 1 Corinthians 15:20-23:

> [20]But as it is, the Anŏinted had been getting raised from the dead, the first fruits[χ] of those who have been falling asleep. [21]For since by a man came death, by a man also came the resurrection of the dead. [22]For as in Adam all die, so also in the Anŏinted all will be made alive.
>
> [23]Yet, each in his own order: the Anŏinted, the first fruits, after that those who are the Anŏinted's at his presence, [24]then *is* the ending, when he shall be delivering the kingdom for the Almĭghty and Făther, when he shall have destroyed all contrary rule and all authority and power.

The first-fruits offering was a quantity of new grain that was offered near the beginning of the year on a specific day, "in the day after the Sabbath" (Lev. 23:11). There was and is a dispute among the Jews as to which day this is. Anciently it was a *theological*[170] dispute between the Pharisees and Sadducees. Currently it is a *theological* dispute between the Karaite Jews and Rabbinic Jews. The majority party were the Pharisees and later Rabbis, for whom "in the day after the Sabbath" meant after the first Rest-Day[171] of Passover, which was Nisan 16. The Boethosees (a variety of Sadducee) maintained that the wave-offering of first-fruits should be on the day after the weekly Sabbath.[172] Now the proto-Catholics, who placed the resurrection on Sunday, immediately latched onto this *Sunday Pentecost* view as a support of the Sunday resurrection, and this view has been maintained by the masses of Christians ever since.

---

[170] It was a *theological* dispute because it is clear that in practice the Pharisees' views were carried out in the Temple. This will be shown later in this chapter. It will remain a theological dispute, because when the future temple is rebuilt there is little doubt which method will be used.

[171] The Rabbis interpret "Sabbath" according to its literal meaning "cessation"/"ceasing" or "rest-day," and translate it as such in Lev. 23:11 and 15. The Sadducees connect the term exclusively with the "seventh day," which they think is more literal.

[172] pg. 37, §26. Pharisees and Sadducees, *A History of the Jewish People in the Time of Jesus Christ*, Schürer, II.ii.37.

Typically these Christian masses argue that the resurrection must occur at the time of the wave-offering on the *first Sunday* after Passover (which they call Easter). However, for the most part, they have been abandoned by Christian scholars[173] who maintain that the sheaf waving on Nisan 16 has the better support and is correct. This view puts the wave offering on the *day after Passover.*

First, it should be explained that according to the *Sunday Pentecost* this type is mismatched with the Wednesday-Sabbath afternoon theory. For it requires the women to go to the tomb on Sunday morning, by which time the resurrection was over. The wave offering would be after sunrise, and the *Sunday Pentecost* consensus was that this was about 9 a.m. in the morning. Therefore, proponents of the Sabbath afternoon resurrection have a disconnect between the wave offering and the *Sunday Pentecost* timing. An attempt is made to repair the mismatch by linking it with Messiah's ascension, but this too must have been complete before the *Sunday Pentecost* timing.[174] And Paul explicitly links the first-fruit offering with the resurrection.

Second, the Friday-Sunday view has the same mismatch unless it posits that the resurrection occurred well after sunrise, which seems unlikely according to John 20:1 since it says that Miriam came to the tomb "while still dark" and found the stone removed. Indeed, by all accounts the *Sunday Pentecost* wave-offering (in theory) would not have been offered in the Temple yet. To say the least, both theories are stretching matters by claiming that the *type* matches reality.

The solution then is to get the timing of the first-fruit offering correct. The first-fruit offering operates on the same principle as all

---

[173] Some Christian scholars tend to show some inconsistency here. When discussing Leviticus they side with the Pharisees. When discussing the resurrection of Paul's typology they side with the Sadducees.

[174] Yeshua would not let the women touch him until he had ascended to the Father (John 20:17), but then later he allows it (Mat. 28:9). This was all during the dawning (Mat. 28:1) and thus was before the wave-offering according to the *Sunday Pentecost* theory. What was happening in the temple during the dawning was the continual (tamid) offering. In all views the wave offering cannot be offered before the tamid. So, even Yeshua's presentation to the Father occurs before the wave offering—according to the *Sunday Pentecost* argument. There is another interpretation of "touch me not," but it is not in favor of the *Sunday Pentecost*. *The Good News of Messiah* renders the passage, "Don't be clinging to me, because not yet have I been ascending to the Father...." His point was that he was not yet saying goodbye, he had things to do, and Miryam would see him again before he ascended.

the other sacrifices. Indeed, there was a male lamb offered with it. The part of the first-fruit offering that was for Yahweh was thrown on the altar along with the lamb. The other part of the first-fruit offering was eaten by the Priests. This all began in the morning after the tamid (continual) offering at dawn.

The continual offering marked the beginning of the new day. For the temple day was from daybreak to daybreak. The priests portion was to be eaten that same day, which is to say before dawn the next morning (cf. Lev. 7:15). Further, the Torah required the offerings for Yahweh to burn on the altar all night (cf. Lev. 6:9), and the whole of this time the smoke of the offering was ascending. So then, the offering is made on Nisan 16 in the morning, and continues to burn on the altar all the following night. The resurrection, then, is timed with the last remnants of the wave offering ascending toward dawn. The following chart shows this:

Figure 34: The Three Offerings and Three Days

	Annual Sabbath		Weekly Sabbath
Wed	Thu	Fri	Sat
First Passover Offering	Exodus Chaggiah offering	First-fruit Offering Nisan 16	
1	2	3	

three days and three nights

So there are three offerings on three days, and each offering is according to the Temple day from daybreak to daybreak. Each offering has a limit of morning for consumption. Yeshua ascends in the last remnants of the *olah* of the wave offering and its lamb (cf. Judges 13:15-24, specifically vs. 20). So the resurrection occurred on the Sabbath just before dawn, and likewise the ascension mentioned in John 20:17.[175] Both the resurrection and the presentation to the

[175] See note 174. That is, if an ascension occurred that day. The alternative possibility is that Yeshua was assuring Miryam that he was not leaving for at least another month.

Father fit the type.

Now that the relevance of the timing has been made clear, the case for offering the first-fruits in the *day after the Passover* must be proved. First I will cover the historical arguments.

Shavuot according to history

Josephus tells us the actual practice in the Temple:

> But on the second day of unleavened bread, which is the sixteenth day of the month, they first partake of the fruits of the earth, for before that day they do not touch them.[176]

Philo confirms this:

> There is also a festival on the day of the paschal feast, which succeeds the first day, and this is named the sheaf, from what takes place on it; for the sheaf is brought to the altar as a first fruit both of the country which the nation has received for its own, and also of the whole land;[177]

Jewish Historian Emil Schürer further explains:

> The price at which the Sadducees had to secure themselves power at this later period was indeed a high one, for they were obliged in their official actions actually to accommodate themselves to Pharisaic views, "Nothing is, so to speak, done by them, for whenever they obtain office they adhere, though unwillingly and by constraint, to what the Pharisees say, as otherwise the multitude would not tolerate them."[178]

Schürer's quotation is from Josephus (*Ant.* 18:17 [xviii. 1.4]). This shows that though the Sadducees held on to the political power

---

[176] Josephus *Ant.* 3:250.
[177] De specialibus legibus 2:162.
[178] pg. 42, §26. Pharisees and Sadducees, *A History of the Jewish People in the Time of Jesus Christ*, Schürer, II.ii.42.

that in religious affairs they were compelled to abide by the rulings of the Pharisees. Schürer also remarks:

> Quite apart from the fact, since the time of [Queen] Alexandra[179] they had no longer carried out their views into practice, they also theoretically agreed with Pharisaic tradition in some, perhaps in many particulars. They only denied its *obligation*, and reserved the right of private opinion.

Alfred Edersheim states:

> The nine years of Queen Alexandra's (in Hebrew Salome) reign [beginning in 78 B.C.] were the Golden Age of the Pharisees . . . But as, *Josephus* puts it (Ant. xiii. 16. 2)[180] although Salome had the title, the Pharisees held the real rule of the country. . . First, all who were suspected of Sadducean leanings were removed by intrigue or violence from the Sanhedrin. Next, previous ordinances differing from Pharisaical views were abrogated . . . So sweeping and thorough was the change wrought, that the Sadducees never recovered the blow, and whatever they might teach, yet those in office were obliged in all time coming to conform to Pharisaic practice (*Jos. Ant.* xviii. 1.4; Tos. Yoma i. 8).[181]

Lawrence H. Schiffman:

> With new evidence from the Dead Sea Scrolls it is now possible to demonstrate that for much of the Hasmonean period Pharisaic views were indeed dominant in the Jerusalem Temple. In short, the reports of the religious laws, or halakhah, attributed to the Pharisees in later Talmudic texts are basically accurate. Moreover, we can now prove that some of the teachings attributed to rabbinic sages who lived after the Roman destruction of the Temple actually go back to earlier, pre-destruction, Pharisaic traditions.[182]

---

179 Jewish Queen Salome who inherited her husband's power upon his death.
180 See 13:405, 408.
181 pg. 678, Appendix IV, vol. II, *The Life And Times of Jesus The Messiah*, Edersheim.
182 "New Light on the Pharisees—Insights from the Dead Sea Scrolls," June

Joshua 5:10-12 to indicates that the first-fruits were eaten after the Passover:

> While the sons of Israel camped at Gilgal, they were doing the Passover during the setting of the fourteenth day of the month on the desert plains of Jericho. And they were eating from the produce of the land in the day after the Passover—unleavened bread and roasted grain in the same day. And the manna took a sabbatical in the day after, when they ate from the produce of the land, so that the sons of Israel no longer had manna, but they ate some of the yield of the land of Canaan during that year.

In order to comprehend this text, we must understand that Passover offerings were eaten on two days. The first was for the Passover in Egypt. And the second Passover offering was a festive offering to memorialize the Exodus. This second Passover offering is described in Deut. 16:1-8. It is clearly on the 15th of Nisan because only six days remain in the feast when it is finished. So the picture is as follows for Joshua 5:10-12.

Figure 35: New Grain Eaten After Second Passover Offering

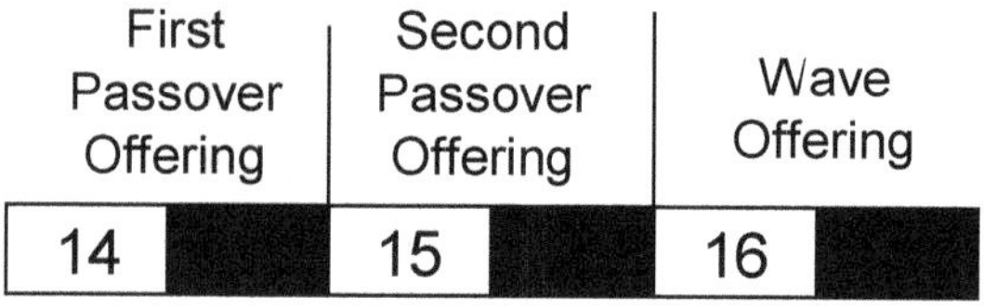

First Passover Offering	Second Passover Offering	Wave Offering
14	15	16

"The day after the Passover" is the 16th day of the month. Now one group of Karaite skeptics says that that the 15th day must have been the weekly Sabbath, and other Karaite skeptics say that the 14th day was a weekly Sabbath and that the sheaf was waved on the 15th. However, in the year of the entry into Canaan, neither the 14th nor the 15th was the weekly Sabbath that year. The most direct proof of this is within the text itself:

1992, *Bible Review*, Schiffman.

And the manna took a sabbatical [וַיִּשְׁבֹּת] in the day after, when they ate from the produce of the land, so that the sons of Israel no longer had manna, but they ate some of the yield of the land of Canaan during that year

Now, the manna either came or it didn't come. The text is saying that the manna didn't come this day. It was the day of its ceasing. If it is claimed that the 15th day came on the weekly Sabbath, then the 16th is claimed to be the day of ceasing. But then this would not be true, because the 15th day would be the day of the ceasing, since there was never any manna on the Sabbath. Or if it is claimed that the 15th day was a Sunday and that the sheaf was waved on Sunday, then it is claimed that Sunday was the day of ceasing. But since the manna already ceased on the preceding Sabbath, this too would not be true. The following diagrams illustrate:

Figure 36: Joshua 5 Karaite Scenario #1

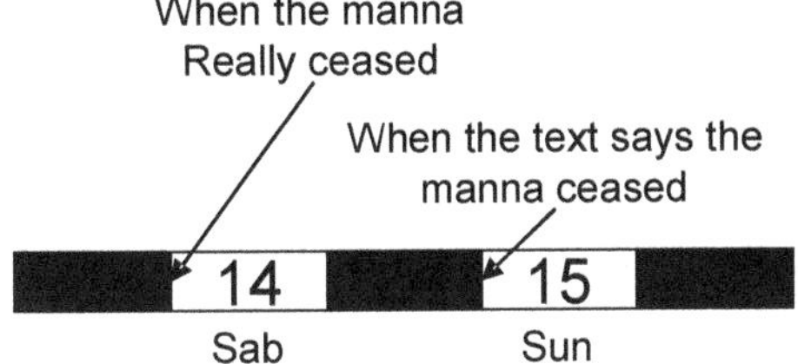

Figure 37: Joshua 5 Karaite Scenario #2

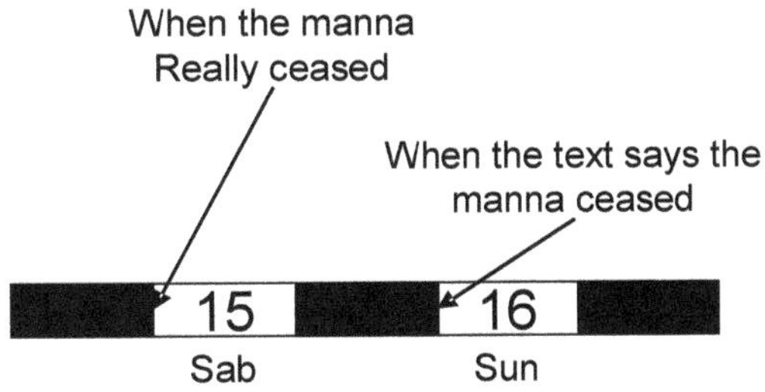

In these cases, would it not be said that the manna ceased on the Sabbath instead of the day after it? But if the manna ceased in the middle of a week when it was not customary for it to cease, then it would make sense to say that it had ceased on that day, such as the day after an annual Sabbath, because the manna did not cease for the annual Sabbath.

How it really was:

Figure 38: The Real Joshua 5 Chronology

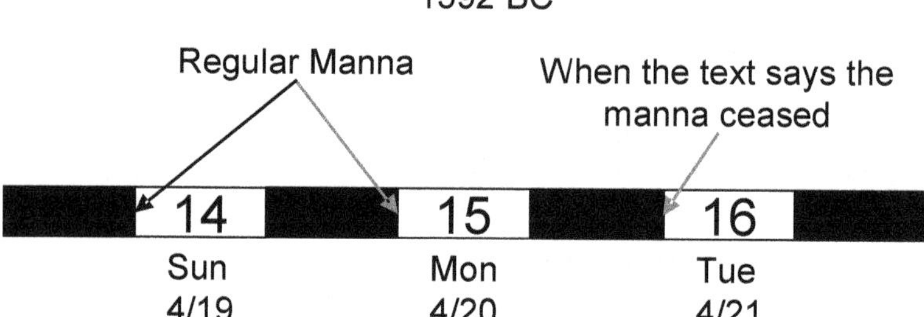

Proving the year and calendar dates is rather complicated and beyond the scope of this book.[183] But as shown above, the text itself says that the manna could not have ceased on Sunday. For it makes no sense to say it ceased then, if it already ceased on the Sabbath.

The calendar date proof starts with the subject of this book and uses the results to reconstruct all of Biblical Chronology giving us 1592 B.C. as the year they entered the land. The calendar for the first month looks like this:

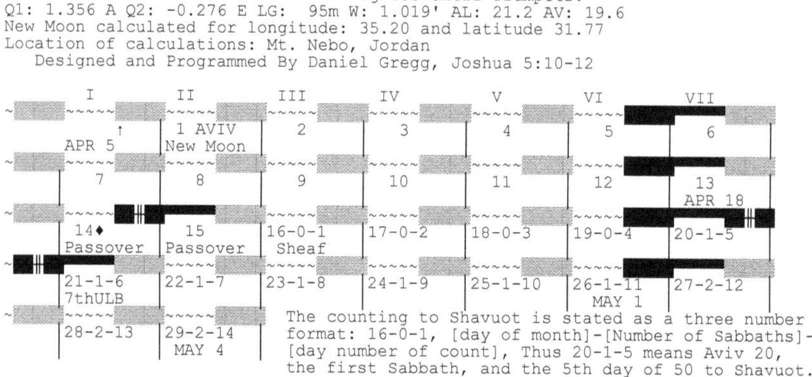

Month: I AVIV, 1592 BC 2548 A.M. Sab. Cyc: 7. Jub. Cyc: 49 Cycle No: 52
Sabbatical Year in Progress until Trumpets.
Q1: 1.356 A Q2: -0.276 E LG: 95m W: 1.019' AL: 21.2 AV: 19.6
New Moon calculated for longitude: 35.20 and latitude 31.77
Location of calculations: Mt. Nebo, Jordan
Designed and Programmed By Daniel Gregg, Joshua 5:10-12

I	II	III	IV	V	VI	VII
↑ APR 5	1 AVIV New Moon	2	3	4	5	6
7	8	9	10	11	12	13 APR 18
14♦ Passover	15 Passover	16-0-1 Sheaf	17-0-2	18-0-3	19-0-4	20-1-5
21-1-6 7thULB	22-1-7	23-1-8	24-1-9	25-1-10	26-1-11 MAY 1	27-2-12
28-2-13	29-2-14 MAY 4					

The counting to Shavuot is stated as a three number format: 16-0-1, [day of month]-[Number of Sabbaths]-[day number of count], Thus 20-1-5 means Aviv 20, the first Sabbath, and the 5th day of 50 to Shavuot.

---

[183] See *The Scroll of Biblical Chronology and Ancient Near Eastern History*, Daniel Gregg, 7th edition. The year of the entry into the land is an independent result of the chronology, and so also the astronomical calculations of the weekdays in the first month. The chronology cannot be recovered without correclty understanding the Passion or Daniel 9. On the other hand, I had no control over the resulting weekdays for various events. They are what they are, and in every place agree with that indicated by biblical texts.

The Karaites claim that Lev. 23:11 "morrow of the Sabbath" means the day after the weekly Sabbath, and that Lev. 23:15 refers to the same. However Joshua 5:10-12 says that they ate the new grain "on the day after the Passover." According to Karaite calculation this would be Sunday, 4/19, 1592 B.C. which is not the "day after the Passover." So the Karaite opinion is conclusively dis-proven by the overall chronology as well as the ceasing note in Joshua 5:12.

The Karaite opinion is translated into the text of the King James Version:

> KJV **Leviticus 23:11** And he shall wave the sheaf before the LORD, to be accepted for you: on the morrow after the sabbath the priest shall wave it. . . v15 And ye shall count unto you from the morrow after the sabbath, from the day that ye brought the sheaf of the wave offering; seven sabbaths shall be complete: v16 Even unto the morrow after the seventh sabbath shall ye number fifty days.

One will find that the Rabbinic position is translated into the RSV and the NIV, and the Karaite position in the NASB. One will find the Rabbinic position translated in the JPS Tanakh (1985), and also in the *Stone Edition Tanakh*:

> On the morrow of the rest day the Cohen shall wave it. . . You shall count for yourselves—from the morrow of the rest day. . . seven weeks. . . until the morrow of the seventh week you shall count fifty days.

One will find the Rabbinic position translated into the LXX (Septuagint):

> LXX Lev. 23:11 on the day after the first (τῆς πρώτης) the priest shall raise it up. . . And you shall count from the morrow of the Sabbath. . . seven weeks (ἑβδομάδας) whole. . . until the morrow of the seventh week (ἑβδομάδος) you shall count fifty days.

The translation issue cannot be decided by simply choosing between a Rabbinic version and a Karaite version. The Rabbinic version is only 1/3 right and the Karaite version is only 1/3 right. Choosing the best of both gets us 2/3 right. The missing 1/3 has to be supplied from a correct understanding the Hebrew text and a new translation, which I will come to in the following pages.

Meanwhile, there are those willing to admit that the Pharisees are correct in counting from Nisan 16, yet who say anyway that in the year of the crucifixion that the annual Passover Sabbath fell on the weekly Sabbath negating the difference. For if the 15th of the month by chance lands on the weekly Sabbath, the Karaite and Rabbinic interpretation both yield the next Sunday as the day for the waved grain offering.

I am not mainly concerned with this group that says Nisan 16 by chance that year was Sunday because they still believe in the Friday-Sunday scenario. They dismiss Matthew 12:40. I will explain later that the chronology only works with the death and resurrection of Yeshua in A.D. 34, i.e. with things like Daniel 9 and the sabbatical year. So in fact, the 15th of Nisan did not land of the weekly Sabbath that year.

What I am going to address here is the contention of many that Shavuot (Pentecost) always must land on a Sunday according to the Karaite interpretation. They say the "Sabbath" in Lev. 23:11 is the weekly Sabbath, and that the waved grain offering must be on the first day of the week. The interlocutors of this position also demand that in Leviticus 23:15-16 the words for "Sabbaths" be translated as *Sabbaths*. This is as it should be, and I show it in the GNM translation:†

> "AND YE *WILL* HAVE COUNTED FOR YOURSELVES IN THE TOMORROW OF THE ȘABBAȾH, FROM THE DAY OF YOUR BRINGING THE SHEAF OF THE WAVE OFFERING: SEVEN REGULAR ȘABBAȾHS SHALL BE UNTIL IN THE TOMORROW OF THE SEVENTH ȘABBAȾH YOU *WILL* HAVE COUNTED A FIFTIETH DAY."

What the interlocutor [who believes in Yeshua] does not know is that this Karaite position is hugely inconsistent for those who think the resurrection was on the "first day of the week." Here is the *Jewish*

† *The Good News of Messiah*, pg. 162.

Publication Society's translation of Lev. 23:15-16, which expresses the Pharisees' position:

> JPS **Leviticus 23:15** And ye shall count unto you from the morrow after the **day of rest**, from the day that ye brought the sheaf of the waving; seven **weeks** shall there be complete; [16] even unto the morrow after the seventh **week** shall ye number fifty days; and ye shall present a new meal-offering unto the LORD.

Now they say these occurrences should be translated "sabbath" , "sabbaths" and "sabbath" and not "day of rest," "weeks" and "week." They say we should count actual "sabbaths" "first of the sabbaths," "second of the sabbaths," "seventh of the sabbaths." Yet, inconsistently, when we come to the New Testament Greek Texts they accept the "first day of the week" translation:

> KJV **Matthew 28:1** In the end of the sabbath, as it began to dawn toward the first *day* of the **week**, came Mary Magdalene and the other Mary to see the sepulchre.

> KJV **Mark 16:2** And very early in the morning the first *day* of the **week**, they came unto the sepulchre at the rising of the sun.

> KJV **Luke 24:1** Now upon the first *day* of the **week**, very early in the morning, they came unto the sepulchre, bringing the spices which they had prepared, and certain *others* with them.

> KJV **John 20:1** The first *day* of the **week** cometh Mary Magdalene early, when it was yet dark, unto the sepulchre, and seeth the stone taken away from the sepulchre.

> KJV **John 20:19** Then the same day at evening, being the first *day* of the **week**, when the doors were shut where the disciples were assembled for fear of the Jews, came Jesus and stood in the midst, and saith unto them, Peace *be* unto you.

[KJV] **Acts 20:7** And upon the first *day* of the **week**, when the disciples came together to break bread, Paul preached unto them, ready to depart on the morrow; and continued his speech until midnight.

[KJV] **1 Corinthians 16:2** Upon the first *day* of the **week** let every one of you lay by him in store, as *God* hath prospered him, that there be no gatherings when I come.

[KJV] **Luke 18:12** I fast twice in the **week**, I give tithes of all that I possess.

How can they tell us that it means to count seven Sabbaths in Lev. 23:15-16 while telling us that it does not mean the "first of the Sabbaths" in the resurrection passages but only "first day of the week"? The word for Sabbath (σαββάτων, שַׁבָּתוֹת) is used in the original language of the resurrection passages just the same as in Lev. 23:11-16!

If they think that "week" is correct in the New Testament, then they have no basis for refuting the Rabbinical translation of "weeks" in Leviticus. By allowing "week" in the resurrection passages (Mat. 28:1; Mark 16:2, 9; John 20:1, 19) or anniversary passages (Acts 20:7, 1 Cor. 16:2) or Luke 18:12 they undermine their objection to the same in Lev. 23:15-16.

But if they admit that the resurrection passages should also be translated "Sabbaths" so that no excuse is afforded to translate Lev. 23:15-16 with the word "week," then they destroy their own position that the Sabbaths should be counted from the day after the weekly sabbath. How is this so? If the Karaite admits that "sabbath" is literal in the resurrection passages, "first of the Sabbaths," then it is evident that this "first of the Sabbaths" was the weekly Sabbath after the 15th of Nisan. However, the Karaites only begin to count days after this Sabbath, and do not count the "first of the Sabbaths" until seven days after the "first of the Sabbaths" mentioned for the resurrection passages. Hence the Karaite first Sabbath is one week after the biblical first of the Sabbaths.

For in counting after the weekly sabbath, their counting will always be a week late for “the first of the Sabbaths.” In the case of Yeshua’s resurrection, their “first of the Sabbaths” will come a whole week after the resurrection Sabbath. Therefore, the Karaite cannot translate the New Testament Literally. He or she must become a Rabbinic translator and render the resurrection passages with the word “week.” How is that for inconsistency?

So to count Sabbaths like the Karaites and observe Shavuot that way, and then to be a believer in the translation “first day of the week” means believing mutually exclusive things, 1. translating in Lev. 23:15 so that Sabbaths can be counted, and 2. refusing to allow counting with the resurrection passages in an identical context. We call something like this a “self refuting position.” They agree with those who cover up the counting in the New Testament, but disagree with those who cover it up in the Torah.

And the context is identical. All of the evangelists place the resurrection right after Passover. And further the usage in Acts 20:7 is right after Passover, and likewise the usage in 1 Cor. 16:2 is before the feast of Shavuot (Pentecost) mentioned later in the chapter.

The 1/3 correctness of the Rabbinic translation is rendering Lev. 23:11 “the rest day,” and the same in Lev. 23:15. This is because the word “Sabbath” (הַשַּׁבָּת) in fact means “cessation” or we may translate it as a participle: “ceasing” (הַשֹּׁבֵת). The Rabbis are also correct on the timing. They are incorrect with the translation “weeks” and “week.” The 1/3 correctness of the Karaite translation is merely with “Sabbaths” in vs. 15, and “seventh Sabbath” in vs. 16.

Both versions are incorrect on the rendering of the word “morrow” (מִמָּחֳרַת), which is the 1/3 that must be corrected from the Hebrew. And unless this last bit is corrected that neither the Karaites or Rabbis have it right. The Karaites and the Rabbis are at a standstill over the word Sabbath. If either side budges toward “weeks,” or toward “Sabbaths,” then they loose the argument. You can see that if *week* is put into Lev. 23:16 that the Rabbis can have the week end on any day, but that if Sabbath is required, then the day after will be Sunday:

> KJV **Leviticus 23:16** Even unto the morrow after the seventh sabbath [or week] shall ye number fifty days; and ye shall offer

a new meat offering unto the LORD.

In plain English, it is clear enough that the "morrow after the seventh sabbath" can only be the "first day of the week." And that would settle the issue if the English translation were correct. However, it would not dispense with the inconsistency of translating "first day of the week" in the New Testament. This logjam can only be broken by correcting the text from the Hebrew in a way that neither the Rabbis nor the Karaites have cared notice since the word "week" was introduced as a meaning for the word שַׁבָּת sometime after the Bar Kochba Revolt (A.D. 131-135).

As mentioned before, we have to go behind all the traditions and dogmas and discover the truth on a purely linguistic and factual basis. Conflicted traditions cannot be trusted, and if Yeshua rose on the "first of the Sabbaths" after Passover, then we can be certain that Judaism would want to deny it because it leads to proof that Yeshua is the Messiah. So Judaism will adapt so as to avoid the conclusion. They adapted by corrupting their timing and/or apologetic and translations of Lev. 23:11-16.

It is no secret that Jewish translations regularly corrupt what the Hebrew actually says on Messianic Prophecies.* It is also true that in a few cases they have altered the Hebrew text itself to foil Messianic Prophecies.† Yet, Jewish Scholars like textual expert Emmanuel Tov point out that the LXX often preserves the sense of the original Hebrew. Now we know the tendency of Judaism we should be suspicious of translations that support it, and demand our proofs based on evidence before the period when Judaism rejected Yeshua as the Messiah.

On the other hand, when it comes to texts that might tend to support Torah observance, the Church regularly and habitually changes the texts so that they are against Torah observance. That is the disposition of the Church, and so when we find these texts, we should be suspicious of them, and demand proof based only on evidence that comes from a period before the Church existed to contaminate it.

The paradigm is quite simple. 1. ignore everything the Church supports against Torah by its own traditional arguments from about

* For example, the more literal Stone Edition Tanach has "the maiden" in Isa. 7:14. Maiden is the more polite word for virgin (בתולה). But the Hebrew word used in Isa. 7:14 is the clinical form, meaning "the virgin" (עלמה). In Isa. 9:5 this version rearranges the words: "the Wondrous Adviser, Mighty God, Eternal Father, called his name Sar-shalom," but the Hebrew order reads, "Then he will call his name Wonderful Adviser, Mighty God, Everlasting Father, Sar-Shalom."

† Psalm 22:16; Dan. 9:25 (the 'Athnach').

A.D. 100 onward, except on Messianic Prophecy.[184] 2. ignore everything Judaism supports against Yeshua being the Messiah from about A.D. 100 onward, except on the subject of the validity of the Torah.

What will keep us from becoming total skeptics and falling into agnosticism is knowing where the actual non-conflicted evidence leads. And indeed, many have tried to find the truth and have failed in their own human efforts and have given up and turned to perpetual skepticism, atheism, or agnosticism. That is the burden of living under the curse of inherited lies.

So now, with the above for background and perspective, I will turn to the third part of the argument that neither the Rabbis nor the Karaites have correct. Nor for that matter does the Church have it correct. The reason is that the Rabbis and Karaites want to avoid evidence that Yeshua is the Messiah, so they leaven their translation and doctrines just enough to make the proofs fuzzy. And the Church wants to have Messiah "fulfill" times and seasons of their own making so that they do not have to follow Torah—like Easter Sunday and Pentecost Sunday. Once we understand the *motives* for the corruptions, it is not hard to see that they *are corruptions* when the non-conflicted evidence is exposed.

Here is the text from the GNM:

> "AND YE *WILL* HAVE COUNTED FOR YOURSELVES **IN THE TO-MORROW OF** THE ȘABBAȶH, FROM THE DAY OF YOUR BRINGING THE SHEAF OF THE WAVE OFFERING: SEVEN **REGULAR** ȘABBAȶHS SHALL BE UNTIL **IN THE TOMORROW OF** THE SEVENTH ȘABBAȶH YOU *WILL* HAVE COUNTED A FIFTIETH DAY" (page 162, End Note No. 2).

I have bolded the portion of the translation that has been corrected vs. the Rabbis and Karaites.

[184] This latter point might appear to be conflicted to Jews, but somebody has to be right some of the time. It will become clear that when you take what is right from both Judaism and Christianity and put them together that what is right is mutually confirmed. There is no danger of circular reasoning on these major points since in fact only part of the evidence has been tampered with and not all of it.

The English translation "morrow after" [185] is incorrect. Let us examine the word in Hebrew. The Hebrew word in the text is מִמָּחֳרַת. Remove the preposition מִן from the word, and what remains is מָחֳרַת. This is the feminine noun form of מָחָר. Now nearly every noun and adjective in the Hebrew language is derived from a verb root. If we go over to the Baumgartner's LEXICON IN VETERIS TESTAMENTI LIBROS we find that the verb root is אחר. If we look the feminine form מָחֳרַת in the same lexicon, it tells us that the root is אחר and to see the entry for מָחָר. The reason that it says to see the masculine entry is that the pair מָחָר / מָחֳרַת is what is known as a gender doublet, and in cases like this the meaning is the same. Only the gender is different.

Gesenius' Lexicon tells us "this word is supposed to be closely connected with the root אחר." Likewise, Jastrow[186] cites the same root.

There are several derivations which have merit. 1. The masculine and feminine forms are contractions from the pual participle where the א is contracted: 1a. מְאֻחָר > מָחָר and 1b. מְאֻחֶרֶת > מָחֳרַת. The meaning would be "*being made to be after.*" 2. or a hufal participle: 2a. 2 מָאֳחָר > מָחָר. מָאֳחֶרֶת > מָחֳרַת. The meaning would be "*being made after.*"

The third derivation 3. The prefixed מִמָּחֳרַת is a contraction of מִמָּחֳרַת < מִיֹּמָּחֳרֶת < מִיּוֹם־מָאֳחֶרֶת. Writing it with a contraction mark: מִ׳מָּ׳חֳרַת. The sense is "*in day being made after,*" or to be less pedantic, "*in day after.*" We could also form the form *מִמָּחָר. The gender difference rests on the fact that a noun form of the adverb was desired and the feminine gender was selected for this. Analogous English to the gender difference would be **in the day after** vs. **in in the day afterward.**

It is worth noting that the verb אחר forms also a gender doublet:

---

[185] "Morrow" is etymologically related to "morning"; **morrow**: "late 13c. *morwe*, shortened variation of *morwen* 'morrow' (see **morn**)." And **morn**, "contracted from M.E. *morwen*, from O.E. (Mercian) margen (dat. marne), earlier morgen (dat. morgne), from P.Gmc. **marganaz*, **murganaz* "morning" (cf. O.H.G. *morgen*, Goth. *maurgins*), perhaps from PIE base **mergh-* "to blink, twinkle" (cf. Lith. *mirgeti* "to blink")."

[186] *Dictionary of the Targumim, the Talmud Babli and Yerushalmi, and the Midrashic Literature.*

a. אַחַר **adv** *after, hinder, following part;* b. **n.f.** אַחֲרִית *after-part, end, hindermost*. This is exactly on the pattern of the **adv.** מָחָר, and **n.f.** מָחֳרָת. On the forgoing considerations, the gender makes no serious difference in meaning other than part of speech:

> Some non-animate nouns have both masculine and feminine forms. Although these so-called *doublets* may have different connotations, it is best not to rely too heavily on their gender distinctions; both forms mean essentially the same thing.[187]

It is possible that the choice of the feminine form was motivated by the need for a construct noun in Lev. 23:11, 15, 16; Num. 33:3; Josh. 5:11 and 1 Sam. 20:27. The feminine form shows a more obvious construct than the masculine which might still be confused as an adverb. And these are the only passages having the construct form מִמָּחֳרַת.

The key to understanding the passages is that מָחָר has two meanings. On first use in Gen. 30:33, the phrase means "in a day to come" (KJV) = בְּיוֹם מָחָר:

> So my righteousness will answer for me in *the* time being after [בְּיוֹם מָחָר], when you come concerning my wages. Every one that is not speckled and spotted among the goats and black among the lambs, *if found* with me, will be considered stolen (my translation).

The word מָחָר is used 13 out of 52 times with this meaning "time to come." Marcus Jastrow gives the definition:

> מָחָר m. *next day, future day*...there is a *mahar* which means *now* (the next day), and there is a *mahar* which means some future time. (ibid. page 764).

Brown, Driver, Briggs defines:

> מָחָר **n.m.** used oft. as **adv., to-morrow, in time to come** . . . 2. = *in future time.*[188]

[187] pg.106, §6.4.3, *An Introduction to Biblical Hebrew Syntax*, Bruce K. Waltke, M. O'Connor.
[188] *The New Brown-Driver-Briggs Hebrew Lexicon.*

The sense of *time* comes from the contracted יוֹם = מ, and *after* from the contracted אַחַר. Thus: "מָ'חָר" = יוֹם אַחַר. Whether the participle derivation is more correct or the *yom* derivation is more correct does not affect the end result. If the participle is correct, then the word means "being after." I think that the yom derivation and the participle derivation blended together: *day being after*. Again, this does not affect the result because the word "day" can mean "time" and not just one literal day:

> In the day of Yahweh Almighty's making earth and heavens, and before any shrub of the field will be on the earth, and before any herb of the field will sprout, becasue Yahweh Almighty had not made rain upon the earth, and no man to work the ground, and a mist goes up from the earth, and had watered the whole face of the ground, then Yahweh Almighty forms the man, dust from the ground....(Gen. 2:4b-7a).

> But from the tree of the knowledge of good and evil you shall not eat, for in the day [בְּיוֹם] that you eat from it death you shall die (Gen. 2:17).

> Like the cold of snow in the time [בְּיוֹם] of harvest is a faithful messenger to those who send him, for he refreshes the soul of his masters. (Prov. 25:13).

> Near is the great day of Yãhweh [יוֹם־יַהְוֶה], near and coming very quickly; listen, the day of Yãhweh! In it the warrior cries out bitterly (Zeph. 1:14).

These examples illustrate that the word "day" can be used to mean "time." And the BDB Lexicon says, "6. יוֹם = time" (pg. 399, ibid.) So this is the reason why מָחָר = *day after* = *time after*. Now this sense is not common. The literal sense of "day" dominates heavily. However, if the context requires, the sense is natural in Hebrew.

The word מָחֳרָת works the same way as מָחָר. The gender difference is like that of "day after" and "day afterward" in English.

Now the word מָחֳרָת is always prefixed with the preposition מִן to form: מִמָּחֳרָת or מִֽמָּחֳרַת (construct). One may be tempted to explain Lev. 23:16 by translating like this:

> Until <u>from</u> the day after the seventh Sabbath counting a

fiftieth day. . .

And then the temptation is to explain "from" as meaning the counting continues "away from" the seventh day until the 50th day is reached. If this seems to be stretching it, then the precedent was set by translators of both Karaite oriented versions and Rabbinic versions of the preceding verse, Lev. 23:15:

> KJV Leviticus 23:15 And ye shall count unto you <u>from</u> the morrow after the sabbath, from the day that ye brought the sheaf of the wave offering; seven sabbaths shall be complete:

> JPS Leviticus 23:15 And ye shall count unto you <u>from</u> the morrow after the day of rest, from the day that ye brought the sheaf of the waving; seven weeks shall there be complete;

The word *from* shows up in Young's Literal Translation also, only this time I quote all three occurrences of, "in the day after":

> מִ <u>On</u> the morrow of the sabbath doth the priest wave it15 'And ye have numbered to you מִ <u>from</u> the morrow of the sabbath, from the day of your bringing in the sheaf of the wave-offering: they are seven perfect sabbaths; 16 unto מִ <u>??</u> the morrow of the seventh sabbath ye do number fifty days (YLT, Lev. 23:11, 15-16).

All the translations follow this pattern like lemmings off a cliff. In vs. 11 "on"; in vs. 15 "from"; and in vs. 16 the translation is omitted. So we have מִן = {on, from, ∅}:

Stone Edition Tanakh, JPS, NAS, NAU, NIV, RSV, TNK, YLT, KJV, ASV, CJB, CSB, DBY, ERV, ESV, GWN, NET, NJB, NKJV, NLT, NRS, RWB, TNIV, WEB = {on, from, ∅}. DRA, GNV = {∅, from, ∅}. Even the LXX = {τῇ in the, ἀπὸ from, ∅}. But the Hebrew is the same in all three cases: מִמָּחֳרַת. Does the contraction of מִמָּחֳרַת = בְּיוֹם־מָחָר have three meanings?

The reason why all these translations translated "from" in Lev. 23:15, "from the day after the Sabbath [ceasing]" is that the translators were 1. too ignorant of Hebrew to recognize that "in the day after" = "in the time after" and could contain seven Sabbaths, or

2. they simply copied the ignorant translator before them without checking the matter out.

An examination of the other 24 usages of מִמָּחֳרַת or מִמָּחֳרַת (construct) will show that the sense of the preposition is never "from"! It is always in agreement with the sense given in the uncontracted first use: בְּיוֹם־מָחָר = *in day after*. Further, an examination of the preposition will show that it must mean "in" and not "from."

There are 25 verses that have this word and include the inseparable prepositional prefix מִ attached to מָחֳרָת. It is clear from examining these other passages that the preposition מ does not mean *from* in an extensive sense, as in English, "I went *from* New York to Philadelphia." Yet, the translators tried to obtain that sense in Lev. 23:15, and we could, in theory exploit the same idea of *from* in Lev. 23:16 and arrive at the same end result with the chronology. However, just because the translators did this (Karaite oriented & Rabbinic alike) in vs. 15 does not make it legitimate. The usage of מ to mean *from* in the extended sense of "away from" is not supported by any other uses of מִמָּחֳרָת.

It is clear that the preposition מ means from in a different sense: It marks the block of time *out of* which, *from* which, or *in* which some time is indicated.

> Temporal uses of *mn* vary in relation to the beginning point, which may be included ('from, on, in,'; #5) or not ('after'; #6). Temporal mn can also mark a block of time ('after'; #7) (11.2.11, *Biblical Hebrew Syntax*, Waltke).

To clarify this for the non-scholar, I will use this illustration. Consider the "day after" a block of time, either 12 or 24 hours. What the preposition does is draw a point in time *from/in/on* that block of time. There is therefore no extension away from the block of time. The *moment* can only be "in" or "from" the block of time.*

So when the translators tried to translate Lev. 23:15 "*from* the day after" they did so because the context required it. However, they went against every other use of ממחרת, in which the moment indicated must be contained "in" or taken "out of" or taken "from" the space of

* I have since the first edition thought of an easy English example to show this, "Take time from tomorrow to finish up that project." "From" clearly means the same thing as "in," i.e. "Take time in tomorrow...."

time called the "day after". So "from day after" is a moment taken "from" the day after, and not a departure beyond the "day after". It is a very subtle difference.

Here are the 25 verses from BibleWorks:

> Gen. 19:34; Exo. 9:6; Exo. 18:13; Exo. 32:6; Exo. 32:30; Lev. 23:11; Lev. 23:15; Lev. 23:16; Num. 17:6; Num. 17:23; Num. 33:3; Jos. 5:11; Jos. 5:12; Judges 6:38, 9:42, 21:4; 1 Sam. 5:3; 1 Sam. 5:4; 1 Sam. 11:11; 1 Sam. 18:10; 1 Sam. 20:27; 1 Sam. 31:8; 2 Kin. 8:15; 1 Chron. 10:8; Jer. 20:3

The inclusion of the preposition in all of these passages argues eloquently for the sense "in the day after", and proves the translators attempt to resolve Lev. 23:15 with "from" in an extended sense errant. The Hebrew מִמָּחֳרָת or מִמָּחֳרַת (construct) has the same senses as: בְּיוֹם־מָחָר, which is "in *the* day after."

Now if a critic were to insist that the preposition means *from* in the extensive sense then he or she cannot explain 24 of the 25 uses. Only the use in Lev. 23:15 would be explained. Further, the critic would thereby disprove that Lev. 23:16 only means the first day of the week. If the skeptic says that it means *from* in vs. 15 and does not likewise read *from* in vs. 16, and renders it *on* in vs. 11, then he or she is being inconsistent. The interlocutor would be arbitrary. Arbitrariness is *ad hoc*. It does not agree with the principle of the simplest explanation (Occam's Razor).

The solution, therefore, lies in the Hebrew understanding of the word *day*. The contextual requirement of Lev. 23:15 for a time period longer than just one *day* in order to count the *seven sabbaths* should point us to an allowed sense of *day* meaning *time to come* as used according to Hebrew, which use is well proved, rather than trying to solve the problem by an *hapax ad* hoc rendering of Lev. 23:15 with extensive *from*, which is contrary to the usage of ממחרת elsewhere. Here is another rendering that gives the Hebrew literally:

> 'And he shall wave the sheaf before Yãhweh, so that you may be accepted. **<u>In</u>** the day after the resting the priest shall wave it 15 'And you count for yourselves **<u>in</u>** the day after the resting (from the day when you brought in the sheaf of the

wave offering) seven restings perfectly regular they shall be 16
until **<u>in</u>** the day after the seventh resting you are counting a
fiftieth day; then you shall present a new grain offering to
Yãhweh.

Let me simplify the sentence, "And you count . . . **<u>in</u>** the day after the resting . . . seven restings." It is clear that "**<u>in</u>** the day after" = "**<u>in</u>** the time after." This is clarified by the parenthetical statement, "(from the day. . .)." This explains that "**<u>in</u>** the day after" means the time period "from the day when," and in this case "from the day when" (מִיּוֹם) is extensive.

Now while the ambiguity remains, and I have sided with the Nisan 16 interpretation here, the important point to remember after all this is that the Karaite argument no longer has a proof text in Lev. 23:16. The skeptic that wishes to remain in this position only has an interpretation, but it is inconsistent with the overall chronology of scripture, and certainly the resurrection passages contradict the Karaite notion of when the "first of the sabbaths" is to be counted.

It is not consistent to insist on the literal translation of Sabbath in Lev. 23:15 and then to accept the mistranslation "weeks" at face value in Mat. 28:1; Mark 16:2; Luke 18:12, 24:1; John 20:1, 19; Acts 20:7; 1 Cor. 16:2). Nor is it consistent to accept the translation "from" in Lev. 23:15 while disallowing it in vs. 16. Nor is it consistent to allow "in the time after" for the masculine מָחָר, but then to insist that the noun looses the possibility of that meaning just because it is feminine. Nor is it consistent to posit that "in the time after" is too rare a sense when all the translators were forced to insert "from" into the text of vs. 15 to prevent the contradiction that seven sabbaths cannot be literally counted "in the morrow" or "in the day after"—except in the Hebrew sense "time after," which clearly is allowed.

The definition given here "in the time after" is explained in Samuel Lee's Hebrew Lexicon this way:

> מָחָר, m. מָחֳרָת, f. } plur. non occ. constr. fem. מָחֳרַת. The primitive notion seems to consist in *proceeding forwards*; which, applied to time, may designate the (a) ***Morrow***, or day following some other day previously expressed *or* implied. (b)

> ***Hereafter***, ***henceforward***, Gen xxx. 33; Exo. xiii. 14; Deut. vi 20; Josh. iv. 6.21: so Matt. vi. 34, εἰς τὴν αὔριον.[189]

Yeshua says, “do not be anxious for tomorrow; for tomorrow will care for itself” (Mat. 6:34). Clearly here he includes the “hereafter” in the meaning of “tomorrow.”

Lee’s definition is excellent. The sense “hereafter” or “henceforward” only needs a bit of modernization to “in the time after,” or “time to come.” So a literal translation of Lev. 23:15-16 using Lee’s gloss:

> 15 ‘And you count for yourselves in the ***hereafter*** of the
> resting (from the day when you brought in the sheaf of the
> wave offering) seven restings *perfect (regular) shall be 16
> until in the ***hereafter*** of the seventh resting you are counting a
> fiftieth day; then you shall present a new grain offering to
> Yãhweh.

OR using “out of”.

> 15 ‘And you count for yourselves out of the ***hereafter*** of
> the resting (from the day when you brought in the sheaf of the
> wave offering) seven restings—complete they shall be— 16
> until out of the ***hereafter*** of the seventh resting you are
> counting a fiftieth day; then you shall present a new grain
> offering to Yãhweh.

KARAITE CRITICISMS REVIEWED

Fixed Date Argument:

A popular Karaite criticism is that if Shavuot always comes on Sivan 6, a fixed day in the Rabbinic calendar, then wouldn’t the scripture have specified the fixed day “Sivan 6” for Shavuot rather than requiring counting? This would be a valid point if the calendar for the biblical period were the same as the modern Rabbinic

---

[189] *A Lexicon, Hebrew, Chaldee, and English*, Samuel Lee, London, 1840; 664 pages. The bold emphasis is mine and the evidence for definition (a) has been omitted as there will be no dispute about it.

* The specification תְּמִימֹת תִּהְיֶינָה has to be surely fatal to the Rabbinic attempt to understand Sabbaths as irregular (or imperfect) weeks. A perfect week would have begin with the first day and end on a Sabbbath. So since perfect weeks do not work out, the sense must be perfect Sabbaths, which would exclude annual Sabbaths. On the seventh day, Creation was declared to be complete.

calendar.

On the modern Rabbinic calendar, Shavuot is fixed on Sivan 6. Now Rabbinic Jews still count 50 days, but the 50th day is always on Sivan 6 giving some validity to the objection. However, we must consider that the Rabbinic calendar was introduced in 359 A.D. by Hillel II, and that it is not the same as the Scriptural calendar. The Rabbinic calendar does not sight the first crescent of the new moon, and as a result of imprecision in their calculations they fixed the length of Nisan at 30 days and the length of Iyar at 29 days. It is these fixed month lengths that result in Shavuot always coming on Sivan 6 in the Rabbinic calendar.

Before A.D. 359, the new moon was sighted. And when the new moon is sighted, the length of Nisan varies between 29 and 30 days, and the length of Iyar also varies between 29 and 30 days. So in the biblical period the following combinations occur:

Nisan 29 days + Iyar 29 days results in Shavuot on Sivan 7
Nisan 29 days + Iyar 30 days results in Shavuot on Sivan 6
Nisan 30 days + Iyar 29 days results in Shavuot on Sivan 6
Nisan 30 days + Iyar 30 days results in Shavuot on Sivan 5

So we see that when the new moon is observed the month lengths vary year to year and Shavuot can come on Sivan 5, 6, or 7. Therefore, there is no way the Scripture could have stated a fixed date for Shavuot. The fixed Rabbinic date is an artifact of not observing the new moon. Nowadays we observe the new moon, so Shavuot regularly comes on Sivan 5, 6, or 7, and not just Sivan 6.

Morrow of the Sabbath Argument:

The main Karaite argument is that the Sabbath in Lev. 23:11 and 23:15 after which the counting begins is the weekly Sabbath. This argument is based on the assumption that "The Sabbath" always means the weekly Sabbath. This argument is inconclusive on the linguistic meaning of the word שַׁבָּת. Shabbat merely means *cessation, ceasing*. Besides Lev. 23:11 & 23:15, two usages that obviously do not refer to the seventh day of the week are found in Lev. 23:32; and another is in Lev. 25:6.

The Karaite is forced to fall back to the word "the" הַ. A festival

Sabbath is never called "the Sabbath" he argues. However, the concept of the definite article (definiteness) does not have the power to tell the difference between a weekly Sabbath and a festival Sabbath. Definiteness only means that the item in question has been referred to before, or that it is known already what his being talked about. Translate literally, "the ceasing" הַשֵּׁבֵת or "the cessation" הַשַּׁבָּת. What is *the ceasing* that was referred to in the preceding context? Try four verses earlier, "In the first day you shall have an holy convocation: ye shall do not servile work therein" (Lev. 23:7).

The definite article refers to something defined before. Hence in 23:7, "בַּיּוֹם הָרִאשׁוֹן" *on the first day* is defined before in vs. 6: "seven days you shall eat unleavened bread." Here no definite article is used: "שִׁבְעַת יָמִים." But "the ceasing" is also made definite by previous mention in Exodus 12:15, "On the first day, you shall cause to cease leaven out of your houses." The words translated "cause to cease" are תַּשְׁבִּיתוּ.*

Thus on the assumption that "the cessation" (Lev. 23:11) refers to Lev. 23:7 and Exodus 12:15, the legislation is unambiguous and speaks of a definite known day. But the Karaites assume that "the Sabbath" refers to a weekly Sabbath. They might explain this as definite by previous reference to Lev. 23:3. In that case the definite article is what is called "generic." A generic definite article refers to a known class of objects, but does not say which one of the class is meant. So which weekly "Sabbath" is meant is not clear by the Karaite interpretation.

Would it be the Sabbath before the feast of unleavened bread? Or the Sabbath in the feast of unleavened bread? Or even a Sabbath after the whole feast of unleavened bread is complete, i.e. a Sabbath after the rest day mentioned in Lev. 23:8? In an attempt to resolve this problem, the Karaites attempt to make the matter definite by specifying that the day after the Sabbath must be one of the seven days of unleavened bread. The result of this requirement is that if the 15th of Nisan lands on a Sunday, then the sheaf must be waved on the 15th of Nisan, and not on the 22nd of Nisan because the 22nd of Nisan would be after the last day of the feast.

The assumption that a weekly Sabbath be chosen such that the

---

* Exodus 12:15. A cause to cease precedes a "ceasing," (so the first day of the seven is regarded as "the ceasing," but the cause of it is on the headmost day (בַּיּוֹם הָרִאשׁוֹן), i.e. one day before the first (cf. Rashi; Mat. 26:17; Mark 14:12; Luke 22:7). Exodus 12:15 may also be interpreted as involving a 'declarative Hiphil,' viz. 'On the first day ye shall declare ceased leaven from your houses' (cf. Exodus 22:9, 23:7; Deut. 25:1; Isa. 29:21; 1 Ki 8:32; Job 9:20; perh. Mat. 5:32; cf. 'declarative Piel.'). Either way the first day may be termed "the cessation" (הַשַּׁבָּת).

wave sheaf falls in the feast is *ad hoc*. It is an assumption added to repair the obvious ambiguity resulting from the Karaite assertion that "the Sabbath" means the weekly Sabbath. This begs the question, "Why must the sheaf be waved in the feast of unleavened bread?" What historical answer can be given for waving the sheaf fixed to the feast of unleavened bread, when the day for waving varies every year† as to which day of the feast it falls on? † In the Karaite system.

And what historical reason can be given for counting 50 days from a starting point that varies? The only answer that makes the remotest sense is TO CONFUSE THE TIMING OF THE ORIGINAL HISTORICAL EVENT by rendering the memorial counting of it arbitrary. I do not say that all in agreement with the Karaites are guilty of this motive. But it appears that the originators are.

I explained before that that "in the day after the cessation means to start with Nisan 16, the day after the annual Sabbath. The true historical reason for this is that Nisan 16 marked the first day that Israel was out of Egypt‡ It marks the day when Israel camped in Succoth* and baked their dough into unleavened bread. It was further explained that the night Israel went out of Egypt and the 16th day following was the weekly Sabbath. Thus, seven sevens of days contained seven completed Sabbaths, and then Shavuot itself was on the Sabbath. * Prob. a district in the Sinai where they camped several times.

Now, for the faithful in Yeshua who accept the testimony of the four Evangelists, we have in John 19:31 the usage of the words "the Sabbath" (τῷ σαββάτῳ); Delitzsch: הַשַּׁבָּת. If we heed Matthew 12:40 at all, then "three nights" requires this Sabbath to be an annual Sabbath,[190] and John says just this: ἦν γὰρ μεγάλη ἡ ἡμέρα ἐκείνου τοῦ σαββάτου = "For that Sabbath was the Great Day." The testimony of the Evangelists rejects the Karaite notion that "the Sabbath" must refer to the weekly Sabbath.

<u>Morrow of the seventh Sabbath argument</u>:

This was covered extensively before, so the Karaite argument will be stated and the solution stated. The proof is elsewhere in this book.

---

[190] Both Wednesday and Thursday chronologies that take Matthew 12:40 truthfully place the annual Sabbath on a weekday other than the weekly Sabbath.

‡ Num. 33:5, "Then they pull out from Ra'meses in the first month, on the fifteenth day of the first month, in the tomorrow of the Passover they went out..... Then the sons of Israel pull out from Ra'meses. Then they encamped in Sukkot." Passover here is the 14th. They began to go out at daybreak (Exodus 12:22), and finished toward dawn starting the 16th day. It appears that, Sukkot and Etham were regions outside of settled Egypt within its sphere of influence, taking a few days each. ⟶

The Karaite argues that the morrow of the seventh Sabbath is necessarily a Sunday (Lev. 23:16), and therefore, one must begin to count on a Sunday. The answer is that "morrow of" is a poor translation. Literally the Hebrew says, "IN THE DAY AFTER." In the Hebraic sense, this means "IN THE TIME AFTER," and according to the usage of "day" in Gen. 2:4 and 30:33 and elsewhere is not limited to just a single literal day. This usage in Lev. 23:16 is proved by the need to translate "from" in Lev. 23:15. Instead of translating "from" in vs. 15, it is correct to translate, "in the day after," and understand that it means "in the time after" to count seven Sabbaths.

Also, instead of counting "until the morrow of the seventh [weekly] Sabbath," which would be Sunday, it is "until in the day after the seventh Sabbath counting a fiftieth day," which means "in the time after." Later in this book, practical directions for doing this will be detailed for each year.

The above, therefore covers the fundamental Karaite arguments for the Sunday Shavuot, and the answers.

Figure 39: Exodus 19-14 Chronology

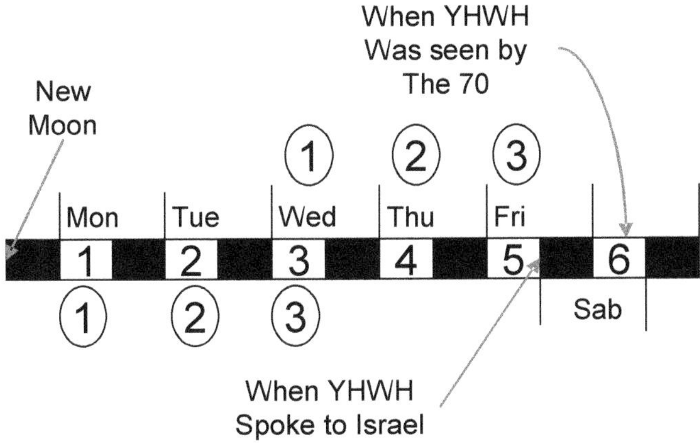

ADDITIONAL BIBLICAL EVIDENCE

Now in the year of the Exodus, the children of Israel traveled around to the back side of Mt. Sinai, a journey of three days (Ex. 3:18; 5:3; 8:27). They sanctified themselves for two days (Ex. 19:10), and were ready the third day. They entered the wilderness of Sinai on the first day of the third month. As usual, the day is from daybreak to

(from previous page) It appears unlikely that Succoth and Etham are simple place names. Rather larger regions, perhaps taking their names from some named location in the district. This is because it must have taken longer than three days to reach the sea where they crossed. There must be several nights in each of these regions. The timing on when Pharaoh's army caught up with them also supports this.

daybreak, chronology is as follows:

First the new moon is seen (see Figure 39: Exodus 19-14 Chronology). Then Israel enters the wilderness of Sinai to travel to the back side of the mountain, taking three days, numbered on the bottom in the circles. They reach their destination sometime on the third day, and are instructed to sanctify themselves "today" הַיּוֹם "and day after" וּמָחָר. Accordingly, numbers 1-2 in the circles over Wed-Thu. They are to be ready for the third day לַיּוֹם־הַשְּׁלִישִׁי. At the beginning of the Sabbath YHWH spoke to Israel out of fire and cloud. The next morning, on the day part of the Sabbath, Moses ratified the covenant. The cloud was cleared off the mountain, and the elders of Israel ascended Mt. Sinai and saw YHWH. The person they saw was Yeshua, YHWH the son of YHWH. The text says:

> Then he said to Moses, "Come up to Yãhweh, you and Aaron, Nadab and Abihu and seventy of the elders of Israel, and you shall worship at a distance.
>
> Exodus 24:1

To this be sure to compare:

> And it shall be from new moon to new moon and from sabbath to sabbath, all mankind will come to bow down before me," says Yãhweh.
>
> Isa. 66:23

We see therefore that this took place on the Sabbath. What happened next is this:

> Then Moses went up to the mountain, and the cloud covered the mountain. And the glory of Yãhweh rested on Mount Sinai, and the cloud covered it for six days; and on the seventh day he called to Moses from the midst of the cloud.*
>
> Exodus 24:15-16

The cloud now returns to the mountain for six days, and out of the cloud YHWH speaks to Moses on the seventh.

See Appendix VI, page 475 for the calendar of the 3rd month.

---

* The timing of the transfiguration requires these six days to be the six working days of the week. Because this is the only way to reconcile Matthew's "after six days" (17:1) with Luke's "And almost eight days after...." (9:28). Both are counting from Sabbath to Sabbath, from the same two points. The Evangelists wanted us to connect the transfiguration with Exodus 24 by these clues.

Figure 40: YHWH speaks on the Sabbath

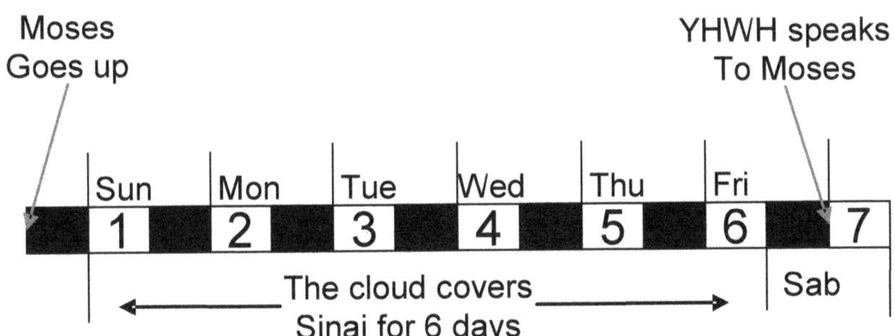

This time the numbers number the days of the week, whereas in the preceding diagram they numbered the days of the month. The principle of the matter is that YHWH speaks to Israel and Moses on the Sabbath. At other times he spoke to Moses on any day, but here YHWH delays till the Sabbath. The reason can be no other than to underscore the importance of the seventh day Sabbath, and is strong confirmation that YHWH appeared to the elders of Israel on Mt. Sinai on the Sabbath.

Now we must consider the typology in all of this for the death and resurrection of Messiah.

1. The people were first told to prepare on the 4th day of the week, which was Wednesday. This matches the fact that Yeshua was then prepared for sacrifice, and the people prepared their passover lambs.

2. YHWH appeared to the elders of Israel on the day part of the following Sabbath. Thus Yeshua appeared to the disciples on the Sabbath day, so also they fell at his feet, and so also they ate and drank with him (John 20:19ff).

3. The three days mentioned in Exodus 19 correspond to the three days of Yeshua's suffering, death, and resurrection. They also clearly show three days and three nights. Moses came down Mt. Sinai at dawn on the Sabbath to ratify the covenant. Therefore, with Yeshua's resurrection on the Sabbath Messiah's covenant renewal with Israel is confirmed through the effect of his death the third day before. The good news about the new made covenant of old is that the Almighty has remembered his covenant despite the sins of Israel and Judah. He is keeping his promises to give the repentant a new made heart.

Populations of Egypt and Canaan

Secular archaeologists assume that the populations of Egypt and Canaan were far less than can be logically deduced from Scripture statements at the time of the Exodus (1632 BC). Conveniently this allows them to dismiss the Scripture as a fairy tale. But are their own conclusions based on sound assumptions and careful reasoning? The answer is no. Their conclusions are based on an alien worldview, an ideology, a system of thinking that allows only favored conclusions. All evidence is first filtered through the worldview and given an interpretation that agrees with the worldview before the evidence and actual logic are allowed to speak for themselves. This worldview is called humanism. In it man is the measure of all things, and there is no Almighty, Creator of all. The first rule of this worldview is to make sure that whatever the evidence is, that it never gets explained so that it agrees with Scripture. Though they attempt to hide this bias so that the unsuspecting will think their conclusions are scientific, those who examine matters will find that their claims are simple dogmatisms. Essentially, they are blindly holding faithful to their anti-biblical worldview in the same sense that pagans blindly hold to their false gods. Whatever the facts are, they frame their story with as many fictional presumptions as needed to keep their false narrative going.

What the reasonableness of an opinion is, is judged by their worldview, and this soon becomes the "expert" opinion presented in all sincerity to Christians who are unaware of the foundations of their own biblical worldview, and unaware that accepting these demigod claims destroys their own foundations. Now, there is no way to escape the fact that Scripture puts the population of Israel at the time of the Exodus over two million even by the roughest of estimates (the actual figure will shortly be computed). There are many going around suggesting to Christians that the biblical numbers can be reduced, because the Hebrew word *elef* (אֶלֶף) might mean "troop" or "unit" rather than 1000. But a closer examination of the census numbers and the half-shekel tax collected shows that reducing the numbers by such means results in mathematical contradictions. Nevertheless, Christians who say they believe the Bible account of matters accept such arguments because it allows them to believe the secular archaeolgists also without examining the claims. But now they are doubly deceived, because they believe two lies and prove hypocrites on their continued claim to believe Scripture. As I said, the attempt to reduce the Scripture numbers may be mathematically exposed for the lie it is, because the numbers do not add up that way. So to believe the numbers may be reduced is not to believe what Scripture says. It is to disbelieve it.

So they say they believe it. But it can be proven they disbelieve it. They believe the secular archaeologists who contradict scripture. And they believe that the numbers in Scripture may be reduced to make scripture agree with them.

But the truth is that the Scripture absolutely disagrees with the secular archaeologists and their worldview! It is probably easier to convince the secular archaeologist that this is so than to convince the Christian, who wants to agree with the secular archaeologist, that the Scripture is not going to go with them on that path. If the Christian wants to stop being a hypocrite and to really follow the Almighty, then he has to stop believing the lies of the world. He has to come to terms with the fact that Scripture will not agree with the secular archaeologist. Then he has to realize he cannot hold to an error as great as saying the population numbers are wrong and reasonably have faith in the accuracy of the rest of Scripture. He has to deny himself and accept the fact that the world will not pat him on the back and treat him as a good boy.

Contrary to the evolutionary assumptions, ancient man multiplied faster than modern man. The earth had more biodiversity, and was more fertile. Small areas could sustain larger populations than assumed. Those who chose to hunt plentiful game multiplied as fast or faster than those who settled and grew crops. Also contrary to modern assumptions, epidemics, wars, and disasters killed far greater percentages of nations that did not practice biblical laws. The Bronze Age Collapse witnessed a significant decline of Middle East populations. Even in the Western Hemisphere, in more recent times, the native population was greatly reduced after 1492, in some places to only 1/10th of its former numbers, by European diseases and other causes. In ancient times population decline and recovery could happen in shorter periods of time. After the deluge a series of climate changes also affected outcomes for many nations, both negative and positive even a thousand years afterward. The bones and graves of 99.9% of ancient Egypt vanished long ago, and Egypt took no written census that has survived. So archaeologists have no idea what the ancient populations of Egypt and Canaan were aside from assumptions based on their world view and what they are not finding in the earth, which vanished long ago, and so is no longer there to find!

At the end of the second intermediate period before the devastation of the ten plagues, the population of Egypt must have been on the order of 15 to 30 million. Afterward they may have died off to as few as 3 or 4 million. The population of Canaan also must have been considerably higher than Israel, because the Scripture says that seven nations in Canaan were greater and mightier than they (Deut. 7:1). Perhaps these seven nations numbered as few as 5 million or as many as 20. The average inhabitant of these lands would have left no trace of their existence behind after a few centuries. The bones of most burials would have turned to unidentifiable dust. Their mud huts, wood homes, and tents would have washed away or rotted and their pottery been broken, crushed, and scattered. Archaeologists have no idea how many such people existed. But calculations based on Scriptural numbers give us an indication because Scripture is a historical record. The archaeologist can only estimate based on extrapolating from what he has found to guess at what has disappeared. And what if his assumptions about the nature of the culture surrounding his artifacts are

(cont. page 209)

After Three Days

Error is the slow and steady accumulation of inconsistencies that lead to the wrong conclusion. Also, a wrong interpretation has the result of introducing more inconsistencies into a theory. The errant theory is believed on the basis of tradition or because its followers want it to be true. They have become emotionally invested in their belief, and this is most hazardous if the foundation of the belief is faulty. But like the Roman Catholic indulgences there comes a point in time when the malpractice becomes so extreme that one can hardly not notice. Only then do men begin to go through the prevailing paradigm with the closest of scrutiny that exposes the magnitude of the error.

We must seek sources of evidence that are not contaminated and conflicted by the paradigm that needs to be tested. For if the chief advocates are allowed to burn all the old books, and rewrite all the new ones, and to redefine the very language that might be used to expose it, then it can never be properly tested or challenged. This means trusting neither Judaism nor Christianity before they parted ways about A.D. 131, nor statements coming from the Gnostic majority of Christians going back to about A.D. 90.

Rabbi Akiba and his contemporaries wanted to push the faithful in Yeshua out of Judaism and into Gnostic Christianity. For as lawless Christians they are harmless to Jews, or so they thought at that time before Hadrian showed them wrong. Meanwhile both sides traded converts in the polemical battle. The Torah observant faithful in Messiah were caught in the middle of it, just as today. Jewish converts to Christianity provided the Church excuses to remain lawless from their knowledge of Judaism, and likewise converts to Judaism provided Jews excuses not to believe in Messiah. They also provided each other excuses to keep separate.

Part of the "agreement" between the Church and Synagogue was the mutual common interest in undermining the true chronology of Yeshua's resurrection. For the true chronology inseparably links Yeshua's claim to being Messiah with typology and upholding of the times and seasons of Torah. Thus, it is necessary to do an end run around these two corrupt institutions to discover the truth.

We will find that the current translations only preserve the statement of Yeshua that he would rise *after three days* in one text:

> [31]And he began to teach them that the Sŏn of Man must suffer many things and be rejected by the elders and the chief priests and the scribes, and be killed, and after three days rise again.

GNM, Mark 8:31

[וְאַחֲרֵי שְׁלֹשֶׁת יָמִים = μετὰ τρεῖς ἡμέρας; MSS: all]

It will be seen at once that this statement is instantly fatal to the Friday-Sunday scenario. The following chart shows why:

Figure 41: Failure of After Three Days with Sunday

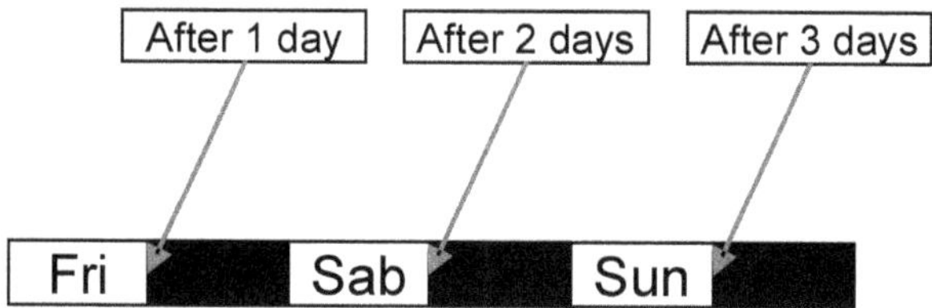

Clearly by Sunday morning only "after two days" has been attained, and there is no way for it to be "after three days." But if Yeshua died on Wednesday and rose on the Sabbath, everything is explained:

Figure 42: After Three Days Explained

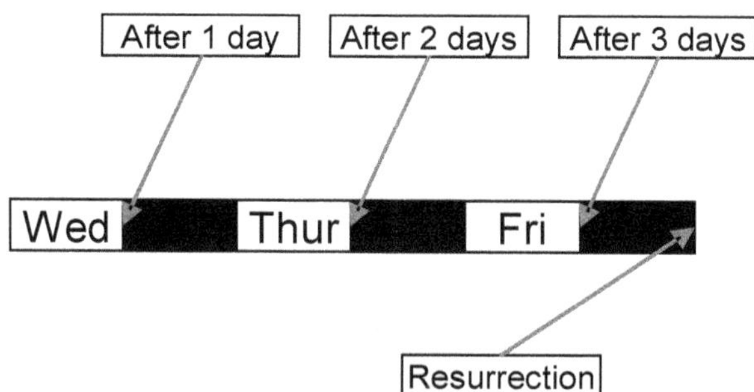

I described the daybreak to daybreak day earlier. In this case, the day may be reckoned to be over at sunset which would fit the shortest chronology, and thus as soon as the sun goes down one may say "after one day." Thus, the Mark passages are counting the end of a literal day (dawn to dusk) at the end of daylight.

Scribes and translators know that these "after three day" texts are hazardous to their Sunday paradigm. So they changed many of the texts in the second and third centuries. What was left over, scribes mistranslated in other languages, simply ignored, or swept under the rug with inclusive counting excuses. Between Scrivener's 1894 Greek New Testament (τῇ τρίτῃ ἡμέρᾳ) and Nestle-Aland 27th (μετὰ τρεῖς ἡμέρας) we can recover Mark 9:31:

> 31For he was teaching his disciples and telling them, "The Sŏn of Man is to be delivered into the hands of men, and they will kill him, and when he has been killed, he will rise after three days" (GNM, Mark 9:31).

MSS Witnesses: (Mark 9:31). [μετὰ τρεῖς ἡμέρας = *post tres dies*; MSS: א B C* D L Δ Ψ 579. 892. 2427 *pc* it sy^{hmg} co]

Also we can recover Mark 10:34. Scrivener has τῇ τρίτῃ ἡμέρᾳ. But the critical text: μετὰ τρεῖς ἡμέρας:

> 34And they will mock him and spit upon him, and scourge him, and kill him, and after three days he will rise again" (GNM, Mark 10:34).

MSS Witnesses: [MSS: א B C* D L Δ Ψ 579. 892. 2427 *pc* it sy^{hmg} co]

Of course these passages have parallels in Matthew and Luke, and when you look at the apparatus of the critical text you will find some variants for "after three days" that match these Mark passages. Parallel to the Mark 8:31 text we have a Matthew text and a Luke text.

> 21From that time Yĕshua the Anŏinted began to show his disciples that it is necessary for him to go to Yerushalayim, and to suffer many things from the elders and the chief priests and the scribes, and to be killed, and ⸀after three days to rise" (GNM, Mat. 16:21).

MSS Witnesses [μετὰ τρεῖς ἡμέρας; MSS: D (*al* it) bo]

> 22"It is necessary for the Sŏn of Man to suffer many things, and be rejected by the elders and the chief priests and the scribes, and to be killed, and after three days to rise" (GNM, Luke 9:21-22).

MSS Wit: [μεθ ημερας τρεις; MSS: D it; Mcion$^{A,(E)}$]

But these variants are not put in the main text of the critical text because there are too few manuscripts supporting the "after three days" reading. However the above parallel texts probably should agree with Mark.* After all, they are recording the same material and the same statements of Yeshua. In Mat. 16:21 "after three days" is in Codex Bezae and more than a few old Latin manuscripts. So if the critical text says that Mark 8:31 should be "after three days" (with no disputes), and Mat. 16:21 is parallel to it, then it should have originally said the same. We can only conclude that Codex Bezae is correct and that the scribes altered the other manuscripts.

The story is the same for the parallel passage to Mark 9:31:

> [22]Yĕshua said to them, "The Sŏn of Man is about to be delivered into the hands of men, [23]and they will kill him, and after three days he will be raised" (GNM, Mat. 17:22-23). Texts: [μετα τρεις ημερας; MSS: D it sy^s bo]

The parallels with Mark 10:34 are not so well supported:

> [18]"Behold, we are going up to Yerushalayim, and the Sŏn of Man will be delivered to the chief priests and scribes, and they will condemn him to death, [19]and they will deliver him to the nations to mock and scourge and fasten him up on an execution timber, and the third day he will rise" (GNM, Mat. 20:18-19).

> [31]And he took the twelve aside and said to them, "Behold, we are going up to Yerushalayim. And all things which have been getting written by the prophets will be accomplished by the Sŏn of Man. [32]For he will be delivered to the nations, and he will be mocked and he will be spit upon, [33]and scourging, they will kill him. And the third day he will rise" (GNM, Luke 18:31-33).

It is the better part of parsimony here to suppose that Matthew and Luke ended their quotations (parallel to Mark 10:34, "after three days") from a separate statement of Yeshua. For Yeshua said both "on the third day" and "after three days" at different times. A comparison of the Greek text of Luke 18:32-33 and Matthew 20:19b show enough significant differences to suppose that Yeshua is being quoted from elsewhere, or that the evangelists are paraphrasing and simply chose

* "After three days" certainly qualifies as *lectio difficilior potior*. The Scribes had every motive to change these texts. But there is no motive for the reverse!

from their inventory of Yeshua's sayings, which included both "after three days" and "the third day."

The skeptic will say that since part of a day can be counted as a whole day that when an hour or two of daylight passes on Sunday morning that said hour can qualify as a day, and that being *after* that hour qualifies as "after three days." To say the least, this is *ad hoc*. People simply do not think this way. If I come to your house at 3 in the afternoon, and say that I will return "after one day," then the earliest you can expect me is sometime the next day. You will not be expecting me at 4 p.m. that day or 5 p.m. If I say I will return "after two days," then you will not expect me the next day, but only the day after it, and if I say I will return "after three days" you will not expect me the next day (for it is only after one day), or the next (for it is only after two days), but you will expect me to skip the next two days and return on the third.

Figure 43: "After N Days" Theory

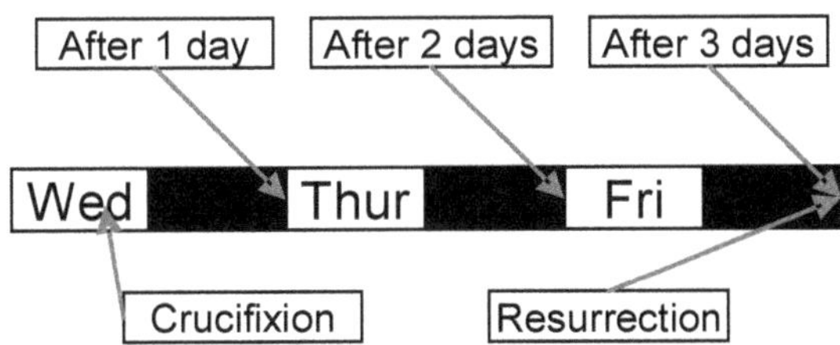

We have "after three days" in Mark 8:31; 9:31; 10:34, and Matthew 16:21, 17:23, and Luke 9:22. The interpretation above is confirmed by Matthew 12:40. For clearly there are "three" literal days, and "three" literal nights, and if "after three days" be shortened by some inclusive counting trickery then it will not fit with Matthew 12:40.

Our conclusion is also confirmed Revelation:

> And after the three and a half days the breath of life from the Almĩghty came into them, and they stood on their feet; and great fear fell upon those who were beholding them (Rev. 11:11).

Here they are dead for "three and a half days." Why the extra half day? The two witnesses are going to demonstrate the sign of Jonah, but Yeshua knows all about the attempt to shorten the period of the sign, and he knows all about the fact that after A.D. 70 Judaism decided to forget about the day for sacrificial offerings beginning at daybreak. So to prevent a mistake, he prophetically states it in terms of the prevailing view of the Jewish day for modern times. Here it is charted out:

Figure 44: After 3 1/2 Days (Just to be sure)

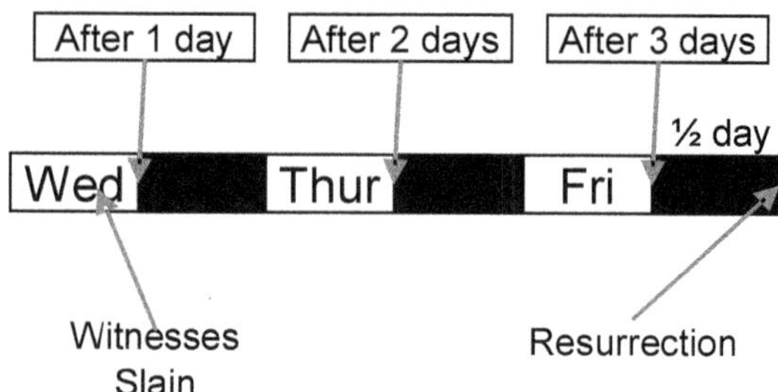

Since the post Temple Jewish day ends at sunset, then "after three days" naturally comes about at sunset, and not dawn. The extra 1/2 day is to get us at least half of the calendar day into the period identified as "after three days."*

THE POSTING OF THE GUARD

62Now on the [θ]morrow which is next to the preparation, the chief priests
and the Perushim gathered together with Pilate, 63and said, "Sir, we remember that when he was still alive that deceiver said, 'After three days I
rise again[κ].' 64Therefore, give orders for the grave to be made secure [λ]past
the third day, lest his disciples, having come, will have stolen him away
and will have said to the people, 'He has risen from the dead,' and the last
deception will be worse than the first" (GNM, Mat. 27:62-64).

It did not occur to the Jewish authorities to be concerned about a stolen body on the first night, nor does it appear that they were concerned about a stolen body after the time of Yeshua's predicted resurrection had passed. The authorities were concerned that the body

* This by the way is good proof for a sunset reckoning to the Sabbath. Mark 8:31, 9:31, etc. refer to the literal day (dawn to dusk) in stating "after three days," but to clarify this as "after three and a half days" makes the night at the end of the third day a "half day." If a sunrise day be used instead, the half day will make the witnesses' example end at sunset at the end of Sabbath whereas we already know Messiah was raised before dawn while still dark on the first of the Sabbaths.

disappear during any time that could be considered "the third day" or "after three days." They did not harmonize Yeshua's separate statements. Rather they took the statements separately and set the beginning and ending points of the prediction separately using the most expansive interpretations possible. In other words, they were playing it safe. They did not want the prediction to come true by any legitimate interpretation.

The phrase "on the third day" affords the potential for the earliest possible resurrection. Counting days inclusively according to a sunset epoch for the day makes sunset Thursday the first point in time of their concern (cf. top half of diagram below). The phrase "after three days" stretched out as far as it can go marks the latest possible point for resurrection, using a sunrise epoch for the day, at sunrise on Sunday. Here is the chart:

Figure 45: Posting the Guard for all Contingencies

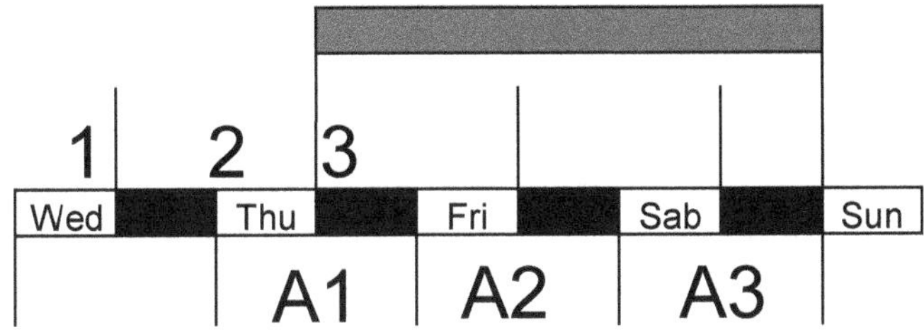

The authorities picked the soonest the third day could be to set the guard. They would have gone to Pilate shortly before or after sunset Thursday near the close of the annual Sabbath. The "morrow"[191] after the preparation is the same as the limits for A1 in the chart. In any case, the time period the tomb needed a guard is shaded out in gray—from the earliest interpretation of "on the third day" to the latest interpretation of "after three days."

The phrase "until the third day" (ἕως τῆς τρίτης ἡμέρας), Mat. 27:64, in Hebrew and Greek can 1. include the endpoint, 2. exclude the end point, 3. or mean going past the end point in Hebrew. That's

[191] The "morrow" means the next day. The *terminus a quo* (beginning point) is sometime after dawn on Thursday. The Greek word used here is ἐπαύριον, which is equivalent to the Hebrew יוֹם הַמָּחֳרָת (See Num. 11:32 for the definition of the "next day").

why I translated “onward past,” to indicate that the whole third day is included in the orders for the watch. The end of A3 marks “onward past the third day.” A3 does not mark the actual third day, but only as the authorities might have interpreted it, so as to make sure that the prophecy did not come true in any sense, and “3” marks the earliest the third day could be by a minimal interpretation. When the data are harmonized, neither “3” or “A3” is the third day.

The first night that the watch watched was Thursday night. This night was the “night” that Israel went out of Egypt (cf. Deut. 16:1).[192] For they began the Exodus at daybreak on the 15th of Nisan, but they finished it during the watches of the night:

> It is a night to keep watch for Yãhweh for having brought them out from the land of Egypt; this night is for Yãhweh, to keep watch by all the sons of Israel throughout their generations (Exodus 12:42).

So likewise the watch is posted by the authorities—to watch for Yahweh. Now as I said, the authorities took the statements separately so that they could cover any extreme interpretation. Harmonizing the statements produces this chart:

Figure 46: The Convergence "on" and "after" three days

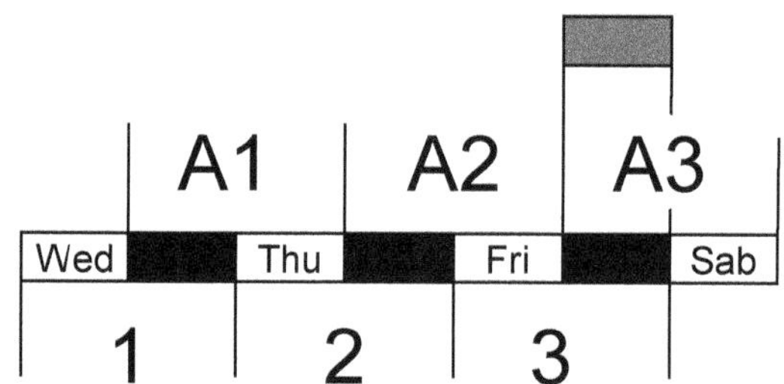

The two statements “after three days” and “on the third day” can only be made to agree at the intersection of the two statements, which is between Friday dusk and dawn on the Sabbath, indicated by the shaded segment.

---

[192] I do not explain this chronology fully here as the point is to make a typological connection. But briefly Israel did not leave their houses until sunrise after the night the destroyer slew the firstborn. The Exodus was thus completed in the night after the day part of the 15th according to Deut. 16:1.

On The Third Day

Using Hosea 6:1-3, it was shown that the resurrection was "on the third day" (בַּיּוֹם הַשְּׁלִישִׁי). Further, it was shown in the below chart that "after two days" (מִיֹּמָיִם)[193] meant that the counting had to be inclusive in the case of "on the third day.":

Figure 27: Hosea's Prophecy of the Resurrection

(From page 147)

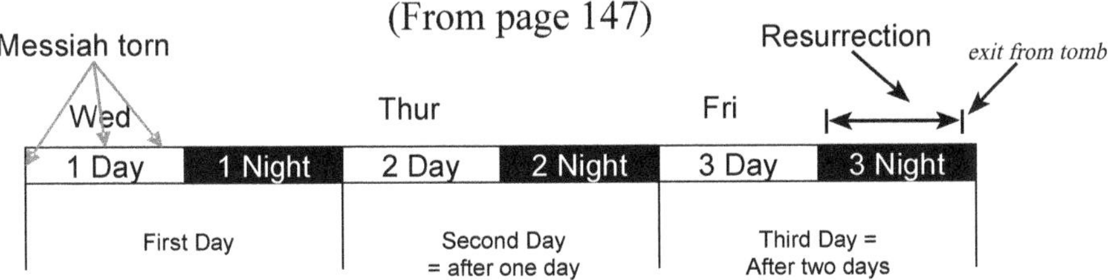

It is for this reason that the resurrection cannot be Sabbath afternoon (say 3 p.m.) or at sunset ending the Sabbath (about 6 p.m.) or a few minutes after the end of the Sabbath. The resurrection must be near dawn on the Sabbath to satisfy the constraint that it is on the third calendar day.

> And he said to them, "Thus it is written, that the Mĕssiah should suffer and rise again from the dead the third day [τῇ τρίτῃ ἡμέρᾳ] (Luke 24:46).

> And they will deliver him to the peoples to mock ... and scourge and crucify *him*, and the third day he will rise [τῇ τρίτῃ ἡμέρᾳ] (Mat. 20:19).

> And scourging, they will kill him; and the third day he will rise [τῇ ἡμέρᾳ τῇ τρίτῃ] (Luke 18:33).

---

[193] "after two days" = LXX: *μετὰ δύο ἡμέρας*. Compare Mark 8:31, 9:31, 10:34, "after three days" (*μετὰ τρεῖς ἡμέρας*). The discrepancy is only apparent, and is solved by realizing that the Hosea passage defines a day from daybreak to daybreak while the Mark passages reckon the end of a day at sunset. Thus from the Hosea passage the third day (= after two days) is Friday sunrise to Sabbath sunrise, but from the Mark passage "after three days" is from sunset Friday to sunset on the Sabbath. The Hosea and Mark reckonings only intersect (or agree) during Friday dusk to Sabbath dawn.

Now in the Luke 24:46 passage, Yeshua himself is speaking, and he says that the "third day" is what is written in the Scriptures. This is confirmed by Paul:

> And that he was buried, and that he was raised on the third day according to the Scriptures [τῇ ἡμέρᾳ τῇ τρίτῃ κατὰ τὰς γραφὰς] (1 Cor. 15:4).

When Yeshua and Paul referenced what "is written" and "the Scriptures" respectively, they did not mean the New Testament. They meant the Torah and the Prophets. I have already shown Hosea 6:2. Here are the other Scriptures:

> On the third day Abraham raised his eyes and saw the place from a distance; [בַּיּוֹם הַשְּׁלִישִׁי], (Gen. 22:4), [LXX: τῇ ἡμέρᾳ τῇ τρίτῃ].

The binding of Isaac is a picture of Messiah's death and resurrection. In the symbolism, the sacrifice is slain on the third day, and the Son of Abraham is received back on the third day—pre-figuring the resurrection. What might be confusing to some is the idea that the sacrifice is slain on the third day. The following two passages explain how this happened:

> You know that after two days the Passover is coming, and the Sõn of Man is *to be* delivered up for crucifixion (Mat. 26:2).

> Now the Passover and Unleavened Bread was after two days; and the chief priests and the scribes were seeking how to seize him by stealth, and kill *him* (Mark 14:1).

I have explained that "after two days" equals "the third day." So we see that the Passover sacrifice was scheduled "after two days," which is to say "on the third day," and this sacrifice was Yeshua who died at the very same time the passover lambs were being offered. The very reason Yeshua said "after two days" was to remind us of the Scriptural connections.

So then at the binding of Isaac, the sacrifice was made on the third day, and the father received his son back on the third day.

Then Joseph said to him, "This is the interpretation of it: the three branches are three days; within three days [בְּעוֹד שְׁלֹשֶׁת יָמִים] Pharaoh will lift up your head and restore you to your office; and you will put Pharaoh's cup into his hand according to your former custom when you were his cup-bearer (Gen 40:12-13).

Then Joseph answered and said, "This is its interpretation: the three baskets are three days; within three days [בְּעוֹד שְׁלֹשֶׁת יָמִים] Pharaoh will lift up your head from you and will hang you on a tree; and the birds will eat your flesh off you.

Thus it came about on the third day, [בַּיּוֹם הַשְּׁלִישִׁי] which was Pharaoh's birthday, that he made a feast for all his servants; and he lifted up the head of the chief cup-bearer and the head of the chief baker among his servants. And he restored the chief cup-bearer to his office, and he put the cup into Pharaoh's hand; but he hanged the chief baker, just as Joseph had interpreted to them (Gen. 40:18-22).

Figure 47: Day Reckonings Synchronized

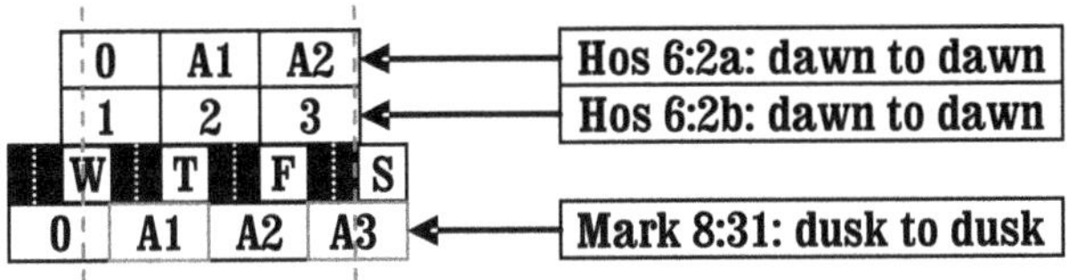

This passage is also a Messianic Prophecy for those with eyes to see and ears to hear. The baker's sentence illustrates the crucifixion of Yeshua on the third day. The cup-bearer's reprieve and restoration illustrates Yeshua's resurrection "on the third day." It should be noted that the Hebrew word *bə'od* בְּעוֹד specifically means *within*, or *while still* three days. The three days are given in the second row of the figure, counting inclusively from red line to red line. The top row is according to Hos. 6:2a, "after two days." The bottom row is according to Mark 8:31, counting "after three days" exclusively. Notice the first two rows assume a day defined from daybreak to daybreak, and the bottom row from setting to setting. The top rows are according to the day for Temple offerings, and the bottom row according to Sabbaths.

End Note: Calendar Days and Literal Days

The reader should keep in mind the difference between calendar days and literal days. A calendar day is a cycle of *time* that comes back to its starting point, that is dawn to dawn, or dusk to dusk. In astronomy a Julian date is from noon to noon. The origin of these kinds of days lies in the Hebrew definition of 'day' as a *time period.*

A literal day is from dawn to dusk, from when the light appears to when the light disappears. The term 'night' does not have this time period definition. A night always refers to literal darkness except when it is being used figuratively, e.g. "those who dwell in the blackest night of deception." When the term 'night' is put alongside 'day,' the indication is that both the day and the night are to be understood literally, and not as a calendar 'day.'

In Genesis 1:3-5, a literal day and a calendar day are both in view. The summary at the end, 'One Day,' is a calendar day from dawn to dawn. When speaking of the "third day" a calendar day is in view, being from dawn on Friday to dawn on the Sabbath. When speaking of "after three days," it is not calendar days in view, but the end of literal days. Therefore "after three days" brings us to the night after the third literal day. But this third night is contained within the third calendar day.

Matthew 12:40 refers to literal days and nights because night is brought alongside the day. The end of Genesis 1:5, "one day," speaks of a calendar day because the night, "then there is setting; then there is daybreak" is included in the "one day." Even those who get this in the wrong order consider it a calendar day! If the night is included in the 'day,' then it is a calendar day. If it is not, then it is a literal day.

Sabbath Days and other special Sabbath Days are also calendar days beginning with the night and ending with the end of day.

The Sign of David and Jonah

Many have heard of the sign of Jonah, but few have heard of the sign of David:

> Then it happened when David and his men came to Ziklag on the third day [בַּיּוֹם הַשְּׁלִישִׁי], that the Amalekites had made a raid on the Negev and on Ziklag, and had overthrown Ziklag and burned it with fire; and they took captive the women and all who were in it, both small and great, without killing anyone, and carried them off and went their way. And when David and his men came to the city, behold, it was burned with fire, and their wives and their sons and their daughters had been taken captive. Then David and the people who were with him lifted their voices and wept until there was no strength in them to weep. Now David's two wives had been taken captive, Ahinoam the Jezreelitess and Abigail the widow of Nabal the Carmelite. Moreover David was greatly distressed because the people [הָעָם] spoke of stoning him, for all the people [כָּל־הָעָם] were embittered, each one because of his sons and his daughters. But David strengthened himself in Yãhweh his Almĩghty (1 Sam. 30:1-6).

David is a symbol of Messiah. "On the third day" David suffers great loss (1 Sam. 30:1). The Scripture does not say "on the third day" here as just some kind of trivia. It says it in reference to Yeshua as well as David. Remember that the crucifixion was "after two days" (Mat. 26:2; Mar. 14:1), and that "after two days" amount to saying the same thing as "on the third day" when counting inclusively. Recall that Abraham saw the place "on the third day." Yeshua saw the same place "on the third day."

Now in a capital case involving blasphemy, all the congregation [כָּל־הָעֵדָה] would be obligated to stone the offender (cf. Lev. 24:16). Likewise a Sabbath breaker was to be stoned (cf. Num. 15:35). The Son of David was accused of both. His final sentence was based on the allegation of blasphemy. For this he had to be stoned. So as the people thought to stone David (1 Sam. 30:6 above), they really did stone Yeshua.

Also it says, "Then David and the people who were with him lifted their voices and wept until there was no strength in them to weep" (1 Sam. 30:4). But Yeshua strengthened himself in Yãhweh his Almĩghty (1 Sam. 30:6), and said, "Daughters of Jerusalem, stop weeping for me, but weep for yourselves and for your children." Then, "all the people [כָּל־הָעָם] were embittered, each one because of his sons and his daughters" (1 Sam. 30:6). For thus says Yahweh:

> And I will have poured out upon the house of Dauid and upon those dwelling in Yerushalaim a spirit of favor and supplication. And they will have looked unto Me whom they have pierced. And they will have mourned over Him as a mourner over an only child and grieve over Him as a griever over the firstborn. In that day will be great the mourning in Yerushalaim, like the mourning of Ḫadad Rimmon in the valley of Megiddon. And they will have mourned the land families by families alone, the families of the house of Dauid alone, and their women alone, the families of the house of Nathan alone, and their women alone, the families of the house of Leui alone, and their women alone, the families of the Shimeites, and their women alone, all the remaining families, families by families alone, and their women alone (Zech. 12:10- 12).

The family of David weeps because they sought to stone the Son of David. The piercing was not just by the Romans (gentiles). The people threw sharp stones at Yeshua and pierced him that way also. Paul said, "for I bear on my body the brand-marks of Yeshua " (Gal. 6:17). This is because Paul was stoned (cf. Acts 14:19), and it left a scar on him. "His appearance was marred more than any man, and his form more than the sons of men" (Isa. 52:14; cf. Ps. 22:16-17). They had tried before to stone Yeshua (cf. John 8:59; 10:31-33; 11:8). Pilate said, "judge him according to your law" (John 18:31).

> On the eve of the Passover Yeshu[a] the Nazarean was hanged…"He is going forth to be stoned " (Sanhedrin 43a).

This shows that Jewish expectation was that Yeshua would be stoned.[194] Continuing the passage:

> Then David said to Abiathar the priest, the son of Ahimelech, "Please bring me the ephod." So Abiathar brought

---

[194] Ernest L. Martin explains more details in his book *Secrets of Golgotha*.

the ephod to David. And David inquired of Yãhweh, saying, "Shall I pursue this band? Shall I overtake them?" And he said to him, "Pursue, for you shall surely overtake them, and you shall surely rescue all." (1 Sam. 30:7-8).

So also, Yeshua will rescue all who are holding faithful to Him. By his blood is the ransom from our enslavement to sin. Thus, when the Son of David gave up His Spirit on that day he said, "It is finished."

So David went, he and the six hundred men who were with him, and came to the brook Besor [נַחַל הַבְּשׂוֹר], where those left behind remained. But David pursued, he and four hundred men, for two hundred who were too exhausted to cross the brook Besor, remained behind. (1Sam. 30:9-10).

The words "brook Besor" signify *wadi-torrent of the good news*, the word בְּשׂוֹר being derived from בְּשׂרָה. Two hundred had to stop at the good news, for they were too weak to fight the big battles of the kingdom. When David returned to collect those who had to stay behind, some wicked an unmerciful men complained that they should not receive the blessings of victory (1Sam. 30:21-31.) So also we must be careful in our knowledge of the kingdom and success in the war of Yahweh that we do not slight those who are too weak to fight because they are weakened.[195] For there are many in their new found knowledge of Messiah who forget where they came from, and who forget who gives them success who play the part of the unforgiving servant.

Now they found an Egyptian in the field and brought him to David, and gave him bread and he ate, and they provided him water to drink. And they gave him a piece of fig cake and two clusters of raisins, and he ate; then his spirit returned [וַתָּשָׁב רוּחוֹ]. For he had not eaten bread or drunk water for three days [שְׁלֹשָׁה יָמִים] and three nights [וּשְׁלֹשָׁה לֵילוֹת]. And David said to him, "To whom do you belong? And where are you from?" And he said, "I am a young man of Egypt, a

[195] The brook may also be explained eschatologically. Those left behind represent the privations of the exile of Israel in the 2000 years between Yeshua's first coming and the restoration of the kingdom to Israel.

> servant of an Amalekite; and my master left me behind when I fell sick [חָלִיתִי] today *is* the third *day* [הַיּוֹם שְׁלֹשָׁה]. "We made a raid on the Negev of the Cherethites, and on that which belongs to Judah, and on the Negev of Caleb, and we burned Ziklag with fire." Then David said to him, "Will you bring me down to this band?" And he said, "Swear to me by the Almĩghty that you will not kill me or deliver me into the hands of my master, and I will bring you down to this band. (1Sam. 30:11-15)

This Egyptian is like unto Joseph. He is a type of Messiah. He falls sick [חָלִיתִי]. The same word is used in Isa. 53:10: הֶחֱלִי,* "to grief." So Messiah was put to grief. In vs. 13, he says "Today is the third day," (הַיּוֹם שְׁלֹשָׁה) or "the third day." The text says that "his spirit returned." Here we have a prophetic hint toward Yeshua's resurrection. Then His Spirit returned: וַתָּשָׁב רוּחוֹ.

Like Joseph the Egyptian, so too here we have Messiah in the guise of an Egyptian. How do they count days in Egypt? They count them from daybreak to daybreak. So then here is the reckoning of "three days and three nights."

Figure 48: The Sign of David

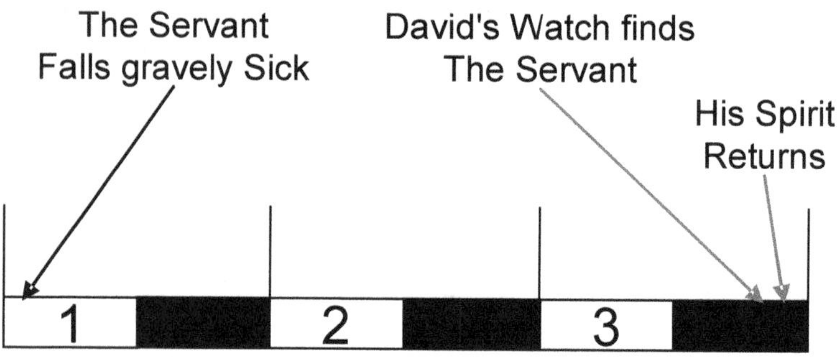

The Servant
Falls gravely Sick
David's Watch finds
The Servant
His Spirit
Returns
1
2
3

The servant is in dire need and cries out, so that David's watch find him in the dark. For they have marched all that day and as late into the dusk as their tracking abilities allowed. They have camped and fallen silent listening. Then they hear the fallen man, and raise him up. What happens next?

> And when he had brought him down, behold, they were

* More accurately, "And Yahweh will have been pleased to make him to be bruised. He will have made [him] suffer when his soul makes a guilt offering" (Isa. 53:10). And "Because I had been suffering illness, today is the third" (1 Sam. 30:13).

> spread over all the land, eating and drinking and dancing because of all the great spoil that they had taken from the land of the Philistines and from the land of Judah. And David slaughtered them [וַיַּכֵּם] from the morning twilight [מֵהַנֶּשֶׁף] even until the setting [הָעֶרֶב] for *the* day after of them [לְמָחֳרָתָם]; and not a man of them escaped, except four hundred young men [אִישׁ נַעַר] who rode on camels and fled. So David recovered all that the Amalekites had taken, and rescued his two wives. But nothing of theirs was missing, whether small or great, sons or daughters, spoil or anything that they had taken for themselves; David brought it all back. So David had captured all the sheep and the cattle which the people drove ahead of the other livestock, and they said, "This is David's spoil." (1Sam. 30:16-20,).

David and the 400 attacked at first light of dawn. Only the young men who were not drunk or stuffed full escaped. There must have been thousands of enemy troops. For they had ravaged the land. They did not know that they had lost until the very end. For the battle raged on for more than twelve hours. But they were too weak to best the skill of David and his men whose battle rage was unquenchable.

When they battled Amalek, Moses held his hands up "until the sun set" [עַד־בֹּא הַשָּׁמֶשׁ].

> And Moses built an altar, and named it Yãhweh is my Banner; and he said, "because an arm was raised over the throne of Yãh, it shall be the war of Yãhweh with Amalek from generation to generation. (Exodus 17:15-16).

Now, there is a curious phrase in the passage, "Then David slaughtered them [וַיַּכֵּם] from the morning† twilight [מֵהַנֶּשֶׁף] even until the setting [הָעֶרֶב] for *the* day after of them [לְמָחֳרָתָם];" or "until their next day." This confirms that the "three days and three nights" are from daybreak to daybreak,‡ according to the Egyptian reckoning, which David and his men shared, but the Amalekites reckoned their day from sunset.[196] The text could have merely said,

---

[196] See Nina L. Collins, "The Start of the Pre-Exilic Calendar Day of David and the Amalekites: A Note on 1 Samuel xxx 17', *Vetus Testamentum* 41 ⟶

† As only it can be coming before the setting of the day. Cf. LXX.

‡Also, "I [the] third, the arrow off to the side will shoot as sending for myself toward a mark" (1 Sam. 20:20). The new moon days were reckoned till daybreak. Cf. 1 Sam. 20:35.

"until night." It doesn't. It says "until the setting [הָעֶרֶב] for *the* day after of them" [לְמָחֳרָתָם]. The letter marked in grey is the Hebrew suffix meaning "them." So it looks like this:*

Figure 49: The War of YHWH with Amalek

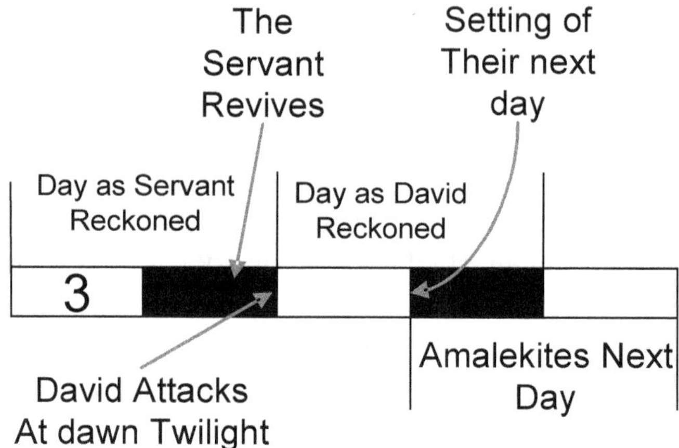

This makes precise sense of the Hebrew text. Why would it be pointed out that the servant was an Egyptian? Why would the suffix by added to show that it was the Amalekites next day when the battle ended? These details, which would normally be incidental to the story, are added to teach us the structure of Yeshua's prophetic fulfillment of the passage.

So as the servant was "three days and three nights" in sickness, so the Servant of YHWH spent "three days and three nights" from suffering till the return of His Spirit. Then the Servant of YHWH leads the way to complete the war of YHWH upon Amalek.

THE SIGN ACCORDING TO JONAH

There is more to notice in the story of Jonah than just the "three days and three nights." "So they cast lots and the lot fell on Jonah" (Jon. 1:7). "And for my clothing they cast lots" (Psa. 22:18; cf. Mat. 27:35; Mark 15:24; Luke 23:34; John 19:24). "What is your country? From what people are you?" (Jon. 1:8) "I am a Hebrew." "You are My Servant, Israel, in whom I will be glorified" (Isa. 49:3; cf. John 12:23). "For you, Yãhweh, have done as you have pleased" (Jon.

(1991), 203-10. Collins comes to the same conclusion.

* There is no doubt that the pronoun refers to Amalek, because the same pronoun is used in "Then David struck them" just before "until...their next day."

1:14). "But Yãhweh was pleased to crush him" (Isa. 53:10). "And they offered a sacrifice to Yãhweh" (Jon. 1:16.) "He will have made [him] suffer when his soul makes a guilt offering; he will see [his] seed; he will make long [his] days. And Yãhweh will have been pleased. By his hand he will advance" (Isa. 53:10).*

> "Yãhweh appointed a great fish to swallow Jonah, and Jonah was in the belly [בִּמְעֵי, κοιλίᾳ] of the fish three days and three nights." "Then Jonah prayed to Yãhweh his Almĩghty from the belly [מִמְּעֵי, κοιλίας] of the fish, and he said, "I called out of my distress to Yãhweh, and he answered me. I cried for help from the belly [מִבֶּטֶן, κοιλίας] of the grave [שְׁאוֹל]; you did hear my voice" (Jon. 1:17-2:3).

Notice that the Hebrew word on the last use of "belly" changes to מִבֶּטֶן. From this we are not to regard the whole of the *sheol* experience as inside the fish. There is, so to speak, an outer *sheol* here and an inner *sheol*. The seas represent the outer sheol, which is the threat of death, and suffering, and so is not to be strictly equated to inside the fish. Hence the different Hebrew word. The belly of the whale represents the inner *sheol* which is death itself. So Jonah was in the inner *sheol* "three days and three nights," in which part of the first day is counted as a day. On the other hand, he is in the outer sheol for the other part of the first day. I assume that they threw him in at dawn because that is when the storm broke, and meets the types. So if the time in the outer sheol is added to that in the inner sheol, then the time is a full seventy-two hours.

So, the belly of *sheol* is to be regarded as adding Yeshua's suffering to his actual death. The Psalmist writes:

> "The cords of Sheol surrounded me; The snares of death confronted me" (Psa. 18:5). And, "Yãhweh, you have brought up my soul from Sheol; you have kept me alive, that I should not go down to the pit" (Psa. 30:3).

It is plain that one can be surrounded by "Sheol" by being under the mere threat of death. For if one is surrounded by something, then one is in it. In English the idiom "Hell on earth" describes this. So this can be regarded as "in the belly of Sheol." That a distinction is made between outer and inner Sheol is made plain in this text, "For great is thy mercy toward me: and thou deliverest my soul from the

---

* I have taken the second use of חפץ to be a perfect verb. The Stone Edition Tanach commits folly here, "if his soul would acknowledge guilt." So does CJB.

lowest hell [מִשְׁאוֹל תַּחְתִּיָּה]" (Psa. 86:13; cf. Deu. 32:22). For other uses of Sheol that indicate a state near to death but less than death see Prov. 7:27, 9:18 [בְּעִמְקֵי שְׁאוֹל]; Is. 38:10; Amos 9:2; Job 17:13; 2Sam. 22:6. "So they and all that belonged to them went down alive into Sheol [חַיִּים שְׁאֹלָה], and the earth closed up over them" (Num. 16:33). So we see that briefly they were alive in Sheol before it finally killed them.

We have the English idiom, "One foot in the grave" and further to consider, is that in the middle east graves were typically caves into which one could enter. So it is literally possible to enter into a grave [שְׁאֹלָה], and then to come out alive again, and clearly being under the threat of death can be considered "in Sheol." "War is hell" they say in English.

These considerations allow us to complete the "three days and three nights" to seventy-two hours:

Figure 50: A Seventy-Two Hour Interpretation

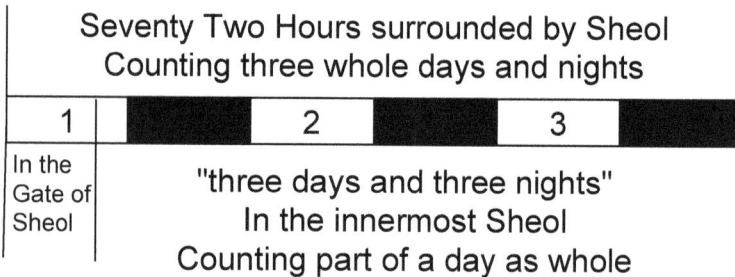

Seventy Two Hours surrounded by Sheol Counting three whole days and nights							
1			2		3		
In the Gate of Sheol	"three days and three nights" In the innermost Sheol Counting part of a day as whole						

Yeshua began to suffer at dawn and he was raised from the dead at dawn.* Now we must examine the meaning of Yeshua's phrase "heart of the earth" (ἐν τῇ καρδίᾳ τῆς γῆς), translated into Greek for us by Matthew. This actual phrase does not occur all together in Jonah. The key words "heart" and "earth" occur separately.

Yeshua is combining two elements from Jonah, "heart of the seas" [בִּלְבַב יַמִּים] (Jonah 2:3), and "The earth with its bars shut behind me to time immemorial" [הָאָרֶץ בְּרִחֶיהָ בַעֲדִי לְעוֹלָם] (Jon. 2:6). The "earth" part of the phrase obviously corresponds to the actual grave, which is the inner sheol. The "heart" part corresponds to the "seas" of suffering. The earth part corresponds to death:

For you hadst cast me into the deep, into the heart of the

*According to the Scripture he exited the grave at deep dawn (cf. Hos. 6:3). The resurrection was before his exit. A 72 hour interpretation is not required, but if it is assumed then the resurrection would have to be at the very end of night, or being alive but still in the tomb would have to count in the 72 hours. Strictly speaking, the resurrection was possibly earlier in the night.

seas, and the river surrounded me. All your breakers and waves crossed over me. So I said, 'I have been driven out from in front of your eyes. But I will look again toward your holy temple.' Water encompassed me as far as the soul of the deep. Kelp was surrounding being bound to my head. I descended to the cuts of the mountains. The earth with its bars shut behind me to time immemorial, but you caused my life to ascend from the pit, Yãhweh my Almĩghty. Jonah 2:3-6

The river of suffering and the sea of tribulation surrounded Yeshua. So he was the "heart of the seas." He was beaten by the waves and his back crossed over with a whip. He was driven outside the camp, but he looked toward the Temple in hope. Notice that "kelp was ... bound to my head." So Yeshua was wrapped in linen. He descended into the mountain, into the grave. The stone barred the way out to time immemorial they thought, but YHWH made Yeshua's life to return and ascend from the pit. We may think of "heart of the earth" in two ways. One way is to describe being inside the grave. And the other way is to describe his suffering "in the heart of the land." For Jerusalem is the heart of the land of Israel. The Hebrew word "הָאָרֶץ" means both "land" and "earth." So the phrase "heart of the earth" sums up the whole experience of death and suffering.

In conclusion, then, the sign of David and the sign of Jonah account for all the Scriptural uses of "three days and three nights," in the order of "day" and then "night." The servant of Yahweh is raised at the end of the third night, the third calendar day. It was also shown how seventy-two hours fit into the picture.

(continued from page 188)
incorrect? Further, the archaeologist can in no way prove that it is impossible for the evidence to fit into a model that agrees with the Scripture also. Rather, he is busy trying to construct contrived models based on opinion and assumption that are dogmatically designed to exclude Scripture. This is because secular archaeology is at war with God, and their contrived models are part of the propaganda.

Meanwhile, so called biblical scholars are trying to deceive Christians into thinking their Bible can be made to agree with the secular world view. The watershed article on this was authored by Colin J. Humphreys: THE NUMBER OF PEOPLE IN THE EXODUS FROM EGYPT: DECODING MATHEMATICALLY THE VERY LARGE NUMBERS IN NUMBERS I AND XXVI (Vetus Testamentum, vol. 48, no. 2, 1998, pp. 196–213.) In a footnote on the first page he thanks K.A. Kitchen for detailed comments on his paper. Kenneth Kitchen is supposed to be a respected Evangelical Egyptologist.

Humphreys begins by assuming the 22,273 firstborn in Numbers 3:43 were all the firstborn of Israel. From this he reasons the number is too small for a population of several million. Therefore, the other numbers must be "decoded" into much lesser figures. But he never understood the text. The text is counting all the new firstborn Israelites from a month old and upward who were born from the day of the Exodus until the time of the census a year later. In Exodus 13:2 Yahweh claims that every "opener of the womb" belonged to him. Later he decides to allow his claim on these new firstborn to be transferred to the tribe of Levi, which numbered 22,300. 300 of the Levites, however, were themselves new firstborn, and so would have to redeem themselves by serving. As such they could not be counted in place of the other new first born of Israel. This means there were only 22,000 Levites that could compensate for Yahweh's loss of future service from 22,273 Israelite firstborn. The imbalance was 273, and these were required to pay a monetary compensation to be released from service.

If we double 22,300 for the males of Levi, then we get a total figure for the tribe of 44,600. At a 5.2% annual increase, the population will grow by 2319 in one year, or by half that number in males: 1160. Since 300 of these are new first born, they make up 1/4 of the population of males. The number of males in the average completed family is therefore 4 and the total average family size with 4 girls is 8 children plus 2 parents.

The ratio of Levite newly firstborn in the last year to the total non firstborn and older firstborn is 300 to 22,000, or 1 to 73. The number of Israelite new firstborn was 22,273. For a total population of non-firstborn and exempt firstborn, scale this up by x 73: 1,625,929. Add back again the new firstborn: 1,648,202. For a total population double the number: 3.3 million. In such a population about 18.5% of the population is male between 20 and 50, of military age: 609,834. And this last figure is close to the census figure, which was: 603,550. So we see that by using demographic figures for a fast growing nation, and taking 22,273 to be all the new firstborn born in just one year we can come real close to the census total for the men of war.

Humphreys assumes that the 22,273 count all the elder firstborn who were born before the Exodus and then he proceeds to show that contradictions result from this figure if the 603,550 man figure for the men of war is taken seriously. Humphreys then gives a list of proposed solutions according to different theories. The solution just mentioned above is not on his list, i.e. that the 22,273 counts all the *new* firstborn since the Exodus. After failing to mention the actual solution, Humphreys presents his own solution as if it were now reasonable. He takes the Hebrew word for 1000 to mean 'a troop.'

Thus 603,550 men is 603 troops, 550 men, but since these figures do not work, Humphreys changes them to "598 *'lp* (troops) and 5 *'lp* (thousands) and 550 men, and the original readers understood that there were 598 troops containing 5550 men. At a later date, the original meaning was lost, a scribe conflated the numbers and ran together the two *'lp* figures (598+5), to yield 603 thousand" (page 207). So we see that Humphreys must resort to saying the actual text is in error.

Humphreys concludes the total population at the Exodus was about 20,000. But if the population of lower Egypt as assumed by archaeologists was about 2 million, then Israel would have been only 1% of the population (and a tiny fraction of the total slave population), and hardly the threat described in Exodus. Pharaoh would have let such a small part of his slaves go long before Egypt was ruined by the final plagues.

Humphreys' clever theory requires him to assume that the average family contained 11 boys (page 212). If we add girls, then the family size becomes 22 children and 2 parents. This average family size is much larger than the geneological lists suggest. Further, Humphreys' theory results in the definition of a troop size being {11, 5, 14, 8, 7, 7, 12, 6, 11, 11, 12, 8} for each of the tribes, but he has to use the numbers {71, 38, 33} for the 'troop' sizes of the three clans of Levi, where he defines *'lp* (אֶלֶף) as 'teams,' page 213, and he averages these to 48. At the second census, Humphreys' troop sizes change yet again to {16, 9 , 12, 7, 5, 8, 15, 13, 13, 6, 8, 9}. If one looks closely at Humphreys' data one will see that even within a tribe the troop size has to vary, e.g. Reuben, 46 troops (500 men), size 11: but 500/11 = 45.45.

According to Exodus 38:25-26, "And silver of those being accounted of the congregation: one hundred talents, and a thousand and seven hundred and five and seventy shekels, by the shekel of the holy place, a beqa for each head, half of a shekel, by the shekel of the holy place, for for all who were being passed over by the accountants from a son of twenty years and above, for six hundred thousand and three thousand and five hundred and fifty." An Israelite talent is **3000** shekels. But to make Humphreys' 5,550 number work out, a talent should equal **10** shekels (5550 = (100 × **10** + 1775) × 2). But in Exodus 38:27 we find a talent used in each of 100 "sockets" used as weighted bases for the Tabernacle. Since a shekel was 11.33 grams, these bases according to Humphreys' numbers used only 113.3 grams of silver or about 3.9 ounces. But the true weight was about 75 pounds. The numbers are even greater if a Babylonian talent is used (1 Talent = 3600 Shekels).

"And Bil'am lifted up his eyes. Then he sees Yisra'el camping by its tribes.... 'How lovely are your tents Ya'aqov, your dwellings Yisra'el. Like streams they have stretched out, like gardens by the river, like aloes Yăhweh has planted, like cedars by the waters" (Num. 24:2, 5-6).

*Other figures make no sense if אֶלֶף means a "unit" instead of **1000** (Bryant Wood's translation), which Humphreys averages to be 9.3 men per unit for the first census and 9.6 men for the second census. Did Israel only send 12 units (12 × 9.6 = 115 men) to fight Midian or "**12,000** out of the thousands of Yisra'el" (Num. 31:5)? If 115 men does not make sense, then **12,000** exceeds Humphreys 5,550 man figure for the whole army of Israel! Do they acknowledge that 3,000 were killed at Sinai (Exo. 32:28), or 14,700 besides 250 leaders in Korah's rebellion (Num. 16:2, 49)? Or that 24,000 died in a plague (Num. 25:9; 1 Cor. 10:8, χιλιάδες)?

I could go on to examine the use of אֶלֶף in other places to show that the alledged sense of "a unit" on the order of 10 men is ridiculous. Based on the Scripture numbers, ancient populations must have been multiples greater than secular archaeologists assume. The population density of ancient Rome (13.7 km²/1 million) was 294 persons per acre. A similar estimate for Ebla brings us to 43,000 people in 60 hectares (60 × 2.47 × 294). If we use these densities (based on written documents) for Hazor, then the 80 hectare site would have had a population of 58,000 (80 × 2.47 × 294) rather than the 20,000 usually supposed. If MB II Israel had 552 hectares† of administrative (walled cities) then 552 × 2.47 × 294 = 402,000. But how many dwelled outside walled cities in tents and wood structures or huts? Perhaps 97% of the population contrary to the assumption that most of the population was urbanzied. The western British Mandate was 26 thousand km² (6.4 million acres). A population of 12 million would be 1.8 persons/acre ruled over by the 3% in the cities, less than the density of Holland. But Broshi and Gophna assumed, "It seems quite safe to assume that it [the nomadic population] was not large."‡

---

* See *Patterns of Evidence*, Mahoney, pg. 321. The content previous to this paragraph was researched and written before I read Mahoney's "Bonus Chapter C." I was stunned by the similarities afterward. What now follows is my summary of the additional arguments that Mahoney makes. †BASOR No. 261, p. 86. ‡p. 74.

The Year and Day of Messiah's Birth[197a]

The Friday crucifixion and Sunday resurrection traditions require AD 30 or 33 to work out. But we can eliminate AD 30 by correctly placing the birth of Messiah in 2 BC, and then taking account of Yeshua's age leading up to those years, according to Luke 3:23, when he was "nearly thirty years" (GNM).

Figure 51: Messiah's Age in AD 29/30

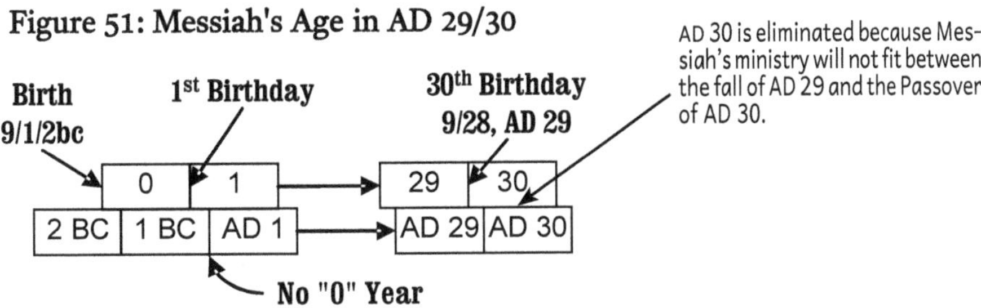

Messiah was born on Tishri 1, 2 B.C.* Therefore, his first year is counted by months, and his first birthday only after the year is complete. In the second year, we say that Yeshua is one whole year of "age," which really means at least one year old plus a fraction of the second year. (This is the way "age" is always counted in the Scripture, and never from conception. This can be proved using pre-deluge chronology, and noting that this assumption is required to prevent Methuselah from dying several years after the flood.) As a result, Yeshua's 30th birthday would be on September 28th A.D. 29.[197b] Leading up to that date, perhaps a month before, Yeshua is "about thirty," or as we might say "twenty-nine going on thirty."

If we back up a bit, we will discover that in Luke 3:1, just before Luke reports that Yeshua was "nearly thirty," that it was the 15th year of Tiberius Caesar. In the next chapter, it will be shown that the 15th year of Tiberius was August 19, A.D. 28 to August 18, A.D. 29.† The following figure shows how this relates to the beginning of John the Baptist's ministry:

In Editions 1-2.

[197a] This chapter originally included a theory of priestly divisions that proved later to be incorrect. This revised edition corrects the error. The opening of Solomon's Temple, the precept that priests serve equally, and DSS 4Q320-321 show that the divisions rotated continuously in unbroken cycles, and not annually as previously supposed. This discovery greatly improved the argument for Messiah's birth date, which remains unchanged. My new research reveals the conception dates of both Yoḥannan the Immerser (John the Baptist) and Yeshua, as well as the very likely date of Yoḥannan's birth.

[197b] Parker and Dubberstein. But Elul that year was 29 days, so there is a possibility that Tishri 1 was on Sept. 29th. *Sept, 1 (7th month, day 1)

†However, the official date he was voted to take the title Princeps by the Senate was Sept. 18, AD 14, so the previous month he was legally ruling in an unofficial capacity.

Figure 52: Almost 30 Years Old

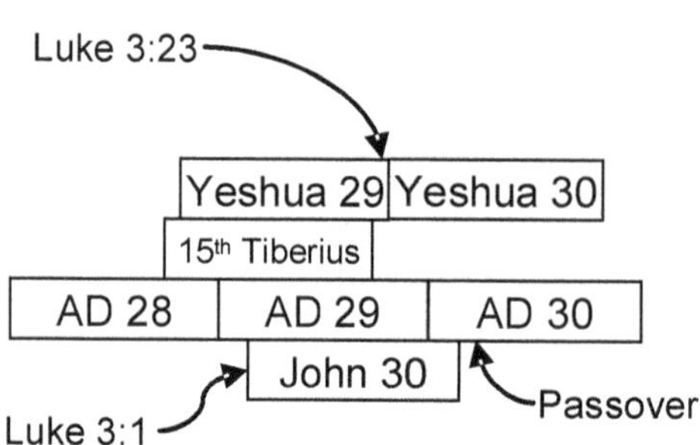

Yoḥanan turned 30 himself after Passover of AD 29 and was installed as a priest. After this he began his ministry. This all took place in the 15th year of Tiberius. Before the end of this regnal year of Tiberius, counting from when the Senate conferred upon Tiberius the title of Princeps, Messiah was immersed in the Jordan River, being almost 30. He then turned 30 on Tishri 1 that year. The first Passover of his ministry in John 2 followed the next spring in AD 30.

According to Luke 3:23, "And, Yeshua was nearly thirty years old when beginning, as it was getting customary to be" (GNM). We see that Luke qualifies his statement, "nearly thirty years" (ὡσεὶ ἐτῶν τριάκοντα). The most parsimonious explanation is that Luke actually knows when Yeshua's birthday is, and how old he will be, and that by "about" (ESV) he means almost thirty, or as we say, "twenty-nine going on thirty." Luke is not some historian writing centuries after the fact and trying to guesstimate Yeshua's age. He was close to events and researched and investigated the matters from living witnesses, so it would be unparsimonious to construct a chronology that assumes Luke's ignorance (cf. Luke 3:1-4).[198]

In Luke 3:1, John begins his ministry in the 15th year of Tiberius (which is a fixed year in Roman history), when as a qualified priest he could enter the ministry at the age of thirty (Num. 4:3). This confirms that John turned 30, and not 31 in the 15th year of Tiberius, and fixes the year of his birth as early spring 2 B.C., and that of Yeshua in the fall of 2 B.C. The word of Yahweh came to John in the wilderness (cf. Luke 3:2), and so it was the Almighty that picked the time to start his ministry, according to the legal time for his service as a priest to go before Yahweh's Anointed. The course of Abijah would have been on duty in A.D. 29 for

[198] Many suppose that Luke is using round numbers, wherein "about thirty" means 30±5 years. But since Luke knew how old Messiah was and when his birthday was, we would have to accuse Luke of deliberately obscuring the matter by speaking such. Furthermore, a figure such as 30±5 years assumes a modern concept of one significant digit. The ancient concept of rounding here with "about" is no greater than 30±½ year. And further "ωσει" is typically used for "almost" and not thirty and then some. For in that case Luke could have just said "thirty." Also, there would be no point in supposing that he was a little over 30 on Tishri 1 AD 28 (Sept 9), since this date would require all the events in Luke 3:1-18 to be cramped into a time period after Messiah turned 30, and also prevent Messiah from fasting after his immersion during the traditional period 40 days of repentance starting in the 6th month.

the fifth week of Nisan (April 30-May 7) [Nisan 26 to Ziv 4], and this is when John could have received his anointing at thirty years of age.†

On Nisan 29 (Tue., May 3), assuming he was born 266 days after conception, was his 30th birthday. See chart on last page of this book. Then he could go through his ordination.

It would be toward the end of the 15th year of Tiberius, or perhaps sometime in the days from August 19th to September 27 that Luke was referring to when he said Yeshua was "about thirty." [The most likely date is Av 30 (Aug 29, AD 29), since this would be a customary time to begin a 40 day fast.] This time period was in late summer of A.D. 29, just before his thirtieth birthday on Tishri 1. It also means that the first Passover of Yeshua's own ministry was that of A.D. 30, and completely rules it out as the year of the crucifixion. Also ruled out is A.D. 31 since John mentions at least three Passovers, and A.D. 32 is also ruled out by the lack of suitable dates for Nisan 14.

†He was a full 30 solar years old by Nisan 1, AD 29.

Now, if an attempt is made to shift Messiah's thirtieth birthday to Tishri 1, A.D. 28, then this implies that John began his ministry outside of Tiberius' fifteenth year (i.e. before Sept 18 A.D. 28). The only way to overcome this is to move the start of John's ministry to within a few months before Messiah's ministry started. But doing this would not explain how John gained such a large following at first, and why Yeshua only caught up to him in numbers of disciples a year later (John 4:1). So, John the Immerser began his ministry in the spring of A.D. 29. Yeshua was immersed close to, but not after Tishri 1, A.D. 29, and the Passover of John 2:13 was A.D. 30, which is when Yeshua's ministry really got going, almost a year after John's.

Some translations, and a few Greek texts, try to make Luke 3:23 say, "beginning to be about thirty," and so imply that the passage refers to a time after Yeshua's thirtieth birthday (but not too far past it). The King James says, "began to be about thirty years of age," but the New American Standard says, "when He began His ministry... was about thirty years of age," which suggests "almost" thirty. Since Luke 3:1-2 tells of the start of John's ministry, it is probable that "when He began His ministry" is what he means in 3:23, and that we should take the meaning as "almost" thirty.

Obviously the scribes that edited the variations to imply that Yeshua was already in the beginning of his thirtieth year felt the difficulty of squeezing Messiah's starting point too close to John's. The variants give them another five months to work with. However, I suggest that Messiah was immersed in preparation for ministry "almost thirty," but that he did not begin it until after the forty days of temptation, which takes us past his thirtieth birthday. The word's "began His ministry" are not strictly accurate in the New American Standard. The Greek ἀρχόμενος actually means "making a beginning," and arguably his baptism was the first step of preparation, but Messiah was not looking to call disciples or minister publicly before his thirtieth year. He was immersed by John and anointed by the Holy Spirit, and then tested for forty days and forty nights.† Then he was ready for service on his thirtieth birthday. And this is the standard procedure according to Torah. †Prob. Av 30-Tishir 10.

The Star of Bethlehem

Millennia before Messiah's birth, the Almighty guided the heavenly bodies into their courses, and subsequently arranged the chronology of his Son's birth to agree with their movements and their symbolical meanings. He had even influenced the metaphors of ancient star watchers, and the Hebrew names of the stars and constellations so that, at least once, associations would place the correct meaning on astronomical events surrounding Messiah's birth.

Not all Magi practiced divination, the forbidden, and unscientific art of foretelling the future with the stars. In those days, astronomy (star laws) and astrology (star study) were combined. Those who did not cast horoscopes went to the same schools with those who did. Arguably, astronomers still practice divination with cosmic evolution and deep time, but not all of them. It is just possible some, who did not practice divination, had faith the Almighty would put on some kind of stellar show for the coming of Messiah. There *were* scripture texts that hinted at this possibility that the stars would bring a redemptive analogy to Messiah's birth, like the *Peace Child*. There was no harm in looking to see if there would be a show so long as it could be scientifically and historically confirmed.

How did the Magi know when to look for a divine show? Astronomical events repeat periodically, and the same messages could be obtained at different times, making it all subjective. What convinced them to look and see at the time they did? The answer is in Daniel 9:24-25. They could have calculated that the Messiah would be cut off after the terminal sabbatical year in AD 32/33. Since the Messiah would be Anointed before then, they could have reasoned that David became king at at 30, and that priests were anointed at age 30. Reducing AD 32/33 by 30 brings them back to AD 2 or 3 at the latest dates they should check their calculations for birth signs. When they looked over the years 3 to 2 BC they found that Tzedeq was in Leo, which only happens once in a 12 year window. They found some amazing conjunctions with Regulus in Leo, and some amazingly close and rare conjunctions of Jupiter and Venus. Could there be something to this? They had to check it out. And they were not to be disappointed. No doubt, they only noted enough at first to get their search going, to justify their journey. So what follows here is not what they discovered at first, but as much as can justly be said to be part of the divine show in hindsight. And likely the Spirit had a role in getting them going. A show was planned. It should not be missed.

On July 13th, 3 BC, at noon, Zechariah was released from his Temple service. On July 14, the new moon day for Av, he was returned home and mutely confirmed matters to his wife, with the support of fellow priests. That night, the evening of July 14th (1 Av), the moon was found in conjunction with Mercury (the *wisdom star*; Panarion 1.1.16; cf. Luke 1:17) in Leo, the so-called messenger of the gods. It would be fair to say that the messenger of ha-Elohim was conceived that night. John is the messenger. The lion is the hill country of Judah. The moon is Elizabeth begetting a child (cf. Gen. 37). For her part, she must have been seized with fear upon hearing of her husband's curse, and hopeful joy upon hearing a prophecy that she would conceive a son that would break the curse. As a result, it would only be natural for her to make haste to conceive the Most High's messenger. Yoḥannan was quick in the womb, and burned brightly in ministry. No prophet arose more popular than he. He was loved, respected, and hated, and his mission accomplished quickly, and quickly he perished, a martyr for Messiah.

That same month, on August 1st, *Tzedeq* (Jupiter) was born a dawn star by a helical rising in Leo using the standard 12 degree separation from the sun rule, attended by Venus. With 20-20 hindsight, this event was just an announcement that a righteous king would be born in Judea. Venus (Nogah, brightness), Jupiter (Tzedeq, righteousness), and Regulus (Melech, king star), were all aligned at the face of the Sun. "For we saw his star in the rising" (Mat. 2:1). This was the first appearing of the star the Magi thought significant, which they reported to Herod, and based upon which Herod calculated he should murder all the boys in the second year and under, since it was the 18th month from then that the Magi arrived at his court.

That same month of Av, a half day before the new moon, Aug 12, 3 B.C. Jupiter conjuncts with Venus (Nogah, 'brightness') (closest approach 0.07°) in Leo (Ari), between its front legs. But observers would see them just 0.15° apart at dawn. Also, the helical rising of Regulus was this morning. Perhaps Gen. 49:10 was known to the Magi. These events are a metaphor for conception, that the power of the Most High will overshadow the virgin, who will beget the king of Israel. The Magi would also have foreseen upcoming events in Virgo and have considered Isa. 7:14. Bethulah would be on their minds.

Yet another announcement: Sept. 14, 3 B.C. Jupiter, (Tzedeq) moves into conjunction with Regulus (Melech), the king star, in the sign of Leo, the Lion. A just king will be born in Judea. Regulus means king in Latin, and Leo means Lion. Tzedeq means justice. Judah's symbol is the Lion. Melechi-Tzedek. Psalm 110:4, "my king of justice." See also Jer. 23:6.

The sixth new moon after Zechariah finished his service was seen on December 9, 3 BC. The following new moon day was the date of the Messenger's announcement to Miryam, and it was the conception date of Messiah. That new moon day was the sixth day of Hannukah. It is fair to say that the evening of the new moon day, that Venus (Nogah) made its first appearance out of the sun as an evening star. This was in Sagittarius, and the moon in Capricorn. It is fair to say, according to the symbolism, that both signs involve combined natures (goat-fish, man-horse). But we need not depend on it. The equivalent symbolism is in Hannukah! The sixth day conception is the day of the incarnation combining the divine with the human. And six is the number of man. Venus is Nogah in Hebrew, meaning brightness, and on this day seven lamps of the Hannukah menorah are lit, six for the number of man, and the seventh as the servant of the Most High. The divine put on the human and became a servant to ransom men.

Yet another announcement: Feb. 17, 2 B.C. Jupiter conjuncts with Regulus (0.85°) a second time. The moon covers then uncovers Regulus, as if to suggest the king is hidden in the womb, or crowned in the womb, as did happen to the Parthian king Shapur II, who reigned for 70 years.

March 28, 2 B.C. Jupiter reaches a stationary point and resumes its proper eastward motion against the background of the stars. May 8, 2 B.C. Jupiter conjuncts with Regulus the third time (0.72°). This last conjunction completes a loop d' loop of Jupiter over Regulus. It is a rare triple conjunction, three times shining down upon a king of justice in the womb, melchenu-tsedeq.

On April 5, 2 BC was the last day of Aviv (Nisan), the 15th day from the spring equinox. The conception date for John was Av 1, 3 BC, which was the 115th day of the old year. Days in old year = 365 − 115 + 1 = 251. And 251 plus 15 days of the new year = 266 (38 weeks). So April 5, 2 BC was Elizabeth's due date. On this date Mercury appeared as the morning star, and the new moon appeared in the evening for Iyyar. The messenger is new born with nine lunar months complete from the day of conception.

On June 17, 2 B.C. Jupiter (Tzedeq) and Venus (Nogah) conjunct again in the midst of Leo in a spectacular double star, only this time they actually appear to join, partially merging to the human eye (0.01°: DE406 26.2 arcseconds). The double star is formed in the sign of Leo (*Ari*, the Lion) on the night of the full moon. No stellar object in the sky would be brighter then this conjunction. If one is willing, this illustrates the power of the Most High overshadowing the virgin in Judea, who is full with child. An alternate name the Pharisees used for Jupiter was "the husband star" (כוכבה בעל, Panarion, 1.1.16). And, Venus, called "brightness" (Nogah) was associated with the female aspect due to its brilliant beauty.

August 26, 2 B.C. Six days before Messiah is born, Nogah, Kochav Chochmah, Tzedek, and Ma'adim (Mars) assemble in the sign of Leo. The sun is in Virgo, and the moon about to enter Leo. Thus six heavenly bodies assemble before the king, one behind, one in front, and four at his feet to await the birth of the second Adam. And the number of man is six, and counting inclusively from the assembly of the stars to his birth is seven days, and the number seven is the number of the Almighty. So the Almighty is born into the form of a man, and the stars lined up for his birth. But Saturn (Shabbatai) was ceased from them. The seventh sphere, looked down on the other six bodies from its high position for seven days. And at the moment of Messiah's birth it looked down from high heaven on the festival Shabbat as the others were rising.

Aug. 31, 2 B.C. In six days, at evening the new moon is under the feet of Virgo, clothed with the sun, and crowned with twelve stars. Rev. 12:1-3. And at dawn on the new moon day was the helical rising of Jupiter, the morning star. This is when the Tsedeq (righteous one's) star first reappears after being in the womb of the sun. This is the dawn star of Messiah's birth. The birth was also attended by Venus. Both stars, therefore, may be justly claimed by Messiah as his stars, Venus (brightness) as the evening star at his conception, and Jupiter (righteous one) at his birth as the morning star. He was conceived during the festival of lights and born on the feast of Trumpets, the new year day for the kings of Judah.

To complete the symbolism, Revelation 12 tells us that the "dragon," which is really a great serpent, the *Tannim* (cf. LXX *δράκων* for תָּנִּין) stood before the woman. This is Hydra, which was a many headed serpent. This constellation is adjacent to Virgo, and its tail spans a third of the twelve zodiacal constellations, Libra, Virgo, Leo, and Cancer. The serpent casts a third of the stars to earth, the virtues of Justice, Purity, Sovereignty, and Nurture. The Hydra is the largest and longest of the constellations laying parallel to the zodiacal constellations, spanning over 100 degrees. The symbolism reaches to the end of days, and speaks of the devil and his messengers being cast down to earth. In the Greek myth, Hercules battles the Hydra. He was half god and half man. In reality it is Messiah, the Almighty Son who will battle the many headed serpent. Can a horoscope or astrologer top this? I think not.

After its helical rising on 9/1, 2 BC, the Magi continue to make predawn observations of Jupiter's progress about an hour before sunrise. Jupiter moves further west at each morning observation, in the direction of Judea, as well as moving west in the daily motion. On Nov. 6, 2 BC Jupiter had moved under the branch of Virgo, and Venus was in conjunction with Spica.

They reached Jerusalem, where they heard the prophecy that Messiah was to be born in Bethlehem. Leaving Herod after the Sabbath, they set out on the evening of the 27th, camping in the dark for their customary observations. Then Jupiter reached a stationary point on Dec. 27, 2 BC a few hours before midnight in the constellation of Virgo. It says of the star, "till it came and stood over where the young child was" (Mat. 2:9). This refers to Jupiter reaching its stationary point (when it changes from proper eastward motion to retrograde westward motion). Then 2 hours before sunrise on the 28th (around 5 a.m.), Jupiter would be seen at 200 degrees Azimuth, i.e. SSW, and 65 degrees over the direction of Bethlehem having made no detectable movement against the stars. They connect this with the prophecy and make haste to Bethlehem in the morning, while they rejoice over seeing His star in that direction. They found the child before the 28th day ended, the day Tzedeq stopped. (In Babylon one calendar day is a night and a day). Then in the evening, at the time of the new moon they presented their gifts. That night they learn the dates that Messiah was conceived and born and are filled with joy. They turn in late and are warned in a dream. They depart at the early observation hour. Meanwhile Joseph has a dream, and he also departs by night with the family. In the morning of the 29th, Herod, having waited for news of the Magi longer than he wished, his patience having held barely over a day, has sent his soldiers who arrive and slaughter the boys under 24 months old. Various Churches mark a Feast of the Holy Innocents from 27 December to 29 December. The correct time is no earlier than dawn on the 29th.

To sum up the show, Mercury is in conjunction with the crescent moon at John's conception, and Mercury is the morning star at his birth in 266 days, and the new moon appears that evening. Venus first appears as an evening star at Yeshua's conception, and Jupiter first appears as a morning star at his birth in 266 days. Venus and Jupiter make a close conjunction four months before Messiah's conception in Leo. Venus and Jupiter make a second even closer conjunction three months before Messiah's birth in Leo at the face of the full moon. On the day of Messiah's birth, Tzedeq is born as a dawn star in Virgo, while the sun is in Virgo, the morning after the moon was under her feet with Nogah also as a morning star. After four months are completed, Herod, represented by Hydra tries to murder the Messiah, but the child is caught away.

Scripture Texts

I see Him, and not now. I behold him, and not near. A **star** will have made way from Ya'aqov, and will have risen a *scepter from Yisrael (Num. 24:17, *or *rod*).

Therefore, Adonai himself will give to you a **sign**. Behold the virgin is pregnant, and is bearing a son. And you will have called his name Immanuel (Isa. 7:14).

Where is He who has been born king of the Yehudim? Because, we have seen his **star** in the ***rising** (Mat. 2:2, *or *branch*).

Herod ascertained from them the time the **star** manifested itself (Mat. 2:7).

And behold the **star**, which they did see in the ***rising**, was going before them till, having arrived, it was stationed up above where the child was, and when they saw the star they themselves rejoiced (Mat. 2:9, *or *branch*).

> As I also have been receiving authority from my Father, also I will give to him the morning **star** (Rev. 2:28). I am the root and kindred of David, the bright dawn **star** (Rev. 22:16).
>
> And will have risen for ye fearers of my name the sun *toward* ***Tzekeq*** (צְדָקָה) with healing in her wings (Mal. 4:2).
>
> Behold the man, **riser** is his name, and from under it he will rise up, and he will have built the Temple of Yahweh (Zech. 6:12).
>
> *The* **RISER**[μ] from on high, [79]TO APPEAR TO THOSE WHO SIT IN DARKNESS (LUKE 1:78, GNM)
>
> Who will have raised up **Tzedeq** from the sunrise; he will call him to his feet. He will set at his face nations. And kings he will tread down. His sword will make them as dust (Isa. 4:2; cf. Shabbat 156b:1; FOR THE LION OF YEHUDAH WILL BE A YEAR OF JUBILEE).

Matthew 2:9 presents the star as a divine sign, validating in the narration the statement of the Magi in 2:2. We cannot say that he merely reports on a superstition and then dismisses it as such, because Matthew's words in 2:9 assume the truth of the words in 2:2. The Magi had the faith to take Numbers 24:17 very literally that a birth star was appointed for Messiah. Their waiting and watching did not disappoint. In Rev. 22:16 Messiah owns this star along with its royal implications.

The texts refer to the first appearing of the star, and the last, which Herod calculated to be more than a year of days, but less than two years of days. The actual time was 18 months. We learn that the star is the morning star from Yeshua's remark in Revelation. In the context of Rev. 2:28, Messiah speaks of granting authority to the faithful for the administration of justice, and then he illustrates this point with the morning star. Which morning star is it? The usual Hebrew name of the largest planet is *Tzedeq*, which means "justice" (Shabbat 156b:1; Eruvin 56a:11). And there is every indication that this name is very ancient.

Tzedeq, therefore, fits all the known behaviors ascribed to the star in Scripture. Aside from astrology, Scripture gives good reason to believe that the Almighty put on a stellar show for his Son's birth using the most basic of symbolism associated with the stars. Could any astrologer could design a horoscope better than the show that did occur? They are typically happy with subjective opinions when helical risings and other alignments occur near a person's birth, say two weeks before or after it. But we see that everything lined up more exactly than the most stingy astrologer could justly demand. We have also seen that the symbolism is adequately explained by falling back to Hebrew symbolism and logical symbolic connections that probably predate the corruptions of astrology.

It was only after wondering about the precision of the astronomy that I wondered if the birth was at dawn. With the evidence of a helical rising? I asked, what time of day was Messiah born? The answer was found in Luke 2:8. They were keeping the "watches of the night," stated in the plural as Miryam was in labor with her firstborn from the previous evening (Rev. 12:1-2). It was therefore at the end of the morning watch. It was at the moment of dawn when *Tzedeq* and *Nogah* were seen. Then the messenger appeared and announced that "today" the Savior has been born. Then the angelic host appeared.

Chronological conclusions: Yoĥannan was conceived on Av 1 in 3 BC and born on Nisan 29 in 2 BC, at nine full months and 266 days. Yeshua was conceived on Tebeth 1 in 3 BC and born on Tishri 1, 2 BC, in 266 days. The conception and birth dates are both marked by meaningful astronomical events. For John, appearances of Mercury, and for Messiah helical risings.

The Biblical Months of 2 BC

Most interpreters that deal with 2 BC calculate the month of Aviv (aka Nisan) incorrectly, because they calculate it a month late. The easiest way to err on this is to use a modern method of determining the spring equinox without realizing that ancient peoples employed different methods such as (1) the sun at the midpoint between the solstice points on the horizon, or (2) the middle date between two solstice dates, or (3) the tip of a shadow traces as near a straight line as possible, or (4) a traditional date that has drifted away from any strict observational criteria, or (5) the sun rising due east or (6) setting due west. All the methods are not mentioned here. It is only necessary to know that different methods were used, and we should not assume that familiar modern methods were used in ancient times. All these methods may produce dates of the equinox varying by a few days.

The scripture requires Passover to be observed from *days to days* (Exodus 13:10). This is a Hebrew idiom for a solar year measured by the sun's cycle of days, which is the time the sun takes to move through all its variations of the day until it begins to repeat again. The Hebrew word 'days' *yamim* is an idiom meaning "a year." The reason this idiom came about is because a year was defined as so many "days" it took for the sun to complete a cycle of days. We know this as the solar year, a period of 365 or 366 days. Like the month, it's length can vary by one day. A regular year is 365 days. A leap year is 366 days. Likewise a month is either 29 or 30 days, called a hollow or full month.

The precept is that Passover is to be observed once per year, and it should not be observed in the old year. Scripture calls for three pilgrim feasts per year. Keeping Passover in the old year would cause one year to have four feasts, and the next to have only two! The day upon which the new year begins, therefore, is critical to determining whether a potential Passover date falls in the new year.

A strictly observational method is consistent with all the biblical facts. The priests who specialized in the calendar observed the sun each day. The date upon which the sun set west or just north of due west was fixed as the first day of the year. Also the day upon which the sun rose due east or just north of due east would qualify. Whichever happened first could determine the day. If the sun set south of west on one day and rose on the next due east, then that day would be the new year day. Or if the sun rose south of due east but set north of due west on the same day, then that day would be the first day of the new year.

Strictly speaking, in a close call situation, the priests had to rely on counting 365 days from the date of the last observation. Their last observation would have been on 3/22 in 3 BC. The first day after 365 days from this is 3/22 in 2 BC. If no mistake were made, the lengths of the years are thus:

Vernal Year	Length	Ended	Next Year
7 to 6 BC	365 days	March 21	March 22
6 to 5 BC	365 days	March 20	March 21
5 to 4 BC	366 days	March 21	March 22
4 to 3 BC	365 days	March 21	March 22
3 to 2 BC	365 days	March 21	March 22

The last leap year was the spring of 4 BC, and the spring of 2 BC was only the second year afterward. Therefore the priests would not assume that 366 days were needed in the spring of 2 BC. They would guess correctly that the year would be 365 days. Sometimes when the case was a close call, the priests had to make the best guess possible. For it would not be possible to observe if the first day of the year that year was correct in time for Passover. The new year day had to be estimated from the observations of the prior year in a close call. The tendency of the priests was to set the new year date as early as evidence would allow because they were not to give cause for delaying offerings, and also their income depended upon keeping the harvest season as long as possible.

The new moon for the first month in 2 BC fell such that the 15th day of the month was the day of the spring equinox. For on that day the sun set just north of due west as observed. Now it is in keeping with the biblical practice of inclusive counting to reckon the whole of the Great Sabbath with the beginning of the year. The beginning of the feast is reckoned from sunset on the 14th to sunset on the 15th. The feasting that day, therefore, is accounted to be on new year's day (March 22, 2 BC). Naturally the priests would not be able to make the 2 BC observation before the feast occurred that year. They would have to make their decision based on the number of regular 365 day years that had gone by since the last leap year. If it was only the second regular year, then no leap year would be presumed. For there would usually be three regular 365 day years before a leap year would be assumed, and it was only the third regular year that was at risk of being so presumed. The priest's would not use the leap day unless observations compelled them to.

Even if someone should be a stickler for a modern equinox method, I have one more trick up my sleeve that can silence their dogmatism. According to Jewish tradition, if the moon was not seen on the 29th of a month, it would automatically be given 30 days. An otherwise visible new moon might be missed on account of bad weather and the lack of witnesses to say they saw it. It so happens that the month of Adar in the spring of 2 BC had only 29 days. If a 30th day were added to the month, as allowed for by traditional circumstances, then the dispute over the equinox date in 2 BC becomes a moot point. The critics of the method of observation I outlined above would thus be unable to prove that an Adar II was added in the spring of 2 BC.

Some would like to follow the Babylonian method, which normally calculated the first month of Nisanu so that the whole month was after the spring equinox. But the Babylonians themselves demonstrate that at one time they were much closer to the biblical method. Parker and Dubberstein show a remarkable number of Nisanu's dated with Nisanu 1 before the spring equinox. In the reign of Nabopolassar, years 1, 2, 4, 5, 7, 9?, 10, 12, 15, 18, 19, and 20. In the reign of Nebuchadnezzar, years 2, 5, 7?, 21, 26?, 40, and 41. Also for the reign of Kandalanu, just prior to that of Nabopolassar, Saturn observations in British Museum tablets show regular intercalations of Nisanu 1 before and after the spring equinox consistent with the use of a fixed date in the middle of Nisanu for determining the intercalation of the year.

Kandalanu	Nisanu 1
Year 2	3/18
Year 4	3/25
Year 5	3/14
Year 7	3/21
Year 8	3/11
Year 10	3/20
Year 13	3/16

Heliacal Rising

The faithful in Messiah should not fear word metaphors involving light or the sun as applied to the Almighty. The scripture is full of them. For example:

> For a sun and a shield is Yahweh (Psalm 84:11). And the light shines in the darkness, and the darkness grasps it not (John 1:5.). I am the root and the offspring of David, and the bright and morning star. (Rev. 22:16). But unto you that fear my name shall a sun of righteousness arise with healing in his wings (Mal. 4:2).

The scripture expressly forbids the use of images, engravings, and pictures as representations of the Almighty. However, it does not forbid "word" pictures, poetry, metaphors or similes. And a good deal of human creativeness is expressed this way. It is one of the attributes of being created in the image of God.

But surely there is such a thing as "word" idolatry. Any time the Almighty's character is misrepresented by words, this is idolatry.

And some words by constant association with image idolatry and false worship evoke the idolatry. The word *Ba'al* is one of them. It means "lord" or "husband," but by constant association with evil it has been essentially ruined, a point recognized by the Scripture (Hos. 2:16). The "days of Ba'al" misrepresent the Almighty, and are associated with pagan deities. However, we should be careful not to let abuses prevent us from seeing the message in legitimate biblical metaphors and figures of speech. For this is a powerful way to communicate and the Scripture indulges in it in spades.

Some things do go too far, like the King James Bible capitalizing "Sun" in "sun of righteousness," (Mal 4:2) and I do think that this metaphor has been ruined by the marriage of Mithraism and Rome, and therefore is not without good reason shunned in any worship context. However, this should not keep us from discovering what the Scripture is trying to communicate by the metaphors it uses. And, indeed there are some powerful messages, and truths that can be revealed this way.

We should also not fear to use constellation names. For they appear in Scripture. Job is asked if he knows the constellations (Job 38:32). They are called *mazzaroth* (מַזָּרוֹת). Also mentioned are, "the Bear, Orion, and the Pleiades" (Job 9:9; 38:31; Amos 5:8). The *mazzaroth* is what is commonly called the Zodiacal signs, and agrees with Genesis 1:14 that the stars are also to be for "signs." Rev. 12:1-3 is certainly the greatest of all the signs, and the birth of Messiah is called a sign in Isaiah 7:14.

The Magi tell us that they "have seen his star in the rising, and are come to worship him" (Mat. 2:2). Matthew adds a second time, "which they saw in the rising." (Mat. 2:9). And this was a matter that greatly disturbed "all Jerusalem." The key words are "ἐν τῇ ἀνατολῃ" in both passages. This Greek *anatolei* word means "rise up," "dawn," "east," "rising," "growing," "branch," "sprout." The Hebrew term is from the root "צָמַח." Jastrow supplies us with the following definition:

> צָמַח (b.h.) to break forth, shine; to bloom, sprout, grow.[211]

[211] pg. 1287, *Dictionary of the Targumim, the Talmud Babli and Yerushalmi, and the Midrashic Literature*, Marcus Jastrow.

To this I add the statement of Zechariah in Luke:

> Because of the tender mercy of our Almighty, with which a rising from on high will visit us, to appear to those who sit in darkness and the shadow of death, to guide our feet into the way of peace" (Luke 1:78-79).

The word Zechariah uses for "a rising" is "**ἀνατολη**." The reason Zechariah uses this word is that it stands for the word: צֶמַח ,צֶמַח. The verse could even be translated, "Because of the tender mercy of our God by which the Branch from on High shall visit us."[212] The Septuagint, in Zech. 6:12, "the man whose name is Branch" (ἀνήρ **Ἀνατολὴ** ὄνομα). Also Zech 3:8, "**Ἀνατολήν**"; Jer. 23:5, "**ἀνατολὴν**"; Isa. 4:2, "ἐπιλάμψει" (*shine forth*). Thus one of the meanings of צֶמַח is explained to be "shine forth," or by the Greek term even, "dawn," "east," "rising."

The magi were connecting the appearance of the star with the Messianic title, "we saw his star in the Branch" or "we saw his star in the dawn" (at the heliacal rising). Both interpretations are the truth. I have mentioned the heliacal rising of Jupiter on 9/1, 2 B.C, and also 8/1, 3 B.C. 8/1, 3 B.C. is when the star first appeared, and then conjuncted with the morning star on 8/12, 3 B.C. This is why Herod killed all the boys under two years. He was covering all possible interpretations of conception and birth.

Now there were two stars which could be called "his" star after the conjunction of Jupiter and Venus. Venus is the brightest of the stars, and is called the "bright and morning star" (ὁ ἀστὴρ ὁ λαμπρὸς ὁ πρωϊνός), and is a metaphor of Messiah (Rev. 22:16). On the other hand, Jupiter is called *Tsedeq* (Isa. 41:2), "He causes the righteous one to rise from the east" (הֵעִיר־מִמִּזְרָח־צֶדֶק), or "He makes Jupiter rise from the east." So both these stars are being used as prophetic metaphors. The magi said, "We saw his star *in the branch*" (ἐν τῇ ἀνατολη).

So it was on November 6, 2 B.C. that Venus, representing the mother conjuncted with the star *Spica*. Spica means an ear of corn in Latin, which we can connect with "seed," as in the promised seed.

---

[212] pg. 1929, *Theological Wordbook of the Old Testament*.

However, in Arabic it is *Al Zimach*, and corresponds to the Hebrew *Tsemech* (צֶמַח), and means "Branch," translated by ἀνατολη in Greek (LXX: Zech. 3:8, 6:12, Jer. 23:5). The *Tsemech* star is the brightest in the constellation of Virgo and in the sheaf of grain in the left hand.

In the right hand of Virgo is a larger more definite branch, held upright. The star there is called "*Al Mureddin* which means *who shall come down* (as in Psa. lxxii. 8), or *who shall have dominion*. It is also known as *Vindemiatrix*, a Chaldee word which means *the son*, or *branch, who cometh*."[213] In the right hand, the traditions have the virgin holding a branch, vine, or rod. In the Latin Vulgate Isa. 11:1 renders נֵצֶר with the term *virga*, which means in Latin a "branch" or "twig." Also in Arabic the root *Batūl* means "A shoot or offset of a palm-tree…Heb. בְּתוּלָה *Bethūlāh*."[214] "The word means "palm shoot or palm scion; one consecrated to God; virgin."[215] And Bullinger translating loosely, "The name of this sign in the Hebrew is *Bethulah*, which means *a virgin*, and in the Arabic *a branch*."[216]

The Magi said, "we saw his star in the branch." Could this mean that they saw Messiah's star in Virgo? I have already mentioned this for Venus. But also on November 6, 2 B.C. Jupiter appeared in Virgo at a point on the ecliptic perpendicular to the "branch" in the right hand of Virgo:

....

> And you will have taken silver and gold. And you will have made a great crown. And you will have set it on the head of Yehoshua Ben Yehotsadaq, the high priest. And you will have said unto him, saying, 'Thus says Yahweh of Hosts, saying, behold the man, BRANCH is his name, and from his place he will branch out. And he will have built the Temple of Yahweh. And he will build the Temple of Yahweh. And he will bear the glory. And he will have sat, and he will have ruled upon his throne. Also there will have been a priest on his seat, and the counsel of peace will be between the two of them (Zech. 6:11-13).

---

[213] Bullinger, *Witness of the Stars*, pg. 33. I have been unable to confirm the Chaldee meaning of *Vindemiatrix*.
[214] *A Dictionary of Islam*, Patrick Hughes. pg. 39.
[215] pg. 340. *Theological Dictionary of the Old Testament*, Vol. 2, Botterweck.
[216] pg. 30, note 211.

Figure 56: The Star in the Branch

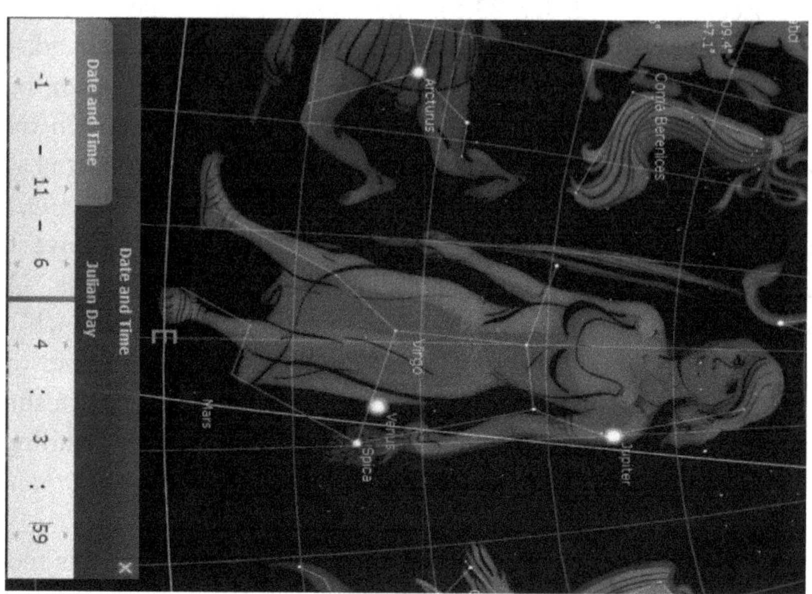

The branch in the right hand of Virgo goes in the space just above "Zaniah" (ε), i.e. Vindemiatrix/Al Mureddin, and stretches most of the way to Denebola. Jupiter is exactly in conjunction with the middle of the branch, rod, or scion as usually drawn. Meanwhile, Venus was in conjunction with Spica, called Al Zimach in Arabic or Tsemech in Hebrew (Compare with Figure 53). These are the same two stars that joined twice before, once on Aug. 12, 3 B.C. in Leo to the east of Regulus, and once again in Leo, to the west of Regulus. In between these two conjunctions, Jupiter makes a triple conjunction with Regulus and then rises helically on August 1, 3 B.C. and moves under the Branch in Virgo while Venus moves under the Branch Star.

The Magi declared in Jerusalem, "We have seen his star in the Branch/dawn." This refers to the helical risings of Jupiter and the latest event in their observations on Nov. 6, 2 B.C. shown above in the figure. The star was made of two stars, and both appeared "in the Branch" (ἀνατολη, צֶמַח) at the same time.

These revelations, without a doubt, would have thrown Jerusalem into a tizzy of trouble and agitation.

Luke's mention that Zechariah was from the priestly division of Abijah agrees perfectly with the Tishri 1, 2 BC date for Messiah's birth.[217] When Zechariah finished his priestly duties then his wife Elizabeth conceived. After five months Miryam, the mother of Messiah, conceived (Luke 1:24, 26).* And then after nine months Messiah was born. If we can ascertain the date Zechariah finished his duty period in 3 BC, then we can check the timeline against the Tishri 1 date of Messiah's birth, which was Sept. 1, 2 BC according to the Revelation 12 synchronism. If the time between the two points is just the right amount of time, implying neither a premature or overdue birth, then the Tishri 1, 2 BC birth date of Messiah will be confirmed by a third witness. We ascertain the 2 BC date from Luke 3, and the Tishri 1 date from Rev. 12:1-2. The priestly data give a third cord confirming both the year and date.

A key fact is that Luke 2:6 informs us that Messiah was not born premature. Luke 2:5 further informs us that their purpose in going to Bethlehem did not require more than one business day. It is implied by this fact that they would have left again once the registration had been completed if the birth had not detained them. It is further implied by the circumstance that Messiah was laid in a feeding trough that no plans had been laid to stay in their present accommodation until the child was born. For if that had been the case, the accommodations would have been more suited. It appears that the accommodation they had was retained only for the short term purpose of waiting till the first business day to go before the magistrate to complete the registration. They did not rent the whole building and their use of the common room was thrust upon them by the onset of labor.

From these observations, we may conclude that Messiah was not born overdue by two weeks or even a week. The due date arrived as soon as they arrived. A longer stay is refuted by the stated purpose of the visit. The unsuitable accommodation implies they were hoping to get away again before the birth and not planning for it to happen when it did.

One might suppose that the day of the 6th month on which Miryam received the announcement from the heavenly messenger is not knowable, but the circumstance of knowing that Miryam reached her term date with Messiah and the end of Zechariah's service as just so that the announcement was on the first day of the 6th month. For any other arrangement would imply that Messiah was born premature on Tishri 1, 2 BC or that Elizabeth had not reached her sixth month. Furthermore, I

---

[217] Luke 1:5. See also 1 Chron. 24:1-19, and 24:10.

* On the first day of the sixth month.

have now been able to show חֹדֶשׁ means *renewing*, either in the sense of the renewing period, a month, or the renewing point, the new moon, and when the context does not show it to be a month, it is a new moon, as in Exodus 12:2, 19:1 and Deut. 16:1. So Luke means the new moon.

The workings of the priestly divisions are such that there were 24 divisions of priests, and each division served in turn for one week, starting at noon on the Sabbath and serving till noon on the next Sabbath. When the 24 divisions had all served covering 24 weeks, the rotation began again with the 1st division. The Torah required all the priests to receive equal shares (or portions). A priest could only receive his allotment if he were serving and therefore the measure of equal shares is equivalent to equal time in service. Therefore similar to the clock of the seven day week each priest could expect to serve once every 24 weeks. And they did not want to miss their service period, so they counted weeks as religiously as other Jews counted seven days to the Sabbath.

Many have supposed that the priestly rotations were reset every year on Nisan 1 or Tishri 1. But this kind of system would result in some divisions serving three times a year when the rest only served two. Others have supposed that all the priests served during feast weeks delaying the regular rotation by a week each time. But only one feast lasts exactly a week, and this is the feast of unleavened bread. For Pentecost, which lasts one day, all the divisions are competing for six more days for the proceeds normally received by one division. After Tabernacles the last great day falls on the 8th day. It would be better to assume that all divisions were allowed to serve anytime there was extra work to be divided up and that the regular division went on with the regular work also taking 1/24th of the extra work as overtime. Every division would get its turn at regular work and extra work by a strictly repeating pattern of 24 weeks with no skipped weeks and no annual reset.

One may wonder how Solomon, the wisest man in the world, set up a 12 month rotation to provision his table. Obviously he did it by setting up his taxation year without a 13th month. Thus the turns of his provinces rotated continuously and wandered through the seasons. This was the most equitable way to divide the tax load. Each province would find its duty load rotating between seasons of plenty and scarcity, and winter and summer.

Besides the Torah requirement for equal portions, the Dead Sea Scrolls 4Q321 and 4Q320 show a system of continuous rotations in place. The Torah also shows that the rotations did begin in the 12th year of Solomon on the 2nd week of Tishri, after the first Temple was inaugurated. This fact alone proves a system of continuous rotations was used when we take the events of AD 70 into account when the first division was serving on Av 9. According to Seder Olam (ca. AD 150) when the Second Temple was destroyed, the first division was serving on Av 9, on the first day of the week (August 5, AD 70). This timing note gives us an additional synchronization point anchoring the continuously rotating system of priestly divisions to known a known date. Does this fact work with any of the other systems?

Beckwith proposed that the system reset with the week of Tishri 1 in AD 69 (and every week of Tishri 1 prior to AD 69). But it is simply a coincidence that the first division lands then, when counting back from Av 9, AD 70. The continuous system predicts the same division for the week of Tishri 1, AD 69. In Solomon's 12th year, all the divisions were sanctified without respect to divisions on the week of Tishri 1. Thus, the first division was not serving then. By this contrary example Beckwith's assumed Tishri 1 reset system is refuted since it requires the divisions to always begin with the week of Tishri 1. Prior to Beckwith, Thomas Lewin (1805-1877) had already figured out the proper dates for the rotations.

Others proposed the divisions began with the week of Nisan 1. If we use AD 70 to likewise count back to Nisan that year we find the seventh division serving during the week of Nisan 1. So this system is also refuted by Seder Olam besides by their inception in the first Temple.

As mentioned before, others propose that feast weeks were skipped over. But the Seder Olam data for AD 70 refutes all such systems. There is simply no way the Av 9 synchronism for the first division can be obtained by any proposed system of week skipping. The Qumran data also independently refutes week skipping besides unequivocally demonstrating that the rotations were continuous. So besides Torah's requirement for equal service periods, our other sources also confirm continuous rotations.

Using astronomical data in the Qumran sources John Pratt was able to single out 42 BC as the probable synchronization year, and he showed also that this agreed with the Seder Olam note.* Pratt's other candidates were 45, 39, and 28 BC. I am able to eliminate all of these because the division times are so far off that they do not lay within the window of wiggle room when the second Temple was finished in 515 BC. The Temple was finished on 3 Adar I, 515 BC. The first Temple was destroyed while division 14 was serving in 587 BC. The rotations pick up with No. 15 in the first week of Nisan just before Passover. Pratt's other years require +12, +12, and -10 division offsets to work in this window, but there are not sufficient weeks to do so and renew the rotation with No. 14 or No. 15. It is obvious that treating the priests fairly requires them to pick up where they left off, so any system that proposes they maintained

* https://www.johnpratt.com/items/docs/lds/meridian/2003/qumran.html

a theoretical count through the exile would also contradict Deut. 18:6-8.

Here is the 2nd Temple period numerical recipe for finding a division number for a given week from the whole number part of the Julian Day Number for sunset at the end of the day part of the first day of the week (JD) in Jerusalem. **Add 1. Divide by 7. Add 3. Find the remainder after dividing by 24. Add 1.** Thus for Sun, March 21, AD 34, JD = 1,733,556 (**+1**) = 1,733,557 (**/7**) = 247,651 (**+3**) = 247,654 (**MOD 24**) = 22 (**+1**) = 23 (Delaiah). Delaiah's service would be noon March 20th (Sabbath) to noon March 27th (Sabbath). For July 7, 3 BC, JD = 1,720,515 (**+1**) = 1,720,516 (**/7**) = 245,788 (**+3**) = 245,791 (**MOD 24**) = 7 (**+1**) = 8. For Sun, Aug. 31, 2 BC, JD = 1720935 (**+1**) = 1,720,936 (**/7**) = 245,848 (**+3**) = 245,851 (**MOD 24**) = 19 (**+1**) = 20 (Jehezkel). Stellarium 0.19.2 can be used for this. Use the "configuration" window to set it to show the weekday.

In 3 BC Zechariah's division was serving noon July 6 to noon July 13. This puts him back at home on July 14th, the first day of the week, and also the new moon day for month V (Av). This was the day that Elizabeth conceived. The five months are V, VI, VII, VIII, and IX. On the first day of month X was the announcement to Miraym, this being the 6th new moon for Elizabeth. The date was 1 Tevet, 3 BC (December 10). The new moon was seen on Julian date 1,720,670. The following Tishri 1 new moon was seen on Julian date 1,720,935. The difference by inclusive counting is (935 – 670 + 1 = 266).

The due date for a child is figured from the beginning of the last menstrual cycle at 280 days. But to measure from conception 14 days must be subtracted for the average conception date. Therefore 280 – 14 = 266. This is because maximum fertility happens at the end of day 14 in the average 28 day cycle.

If we keep counting backwards we arrive at division 15 for the week of Nisan 1 in 515 BC when the Temple services were restarted after the Babylonian exile. In 587 BC the last division to come on duty before the First Temple was burned was No. 14. Counting back to the second week of Tishri in the 12th year of Solomon (1012 BC) we arrive at division No. 1, the commencement date for the 24 division system.

> And when the Levite comes from one of your gates, from all Israel, where he is sojourning, and he will have come with all the desire of his soul to the place which Yahweh will choose, then he will have ministered in the name of Yahweh his Almighty equal to all his brothers the Levites, those standing there at the face of Yahweh. Portion equal to portion they will eat, besides his sales from his fathers' estates (Deu. 18:6-8).

> And it happened in those days that a decree went out from Caesar Augustus to register all the inhabited earth. [2]This first registration happened—of Quirinius' governing Syria. [3]And everyone was going to register, each to his own city. [4]But Yosef also went up from Galil, from the city of Netsereth, into Yehudah, into the town of David, being called Beth-lehem, because of his being of the house and family of David, [5]in order to register along with Miryam.

"In those days," is broadly used (cf. Luke 1:78). It is likely that Augustus decreed this plan before Quirinius entered office, but it was finally a success when under Quirinius' direction, Herod was able to obtain compliance. This was the first registration during Quirinius' two terms as governor split between 2 BC and AD 6. But, the initial attempt under Saturninus to enroll the people met with failure:

> These are those that are called the sect of the Pharisees, who were in a capacity of greatly opposing kings. A cunning sect they were, and soon elevated to a pitch of open fighting and doing mischief. Accordingly, when all the people of the Jews gave assurance of their good-will to Caesar, and to the king's government, these very men did not swear, being above six thousand; and when the king imposed a fine upon them, Pheroras's wife paid their fine for them (Ant 17.41-42).

Shortly after this, Antipater went to Rome for seven months (17.52-57), Saturninus still being mentioned as the governor. It was about April 13th, 2 BC when we last read of him. Seven months later we meet Varus, it being unclear from Josephus who filled the gap, but as we shall see, it only became unclear after the Church rearranged matters.

In general the Jewish people were opposed to this oath to Caesar, but Joazer, Son of Boethus (a Sadducee), one of the chief priests, and brother-in-law to the High Priest Matthias, through the summer of 2 BC, persuaded most of the people to take the oath, even though oath was opposed by Judah the Galilean, a Rabbi of the Pharisees (*Ant.* 18.3), and those who listened to him. It was this very Rabbi who incited the removal of the golden eagle from the Temple gate, and who was promptly burned alive by Herod on Jan. 9, 1 BC (cf. 17.167). At that time Joazer was appointed high priest, because Matthias had been complicit with Judah. Matthias was spared out of respect for the institution, and because Herod, though a despot, was not so politically witless as to burn a high priest. Nevertheless the seeds of revolt were sown by Herod, and a revolt in the name of Judah the Galilean followed in the spring of 1 BC after Herod's death (18.4; Acts 5:37). The Roman governor, Varus, put down the revolt.

The Pharisee's refusal to take the oath, Joazer's advice to comply during Quirinius' short tenure, and finally the people agreeing to go to register, all fit into the window of time roughly contemporaneous with Antipater's seven month journey to Rome from the spring to the fall of 2 BC (April to October). Saturninus was governor when he left, and Varus was governor when he returned. These are the bookends of Quirinius' short term as governor.

These are how matters stood in the original sources and the minds of the people, who knew the events well, but the timing later became unacceptable to the Church, because it wanted to assume Messiah was conceived in the spring, and born in the winter. So they edited Josephus after they at first had moved the birth of Messiah back to the winter of 2 BC, and then later back to the winter of 3 BC. For this reason Josephus was edited at a later date to allow it to be assumed Quirinius governed in the winter as a deputy of Saturninus. And so all mention of Quirinius' first term, and associated items, were conflated with Quirinius' property census in AD 6. The Almighty allowed this corruption to happen as the result of their blindness, and because the truth was secure in the literary parables placed into the Scripture, safe for a later generation, who would have their eyes opened to his Law, and then be able to understand.

The mess the Church made out of Josephus has not gone unnoticed. After Herod appointed Joazer on Jan 9, 1 BC, and Herod died, Archelaus accused him of aiding the revolt and removed him. But VanderKam notes:

> One would think the removal of Joazar, the son of Boethus, would have been the last we would hear of him as high priest, but it is not. In a puzzling reference, Josephus mentions him again [as high priest] as he writes about events that happened in 6 CE" (From Joshua to Caiaphas, pg. 417; cf. Ant. 18.3).

So do we conclude that Archelaus, struggling for the kingship, had pity and reappointed Joazer when the people were ostensibly on the point of sedition again only to be deposed by Quirinius in AD 6? Hardly! But the account of Josephus was corrupted by the Church by removing Quirinius, Joazer, and elements of the associated revolt to AD 6, duplicating Joazer's high priesthood, and Judah's revolt. Josephus must have originally stated that Joazer, while a chief priest, and brother-in-law of Matthias, advised the people to comply with the registration of Quirinius somewhere during the months of Antipater's seven month sojourn to Rome. So Quirinius and the census was lost because it did not happen in the winter. It was lost when the Church conflated it with Josephus' account of the second registration in AD 6, which was a registration of property, so that Archelaus' estate could be sold, and the tax base be reassessed. And this is exactly what the people wanted, to be rid of Archelaus, and to be joined to the province of Syria (17.314). So also there was no revolt in AD 6. There was no Joazer in AD 6, nor any refusal of the people.

Even with Joazer's urging, the registration of the holy family was delayed. Yosef and Miryam were registered in Nazareth, but upon discovery that they were of the royal family of David, they were given a letter, and required to complete their oath of loyalty at a later date at a special court in Bethlehem. Possibly, with compliance in view, they were even given a travel allowance. They were required to show up just before Tishri 1, 2 BC, with the threat of a princely fine if they failed to do so. It is probable that the extra requirement for the house of David was in addition to the Roman requirement. It was more so Herod's concern.

Table 3: Governors of Syria[226]

M. Titius	7 B.C. and before
Q. Varus	7 or 6 B.C. to 4 B.C.
S. Saturnius	4 B.C. to 2 B.C., ? month,
P. Quirinius	2 B.C. (? month thru Sept)
Q. Varus[227]	2 B.C., October to A.D. 1
G. Caesar	A.D. 1 to A.D. 4

The Church "Fathers" Testimony

The testimony of the so called "Church Fathers" is not worth a whole lot as almost all of them knew far less than we do about ancient chronology. In those days, any person removed more than a lifetime from events is likely to make sophomoric errors. This tendency toward error is increased when they are trying to avoid chronology leading to unwanted conclusions. The reason that we know what we do today is not because we were able to piece things together from their records written centuries later. Rather it is because of archaeology, sources contemporary to dates giving witness of them, and astronomy, as well as honest reading of Scripture passages, after coming to realize that the Almighty did not abolish his Law. In the time of restoration, we make an end run around them.

If the devil and his human accomplices were to have their way, all of the truth would be erased, but the Almighty preserves enough of the truth so that the corrupt tradition may be exposed. Traditionalists object when the truth is not found in the tradition. But this is self serving since it is they who erased it. When anyone repents of rebellion against the divine Law, then they can begin to see where the truth was truly preserved, not by men, but by the Almighty.

It is well known that these men had a predetermination for anti-Judaism, and not just anti-Judaism, but anti-Torah observance. They thus aimed to steer as far away from the 14th-15th Passover celebration as possible, and as far away from other Jewish observances, which were really scriptural observances. This included the feast of Trumpets, otherwise known as Yom Teruah, or Rosh Hashana. Knowing that Messiah was born on Tishri 1, 2 B.C., we can understand that the most parsimonious error made by the Church was to shift the birth of Messiah back to Jan. 6, 2 B.C., so as to make it as close to the winter solstice as possible without departing from the year in which Augustus Caesar placed his XIIIth consulship.* Probably later, the change was made to move the birth from Jan. 6, 2 B.C. back twelve days to Dec. 25th, 3 B.C.

It is for this reason that these men give us a constellation of dates in 3/2 B.C.

Source	Birth Date	Source Date
Irenaeus	3 B.C.	A.D. c. 180
Clement of Alexandria	Nov. 18, 3 B.C.	A.D. 194
Tertullian	3/2 B.C.	A.D. 198
Africanus	3/2 B.C.	A.D. c. 170- c. 240
Hippolytus of Rome	3/2 B.C.	A.D. c. 170-236
Hippolytus of Thebes	3/2 B.C., 2 B.C.	after Hipp. of Rome
Origin	3/2 B.C.	A.D. c. 185-253
Epiphanius	Jan. 6, 2 B.C.	A.D. c. 315-403
Eusebius	3/2 B.C.	A.D. c. 325
Cassiodorus Senator	3 B.C.	A.D. c. 490-585
Orosius	2 B.C., 752 AUC	A.D. 418
Dionysius Exiguus	1 B.C.	A.D. 525

Generally, the sources that state 3/2 B.C run from Jan. 1, 3 B.C. to the spring or summer of 2 B.C. They thus exclude the fall of 2 B.C. To help us evaluate the credibility of these men's estimations is Sir Isaac Newton:

> "The Christians who first began to inquire into these things, as Clemens Alexandrius, Origen, Tertullian, Julius Africanus, Lactantius Jerome, Austin, Sulpicius Severus, Prosper, and as many as placed the death of Christ in the 15th or 16th of Tiberius, make Christ to have preached but one year, or at most but two" (*Observations on Daniel*, pg. 145, Joseph Priestly, *Harmony of the Evangelists*, pg. 38).

This tells us that these men paid no attention to the book of John,

* The *pater patriae* award (Feb 5, 2 BC) required no census or registration to be given, but 3 BC advocates assumed one was required beforehand. As a result, they assume Quirinius was a lesser co-president, but as a rule, when only one is mentioned, it is the top authority. There may be examples of provincial oaths, yet we should not equivocate dates for them with a decree for an Empire wide oath, which may have been conducted over a span of years in different provinces.

or very little, and it underlines the danger of assuming that just because Matthew, Mark, and Luke, or even John do not directly mention so many Passovers, that all the feasts are mentioned, or all are accounted for. Clearly these men were no better at interpreting the biblical evidence before them than many modern scholars, and here Murphy's law applies: if there is a way to err, then they will certainly err.

Fall 2 b.c. vs. Fall 3 b.c. Date

The Tishri 1, 2 b.c. date, and the 30th year of Yeshua, relates the 15th year of Tiberius correctly to his age, and explains all the other facts. However, in a bid to stop this truth, some argue that Yeshua was more than a few months old when the wise men visited, and they propose a difference between the Greek word "παιδίον" (Mat. 2:11; Luke 1:59), and "βρέφος" (Luke 2:16), like the difference between "baby" and "toddler" in English, to help create a dogmatism for their conclusion. They want to create the impression that the visit of the wise men was more than a year later, and say he was a "toddler." No such difference exists in Greek, as is proved by the use of the two words for an infant, on the day of birth in one case, and only eight days old in the other. It is only necessary to check the Greek word used in Luke 1:59 and 2:16 to falsify the claim.*

Yeshua was exactly 4 months old on the day that Jupiter stopped over his birthplace. He was born on Tishri 1, the 7th month, and Jupiter stopped (Mat. 2:9) and changed to retrograde motion on Shebat 1, the 11th month. And this is when the wise men visited. That day was Dec. 27/28 in the Julian calendar. And the new moon is a holy day in Scripture (Isaiah 66:23; Mat.2:11) on which Yahweh is worshiped, and this is when the wise men worshiped Yeshua.

* I have since traced this error back to Adam Rutherford, *Treatise on Bible Chronology*, 1957, page 433, a personal friend of Thiele (pg. 11), and opponent of the Resurrection Sabbath (pg. 479ff). Rutherford claims that "all advocates of all theories agree that the extreme limits of possibility for the correct date of the Crucifixion lie within the 7 years from A.D. 27 to A.D. 33 inclusive" (pg. 482). But this is shown to be false on page 211, End Note No. 2, in *The Good News of Messiah*. AD 34 can name Bede, Mercator Scaliger, and Newton among its advocates.

In the night of Dec., 29, just before dawn on the first day of the 11th month, the Almighty sent dreams that they should be fleeing away to safety on the new moon day.

Now that we know when the priestly rotations were based on Qumran in 42 BC, Seder Olam in AD 70, the inception of divisions in the second week of Tishri in 1012 BC to 587 BC, and their continuance in 515 BC, also as explained by Thomas Lewin in the 19th century, it is clear that Sept. 11, 3 BC is an impossible date.

Luke 1:36 states:

> And behold, your kinswoman Elisheva, even she has been conceiving a son in her old age. And this new moon, the sixth is, for her being called barren.

The Messenger is counting the duration of Elizabeth's pregnancy as reaching the sixth new moon. Luke 1:26 said it was the sixth month, that is the sixth new moon. But Luke 1:36 says it is the sixth new moon for her being called barren. Now the norm is for women to count days and weeks to their term, and not to count months in an inclusive fashion as we do with other chronological terms. When a woman counts months for herself, she is counting irregular months, like the irregular seven day periods counted to Shavuot. So the Messenger is counting for her, since she did not really know the day of her conception. He thus must mean at least 5 whole months and one day, either five irregular 29/30 day periods and at least one day, or 5 actual whole months, and one day. That is, supposing she conceived on the 15th day of a month, then on the 15th day of the next month would be the second month of the pregnancy, without regard to whether the old month ended at 29 or 30 days. It turns out that Elizabeth's irregular months exactly matched the actual months. But in no case may the text be interpreted such that a part month is counted as a month. Women don't do this, and the Messenger counting for this woman do not do this either. Women want to know when they can expect to deliver.

Now in 4 BC, Abijah finished on 11 August (18 Av). So the soonest a conception date could be is 19 Av. Thus a sixth irregular month would begin on 19 Tebeth (Jan 7, 3 BC), day 292 by the sun. So the balance of the year has 74 days. Now Sept. 11, 3 BC is day 174 in the new year, and 74 + 174 = 248, which is 18 days before a full term of 266 days. But Luke 2:6 says, "Then it happened that while they were there, the days were fulfilled for her to give birth." Accordingly, the correct date is Sept. 1, 2 BC, and the months as pregnant women count them matched the actual months. Messiah was conceived on the sixth, and born on the seventh.

The Year of Messiah's Resurrection

In order to determine the year of Messiah's resurrection, we have to know, using other evidence what the possible range of years are. A good deal of evidence has ambiguities, or what you can call a fuzzy factor. If you allow for all the choices and interpretations of a piece of evidence you will find that it is not totally useless. You just have to allow for all the legitimate interpretations and go find other evidence, which hopefully will confirm the most likely interpretation. If you collect enough evidence you will find the ambiguity of the whole picture decreasing until one day you have so much evidence that it only fits together exactly one way.*

Finding the year of Messiah's resurrection requires a lot of evidence. We have to know which day of the week he died on (Wednesday). We have to know which day of the Jewish month he died on (Nisan 14). We have to know that Jews sighted their new moons and that the month began at the first visible sighting. We have to know that past new moon dates can be calculated by computer. We have to know that the motion of the moon is regular and reliable. We have to know the correction factors for the earth's spin rate. We have to know that the Sabbath as we received it today from Jews and Sabbath keeping Christians is the same Sabbath as Yeshua kept. So this is a summary of things that need to be known.

For the most part the vast majority of Jewish scholarship and Christian scholarship is in agreement on these input factors. But like the wheel and axle they just let the broken cart lay at the side of the road, neither wanting to make the obvious repair, leaving the vast majority of people clueless as to how the pieces go together and making them skeptical that the pieces go together at all. This skeptical mass of people are spread across Christianity, Judaism, and cults of both. I have news for them: the pieces fit together exactly. The validity of some of the pieces have been questioned more than others, so it will be necessary to explain. And I start with when the Sabbath is.

The Sabbath begins after sunset on the sixth day of the week, and ends with dusk on the seventh. The skeptic will ask us how we know

* Originally it was not necessary to tread this path to put everything back together. The Evangelists plainly stated to their audiences that the resurrection was on the first of the Sabbaths, but through time, heretics figured out how to misinterpret the passages. These were promoted by Satan. They bequeathed to the generations that followed a web of lies and deceit which requires some effort to break out of.

which day of the week is the seventh. There are two or three very strong evidences for when the Sabbath is. The first is the collective witness of the Jews, who have been marking the Sabbath continuously for the 3643 years after God restored its observance following the Exodus (1632 B.C.). In the first century Yeshua kept the same Sabbath as his fellow Jews, and thus confirmed that they had maintained the correct time down to his first coming. Since then a million (or more) Jews have continuously noted when the Sabbath was, even if they did not all keep it. When a large body of people collectively witnesses when something occurs, and on a weekly basis mentally reviews, recalls, or renews that knowledge, then the knowledge cannot be forgotten. Evil would have to exterminate all Jews to erase the knowledge of the Sabbath; so far it has never succeeded in this goal.*

Likewise, since about A.D. 140 or so we have the collective witness of Christians neglecting the Sabbath by meeting on the first day of the week, and agreeing that the Sabbath of the Jews is the day before. This anti-witness also bears testimony to when the Sabbath really is. If these two evidences are not good enough for the skeptic, then it is unlikely that any amount of evidence will convince them of when the Sabbath is. It is more likely that they have fallen prey to the disease of perpetual doubt called skepticism, which is a way-point on the road to agnosticism.

Additionally, about 160 languages of the world contain evidence of when the Sabbath is because these languages name this day with derivatives of the number "seven" or "rest." The word "seven" or "rest" entered many of these languages through either Jewish influence or Christian missionaries who kept the Sabbath. However, in some of the languages, the introduction of the word "rest" or "seven," for the seventh day, entered the language long before Yeshua confirmed it in the first century, and may indeed go back before the Almighty confused the world's languages at the tower of Babel.

So it is reasonable to conclude that the Sabbath as we have it identified today is the same Sabbath that Yeshua observed, and which He as Creator rested on. Now let us discuss astronomical calculation. In ancient times the common people were able to predict that the next new moon would come in 29 or 30 days, and they would be able to

* Some argue the 7th day is another day. Such are the calendars of continental Europe, but ancient languages from all parts of the Middle East show which day is the seventh day. Some wish the Sabbath to go through Saturday night to dawn on Sunday. Some wish to exclude the night before the seventh day and make the Sabbath be only from dawn to dusk. See page 290 for reasons why these positions are not compelling.

tell you that the last new moon was 29 or 30 days before the current new moon. If you knew the week day the current new moon was on, then you could tell that the last new moon was on one of two weekdays simply by counting backwards. The reason for this is that the moon follows cyclical mathematical laws determined by mass and gravity. The common people were able to get a rough idea of those laws just by simple observation and counting days, which is the most basic form of astronomical calculation.

In ancient times, above the common people was a class of astronomers and priests, who were often astrologers. These people knew more of the mathematical laws that governed the moon and could predict eclipses and other astronomical events in advance, or they could use the same laws to tell you when something happened in the past. Compared to our modern knowledge this ability was primitive, and it was limited. For they did not understand how to compute the laws with enough precision to go many years back or forward.

All this changed with the discovery of a way to calculate the law of gravity using mass and distance by Sir Isaac Newton. Newton grasped the concept well enough and then invented a mathematics to calculate it with the help of a Frenchman. That math is now called calculus. Calculus enabled the astronomer to compensate for the regular but small variances in the laws of motion. It was now possible to calculate the positions of the moon thousands of years into the future and thousands of years into the past. The validity of the new astronomical calculation was quickly confirmed. It was able to reproduce by current observations and mathematical calculation alone what was recorded in historical records thousands of years before.

This science took a huge advance with the discovery of old Babylonian records from the period 604-539 B.C.* The Babylonian priests kept detailed observational records of planetary bodies and numerous eclipses, which could now be confirmed by astronomical calculation. It could also be determined which years those observations took place in, and which dates they occurred on, and indeed, astronomers can tell you which weekday most of the new moons would have been seen on.

* This has been extended back to Kandalanu (648 BC), and forward to AD 75. For example, we can figure out that Nisannu frequently began before the spring equinox during Kandalanu's reign using Saturn observations.

So, a modern astronomer makes current observations of the moon and earth. He even has a laser range finder on the moon that gives the exact rate of change in the earth's spin. You ask him to write a computer program that calculates the new moon and what weekday it was on back to 604 B.C. It does not matter whether the astronomical expert is Catholic, Protestant, Atheist, or Hindu. They can all tell you which weekday the lunar conjunction occurred on. And if you tell them you want to calculate for the sighted moon they can do that too.

As for which days Nisan 14 came on a Wednesday between A.D. 30 and A.D. 34, that work has already been done. Finegan's *Handbook of Biblical Chronology*[229] lists the dates with their corresponding weekdays:

Table 4: Weekdays of Nisan 14/15 in A.D. 30-34

A.D.	Nisan 14 fell on	Nisan 15 fell on
30	Friday, April 7	Saturday, April 8
31	Tuesday, March 27	Wednesday, March 28
32	Monday, April 14	Tuesday, April 15
33	Friday, April 3	Saturday, April 4
34	Wednesday, March 24	Thursday, March 25

Richard A. Parker and Waldo H. Dubberstein list the corresponding dates of the new moons.[230] The Roman weekday of the sighting of the moon corresponds to Nisan 14 also.[231]

---

[229] Revised Edition, page 363, 1998, Table 179.

[230] pg. 46, *Babylonian Chronology* 626 B.C. — A.D. 75. Parker and Dubberstein always give the day after the new moon is seen as the new moon day, "The dates as given are civil days, from midnight to midnight, although in actual practice the Babylonian day began in each case with the preceding sunset" (pg. 26). The calculations when run for the location of Jerusalem give the same results most of the time.

[231] The Babylonian calendar does not use the correct rule of the equinox. So in some cases Parker and Dubberstein list the month as Adar II. My use of Parker and Dubberstein is meant to confirm the new moon date—not to settle the dispute about how to intercalate the year.

Table 5: New Moon in A.D. 30-34 for Nisan 1

A.D.	Julian date	New Moon First Seen on:
30	March 25	(seen Friday, March 24)
31	March 14	(seen Tuesday, March 13)
32	April 1	(seen Monday, March 31)
33	March 21	(seen Friday, March 20)
34	March 11	(seen Wednesday, March 10)

Roger T. Beckwith, states, "In A. D. 34 . . . the 14th day of the lunar month next after the equinox would have been a Wednesday (March 24th)."[232] Another writer says, "In A.D. 34, Nisan 14 would have been on Wednesday, March 24, according to the computations of Humphreys and Waddington."[233]

Two famous men, one Jewish, and one Christian have said that the crucifixion was in A.D. 34. The Christian is Sir Isaac Newton,[234] and the Jew is Solomon Zeitlin. Zeitlin wrote articles for the *Journal of Biblical Literature* and the *Jewish Quarterly Review* in the first half of the 20th century.

How can we be certain of a date in the past? How can we be certain that A.D. 34 is a valid date? In ancient times era's were enumerated according to the years ruled by kings. Biblical records state the term of a king, prophet, or judge after the settlement of Israel (1592 B.C.). Before the Exodus, years were generally stated according to the age of a biblical figure. As long as there is a valid matching and synchronization (or succession) between records using an older era and that of the newer era, no years are lost. As long as the synchronization or succession between eras is valid, then any system can be extended forward or backward in terms of the other. All that is needed is one valid matching date.

For example our current A.D. system of dating was introduced in A.D. 525 by Dionysius Exiguus.[235] Dionysius' new system makes the

---

[232] "THE DATE OF THE CRUCIFIXION," pg. 289, *Calendar & Chronology, Jewish & Christian.*

[233] Duncan Steel, *MARKING TIME: THE EPIC QUEST TO INVENT THE PERFECT CALENDAR*, pg. 338.

[234] If the month was postponed in A.D. 34 by a Karaite method then Nisan 14 would be on a Thursday. Newton seems to have favored further Rabbinical "postponements" to achieve a Friday date in this year. Newton settled on A.D. 34 for other historical reasons that point to that year.

[235] A.D. 525 was synchronized by Dionysius in "the consulship of Probus Junior." See the consul list on page **443**, "Flavius Anicius Probus iunior."

year A.D. 532 in his new system follow year 247 of the Diocletian Era.[236] The Diocletian Era is in turn dated in terms of the Roman consuls between 509 B.C. and A.D. 541.[237] Dionysius also dated A.D. 525 in terms of the consular list. The complete consular lists can be found at: en.wikipedia.org/wiki/List_of_Roman_consuls and in this book.

Since there is a valid succession of consuls, the old system can be converted to the new without loss of any years or addition of any years that do not belong. Such conversions can be done with any ancient author that double dates at least one event using a newer system and an older system, or provides enough documentation to figure out the connection between the old and new system.

So when a date A.D. or B.C. is stated before A.D. 525, it has actually been converted from a system older than A.D. 525. However, there is no gain or loss of years since the makers of newer eras were careful to synchronize (or otherwise document) them with the older eras. This was necessary during the transition so that those still using the older era could "translate" between the two eras, the newer and the older.

A lot of people think that Dionysius Exiguus made a mistake which causes A.D. dates before 525 to be invalid. This is not the truth. While Dionysius set out to fix year 1 of the A.D. system according to the birth of Messiah, the actual synchronization of the A.D. system was made with the Diocletian Era and the consular list in the time of Dionysius. This fact ensures that older historical records were correctly stated in terms of the new A.D. system. So when the Roman Era (AUC[238]), or consular lists were translated into the A.D. system it was no different than if the consular lists, or AUC systems had been continued. All dates in those systems are just as valid as when stated in terms of A.D. or B.C. dates. Now if the original AUC or consular date

---

[236] See the appendix on page **443** showing A.D. 532 right after year 247 of the Diocletian Era. This is one of several points where the A.D./B.C. system is anchored to the Roman consular list.

[237] The consular lists were kept in multiple records and regularly updated with the new consuls for each year. And then they were widely used as the standard method of dating events by Roman historians. There are orders of magnitude more redundancy in the consular lists of Rome than the eponym lists of Assyria which are not trustworthy.

[238] *A.U.C.* = *ab urbe condita* = from founding of the city (of Rome).

was an error for a particular event, then its corresponding B.C./A.D. date would be in error for just that one event. But an error in a particular date does not invalidate the whole systems of A.U.C., consular dating, or B.C./A.D.

I will detail the birth of Yeshua more later, and show how it fits with his death and resurrection in A.D. 34. Here I will relate it to the common era, without at the moment proving the birth date. Yeshua was born Sept. 1, 2 B.C:

Figure 58: Dionysius Right 3/4 of the time

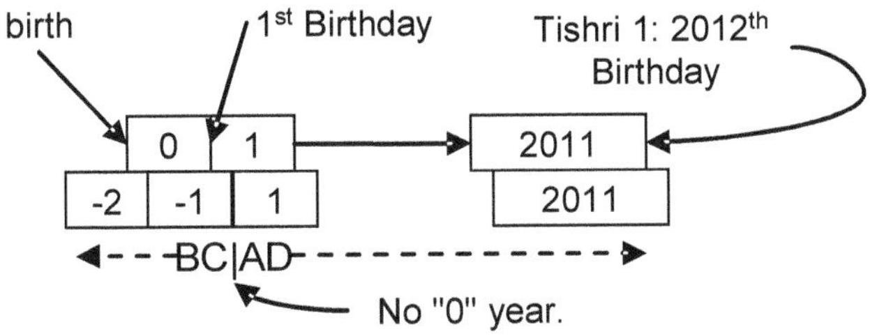

After accounting that Yeshua's first twelve months as a baby are counted in months, and that his first birthday is a year later, and considering that there is no zero year, it is clear that the common era gives the correct "age" of Yeshua from January 1 to Tishri 1 each year. Thus, Yeshua's age from his birth in Bethlehem is 2012 years since we have just passed Tishri 1, 2011. So Dionysius so called mistake is no mistake at all in terms of Messiah's age.

The common era system itself was anchored by Dionysius' and his successors such that A.U.C. 754[239] = A.D. 1. However, Messiah was born in A.U.C. 752. A new system of dating can be introduced at any time using an arbitrary sequence of numbers, and so long as the numbers increase sequentially by one each year, and so long as when the new system was started, it was accurately synchronized with

---

239 The Romans dated records with their consular lists. Suetonius (Augustus 1. 2. c. 100-104. s. 1. 1:303;) tells us that Augustus died "in the year in which the two Sextuses, Pompeius and Appuleius, were consuls, on the 19th of August, at the ninth hour of the day, in the seventy sixth year of his life, thirty five days before his birthday." This is matched to A.U.C. 767 and A.D. 14 in the Roman consular lists. The consular lists are complete for every year from A.D. 1 to A.D. 541. So the date of Dionysius' letter is A.D. 525 in the consulship of Anicius Probus iunior.

contemporary records, then there is no loss of data, and no loss or addition of years. All the older dates can be simply translated into the newer system. And all calculations done in the newer system will be just as valid as any done in the older. Dionyisius' system can be simply regarded as an arbitrary system, with only a close relation between its starting point and the birth of Messiah, and a more exact one with his stated age, for 8 or 9 months of every Roman year.

In the case of Roman consular lists, copies of these lists were kept by Romans, stating the two consuls and replacement consuls for any given year. The consular lists were numbered according to the year of Rome, but Roman historians normally stated dates by naming the two consuls.

Tiberius' Fifteenth year

The important date, for passion chronology, is the 15th year of Tiberius Caesar (Luke 3:1). Two Roman Historians tell us when Tiberius reign began. The first is Tacitus:

> Now at Rome, Consuls, Senators, and Roman Knights, were all rushing with emulation into bondage, and the higher the quality of each, the more false and forward the men; all careful so to frame their faces, as to reconcile false joy for the accession of Tiberius, with feigned sadness for the loss of Augustus: hence they intermingled fears with gladness, wailings with gratulations, and all with servile flattery. Sextus Pompeius and Sextus Apuleius, at that time Consuls, took first the oath of fidelity to Tiberius (*The Annals of Tacitus*, Book I, A.D. 14 and 15).[240]

The date indicated is A.D. 14. This is marked in the consular list on page **423**. Another Roman Historian, Dio Cassius confirms the dating:

> For in the following year, when Sextus Apuleius and Sextus Pompeius were consuls, Augustus set out for Campania, and after superintending the games at Neapolis, passed away shortly afterward

[240] Publius Cornelius Tacitus (A.D. 56 - A.D. 117) was a senator and historian of the Roman Empire. He wrote in Latin.

> at Nola. ... So Augustus fell sick and died. Thus on the nineteenth day of August, the day on which he had first become consul, he passed away, having lived seventy-five years, ten months, and twenty-six days (he had been born on the twenty-third of September), and having been sole ruler, from the time of his victory at Actium forty-four years lacking thirteen days.[241]

The date Augustus died was 19 August, AD 14. But Tiberius did not automatically become the official Emperor. In Rome they viewed things differently. The Senate had to elect Tiberius to be the head of state, and this they did on 18 September, AD 14. Before he was appointed, Quintus Haterius asked, "How long, Caesar, will you permit the state to lack a head?" (Tacitus Annals 1.13) The formalities of the old republic were still followed (cf. 1.7). So his first regnal year began Sept. 18, AD 14., and his 15th year spanned Sept. 18, AD 28 to Sept. 17, AD 29. But it may be rightly supposed that unofficially, Tiberius was *de facto* emperor upon the death of Augustus. But since everything in Rome was done according to official legality to maintain the appearance of the republic, Tiberius' reign began on Sept. 18. A proper Roman would do Tiberius the honor to saying Tiberius was Emperor because the Senate had conferred the power to him, and not because he had inherited it.

Some may still be skeptical of Tiberius' date, however, the scripture only refers to the reigns of foreign kings when the reign is accurately remembered by history. For example, the Scripture dates events in terms of the Neo-Babylonian Kings and Persian Kings. The reigns of these kings are anchored by astronomy[242] just as the Roman reigns are anchored by the consular lists. On the other hand, the Scripture never uses Assyrian reigns to date anything, or Egyptian dates, nor does it even use the Greek period dates. This is because Assyrian dates are wildly unreliable,[243] and

---

[241] Dio Cassius, Book LVI, 28-30. Lucius Cassius Dio Cocceianus (ca. A.D. 155-after A.D. 229) wrote 80 volumes of Roman History in Greek.

[242] The reign of Nebuchadnezzar is so anchored, and so also Artaxerxes I, and the latter is especially important for Daniel 9.

[243] The Assyrian eponym lists are missing some 52 years according to biblical chronology. This however does not stop some chronologers from contradicting the biblical synchronisms between Hezekiah and Hosea in favor of the faulty Assyrian numbers.

some Greek dates could be off by 1-2 years.[244] The Scripture is telling us by using Neo-Babylonian, Persian, and Roman dates, that these dates are accurately preserved. Or to put it another way, the Scripture does not use dates open to inaccuracy or question, and only uses foreign dates when absolutely necessary.

The date of Augustus' death and Tiberius accession is noted by two witnesses, by two Roman Historians. The third witness is that the Scripture condescended to use the foreign date "the 15th year of Tiberius." We may be assured that by using this date, the Scripture is also telling us that this date is reliable in Roman history. The Scripture is always concerned with exact accuracy in dating. Long before any other world history was written or concerned with chronology, the Scriptures were giving detailed and accurate records.

Now the supposed Friday Crucifixion and Sunday resurrection led to the confusion of Christian chronology, which, at first, required the crucifixion on a Friday in A.D. 30. In order to do this, the start of Tiberius' reign in A.D. 14 must be rejected for an earlier one in A.D. 11-12. So ecclesiastical chronologists, since the sixteenth century, when astronomical calculation became possible, propose a "co-regency" with Augustus. The reason for this is that the received catholic date for a Friday in A.D. 30 simply does not fit. Rather than fix the problem according to "three days and three nights" and "the first of the Sabbaths," they decided it was more expedient to break Roman chronology.

While Tiberius did share power with Augustus earlier than A.D. 14, he would not have the honor of having regnal years for those years. And no Roman historian mentions any, nor do monuments or coins agree:

> Augustus died the 19th of August, A.D. 14, and the "Anni Augusti†" which we have seen were computed from January the 1st, B.C. 27, ceased in the forty-first year,—the latest date of which we possess procuratorial coins struck during the reign of this emperor.
>
> The new coins issued under Tiberius (as far as at present known)

---

[244] This is due, in part, to various ways of counting the Seleucid Era. The scripture never uses this era, however.

†Triumvir from 43 BC, de-facto sole ruler from 27 BC.

bear dates from 1 to 18 (L. A to L. IH), *i.e.* from A.D. 14-15 to A.D. 31-32.

It is almost certain that the regnal years of Tiberius were computed from the 19th of August (xiv. *Kal. Sept.*);* A.D. 14, after the death of Augustus, and his tribunitian years from June 27th (v. *Kal. Jul.*), A.D. 4, the year of his adoption. His second year would therefore commence on the 19th of August, A.D. 15, and Valerius Gratus, as we have seen, was sent by Tiberius as procurator in A.D. 15.

The Rev. H. Browne (Kitto's "Cyc. of Bibl. Lit." ed. Alexander, *s.v.* Chronology, vol. i. p. 515) … states, "St. Luke's dated 'fifteenth of Tiberius' (iii. 1) [as] interpreted by the constant rule of the Imperial annals (and also of the Canon), denotes the year beginning August, A.D. 28, and ending in the same month of A.D. 29.

The hypothesis of a dating of the years of Tiberius from an epoch earlier by three years than the death of Augustus, which from the sixteenth century downward, has found favor with many learned men, <u>will not bear examination</u>; it is unknown to the early ecclesiastical writers, and nowhere in the histories, on monuments, or coins, is a trace of any such epoch of Tiberius to be met with."[245]

Further, whenever there is a question of counting co-regency years, the Scripture is careful to document it as in 2 Kings 8:16 and by cross dating with the Northern Kingdom. Other claims of "co-regency" are *ad hoc* arguments to give those who build incorrect chronologies the flexibility to avoid contradicting their own erring assumptions. Normally, when a co-regency occurs, regnal years are not assigned to the co-regent, and the first year of reign means the first year of the sole reign after the previous ruler dies. There are cases of confusion, but the Scripture never depends on them.

If Tiberius' association with Augustus in the administration of the provinces in A.D. 12 is supposed to be a co-regency, the usual method of reckoning things is not to count years for the co-regent until the

---

[245] Page 176-177, *International numismata orientalia*, Vol. 2, William Marsden; "Coins Of The Jews". Frederic W. Madden, M.R.A.S. 1881. Underlined emphasis mine.

*So he says, but this can only be *de facto* power, and not official. The correct date is 18 September.

first year of sole rule. This is what the coins show. So to say that Luke 3:1 was reckoned from A.D. 12 or earlier, so as to allow for an A.D. 30 Friday crucifixion, is out of the question, and on the same level of speculation as simply saying that Luke's number is wrong.

Roman historians, in fact, all total up the number of years of Tiberius close to the actual figure: 22 years 6 months 26 days,[246] and end it in A.D. 37. These years fit neatly from A.D. 14 to A.D. 37. And never before A.D. 14 is Tiberius Emperor.

> One would suppose that here no door was open to controversy, and yet some chronologers … have endeavored to evade the express testimony of Luke as to the fifteenth year of Tiberius, by surmising that the reign of Tiberius was computed by him not in the ordinary mode from 19th Aug.* A.D. 14, the death of Augustus, but from some point of time two years earlier, in A.D. 12; and they rely upon certain passages in Tacitus, Suetonius, and Vell. Paterculus, but which, when taken together, show only that in A.D. 12 large powers were conferred on Tiberius, but not that he was then emperor jointly with Augustus, or that his reign was ever supposed to commence from that period. Other chronologers, as Burton, admit that the fifteenth year of Tiberius must begin in [be reckoned from] A.D. 14, but then they maintain that instead of being computed from 19th Aug.* of that year, it must be referred back to 1st January of the same year; for as the Romans reckoned their year from one first of January to another, the whole year within these limits was, according to Burton and his followers, considered the fifteenth year of Tiberius.[247]
>
> These hypothesis are open to one overwhelming objection, viz. that the reign of Tiberius, as beginning from 19th Aug.* A.D. 14, was as well-known a date in the time of Luke as the reign of Queen Victoria

---

[246] Theoph. Ant. 22 years; Dio Cassius 22 yr. 7m. 7d; Cassiodorus 23 yr. Pascal Chronicle: 22 yr. This is no more than rounding off 22 years and a fraction, or rounding up to 23, or the historian making the best estimate as he can of 22 years and the fractional year. See page 2, *Fasti Romani*, Vol. II, H.F. Clinton, 1850.

[247] For the 15th year, the difference is between the consular year Jan 1, A.D. 28 to Dec 31, A.D. 28, and the 15th factual year of Tiberius' reign (Aug 19, A.D. 28 to Aug 18, A.D. 29. This is some eight months earlier, but such a supposition is devoid of any proof.

*18 Sept.

in our own day [20 June 1837], and that no single case has ever been or can be produced in which the years of Tiberius were reckoned in any other manner.

Tacitus opens the fourth book of his Annals with these words, 'C. Asinius and C. Antistius being consuls, it was the *ninth* year of Tiberius;'[248] that is, the consulship of Asinius Pollio and Antistius Vetus, reckoned from 1st Jan. A.D. 23, fell in the ninth year of Tiberius up to 19th Aug. A.D. 23, when the tenth year would commence. Dion Cassius again reckons in the same way, for in speaking of the year A.D. 24 he mentions, that in the course of it (viz. on 19th Aug.) 'ten years of the reign of Tiberius expired;'[249] and again, he places the consulship of Licius Vitellius and Fabius Persicus on 1st Jan. A.D. 34, in the twentieth year of Tiberius.[250] So Philo computes the reign of Tiberius in round numbers at twenty-three years; and as Tiberius died in A.D. 37, Philo, of course, dated the commencement of the reign from 19th Aug. A.D. 14.[251] ... And again, Josephus reckons the reign of Tiberius at 22 years, 5 months, and 3 days;[252] or , as in another place, at 22 years, 6 months, and 3 days;[253] and as the death of Tiberius occurred on 16th March A.D. 37, Josephus refers the commencement of the reign to 19th Aug. A.D. 14.

There are two coins of Antioch, however, which have been thought to countenance the notion that Tiberius began to reign in A.D. 12. One of them has the head of Tiberius, with the inscription Καισαρ Σεβαστος, ΓΜ, i.e. in the 43rd year of the Actian era, commencing from 2nd Sept. B.C. 31, and therefore struck in A.D. 13-14;[254] and as the head of Tiberius is found on these coins with the title of *Augustus*, it

---

[248] C. Asinio, C. Antistio consulibus nonus Tiberius annus erat. Tac. Ann. iv. 1.

[249] Διελθοιτων δε των δεκα ετων της αρχης αυτου. Dion, lvii. 24; and so Dion, lviii. 24.

[250] Dion, lviii. 24. See page **424** to locate these two consuls in the list.

[251] τρία πρὸς τοῖς εἴκοσιν ἔτη γῆς καὶ θαλάσσης ἀναψάμενον τὸ κράτος. Philo, Legatio ad Gaium 1:141.

[252] Jos. Ant. 18:224.

[253] Jos. War 2:180.

[254] Eckhel, iii. 276.

has hence been argued that he was emperor as early as A.D. 12. The genuineness of these coins has been questioned by Eckhel, iii. 277. But even admitting them to be free from suspicion, they prove only that Tiberius had then been honored with the title of Augustus, not that he had then begun to reign as emperor. Besides, there are other undoubted coins of Antioch which show conclusively that the Antiochians (and Luke himself was a native, or at least an inhabitant, of that city) dated the reign of Tiberius not from A.D. 12, but from the death of Augustus in A.D. 14. Thus we have one coin of Antioch with the head of Tiberius and the letter A, i.e. the first year of his reign, and coupled with the Actian year EM, or 45, and therefore equivalent to A.D. 14-15. Again, there are other coins with the head of Tiberius, and the letter Γ, i.e. that is, in the third year of his reign, and coupled with the Actian year ZM, or 47, and therefore equivalent to A.D. 16-17.[255], [256]

Why were the Roman dates "revised" by Christian chronologists? They were revised because the Church of Rome advocated a Friday date in A.D. 30. However, this date is contradictory to the normal Roman chronology when put together with the required length of Messiah's ministry. The Church started out with the wrong assumptions. First they assumed that Messiah's ministry was only one year, then finding otherwise, revised Tiberius' reign backward according to a Friday in A.D. 30. This then was "corrected" to A.D. 33. But the correction too was mistaken as it did not account for the true length of Messiah's ministry, and missed it due to the commitment to Friday-Sunday.

For now, I am simply pointing out that all of the "mistakes" made by the Church have motives behind them that find their origin in either ignorance of Torah or rebellion against it. And when history contradicts their "mistakes," things are revised in another mistaken direction due to the desire to avoid the correct conclusion.

One of these mistakes I should repeat here is the dating of Messiah's birth before 4 B.C., and the dating of Herod's demise in that

---

[255] Eckhel, iii. 278.

[256] Page liii-lv. *Fasti Sacri or A Key to the Chronology Of The New Testament*, Thomas Lewin, Esq., 1865.

year. This came about due to the Church commitment to the Friday date in A.D. 30. The Church was trying to "fix" a problem, and that was that Luke tells us that Yeshua was "thirty years"† old in the 15th year of Tiberius. If the A.D. 30 date is to be defended, then the ministry of Yeshua must begin around A.D. 25-27. But this implies a 15th year of Tiberius in A.D. 26/27 instead of the correct A.D. 28/29. This in turn forces the birth year to just before 4 B.C. It is important to know that this chain of reasoning occurred because of the prior commitment to a Friday crucifixion date in A.D. 30.

But now, it has been discovered that Herod did not die in 4 B.C. He died in 1 B.C! Thus, we have to unwind all the damage caused by the Friday crucifixion commitment in A.D. 30. David W. Beyer explains what went wrong:[257]

> A central argument offered by scholars supporting 4 B.C. as the year of Herod's death focuses on the dating of his son Philip's reign. Modern editions of Josephus' *Antiquities of the Jews* unanimously state that Philip died in the twentieth year of Tiberius, that is, in A.D. 34, after ruling thirty-seven years. Therefore: A.D. 34 - 37 years = 4 B.C.
>
> The logic seems concise and irrefutable. Nevertheless, it is flawed by a contaminated evidentiary source....

What Beyer is referring to here is that when the hand copied manuscripts of Josephus were first type set to be printed a mistake was made in *Ant.* 18:106.* The word "second" was dropped out of the text. Herod Philip died in the "twenty-second year of Tiberius" and not in the "twentieth." This means that the 37th year numismatic evidence implies the reign beginning in B.C. 1 for Herod's son, and thus the death of Herod the Great in that year.

He says:

> My visits to the British Library in April 1983 uncovered evidence that substantiates Filmer's thesis. Out of the forty-six early editions of Josephus' *Antiquities* published before 1700 that were examined, twenty seven demonstrate the uncommon "twenty-second year of

[257] "Josephus Reexamined: Unraveling the Twenty-Second Year of Tiberius," *Chronos Kairos Christos II*, Ray Summers.

* Or rather later MSS with the error in it were used.

† "almost 30 years."

> Tiberius." Of these twenty-seven texts, all but three were published prior to 1544, some dating back to the twelfth and thirteenth centuries. Of greatest importance, however, is the fact that, in the British Library, not a single edition published prior to 1544 was uncovered bearing the "twentieth year of Tiberius." In 1994 I conducted further research in the Library of Congress. Their collection offered further confirmation of these original findings. Five more editions supported the "twenty-second year." Among the others, none prior to 1544 recorded the "twentieth year."
>
> Timothy Barnes's articulate response to W. E. Filmer's thesis is hereby challenged—not by another theory—but instead by thirty-two editions of Josephus' *Antiquities* still extant in the British Library and the Library of Congress. The work of Filmer is vindicated—Herod did die in 1 B.C....

And since Herod died in 1 B.C. the eclipse mentioned in Ant. 17:167 was the total lunar eclipse of Jan 9/10, 1 B.C., and not the partial magnitude 0.37 eclipse of March 4 B.C. The 15th of Tiberius immediately precedes Messiah's thirtieth. Luke 3:1 and 3:23 together require the birth of Messiah in 2 B.C., and other factors put it on Sept. 1 (cf. Rev. 12:1-3). Further, the War of Varus, and many other factors make sense this way, both historical and archaeological. The 29th year of Yeshua and 15th of Tiberius span the fall of A.D. 28 to the fall of A.D. 29., which confirms that a Friday in A.D. 30 is out of the question for the crucifixion, and Messiah's 30th year commences with the fall of A.D. 29.[258]

There are other time notes relating to the year, but none so important as the one's already mentioned. The procuratorship of Pontius Pilate does not narrow down the range any more than other factors under consideration. So I give only a brief account. The dates for Pontius Pilate being in office are derived from old records and these are translated into A.D. dates: A.D. 26-36. It has already been seen that Luke dates the beginning of John's ministry to the 15th year of

[258] Also weighing in against A.D. 30-31 is that this was prior to the fall of Aelius Seianus (Sejanus), co-consul with Tiberius in A.D. 31 till May (see consular list, page **424**). Pilate's weakness viz. a viz. the Jewish authorities is best explained in the wake of Sejanus' fall. See *A.D. 33: The Year That Changed the World*, Colin Duriez.

Tiberius Caesar (Luke 3:1), which we know from Roman records was fall A.D. 28 to fall A.D. 29. Pilate's rule, thus, only restricts the upper bound to A.D. 36. The start date for his rule is superseded by Tiberius' 15th year as a restricting factor.

Forty Six Years Be'eth Built This Temple

In John 2:20 the Jewish authorities say, "forty and six years be'eth built this sanctuary," which is to say that it was standing completed for 46 years. I have translated the aorist passive "be'eth built" (οἰκοδομήθη). It refers to the inner timple (ναὸς) being in a state of completion.

Figure 59: John 2:20, "Forty and Six Years"

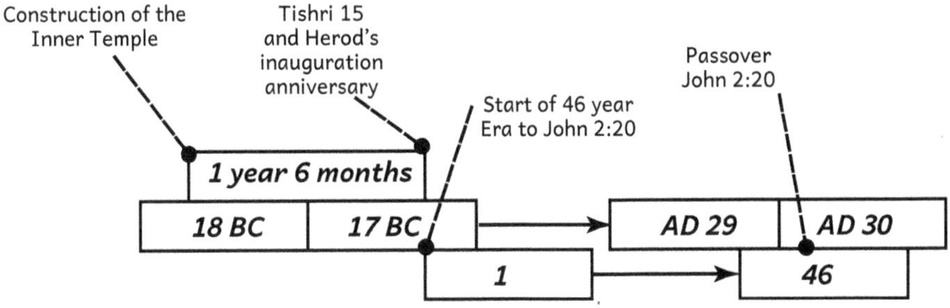

Construction of the Inner Temple
Tishri 15 and Herod's inauguration anniversary
Start of 46 year Era to John 2:20
Passover John 2:20
1 year 6 months
18 BC
17 BC
AD 29
AD 30
1
46

Josephus tells us that Herod's proposal to rebuild the temple was made in his 18th year (*Ant.* 15:380) and the 15th year (*War* 1:401; cf. *Ant.* 15:420). Deciphering this is complicated by the fact that Herod had three different reckonings to his reign in the sources, one factual by Nicolaus of Damascus, one Roman, and one Judean by the priestly aristocracy, and further, Josephus confused the sources' dates and arranged his narrative incorrectly conflating the two beginning points, a beginning point for building the temple as a whole including the outer structures, and the beginning date for construction of the inner temple. (See *The Scroll of Biblical Chronology and Ancient Near Eastern History*, Vol. II for details.) With respect to the 8 years it took to build the whole complex, the Roman 18th year was the same as the factual 15th year for beginning this work. The factual 15th year was 24.t/23.t BC. The eight years are counted from the spring epoch: the part year 24.t/23.n BC is the first, and 18.n/17.n is the 7th, and the part year 17.n/17.t BC is the 8th. None propose that Messiah's ministry began any later than AD 30 (all other proposals being earlier), and the 8th year cannot be made any earlier than 17.n/17.t BC. Neither can Herod's factual reign be put earlier, it being clear that the 7th year was current for the same year as Caesar's victory at Actium in 31 BC. It just so happens that the exact number of years between 17.t BC and AD 30.t is 46.

A further confirmation comes from Josephus:

Josephus reports, "for at the same time with [the] celebration for [completing] the work about the temple, fell also the day of the king's inauguration, which they kept by custom as a festival, and it now coincided with the other; which coincidence of them both made the festival most illustrious (Jos. Ant. 15:421-423)."

Edward Greswell (*Dissertations upon a Harmony of the Gospels*, vol. 1, 1830, page 210) assures us that Herod's crowning day in Rome was certainly after September 25th in 40 BC, but not more than a week later, thus from Sept 25 to Sept 30. And in 17 BC the 15th of Tishri fell upon September 30th! In 18 BC it was Oct 4, and this does not allow for the 8 years from Herod's 15th year. In 16 BC, the feast was on Sept 20th, which is too early for Herod's inaguration date, and makes the 46th year commence in AD 30.t. No one proposes to begin Messiah's public ministry as late as Passover in AD 31. The 46th year demonstrates that Messiah's public ministry began in AD 30 at the Passover.

The Length of Messiah's Ministry

I have before cited Sir Isaac Newton's remark about the impossibility of the one and two year ministry lengths. This leaves the three year ministry, bounded by four Passovers, and the four year ministry, bounded by five Passovers to be considered. Newton and others of his time reasoned that five Passovers were required. This was revised to four Passovers, and a three year ministry when more accurate astronomical calculations, and pre-rabbinic intercalation, showed that A.D. 34 could not produce a Friday date. This does not mean however, that the arguments supporting five Passovers suddenly became invalid. It simply means that no one wanted to consider them anymore due to the fact that the required Friday crucifixion could not

[259] Also those who would argue for A.D. 29 are faced with the prospect of making Yeshua's ministry too short, or running afoul of Daniel 9.

[260] Finegan, *Handbook of Biblical Chronology*, rev. ed. pg. 349, §595.

be worked out with five Passovers.

The first Passover is pretty obvious. It is mentioned in John 2:13 and corresponds to A.D. 30. So also the third in John 6:4, and the fifth during which Messiah died. It remains to be shown then where the second and fourth Passovers fall. The fourth passover is the one that we really need to prove, but first the proof of the second one as given by three year ministry advocates:

> There needs to be an additional year of his ministry between the Passovers of John 2:13 and 6:4. The Passover of 6:4 took place around the time Jesus fed the five thousand, the only miracle mentioned in all four Gospels. Previous to this feeding miracle the Synoptic Gospels mention the disciples plucking grain in Galilee (Mat. 12:1; Mk 2:23; Luke 6:1), and this must have taken place after the Passover of John 2:13. The reason for this is that the Passover of John 2:13 occurred shortly after Jesus' baptism and the locale of his ministry was in Judea, whereas the plucking of the grain occurred a considerable time after Jesus' baptism and the locale of his ministry was in Galilee. Therefore, the plucking of the grain would fit well around the Passover between the Passovers recorded in John 2:13 and 6:4.
>
> John provides two other indications of time that would indicate an additional year between these two Passovers. First, after the Passover of John 2:13 Jesus ministered in Judea and then went to Samaria. There he mentioned that there were four months until harvest (John 4:35), which would mean the following January/February.[261] While some would read this as a proverbial statement, it seems best to take this as a literal chronological reference.[262] The second time-note is in John 5:1 where there is

[261] I should point out that four months ended in March. In A.D. 31, the date to begin the harvest was March 29th (Nisan 16). There was no Adar II this year, so counting exclusively backward: Adar, Shebat, Tebeth, Kislev are the four months. Kislev began on Nov. 16, A.D. 30. Supposing that Yeshua went to the feast of Hanukah that year, we may place his return to Galilee via Samaria at the end of the month, and indeed he may be counting inclusively, so that it was possibly as late as January when he made the statement.

[262] I concur. Why would anyone invent such a proverb? Why not some other number of months and then the harvest as a proverb? No one planted in November to January, why would there be such an exclusive proverb applied at a random time of year? An agricultural community would then invent a proverb that met the actual case according to the actual countdown of months, and apply the proverb that actually fits. Thus pleading that "four

mention of another feast. Although not specified, some interpreters understand it to be another Passover, although it is more likely to refer to the Feast of Tabernacles. [Either way, there has to be a Passover between the midwinter statement and Tabernacles]. These two times notes would substantiate that there was another passover between those of John 2:13 and 6:4.[263]

Further, I note that the feast of John 5:1 was one of the three pilgrim feasts. For it says Yeshua "went up" (John 5:1). From midwinter 30/31 A.D. onward, the first pilgrim feast is Passover, then Shavuot, and then Sukkot (Tabernacles). So no matter how it is computed, an extra Passover is required. The John 5:1 feast may be Tabernacles.* However, Luke 6:1-5 (cf. Matthew 12:1-8; Mark 2:23) directly refers to Passover week, as explained earlier in this book. The "second first Sabbath" is the first of the Sabbaths falling after the first Sabbath of the feast of unleavened bread. It is the weekly Sabbath after Nisan 15.

So the above is the second Passover in A.D. 31. The third Passover is mentioned in John 6:4, and this occurred in A.D. 32. Now to the proof of the fourth Passover, which is the Passover of A.D. 33. I will quote from Thomas Lewin, *Fasti Sacri*. Thomas has the sequence and number of Passovers correct, except that he is early by one year in order to match a Friday date in A.D. 33. I thus correct his year dates in [ ][264] as it has already been amply shown that the sequence of Passovers began in A.D. 30:

> The duration of the ministry may be collected from the number of successive Passovers. The *first* was...A.D. [30], and is mentioned in John, ii. 13, and was *before* John the Baptist was cast into prison, John, iii. 24. The *second*, A.D. [31], was that which a little preceded the incident recorded by the three first Gospels, when Our Lord passed through the corn-fields on the δευτεροπρῶτον σάββατον ["second-first Sabbath"], Luke, VI.1; Matt. xii. 1; Mark, ii. 23; for this must have been soon after some Passover when the harvest began, and was *after* John the Baptist was cast into prison. Matt. iv.

---

months" is a proverb not related to the actual time is simply a special pleading for those who want to avoid putting the woman at the well episode in midwinter, to be followed by a Passover.

[263] *Dictionary of Jesus and the Gospels*, Joel B. Green, pg. 119.

[264] Lewin's dates were one less than that in the [ ]'s.

* It now turns out that this was Purim in AD 32. See Vol. I and II, SBC.

12. Mark, i.14. A *third* A.D. [32], occurred when the corban, or Temple-tax, was demanded of Our Lord at Capernaum, Matt. xvii. 24: for the corban, or Temple-tax, was usually demanded at the Passover. And the *fifth*, A.D. [34], was the Passover of the Crucifixion.[265]

Lewin expands on page xlvi of the same work:

A *fourth* Passover is attended with more difficulty, but still can be distinctly proved. In that first place, a Passover seems to be implied by the call made upon our Lord at Capernaum to pay the half siclus or didrachm, the tribute-money or Temple rate due to the Temple exchequer, called the corban;[266] for, on the authority of the Mishnah, the tribute was collected on 15th Adar, i.e. a little before the Passover;[267] and if a Passover can be assumed at this time, it was certainly not the Passover when Jesus went up to Jerusalem from Capernaum, or the Passover when Jesus passed through the cornfields. The only question is, whether it could have been the Passover which was at hand when the 5,000 were fed or the Passover of the Crucifixion, or whether in fact it was some intermediate Passover. It could not have been the Passover at the feeding of the 5,000, for at the time of that miracle the Passover was nigh, ἐγγὺς,[268] i.e. only a few days off. But between this miracle and the payment of the tribute-money, our Lord visited the borders of Tyre and Sidon, and Caesarea Philippi, which He could not have done before the actual arrival of the Passover, if nigh at hand when the miracle was wrought. Neither could the tribute-money have been demanded on the 15th of Adar, before the Passover of the Crucifixion, for in that case there would not remain sufficient time for the long journey from Galilee to Jerusalem, related as a subsequent event by Luke ix. 51—xix. 28.

However, we cannot assume with certainty that the tribute was in fact demanded and paid by our Lord on 15th Adar. No doubt as the Passover was the first feast of the sacred year, the tribute properly

---

[265] *Fasti Sacri; or A key to the chronology of the New Testament*, Thomas Lewin, pg. 182-183.
[266] Matt. xviii. 24.
[267] XV Adar ubique sederunt nummularii extra Hierosolymam, et pridie a quovis semisiclum expetierunt, nec tamen adegerunt, qui tunc nondum obtulerat. A die xxv vero, cum in sancta urbe sedissent, tamdiu quemvis urgebant donec tradidisset, et si longas moras nexisset nec dedisset in pignus, vel vesto retenta oppignerabant. Tractat. Talmud. Schekalim.
[268] John vi. 4.

became due, as we have seen from the Mishnah, just before that feast. But there was constantly large arrears, arising from the absence of some ratepayers and the inability of others, and in consequence the tax was gathered from the defaulters as opportunity offered, and particularly a little before the Pentecost, and again a little before the Tabernacles,[269] at which times these arrears called *sicli veteres* could be conveniently carried up by the pilgrims to the Temple. Still here, on the hypothesis that the corban was occasionally collected previously to the Feasts of Pentecost and Tabernacles, as well as before the Passover, the very circumstance that our Lord paid the tribute at all leads to the presumption that a year had intervened between the Passover when the 5,000 were fed and the Passover of the Crucifixion; for as our Lord had been at Capernaum just before the miracle of the 5,000, and was again there just after it, we must conclude that He had long ago paid the tribute for that year on one of those occasions. Neither on the other hand could the tribute now demanded have been that for the Passover of the Crucifixion, as our Lord must have quitted Capernaum, and commenced the journey recorded by Luke ix. 51 long *before* 15th Adar, i.e. long before the tribute for the year of the Crucifixion had even become due.

If the Temple tax then was demanded at the usual time, i.e. a little before a Passover, it is clear that such Passover could not have been the first, second, or third Passover of our Lord's ministry, nor the Passover of the Crucifixion, and must therefore have been some other Passover not particularly mentioned by the Evangelists. And even supposing that the tax was not demanded before a Passover at all, it would still appear highly probable from the foregoing remarks, that a fourth Passover, omitted by the Evangelists, just have occurred.

We shall now proceed to show, from a careful analysis of the long journey recorded by Luke, from ix. 51 to xix. 28, that in fact a fourth Passover did intervene between the Passover when the 5,000 were fed and the Passover of the Crucifixion, so that the Passovers

[269] Ter in anno curant de conclavi—in spatio semestri (fifteen days) ante Pascha—in spatio semestri ante Pentecosten—et in spatio semestri ante Scenopegiam. Mishna ii. 184, 3; which Maimonides interprets thus: — Tempore Festi Paschatis publicabatur adducendam oblationem priman de loco propinquiori; et illi, qui remotiores erant adducerent tempore Pentecostis; et illi, qui remotissimi errant, adducerent tempore Festi Tabernaculorum. See 2 Gresw, Diss., 342.

during our Lord's ministry were, in all, five in number. The details of this journey are as follows: —

It was in the neighbourhood of Caesarea Philippi that our Lord first openly announced to His disciples that He was the Messiah, and as such that He must be betrayed and put to death, and on the third day rise again, Matt. xvii. 22; Mark viii. 31; Luke ix. 22. Thus at the very outset, before the journey begins, an impression is created that our Lord from this forewarning was about to suffer shortly. Eight days after this was the Transfiguration, when Moses and Elias were seen conversing on the subject of His approaching death, τὴν ἔξοδον αὐτοῦ, ἣν ἤμελλεν πληροῦν ἐν Ἰερουσαλήμ, ["the glory of Him, which was he was about to fulfill in Jerusalem"], Luke ix. 31; and as Jesus and His three disciples were descending from the mountain, our Lord in explaining [a type of] Elias to be John Baptist again referred to His passion, οὕτως καὶ ὁ υἱὸς τοῦ ἀνθρώπου μέλλει πάσχειν,["so also the Son of man is about to suffer"] Matt. xvii. 12. What could be the meaning of these repeated warnings, but to prepare the minds of His disciples for the scene at Jerusalem at His next visit there.

Jesus then passed passed through Galilee to Capernaum, but the journey was a private one, and why? Mark tells us that it was for the purpose of instructing His disciples by the way, on the subject of His betrayal and death at Jerusalem, Mark ix. 31.

On arriving at Capernaum, the corban, or Temple tax of a half siclus or didrachm a head, was demanded of Him, Matt. xviii. 24.[270]

I interrupt Lewin here to provide more information on the Temple dues, as his footnotes are in Latin:

---

[270] Since this indicates that the *fourth* Passover was but a few weeks away, or even already past, the question is how Yeshua and his disciples were justified in staying away. The answer is that Yeshua was already under the threat of death, and his disciples under threat of persecution from Pilate, and that since it was not his time yet, the higher law for preservation of life superseded that of the command to bring the passover lamb at the appointed time.

A warning was given on the first day of Adar (around the month of March) that the half- *shekel* was due (*Mishnah Shekalim* 1:1). On the 15th of the month, the tables were set up in the provinces in order to collect the tax. One might assume, since Capernaum was a major Jewish center in Galilee that one of the tables was in that city. By the 25th of Adar, the tables were set up in the Temple (*Mishnah Shekalim* 1:3). If one chose to pay the tax in the Temple, there were 13 *shofar*-chests in the Temple court which were used to collect different offerings (*Mishnah Shekalim* 6:5). One was inscribed "New *Shekel* dues: which was for that year. Another was inscribed "Old [*shekel* dues]" in order to collect the tax from the previous year if it had not been paid.

Every Jewish male, 20 years old and up, voluntarily paid this tax once a year. He was to pay the tax either in his province or in the Temple in Jerusalem (*Mishnah Shekalim* 1:3). The tax was always paid in the Tyrian coinage (*Mishnah Bekhoroth* 8:7; *Babylonian Talmud Kiddushim* 11b). These coins average 14.2 grams in weight and were minted with near pure silver.

Leo Kadman describes an important discovery relating to these Tyrian shekels. He reports: "In the spring of 1960, a hoard of about 4,500 ancient coins was discovered near Isfiya on Mount Carmel; 3,400 of the coins were Tyrian Shekels, about 1,000 Half-shekels, and 160 Roman Dinarii of Augustus. The Shekels and Half-shekels are dated from 40 B.C.E. to 52/53 C.E. … the bulk of them from 20-53 C.E. … In the middle of the first century C.E., there was only one purpose for which the exclusive use of Tyrian Shekels was prescribed: the Temple-Dues of half a Shekel, which every male Jew of 20 years of age and above had to pay yearly to the Temple in Jerusalem. … The disproportion between the 3,400 Shekels and the 1,000 Half-Shekels is to be understood from the prescription of the Mishnah that each payment of a Half-Shekel for one person was liable to an agio of 4-8%, while the payment of a Full-Shekel for two persons was exempt from the agio. … The 160 Dinarii exactly represents the agio of 8% on the 1,000 Half-Shekel found in the hoard (1962:9, 10).

> This hoard of coins was probably from a community of 30,000 Jews living in Phoenicia. The coins were most likely hidden on Mount Carmel when the caravans realized they could not make it to Jerusalem in May AD 67, because the Romans controlled the road from Megiddo to Jerusalem (Kadman 1962:11).[271]

Now Yeshua paid His and Peter's half-shekel tax with one coin, which is to say that neither of them paid the exchange rate called the *agio* above charged of those individuals that paid a half shekel. But before this was the Transfiguration (Matthew 17:1-23), which as shown, was on a Sabbath, and this likely March 14, A.D. 33. So the temple-tax collectors showed up sometime in the next week of Adar 24 when they had got back from the mountain.

Continuing with Lewin:

> Our Lord then bade adieu to Capernaum and set out for Jerusalem; but the words of Luke are remarkable: Ἐγένετο δὲ ἐν τῷ συμπληροῦσθαι τὰς ἡμέρας τῆς ἀναλήμψεως αὐτοῦ καὶ αὐτὸς τὸ πρόσωπον ἐστήρισεν τοῦ πορεύεσθαι εἰς Ἰερουσαλήμ. ["And it happened in the completing of the days of His ascension, that He set His face to go up to Jerusalem."], Luke ix. 51. After all the distortions to which this passage has been subjected in the hands of commentators and harmonists, there cannot be a shadow of a doubt that the natural meaning is the true one, viz. that, when the days of our Lord's assumption were accomplishing, He set His face resolutely to go to Jerusalem. The words ἀναλήμψεως [ascension] and συμπληροῦσθαι [completing] must be interpreted from the use of them by the same writer. Thus in the Acts we have ἄχρι ἧς ἡμέρας ... ἀνελήμφθη. (i. 2) ["until which day ... he was ascended"], and ἐν τῷ συμπληροῦσθαι τὴν ἡμέραν τῆς Πεντηκοστῆς (ii. 1) ["at the completion of the fiftieth day"]. Luke then tells us in the plainest terms, that Jesus was now going up to Jerusalem to His death; in other words, that this was His last journey.

Lewin does not do complete justice to Luke 9:51. "The days of his ascension" (τὰς ἡμέρας τῆς ἀναλήμψεως αὐτοῦ) refer to

[271] Gordon Franz, "Does Your Teacher Not Pay the [Temple] Tax? (Mt 17:24-27)."

the whole time period between Passover and Shavuot, so that Luke is saying that Yeshua at that time set his face to Jerusalem one year before those final days of ascension. Luke's literary use of the phrase suggests, (1) ascending to Jerusalem, (2) ascending to die on the cross, (3) ascending by resurrection, and (4) ascending back to heaven some forty days after his resurrection. So "days of his ascension" can properly refer to this time period as a technical term of the Nazarenes. Therefore, Luke is dating this passage after the temple tax was collected sometime between Passover and Pentecost A.D. 33.

> On entering a Samaritan village by the way, Jesus was repulsed by the inhabitants, and then changed His route, and appointed seventy disciples to make ready before Him in the new line. The seventy went two and two, and therefore to thirty-five different places. It is not said whether they all started together while our Lord waited for their return, or whether they were dispatched from time to time and returned to Jesus, or were overtaken by Him, according to circumstances. In the first case a long interval would elapse before our Lord could resume His progress; but even on the latter supposition it is evident that our Lord contemplated teaching Himself in thirty-five different localities between the appointment of the seventy and His arrival at Jerusalem. If we allow only a day's sojourn at each place, we should thus have thirty-five days, but which of course would fall very far short of the time actually consumed including the delays of traveling from station to station.

I should make more explicit here what Lewin simply supposes. Luke tells us, that "the Master appointed seventy others, and sent them in pairs before his face, to every city and place where he was himself about to come" (Luke 10:1). The words "where he was himself about to come" (οὗ ἤμελλεν αὐτὸς ἔρχεσθαι) show that he wanted them to find all the places worthy of his coming, and stay there until he arrived. Yeshua was planning to harvest as much as he could (Luke 10:2). These words are indicative of the late spring and summer season, and indeed, it was, for he sent his emissaries out barefoot.

It cannot be supposed that he sent more than two to each place. Thus they would find thirty-five places for him to go, and likely he was planning to be in each place over the Sabbath and other places during the week. We may suppose this mission went on until late fall.

> The next incident is of considerable importance, and one which has not hitherto received the attention it deserves. While our Lord was upon the road to Jerusalem, intelligence was brought to Him that Pilate had mingled the blood of the Galileans with their sacrifices, *τῶν Γαλιλαίων ὧν τὸ αἷμα Πιλᾶτος ἔμιξεν μετὰ τῶν θυσιῶν αὐτῶν*, ["the Galileans whose blood Pilate mixed with their sacrifices"] Luke xiii. 1. Now, sacrifices, could be performed nowhere but at Jerusalem, which therefore, as we should have otherwise concluded, was the scene of the massacre. But the Galileans resided at a distance from Jerusalem, and only went up thither at the principal Feasts. On these occasions vast multitudes flocked to Jerusalem, and, as we learn from Josephus, tumults, often accompanied with bloodshed, were of frequent occurrence, notwithstanding the occupation of the western cloister by the Roman soldiery for the purpose of keeping the peace. The massacre of the Galileans, therefore, over their sacrifices implies that one of the great Jewish Festivals occurred while our Lord was on His way to Jerusalem.
>
> Again; while He was still en route along the borders of Samaria toward the Jordan, we find Him preaching in a synagogue on one sabbath, and eating bread with a Pharisee on another Sabbath. We have here, then, an interval of a week at least which we do not dwell upon as material in respect of time, but as evidencing the deliberate manner in which our Lord was progressing; for, from the point at which He had been repulsed by the Samaritans, the journey to the Jordan would, by the direct route, occupy at the most two days only; but we have here an interval of a week mentioned incidentally on the road. Plainly, therefore, our Lord was not traveling with the sole view of reaching His final destination, but was exercising His ministry amongst the cities and villages within His reach. Indeed, Luke tells us this in express terms, *καὶ διεπορεύετο κατὰ πόλεις καὶ κώμας διδάσκων, καὶ πορείαν ποιούμενος εἰς Ἱερουσαλήμ*, ["And He was going

through cities and villages, teaching, and proceeding on His way to Jerusalem."] Luke xiii. 22.

After this some Pharisees, emissaries of Herod, came to our Lord, and told Him, with the view of getting Him out of Galilee, that Herod was seeking His life. Our Lord answered that He was traveling from day to day until He should reach Jerusalem; for that, like every prophet, He must suffer at Jerusalem, Luke xiii. 31. What possible inference can be drawn from this but that Jesus was now on the road to Jerusalem to meet his death, and consequently that this journey was the last. But further, our Lord, apostrophising Jerusalem, adds that the Holy City should see Him no more until they should say, 'Blessed is He that cometh in the name of the Lord;' that is, I am now on my way for the last time to Jerusalem, and henceforth (i.e. after this my final visit) they shall see Me no more till my triumphant appearance at the day of judgment!

A little further on we find our Lord still pursuing His journey along the borders of Samaria and Galilee toward Jerusalem, *Καὶ ἐγένετο ἐν τῷ πορεύεσθαι αὐτὸν εἰς Ἱερουσαλήμ, καὶ αὐτὸς διήρχετο διὰ μέσου Σαμαρείας καὶ Γαλιλαίας*, ["And it came to pass, in his going on to Jerusalem, He was passing between Samaria and Galilee"] Luke xvii. 11. We shall only observe upon this, that Luke very pointedly throughout lays a stress on the word Jerusalem. Our Lord was to suffer at *Jerusalem* (Luke ix. 31); He sets His face to go to *Jerusalem*. (Luke ix. 51); He is seen advancing from place to place on His way to *Jerusalem* (Luke xiii. 22); and here again He is said, though traveling eastward, to be on His way to *Jerusalem*. His object throughout, therefore, was to go up to Jerusalem. These remarks are made with reference to the theory advocated by some, that this journey was merely to Judea, and that after his arrival in Judea, he went up to Jerusalem at the *ἐγκαίνια*, ["Dedication/Hanukkah"] and returned to Galilee, and then again went up to Jerusalem at the Passover at which he suffered. Such a view is at variance with the whole character of the journey as described by Luke, which is repeatedly said to have had, not Judea, but Jerusalem, for its object; and Jerusalem not as an arena for the exercise of his ministry, but as the terminus or goal at which he was to close his life at the hands of his enemies.

Our Lord new crosses the Jordan into Perea, where he resumes his labors as usual, and was therefore occupied for some considerable time, *καὶ ὡς εἰώθει πάλιν ἐδίδασκεν αὐτούς* (Mark x. 1) ["And as he had been accustomed, again He was teaching them."]

From Perea He crosses the Jordan, and then, passing through Jericho, arrives at Bethany six days before the Passover, and on the day of the paschal sacrifices is betrayed, and the next [SIC][272] day suffers death.

As this journey of our Lord occupies from Luke ix. 51 to xix. 28, or about ten chapters out of the twenty-four comprised in the gospel, this alone tends to show that the time thus occupied must have been no brief interval.

The conclusions, therefore, to be drawn from this lengthened journey are—1. That it was *one* continuous journey; 2. That it was our Lord's *last* journey to Jerusalem; and, 3. That it must have occupied at least several months. We now proceed to build some arguments on the foundation which has thus been laid.

The question is, Whether, between the Passover at the feeding of the five thousand (John ii. 13) and the Passover of the Crucifixion, another Passover did or did not intervene?

1. The first argument is of a negative character, and arises from the unreasonableness of a contrary supposition [that there was no extra Passover]. Let us assume…that the Crucifixion occurred at the

[272] Not on the next day, but on the same day as the Passover offerings. Lewin's err here, however, does not harm his explanation of five Passovers.

Passover A.D. 33,[273] ...on 3rd [274] April of that year, ...[given] that the Passover at the feeding of the five thousand was in A.D. 32, which fell on 14th[275] April of that year. Now John tells us that after this miracle of the five thousand Jesus attended the feast of Tabernacles, and after that the feast of ἐγκαίνια, ["Dedication/ Hanukah"] at Jerusalem. The latter feast in A.D. 32 was on [18th] December...and lasted eight days, and therefore ended on [25th] December A.D. 32. After this Jesus went over Jordan to Bethabara, and there abode, [καὶ] ἔμεινεν ἐκει (John x. 40) ["and remaineth there"], and that long enough to make many converts there (John x. 42). We cannot well allow less than a fortnight for this retirement, which will bring us to [8th] January, A.D. 33. Then Mary and Martha, the sisters of Lazarus, send a message from Bethany, and two days after Jesus returns and raises Lazarus (John xi. 6), and then retires to Ephraim (John xi. 54). For this we should add mother week, which will reach to [15th] January, A.D. 33. At Ephraim he made a sojourn, κἀκεῖ διέτριβε (John xi. 54) ["there he remained", ἔμεινεν], which would require about a fortnight, and, if so, we come to [29th] January. As the Passover of A.D. 33 was on [3rd] April and our Lord arrived at Bethany six days before, he would reach that place on [28th] March. From [29th] January to [28th] March would be just two months, and if we further deduct the time required for his return to Galilee, viz. another week, the remnant will be seven weeks only. As the journey recorded by Luke was one continuous journey, and that the last, all the events comprised within its limits must have

---

[273] Lewin treats A.D. 33 as given, and A.D. 32 as the test hypothesis for the third Passover, and backs up the beginning of the ministry to A.D 29 upon finding he cannot fit Luke's Travelogue. So he makes A.D. 32 the fourth Passover. But the real solution is to keep the beginning at A.D. 30. I have recomposed his argument so that A.D. 33 is the test hypothesis and that A.D. 32 is the given as the third Passover. I find that the test hypothesis cannot accommodate Luke's Travelogue, and therefore A.D. 33 is the fourth Passover, and the crucifixion at the fifth is in A.D. 34.

[274] Lewin says 2nd. Lewin gives the correct "3rd" on page 238. His other figures are frequently early by a day or two owing to the inability to accurately calculate the first crescent at a range of 2000 years in 1865. Typically numbers are given for the astronomical "new moon" (dark moon) in cases where scholars just want a quick figure.

[275] Lewin has 13th April, and 16th Dec. to 23rd Dec. for the Dedication Feast dates, and 6th Jan., 13th Jan, 27th Jan.

occurred within this short compass of seven weeks; and looking to the variety of the incidents and the time they must have occupied, more particularly the mission of the seventy, two and two, and therefore to thirty-five different places, we must conclude that, instead of a few weeks, many months must have been consumed, and consequently [the supposed A.D. 33 Crucifixion cannot immediately follow the A.D. 32 ἐγκαίνια, "Dedication/ Hanukkah" referred to by John, but A.D. 33 must be an extra year, and the Crucifixion in A.D. 34 to allow for Luke's Travelogue.][276]

2. A second argument is this. We have seen that, during our Lord's last journey, Pilate mingled the blood of the Galileans with their sacrifices; in other words, that one of the great festivals of the Jews had been celebrated; for at a feast only could such a massacre have been committed. What feast then could this be, on [given] that the Passover at the feeding of the five thousand was in A.D. 32, and [supposing] the Passover of the Crucifixion in A.D. 33? Was it the Pentecost of A.D. 32? Impossible; for between the Passover and Pentecost were fifty days only, and from the miracle of the five thousand to the news of the Galilean massacre the following events happened. Our Lord returns to Capernaum, retires to the borders of Tyre and Sidon, exercises his ministry in Decapolis, crosses the lake to Bethsaida, retreats northward to the villages of Caesarea Philippi, returns to Capernaum, enters a Samaritan village, and, being repulsed by the inhabitants, takes the road to the Jordan; sends the seventy, two and two, and therefore to thirty-five different places [to which He himself followed in turn (see above)], &c. It is evident at first sight, that all this cannot on any hypothesis be compressed within the compass of fifty days; and, if so, the feast when the Galileans were slain could not be the Pentecost of A.D. 32. Was it then the Tabernacles of A.D. 32? Certainly not, for John tells us that after the miracle of the five thousand Jesus was at a feast of Tabernacles at Jerusalem, and if the Passover of the Crucifixion was in the year which followed that of the miracle of the five thousand, the Tabernacles referred to by John could only be that of A.D. 32; and at

[276] I have adapted Lewin's argument and finished it correctly.

the Tabernacles of A.D. 32 our Lord was at Jerusalem itself, and therefore not in Galilee, which was his whereabouts when intelligence was brought to him of the outrage committed by Pilate against the Galileans. Was the feast in question, then, the feast of ἐγκαίνια, "Dedication/ Hanukkah"? We answer no, for the like reason, viz. that at the ἐγκαίνια, "Dedication/ Hanukah" also Jesus was at Jerusalem, and not in Galilee. There remains only one other feast, viz. the feast of Purim; and as to this we would observe, in the first place, that this festival was not of sacred institution, and was of secondary importance. Besides, the Purim did not require the Jews to go up to Jerusalem at all, but was celebrated at their own homes. But on another ground also the massacre could not have befallen at the feast of Purim [and also because there were no sacrifices for it]. The days during which it was celebrated were 13th Adar, which was a fast, and the 14th and 15th Adar, which were feasts. The season, therefore, was just one month before the Passover; and as our Lord reached Bethany six days before the 'Passover, three weeks only would intervene between the massacre, if enacted at the Purim, and the arrival at Bethany. But, after our Lord received intelligence of the massacre, two sabbaths are mentioned as having happened while he was still in Galilee (Luke xiii. 10 and xiv. 1), and he preached in cities and villages καὶ διεπορεύετο κατὰ πόλεις καὶ κώμας διδάσκων, ["And He was going through cities and villages teaching"], Luke xiii. 22, and is found traveling along the borders of Samaria and Galilee towards the Jordan, Luke xvii. 11; then crosses the Jordan and exercises his ministry as usual in Perea, καὶ ὡς εἰώθει πάλιν ἐδίδασκεν αὐτούς (Mark x. 1) ["And as he had been accustomed, again He was teaching them."]; and finally passes through Jericho to Bethany. Considering the slow rate of our Lord's progress while he was thus preaching in the numerous cities and villages which lay within reach, and to which he had sent the seventy disciples to prepare for him, it seems in the highest degree improbable, and all but impossible, that three weeks only should have been consumed. The inference is that the feast at which the blood of the Galileans was shed cannot be accounted for at all on the hypothesis, that the Passover of the Crucifixion followed next after that of the feeding of the five thousand; but if we place [the

Crucifixion one year later, i.e. in A.D. 34], then all runs smoothly. There is time enough for the intervening events, and all these difficulties vanish.

The general result of the preceding discussion is, that the ministry of our Lord comprised five distinct Passovers, and therefore lasted four complete years.[277]

So which feast was the massacre related in Luke 13:1 at? It appears that the only choice is Tabernacles of A.D. 33. This massacre must have happened in the Temple courts. Josephus relates the likely circumstance:

> But Pilate undertook to bring an aqueduct Jerusalem, and do'eth it with the sacred money [temple-tax revenue], taking the water of the stream from the distance of twenty-five miles. However, they were not pleased about this water undertaking; and many ten thousands of men got together, and made a clamor against him, and insisted that he should stop that design. Some of them, also, used reproaches, and abused the man, as crowds of such people usually do.
>
> So he outfitted [disguised] a great number of his soldiers in their clothes, who carried daggers under their garments, and sent them where they might surround them. So he bade the Jews himself go away; but they boldly casting reproaches upon him, he gave the soldiers that signal which had been beforehand agreed on; who laid upon them much greater blows than Pilate had commanded them, and equally punished those who were tumultuous, and those who were not, nor did they spare them in the least; and since the people were unarmed, and were caught by men prepared for what they were about to do, there were a great number of them slain by this means, and others of them ran away wounded; and thus an end was put to this sedition (*Ant.* 18:60-62).

The sedition took place in the temple, for it was the place where a Jewish crowd of men could retreat to for a rally, and this is why the

[277] "Duration of Our Lord's Ministry," pg. xlvi-li, *Fasti Sacri*, Thomas Lewin, Esq., 1865.

massacre took place in the temple (Luke 13:1). For Pilate's soldiers had to disguise themselves to enter the courts, and Pilate exhorted them from the fortress of Antonia, which was joined to the corner of the Temple complex. The aristocratic (and liberal) ruling priests were probably complicit in the design to use the temple revenue. For after the fall of Sejanus, Pilate was disposed to please them. But what was pleasing to them was not pleasing to the more conservative Galileans. The Temple dues were sacred money. They were consecrated and offered to the Almighty. So they mounted a protest, which Pilate put down with bloodshed. And he thereby made himself an enemy of king Herod (cf. Luke 23:12), whose subjects he had killed. Josephus' account of this massacre is related immediately to his account of Messiah (cf. *Ant.* 18:64), and Luke relates it after the seventy were sent out.

Key Points:

A.D. 30	John 2:13	1st Passover
A.D. 31	John 4:35	2nd Passover in "four months"
	Luke 6:1	Passover+second-first Sabbath
A.D. 32	John 6:4	3rd Passover
A.D. 32	John 7:2	Tabernacles
A.D. 32	John 10:22	Hanukah
A.D. 33	Matthew 17:24	Temple Tax (Adar 15)
	Luke 9:51-18:14	
A.D. 34	John 11:55	5th Passover

Luke 13:7-8 gives us a further chronological parable:

> And he said to the vineyard-keeper, 'Behold, for three years I have come looking for fruit on this fig tree without finding any. Cut it down! Why does it even use up the ground?' "And he answered and said to him, 'Let it alone, sir, for this year too, until I dig around it and put in fertilizer; and if it bears fruit next time†, fine; but if not, cut it down.'

† εἰς τὸ μέλλον = 'into the coming.' Probably *year* is to be supplied. It is possible that a Sabbath year inspection is omitted. Each inspection was conducted in the spring and summer of AD 30, 31, and 32. AD 33 was skipped on account of being the Sabbath year. So the next inspection would be spring and summer of AD 34. The tree's failure was plain going 'into' the spring of AD 34. The scene in Luke 13 takes place in the fall of AD 33 after the close of the Sabbath year.

The parable is according to Yeshua's four year ministry from A.D. 30-34, which was bounded by five Passovers. The years of the parable are:

Fall AD 29 to Fall AD 30	Year 1
Fall AD 30 to Fall AD 31	Year 2
Fall AD 31 to fall AD 32	Year 3
Fall AD 32 to fall AD 33	Sabbath Year
Fall AD 33 to fall AD 34	Year 4

The time from Passover in AD 30 to Passover in AD 34 is four full years.

So the fig tree (Israel) was given a chance to produce a harvest for a fourth year—the one following the Sabbath year in AD 34. This was four full years counting from Passovers, or five if counting from Tishri.

There is one more item that shows a four year ministry, bounded by five Passovers. Luke 9:51-19:28 constantly repeats that Messiah is "going to Jerusalem" (9:51; 13:22; 17:11; 18:31). It is therefore impossible for Messiah to turn back. He did take a very zig zag route preaching and teaching along the way. However, it is also not possible for him to raise Lazarus from the dead after reaching Jerusalem and then to retreat from Judea to the wilderness to a city called Ephraim (John 11:54) in the face of death. For then he would be retreated from that very thing which he "set his face toward Jerusalem" to do! (Luke 9:51). So Lazarus must have been raised before Yeshua set his face to go up to Jerusalem to die.

In John 10:39-42, Yeshua retreats beyond the Jordan, where John first baptized, and this is just after the Hanukah festival in A.D. 32 (John 10:22), which was Dec. 18th to Dec. 25th that year. Messiah could not have been more than one day trip away from Bethany. For the message would take a day, the return trip a day, and He stayed two days after getting the message where he was. So that is a total of four days, and that is how long Lazarus was dead when he arrived (John 11:17; 39). When Yeshua announced his plans, the disciples reminded him that the authorities had just tried to stone him (John 11:8; 10:31-33). So in the four year ministry chronology I have given, the raising of Lazarus must come before Yeshua returns to Galilee in the spring of A.D. 33.

There is, in fact, confirmation that Lazarus was raised between Hanukah of A.D. 32 and Passover of A.D. 33. In Luke's Travelogue, after Yeshua set his face to Jerusalem, where do we find Mary and Martha? In Luke 10:38, Luke briefly tells us that they are in a "certain village" (κώμην τινά), which clearly cannot be Bethany.* For in Luke 13:31-35, Yeshua is still in Galilee, and in 17:11 between Samaria and Galilee. He is taking the slow road to preach and maximize the time he has left. So why are Mary and Martha in an unnamed village in Galilee? The answer is that they moved there after the raising of Lazarus.

Lazarus is not mentioned in the Luke passage, but it is likely that he was there too. Lazarus or his sister was not poor. For Mary could afford the costly perfume in John 12:3, worth 300 denarii, which is 300 days wages. Mary, Martha, and Lazarus would not have made their permanent relocation public after Lazarus' resurrection. They would have had to find a new place and keep it quiet, hence the unnamed village in Galilee. The threesome are found in Bethany in John 11:55-12:11 because they had come up for the Passover, but as Lazarus was under the threat of death, and for certain investigation from the authorities, and his sisters as well, it is certain that they had made arrangements with Yeshua while he visited them at their undisclosed location (Luke 10:38-42). Indeed, that was likely when the dinner appointment was made, and when Mary resolved to anoint Yeshua. It is clear that their testimony would be to those of the Jews that they agreed to let them see, and then they were going back to the unnamed village after the Passover. Mary had private conversations with Yeshua. It is quite possible that she was one of the few people who knew he would die for Israel's sins and rise again.

Table 6: Nisan 14 Weekdays, A.D. 30-36

AD	Reference	Date of Passover
30	John 2:13	Nisan 14 on Friday
31	Luke 6:1	Nisan 14 on Tuesday
32	John 6:4	Nisan 14 on Monday
33	Matthew 17:24	Nisan 14 on Friday
34	John 11:55	Nisan 14 on Wednesday
35	—	Nisan 14 on Tuesday
36	—	Nisan 14 on Monday

The extra two years are provided to show that no suitable dates

* See Meyer's NT Commentary, Luke 10:38. Meyer notes the difficulty of identification with Bethany and supposes some sort of error in Luke in the order of the narrative, but Luke is the most careful of the Evangelists to put things in chronological order! And he was acquainted with the participants in the story.

remain within Pilate's term in office, which ended in A.D. 36.

Now some may wonder if it is possible if the new moon day for Nisan A.D. 34 could have been postponed due to cloudy weather on the last day of Adar. This would result in Nisan 14 landing on a Thursday instead of a Wednesday. The answer to this question is no, and this is due to the fact that Adar was a full month that year. The month of Adar was already 30 days long. The new moon would not appear at the end of Adar 29, and it would only appear at the end of Adar 30. In cases where the new moon was obscured at the end of Adar 30, the first day of Nisan would be proclaimed regardless of the weather, and regardless of whether the moon was seen or not.

Parker and Dubberstein have the new moon first visible on February 8, and so this would be the first day of the month. The new moon for Nisan was seen on March 10 after sunset. Here is the calendar for Adar A.D. 34:

Table 7: Adar, A.D. 34

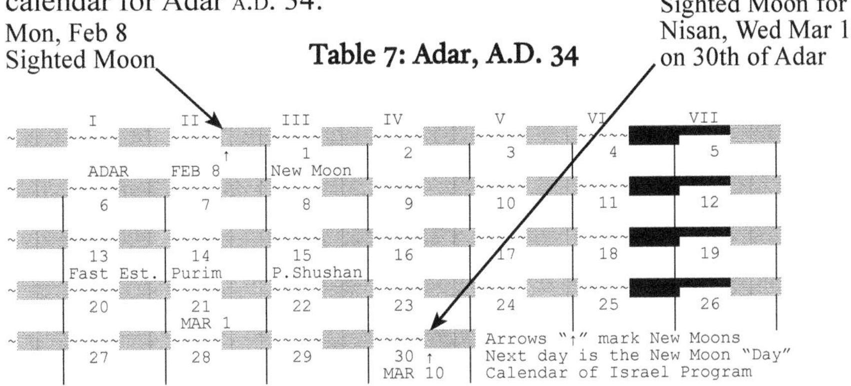

Mon, Feb 8
Sighted Moon
Sighted Moon for
Nisan, Wed Mar 10
on 30th of Adar
I
II
III
IV
V
VI
VII
1
2
3
4
5
ADAR
FEB 8
New Moon
6
7
8
9
10
11
12
13
14
15
16
17
18
19
Fast Est.
Purim
P.Shushan
20
21
22
23
24
25
26
MAR 1
27
28
29
30
MAR 10
Arrows "↑" mark New Moons
Next day is the New Moon "Day"
Calendar of Israel Program

The new moon did not appear until the end of the 30th day, so the next day automatically becomes Nisan 1. Since Nisan 1 would be on the same day that calculations show for the new moon and at the same time after the 30th of Adar, there is no way to "postpone" or delay Nisan 1 another day. Naturally, the scripture does say the resurrection was on the "first of the Sabbaths", and that this was the "third day" according to the Temple calendar. So it follows that the crucifixion was on the fourth day of the week, Nisan 14, and that the new moon for Nisan 1 was also seen just after sunset on 3/10/34. So besides being extremely probable* from astronomy, the Scripture makes it perfectly plain. That is, the Scripture's direct statement means that no improbable human factors interfered with the expected reckoning.

* The Adar moon is rated B on the Yallop scale, meaning conditions had to be good for the sighting. The Nisan moon is rated A, Q=1.501, a very easy sighting.

The historical statement of the text lines up exactly with the science of the matter.

Others may wonder if there may have been a second Adar in A.D. 34 causing a postponement of Nisan by one month, which would result in different dates.* However, the postponement rules are based traditions that crept into Judaism after the destruction of the Temple in A.D. 70. I take it for granted Messiah never broke the Law, so we may assume that when he kept and fulfilled the Passover that he did it at the biblical times. So Messiah would not have fulfilled the Passover according to tradition. He would have kept it according to the Torah. So now I will explain why.

The Law does not permit a postponement of the first month beyond its proper time. The reason that skeptics think that Nisan might be postponed is that they have been learning from Jewish traditions and not from the Law. So it is here necessary to outline the instructions of the Law:

First it is written, "Three times [שָׁלֹשׁ רְגָלִים] you shall go on foot to feast unto me in the year [בַּשָּׁנָה]" (Exodus 23:14; cf. Ex. 23:17, Deut. 16:16; 2Chron. 8:13; 1 Kings 9:25). This means that a year must contain exactly three pilgrimage festivals: Passover, Shavuot [Pentecost], and Sukkot [Tabernacles]. No more than three. No less than three. It would not be allowed to have four feasts in one year and two in the next.

Also, "Thou shalt not delay [לֹא תְאַחֵר] *to offer* the first of thy ripe fruits [בִּכּוּר]" (Ex 22:29). The Passover was a set time for offering first fruits:

> Speak to the sons of Israel, and say to them, 'When you enter the land which I am going to give to you and reap its harvest, then you shall bring in the sheaf of the first fruits [רֵאשִׁית] of your harvest to the priest. And he shall wave the sheaf before Yãhweh for you to be accepted; in the day after the ceasing the priest shall wave it (Lev. 23:10-11).

The time of this offering was on the day after the annual Sabbath [literally, "ceasing"]. The annual Sabbath[278] was the 15th of Nisan.

---

[278] Literally, "ceasing" because this Sabbath was a "cessation" from work →

* Considering AD 34 alone in light of Daniel 9, the third week of March figures heavily in ancient datings of the Passion, e.g. Bede: 25 March, AD 34; Paderborn: 26 March, AD 34; Albert the Great: 25 March, AD 34; Claudius of Turn: 21 March, AD 34; Panvinio: 26 March AD 34. Only after matters did not land on assumed weekdays was shifting the month thought of: Mercator: April 2, AD 34; Scaliger: April 23, AD 34. Likewise Newton picked a late date in AD 34. See The Good News of Messiah, pg. 211, and Nothaft, *Dating the Passion.*

The commandment is not to delay this offering. Additionally, the law prohibits eating the new produce until the offering is made (Lev. 23:14). So the commandment not to delay the offering is in the interests of mercy (Hosea 6:6), so that the people would be allowed to eat. As long as it is possible to call the first day of the feast, "Sabbath," as Yom Kippur is called "Sabbath" (cf. Lev. 23:32) and Passover (cf. John 19:31), then it should be noted that the commandment not to delay the offering agrees with the earliest possible time, which would be after the annual Sabbath. Otherwise, the people might have to wait until after the feast to enjoy their bounty. So this offering is "in the day after" Nisan 15.

Now, Nisan 15 itself should be as early in the year as possible to satisfy the commandment. The offering should not be delayed so that Nisan 15 falls later in the year than necessary. If Nisan 15 falls in the old year, then it is too early and violates the commandment to observe three feasts per year. So to satisfy this commandment it must wait till the year starts. But it must wait no longer than necessary.†

So, when does the year start? Here is the general instruction for the calendar:

> Then the Almĩghty says, "Let there be lights within the vault* of the heavens to separate the day from the night, and let them be for signs, even for fixed times and for days and years; and let them be for lights within the vault of the heavens to give light on the earth"; (and it is so). Then the Almĩghty makes the two great lights; the greater light to govern the day; and the lesser light to govern the night; and the stars. (Gen. 1:14-16).

We see that the greater light, which is the sun, is supposed to govern the days (יָמִים) and years (שָׁנִים). With respect to the Passover feast, the Scripture says this:

> Therefore, you shall keep this ordinance at its appointed time <u>from days to days</u> [מִיָּמִים יָמִימָה] (Ex. 13:10).

What this means is from year to year, but it is stated as "from

---

and in this case also the beginning of cessation from leaven. The same verb root is used in Ex. 12:15, "you shall make cease leaven from your houses."

† I also make the observation that the Levitical incomes depended on the people bringing their offerings, their tithes and the firstfruits. Naturally, they would not have wanted to delay the first produces of the new year after winter, because this means a delay in the time it takes a portion of the best of the land to feed their families.

* Or 'expanse.' The language is that of appearance, such as we call the part of the galaxy we can see 'the Milky Way.' People often realize that the names they give things from a distance are based on appearance and that they do not have those literal properties when examined up close.

days to days" because a year is determined by a complete cycle of *days*. That is, the Passover must be observed once in each complete cycle of days. And to keep the commandment not to delay the first fruits, the Passover must be observed as soon after this cycle begins as possible.

When does the cycle of days begin? The following scriptures answer the question:

> Now that man went up from his town from days to days [מִיָּמִים יָמִימָה] to worship and to sacrifice to Yãhweh of hosts in Shiloh ...Then it was at the great circuit of days ‡ [לִתְקֻפוֹת הַיָּמִים] And when Hannah had conceived she bore a son; then she called his name Samuel, saying, "Because I have asked him from Yãhweh." Then the man Elkanah went up with all his house to sacrifice to Yãhweh the sacrifice of the days and his vow. But Hannah did not go up, for she said to her husband, "—until the lad is weaned; then I will bring him, that we may appear together before Yãhweh. Then he will stay there onward forgetting time." (1 Sam. 1:3, 20-22).

> Now it came about לִתְקוּפַת הַשָּׁנָה at the circuit of the year that the army of the Arameans came up against him; and they came to Judah and Jerusalem, destroyed all the officials of the people from among the people, and sent all their spoil to the king of Damascus (2 Chron. 24:23).

> Then the prophet came near to the king of Israel, and said to him, "Go, strengthen yourself and observe and see what you have to do; for at the turn of the year לִתְשׁוּבַת הַשָּׁנָה the king of Aram will come up against you (1 Kings 20:22).

Observe that Samuel uses the exact same phrase as Exodus 13:10, "from days to days" to refer to the start of the year and feast cycle. After the feast of Shavuot, because it was a one day feast (cf. 1 Sam. 1:19), when Hannah had conceived, then she born a son "at the great circuit of days (or circuits)." This is when two yearly cycles join, the day on which the old ends and the new begins. The Scriptures use this phrase in parallel with "circuit of the year" and "turn of the year."

‡The Hebrew is a plural of number or intensification, either "circuits of the days," or "great circuit of the days." The point is that this miraculous birth was exactly on the day which the old days of the year ended and the new began.

Figure 60: Cardinal Points of the Solar Year

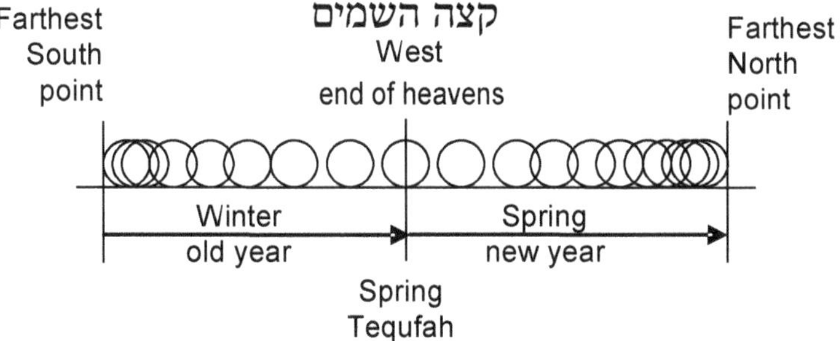

If one watches the sun set for each day during the year, one will notice that for three days in the summer it sets at an extreme point along the western horizon toward the north, and that during the winter it sets at an extreme point on the western horizon toward the south. This works for the northern hemisphere and the land of Israel.[279]

Then one will observe when the sun sets at the westernmost extreme of the heavens (or just barely past it in the direction of travel), between the extreme summer and winter points, that it is either the beginning day of the spring or the fall. Also on these days the sun appears at first sight to trace a half circle horizon to horizon, but in fact it is slightly bent by refraction.

So on the day before the sun sets at the westpoint it traces $< 180°$. On the day it rises at the westpoint it traces 180°, and on the day after $> 180°$. On the westpoint day, the sun is visible for exactly or just over half of its complete circuit. Its distance in the night half is equal counting the twilight periods with the night period. Ancient peoples used observation only. They had no accurate clocks. The sun's path is in fact slightly bent at sunrise and sunset.[280]

---

[279] Additional details: the sun's position changes slowly at the extreme points, but near the midpoint the sun moves a whole diameter each day. From the winter extreme the sun moves in the direction of the arrow to the midpoint, marking the new year, and then continues from left to right until it reaches the extreme north point, marking the end of spring and the start of summer. Then the direction reverses.

[280] Refraction bends an otherwise ideal circle traced by the sun during sunrise and sunset. This causes the sun to appear longer during the day than it does not appear after setting or before rising, as measured by accurate clocks (which ancient peoples did not have). The theory here is based on local observational geometry and not theoretical methods or clocks.

The point in the year when this event occurs is called the "circuit of the days," "circuit of the year" or "turn of the year." It marks the boundary of the year between "days" and "days." So in the text "from days to days," the dividing point is the *tequfah*, [תְּקוּפָה].

The word *tequfah* means either the whole *circuit* or a circuiting point—a *coming round* point on the circuit:

> In them he has placed a tent for the sun, which is like a bridegroom going forth from his chamber; he rejoices like a strong man to run his course. From the extremity [מִקְצֵה] of the heavens is his going forth, and his coming round [תְקוּפָת] is at their extremities [קְצוֹת], and nothing is hidden from his heat (Psalm 19:4b-6).

The heavens are spread out like a tent (Isa. 40:22). The sun runs its course through this tent (the constellations) each year. It goes out of its chamber at the start of the year. At the start of the year it goes out at the extremity of heaven (east), and at the end of the year it comes round upon their extremities again (east and west). The extremities, or ends of heaven, קְצוֹת, are four. There are "four winds from the four extremities of the heavens" (Jer. 49:36), which are the four compass directions, e.g. Ezekiel's Temple (Eze. 42:20), and the gates (1 Chron. 9:24), "to the four winds...east, west, north, and south."

The Hebrew word קָצֶה refers to an 'end' 'limit' or 'extreme point' of the heavens. In Hebrew idiom it is used as a technical word to mean one of the compass points, east, west, north or south. This is why Jeremiah 49:36 numbers them in the plural at four: אַרְבַּע רוּחוֹת מֵאַרְבַּע קְצוֹת הַשָּׁמַיִם, "Four winds from the four end-points of the heavens." Only in modern usage we would say "compass points." The "four winds" are further equated to "east, west, north, and south" 1 Chron. 9:24.

Most commentators ignorantly suppose that Psa. 19:4-6 is referring to just a daily circuit of the sun. There are several elements in this text to disprove this. First the sun's coming round is "upon their end-points" (קְצוֹתָם). The word here is either a plural of intensification or number. If a plural of number, then it refers to coming back to due east and due west at the end of the year. The plural would refer to both east and west at the 'end of days.' If the former, it means that the sun comes round back to the 'most extreme end point' which would simply mean its starting point due east after one year. The year is renewed when the sun crosses either of two extremity points, east or west.

Now, while the sun reaches an extreme point in the fall, this point is not the coming round of the circuit. It is, in fact, the half of the circuit. This is another reason why a whole year is in view in this text.

Next we have to consider that the 'tent" through which the sun runs its course is not a vague metaphor. The "tent" is defined in Isaiah. 40:22. The tent is the constellations, the starry hosts. The text also refers to the constellations as a 'curtain.' Next look at the word "chamber" in Psa. 19:5, מֵחֻפָּתוֹ. This may mean "from his canopy," but it is virtually synonymous with "chamber" in Joel 2:16, "Let the bridegroom go forth from his chamber (מֵחֶדְרוֹ), and the bride from her canopy (מֵחֻפָּתָהּ). What kind of house is this? The answer is in Job 9:9: "He makes the Bear, Orion, and the Pleiades, and the chambers (וְחַדְרֵי) of the south." We see then that the chambers are the same as saying the "houses" of the constellations, or Zodiac in the special case of the sun. Note that in Job the bridegroom goes forth from his "chamber" (מֵחֶדְרוֹ) and in Psa. 19:5 he goes forth from his canopy (מֵחֻפָּתוֹ).

So the sun goes forth at the start of the year from its spring constellation. It then runs its way or path (אֹרַח) until it returns to its starting point at the extremities, east and west.

Albert Barnes comments:

> Is from the end of the heaven - From one end of the heaven; that is, from the East, where he starts. And his circuit - The word used here - תקופה teqûphâh - means properly *a* coming about, or *a* return, as of the seasons, or of the year. The word [תקופה] here does not refer to the fact that the sun comes round to the starting-point on the following day, but to the sweep or circuit which he makes in the heavens from one end of it to the other - traveling over the entire heavens. Unto the ends of it - That is, to the other side of the heavens. The plural term is used here perhaps from the idea of completeness, or to denote that there was nothing beyond. The complete journey was made.

This comment is not inconsistent with the use of tequfah elsewhere. For example in Exodus 34:22 almost all interpreters have mistaken the words: "וְחַג הָאָסִיף תְּקוּפַת הַשָּׁנָה," to mean the fall equinox, "... and feast of the ingathering * circuit of the year." Every version either translates * as "at the" or interprets it with the same meaning using other words. But there is no preposition "at" in the text. It should simply be rendered "....; a circuit of the year." It refers all the way back to vs. 18 and everything following up to "a circuit of the year." It refers to the whole circuit. Likewise Exodus 23:16 is to be taken, "in a going forth of the year, during your ingathering from your labor from the field." It is evident that they gathered from the field during the whole circuit of the year.*

So it is now demonstrated above that the year begins when the sun sets forth from the day on which it rises east or sets west. If it sets west, then it must have begun the year before setting. Now the sun may not set west, but it may rise east. In both cases the first day of the year is counted back to the previous sunset. This is the inclusive principle. If the circuit is completed at any time on a given day, then the whole of the day is the first day of the new year. In this case the day is reckoned from sunset to sunset instead of the ordinary dawn to dawn reckoning, and we shall shortly see why.

Three feasts are to be kept in a year. The feast of unleavened bread began with sunset on the 14th day of the month. The Passover was sacrificed in the afternoon, and prepared, and then the feast was that night. Therefore, the feast must be counted in the new year. For this reason the sun must rise east on (or before) the 15th day of the month or set west on or before the 15th. Either condition will work. And the first day of the feast, having the character of a Sabbath, is counted between sunset on the 14th day and sunset on the 15th day. **

As mentioned before, the Law did not allow any delay once these conditions were met. As mentioned before earlier in this book (pg. 220-223), in practice the priests counted 365 days from the last new years day, and forward from the new moon day of the first month, in a close call, before making a decision to intercalate the year. So long as the 15th of the month came on or after the new years day, the year would not receive an extra month. Perhaps if three 365 day years had gone by then they would make their estimate with 366 days. This uncertainty is on the same order as that a month has 29 or 30 days in a close call.

*Possibly Exodus 34:22b and 23:16b are to be joined to the following verse: "[22b][In] the circuit of the year, [23]three times in the year, every male of you shall see the face of the Lord Yahweh Almighty of Yisrael." And, "[16b]In the going forth of the year, when you are gathering your labor from the field, [17]three times in the year, every male of you shall see *unto*† the face of the Lord Yahweh."

---

† The MT reads אל here, which is clearly an attempt to soften "see the face of Yahweh." But the SP reads את like the MT over in Exo. 34:23. The SP likewise tries to soften the same phrase by putting "the face of the lord Ark" suggesting we should take it as a possessive, "the Lord's Ark." See BHS.

* I am now certain that the clauses should be joined to the next verse. See below.

** If part of the day is in the old year, this is permitted, because the year timing is specifically connected to the second (festive) passover offering at the going down of the sun on the 15th day of the month, and this may be eaten till daybreak for the 16th, the night of the watches.

The first day of the year happened on the day that the sun either passed just north of east at sunrise or just north of west at sunset. On the previous day neither condition would be met. The first day of the year is reckoned backwards to the previous sunset. The top of the sun is used for this. So the top of the sun is seen at 90 degrees or just less than 90 degrees of Azimuth at the moment of sunrise, and the first day of the year is counted with the previous night. Or the top of the sun is seen at 270 degrees or just over 270 degrees at the moment of sunset, and the first day of the year is counted to begin with the previous sunset.

If we suppose then that an infrequent case of having the first day of the year on 15 Nisan occurred, then the northward crossing would have been noted at sunrise or sunset on the 15th day. This would be the first day of the feast, and the first day of unleavened bread. The feast would be just inside the new year satisfying the precepts, and there would be no delay of the new year's offerings a month.

This was certainly the case in 2 BC so long as Adar was not prolonged from 29 to 30 days by poor weather. If such was the case, though, only the month of Nisan would have been one day later, and not a whole month later. In AD 34 the first day of the year happened on March 22 or Nisan 12 after a year 366 days long. The first day of the feast March 25, beginning at sunset on the 24th was Nisan 15. In the Exodus year, 1632 BC, the first day of the year was on Nisan 8 (April 4) after a year of 365 days, and accordingly, the next 15th of the month was after the beginning of the year.

So by these three witness and Psalm 19 we have the method explained and confirmed along with proper Hebrew definitions of "the four winds of the heavens," and "the four extremities of the heavens." These things have all worked out miraculously perfectly.

Now there were two Passover offerings, one on the 14th of Nisan (for the Passover in Egypt), and one on the 15th of Nisan (for the Exodus):

> And you shall tell your son on that day, saying, 'It is because of what Yãhweh did for me when I came out of Egypt.' "And it shall serve as a sign to you on your hand, and as a reminder on your forehead, that the Law of Yãhweh may be in your mouth; for with a powerful hand Yãhweh brought

you out of Egypt. "Therefore, you shall keep this ordinance at its appointed time from days to days. (Ex 13:8-10).

Israel did not go out of Egypt on the 14th of Nisan. It was on the 15th of Nisan. So the set time is for the day of the Exodus. Israel stayed in their houses until dawn of the 15th of Nisan, and then they went out. A second Passover offering is legislated to memorialize the Exodus:

> "You are not allowed to sacrifice the Passover in any of your towns which Yãhweh your Almĩghty is giving you; but at the place where Yãhweh your Almĩghty chooses to establish his name, you shall sacrifice the Passover in the setting as the sun goes down, at the set time that you came out of Egypt. "And you shall broil and eat it in the place which Yãhweh your Almĩghty chooses. And in the daybreak you are to return to your tents. "Six days you shall eat unleavened bread, and on the seventh day there shall be an assembly to Yãhweh your Almĩghty; you shall do no work on it (Deut. 16:5-8).

It will therefore be noted that this offering was for the afternoon of the 15th of Nisan. Observe the fact that only six days of unleavened bread remain the following morning. Observe also that this sacrifice could be from the "herd" בָּקָר (Deut. 16:2) unlike the 14th Passover offering which had to be from the "flock" (צֹאן) only. This offering could be broiled in water (cf. Exo. 12:9; Deut. 16:7; 2 Sam. 2:13) unlike the Passover offering. This was the second Passover offering that memorializes the Exodus. It was offered "in the setting as the sun goes down." It was during this day and the night following that Israel went out of Egypt.

Therefore, the precise legal point that must come after the spring *tequfah* is sunset on the 15th of Nisan. So Israel would sight the new moon following the 12th month of the year. Israel would count forward 15 days. From the last years *tequfah* observation they would know if the 15th day would fall before the *tequfah*. If the 15th day was to fall before the *tequfah* then that month was declared intercalary. It was the 13th month, later called Adar II. If the 15th day was to fall on or after the circuit of the year, then the month was declared Nisan, the first month, and the 15th day was marked as the annual "ceasing" (הַשַּׁבָּת , הַשֹּׁבֶת)[286] for the feast of unleavened bread. The whole night of the calendar 15th (dawn to dawn) had to be in the new year.*

The consideration of when the year begins sets an early limit which the feast date cannot precede. Likewise, the precept that the first fruits be not delayed forbids the Passover from being delayed a month. The 15th day that lands first on or after the tequfah is the legal time. Postponing the feast to a second month where a second 15th of the month came after the *tequfah* was not legal—unless one was a private individual on a journey and had missed the proper time (cf. Num. 9:10-13). Exodus 13:10, "from days to days" (מִיָּמִים יָמִימָה) and Gen. 1:14 provide the cycles of the sun (daily, and yearly) to determine the time of the feast.

Therefore, we may say that it was not possible that the feast of Passover was postponed to the second full moon after the spring equinox—not while Yeshua observed and fulfilled it. For he kept the Torah perfectly.

Also, Nisan 1 cannot be postponed one day due to inclement weather in A.D. 34 since Adar was already 30 days. Nor can the month of Nisan be postponed skipping the first 15th after the *tequfah*. Furthermore, such postponement cannot be made for any of the other years for which I cited the valid Passover dates:

Table 8: The Five Passovers in the Evangelists

A.D.	Reference	Date of Passover
30	John 2:13	Nisan 14 on Friday
31	Luke 6:1	Nisan 14 on Tuesday
32	John 6:4	Nisan 14 on Monday
33	Luke 13:1-8	Nisan 14 on Friday
34	John 11:55	Nisan 14 on Wednesday

It should be noted further that Adar, A.D. 31 had 30 days.[287] Therefore a Wednesday date cannot be obtained in A.D. 31 by inclement weather.[288] These considerations leave only one year in

---

286 cf. Lev. 23:11, 15. Note: notes 281-285 were deleted in the revision.

287 See also Parker and Dubberstein for confirmation.

288 When the new moon was not seen just after sunset on the 29th day, then an extra day would be added to the month. If the weather was too cloudy

* This agrees with the exact Rabbinic definition, viz. that all of Nisan 16 by sunset reckoning (a night and a day) must be in the new year.

which the crucifixion could be on the fourth day of the week! That year is A.D. 34. It should further be noted that there are no years on which to base a Thursday-Sunday explanation.

The biblical principles and the outworking of chronology are confirmed by both Church tradition for Easter[289] and the Rabbinic Calendar for Passover. First the Church tradition, though it contains much error (not to mention idolatry) did inherit its principles from the Jews. The Church tradition states that Easter should fall on the Sunday that comes after the first full moon after the spring equinox. This custom preserves the biblical precept that the feast should not be postponed by an improperly added extra month. It has to occur with the first full moon after the equinox. This ruling solidly tied the timing of Easter with the 15th of Nisan. For the full moon after the equinox did occur about the 15th of Nisan. Thus, it preserved in the Church custom a remnant of the precept that the first fruits should not be delayed, and a remnant of the precept that three feasts be kept in one year.

Second, the Rabbinic principle, that the 16th of Nisan must fall after the day of the spring *tequfah,* is simply a restatement of the rule that the 15th of Nisan must fall on or after the *tequfah*. For in the case when the 16th of Nisan falls immediately after the *tequfah* day, then the *tequfah* day is the 15th of Nisan.[290] The Rabbinic calendar admits no other principle for intercalating the year.[291] It is therefore in

---

then the new moon might have been seen on the 29th. The new moon can be calculated using modern methods, but clouds cannot be calculated. But if the calculation says that Adar is 30 days, then the possibility of clouds do not need to be taken into consideration as Nisan 1 would begin automatically after the 30th day in the case of clouds.

[289] A name for the Passover used by many Christians derived from a goddess of spring, which is the equivalent of Ishtar or Ashtoreth.

[290] The difference in the two ways of stating the rule are simply that between inclusive reckoning and exclusive reckoning.

[291] However, the Rabbinic "date" for the *tequfah* itself is fictitious (being about a week too soon), since they have too long relied on calculation, and have failed to confirm the calculation with a fresh observation of the *tequfah* for some 15 centuries! Also, Rabbinic "new moons" suffer from the fault that they too are calculated and not confirmed by observations. The Rabbis have forgotten that the observations the calculations were supposed to predict are more important than the calculations. The only consolation is that Christian Europe also had a fictitious equinox problem until the Church corrected it in

*agreement with the biblical legislation and also in agreement with the Church's witness to the timing of Easter. *close, but not exact.

Karaite Intercalation

Many will say that that ancient Israel fixed the first month according to the doctrines of the Karaites. The Karaites believe that the first month is to be fixed by the appearance of barley ears that are sufficiently mature to be roasted in the fire, and then turned into flour.[292] Just before the new moon they inspect the barley in Israel to see if it has reached the 'proper stage,' and also if the fields have 'proper percentages' at this stage to meet their definition of "aviv." If they find the required barley, they declare the next new moon the first month, but if not they add a thirteenth month. This procedure makes the calendar subject to the fickle vicissitudes of weather, climate, and human authority,[293] and if correct would open Yeshua's prophetic fulfillment to question and doubts.

Here is *the chief* text from which they extract a commandment to inspect barley:

Observe the month of <u>the</u> Aviv [הָאָבִיב] and celebrate the Passover to Yãhweh your Almĩghty, for in the month of <u>the</u> Aviv Yãhweh your Almĩghty brought you out of Egypt by night (Deut. 16:1).*

What the Karaites suppose is that the text means they are supposed to go out in the fields before the *new moon* and check the barley. But does the text mean "observe the new moon [when] the aviv [appears]"? This is a fair question. And in this new edition, the previous answer must be modified, because in this instance, the word *hodesh* means "the new moon," but *ha-Aviv* is a month.

1582.

[292] Grinding the barley into flour may have been the case with a specialized form of the wave offering for all the people, but the reality is that each farmer cut a sheaf from his field before the wave sheaf day, and brought it to the priest on the 16th of Nisan. The farmer cut the barley in whatever stage it was in. (It would always have ears of some sort.) It was waved as is, and part put on the altar. The rest was given to the priest.

[293] The principles of the day, month, and year set forth in Genesis 1:14 do not involve human authority. For the sun and moon determine the beginnings of the years, days, and months.

* Compare "Observe the day of the Sabbath" (Deut. 5:12). In theory, using the same argument, one could focus on the meaning of "the Sabbath" as "the ceasing", and then claim that one must determine which day is the Sabbath by watching for a day when ceasing could be observed in sufficient quantity. But since this is absurd, and the syntax and grammar the same as in Deut. 16:1, it follows that there is no compelling reason to take Deut. 16:1 the way Karaites do.

In all other cases, it means "the month of the Aviv": *

This day you are going forth in the month of the Aviv [בְּחֹדֶשׁ הָאָבִיב]. (Exodus 13:4, MISB).

You shall observe the Feast of Unleavened Bread. Seven days you are to eat unleavened bread, as I commanded you, at the appointed time of *the* month of the Aviv [חֹדֶשׁ הָאָבִיב], for in it you came out of Egypt. (Ex. 23:15)

You shall observe the Feast of Unleavened Bread. For seven days you are to eat unleavened bread, as I commanded you, at the appointed time of *the* month of Aviv, [חֹדֶשׁ הָאָבִיב] for in *the* month of the Aviv [הָאָבִיב] you came out of Egypt. (Exodus 34:18).

In all these cases, the words חֹדֶשׁ הָאָבִיב *hodesh ha-aviv* mean "month of the Aviv" and not "new moon of the Aviv" as this would contradict the contexts. Israel did not go out of Egypt in the "new moon" day, but in the "month" of "the Aviv." Therefore, it would not be just to claim in these other uses that "in the month of the Aviv" meant "in the new moon day of [finding] green ears." So, the dogmatism is flawed!

Now what does the word observe שָׁמוֹר *shamor* mean? This word also occurs in the other contexts. In Exodus 23:15 and 34:18, "You shall observe [תִּשְׁמֹר] the Feast of Unleavened Bread." This explains the meaning of "observe" before it appears in Deut. 16:1. "Observe" means to *guard, keep, watch for* the feast. Where "feast of unleavened bread" [אֶת־חַג הַמַּצּוֹת] appears with the word "observe" in Exodus, a substitution is made in Deuteronomy with the word "observe": [אֶת־חֹדֶשׁ הָאָבִיב], and then instructions to keep the Passover are appended: וְעָשִׂיתָ פֶּסַח.

"Observe the month of the Aviv" is a summary of Exodus 23:15 and 34:18: "You shall observe ... at the appointed time [לְמוֹעֵד] of *the* month of Aviv, [חֹדֶשׁ הָאָבִיב]. The words "at the appointed time" [לְמוֹעֵד] must be supplied from the two texts (given by Yahweh before Deut. 16:1) to explain the summary in Deut. 16:1. Further, the meaning of "appointed time" is explained in Exodus 13:10:

* "Watch for the new moon of the [month] Aviv" (Deut. 16:1). Since it means "new moon" the manner of the watching or observing has to do with sighting first visibility of the moon, and then calculating how many days remain in the old year (if any) such that sunset on 15 Aviv falls in the new year. The etymology of "the Aviv" has no more to do with the manner of watching, observing, or guarding than it does in the other verses where the new moon day is not the focal point, where it is a month. As noted before, the Karaite logic applied to Deut. 5:12 also suggests that they erred in their interpretation of the text.

Therefore, you shall keep [וְשָׁמַרְתָּ] this ordinance at its appointed time [לְמוֹעֲדָהּ] from days to days.

This passage explains how to observe [שָׁמוֹר] the appointed time. It is to be "from days to days" מִיָּמִים יָמִימָה. The phrase "from days to days" is a technical specification from year to year. For a year was counted as 365 or 366 days from the preceding *tequfah*. Thus as soon as the 15th of the month was to land on or after the *tequfah* it would be the appointed time. For the 15th of the month was the anniversary of going out of Egypt. So, *Observe the new moon of Aviv,* means "Observe [the appointed time for] the new moon of the [month] Aviv," that is *ha-Aviv* is a month.* page 288

Now why is the first month given the name "month of the Aviv" [חֹדֶשׁ הָאָבִיב]? I have explained the meaning of "month" and the meaning of "observe." Is the naming of a month with the definite article and a descriptive phrase without parallel? Not at all:

> And all the men of Israel assembled themselves to King Solomon at the feast, in the month of <u>the</u> Ethanim, which is the seventh month (1 Kings 8:2).

The seventh month is called: יֶרַח הָאֵתָנִים. This means "month of <u>the</u> ever-flows." The seventh month was so called because typically only the most hearty streams continue to flow in that month. This indicates that the month name is given according to something that typically happens in the named month. The descriptive name "month of the Aviv" [חֹדֶשׁ הָאָבִיב] refers to what is typical of that time of year—the barley will be in the ear.†

Now it has been defined what "observe" שָׁמוֹר means, and what "month" *hodesh* חֹדֶשׁ means. The full title *hodesh ha-Aviv* is simply the descriptive name of the month. The etymology has nothing to do with fixing the time of the month itself. It only describes the condition of the crop in "ears" when the month comes around—a month in which Passover is to be fixed "from days to days" without any delay of first-fruits. So, "Watch for the new moon [of the month]* of the Aviv."

Now the state of *aviv* meaning "ear" means any time the barley has the appearance of ears. This is a much broader definition than the

---

† Eblaite and other ancient near eastern calendars show a tendency to name months after some phenomenon occurring in the season of the month. See "The Calendars of Ebla Part I. The Old Calendar," William H. Shea, *Andrews University Seminary Studies*, Autumn 1980, Vol. XVIII. No. 2, 127-137. *Implied, because Ha Aviv is a month, not a new moon.

Karaites. The Karaites narrowed the definition down to suit their purpose, otherwise they would always find aviv according to the broader definition, and it would be useless for dictating the calendar. Their narrower definition is in reality the insertion of human authority —tradition—to enable them to declare when the new moon is as they like.[294]

---

[294] The only issue that might seem to be unresolved is the location from which the observations should be made. According to precedent, when Israel was in the wilderness the location of the observations was in the wilderness. Therefore, it seems that wherever the camp of Israel is, then that should be the location. For this reason local observation of the new moon by Israel in exile cannot be ruled improper as long as the Temple is not functioning.

— — — — — — — — —

Timing of the Sabbath

Every example we are given where "Sabbath" is defined indicates it is from 'evening to evening.' Firstly, there are the Jews, with whom Messiah did not so much as make a comment to differ on this matter, though he did differ with them when wrongly interpreting the commandment to honor father and mother. Josephus said the trumpets were blown in the evenings to mark the start and end of the Sabbath (War 4:582). Also, when the word is used for the Day of Atonement, it is given from evening to evening, beginning on the 9th day at evening and ending on the 10th day at evening. Moreover, the first day of unleavened bread is called 'the Sabbath' because on it we cease from leaven, and six more days, for seven days. The time is defined from the evening of the 14th day to the evening of the 21st day. And the first and last days no work is to be done. Thus the Sabbath in Lev. 23:11, 15 is from evening on the 14th day to evening on the 15th day. And the final Sabbath is evening on the 20th day to evening on the 21st day. The Sabbatical year is necessarily defined as starting in the 7th month due to the sowing and harvesting cycle, which is the evening of the year. By analogy, the weekly Sabbath begins in the evening of the day.* So we see that all examples indicate a Sabbath begins in the evening or ends in it. Nehemiah then closed the gates. The Jews brought the sick to Messiah after Sabbath also.

So while there are many texts showing a day is reckoned as a day and a night, when the day is a Sabbath, the night before the day is counted as part of the Sabbath. There are no situations in Scripture that teach the night after the Sabbath is part of it, nor any situations that require the night before the day to be excluded from it. *of the day before.

Nisan 16 Chart

The following chart gives the date of Nisan 16 for the next 101 years, and the weekday upon which it occurs. The wave sheaf day must be after the equinox (Tequfah), so that data is also supplied. The table was generated by computer to ensure accuracy.*

Table 9: Nisan 16 Dates 2012-2112

Year	Nis 16		equinox	
2012	4/ 8	SUN	3/20	5:12
2013	3/29	FRI	3/20	10:59
2014	4/16	WED	3/20	16:56
2015	4/ 6	MON	3/20	22:45
2016	3/26	SAT	3/20	4:28
2017	4/14	FRI	3/20	10:26
2018	4/ 3	TUE	3/20	16:15
2019	3/24	SUN	3/20	22: 0
2020	4/10	FRI	3/20	3:53
2021	3/30	TUE	3/20	9:39
2022	4/18	MON	3/20	15:33
2023	4/ 7	FRI	3/20	21:22
2024	3/27	WED	3/20	3: 2
2025	4/15	TUE	3/20	8:58
2026	4/ 5	SUN	3/20	14:45
2027	3/25	THR	3/20	20:25
2028	4/12	WED	3/20	2:16
2029	4/ 1	SUN	3/20	7:59
2030	3/21	THR	3/20	13:50
2031	4/ 9	WED	3/20	19:41
2032	3/28	SUN	3/20	1:22
2033	4/16	SAT	3/20	7:23
2034	4/ 6	THR	3/20	13:17
2035	3/27	TUE	3/20	19: 2
2036	4/14	MON	3/20	1: 0
2037	4/ 3	FRI	3/20	6:48
2038	3/23	TUE	3/20	12:40
2039	4/11	MON	3/20	18:31
2040	3/30	FRI	3/20	0: 9
2041	4/18	THR	3/20	6: 3
2042	4/ 7	MON	3/20	11:51
2043	3/28	SAT	3/20	17:29
2044	4/15	FRI	3/19	23:22
2045	4/ 4	TUE	3/20	5: 8
2046	3/25	SUN	3/20	10:57
2047	4/12	FRI	3/20	16:50
2048	3/31	TUE	3/19	22:30
2049	3/21	SUN	3/20	4:26
2050	4/ 9	SAT	3/20	10:20
2051	3/29	WED	3/20	16: 0
2052	4/16	TUE	3/19	21:55
2053	4/ 6	SUN	3/20	3:45
2054	3/26	THR	3/20	9:33
2055	4/14	WED	3/20	15:29
2056	4/ 2	SUN	3/19	21:11
2057	3/22	THR	3/20	3: 7
2058	4/10	WED	3/20	9: 3
2059	3/31	MON	3/20	14:42
2060	4/18	SUN	3/19	20:36
2061	4/ 7	THR	3/20	2:24
2062	3/28	TUE	3/20	8: 7
2063	4/16	MON	3/20	13:58
2064	4/ 4	FRI	3/19	19:35
2065	3/24	TUE	3/20	1:25
2066	4/12	MON	3/20	7:19
2067	4/ 1	FRI	3/20	12:57
2068	3/21	WED	3/19	18:51
2069	4/ 9	TUE	3/20	0:45
2070	3/29	SAT	3/20	6:33
2071	4/17	FRI	3/20	12:31
2072	4/ 6	WED	3/19	18:17
2073	3/26	SUN	3/20	0:10
2074	4/13	FRI	3/20	6: 8
2075	4/ 3	WED	3/20	11:46
2076	3/22	SUN	3/19	17:37
2077	4/10	SAT	3/19	23:29
2078	3/31	THR	3/20	5:11
2079	**3/20**	**MON**	**3/19***	
2080	4/ 7	SUN	3/19	16:45
2081	3/27	THR	3/19	22:33
2082	4/15	WED	3/20	4:30
2083	4/ 4	SUN	3/20	10: 8
2084	3/23	THR	3/19	15:58
2085	4/11	WED	3/19	21:53
2086	4/ 1	MON	3/20	3:35
2087	3/22	SAT	3/20	9:27
2088	4/ 9	FRI	3/19	15:13
2089	3/29	TUE	3/19	21: 2
2090	4/17	MON	3/20	3: 1
2091	4/ 6	FRI	3/20	8:43
2092	3/25	TUE	3/19	14:35
2093	4/13	MON	3/19	20:34
2094	4/ 2	FRI	3/20	2:20
2095	3/23	WED	3/20	8:12
2096	4/10	TUE	3/19	14: 0
2097	3/31	SUN	3/19	19:47
2098	**3/20**	**THR**	**3/19***	
2099	4/ 8	WED	3/20	7:18
2100	3/28	SUN	3/20	13: 2
2101	4/15	FRI	3/20	18:55
2102	4/ 5	WED	3/21	0:37
2103	3/25	SUN	3/21	6:25
2104	4/12	SAT	3/20	12:15
2105	4/ 2	THR	3/20	18: 4
2106	3/22	MON	3/21	0: 2
2107	4/10	SUN	3/21	5:48
2108	3/30	FRI	3/20	11:38
2109	4/17	WED	3/20	17:36
2110	4/ 6	SUN	3/20	23:23
2111	3/27	FRI	3/21	5:11
2112	4/14	THR	3/20	11: 1

Some cases may need confirmation by live witnesses.

* When the first edition of this book was published, I was using a modern equinox definition, and that is what you see here for all the figures except those in bold. But as noted in the chapter on the birth of Messiah, the ancient method was observational. Accordingly, two intercalations in this 101 year block need correction because the day previous to the modern equinox met the ancient observational definition for the *tequfah*. In all but these two cases, the modern equinox did not make a difference because the cases were not close, and the methods chosen only make a difference in a few very close cases.

Liturgy for Counting the Omer

On the facing page to the right is a table for figuring the counting to Shavuot. Look up the date of Nisan 16 on the preceding page for the current year, and note the weekday that it falls on. Then locate that week day on the chart on the next page. Under that weekday locate column ***N***. Count forward on your calendar starting with Nisan 16 until you reach the current day. When you reach the current day number (***N***) read the figures in Columns ***A***, ***B***, and ***C*** at the far right, then substitute in the blessing that applies:

If before the first of the Sabbaths after Passover (***C*** =0):

> Blessed are you Adonai YHWH who sent your Son as the first-fruits of the resurrection and enjoined on us to count the Omer. Today is the __***A***th day of the __***B***th Shavua IN THE DAY AFTER THE CEASING, even the __***N***th day IN THE DAY AFTER THE CEASING.

When the count is on a weekly Sabbath before 50 (***C*** is shaded gold):

> Blessed are you Adonai YHWH who sent your Son as the first-fruits of the resurrection and enjoined on us to count the Omer. Today is the __***A***th day of the __***B***th Shavua IN THE DAY AFTER THE CEASING, even the __***N***th day IN THE DAY AFTER THE CEASING, and today is the __***B***th of the Sabbaths that are perfect IN THE DAY AFTER THE CEASING.

When the count is on a weekday before 50 after the first of the Sabbaths (C is not gold and is not 0):

> Blessed are you Adonai YHWH who sent your Son as the first-fruits of the resurrection and enjoined on us to count the Omer. Today is the __***A***th day of the __***B***th Shavua IN THE DAY AFTER THE CEASING, even the ***N***th day IN THE DAY AFTER THE __***C***th of the Sabbaths which is/are complete and perfect.

When the count is 50:

> Blessed are you Adonai YHWH who sent your Son as the first-fruits of the resurrection and enjoined on us to count the Omer. Today is the 50th day IN THE DAY AFTER THE CEASING, even the 50th day IN THE DAY AFTER THE SEVENTH SABBATH making seven Sabbaths perfect.

Table 10: Shavuot Countings

Sun			Mon			Tue			Wed			Thu			Fri			Sab			
N	*A*	*B*	*N*	*A*	*B*	*N*	*A*	*B*	*N*	*A*	*B*	*N*	*A*	*B*	*N*	*A*	*B*	*N*	*A*	*B*	*C*
1	1	1																			0
2	2	1	1	1	1																0
3	3	1	2	2	1	1	1	1													0
4	4	1	3	3	1	2	2	1	1	1	1										0
5	5	1	4	4	1	3	3	1	2	2	1	1	1	1							0
6	6	1	5	5	1	4	4	1	3	3	1	2	2	1	1	1	1				0
7	7	1	6	6	1	5	5	1	4	4	1	3	3	1	2	2	1	1	1	1	1
8	1	2	7	7	1	6	6	1	5	5	1	4	4	1	3	3	1	2	2	1	1
9	2	2	8	1	2	7	7	1	6	6	1	5	5	1	4	4	1	3	3	1	1
10	3	2	9	2	2	8	1	2	7	7	1	6	6	1	5	5	1	4	4	1	1
11	4	2	10	3	2	9	2	2	8	1	2	7	7	1	6	6	1	5	5	1	1
12	5	2	11	4	2	10	3	2	9	2	2	8	1	2	7	7	1	6	6	1	1
13	6	2	12	5	2	11	4	2	10	3	2	9	2	2	8	1	2	7	7	1	1
14	7	2	13	6	2	12	5	2	11	4	2	10	3	2	9	2	2	8	1	2	2
15	1	3	14	7	2	13	6	2	12	5	2	11	4	2	10	3	2	9	2	2	2
16	2	3	15	1	3	14	7	2	13	6	2	12	5	2	11	4	2	10	3	2	2
17	3	3	16	2	3	15	1	3	14	7	2	13	6	2	12	5	2	11	4	2	2
18	4	3	17	3	3	16	2	3	15	1	3	14	7	2	13	6	2	12	5	2	2
19	5	3	18	4	3	17	3	3	16	2	3	15	1	3	14	7	2	13	6	2	2
20	6	3	19	5	3	18	4	3	17	3	3	16	2	3	15	1	3	14	7	2	2
21	7	3	20	6	3	19	5	3	18	4	3	17	3	3	16	2	3	15	1	3	3
22	1	4	21	7	3	20	6	3	19	5	3	18	4	3	17	3	3	16	2	3	3
23	2	4	22	1	4	21	7	3	20	6	3	19	5	3	18	4	3	17	3	3	3
24	3	4	23	2	4	22	1	4	21	7	3	20	6	3	19	5	3	18	4	3	3
25	4	4	24	3	4	23	2	4	22	1	4	21	7	3	20	6	3	19	5	3	3
26	5	4	25	4	4	24	3	4	23	2	4	22	1	4	21	7	3	20	6	3	3
27	6	4	26	5	4	25	4	4	24	3	4	23	2	4	22	1	4	21	7	3	3
28	7	4	27	6	4	26	5	4	25	4	4	24	3	4	23	2	4	22	1	4	4
29	1	5	28	7	4	27	6	4	26	5	4	25	4	4	24	3	4	23	2	4	4
30	2	5	29	1	5	28	7	4	27	6	4	26	5	4	25	4	4	24	3	4	4
31	3	5	30	2	5	29	1	5	28	7	4	27	6	4	26	5	4	25	4	4	4
32	4	5	31	3	5	30	2	5	29	1	5	28	7	4	27	6	4	26	5	4	4

Sun			Mon			Tue			Wed			Thu			Fri			Sab			
N	*A*	*B*	*N*	*A*	*B*	*N*	*A*	*B*	*N*	*A*	*B*	*N*	*A*	*B*	*N*	*A*	*B*	*N*	*A*	*B*	*C*
33	5	5	32	4	5	31	3	5	30	2	5	29	1	5	28	7	4	27	6	4	4
34	6	5	33	5	5	32	4	5	31	3	5	30	2	5	29	1	5	28	7	4	4
35	7	5	34	6	5	33	5	5	32	4	5	31	3	5	30	2	5	29	1	5	5
36	1	6	35	7	5	34	6	5	33	5	5	32	4	5	31	3	5	30	2	5	5
37	2	6	36	1	6	35	7	5	34	6	5	33	5	5	32	4	5	31	3	5	5
38	3	6	37	2	6	36	1	6	35	7	5	34	6	5	33	5	5	32	4	5	5
39	4	6	38	3	6	37	2	6	36	1	6	35	7	5	34	6	5	33	5	5	5
40	5	6	39	4	6	38	3	6	37	2	6	36	1	6	35	7	5	34	6	5	5
41	6	6	40	5	6	39	4	6	38	3	6	37	2	6	36	1	6	35	7	5	5
42	7	6	41	6	6	40	5	6	39	4	6	38	3	6	37	2	6	36	1	6	6
43	1	7	42	7	6	41	6	6	40	5	6	39	4	6	38	3	6	37	2	6	6
44	2	7	43	1	7	42	7	6	41	6	6	40	5	6	39	4	6	38	3	6	6
45	3	7	44	2	7	43	1	7	42	7	6	41	6	6	40	5	6	39	4	6	6
46	4	7	45	3	7	44	2	7	43	1	7	42	7	6	41	6	6	40	5	6	6
47	5	7	46	4	7	45	3	7	44	2	7	43	1	7	42	7	6	41	6	6	6
48	6	7	47	5	7	46	4	7	45	3	7	44	2	7	43	1	7	42	7	6	6
49	7	7	48	6	7	47	5	7	46	4	7	45	3	7	44	2	7	43	1	7	7
50			49	7	7	48	6	7	47	5	7	46	4	7	45	3	7	44	2	7	7
			50			49	7	7	48	6	7	47	5	7	46	4	7	45	3	7	7
						50			49	7	7	48	6	7	47	5	7	46	4	7	7
									50			49	7	7	48	6	7	47	5	7	7
												50			49	7	7	48	6	7	7
															50			49	7	7	7
																		50			

Example. In 2024 A.D., Nisan 16 will be on Wednesday, March 27 (as shown on the NISAN 16 CHART). In the chart on the preceding page, I have shaded the column N under Wednesday. Let's say the count is on day ***N***=27. The corresponding numbers are ***A***=6, ***B***=4, ***C***=4. The blessing then goes as follows:

> Blessed are you Adonai YHWH who sent your Son as the first-fruits of the resurrection and enjoined on us to count the Omer. Today is the 6th day of the 4th Shavua IN THE DAY AFTER THE

CEASING, even the *27*th day IN THE DAY AFTER THE 4th of the Sabbaths which are complete and perfect.

The blessing is based on Lev. 23:11-16 and Deut. 16:9. It is designed to cover every aspect of the commandments to count.

> You shall count seven sevens[1] for yourself—from when the sickle is made halal[2] in the standing grain, you shall begin to count seven sevens[3]. (Deuteronomy 16:9)

(1) "Seven sevens" are to be counted. This could also be translated "seven weeks." But the Hebrew word is "שָׁבֻעֹת," which is really a passive plural of "seven," שֶׁבַע. So it means a period of seven of something. In this case periods of seven days. See also Ex. 34:22; Num. 28:26. So to count seven sevens means to count seven days seven times. And it also means to count "sevens" (weeks) unit wise. Thus, 1st day of 1st seven unto 7th day of 7th seven (i.e. the 49th day). Then after the 7th day of the 7th seven is complete, the 50th day is the feast of Shavuot (sevens/weeks).

(2) The hiphil infinitive construct הָחֵל means "to make profane," or "to make common." The same root also means "to begin," and is used that way in the second clause of the verse. The Arabic cognate means "free from obligation," which is used by Arabs as roughly equivalent to, "Kosher." Sometimes in Jericho or other dry places in Israel it was necessary to harvest the grain before Nisan 16. However, it was not legal to eat it (cf. Lev. 23:11-14) until a sheaf of it was waved in the Temple by the priest. Thus before Nisan 16 the grain was not "common." It was not "free from obligation." When the sheaf was waved, it became "common" or "profane" . . . that is legal for human consumption.

(3) The grain becomes common for eating after the sheaf is waved in the morning of Nisan 16. Thus we know that the counting begins in the morning, and not the night before as the Rabbis explain. The sickle does enter the grain before this time, but it may not be eaten. Farmers bring a sheaf to the feast to be waved by the priest, and as soon as the waving is done, the grain market in Jerusalem opens. So from the moment of the waving in Nisan 16, it is time to count the 1st day of the 1st seven (week).

The starting date was proved earlier, so the following will explain how the counting is codified:

> And ye will have counted for yourselves in the time after† the Sabbath, from the day that ye bring the sheaf of the waving, seven Sabbaths. They shall be regular.‡ (Lev. 23:15).

From this text is derived the precept to count Sabbaths in addition to seven seven-day periods (Deut. 16:9). Hence the clause counting the Sabbaths is inserted into the blessing. These are "weekly" Sabbaths or "seventh day" Sabbaths. This is the significance of the word "regular." For in English we say weekly Sabbath or seventh day Sabbath to indicate a regular Sabbath as opposed to a festival Sabbath. The Hebrew uses the word meaning "perfect" or "complete" as this is the other sense of the word "seven."

The recitation is done shortly after sunrise, but any time between that and sunset fulfills the Torah—as the counting was to begin as soon as the sheaf was waved in the morning. Rabbinic Jews recite the blessing after previous sunset, but this is based on a post Temple reckoning of the day, and is not exactly correct according to Deut. 16:9. One should notice the repetition of IN THE DAY AFTER. This is specifically designed to teach the Hebrew sense of this phrase—which Israel having forgotten is one of the major causes of confusion on how to count. Similar usage is found in Gen. 2:4 and Gen 30:33.

> Yet in the time to come after the seventh Sabbath you are counting a fiftieth day; then you shall present a new grain offering to Yãhweh. (Lev 23:16).

From this text is derived the precept to count all the days in sequence, from one to fifty. So this too is included in the blessing for each day.

† Or, 'in the tomorrow of,' where tomorrow is extended by Hebrew idiom beyond the literal next day as sometimes occurs in English.

‡ Or 'perfect,' See for example Lev. 25:29, "And will have been his redemption of it as far as a perfect year of days." This means a year of 365 days, which is the regular year, not a leap year, not a lunar year, not some other kind of tax year. Likewise תְּמִימֹת means perfect Sabbaths, that is on the seventh day, as opposed to some other kind of Sabbath such as the last day of unleavened bread. By the same reasoning 'Sabbaths' cannot mean "weeks" of an irregular sort

Figure 62: Nisan Visibility Plot for 3/10 AD 34

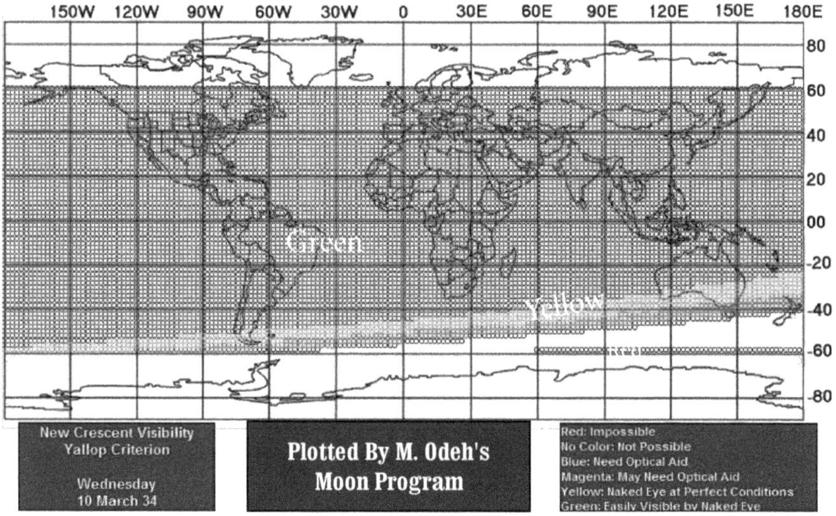

150W 120W 90W 60W 30W 0 30E 60E 90E 120E 150E 180E

80 60 40 20 00 -20 -40 -60 -80

Green

Yellow

Red

New Crescent Visibility
Yallop Criterion

Wednesday
10 March 34

Plotted By M. Odeh's Moon Program

Red: Impossible
No Color: Not Possible
Blue: Need Optical Aid
Magenta: May Need Optical Aid
Yellow: Naked Eye at Perfect Conditions
Green: Easily Visible by Naked Eye

```
Month: I AVIV, AD 34   4173 A.M. Sab. Cyc: 1. Jub. Cyc: 8 Cycle No: 85
Q1: 1.501 A Q2: -0.493 F LG: 102m W: 1.068' AL: 20.8 AV: 20.8
New Moon calculated for longitude: 35.17 and latitude 31.77
Location of calculations: Jerusalem
   Designed and Programmed By Daniel Gregg, ↑ Arrows show when moon is sighted
```

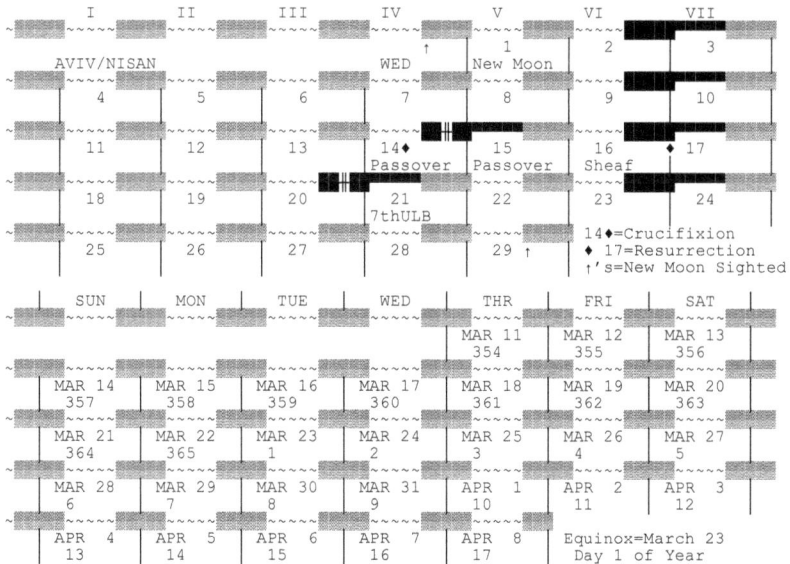

I	II	III	IV	V	VI	VII
			↑	1	2	3
AVIV/NISAN			WED	New Moon		
4	5	6	7	8	9	10
11	12	13	14♦ Passover	15 Passover	16 Sheaf	♦ 17
18	19	20	21 7thULB	22	23	24
25	26	27	28	29 ↑		

14♦=Crucifixion
♦ 17=Resurrection
↑'s=New Moon Sighted

SUN	MON	TUE	WED	THR	FRI	SAT
				MAR 11 354	MAR 12 355	MAR 13 356
MAR 14 357	MAR 15 358	MAR 16 359	MAR 17 360	MAR 18 361	MAR 19 362	MAR 20 363
MAR 21 364	MAR 22 365	MAR 23 1	MAR 24 2	MAR 25 3	MAR 26 4	MAR 27 5
MAR 28 6	MAR 29 7	MAR 30 8	MAR 31 9	APR 1 10	APR 2 11	APR 3 12
APR 4 13	APR 5 14	APR 6 15	APR 7 16	APR 8 17		

Equinox=March 23
Day 1 of Year

Notice that everything is shaded Green here. This means that the new moon for Aviv/Nisan A.D. 34 was easily visible all over the world. The visibility map for the preceding day, March 9, A.D. shows that visibility was impossible.[295]

ADAR VISIBILITY MAP 2/8/34 AD

Figure 63: Adar Visibility Plot for AD 34

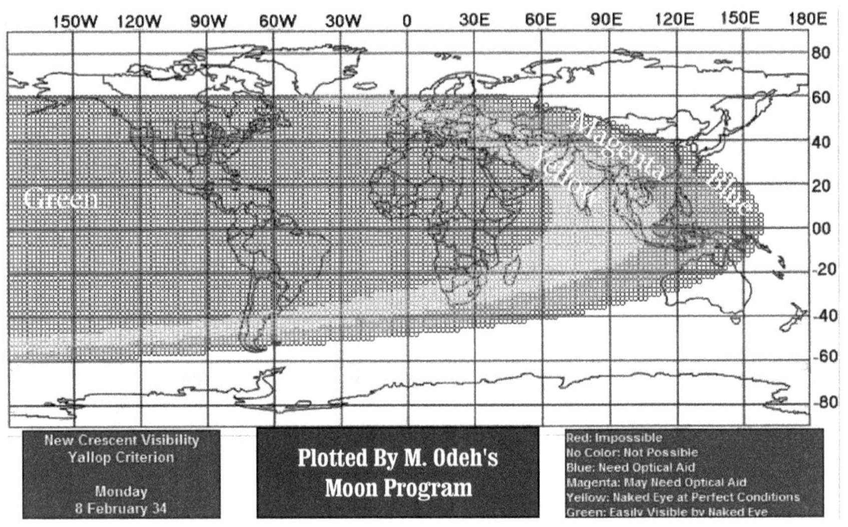


```
Month: XII ADAR, AD 34    4172 A.M. Sab. Cyc: 1. Jub. Cyc: 8 Cycle No: 85
Q1: 0.115 B Q2: -9.000 Z LG:  57m W: 0.332' AL: 11.8 AV: 11.0
New Moon calculated for longitude: 35.17 and latitude 31.77
Location of calculations: Jerusalem
   Designed and Programmed By Daniel Gregg ↑ Arrows show when moon is sighted
```

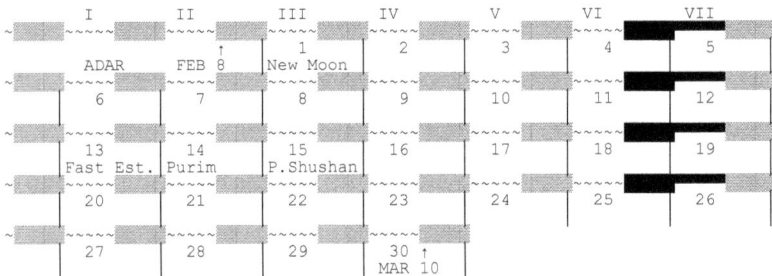

I	II	III	IV	V	VI	VII
ADAR	↑ FEB 8	1 New Moon	2	3	4	5
6	7	8	9	10	11	12
13 Fast Est.	14 Purim	15 P.Shushan	16	17	18	19
20	21	22	23	24	25	26
27	28	29	30 ↑ MAR 10			

[295] The Green zone parabola starts at 80 deg west, Yellow at 30 deg west, and blue at 10 deg east of the prime meridian. Visibility was thus impossible for everything east of 15 deg east.

SUN	MON	TUE	WED	THR	FRI	SAT
		FEB 9 324	FEB 10 325	FEB 11 326	FEB 12 327	FEB 13 328
FEB 14 329	FEB 15 330	FEB 16 331	FEB 17 332	FEB 18 333	FEB 19 334	FEB 20 335
FEB 21 336	FEB 22 337	FEB 23 338	FEB 24 339	FEB 25 340	FEB 26 341	FEB 27 342
FEB 28 343	MAR 1 344	MAR 2 345	MAR 3 346	MAR 4 347	MAR 5 348	MAR 6 349
MAR 7 350	MAR 8 351	MAR 9 352	MAR 10 353			

Notice that Israel is just in the green zone, so the moon was easily visible at sunset on Feb. 8. This calculation makes it clear that Adar was 30 days in AD 34. Providentially, the factors for Adar and Nisan were so arranged as to prevent ambiguity. Since Adar was already 30 days, the new moon for Nisan is at a certain time regardless of any weather factors that may have made seeing the moon impossible. This secures without a sensible doubt that Nisan 14 was on Wednesday, March 24, AD 34.

The Rev. 1:10 Conspiracy

This note goes late into this book. In the Good News of Messiah (GNM) notes I connected Rev. 1:10 to the resurrection day:*

> [9]I, Yoĥanan, your brother and fellow partaker in the tribulation and kingdom and patient endurance in Y'ĕshua, came to be on the island called [θ]Patmos, because of the word of the Almĭghty and the testimony of Y'ĕshua. [10]I came to be in the Spĭrit on [Φ]Yăhw'eh's day, AND I HEARD BEHIND ME[α] A LOUD VOICE AS OF A TRUMPET[β], [11]saying, "Write in a scroll what you see, and send it to the seven assemblies, to Ephesus, and to Smyrna, and to Pergamum, and to Thyatira, and to Sardis and to Philadelphia, and to Laodicea."

I noted:

1:10 ϕ→day; The Şabbaţh. Or this may be read, "Adŏnai's Day" (Lord's Day). The Şabbaţh is the special day for worship and resting unto Him, set apart and made holy for that purpose from creation. The usage came about due to the fact that the special restorative act of the resurrection happened on the Şabbaţh, but Gnostics soon corrupted this use and applied it to Sunday. See "first

---

* Jonah was vomited onto the ground at the face of the ending of the third night. Then he is rising up in the day. As the third night was on the verge of ending, Messiah's spirit had returned from the depth of She'ol, the heart of the earth. Then at the crack of dawn, within the beginning moments of the seventh day he became aware of his body beginning to revive, finding himself laying on the ground. Then he ascended from his bed exiting the tomb (Hos. 6:3). So, what we call the resurrection happened in part before the third night ended, and in part when the day of the Sabbath was just beginning, on the seventh day. On the seventh day, he was ceased from death. On the seventh day, he is getting his breath (cf. Ex. 31:17). To make a proper distinction, his spirit returned from the depth of Sheol by night, but his body was still reviving by day, the whole resurrection event spanning the transition from night to day. His spirit is revived on the third calendar day, in the night of the Sabbath, but he raises his body from the ground on the seventh day, in the earliest part, where the dawn has just become more intense than the moonlight which ruled the night. When the dawn ascends, it overtakes the starlight and moonlight at a critical point. This is the point when the rule of night ends, and the rule of day begins.

of the Ṣabbaṭhs" (Acts 20:7; 1 Cor. 16:2; Mat. 28:1; Mark 16:2; Luke 24:1; Yoĥ. 20:1, 19). Also see Rom. 14:4-6; Gal. 4:10; Col. 2:16. ● **1:10** α Eze 3:12; ● **1:10** β Exo 19:16; ▶ This can be no other than the Ṣabbaṭh day. The Ṣabbaṭh is a day to Yăhweh because he rested on that day after creation. See Exodus 16:25. In the Hebrew there the possessive is formed with a lamed: "הַיּוֹם לַיהוָה *hay-yom le-Yăhweh*" and that is what we see with the dative here: ἐν τῇ κυριακῇ ἡμέρᾳ, which answers to the Hebrew: "בַּיּוֹם לַיהוָה *bay-yom le-Yăhweh*". The Greek text may be re-ordered like the Hebrew: "ἐν ἡμέρᾳ τῇ κυριακῇ." This is not the phrase for the future "day of the Lŏrd" which is "ἡμέρα τοῦ κυρίου" (cf. 2Thess. 2:2). Against this, the book of Revelation is not only about the day of judgment, and indeed the first part is not about it at all. The fact of the resurrection on the Ṣabbaṭh leaves only one possibility for this passage: the seventh day.."

A friend posted a copy of Ranko Stefanovic's paper, "THE LORD'S DAY" OF REVELATION 1:10 IN THE CURRENT DEBATE.* Herein it was brought to my notice that one of the three principle opinions applied the phrase to Easter Sunday. I could not help but think the date may have double reference at that point. As I read on, Stefanovic himself suggested double reference later in the paper for the "DAY OF THE LORD" view and the SABBATH view. I realized that an annual reference to Easter was dismissed because it was presumed to be Sunday and that elevating that day would make no sense in Revelation when a major theme of the book is to draw attention to the appointed times. I also realized that an annual date in such a context makes more sense of the position given to it, and more recently I had come to the conclusion that the chronology of Nebuchadnezzar's restoration also involved double reference along with Ezekiel's 390 days and Luke 13:32. This last text and Rev. 11:11 should then be connected to the first of the Sabbaths, the annual first Sabbath following the Passover feast. While we have no explicit date for which Sabbath, Rev. 1:10 took place on, I now consider it highly probable that it was the anniversary Resurrection Sabbath. Why I did not see it before I do not know.

The world makes it plain that they are conspiring against the truth. So also religion conspires, even Christianity and Judaism (cf. Hos. 5:1-6:11), Ephraim and Judah. I am not hasty to say what the conspiracies are. After all a conspiracy is hidden and often concealed for a very long time. But when the circumstantial evidence is so strong, and the conspiracy hypothesis parsimonious at a key point of history, and so clearly in the service of iniquity, then I think we should not be ashamed to consider it, neither being victims of excessive conspiratorial speculation, nor being those who buy and sell the party line in order to be accepted.

---

* *Andrews University Seminary Studies*, Vol. 49, No. 2, 261-284. 2011.

The Synoptic Problem

In the English texts, John clearly places the crucifixion on Nisan 14,and Matthew, Mark, and Luke appear to place it on Nisan 15. This is called the "Synoptic Problem." It relates to our chronology because we have clearly placed the crucifixion on Nisan 14, whereas it has often been argued that it was on Nisan 15 even until this day. The Nisan 15 view requires a Friday crucifixion and Sunday resurrection to go with it, and therefore has been promoted by those believing in Friday-Sunday as support for that viewpoint.

There are several possible solutions to this problem. Most scholars admit that John places the crucifixion on Nisan 14. And most of those who place it on Nisan 15 are in the unenviable position of believing there is a contradiction between John and the other three evangelists.[296] This dissonant position eventually results in a lowered view of Scripture; that it contains contradictions that cannot be reconciled and eventually leads to regarding the Evangelists as errant.

I will review John's chronology. John 13:1 tells us that the last supper was "before the Feast of the Passover." Then John 18:28 tells us, "they themselves did not enter into the Praetorium in order that they might not be defiled, but might eat the Passover," and John 19:14 says, "it was the day of preparation for the Passover"; also John 13:29, "For some were supposing, because Judas had the money box, that Yeshua was saying to him, 'Buy the things we have need of for the feast;' or else, that he should give something to the poor." On Nisan 15 there would be no buying or selling, so that assumption would not be made. No buying was allowed on a holy day (see Neh. 10:31). John 19:31 says, "The Jews therefore, because it was the day of preparation, so that the bodies should not remain on the cross on the Sabbath (for that Sabbath was a high *day*), asked Pilate that their legs might be broken, and *that* they might be taken away." To make Nisan 15 the crucifixion day is to make it a Sabbath (cf. Lev. 23:11). So why the objection to having bodies on the cross if it was already

[296] The same is true of some who side with John, but to a much lesser extent because these realize that "first day of unleavened bread" in Matthew, Mark and Luke means the 14th of Nisan.

the Sabbath?

John is not the only proof that the crucifixion was on Nisan 14. In Luke 22:15-16 Yeshua says, "And he said to them, 'I earnestly desire this—to eat the Passover with you before I suffer; 16 for I say to you, I shall by no means eat it until it is fulfilled in the kingdom of the Almĩghty.' " He plainly declares that he would not eat it then. Also, there is a basic contradiction between the Torah and the statements in Matthew 26:17; Mark 14:12; and Luke 22:7 if they are taken to refer to Nisan 15. The English texts tell us that the question concerning Passover preparation was asked, "On the first day of unleavened bread." Yet, it was necessary to † choose, slay, and prepare the sacrificial lamb on the 14th of Nisan. Further, it was necessary to remove the leaven before the 15th of Nisan. So it makes no sense to ask about preparing for passover, if in fact the day of preparation passed by.

Additionally, Simon of Cyrene, "coming in from the country" was compelled to carry the cross of Yeshua (Luke 23:26). This would not have been possible on the 15th of Nisan since it was an annual Sabbath. It would be a major violation of Torah to compel a man to do servile labor on this day (cf. Lev. 23:7). Furthermore, Josephus tells us that even the Romans recognized the Jewish exemption, even if they were charged with a crime, "that they be not obliged to go before any judge on the Sabbath day, nor on the day of the preparation to it, after the ninth hour" (*Ant.* 16:163). Even the Jews of Cyrene enjoyed Roman recognition of their rights (cf. *Ant.* 16:168-169).

So it is abundantly clear that something is seriously wrong with the interpretation of the texts that place the disciples question concerning the "first day of unleavened bread" on the 15th of Nisan.

There are several solutions to this problem, all of which (1) correct the chronology, and (2) place the Passover sacrifice in the afternoon of Nisan 14. I will put the best solution first, and then follow it up with mention of the other solutions. The best solution begins with Exodus 12:15:

> 'Seven days you shall eat unleavened bread, but <u>on the day before</u> you shall make cease leaven from your houses; for

† Certain instructions concerning the first Passover were one time commandments for the divine actions during it. Among them, putting blood on the doorposts, and taking the lamb on the 10th day. All the perpetual commandments are repeated or implied in Exodus 12:14-20; 24-27; 42-49. 12:24, "And ye will have guarded <u>this word</u> as a statute" (cf. Num 9:3-5; 11b-12). 'This word,' vid. Exo. 12:26-27a. The 10th day was to make sure everyone was ready for the judgment to pass over.

whoever eats anything leavened from the first day through the seventh day, that person shall be cut off from Israel.†

'On the day before' or 'ahead' or 'head most': the word *rishon*, בַּיּוֹם הָרִאשׁוֹן; Even more literally, 'on the day, the head most one'; in this case it means Nisan 14. The word רִאשׁוֹן is from the noun ראשׁ *head* used as an adjective. See the BDB Lexicon, '3a. = *before, formerly.*' See HALOT '2. *earlier, former.*' '*previous*'; Gesenius, '*former*'; Koehler, '*preceding, former*'; TWOT, '*before*'; Langen-scheidt, '*preceding, before.*'

If the Hebrew word used was *rosh* ראשׁ then the sense 'before' would be natural in all stages of Hebrew. However, it is רִאשׁוֹן. And in later stages of Hebrew putting this sense on the word would at best seem difficult. It could be however, that at an early stage of Hebrew, *bayom harishon* carried both the sense of 'first day' and 'prior day' or 'head most day'. The context of Exodus 12:15 begs for the sense 'on the day ahead,' because there was to be no leaven in the house for seven days, and if one waited to the first day, then one would be in volation of the commandment.

The Rabbis have universally faced the difficulty of Exodus 12:15 by saying that it means leaven is to be removed the day before the first day of unleavened bread. Therefore, it should be noted that the problem interpretations of Mat. 26:17, Mark 14:12, and Luke 22:7 have their counterpart in the Torah itself: Exodus 12:15. So to solve one we solve the Matthew and Mark passages also. The Luke passage has "day of unleavens" (ἡ ἡμέρα τῶν ἀζύμων) "on which it was necessary to be getting the passover sacrificed" (ἐν ᾗ ἔδει θύεσθαι τὸ πάσχα). Obviously this was the 14th of the month (cf. Exodus 12:6). Mark 14:12 also says, "when they sacrificed the Passover" (ὅτε τὸ πάσχα ἔθυον). According to Luke also, there is here a "day of unleavens" prior to the 15th. The sense of the genitive here may be taken as the day on which leaven is removed and unleavened bread baked. The whole of the day need not be unleavened, but only part of it need be, as we may say a "day of" something is the same as a "day for" something that does not take up the whole day. We should note that Luke leaves off the designation "headmost" (πρώτη), probably so that he does not have to explain it to his

† This is the sense that Rashi gives to the text. "'The first day' in this context means the eve of the festival" (Exo. 12:15). "We find that which precedes called 'the first' in other contexts, such as 'Were you born first to Adam?' (Job 15:7: הֲרִאישׁוֹן אָדָם תִּוָּלֵד).

non-Jewish audience. I used to favor Codex Bezae's (**D**) reading of Luke 22:7, "day of the Passover," but it became plain to me that "the headmost day of unleavens" in the other two Evangelists meant there was a "day of unleavens" at that time, and so **D**'s alteration looses its explanatory edge; it has also become clear to me that some of the **D** scribe's alterations were theologically motivated, e.g. Mark 16. So Bezae has to be used with care. It also turns out the Luke 22:7 supplies a corral-cipher key.†

Now I return to Exodus 12:15, Matthew 26:17, and Mark 14:12. The same solution pertains to each of them. (1) בַּיּוֹם הָרִאשׁוֹן = *on the day the-head most one*. The only thing that needs to be mentioned is that is appears that it was acceptable to use the word רִאשׁוֹן in such a way at the time of the Exodus. The word "head" itself may mean at the head of something, which is to say, before it, or it may mean the first part of it. The difference between *rosh* and *rishon* in Hebrew is more akin to the difference between *head* and *header* in English than *head* and *first.* The adjective rishon appears to be formed by the combination of *rosh* + *on*, ון+ ראש . The suffix -on means 'most.' (See the discussion starting on page 315 eg. עֶלְיוֹן, 'most high.') Thus, the literal sense 'head most.'

It is possible that the first occurrence of הרִאשׁוֹן in Exodus 12:15 was pronounced slightly different than the second occurrence (perhaps: רֹאשׁוֹן), or if not, then the ambiguity was then accepted in Hebrew. However, later the literalism, 'head most' gave way to the almost exclusive usage of *rishon* as 'first'; if 'head most' was pronounced different than *rishon* then the difficulty is in ascribing uniform vowel points to an unknown period. So there are logical, though speculative, reasons why this word has a *hapax* sense in Exodus 12:15. It is more likely that a literalism was recognized in the word due to the context and the obvious need to remove the leaven before the first of the seven days, and thus it was taken in the first instance as 'head most;' rather than first of the seven days.

Jewish practice recognizes that the command is to remove the leaven on the day before, and thus ascribes that sense to *bayom ha-rishon* in Exodus 12:15. The explanation of Matthew 26:17 and Mark 14:12 then is nothing more than an archaic throw back to the usage in Exodus 12:15, a sense that may be non-existent in contemporary Greek, but would be explained by the ancient Hebrew in Exodus 12:15.* That the Greek may be bent this way into an ancient Hebrew

† See page 481, note no. 1. *In the worst case we might have to call it a calque.

mold is possible:

> Now on <u>the day before</u> Unleavened Bread the disciples came to Yẽshua, saying, “Where do you desire we should prepare for you to eat the Passover?” (Matthew 26:17).

‘Before, or ‘ahead of’: See Exodus 12:15: בַּיּוֹם הָרִאשׁוֹן, ‘on the day the-head most’; רִאשׁוֹן: ‘earlier, former’ (HALOT); ‘previous’; ‘before’ (BDB 3a). So also the word here, πρώτῃ, ‘earliest’, ‘earlier’, ‘before’ (BDAG, 3rd, 1β). The context also confirms this meaning. It is too late to prepare for Passover on Nisan 15.

> Now the day before Unleavened Bread, (when they sacrificed the passover), his disciples said to him, “Where do you desire us to have gone so we may prepare, that you may eat the Passover (Mark 14:12).

‘Day before or ‘ahead of’: It was Nisan 14 reckoned from sunset to sunset, and it was at the very beginning of it, just after sunset at the end of the daylight portion of the 13th day; ‘before’ (see πρώτῃ 3rd ed. BDAG, 1β). The usage is a Hebraism from a literal, and archaic sense of *rishon,* meaning ‘head’; the same word is used for ‘first’ and for something that is ‘previous’ to the first. John 15:18, ‘ye know that it hath hated me **before** you’ (YLT), ‘γινώσκετε ὅτι ἐμὲ πρῶτον ὑμῶν μεμίσηκεν’; John 1:15, ‘for he was **before** me’ (YLT), ‘ὅτι πρῶτός μου ἦν’; Job 8:8, ‘generation ahead’ or ‘former generation’ (YLT): לְדֹר רִישׁוֹן; LXX: γενεὰν πρώτην. Job 15:7, ‘Ahead of man were you born?’, LXX: πρῶτος ἀνθρώπων, הֲרִאישׁוֹן אָדָם, or ‘before men’, ‘previous to men.’ See Exo 12:15 for the parallel solution. ‘Head-most (of)’ recommended itself as the concordant gloss.

I favor the above solution because it is linguistic, agrees with the context and does not rely on tradition. However, there are several other solutions worth mention, which I will offer with my criticism. The first of these is that according to dispersion tradition the 14th of Nisan was called the ‘first day of unleavened bread.’ Thus we find Josephus saying ‘we keep a feast for eight days, which is called the feast of unleavened bread’ (Ant. 2:317). We also have the circumcstance that the dispersion Jews would have to keep the feast this long on account of doubt as to when the new moon was declared in Jerusalem.

Figure 64: Dispersion Seder Reckonings shows the cases possible. For A.D. 34, it was case 1 for the dispersion. Thus the extra day was Nisan 14, and this was called the 'first day of unleavened bread' in the dispersion, and they would have accordingly rid their houses of leaven on Nisan 13.

Figure 64: Dispersion Seder Reckonings

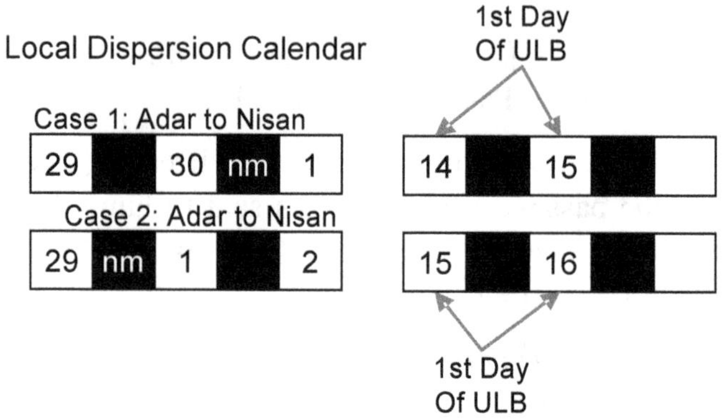

Depending on the local dispersion new moon, either the 14th and 15th (case 1) would be observed in the local calendar or the 15th and 16th (case 2). Both days would be observed as the "first day of unleavened bread." Now in A.D. 34, Adar was 30 days. The crescent visibility map shows that all of the Jewish dispersion would see both the Adar moon and the Nisan moon on the same days as Jerusalem (page 297 and 298). Thus Adar is guaranteed to be 30 days that year. Hence for A.D. 34, it is "Case 1" in the chart. The dispersion would be observing the 14th and 15th as the "first day of unleavened bread."

This is to say that at the same time Yeshua was having supper with his disciples at the start of Nisan 14, the dispersion were observing their first Seder as the 'first day of unleavened bread.' This is shown in Figure 65: Synoptic Problem Solved below.†

The final solution I would like to mention is that of the Anchor Bible:

> Now concerning the first *day* of Unleavened Bread the disciples came to Yẽshua, saying, "Where do you desire we

† I do not favor this solution for the simple reason that the problem already exists in Exodus 12:15. Occam's razor favors one simple solution for all the cases, as does the cipher principle. The other solutions are equally hard to figure out without the benefit of appeal to a cipher.

should prepare for you to eat the Passover?" And he said, "Go into the city to a certain man, and say to him: the teacher says, my time is at hand; with you I will keep the Passover with my disciples." And the disciples did as Yĕshua had directed them; and they prepared the Passover (Matthew 26:17ff).

Figure 65: Synoptic Problem Solved

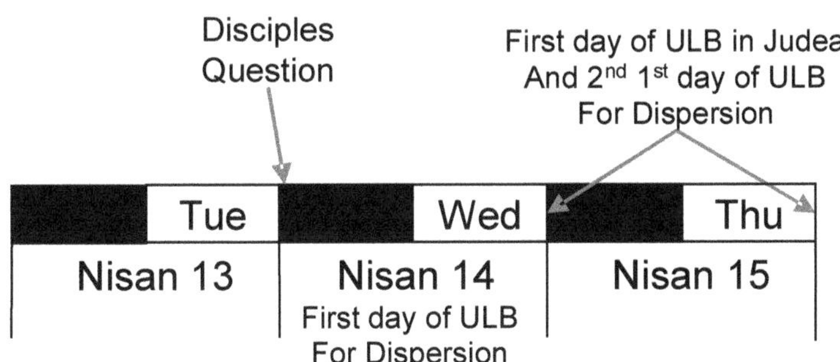

They came 'concerning' that day. This could also be translated 'for the first day of unleavened bread' or 'in regard to the first day of unleavened bread.' The *Anchor Bible Commentary*, one of the few Christian commentaries where the authors' actually consulted Jewish scholars, says this in the "Matthew" volume:

> 17. *On the first day of Unleavened Bread.* This would be Nisan 15, the day *after* the Passover [sacrifice—according to strict Torah reckoning] but Matthew certainly means to indicate that the preparations were being made on the day *before* Passover. Josephus (*Antiquities* II. 317) applies the name Unleavened Bread loosely when he speaks of the feast as lasting "for eight days." (But cf. *ibid.*, III. 249.) Perhaps the expression as we have it here is not as simple as it appears. It is possible to translate the Greek by "With reference to the first day of Unleavened Bread . . ."—i.e., the disciples were asking Jesus for guidance as to the procedures to be followed for the next day.[297]

[297] pg. 319, *The Anchor Bible, Matthew*, W.F. Albright and C.S. Mann, vol. 26, Doubleday, 1971.

The King James Version in this very verse translated the same grammatical case as "for": "Where wilt thou that we prepare <u>for</u> thee to eat the passover." The word "for" translates the dative case of the Greek word *σοι*, "for thee." In Hebrew this is לְךָ. The dative case at the beginning of the verse would likewise be translated, 'And for the first day of unleavened bread...": וְלַיּוֹם הָרִאשׁוֹן לַמַּצּוֹת בָּאוּ. In Greek:*Τῇ δὲ πρώτῃ τῶν ἀζύμων προσῆλθον*. This same idiom occurs in Deut. 4:32, "Indeed, ask now concerning the former days." The Hebrew "לְיָמִים רִאשֹׁנִים" is "concerning days former." Exodus 21:11, "these *three* things for her" (NAS), "*αὐτῇ*", לָהּ.

I do not favor the *Anchor Bible* solution. It is elegant from a linguistic point of view, however it is ugly when one looks at the usage of the dative in Greek. It is always 'on the day'; also Matthew 26:17 and Mark 14:12 are clearly linked to Exodus 12:15. C.S. Mann and W.F. Albright's solution cannot be applied in Exodus, because it clearly says 'on the day-the head most' בַּיּוֹם הָרִאשׁוֹן.

The Synoptic Problem is another corral-cipher,† a parable which may be understood if one first understands the Torah in Exodus 12:15. Observing Passover and paying attention to the fact that there shall be no leaven found in your houses for seven days necessitates removal of it on the headmost day. The Hebrew idiom in Exodus 12:15 uses the word הָרִאשׁוֹן in two different ways. Firstly to mean "headmost" and secondly in מִיּוֹם הָרִאשֹׁן עַד־יוֹם הַשְּׁבִעִי to mean "<u>from the first day</u> until the seventh day." This is the easiest way read Exodus 12:15-20 without making a contradiction out of the text.

Failing to understand these things has opened Christians up to the higher critical attack on Scripture, and has led them into increasing degrees of unbelief and unfaithfulness to the word. There are indeed consequences for rejection of Torah and the adoption of false observances and neglect of Yahweh's appointed times. The consequence is the undermining of redemptive history and a clear understanding of the accuracy of Scripture. But there are many who scorn it as a trivial issue, a side diversion, while they get about the real work of keeping their own traditions. I am telling them they are deceived and will end up being goats for slaughter by he who seeks to change the times and seasons.

† See page 481, note no. 1.

Typical Counter Arguments

"Preparation" only means Friday

In an effort to forestall any investigation of the true timing of Yeshua's death and resurrection, critics typically insist that Friday, and Friday only is ever called a "day of preparation." This dogmatism is a form of circular reasoning because it was the assumption that the preparation meant Friday in the year of Yeshua's crucifixion that was a major factor leading the Gnostic Christians to belief in the Friday-Sunday scenario. The claim that "preparation" means only Friday is therefore a foundational pillar of proving their system. I shall now lay out the weaknesses of this assumption.†

In John 19:14, the Evangelist tells us that it was "the preparation of the passover." Now, the passover could only be prepared on the 14th of Nisan, and in six out of seven years this was on a day other than Friday. However, the explanation of the critic is that it only means "Friday of passover week." The critic is thus suggesting that "passover" means the whole seven days of passover so that a one and only "preparation" on Friday is bound to occur somewhere in it. But this rejects the whole reason for joining the words "passover" and "preparation" in the first place, which is doubtless to refer to the preparation of the passover lamb, the removal of leaven, and preparation of other dishes to go with the passover Seder.

How the Jews could have ever got into the habit of calling Friday of passover week the "preparation of passover" (παρασκευὴ τοῦ πάσχα),[298] and have failed to call the 14th of Nisan the same the other six years when it is not on Friday is not believable. The primary sense of the word "passover" in the scriptures refers the actual offerings. It is thus unparsimonious to expand the sense of the words to "passover week" and argue for the exclusive reference of "preparation of the passover" to Friday against the propensity of Passover keeping Jews. John tells us that it is the "preparation of the Passover" precisely to inform us that it was not the normal weekly preparation day, but a

[298] This is another case where the Greek grammar implies the word "day," hence: παρασκευὴ τοῦ πάσχα = παρασκευὴ [ἡμέρα] τοῦ πάσχα).

† A corral-cipher. See pg. 481, no. 1.

special one for the Passover.

The word "preparation" (παρασκευὴ) is used six times in reference to the day Yeshua died.[299] Therefore in reference to that day, it does not mean "Friday." It means the usual preparations attending the passover lamb for Nisan 14, which is the day before the annual Sabbath that fell between Wednesday sunset and Thursday sunset that year.

(1) Mat. 27:62: ἥτις ἐστὶν μετὰ τὴν παρασκευήν = *which is after the preparation day.*

(2) Mark 15:42: ἐπεὶ ἦν παρασκευὴ ὅ ἐστιν προσάββατον[300] = *since it was a preparation day, that is a before a Sabbath.* The words vary in Scrivener: ὅ ἐστι προσάββατον, and also in other manuscripts: προς σάββατον, and in Codex Bezae: πριν σάββατον.

(3) Luke 23:54: Καὶ ἡμέρα ἦν Παρασκευή = *And it was a day of preparation.* Codex Bezae reads: η ημερα προ σαββατου = *the day before a Sabbath.*

(4) John 19:14: ἦν δὲ παρασκευὴ τοῦ πάσχα = *and it was a preparation day of the passover.*

(5) John 19:31: ἐπεὶ παρασκευὴ ἦν = *since it was a preparation day.*

(6) John 19:42: τὴν Παρασκευὴν τῶν 'Ιουδαίων = *the preparation day of the Jews.*

So long as we understand that the Sabbath mentioned is the annual Sabbath, and that the preparation refers to preparing the passover, to be eaten at the beginning of that "high sabbath" (John 19:31), there is no problem.

The critics who desire an absolute dogmatism on the meaning of preparation, commonly argue that it is a *technical term* for Friday. This is nothing more than an attempt to win the argument with invented jargon that is supposed to have the aura of authority. This claim was rebuked by Solomon Zeitlin in the *Journal of Biblical*

---

[299] Mat. 27:26; Mark 15:42; Luke 23:54; John 19:14, 31, and 42.

[300] The Jewish scholar Solomon Zeitlin reported that "some MSS omit the words ο εστιν προσαββατον" (Studies in the Early History of Judaism, New York: KTAV, 1973, vol. 1, pg. 210).

Literature.

Solomon Zeitlin is a famous Jewish scholar known for chronological emphasis in his professional papers. He placed the year of the crucifixion in A.D. 34 even though he was not a believer in Yeshua. So he was right about that along with Sir Isaac Newton. He has this to say about the word "preparation":

> The word παρασκευὴ is not a Jewish technical term at all (pg. 268). Rather, the word παρασκευὴ, which has in Greek the meaning of preparation, became a *pagan* technical term for the Eve of Sabbath, as well as for the Eve of other holidays.[301]

Zeitlin shows his bias here somewhat failing[302] to recognize that Greek speaking Jews used παρασκευὴ. For Judaism gave up the Septuagint and forgot that a Greek Jewish dispersion existed, and such Greek usage was relegated to the 'minim' Christians.

However, Raymond E. Brown[303] agrees with Zeitlin and rebuts Torrey:

> Torrey's theory [on John 19:14] (JBL 50 [1931], 227-41) that Passover should be understood as the festival period of seven days and that John is speaking of Friday within Passover week has been refuted by S. Zeitlin, JBL (1932), 263-71.[304]

Critics trying to sell the Friday-Sunday myth will try to demonize men like Zeitlin and Brown for their supposed liberal or unbelieving views. But the fact is that neither Zeitlin nor Brown were saying that "preparation" in the Evangelists meant any day other than Friday. They were just pointing out the truth that it could mean a day other than Friday. This fact alone shows that they had no bias on the side of the view of this book, yet what they say exposes the lack of integrity in the dogmatic view that "preparation" only means Friday.

---

[301] pg. 269, *Journal of Biblical Literature*, Vol. 51-52, 1932-33, pp. 263-271. In all fairness, Zeitlin's article is listed in the 3rd edition of BDAG, "against Torrey," just after the Lexicon admits "as the day of preparation for a festival." The Lexicon is clearly biased to Friday, pg. 771.

[302] Though he does admit elsewhere that Hellenistic Jews used the term.

[303] Accomplished Roman Catholic Scholar.

[304] Raymond E. Brown, *The Anchor Bible: The Gospel According to John.* Garden City, NY: Doubleday & Co., Inc., 1970, John 19:14, pg. 882.

Thayer's Lexicon also says that παρασκευὴ, is "the day on which the Jews made the necessary preparation to celebrate a sabbath or a feast."[305] F. F. Bruce remarks, "The first clear occurrence of Gk. παρασκευὴ in the sense of "Friday" is in the Martyrdom of Polycarp 7.1 A.D. 156.[306] C.C. Torrey was a zealous promoter of the theory that Yeshua spoke Aramaic.[307] Yet, even he admits that the Aramaic equivalent παρασκευὴ of can refer to the day before a feast day:

> . . . but the possibility may be admitted that it was given an equally early application to the principal festal days. It is thus used frequently in the later rabbinical Aramaic, sometimes in the construct relation. . ., sometimes after the pattern *arubta deshabbatha*. There is in the *Midrash* Ruth (one of the latest of the midrashim), near the end of the section "qaton wegadol," an example of arubta pescha meaning, "the day before the paschal feast" (pg. 237, JBL 50, '30).

Hence *arubta* (עֲרוּבְתָּא) does not always mean "Friday." It simply means the "eve" of a given day, no matter what day of the week it might precede (except in the Syriac Church's Syriac Aramaic which dates later than the second century). However Torrey argues that *arubta* was not used this way in the first century. How convenient for him. You can just hear the resounding *ad hoc* argument from silence here. He escapes into unknown Aramaic to prove his case. However, the Hebrew equivalent *erev* (עֶרֶב) did apply to the "eve" of the Passover, and this is attested in the Mishnah. The Dead Sea Scrolls, discovered in 1947, have put to rest the theory that Mishnaic Hebrew was an artificial language of the Rabbis, and have shown instead that it was the form of Hebrew spoken in Judea in the second Temple period,[308] and not Aramaic.

Torrey's exclusion of the first century, is therefore invalid, and his theory that it means only Friday is exposed. Solomon Zeitlin wrote elsewhere:

---

305 *A Greek-English Lexicon of the New Testament*, J.H. Thayer.

306 pg. 381, note 12, *The Gospel of John*, F.F. Bruce.

307 Aramaic was one of the languages spoken in first century Galilee along with Hebrew and Greek, but this Aramaic is termed Galilean Aramaic, and is different than the Aramaic that became Syriac centuries later.

308 With the exception of late words like the sense of "week" for "Sabbath."

The words in verse Mark 15.42, "And when even was now come, because it was the preparation, that is, the day before the Sabbath" do not prove at all that the word *parasque* was used to designate Friday only, but not the eve of holidays. We clearly see from John 19:14, "and it was the *parasque* of the Passover" that the word *parasque* may refer also to the eve of the holidays.[309]

On pure linguistic grounds παρασκευὴ means nothing more than "preparation day." The word "day" is to be supplied according to the gender of the word. The meaning must be determined from context, and the context of usage in the Evangelists shows that it was used for the day before the Passover, and in A.D. 34 this was Wednesday, March 24. The attempt to restrict the word's meaning to "Friday" is based on nothing but the need for a dogmatic response by its opponents.*

Annual Sabbaths Don't Exist

In John 19:31, the Evangelist says:

> The Jews therefore, because it was the day of preparation, so that the bodies should not remain on the cross on the Sabbath (for that Sabbath was great), asked Pilate that their legs might be broken, and *that* they might be taken away.

The key words were are: ἦν γὰρ μεγάλη ἡ ἡμέρα ἐκείνου τοῦ σαββάτου = *For was great that day of the sabbath*. That is to say, this Sabbath was the annual Sabbath. What makes this Sabbath Great?

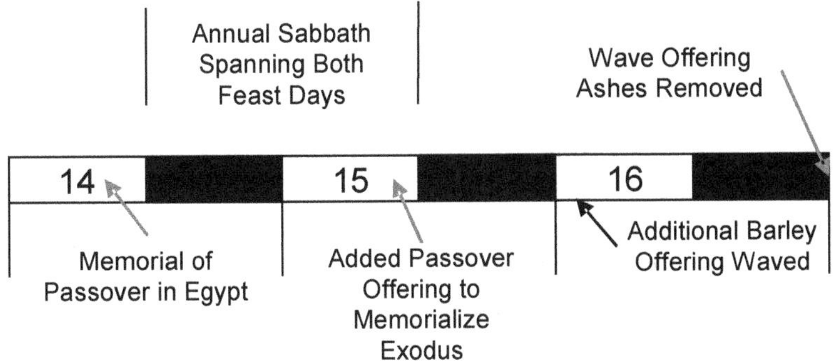

* This dogmatism only works well for putting generally ignorant inquirers back to sleep, to forestall them from investigating further. And that is the design of their argument. It depends claiming a word has an exclusive technical sense more restricted than its lexical sense, without any proof, and then making the argument from Aramaic to escape most cross-examination, and to appear wise to those who cannot. The argument was deception at the beginning, and cracks apart upon closer examination.

[309] *The Jewish Quarterly Review*, Vol. XLII, 1952.

Counter Arguments — *Great Sabbaths*

This chart is from earlier in this book. The annual Sabbath has the distinction of being called, "the Sabbath" in Lev. 23:11 and 15: הַשַּׁבָּת. The meaning of the word "the Sabbath" is "the Cessation" or "the Ceasing" (הַשַּׁבָּת), often translated "Rest Day." What makes it great is that it is the most important annual Sabbath of the year, with Yom Kippur not too far behind it. This Sabbath unites two feast days, the 14th of Nisan upon which the memorial of the Passover in Egypt is slain and eaten, and the 15th of Nisan upon which the memorial of the Exodus is slain and eaten. There are a day and a night for each feast. The annual Sabbath overlaps the memorial of the passover in Egypt in the night part of the Sabbath, and the memorial of the Exodus in the day part of the Sabbath.

The Cessation marked the first day of unleavened bread and the first day of the ceasing of leaven (Ex. 12:15). Also on it there is to be a ceasing from all servile work (Lev. 23:7). It is also a Sabbath of remembering. But the Church, and the critics that agree with the Church want to make this into the "forgotten" Sabbath. So the Friday-Sunday critic makes dogmatic claims to deny this. First no less a scholar than Samuele Bacchiocchi[310] asserts:

> A Ceremonial Sabbath. The reasons given in support of this conclusion [that Nisan 15 is called "the Sabbath"] rest on three major mistaken assumptions. First it is assumed that since certain annual feasts such as the Day of Atonement are designated as "sabbath" (Lev. 23:24, 32, 39), then all the references to the Sabbath found in the Passion narratives must refer not to the weekly Sabbath but to the annual ceremonial Passover Sabbath.
>
> This assumption is discredited by the fact that the day of atonement is designated by the compound expression *shabbath shabbaton*, meaning "a sabbath of solemn rest" (Lev. 23:32; 16:31). But this phrase is rendered by the Septuagint by the compound Greek expression "*sabbata sabbaton,*" which is different from the simple "*sabbaton*" used in the Passion narratives. It is therefore linguistically impossible to interpret the latter as a reference to the day of the

---

[310] Late Seventh Day Adventist Scholar. I had personal conversations with Dr. Bacchiocchi on this very subject in the 1980's, but was only at the very beginnings of researching it when these conversations occurred.

Passover or to any other annual feast day, since these are never simply designated simply as "*sabbaton.*"[311]

Dr. Bacchiocchi's argument is simply a case of errant anti-equivocation and overstatement.† No, not all references to the Sabbath in the passion narratives refer to the annual Sabbath. One would only say this because they accept the mistaken "first day of the week" translation rather than correcting it to the "first of the Sabbaths." And these refer to the weekly Sabbath in Matthew 28:1; Mark 16:2; Luke 24:1, and John 20:1, 19. So he overstated his objection. Further, a distinction between an annual Sabbath and the weekly Sabbath based on the expression *shabbath shabbaton* is easily refuted. Yom Kippur is called this. So also is the weekly Sabbath in Lev. 23:3 שַׁבַּת שַׁבָּתוֹן. But equally clear is that the Septuagint does call the day of Atonement simply Σάββατον[312] at the end of Lev. 23:32, "your Sabbath," for which the Hebrew uses the word שַׁבַּת. Thus the distinction between an annual Sabbath and the weekly one based on שבת is refuted.

How is שַׁבָּתוֹן different from שַׁבַּת?

There are eleven occurrences of שַׁבָּתוֹן in the Torah in the following combinations:

Table 11: Usages of שַׁבָּתוֹן in the Torah

Text	Phrase	Occassion
Exodus 16:23	שַׁבָּתוֹן שַׁבַּת־קֹדֶשׁ	seventh day
Exodus 31:15	שַׁבַּת שַׁבָּתוֹן קֹדֶשׁ	seventh day
Exodus 35:2	קֹדֶשׁ שַׁבַּת שַׁבָּתוֹן	seventh day
Leviticus 16:31	שַׁבַּת שַׁבָּתוֹן	Yom Kippur
Leviticus 23:3	שַׁבַּת שַׁבָּתוֹן	seventh day
Leviticus 23:24	שַׁבָּתוֹן	Yom Teruah
Leviticus 23:32	שַׁבַּת שַׁבָּתוֹן	Yom Kippur

[311] *The Time of the Crucifixion and the Resurrection*, pg. 43, Samuele Bacchiocchi, pg. 43.
[312] The lexical form of the word Sabbath (Σάββατον) in Greek is declined in the nominative neuter singular. † Straw man argument.

Leviticus 23:39a	שַׁבָּתוֹן	First of Sukkot
Leviticus 23:39b	שַׁבָּתוֹן	Last Great Day
Leviticus 25:4	שַׁבַּת שַׁבָּתוֹן	seventh year
Leviticus 25:5	שְׁנַת שַׁבָּתוֹן	seventh year

The archaic ending ־וֹן *on* is poorly explained in Hebrew grammar books. It means "great" or "high." It is often called an "intensive plural," not to be understood in a numerical sense, but as multiplying or intensifying the word to which it is attached. For example דָּגוֹן *Dagon* means "great fish" or "exalted fish"; עֶלְיוֹן *'Elyon* means "high (וֹן) above (עַל)," often translated "Most High." The word *Ammon* עַמּוֹן means "great (וֹן) people (עַם)."

Lexicons have assigned the meaning "complete sabbatism" or "solemn rest" to the word שַׁבָּתוֹן. This is only partly correct. But it is also confusing. Yom Kippur is a "solemn rest," but the weekly Sabbath is not a day for a "solemn" affliction of the soul. Further, Yom Kippur and the weekly Sabbath are "complete rests," but what about the other feast days? They only prohibit "servile labor" (עֲבֹדָה). Thus, it is clear that the words "solemn" and "complete" are inaccurate renditions of the intensive ending וֹן. While the English terms "solemn" and "complete" do "intensify" the meaning of שַׁבָּת they result in discordance and inconsistency. There must be some other "intensive" sense that allows all the contexts to make sense.

That other sense is "great" or "high," but before we jump too quickly to our conclusions to say that שַׁבָּתוֹן always means "Great Sabbath," and clearly the weekly Sabbath is not one of the "Great Sabbaths," I must explain the difference between the adjectival use and the nominal use of the same word. Generally the noun use of a word comes first in Hebrew, and then it is modified by an adjectival word after it or some construct phrase, but not always. The word "great" is itself an adjective. However, to get the whole notion, all the adjectives must be compounded together. There are eight unique combinations:

שַׁבָּתוֹן שַׁבַּת־קֹדֶשׁ	1 **A great ceasing Sabbath of holiness** (7th day)
שַׁבַּת שַׁבָּתוֹן קֹדֶשׁ	2 **A Sabbath of great-cessation~holy** (7th day)
קֹדֶשׁ שַׁבַּת שַׁבָּתוֹן	3 **A holy Sabbath of great-cessation** (7th day)

שַׁבַּת שַׁבָּתוֹן	4 **A** Sabbath **of great-cessation** (10 Tishri)
שַׁבַּת שַׁבָּתוֹן	5 **A** Sabbath **of great-cessation** (7th day)
שַׁבָּתוֹן	6 **Great** Sabbath (1, 15, 22 Tishri)
שַׁבַּת שַׁבָּתוֹן	7 **A** Sabbath **of great-cessation** (7th Year)
שְׁנַת שַׁבָּתוֹן	8 **A** Year **of great-cessation** (7th Year)

The nominal word is grey faced in the English and likewise in the Hebrew. In cases 1-3 & 5 for the 7th day, it is clear that *Shabbat* is the noun and the remaining words adjectives describing the character of the Shabbat. In these cases the intensive "great" is "great rest" or "complete rest." The following translations are then proper:

1. A complete resting Sabbath of holiness.
2. A Sabbath of complete resting—holy.
3. A holy Sabbath of complete resting.

The 4th applies to Yom Kippur, also "A Sabbath of complete resting. And case 7, "A Sabbath of complete resting," means that no agricultural planting or sowing is to be done at all in the 7th year. Likewise for case 8: "A Year of complete resting."

In the 6th case things change. The word שַׁבָּתוֹן stands alone, and therefore has the nominal position. The word part שַׁבָּת is no longer a mere description of a day. It is the day itself. It is no different than if the intensifier stood separately: שַׁבָּת וֹן. It is the word *Shabbat* with an ending added to it. Therefore, it is still a *Shabbat*. The ending cannot make it "not a Shabbat". The ending can only tell what kind of *Shabbat*.

Thus the totality of the description phrase is just "great," and not "great cessation." The word "great" characterizes the day in another way than a great cessation. Clearly 1, 15, and 22 Tishri are not complete rests. Only servile labor is prohibited (כָּל-מְלֶאכֶת עֲבֹדָה), Lev. 23:7. So the intensifier ending is not aimed at intensifying cessation. Rather it intensifies in the sense that it is an special Sabbath or annual Sabbath, i.e. "High Sabbath" or "Great Sabbath." So the only difference between שַׁבָּת and שַׁבָּתוֹן when both stand in the main noun position is that the latter is called "Great" or “High.” What I mean by nominal is that the word “Sabbath” in a descriptive sense means “cessation,” but in a nominal sense it becomes a Proper Noun, and we have to look elsewhere other than the etymology of the word to find out why the Proper Noun is “great”:

> In the seventh month, on the first of the month, it will be for you a Great Sabbath—a Great Memorial of blowing, a holy convocation (Lev. 23:24). (*or* a special memorial)

> On the fifteenth day of the seventh month…the feast of Yahweh, seven days; on the first a Great Sabbath and on the eighth day a Great Sabbath (Lev. 23:39).

With these three precedents, it is no surprise that three other Sabbaths may be called שַׁבָּתוֹן “Great Sabbath,” not relating to complete rest, but relating to the their annual importance. It should also be noted that in Lev. 23:24 זִכְרוֹן follows שַׁבָּתוֹן. Once more the intensive shows, “a Great Memorial.” So also the cessation of Passover is a Great Sabbath and a Great Memorial. It is in fact the greatest as proved in John, “ἦν γὰρ μεγάλη ἡ ἡμέρα ἐκείνου τοῦ σαββάτου” “For that day of the Sabbath was Great” (John 19:31).[313]

Now I shall tie up the loose ends:

While Dr. Bacchiocchi is using the Septuagint to make his case, he missed the fact that in Lev. 23:15, the simple Σάββατον is used to designate the first day of unleavened bread, and that the Septuagint defines this as the “first day” (τῆς πρώτης) of the feast of unleavened bread in 23:11. Dr. Bacchiocchi’s insistence on the ‘linguistic impossibility’ of Σάββατον referring to the first day of unleavened bread in the Evangelists is thereby refuted. The Pharisees, Philo, Evangelists, Josephus, Rabbis, Septuagint, and Targums thus disagree with the Doctor.†

But the critics cannot give up this dogmatism. For once it is suspected that the main Jewish view designates Nisan 15 as “the Sabbath” then the Friday-Sunday view begins to be suspected of error. Adding to his prevaricating myth is Harold Hoehner:

---

[313] The inspiration for this section started with, *The Biblical and historical background of Jewish customs and ceremonies*, Abraham P. Bloch, “Definition of Shabbat and Shabbat Shabbaton,” pg. 164-168.

† See page 481, no. 2.

> The argument that since Nisan 15 is a holy convocation on which no one works and thus conclude that it was a Sabbath is a *non sequitor* [not a logical conclusion]. There is no evidence for this anywhere. This is a creation of those who hold this theory only to fit their theory.[314]

Don't let your eyes glaze over when Harold uses a word like *non sequitor.* It is simply dressing to divert you from the fact that the case is the exact opposite. The Jewish traditional evidence and textual evidence is to the contrary, which I need not repeat. Harold's statement is simply designed to put off further investigation by erecting a dogmatic wall. It is made for those who would be led astray by trusting him as an authority, and taking his word for it.

The dogmatic certainty of Dr. Bacchiocchi and Harold Hoehner belie what scholars on their own side of this issue say. For instance, the famous Hebrew Scholar's Keil and Delitzsch write on Lev. 23:11:

> The "Sabbath" does not mean the seventh day of the week, but the day of rest, although the weekly Sabbath was always the seventh or last day of the week; hence not only the seventh day of the week (Ex. xxxi. 15, etc), but the day of atonement (the tenth of the seventh month), is called "Sabbath," and "Shabbath shabbaton" (ver. 32, chap. xvi. 31). As a day of rest, on which no laborious work was to be performed (ver. [7-]8), the first day of the feast of *Mazzoth* is called "Sabbath" irrespective of the day of the week upon which it fell: and "the morrow after the Sabbath" is equivalent to "the morrow after the Passover" mentioned in Joshua 5:11.[315]

And now the Lutheran, J.P. Lange:

> The better view is that found in the LXX, Philo, Josephus, the Targums, and the Rabbinical writers generally, and which seems most in accordance with the text itself, that the Sabbath was simply the festival Sabbath, the 15th of Abib [Nisan], on

[314] *Chronological Aspects of the Life of Christ*, pg. 69. Harold Hoehner.
[315] C.F Keil and Franz Delitzsch, *Commentary on the Old Testament-The Pentateuch*, Eerdmans, rp. 1981, Lev. 23:4-14.

whatever day of the week it might happen to fall.[316]

The faults of the LXX, Targums, and Rabbinical writers have been mentioned before, viz. they translated the word "Sabbaths" as "weeks." The purpose here is not to endorse those translations (whose beginnings lie in the second century), but to show that the foundation of the dogmatic argument against the feast day being called the "Sabbath" is full of holes, and that critics who take the dogmatic view have plenty of fellows to deflate their certitude.

The dogmatism of the critics, and in this case the Church and Judaism, leaves the question of what to do with the "Great Sabbath" (μεγάλη ἡ ἡμέρα ἐκείνου τοῦ σαββάτου). Franz Delitzsch translates this for us: וְגָדוֹל יוֹם הַשַּׁבָּת = V'Gadol Yom Ha-Shabbat. "And great *was the* day† of the Sabbath." The explanation of the Church is that the Sabbath is "Great" whenever a feast day happens to coincide with the weekly Sabbath. If the ad hoc nature of this apologetic is not clear, then consider that the feast day would not be "great" in the six out of seven years that it does not coincide with the weekly Sabbath. The explanation they give is simply to rid themselves of the annual Sabbath occurring between Wednesday sunset and Thursday sunset in that year, and the fact that it is called "great" because it joined together the Passover in Egypt and the Exodus on the first day of unleavened bread, and therefore is an extraordinary (great) Sabbath.

But the Church did not stop with this explanation. They decided to redefine the whole issue. The Greek Orthodox say the Great Sabbath is the weekly sabbath between the Friday crucifixion and Sunday resurrection in every year. Thus, the need for a Jewish feast day to land upon it to make it Great is forgotten. It is great simply because it lies between the crucifixion and resurrection. The Roman Catholic Church agrees, but usually calls this day "Holy Saturday":

> The Saturday, or Sabbath, in Passion Week, was commonly known by the name of the Great Sabbath. It was the only Sabbath throughout the year that the Greek churches, and some of the Western, kept as a fast.[317]

---

[316] Commentary on the Holy Scriptures, Grand Rapids: Zondervan, 1960, vol. i. "Lev 23:11ff," pg. 175).

[317] *Cyclopaedia of Biblical, Theological, and Ecclesiastical Literature,*

† But it should be noted that John does not use the idiomatic words, "day of the Sabbaths" (ημερα των σαββατων) for the festival.

Thus Israel's greatest Sabbath and feast day was moved onto the weekly Sabbath and turned into a fast! Of course when John called the annual Sabbath the "Great Sabbath," it was not a fast, and it was not perpetually placed on the weekly Sabbath. It was great because it was Israel's greatest day.

Judaism, however, was not to be outdone by the Church. They also had an interest in ridding themselves of the "Great Sabbath" attested to by John. For to acknowledge the Evangelist is too much, and to certify his correctness too dangerous. The Jewish masses might figure things out. So the Rabbis decided sometime after the second century that the "Great Sabbath" for them would now be the Sabbath before the Passover:

> It is extremely doubtful whether the Jews described any Sabbath as "the great Sabbath" until later. The only argument in favour of an early date is its occurrence in John xix. 31. The entire absence of the term from the early Rabbinic sources led Zunz to the view that the Synagogue adopted it from the Church Much later the Jews applied the title to the Sabbath before Passover, Pentecost, New Year, and Tabernacles.[318]

So we see that the "great Sabbath" has been moved out of its place by both the Synagogue and the Church.

It Isn't Possible On Sabbath

One of the charges that the authorities wanted to try Yeshua on was Sabbath breaking. It seems that Yeshua's definition of work on the Sabbath was nowhere so stringent as the Scribes and Pharisees. Yeshua healed on the Sabbath. He instructed a man to carry his bed. He allowed his disciples to "harvest" (Luke 6:1). He made mud on the Sabbath. And he said he was working. Of course it was redemptive work—a work of rescuing. And the Torah permitted rescuing on the Sabbath. Yeshua justified his disciples by citing the fact that the Priests do work in the Temple during their service to YHWH, and he also cited exceptional circumstances sometimes justified ignoring the

---

volume 7. John McClintock, James Strong, pg. 732, "Passion Week."

318 *Studies in Pharisaism and the Gospels*, pg. 69, Israel Abrahams.

letter of a torah for the sake of a greater Torah, like when David and his men ate the bread of the presence.†

When faced with all the chronological facts for the resurrection on the "first of the Sabbaths," it seems that critics make a quick conversion to orthodox Judaism. Now we learn that the women cannot perform the final anointing out of respect for the dead on the Sabbath. We learn that Cleopas and his fellow disciple are not allowed "get out of Dodge" (flee from the authorities) before they are implicated on the Sabbath. We learn that Yeshua cannot ride a donkey to His House of prayer on the Sabbath, and we learn that the crowds cannot cut down branches or lay cloaks in his way as an act of worship for the King—all because it does not agree with Orthodox Judaism's notion of Sabbath observance as defined in the Talmud or assumed to be defined by first century Judaism.

Now as it turns out, Nisan 10 (the Sabbath before the crucifixion in A.D. 34) was the day on which the original Passover lamb had to be picked and examined. So the work to pick and examine the lamb of *Elohim* would justified. Indeed, the priests did this every morning for the daily sacrifice—even on the Sabbath. But every lamb had to have its initial examining, and Nisan 10 was just the prophetic day for <u>The Lamb</u> to be examined (cf. Ex. 12:3-5). So everything done on Nisan 10 was for the purpose of examining <u>The Lamb</u> and bringing Him to the Temple. He was examined by the crowds and then by the Scribes and Pharisees, and found faultless. The people and the donkey were performing a sacred service of worship on that Sabbath (cf. Zech. 9:9). So like the Priests who work in the Temple, they were faultless on that day (Mat. 12:5).

A good deal of the material in the Evangelists is precisely to free the faithful in Yeshua from overbearing Sabbath regulations. It might be that riding a donkey on the Sabbath is permitted under ordinary circumstances to see a prophet or to transport one to a place of instruction (see 2 Kings 4:23-24). The Pharisees may have wanted to accuse Yeshua of Sabbath breaking on that day, but did not find it politically expedient to do so. The Torah only says that animals should not work, but it does not define work. Obviously using the animal as a power source for plowing, mills, or pulling is prohibited.

† See page 481, note no. 3.

But is riding prohibited? Even the Talmud indicates that riding of itself is not prohibited, but may only be prohibited because it may lead to other incidental work or crossing the Sabbath limit. So the ban on riding was only a fence. Riding itself was not a violation.

In Matthew 21:8, the people cut branches to line Yeshua's path or they threw their cloaks on it. Ask the Rabbi, if the Messiah is coming and the Spirit of the Almighty bids you cut a branch to smooth his path, then is it permitted? There is no prohibition in Torah against cutting a branch to throw in the king's path. This was the ancient form of throwing confetti down on a celebrity. Nor is there a prohibition against cutting your asparagus on the dinner plate. Yeshua explained that the "harvesting" in Luke 6:1-5 and Matthew 12:1-8 as the Pharisees called it was not a violation of Torah.

Prohibitions against carrying burdens—like mothers do not carry their infants or people the clothes on their back—that go beyond the obvious intent of the prophetic ruling (cf. Jer. 17:27) are not the intent of Torah. The prohibited burdens are clearly what people carry to engage in work or commerce, tools, wares, etc.

<u>The Sabbath limit</u>: The Pharisees obviously had a rule, but was it enforced and did the people follow it? There is no evidence that it was uniformly enforced or even followed everywhere, or in every situation. It was known enough to be used as a measuring distance. And the distance itself is rather arbitrary. What is one foot more or one foot less? The prohibition in Torah was specifically connected with seeking manna that would not be found on the Sabbath. When the Torah was given, the seventy went up Mt. Sinai on the Sabbath, and this was most certainly outside the camp, and more than the Rabbinic limit. So clearly the Rabbis contradict themselves on that point.

The Scribes and Pharisees sit in the seat of Moses (cf. Mat. 23:1-3). Were not the four Evangelists Scribes? And did they not write examples of how Yeshua liberated the Sabbath? So then it is Scribe vs. Scribe. And I'll take Yeshua's scribes any day of the week over the Rabbis.‡

‡ On pages 149-150, additional reasons are given from the Mishnah. The the dead, according to Jewish custom, were treated with all due respect, as if they were an elderly ill person that was still alive, and therefore a limited amount of work in tending them was allowed. According to custom, the spirit was not regarded as departing from the body or near it until after three days had passed. This belief may have been superstitious, but it helps explain why loving care was bestowed upon the bodies of the dead for three days.

First of the Sabbaths Revisited in Hebrew

I have given the Hebrew gloss בְּאַחַת הַשַּׁבָּתוֹת as 'on #one of the sabbaths,' as equivalent to (τῇ) *μιᾷ τῶν σαββάτων*. There are a number of issues with the putative Hebrew translation. Firstly, not just one Hebrew translation is possible, but several. Some are more literal to the Greek. And we could render into Hebrew woodenly by breaking the Hebrew grammar rule for the construct which is not obeyed by Greek. Second, in Hebrew there is a choice of gender with the adjective. It could be rendered into the feminine to agree with Sabbaths. Or it could be rendered in the masculine to agree with the latent Hebrew word for day. Thirdly, there is the ambiguity of the indefinite use of the word "one." After observing the possibilities, it will become evident that בְּאַחַת הַשַּׁבָּתוֹת is the most likely source of the Greek.

In the chart "Inception" means the period in the Hebrew language at which the supporting grammar is first attested for the form. "Gender" indicates the word which the gender of the adjective agrees with. Comment notes a potential fault.

Hebrew	Inception	Comment	Gender
1. בְּאַחַת הַשַּׁבָּתוֹת	early Hebrew	ambiguous	שַׁבָּתוֹת
2. בְּאַחַד הַשַּׁבָּתוֹת	early Hebrew	ambiguous	יְמֵי
3. בְּרִאשׁוֹן הַשַּׁבָּתוֹת	early Hebrew	≠ μιᾷ	יְמֵי
4. בְּרֵאשִׁית הַשַּׁבָּתוֹת	early Hebrew	≠ μιᾷ	שַׁבָּתוֹת
5. בָּאֶחָד לַשַּׁבָּתוֹת	early Hebrew	wooden	יוֹם
6. בָּאֶחָת לַשַּׁבָּתוֹת	early Hebrew	wooden	שַׁבָּתוֹת
7. בְּאֶחָת לַשַּׁבָּתוֹת	early Hebrew	ambiguous	שַׁבָּתוֹת
8. בְּאֶחָד לַשַּׁבָּתוֹת	early Hebrew	ambiguous	שַׁבָּתוֹת
9. בְּרִאשׁוֹן לַשַּׁבָּתוֹת	early Hebrew	≠ μιᾷ	יוֹם
10. בְּרִאשׁוֹנַה לַשַּׁבָּתוֹת	early Hebrew	≠ μιᾷ	שַׁבָּתוֹת
11. בָּרִאשׁוֹנַה לַשַּׁבָּתוֹת	early Hebrew	≠ μιᾷ	שַׁבָּתוֹת
12. בָּרִאשׁוֹן לַשַּׁבָּתוֹת	early Hebrew	≠ μιᾷ	יוֹם
13. הָאֶחָד שֶׁל הַשַּׁבָּתוֹת	late Hebrew	wooden	יוֹם
14. הָאֶחָת שֶׁל הַשַּׁבָּתוֹת	late Hebrew	wooden	שַׁבָּתוֹת
15. הָאַחַד הַשַּׁבָּתוֹת	non Hebrew	wooden	יוֹם

We can dispense with No. 15 because it is non-grammatical in Hebrew. But it does woodenly imitate the Greek. So it might be useful as

(continued page 386)

Daniel's Prophecy of Seventy Sevens

Daniel 9:24 contains an exact and precise prediction of when Yeshua would die for the sins of the world. This prediction is combined with the Torah, Temple, and Messiah. Jews reject it and corrupt it because of Messiah, and Christians reject it and corrupt it because of the Torah and Temple. It should then be no surprise that neither Synagogue nor Church fully understand this prophecy. For corrupting it lies at the intersection of their mutual interests. Jews either forbid the reading of the book of Daniel or trot out anti-Messiah interpretations. Christians demonize the Temple and the sabbatical year institution. The price of these transgressions is high, as it leaves interpretation full of contradictions and inconsistencies.

The reason that I discuss this prophecy in a book about the death and resurrection of Messiah is that it is the final independent piece of confirming evidence that proves a Wednesday crucifixion and Resurrection Sabbath. Unlike the errant interpretations of Daniel 9 put out by the Church and the Synagogue, this one, that goes with the true date of the crucifixion and resurrection, works out perfectly. For it only works with A.D. 34. And A.D. 34 only provides Nisan 14 on a Wednesday as was shown. And as Yeshua was not in the grave more than three days, but at least three days and three nights, the resurrection is fixedly determined to be on the Sabbath day at dawn by the most absolute reckoning possible. The chart on page **331** gives an overview of how things fit together.

To translate the prophecy into modern terms of the simplest form, the prediction of Daniel 9 is that between a commandment to rebuild Jerusalem and the death of Messiah would be seven sabbatical years plus sixty two sabbatical years, with one sabbatical period being reserved for the end of days. The commandment was made in 445 B.C. and the crucifixion was in A.D. 34. So between those two dates are the sum total of sixty-nine sabbatical years.

Now, it will be important to detail the beginning point, the end point, and the measuring stick we are using. The end point is established by the passion chronology in A.D. 34. So to confirm the end point and the rest of the prophecy we have to explain how the measuring stick and the beginning point fit. If these two elements are confirmed, then the end point date is also confirmed.

First, let us work on the measuring stick. The prophecy is measured in terms of so many sabbatical years. To this Jewish tradition admits, and Christian tradition ignores. The Jewish tradition has a solid biblical foundation. The units of measurement are called "sevens" (שָׁבֻעִים). In the consonant text of Daniel 9:24-26, this is simply the word for seven (שבע) with a plural ending (ים). Now it is necessary to understand that the word "seven" (שֶׁבַע) in Hebrew is used in both a cardinal sense "seven" and ordinal sense "seventh." Deut. 15:9 speaks of a Sabbatical year as "year of the seven" (שְׁנַת־ הַשֶּׁבַע), using the cardinal number, but the meaning is "seventh year" and so the New American Standard Bible translates it "the seventh year."

Thus, the "sevens" are sabbatical years. A "seven" need not be the whole seven years. It only needs to be the seventh year of rest. At the same time, a "seven" can also be the whole period, but if we count "sevens," we may count unit-wise. To count three sevens, thus, can be part of a whole seven, a whole seven, and part of a seven. The prophecy works both by inclusively counting seven year periods and by counting all the "seventh" years. It works both ways. Here is an illustration of different ways to count "sevens":

Figure 66: Various Ways To Count a "Seven"

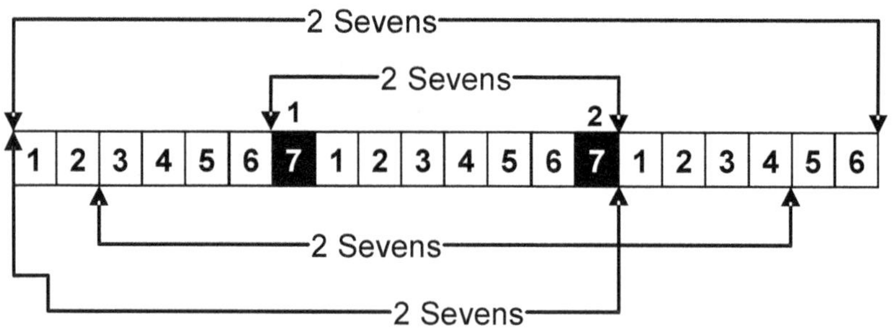

By using inclusive counting, we see that the only essential requirement is that the period of time in question contain the stated number of sabbatical years. For "two sevens" is the same as "two seventh years." Inclusive counting allows us to say that "seven sevens" and "sixty two sevens" come in the period between 445 B.C. and A.D. 34 even though the whole period is less than 483 years. The sevens are shown in the chart on page **331**.

A key point is that Daniel 9:26 says, "And after sixty and two sevens Messiah will be cut off" (וְאַחֲרֵי הַשָּׁבֻעִים שִׁשִּׁים וּשְׁנַיִם). This predicted that Messiah would die after the 62nd sabbatical year was finished. The word "after" (אַחֲרֵי) means that it must be after the 62nd sabbatical year, and not during it. So the sixty-second sabbatical year after the seven sabbatical years (or 69th if you total them till Messiah) must be complete before Messiah dies.

Going back to the first sabbatical year, we find that the city must be built before it begins. This is because Nehemiah caused the debts to be canceled at the start of the seventh year, and the wall was finished before the Torah was read at the feast of Tabernacles. According to Deut. 31:10, this happened at the start of the seventh year:

> Then Moses commanded them, saying, "At the edge of[319] seven years (מִקֵּץ שֶׁבַע שָׁנִים), in the set time of the year of the release, in the Feast of Booths, when all Israel comes to appear before Yãhweh your Almĩghty at the place which he will choose, you shall read this Law in front of all Israel in their hearing.

Moses says that the Torah must be read "in…the year of release"; this also proves that the reading cannot be in the eighth year after the close of the feast of Tabernacles. Rather, it must be at the feast of Tabernacles "in" (בְּמֹעֵד שְׁנַת הַשְּׁמִטָּה) the year of release. This is a

---

[319] Follow the translation of Eben Ezra, "At the edge of seven years" (Deut. 31:10). The proof that the Hebrew word means the beginning edge of the seventh year is provided by the use in Jeremiah 34:14 with respect to Exodus 21:2. The Rabbinic Jews have the matter backwards when they say that the Torah should be read after the Sabbatical year in the eighth year. Eben Ezra corrected them, and proved that it was at the beginning point. The Rabbinic miscalculation finds its origin in the need to confuse Daniel 9 with respect to Messiah. The Hebrew word *miqqaets* (מִקֵּץ) means at the "boundary" or "edge" of something, and not strictly the "end" of it. It is a word meaning "extremity," and may apply to a near extremity, or boundary, or a far boundary.

very important point. The seventh year is the year of release. The eighth year is not the year of release. The seventh year is a Sabbath year, and is for the purpose of ceasing from debts as well as working the land.

Nehemiah compelled Judah to obey the law of release, as recorded in Nehemiah chapter five. And then a scribe with the personal name of Ezra, but of the family of Seriah, read the Torah at the feast of Tabernacles in chapter eight. This means that the walls of the city were completed in 52 days,before the Sabbatical year began.

Table 12: Artaxerxes I Summary (Parker & Dubberstein)

ARTAXERXES I[320]

YEAR	B.C.	NIS 1	YEAR	B.C.	NIS 1
1	464	4/13	11	454	4/23
2	463	4/3	12	453	4/12
3	462	4/22	13	452	4/2
4	461	4/11	14	451	4/20
5	460	3/31	15	450	4/10
6	459	4/19	16	449	3/29
7	458	4/8	17	448	4/16
8	457	3/27	18	447	4/6
9	456	4/15	19	446	3/26
10	455	4/4	**20**	**445**	**4/13**

Now the beginning point was in 445 B.C. This is matched with the rebuilding of Jerusalem in the book of Nehemiah, who states that it was in "the month of Nisan, in the twentieth year of King Artaxerxes" (Neh. 2:1).[321] Now what was impossible before 1900 and unavailable except to experts before 1950 is now made plain by archaeologists and astronomy. And that is exactly when the 20th year of Artaxerxes was, and exactly when the month of Nisan was. This is shown in

---

[320] pg. 32, *Babylonian Chronology, 626 B.C. —A.D. 75,* Richard A. Parker and Waldo H. Dubberstein, 1956.

[321] That the reference is to Artaxerxes I is confirmed by the Elephantine Papyri which "show that the sons of Nehemiah's arch-foe, Sanballat, were active in the last decade of the fifth century [410-401], Sanballat being then apparently advanced in years. They also show that the high priest at the time of Ezra was Johanan, grandson of Nehemiah's contemporary, Eliashib (cf. Neh. 3:1; 12:10f., 22). John Bright, pg. 391, *A History of Israel.* See Pritchard, ANET, pg. 492.

Table 12 above, from Parker and Dubberstein.

Thus it is known that Nisan 1 of Artaxerxes 20th year began on April 13th (Julian) 445 B.C. The reign of Artaxerxes I is also astronomically fixed by tablet VAT 5047, dated to the 11th year of Artaxerxes and recording the positions of Mercury, Jupiter, Venus, Saturn, and two lunar positions. From this information astronomers can fix Artaxerxes reign in absolute time.[322] This means the decree to rebuild the city walls was in the spring of 445 B.C. And as explained before, the walls were built next, and then the Sabbatical year began in the fall. This is the first "seven."†

To repeat, the year between Tishri 1, 445 B.C. and the last day of Elul 444 B.C. is confirmed to be the seventh year by two witnesses. First Nehemiah caused all the debts to be remitted at the beginning of this year, and second a scribe named Ezra read the Torah. For the Torah commands that it be read at the beginning of every seventh year (Deut. 31:10) and that debts also be canceled then. The year expressed above is summarized 445/444 B.C. This year was the seventh year, as proved by the two witnesses. The first seven year period includes the first sabbatical year.† The commandment was given just before it began in 445 B.C. We thus count part of the first Sabbatical period inclusively, there being part of year six and all of year seven left. Or we merely count the "seventh" years. Counting out <u>seven sevens</u> and then <u>sixty two</u> sevens moves us forward to AD 32/33. The prophecy says, "then after the sevens sixty and two Messiah will be cut off" (Dan. 9:26). So after AD 32/33 would be AD 34. The measuring stick is thus perfect.

There is no way that the crucifixion could be in A.D. 33. This is because it is still during the Sabbatical year in A.D. 33, and the prophecy says Messiah would be "cut off" "<u>after</u>" the Sabbatical year. Further, it is quite impossible to shift the seventh year back one year because then Nehemiah would be canceling debts at the end of the seventh year, and Ezra would be reading the Torah after the end of the seventh year. And this would contradict the instructions to do these things at the start of the seventh year! So, A.D. 33 cannot be

---

[322] Further details on this prophecy are given in *The Scroll of Biblical Chronology and Ancient Near Eastern History*, vols I and II.

† As a day (containing hours) may be inclusively counted, so also a Sabbath year period (containing years) may be inclusively counted, one part thereof as a whole #. The first seven = 451.t to 444.t

accommodated (with its Friday date) by shifting the seventh year backward.

There are no loose ends in this prophecy. The technical details of all of biblical chronology are dealt with in *The Scroll of Biblical Chronology and Ancient Near Eastern History*, Vols I & II. Here I will summarize some technical points. (1) Ezra came to Jerusalem in the 7th year of Artaxerxes II, but it was not his first time in the city. (2) His second appearance in Jerusalem corresponds to the "seven sevens" in the prophecy. (3) If a Tishri epoch is applied to Neh. 1:1, it should be backdated and not forward dated. This is proved by the time of Xerxes' death. More on this later. (4) "Cyrus" is a surname, or "throne name" according to history and Isaiah 45:4, and was thus inherited by Artaxerxes. (5) Josephus gives the title "Cyrus" to Artaxerxes.[323] Thus it is explained how "Cyrus" gave orders to rebuild the city and the temple spanning over three kings who inherited the title, and it is clear that the prophecy began with Nehemiah under Artaxerxes I.

It is confirmed that Daniel 9:24-26 teaches sixty-nine sabbatical years from 445/444 B.C. to AD 32/33, and that Messiah was "cut off" after these in AD 34. And AD 34 is the only year that works such that Yeshua died on the 4th day of the week and rose from the dead on the 7th day of the week.*

The Failure of A.D. 33 and Daniel 9

AD 33 advocates fully realize that other chronological data exclude the Friday date in AD 30. That is why I explained that

[323] *Jos. Ant.* 11:184. We cannot trust Josephus here entirely because he has generally mixed everything up in this period of time. The title was first held by Artaxerxes brother Cyrus, who was crown prince. Both Xerxes and Cyrus were murdered by Artabanus leaving the throne and title to Artaxerxes, who successfully uncovered the plot and punished the crime of Artabanus. Artaxerxes chose to use the title "Artaxerxes" rather than Cyrus, possibly for personal reasons connected to the murder of his brother. The title was nevertheless his. Royal persons often have many titles that cannot be remembered by everyone. I do not see any reason to suppose that Artaxerxes was willingly complicit in either his father's or brother's death. Such guilt is exactly what a Greek propagandist would have us believe to tarnish the rule and legitimacy of Artaxerxes.

* The resurrection began before night ended and ended after day began, so that Messiah was in the heart of the earth only three days and three nights, i.e. the depth of She'ol, yet it was also on the seventh day, as written, "his going forth is according to deep dawn" (Hos. 6:3).

Figure 67: Master Chart of Daniel 9:24-27

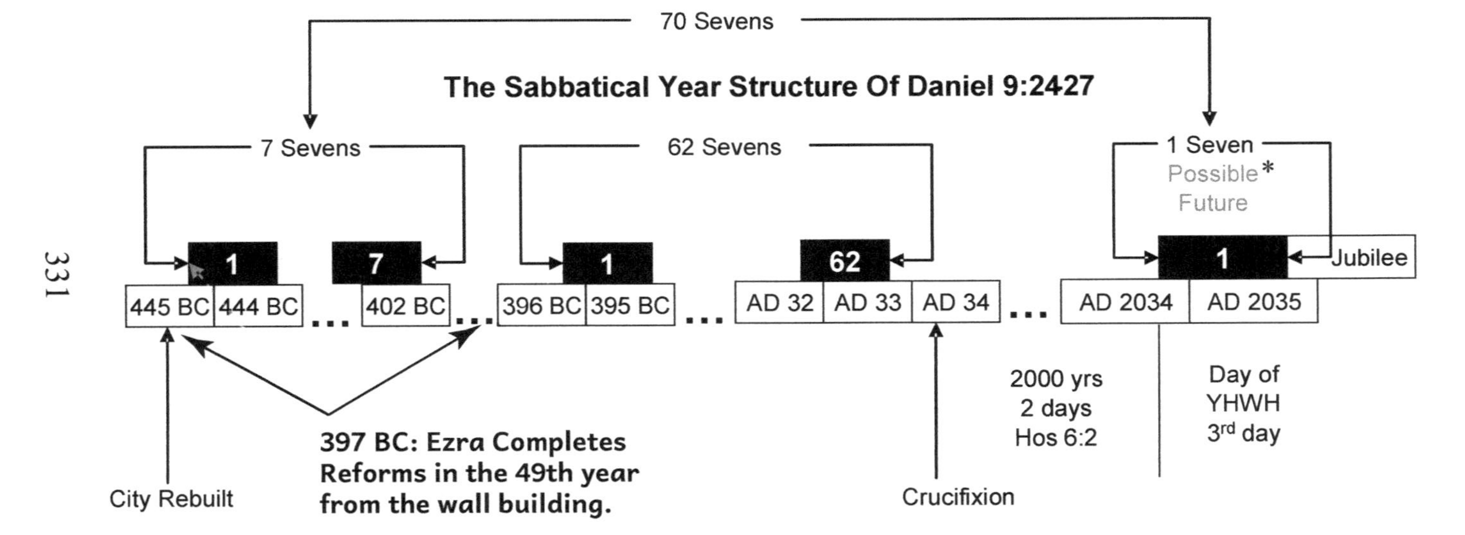

* For quite a long time I have not considered this Jubilee the ending Jubilee of this age. That said, however, I still consider it the beginning of the third millennium after the Resurrection Sabbath (cf. Hos. 6:1-3). I consider that the end of this age will come at a Jubilee in this third millennium. I have sought to understand the numbers in Daniel and Revelation for all the Jubilees of the third millennium. The most elegant solution is for the third, the 2133 Jubilee, more than one hundred years into the future, and no Jubilees after that come even close. To keep things simple, certain patterns detailed in this book will recur in a hundred years, both in terms of chronology, and in terms of the heavens. As I write this the Beast which was is trying to bring the world under its despotic rule, but with much spilled blood and wasted treasure it will be confined to the abyss until the very end. It will be the Beast that "is not," with a fatal wound. Then it "will be" for a short time. In the meantime, the wounding of the beast will entail the technological collapse of our current global civilization. Some regions of the world will be taken back to the age sword and horse with others hanging on to a very local technology. When the world recovers, then the beast will have its wound healed. In the space between now and then, the Almighty will keep the remaining promises of this age for Israel, and a refuge will be set up for Israel to survive the second coming of the beast.

Tiberius' 15th year was completely reliable, and is not to be backdated by a fictitious co-regency. That leaves only A.D. 33, which I will now show,(besides contradicting Matthew 12:40 and the "first of the Sabbaths;")also fails the test of the Daniel 9 prophecy.

The classic calculation was developed by Sir Robert Anderson in *The Coming Prince*† for A.D. 32. This position has been abandoned due to the fact that A.D. 32 lacks any possible Friday, Thursday, or Wednesday dates for Nisan 14. When it was discovered that astronomical calculation disproved A.D. 32, evangelical fundamentalists revised the argument for A.D. 33.‡ Anderson's original argument proposed that the decree was given in 445 B.C., which was the correct starting year,[324] however the evangelical argument for A.D. 33 revised the start date to 444 B.C. This change of the 20th year of Artaxerxes from 445 B.C. requires the assumption that Nehemiah imposed a Tishri 1 new year on the Nisan 1 new year of the Persians, and then forward dated the Tishri year by six months.

In the top row of **Figure 68: Tishri Translation of Artaxerxes I's Nisan Year,** below, year 20a represents the standard Babylonian reckoning of Artaxerxes 20th year, as given in Parker and Dubberstein, and starting in the spring. See **Table 12: Artaxerxes I Summary (Parker & Dubberstein)** page 328. If Neh. 1:1

---

[324] But he also incorrectly put the new moon on March 14 (Julian). Nevertheless, Parker and Dubberstein place this month as new moon Adar II, making the day part of March 15, 445 B.C. the 1st of Adar II; my calculations based on Steve Moshier's public domain Jet Propulsion Laboratory code for the Astronomical Almanac give the same day for the new moon, only on the biblical calendar as Nisan 1, as the Scripture treats the *tequfah* differently than the Babylonian/Persian calendar. Anderson also asserted that the day part of the 10th of Nisan in A.D. 32 was April 6th (Julian). This day is a Sunday on the Julian reckoning. However, the new moon was seen on March 31st just after sunset that year, and so the day part 10th of Nisan needs to be corrected to Thursday, April 10th. Also, as stated before in this book, the day part of 14th of Nisan was Monday, April 14th, which is the key fact that makes A.D. 32 impossible for the crucifixion. In Anderson's day, retro-calculation at the range of -2000 years was still in its infancy and fraught with errors, and this was costly to Anderson, because both his calculations for the new moon in 445 B.C. and A.D. 32 are incorrect. The 445 B.C. miscalculation was a minor error, correctable by realizing the new moon was just a day later. The A.D. 32 err was completely fatal for his ending point.

†1894. ‡ Beginning with Roger Bacon (ca. AD 1250) making use of the Almagest, some began to realize that AD 34 would not work out for them, and so proposed AD 33. But matters remained confusing and controversial through the end of the 19th century. With the discovery of Babylonian Astronomical diaries, it became increasingly clear that astronomical calculation was very accurate.

places Chislev before Nisan in the same year as Neh. 2:1, he would be using a definition of the 20th year beginning in the fall.* The left and right sides of the figure represent two ways to translate the Babylonian spring epoch into a fall basis (20b or 20c).

Figure 68: Tishri Translation of Artaxerxes I's Nisan Year

Thus, A.D. 33 advocates want to translate 20a to 20b on the basis of Nehemiah 1:1, which mentions "Chislev," the 9th month, which falls before Nisan. The only problem with this assumption is that 20a to 20c also satisfies the text. It does not matter whether the translation is to a Tishri year after *or* before. Chislev comes after Tishri in both cases and meets the presumed requirement of Neh. 1:1 and 2:1.

The question then, is which way would a translation be done to a Tishri year? Whether such translation followed the Nisan regnal year or preceded it by six months with any particular king depended upon whether the accession date was between Nisan 1 and the following Tishri, or between Tishri 1 and the following Nisan. British Museum Tablet BM 32234 sheds some light on this: "V/14?–18?/21 (Aug. 4?-8?, 465), death by murder of Xerxes."[325] This shows that Xerxes died between Nisan 1 and the following Tishri in the year 465, and allowing all interpretations of the tablet, between August 4 and August 8, 465 B.C. The month figure is clearly intact.

This demonstrates that Xerxes' successor would have a short accession year about a month and a half to Tishri, and that the first year of his reign would start with Tishri 465 B.C. in the Jewish

[325] *Babylonian Chronology*, 1956, pg. 17. The translation to modern dates in the ( ) was done by Parker and Dubberstein. Parker and Dubberstein add, "The day number is imperfectly preserved, and all numbers from 14 to 18 are possible [Sachs]" which is to say the possible dates range between August 4 and 8, 465.

* The "if" is because I now regard this as a Jubilee cipher for the 20th year of the Jubilee, and that we should interpret the Persian year from its normal spring epoch rather than converting it. The potential for a Jubilee was mentioned in the original edition on page 335. Conclusive reasoning for this possibility is given on page 348ff.

reckoning.[326] The Babylonian tablets know no successor except Artaxerxes I, and the Egyptian documents know only of Artaxerxes as succeeding Xerxes.[327] BM 32234 is solid archaeological evidence that renders all attempts to date Artaxerxes accession after Tishri 465 B.C. unparsimonious. The usual Judean rule then is that up to Tishri 1 that year is Artaxerxes accession year, which is not counted, and is rather assigned as the 21st of Xerxes, even though the new king completed this year.

---

[326] That a Tishri reckoning existed outside of Nehemiah is shown at Elephantine, Kraeling 6, pg. 137, Horn, *The Chronology of Ezra 7*, 1953, and by evidence from Solomon, Josiah, and Nebuchadnezzar's reigns as reported in the book of Kings.

[327] *From Cyrus to Alexander: A History of the Persian Empire*, Pierre Briant, pg. 566, 2006. In the archaeological record Artaxerxes directly succeeds Xerxes with no one else mentioned. Centuries later (ca. A.D. 160-240) Africanus tells us Xerxes' murderer Artabanus reigned for seven months. So also Eusebius (A.D. 263-339). And these two seem to rely on Manetho from the second century B.C. Briant tells us that this is not credible. Artabanus was not from the Achaemenid royal line, and could not be considered an heir, nor did he lead an open revolt against the Archaemenids. His plotting was in secret and was brought to justice by Artaxerxes' discovery of it. A secret plotter does not claim regnal years or months. So Briant has to be correct. There was no seven month rule of Artabanus recognized by the people. Furthermore, Africanus' king list is elsewhere unreliable. He assigns 42 years for Artaxerxes II rather than the correct 46, a most glaring err, and he puts the first year of Cyrus in 560/559 B.C., failing to count from Cyrus' accession in Babylon in 539 B.C. Eusebius' list also includes Artabanus but he likewise errs with Artaxerxes II (40 years). And Manetho is horribly inaccurate. From BM 32234 to AP (Aramaic Papyri) #6 from Elephantine, that is Aug. 465 to Dec. 465 are only five months. Since there are not seven months needed for Artabanus, the whole conjecture of Artabanus' seven months "rule" must be dismissed. It could be that Artabanus' plot was turned into a seven month reign in Egypt as a piece of political propaganda to justify Egypt's plans to revolt against Persia, that is to embolden the rebels in Egypt. Egypt was supported by Greece during the revolt, and we may expect the Greek sources of the palace plot in Susa to be sympathetic to Artabanus' treason.

That Artaxerxes 1st year began with Tishri 465 B.C. by Jewish reckoning is also confirmed by Aramaic Papyri 8. The only interpretation of AP 8 that requires no emendation is that November 460 b.c. was the sixth year of Artaxerxes by Jewish reckoning. Again, this suggests that year one begins with October 19, 465 B.C. Horn and Wood, who plead for the Tishri epoch to follow the Nisan epoch, say "the dates as given can be made to agree by no known methods, so that a scribal error must be involved," pg. 128, but then

Figure 69: The Accession of Artaxerxes I

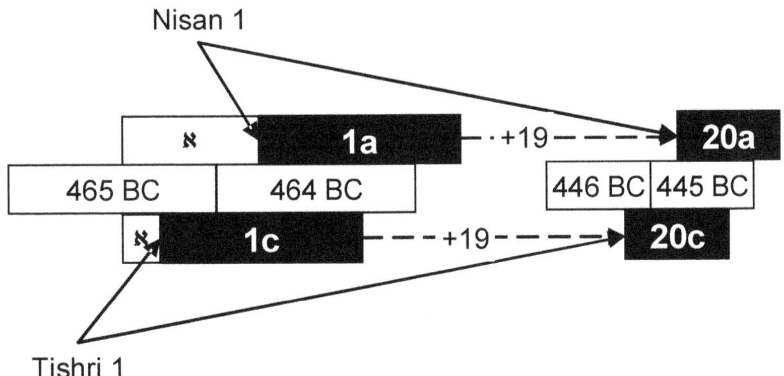

The accession method with the Tishri new year translates 1c to 20c, and the accession method with the Nisan new year translates 1a to 20a. Therefore, the assumption of the A.D. 33 advocates is incorrect. It is only proper for 20c to precede 20a (by six months). This also means that 20c is in fact very close to the anniversary year of Artaxerxes I, and the 9th month of 20c precedes the 1st month of 20c as in Neh. 1:1:

It should be noted that Nehemiah omits "of Artaxerxes" in Neh. 1:1 when he says "the twentieth year." This is because he knew quite well that the official "twentieth year of Artaxerxes" began on Nisan 1 (Neh. 2:1). Neh. 1:1 does not designate the official Persian "twentieth year", but either a Judean translation of it, or possibly a date by anniversary years, or Jubilee cycle. What needs to be noticed,

---

confess on the next page, "If the date line of the papyrus needed no emendation to achieve agreement with the astronomical facts, we should have proof here that the Jews of Elephantine had failed to observe a second Adar in harmony with the Babylonian year." Or I may add failing to follow it as in Judea. It is reasonable that they should so miscalculate because from 463 - 454 Egypt was revolting against the Persian Empire, and with quite a bit of success at first.

The seven months assigned to Artabanus by Africanus and Eusebius have the appearance of being engineered by the chronologers themselves to fill a hole in the chronology left by their assumption that Xerxes reigned only 20 years instead of 21 according to BM 32234. The difference between the quality of BM 32234 and Africanus or Eusebius is that BM 32234 is much closer to the events.

however, is that the translation 20a to 20c keeps Nisan 1 invariant, but (and most importantly) 20a to 20b does not. It changes Nisan 1 by a year. If we look at the chart on page again, it is clear that 464 b.c. begins the first year, and 445 b.c. the 20th year. We are then bound to take Neh. 2:1 as the official Persian reckoning as most parsimonious. The date of the wall building is thus 445 b.c. and not 444 b.c. Nehemiah's method of dating satisfies both Persian and Judean reckoning of the Nisan date and also shows deference to the Persian dating as the official dating.

Figure 70: Agreement of Neh. 1:1 with Neh. 2:1

(Supposing both texts speak of the 20th year of Artaxerxes I)

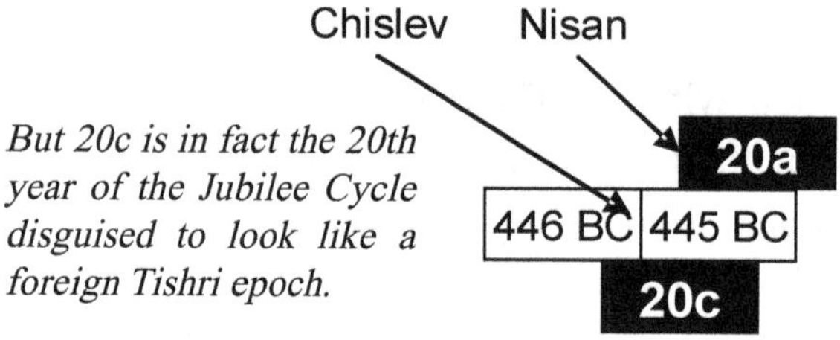

Chislev Nisan

But 20c is in fact the 20th year of the Jubilee Cycle disguised to look like a foreign Tishri epoch.

20a

446 BC | 445 BC

20c

There is one more proof that Artaxerxes' 20th year in the Jewish reckoning would have been 446/445 and not 445/444. And this is from the legitimate reading of Daniel 9. So it counts as absolute biblical proof of which way things would be reckoned if we take the "twentieth year" in Neh. 1:1 according to Jewish regnal counting. Here is the chart:

Figure 71: Judean Counting of the 20th Year

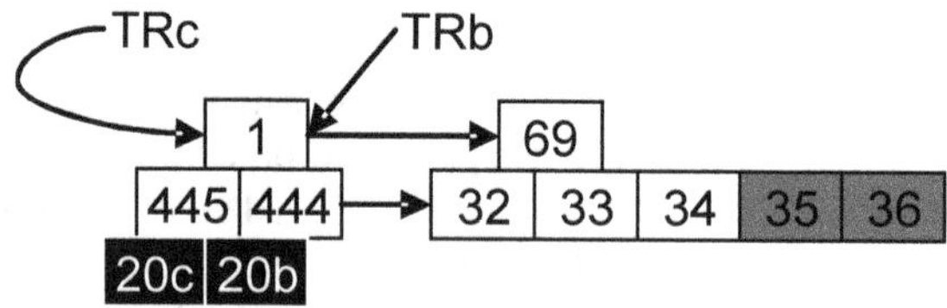

The Tishri year 20c precedes the Nisan year 20a in the previous Figure . I have drawn in 20b in this figure also. We must decide between 20c and 20b for the 20th year of Artaxerxes by the Jewish Tishri epoch. In the top row, 1 represents the first Sabbatical year. If 20c is correct, then Ezra's Torah reading is at the beginning of the

Sabbatical year (TRc), and likewise Nehemiah's usury and debt reforms. If 20b were correct, then the Torah reading and debt release would come at the end (TRb). But Deut. 31:10 teaches that the Torah should be read "at the edge of seven years, in the set time of the year of release, in the feast of the booths." Eben Ezra proved from Jer. 34:14 that the words "at the edge of" (מִקֵּץ) mean the leading edge of the seventh year. For a servant is only to serve six years. Likewise, no one is to be indebted in the seventh year, but only for six years.

We must therefore rule 20b out as the parsimonious explanation. The 69 sabbatical years are the sum of the "seven sevens" and "sixty two sevens" of Daniel 9. Furthermore, there is no chance of shifting the Sabbatical years to the right even one year. The prophecy says "after the sixty two sevens" that Messiah would be cut off. Shifting one year to the right would place the 69th year over Nisan A.D. 34. Then the crucifixion would not be "after" the 69th year. The crucifixion, likewise, cannot be bumped over to A.D. 35 or 36, as the first would put the crucifixion on Tuesday,[328] and the latter on Sabbath.

So we see that the Sabbatical year cannot be moved. This shows that the correct translation of the Babylonian Nisan epoch for the 20th year to the Tishri epoch for the 20th year is 20c. It also shows that the seventh year of Artaxerxes I was 459/458:

Figure 72: Artaxerxes 7th Year in Jewish Reckoning

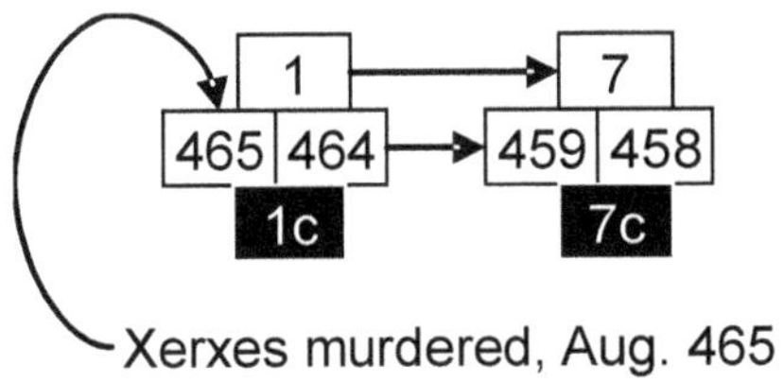

This last diagram shows why the Seventh Day Adventist eschatology beginning in 457 B.C. in invalid. It is apparent that Nisan must be in 458 B.C. if Ezra is taken to come before Nehemiah. (I will

[328] And since A.D. 35 has Adar II of 30 days, postponement to Wednesday this year is not possible. Both these years also open up unacceptable gaps in the length of Yeshua's ministry.

show later that Ezra came in 398 B.C.).

There is one final proof that Nehemiah did not build the walls in 444 B.C. Neh. 6:15 tells us that the wall were finished in 52 days on the 25th of the month of Elul. Please notice that the 25th of Elul was on the 2nd day of the week. This makes the beginning day of the 52 days Av 3 (Aug 1), which was a Sabbath.

```
Month: VI ELUL, 444 BC   3696A.M. Sab. Cyc: 7. Jub. Cyc: 21 Cycle No: 75
            Sabbatical Year in Progress until Trumpets.
Q1: 0.415 A Q2: -0.827 F LG:  48m W: 1.102' AL: 22.0 AV: 9.8
New Moon calculated for longitude: 35.17 and latitude 31.77
Location of calculations: Jerusalem
   Designed and Programmed By Daniel Gregg
```

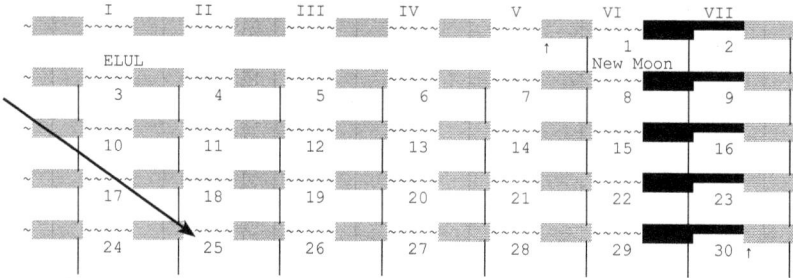

I	II	III	IV	V	VI	VII
				↑	1 New Moon	2
ELUL 3	4	5	6	7	8	9
10	11	12	13	14	15	16
17	18	19	20	21	22	23
24	25	26	27	28	29	30 ↑

Here is the Julian equivalent of Elul, 444 B.C:

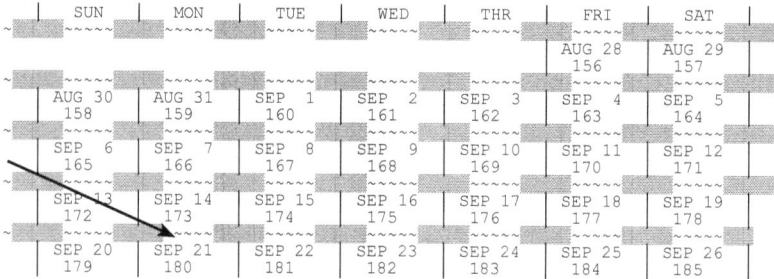

SUN	MON	TUE	WED	THR	FRI	SAT
					AUG 28 156	AUG 29 157
AUG 30 158	AUG 31 159	SEP 1 160	SEP 2 161	SEP 3 162	SEP 4 163	SEP 5 164
SEP 6 165	SEP 7 166	SEP 8 167	SEP 9 168	SEP 10 169	SEP 11 170	SEP 12 171
SEP 13 172	SEP 14 173	SEP 15 174	SEP 16 175	SEP 17 176	SEP 18 177	SEP 19 178
SEP 20 179	SEP 21 180	SEP 22 181	SEP 23 182	SEP 24 183	SEP 25 184	SEP 26 185

Here is the previous month and its Julian equivalent:

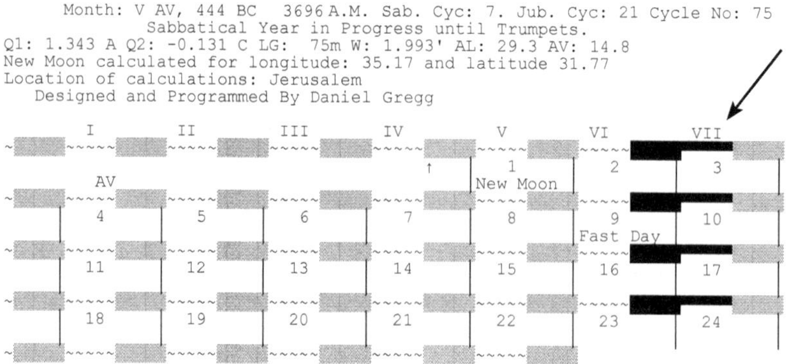

```
Month: V AV, 444 BC   3696A.M. Sab. Cyc: 7. Jub. Cyc: 21 Cycle No: 75
            Sabbatical Year in Progress until Trumpets.
Q1: 1.343 A Q2: -0.131 C LG:  75m W: 1.993' AL: 29.3 AV: 14.8
New Moon calculated for longitude: 35.17 and latitude 31.77
Location of calculations: Jerusalem
   Designed and Programmed By Daniel Gregg
```

I	II	III	IV	V	VI	VII
			↑	1 New Moon	2	3
AV 4	5	6	7	8	9 Fast Day	10
11	12	13	14	15	16	17
18	19	20	21	22	23	24

25	26	27	28	29 ↑		
SUN	MON	TUE	WED	THR	FRI	SAT
				JUL 30 127	JUL 31 128	AUG 1 129
AUG 2 130	AUG 3 131	AUG 4 132	AUG 5 133	AUG 6 134	AUG 7 135	AUG 8 136
AUG 9 137	AUG 10 138	AUG 11 139	AUG 12 140	AUG 13 141	AUG 14 142	AUG 15 143
AUG 16 144	AUG 17 145	AUG 18 146	AUG 19 147	AUG 20 148	AUG 21 149	AUG 22 150
AUG 23 151	AUG 24 152	AUG 25 153	AUG 26 154	AUG 27 155		

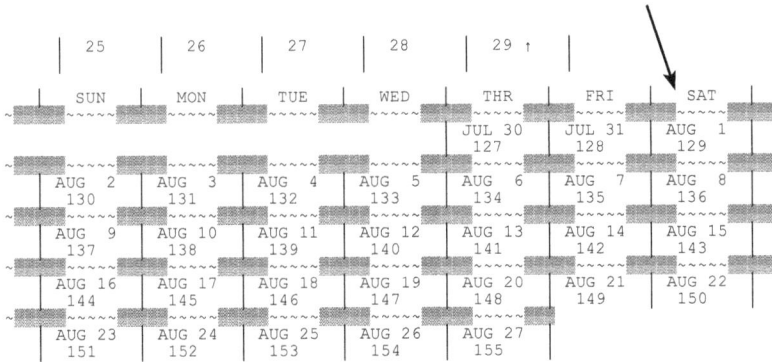

Notice that Av 3 (Aug 1) is the 129th day of the year, and that Elul 25 (Sept 1) is the 180th day of the year. The formula of inclusive counting is to subtract and add 1. Thus 180-129+1 = 52. A.D. 33 advocates should be made aware of the fact that their theory requires the famed wall builder and Sabbath reformer to start his project on the Sabbath.

The second point of calculation A.D. 33 advocates introduce is the 360 day year. They first reduce the actual 365¼ day year length to 360 days claiming that they may do so because a "prophetic year" is 360 days. This is supposed to be justified because the year during Noah's flood is assumed to be 360 days.[329] Clearly the year was not 360 days in the period between Nehemiah and Messiah. Further, they argue that the book of Revelation employs a 360 day year by assuming that 42 months equals 1260 days, and then they divide this to find one month equal to 30 days and then multiply by 12 to arrive at 360. However, Revelation nowhere equates 42 months and 1260 days. 42 months on the scriptural calendar is 29.5 x 42 = 1239 days, give or take a day. So the period of anti-Messiah's rule is shorter than the period of time Israel is protected. Nowhere is exact equation of the time periods stated.

Nevertheless, advocates of A.D. 33 must use a 360 day year, because it is the only way their calculation even comes close. This

[329] For a demonstration that the supposed 360 day year does not explain the Genesis data any better than the current year and month lengths see **Appendix III: Noah's Flood** Year, page **459**. The mean tropical year is 365.2421896698 days. The mean synodic lunation is 29.53058886 days, thus on average any period contains an equal number of 29 day and 30 day months.

360 day year also neglects the Sabbatical years upon which Daniel 9 is based. Daniel 9:2 leads us back to 2Chron. 36:21. And this, in turn, leads us back to Lev. 26:34-35, and 43. Further, the Almighty told Israel he would punish them "seven times" (Lev. 26:18, 21, 24, 28), which matches the broken seventh years with Daniel 9:24, "seventy sevens" and Ezekiel 4:5-6, which mention the 420 years (390 + 40) that contain the actual 70 sabbatical years that Israel broke.[330]

Neglecting all this, A.D. 33 advocates add up the seven sevens and sixty two sevens (7 + 62 = 69) and then treating them as 69 seven year periods, where each year is 360 days, they multiply 69 x 360 x 7, which equals: 173,880 days. We see then that the subtotal for a seven year period is: 2520 days. This is shorter than any proper seven year sabbatical period. Taken 69 times, the total days are 173,880. This is supposed to be the number of days from some point in Nisan 444 B.C. to some point ending just before Nisan 14, A.D. 33.

According to Parker and Dubberstein, Nisan 1, 444 B.C. was April 3 (Julian).[331] Also, as we saw on page **242**, the Friday date for A.D. 33 is April 3. What then is the total number of days from one date to the other? First the Spring Equinox was 3/26/444 B.C. (Julian) at 8h:39m. As the Persians never placed the first month before the equinox, the first month was placed after it on 4/3/444 B.C., just as Parker and Dubberstein state. Further, this date is Aviv 1 for the biblical calendar, as well. For as we have seen, the 15th of Nisan may not fall before the *tequfah* (spring equinox date), which it would, if a date based on the month before the new moon of 4/3/444 B.C. were used. Adar in this year began 3/4/444 B.C., and the 15th of Adar was 3/18/444 B.C., which was before the above mentioned equinox on 3/26/444 B.C. So this year, by both the scriptural method and the Babylonian method, Nisan 1 fell on 4/3/444 B.C. So there is no possibility that Nisan 1 may precede the date of 4/3/444 B.C.

Furthermore, the only Friday date in A.D. 33 is April 3. So there is no chance of changing this date to a later one. Now back to our question. How many days are there from one day to the other? The Julian day number for 4/2/444 B.C., when the new moon was first seen

---

[330] My other book shows that the Jubilee years must be counted also to get a total of 70 broken land Sabbaths in 420 years.

[331] Page 32, "Artaxerxes I," *Babylonian Chronology*.

was 1,559,344. The Julian day number for A.D. 33, April 3 is: 1,733,190[332] + 14 = 1,733,204. To find the inclusive difference, subtract and add one. 1,733,204–1,559,344+1 = 173,861. We see that the number of days is 19 days less than the required number: 173,880. 173,880–173,861 = 19.

But the prophecy says that Messiah would be "cut off" "after" the time period. This time period is 19 days short of the proposed 173,880 days! What did A.D. 33 advocates do about this? Since they could not move the Friday date, April 3rd forward, they moved the date for Nisan 1 backward one month in 444 B.C. This month was really Adar in the Babylonian, Persian, and Scriptural calendars, but they falsely called it Nisan. The A.D. 33 advocates never tell you about this flaw in their system. But it is an absolutely fatal flaw. For it sets a Passover date before the spring equinox in 444 B.C., and flatly contradicts the scripture that says it must be kept "from days to days"[333] (Exodus 13:10).

It is quite clear from the study of chronological systems and pseudo-chronological systems that if you break enough facts and sweep them out of sight that one can make it appear that two events are synchronized with the stated time that transpired between them. But once those facts are brought back and fairly and honestly faced, it becomes evident that such systems are *ad hoc* speculations that disagree with reality.

The A.D. 33 date simply does not hold up to the evidence. Having to place the 20th year of Artaxerxes in 444 B.C. instead of 445 B.C. where archaeology and history place it is a fatal error. The Daniel 9 calculation of A.D. 33 advocates is imperfect, and a near miss is as good as a mile, since biblical prophecy does not deal with near misses, but exact predictions. The 360 day year, in any case, is not according to the scripture in Genesis 1:14 which appoints the sun as the "sign for days and years." Daniel 9 is a "sign" prophecy, since it involves years, and so is the sign of Jonah, since it involves days. If we define a year or a day without regard to the movements of the sun

---

[332] When the new moon was seen. Add 14 days to determine the Julian day number of the 14th of Nisan.

[333] This technical phrase for the period between *tequfot* (equinoxes) is explained earlier in this book.

to indicate the start and end of years, then we are not using the Scriptural sign, but a sign of our own human invention.

The use of the 360 day year in this case is also fatally flawed, as is the ignoring of Sabbatical years, three days and three nights, and finally the plain statement in the resurrection passages that Yeshua rose on "the first of the Sabbaths" after Passover.

The Failure Of A.D. 31 And Daniel 9

Even though A.D. 31 does not allow a suitable Friday date for Nisan 14, it is nonetheless proposed as the year of the crucifixion by many religious leaders. Some claim a Friday crucifixion. But it is contrary to the astronomical evidence. Others claim a Wednesday crucifixion in this year, by placing Nisan a month late after the *tequfah*.[334] Neither of these positions agrees with the astronomical facts or the biblical requirements. The further failure of this year has already been noted in the discussion of Tiberius' 15th year. In this section I will show that this year (A.D. 31) also fails to work with Daniel 9.

Figure 73: Seventh Day Adventist Daniel 9:24-27

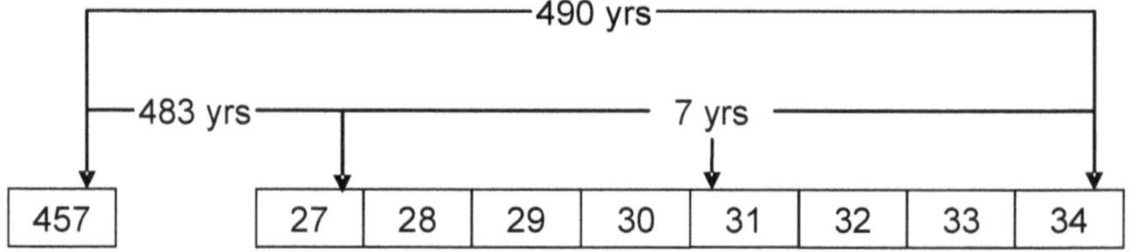

First, in no sense does A.D. 31 work with Nehemiah's building of the walls of Jerusalem in 445 B.C. Just to get A.D. 33 to come close requires A.D. 33 advocates to shorten the year to 360 days. And even this special pleading cannot be used for 445 B.C. and A.D. 31. So there are no proposals to make the correct date for rebuilding the walls work with A.D. 31. But advocates of this year are also required to make it work with Daniel 9. How do they do this? And what can we say of their answer?

In this case the seventieth week of Daniel is structured so that A.D.

[334] The error of postponing the first month past the *tequfah* (equinox) was shown earlier in this book. So a Wednesday date is also impossible in this year.

31 comes in the middle of the seventieth seven, and the starting point is moved back to 457 B.C. See **Figure 73: Seventh Day Adventist Daniel 9:24-27**, above.

The justification for placing the crucifixion in the midst of the seventieth seven instead of "after" the sixty two (which would be spring of A.D. 28 for this case) is their interpretation of Daniel 9:27:

> But he makes strong a covenant of the many seven one, and amid the seven he makes cease sacrifice and grain-offering, and on a wing abominations making desolate— even until an end that is decided will be poured out upon the desolater (Dan. 9:27).

Instead of taking the above text literally, and relating it to the literal cessation of offerings in the Temple, supporters of this doctrine spiritualize the text, and say that Messiah ended the sacrificial system in the middle of the "week," or seven year period. It has to be spiritualized, because in literal fact, the Temple services continued at least 40 years from A.D. 31. Messiah did not actually make the Temple services end.

This position also requires a negative attitude to the Torah and especially the Priestly Levitical Service in the Temple which is contrary to many texts, not the least of which is Jer. 33:17-22. Supporters require us to believe that the "he" at the beginning of the verse makes a covenant for seven years. But we are at a loss to find a covenant that was made for only seven years between Messiah and anyone. It is not the new made covenant because this covenant is not limited to seven years, nor for that matter was the covenant renewal made in A.D. 27, but a remembrance of it was begun at the last supper, and Jeremiah 31:34 clearly indicates that the renewed covenant is not fully implemented. When it is fully implemented, it is to be everlasting.

Another difficulty is that Daniel 9:26 places the "destruction of the city and temple" before the events of Daniel 9:27. If the 70th seven was completed by A.D. 34 then the prophecy is no longer in a chronological sequence that is true to historical fulfillment. The city was destroyed in A.D. 70, and therefore, Daniel 9:27 should happen after A.D. 70. Thus, placing the beginning of Daniel 9 in 457 B.C. is an unparsimonious interpretation.

Additionally, one may note that the person in Daniel 9:27 is responsible for abominations, and that he is destroyed in the end. This is the same person that puts an end to the sacrifices and offerings in the Temple. This is more in character with an Islamic Mahdi or Antiochus Epiphanes, who caused unclean animals to be sacrificed on the altar in Jerusalem. To say the least, interpreting Daniel 9:27 in reference to Messiah is devilish mockery of the Torah and Prophets, and perfectly anti-Semitic.*

Finally, I note that Daniel 9:24 specifies that "everlasting righteousness" be brought in for Jerusalem and Israel by the end of the seventieth seven, and by no means did this happen in A.D. 34, the supposed end of the seventieth week. The Rabbis make the same mistake when they end Daniel's prophecy in A.D. 70 (or incorrectly A.D. 69). Yet, the prophecy does specify that "seventy sevens are decreed …to bring in everlasting righteousness." If they are completed already, then why is there no "everlasting righteousness" for the "holy city." And this is only the start of things that are supposed to be completed in "seventy sevens."

What about "finishing the transgression"? Of course, Christians are going to "spiritualize" the interpretation, and not take it literally for Daniel's "people" and "holy city." They are going to say that all these things were fulfilled by Messiah already. They will say that "everlasting righteousness" refers only to Messiah. They will piously say that he is "everlasting righteousness." He is indeed, but not yet for Israel, and not yet for Jerusalem. The prophecy says that it must be "for your people" (עַל־עַמְּךָ) and "your holy city" (עַל־עִיר קָדְשֶׁךָ), and that is how Daniel, who was looking for the kingdom of the Almighty, understood it.

Daniel 9:27 really speaks of the anti-Messiah. How is it that many have confused the Messiah with the anti-Messiah? The answer is that Satan is a master deceiver and seeks to create groups of people claiming to be "biblical," but who believe the exact opposite of the truth at the most critical points. Yeshua clearly told us that the world will acclaim the anti-Messiah to be the Messiah, and indeed Satan is waiting to become a new Antiochus, the Islamic Mahdi when his time

* In Vol. II of *The Scroll of Biblical Chronology and Ancient Near Eastern History*, pg. 122, I give a corrected translation of Daniel 8:11 which makes it clear that the attack on the sanctuary is an attack on Messiah's Temple in Jerusalem.

comes.

Also, if 490 years end in A.D. 34, then they must begin in 457 B.C., and this requires Ezra's reform to come before Nehemiah 8 (445 B.C.) This rearrangement contradicts the high priestly succession in Ezra, among other details, and most importantly it leaves the "seven sevens" of Daniel 9:25 without the obvious explanation. See the chart on page 331. Ezra came to Jerusalem and completed his reforms exactly 49 years (containing "seven sevens")† after Nehemiah rebuilt the walls. It is no surprise that many have fallen into this trap of mixing up the order of Nehemiah and Ezra. This trap is a pit to fall into. It is a pit for those who do not want to seek and open their eyes to take Yahweh's word literally, and as plainly and parsimoniously as possible. The mix up is a test for those who will not be completely loyal to the Torah and Prophets or Messiah Yeshua.

The next section will further establish that the 458 or 457 B.C. date does not qualify in any sense as the beginning point of Daniel's "seventy sevens."

How Daniel 9 Fails A.D. 30

Essentially the same starting and ending dates are used as for A.D. 31. Only this time the starting year is 458 B.C. and the ending date is A.D. 33, with A.D. 30 right in the middle:

Figure 74: "Catholic" Daniel 9:24-27

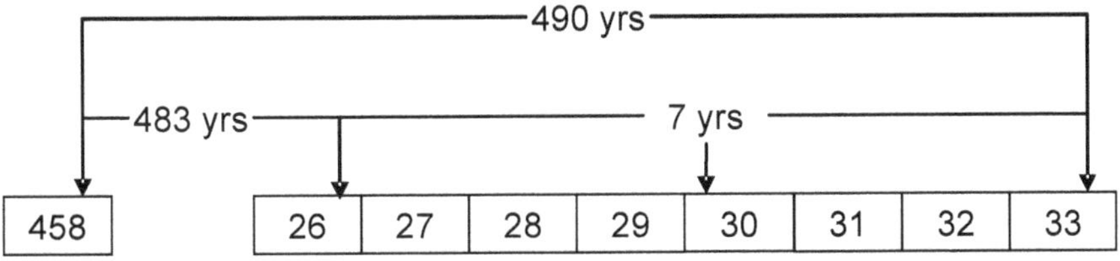

There are many fatal problems with this construction that are covered in preceding sections. At this point I am going to focus on whether 458 B.C. (or 457)[335] is a valid date at all. As briefly

[335] I will not continue to say 457 B.C. , but it must be understood the arguments apply to that year also when I state 458 B.C. 458 B.C. is, in fact, the correct year for the 7th year of Artaxerxes I, using the proper Judean Tishri offset according to Xerxes death in Av 465 B.C., and considering that Nisan 1

† Following the commandment to count seven Sabbaths in the 49 days after the first day of unleavened bread matches the same pattern with the "seven sevens" counted in 49 years. It is as if the text had said, in the tomorrow of the giving of the decree to rebuild Jerusalem you will have counted seven regular Sabbatical years, until in the tomorrow of the seventh Sabbatical year you are noting the coming of the anointed priest Ezra. By the shavuot counting we know that the Daniel 9 reckoning is not strange.

mentioned before, Ezra did not come to Jerusalem in 458 B.C. Ezra 7:7-8 only says the 7th year of Artaxerxes (אַרְתַּחְשַׁסְתְּא). But there is more than one Artaxerxes. There are in fact three:

Artaxerxes I	464-423
Artaxerxes II	404-358
Artaxerxes III	358-337[336]

The 458 B.C. advocates assume Ezra means Artaxerxes I. However, this assumption is an error, which will be shown below. Ezra meant Artaxerxes II. Ezra comes "seven sevens" after the start of the prophecy in 445 B.C., and then Messiah comes "sixty and two sevens" after Ezra, because the prophecy says, "until *an* Anointed Prince, seven sevens; and sixty two sevens…and after the sixty two sevens *the* Anointed will be cut off." As Jewish interpreters argue, this implies *two* anointeds. Indeed, the Hebrew text punctuates the sentence with the greatest major disjunctive after "seven sevens." It is called "atnah." It looks like this: ֑ (upside down "v" or lambda: Λ). I have removed all other vowel points from the text so the reader can see where it is in Dan. 9:25:

עד־משיח נגיד שבעים שבעֽה

until-anointed prince sevens seven;

So the Jewish reader reads the text as: "...until *an* anointed prince seven sevens;" and then ends the clause, here marked with semicolon. Now the atnach may be disregarded and the text read as pointing to one anointed, because punctuation is not part of the original sacred text. However, there really were two anointeds, and this does not upset the prophetic application to Yeshua in the least. Ezra was a priest descended from Aaron. As a priest, he would have been anointed at thirty years of age (cf. Num 4:3; Ex. 30:30). It seems evident that "anointed prince" has a double sense, one for Ezra, and one for Yeshua. That is, the text is to be read both ways, with the disjunctive, and without the disjunctive.

---

in 457 B.C. was the same on the biblical reckoning as Nisan 1 in Parker and Dubberstein, so that Nisan 1, in the 7th year corresponds to the spring of 458 in all cases.

[336] Parker and Dubberstein, *Babylonian Chronology.*

The first anointed is Ezra the Priest and Scribe who completes reforms after seven sevens (שָׁבֻעִים שִׁבְעָה), and the second anointed is Yeshua, who is cut off after (אַחֲרֵי) the end of sixty two more sevens (הַשָּׁבֻעִים שִׁשִּׁים וּשְׁנַיִם). So it turns out that the Jewish interpreters who say there are two anointeds are right.

Ezra represents the Torah, and he was Yahweh's anointed to teach it. Yeshua is Yahweh's Anointed, and he provides redemption for Israel, as spoken in the prophets. Moses represents the Torah, and Elijah the Prophets. These two anointeds come in the last days, during the last "seven" (שָׁבוּעַ) of Daniel 9. The third time is the climax. In the third segment of Daniel's prophecy, Torah and Prophets come together, the two anointings of Torah and Redemption coincide setting the stage for the glorious return of Messiah Yeshua to set up the kingdom of everlasting righteousness (צֶדֶק עֹלָמִים, Dan. 9:24), and so the third day, the day of Yahweh, will bring in the kingdom.

Of course, if the prophecy is supposed to start in 458 B.C, then it is impossible for the first anointed (מָשִׁיחַ), Ezra, to come after "seven sevens." For he would have already come, and the seven sevens would be a non event in 410 B.C. So we must consider Artaxerxes II as the Persian monarch meant by Ezra 6:14, 7:1, 7, 11, 12, 21.

Parker and Dubberstein state the 7th year of Artaxerxes II as 398/397 BC, which would place Ezra's foundation date for aliyah on a Monday, Nisan 1, 398 BC (April 5, 398). This was a well planned date early in the week wherein the local Babylonian calendar intersected the same date for the first day of the first month as the Scriptural calendar.[337]

---

[337] The year 397 is the only other choice here, being much less probable, based on the assumption that Ezra used a Judean Tishri epoch for the 7th year of Artaxerxes, i.e. 398.t/397.t, with 1 Nisan 397 being in the middle of this year. One difficulty with a Judean epoch is that it also implies the use of the Judean method for determining the beginning of the year, and in this case it was a month before the Babylonian Nisanu 1. Furthermore, the biblical date was a Friday (3/24/397), which is somewhat of an inauspicious day to be starting out on an aliyah to the holy land since it was the preparation day for the Sabbath. Another difficulty is the improbability that Ezra would use a Judean Nisan 1 in Babylon. At the very least, it would cause confusion. The departure date could also very well turn out to be a Sabbath since the previous month was only 29 days. While we should concede the use of local epochs for reign years of Persian kings, the Scripture never requires the use of them. All Scriptural datings of regnal years can be reconciled with the norms used by the kings concerned, including Nehemiah 1:1 since no king is named there.

Ezra 7:8 says that they arrived in Jerusalem while it was still the 7th year of Artaxerxes II. Now the wall building took place in the Tishri year 446.t/445.t. Ezra completed his reforms in the year 398.t/397.t. Calculation for inclusive counting is to subtract and add 1. Thus 446−398+1 = 49. Therefore, in terms of actual years Ezra comes in 7 × 7 to complete the separation of the Judeans from the nations. The same period contains exactly seven Sabbath years. The 1 is added because the counting is inclusive, which is to say the year 446.t/445.t is counted as "1" and the year 398.t/397.t is counted as "49." You can prove the math with a simple example. If you count inclusively from 3 to 7, then the count is 5: {3, 4, 5, 6, 7}. Using math: 7−3+1 = 5. So to use subtraction math to count inclusively you have to add 1. (All these details are charted in my other book, *The Scroll of Biblical Chronology and Ancient Near Eastern History*, Vol's I & II.

The way to prove a chart like the above is correct, without having to

Figure 75: Inclusive 49 Year Count for "Seven Sevens"

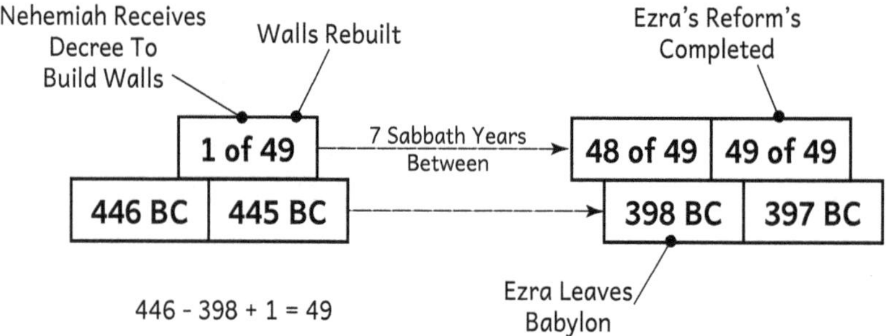

draw out every year on scratch paper, is to notice that the offset between year 1 and 445 BC is the same as that between year 48 and year 398. Then check the sums (445 + 1 = 446 and 398 + 48 = 446). They should be the same. One can also do 445−397+1 = 49.

Since the second edition of this book two changes have occurred that have resulted in corrections. The first is how the priestly divisions are to be reckoned. And the second is a change of Ezra's aliyah from 397 to 398 BC. The first change greatly improves the argument for Messiah's birth date on Tishri 1, 2 BC. The second change counts the 49 years to Ezra's final reform on a Tishri epoch instead of a Nisan epoch, and makes Ezra's local use of Artaxerxes 7th year more parsimonious.

What occurred to trigger this latter change? In short the fall of Horn and Wood's thesis.[338] The kings of Israel used a spring epoch for their reign years, and the kings of Judah a fall epoch. There is a half year in which "equivalent" years do not align. However, in no case is an event ever stated to occur in a year of a king that requires a converted shift into the half year of mismatch for another kingdom to obtain its true date. That is, never at any point did the prophet writers of *Kings* employ a Tishri conversion for the reign years of the northern kingdom or a Nisan conversion for the reign years of the southern. Synchronisms only are stated for the half years in which the two epochs overlap. It is true that outside scripture historical sources state events in terms of these converted years, such as the Elephantine Papyri using a Thoth 1 epoch in Egypt for kings of Persia, but Scripture has a pattern of avoiding this or expecting the reader to assume it.

Figure 76: Tishri Translation for Artaxerxes II

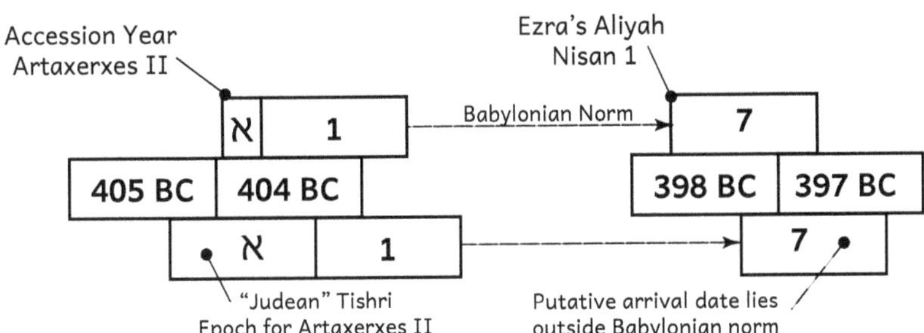

Parker and Dubberstein state "Artaxerxes II was recognized as king before April 404."[339] This means that his Nisan accession year ended in the spring of 404 BC, and year 1 of his reign began (Fig. 76). The figure shows a possible Judean reckoning, but as noted above the Scripture does not set any precedents outside the norm despite the many opportunities that present themselves.

---

[338] *The Chronology of Ezra 7*, Siegfried H. Horn and Lynn H. Wood. Horn and Wood advanced the thesis that the 20th year of Artaxerxes I was referred to in Nehemiah 1:1 and that it was allowable to date events according to a shifted Tishri year that placed the events outside of the normal Persian reckoning. This view is very compelling if another option is not in view, which must be gained from realizing that a number of Scripture passages are ciphers. Most probably, Nehemiah 1:1 is a cipher for the year in the Jubilee cycle at the time and not Artaxerxes. This is why the king is not named in the passage. I have decided therefore not to build on their thesis any foundation, since all matters work without it. It is certain that shifted epochs were used, but no dates are used in Scripture contrary to the norm of the kings named.

[339] *Babylonian Chronology*, pg. 18-19.

This makes Ezra's aliyah and all of his reforms fall into exactly one year and one day (Nisan 1, 398 BC to Nisan 1, 397 BC), which ends on the 49th year counting from the Tishri year of the decree. In the same period, there are seven Sabbath years, "seven sevens," which explain that part of Daniel 9:25-26.

So Ezra is the first anointed, and Yeshua is the second Anointed. In the 49 years between Nehemiah's rebuilding of the walls, and Ezra 10 are seven sabbatical years, and in the time between Ezra and Yeshua's death are sixty two more sabbatical years.

Briefly, the reason that 458 B.C. advocates believe Ezra himself came in that year is that his book comes first in the canon. But this position is naive. Ezra does not discuss himself in the first six chapters. Ezra covers history before himself all the way back to 529 BC. The book of Nehemiah comes after Ezra because it covers only a few years well after Ezra's starting point in history. Since Ezra did not want to completely rewrite Nehemiah's memoirs, he included it as an appendix at the end, and later as the Chronicler, Ezra made a few additions that clearly were not part of Nehemiah's memoirs (such as Neh. 12:26).

At the very worst, Ezra can only be charged with obscuring matters. He could have said that he explicitly meant Artaxerxes II in Ezra 6:14 and 7:1*f*, and he could have cleared up that Nehemiah's memoir which he attached was during Artaxerxes I. So the obscurity is nothing more than failing to explain the matter fully. No one in his time would have misunderstood since they were aware which Artaxerxes was which. It would have been understandable too why Ezra wrote his history starting in 529 B.C., and just simply attached Nehemiah's memoir with a few of his own notes. So the only question is why did Ezra not add extra statements to prevent obscuring matters long after himself. The facts are that Ezra did leave some clues, as the Chronicler, in the final editions. If there is any reason why he only left clues for future generations, it is this:

> And he said, "Go *your way*, Daniel, for *these* words are concealed and sealed up until the end time (Dan. 12:9).

Thus, at the time of the end, the words were meant to be unsealed and understood, but until then they were to be lost in obscurity. Perhaps this does not mean complete obscurity. It only means that the whole importance of the matter, and the precise way things work together is meant to be sealed up. Nevertheless, there are important clues in Ezra and Nehemiah and elsewhere that clear up the order and meaning of matters. And to these clues, I now turn.

Confirmation that Ezra comes after Nehemiah is that "Johanan" was the high priest during Ezra's administration (Ezra 10:6).[340]

The succession is given in Neh. 12:10-11, 22, 23:

> And Jeshua became the father of Joiakim, and Joiakim became the father of Eliashib, and Eliashib became the father of Joiada, and Joiada became the father of Jonathan, and Jonathan became the father of Jaddua....vs. 22: Eliashib, Joiada, Johanan, and Jaddua...vs. 23: up to the days of Johanan the son of Eliashib.

The High Priest "Jonathan" is the same person as "Jehohanan" in Ezra 10:6 and "Johanan" in Neh. 12:22-23.

> Then Ezra rose from before the house of God and went into the chamber[341] of Jehohanan the son of Eliashib. Although he went there, he did not eat bread, nor drink water, for he was mourning over the unfaithfulness of the exiles.

Either the High Priest had two forms to his name, or there is a scribal mistake in his name. The issue does not depend on the exact form of the names (יְהוֹחָנָן vs. יוֹנָתָן). The key point is that a "son of

---

[340] The text mentions the chamber of Johanan in the Temple (יְהוֹחָנָן), and that he was the Son of Eliashib (בֶּן־אֶלְיָשִׁיב). Really, this means he was the grandson of Eliashib in the Hebrew sense of "son," as one would say that David is the "son of Abraham." Eliashib was the High Priest at the time of Nehemiah's administration. By going into the chamber of the High Priest, Ezra was establishing the authority he had been given by Artaxerxes to administrate Judea from the office of Johanan. He did not thereby replace the High Priest, but he established his authority over him to administrate according to the Torah.

[341] That is, "office" or as the "chamber" of a judge in the modern sense. Ezra is asserting his authority as chief magistrate.

Eliashib" was the High Priest. For it was his office in the Temple that Ezra went into. The High Priestly line is also given again in Nehemiah 12:22, only this time, the name is spelled: יוֹחָנָן. And again in Neh. 12:23. The difference between יוֹחָנָן and יְהוֹחָנָן is merely one letter, and is analogous to the difference between *Yeshua* and *Yehoshua*, a short and long form of the same name. So Ezra 10:6 simply employs the correct long form of the High Priest's name. If there is an error in spelling it is in one of Nehemiah's lists (12:11), and not in Ezra 10:6. The Elephantine Papyrus AP 30 spells the high priests' name with the long form exactly as Ezra 10:6 does: יהוחנן:[342]

> The importance of these papyri for the history of the high priesthood is great, indeed. In the first place, TAD A4.7 = AP 30 names the Jerusalem high priest *Johanan* (יהוחנן), gives his Aramaic title (כהנא רבא), and firmly dates one incident in his reign to the year 410 BCE (the date when a letter was sent to him from Yeb). These data are thoroughly compatible with the chronological information in the book of Nehemiah, where Eliashib was high priest in 445 BCE and continued possibly to **433,** though by that time Joiada, Johanan's predecessor, may already have been in office (see Neh 13:28). The least one can say is that Joiada had a son of marriageable age by 433. Consequently, it would not be at all surprising to find his successor serving by 410. The reference to Johanan also demonstrates that his name belongs in the high-priestly list, as Neh 12:22 leads one to believe. Second, the fact that the Jews of Elephantine wrote to the high priest in Jerusalem to ask for his support shows the high regard in which this office was held by at least one group in the Diaspora.[343]

Nehemiah was a contemporary of Eliashib, who was the grandfather of Johanan. This makes it clear that the placement of Ezra before Nehemiah is contrary to the priestly succession. Yet, it was exposed to the public as early as 1888 by Bullinger in *The*

---

[342] *From Joshua to Caiaphas: high priests after the Exile*, James C. VanderKam, pg. 56. The full Aramaic quotation is: "יהוחנן כהנא רבא." This Papyrus is also referred to as TAD A4.7. Another copy of it is TAD A4.8 = AP 31. It dates to 17th year of Darius II, which is to say 407 B.C.

[343] VanderKam, ibid, pg. 57.

Companion Bible. Edwin Yamauchi states:

> [Scholars] conclude that since the Elephantine papyri indicate that Johanan was high priest in 410 BC, it is much more likely that Ezra came…in the seventh year of Artaxerxes II…It must be admitted that if these identifications are correct, this line of reasoning provides one of the strongest arguments for reversing the order of Ezra and Nehemiah.[344]

Provan states the point more directly:

> On last example shall suffice. In Ezra 10:6, Ezra goes to the room of a man named Jehohanan, the son of Eliashib, and the question arises whether the latter, Eliashib, is the same person mentioned in the Elephantine papyrus (AramP 30:18). If so, the latter —we know—lived in 408 B.C., which would make a meeting with an Ezra dated to an earlier period difficult if not impossible.[345]

John Bright adds his objections to the traditional order:

> More seriously, it is difficult to believe that Ezra, though commissioned to teach and impose the law, and filled with zeal, did not even read the law to the people until over thirteen years after his arrival (Neh. 8:1-8)….What is still more serious, any theory placing Ezra's reforms (Ezra, chs. 9; 10) before Nehemiah's inevitably involves the conclusion that Ezra in one way or another failed. One must assume that his reforms were so ineffective that Nehemiah had to repeat them (Neh., ch. 13); or that he aroused such opposition that he had to desist until Nehemiah came to the rescue; or that, having exceeded his authority (say in the affair of Ezra 4:7-23), he was in disgrace or was disciplined by the Persians—for which there is no evidence whatsoever. That Ezra was a failure is, to me, unbelievable. Not only does the Bible not so paint him, the whole course of Judaism was shaped by his work. Would this have been the case, and would tradition have made of him no less than a second Moses, had be been a failure? Yet so he was if his reforms preceded those of

[344] http://www.biblicalstudies.org.uk/pdf/ezra_yamauchi.pdf. Yamauchi himself does not agree with what he states, but he acknowledges it.
[345] *A Biblical History of Israel*, Provan, pg. 299.

Nehemiah.[346]

In Ezra 9:9, the "wall" (גָּדֵר) is referred to:

> For we are slaves; yet in our bondage, our Almĩghty has not forsaken us, but has extended loving-kindness to us in the sight of the kings of Persia, to give us reviving to raise up the house of our Almĩghty, to restore its ruins, and to give us a wall in Judah and Jerusalem.

This wall had to be the one that Nehemiah built in 445 B.C. and that he himself had helped dedicate in 431 B.C. This shows that Ezra 7 comes 49 years after Nehemiah 8, because in 458 B.C. there was no completed wall. Of course, opponents re-explain "wall" to mean some other wall[347] (or spiritualize the idea of "wall" to the concept of unseen protection), but this is not very parsimonious given the fact that the walls which actually succeeded in protecting Jerusalem were those that Nehemiah rebuilt, and here we have Ezra crediting the Almighty with providing these walls as divine providence.[348] There was no divine providence attached to the walls that were torn down prior to Nehemiah. For evidently those walls were not sanctioned by the Almighty for the beginning of the prophetic word in Daniel 9.

John Bright continues:

> In addition, various indexes, though no one in itself decisive, better suit the assumption that Nehemiah arrived before Ezra. Whether Ezra 9:9 refers to Nehemiah's wall or not, Nehemiah certainly found the city largely in ruins (Neh. 7:4), whereas when Ezra arrived it seems to have been inhabited and relatively secure. Further, Nehemiah early corrected economic abuses (ch. 5:1-13) of

---

[346] *A History of Israel*, John Bright, page 393.

[347] Such as the wall in Ezra 4:7-23 (4:12= שׁוּר), and referred to in Neh. 1:3 (חוֹמַת). But Ezra 4:7-23 is part of a parenthetical detail of the opposition placed in the context of chapters 1-6, before Ezra ever mentions himself, and then he begins at 7:1, "And after these things" (וְאַחַר הַדְּבָרִים הָאֵלֶּה). So it does seem that the Artaxerxes of 4:7 is not the one of 7:1.

[348] It may not be doubted that Ezra also implies spiritual protection to go with the physical, and that by "wall" he also means the favor of Artaxerxes and his decree that Yahweh granted Judah at this time. But also Ezra's pointed reference to "Jerusalem" is best understood in light of a literal "wall."

> which there is no hint in the story of Ezra. Would not the godly Ezra have been as shocked at such things as Nehemiah, had they existed when he came (as they would had he preceded Nehemiah)? Again: Nehemiah's reforms (ch. 13), if not milder than Ezra's, were certainly less consequent, having the earmarks of a series of *ad hoc* measures.

And there is another minor point. One "Meremoth son of Uriah" a descendent of "Hakkoz" was a wall builder (Neh. 3:4, 21), and is not called a priest in Nehemiah because the sons of Hakkoz could not prove their priestly status (cf. Ezra 2:61-62; Neh. 7:63-64). Later, in Ezra 8:33 the title is restored: "Meremoth son of Uriah the priest." Evidently the sons of Hakkoz were able to prove their priestly descent after the time of Nehemiah. The omission Meremoth's title in Nehemiah and restoration in Ezra 8:33 only makes parsimonious sense if Ezra 8:33 comes after the wall building, and it is assumed that the records were found, and then the title restored. Not convincing is the assumption that a lay family (with a claim to the priesthood) just happened to have the same father and son name as a different priestly family. Even less convincing is the assumption that Ezra "acknowledged Meremoth" when he arrived, and then deposed him, since there is no record that a priest Meremoth son of Uriah son of Hakkoz was deposed. The last assumption is simply an *ad hoc* attempt to explain why the title is lacking in Nehemiah.

> On a more subtle level, we might note that the figure of Meremoth son of Uriah, who appears to be a vigorous wall builder with Nehemiah (Neh. 3:4, 21), is a mature priestly leader with Ezra in Ezra 8:33-34, which is strange if Ezra is to be placed before Nehemiah chronologically.[349]

Ezra began his reforms as soon as he arrived, yet advocates of a 458 B.C. date posit a 13 year gap until Ezra read the Torah in Nehemiah 8:1. Since Ezra was skilled in the Torah (Ezra 7:6; 10, 12, 21), the Torah would have required one sabbatical year reading <u>before</u> the reading in 445 B.C. (Deut. 31:10). This Torah reading was not optional. It was mandatory. Why then does a 458 B.C. "Ezra" skip over this resulting in the sorrow and ignorance we meet with in Nehemiah

---

[349] *A Biblical History of Israel*, Provan, Long, and Longman, pg. 299.

8:9?

Such a scenario does not explain why the people were weeping in Neh. 8:9 nor why they had to be instructed on the impropriety of mourning on a holy day (8:11). Ezra would have known that he was supposed to normally read the Torah at the feast of Tabernacles (Deut. 31:10-12), but he reads it starting on the first of the month, which is Yom Teruah (blowing) because he knows the people will miss their opportunity to follow the law if they do not know it before the time to obey it comes to build booths. He realizes that he will re-read, or continue reading it at Tabernacles in any case. He does this because they do not know the Torah at all. The people act as if they have never heard the Torah. And clearly what made Ezra's Torah reading and teaching possible was the authority the king had given to Nehemiah.

If he had come 13 years before, then they would certainly know about the feast of Tabernacles, yet Neh. 8:14-18 makes it clear that they were ignorant of the Law, and had not kept it with such rejoicing days of Joshua![*] Ezra came with a complete and total legal mandate from the king of Persia to teach and enforce the keeping of the Torah:

> And you, Ezra, according to the wisdom of your God which is in your hand, appoint magistrates and judges that they may judge all the people who are in *the province* beyond the River, *even* all those who know the laws of your God; and you may teach anyone who is ignorant *of them.* And whoever will not observe the law of your God and the law of the king, let judgment be executed upon him strictly, whether for death or for banishment or for confiscation of goods or for imprisonment. (Ezra 7:25-26).

Ezra was commanded by the king to teach the Torah, yet according to the 458 B.C. advocates he kept the people in ignorance of the most fundamental and important observances and duties so that the people were weeping! To only inform them of their duties 13 years later would be total dereliction of his official responsibility. To so neglect it would be to dare Israel's enemies to strike before reform was possible. That Ezra 7-9 comes before Nehemiah 8, therefore, is unreasonable. Having the power to dissolve marriages, and yet not teaching the Law for 13 years simply wasn't in Ezra's character.

* They mourned because they first heard the Law, then they were instructed to keep the feast with joy, and they really did so with the greatest of joy, because they now knew the Torah, so they could be rescued from sin. It was the joy of repenting and having the feeling of being right with the Almighty for the first time. This is the reason it is said the feast was not kept so since the days of Joshua son of Nun.

For this reason Bright states if Ezra did his work before Nehemiah, then he would have been utterly negligent considering the facts, not worthy of being a second Moses.

The decree puts the lie to the assumption by 458 B.C. advocates that Ezra was teaching the Torah to smaller groups, but not publicly reading it in the seventh year or enforcing it in all Judea. For the King had given Ezra total authority in Judea in this matter.

> A second problem is a theological one. If Ezra spent thirteen years reading the Torah to the people, why is it that Yahweh rewarded Ezra's long—yet successful—mission by bringing disaster upon Jerusalem in the last year of his mission? Nehemiah would have found this disaster difficult to reconcile with Yahweh's past dealings with the nation which was to reward the obedient and bring disaster on the disobedient. Why else does Nehemiah immediately link the destruction of the walls with disobedience? Are we to assume that the national repentance of 445 was brought about by the destruction of the walls, rather than as a result of Ezra's long mission? If so, then we are still left with the problem of an ineffectual, national, spiritual leader.[350]

Nehemiah deals with mixed marriages after 431 B.C. by forbidding any 398 v marriages. He does not require them to be dissolved by divorce, but he does cause certain men to be publicly beaten, no doubt after they disobeyed his orders (Neh. 13:25). Then Ezra comes in 397 B.C. and is informed that the problem of mixed marriages with pagans remained, and was even threatening the priesthood. Ezra, no doubt, knew of Nehemiah's measures against it, and decided that they were not being effective, so he decides that all the cases must be brought before his court and that such marriages must be ended with divorce. For forty-nine years, or seven sevens, the people had been put on notice that mixed marriages were not to be tolerated.† Nehemiah's gracious allowing of those who had already transgressed to remain married expired under Ezra. Further, we may note that Nehemiah's measure was merciful in light of the people's ignorance of the Torah, which ignorance is corrected in Neh. 8:1*f* and 13:1 (445-431 B.C.) By the time we get to Ezra's stricter measures, the people would have known better for long enough to justify the stricter measures.

---

[350] Leslie McFall, *Was Nehemiah Contemporary with Ezra in 458 BC?*

† Forty nine days is the period of redemption, the time allowed between deliverance and responsibility, because the people were delivered out of Egypt, and then with a space of 49 days behind them, they were given the Torah on Mt. Sinai. In the space of 49 years, Ezra brought responsibility to the people.

The traditional order, with Ezra first, makes Ezra a total failure, despite total legal authority to fix the problem, and Nehemiah's measures seem legally impotent by comparison. Ezra had all the legal authority needed to clear up the problem, quite a bit more than Nehemiah had. Yet, according to the traditionalists, he did not solve it, and according to the traditionalists, after the problem had not been solved, the new administration of Nehemiah was even more lenient, and Ezra's authority seems to be nowhere in sight, leaving Nehemiah to deal with the problem. Such a scenario does not make any sense, and it implies that both men were inept, the first overbearing, and the second unable to maintain the status quo.

We may reconstruct things as follows. At the beginning of Xerxes' rule (486 B.C.), the local enemies of Judea wrote an accusation against them, but Xerxes did not listen to it (Ezra 4:6). Then in the 12th year of Xerxes, the Prime Minister Haman plotted to exterminate the Jews from the Persian Empire, from "all the provinces of your kingdom" (Esther 3:8). Haman wrote to "the governors who were over each province, and to the princes of each people" (Esther 3:12). Judea was not exempt.

After Haman's plot was defeated, Mordecai became prime minister of Persia in Xerxes' 12th year (474-473 B.C.) While he was in office, he issued decrees in the kings' name allowing the Jews in all 127 provinces, "from India to Ethiopia," which included Judea, to defend themselves. This resulted in an attitude change toward the Jews, "for the dread of them had fallen on all the peoples" (Esther 9:2), and:

> For Mordecai the Jew was second only to King Ahasuerus and great among the Jews, and in favor with the multitude of his kinsmen, one who sought the good of his people and one who spoke for the welfare of his whole nation (Esther 10:3).

It would seem then that the rebuilding of Jerusalem commenced soon after the 12th year of Xerxes in 473 B.C., and that it prospered under the hand of the High Priest Joiakim till Xerxes 21st year (465 B.C.), and continued into the reign of Artaxerxes I until the complaint in Ezra 4:7-23, which we may place in the summer of 446 B.C. The city would have been in rebuilding for 28 years. However, there was no legitimate decree for this work. It was simply unopposed because of the legacy of Mordecai and Esther until 446 B.C.‡ However, the people were secularized during this time. The Torah was not read at the beginning of the Sabbatical years. The tithes and offerings were neglected, and the Temple operated as sort of a national symbol, yet the people were well compromised. Ezra entered into his priestly service shortly before 446 B.C. as a professional scribe and student of Torah. While his countrymen thought they could be accepted as Jews and Persian citizens, and pay lip service to Yahweh's Torah, Ezra knew better. So when the work was stopped, and the wall broken down by the enemies, he realized it was because the people were neglecting the Temple and their faithfulness to the God of Israel.

Now the Persian king has stated to those who brought the complaint "until a decree is made by me" (Ezra 4:21). But they went in haste to Jerusalem and broke down as much of the wall as was completed and burned the gates with fire. They went too far, and did not realize that the Jews had much support in the Persian court. So the king granted Nehemiah a decree with which to rebuild the walls. Ezra realized that the Jews' secularism had been chastised by Yahweh in allowing the enemies to do what they did, so under Nehemiah's administration he resolved to take the opportunity to teach the Torah to the people.

```
Beginning Year 7 of the Sabbatical Cycle, Year 21 of the Jubilee Cycle
Month: VII ETHANIM, 445 BC  3695 A.M. Sab. Cyc: 7. Jub. Cyc: 21 Cycle No: 75
Q1: 0.380 A Q2: -0.741 F LG:  46m W: 1.115' AL: 22.6 AV: 9.4
New Moon calculated for longitude: 35.17 and latitude 31.77
Location of calculations: Jerusalem
   Designed and Programmed By Daniel Gregg, Ezra reads the Torah ♦
```

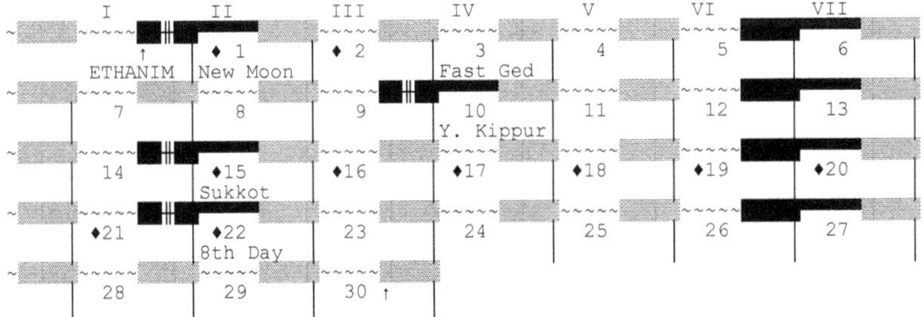

So Ezra under Nehemiah took the unprecedented step to read the Torah in Nehemiah 8 after Nehemiah's work made it safe to do so again, without fear of attack from the enemies (who just before

‡ History repeats itself, and nothing is new under the sun. The book of Esther presents the Jews as secularized and content in their position of exile, with no mention of either the name of the Almighty, nor of Judea. Under Xerxes the Jewish people faced a potential holocaust, but were delivered, and prospered, but there was no spiritual awakening, and so disaster came upon their effort to rebuild Zion. So also it is going to happen again. The Jewish people were delivered from the holocaust in Israel, but they founded it a secular state, with no spiritual awakening. Therefore, a second disaster is coming, and Zion will have to be rebuilt. Gŏd cannot be mocked. Whatever a nation sows, a nation will reap.

Nehemiah had torn down the wall and wrecked the city in their overzealous interpretation of the king Artaxerxes' letter; cf. Ezra 4:7-23; Neh. 1:1-4).[351] The destruction of the unfinished walls was a wake up call to Judea to repent and return more diligently to the Torah. So it is really in 445 B.C. that Ezra's career as a recognized public teacher in Judea became possible. He was ready for the opportunity, and with the destruction of the walls and Nehemiah's coming, was enabled to do what was necessary.†

But at that time Ezra was not in charge. Nehemiah was. Ezra had no mandate from the king of Persia. Ezra was much younger, perhaps just over 30, yet a skilled Torah scholar, anointed to do priestly work. Going to and from Persia was not uncommon for Jewish leaders who needed the support of the dispersion. Ezra returned, and as I will show later from Josephus, after Nehemiah's administration, disastrous things happened under the tenure of another Persian governor, which Ezra came to redress.

The evident ignorance of Torah after the wall is finished only makes sense if during the period between 515 B.C. when the Temple was finished and 445 B.C. when the walls were finished, a period of 70 years, the people were not instructed in Torah, as they should have been. The reason for this is that they were all Persian citizens, and whether a Jew chose to be observant or not was a personal choice. There was no legal authority from the Persian government to compel Judah to follow the Torah on a national scale.

From the 13th year of Xerxes until the 19th of Artaxerxes (473-446 B.C.) Israel enjoyed the favor of the Persian monarchs, but the Jewish leadership had little desire to enforce public Torah observance, and no legal mandate for it. The Persian government had merely

---

[351] The wall was quite a necessary security measure despite the Persian kings' wishes that the Jews be left alone. Artaxerxes I said nothing about wrecking the work. He only said that it should be stopped. The legal wishes of Persia were not enough to control the local hatred against the Jews. As it was Nehemiah had to post his men on guard duty. With this kind of threat, it is clear that before this the people had been bullied into neglecting Torah and the Temple, and that without the wall, they would be further bullied. This means that without the wall decree, and considering the intent of the decree to Ezra, both the king of Persia's intent and Ezra's attempt to implement would be a complete failure.

† A wall represents protection. The Almighty put a "wall" around Iyov (Job 1:10), though it was not a physical wall. When Israel repents, it will be provided a "wall." The nations will be chased away from Israel. See Isa. 17:12-14. If the wall is let down when Israel is obeying him, it is to test Israel, and cause Israel to trust the Almighty and not in their own walls. But a place will be provided for Israel when the hedge comes down.

allowed them to have the Temple service, which did not work well without the observance of the people behind it. They also allowed them to rebuild the city without an explicit decree.

Family Surnames

The name Ezra and Nehemiah appears in the book of Ezra and Nehemiah long before the narrative is concerned about the wall builder and the reformer. Nehemiah appears in Ezra 2:2 and Neh. 7:7. "Seriah" is the original family name of Ezra the reformer in the same texts (Ezra 2:2, 7:1), and both "Seraiah" and "Ezra" appear in Neh. 12:1. Evidently that Ezra, at the time of Zerubbabel, is not the reformer. In fact, it is the family name† of a different family than Ezra the reformer. As Zerubbabel returned in 529-528 B.C., or, worse, as traditionalists have it in 539 B.C. due to another mistaken identity of Cyrus, it is impossible that the same persons were at work in 458 B.C. Assuming Ezra was barely an adult at 20 the first time he was mentioned, this would make Ezra 102 in 458 B.C., and in 445 B.C. over 115 years old. The case is even worse for Nehemiah, who dates his second term in office to after the thirty-second year of Artaxerxes (432 B.C.). So if he returned with Zerubbabel, then he would be at least 128. The solution is that "Nehemiah," and the other names were family names in Ezra 2 and Neh. 7, excepting only the Davidic prince Zerubbabel and the High Priest Jeshua (Yeshua); also Nehemiah the wall builder may not even be from that Nehemiah family mentioned in the lists.

Family names were inherited from famous or prominent ancestors, but could be discarded for new ones if a younger head of a family distinguished themselves. That *Ezra* was the family surname of priests there can be no doubt. Nehemiah 12:13 names the personal head of Ezra in the days of the high priest Joiakim son of Jeshua, "Of Ezra: Meshullam." Notice the list of priestly families that returned with Zerubbabel in the text below. These are all family names, except for the Davidic prince (Zerubbabel) and the High priest (Jeshua).

> Now these are the priests and the Levites who came up with Zerubbabel the son of Shealtiel, and Jeshua: Seraiah, Jeremiah, Ezra, Amariah, Malluch, Hattush, Shecaniah, Rehum, Meremoth, Iddo,

† This name confusion problem is acknowledged by almost all commentators who have considered the timeline. It would therefore only be prudent to guard against the same confusion of kings with the dynastic throne names Cyrus and Artaxerxes.

Ginnethoi, Abijah, Mijamin, Maadiah, Bilgah, Shemaiah and Joiarib, Jedaiah, Sallu, Amok, Hilkiah, and Jedaiah. These were the heads of the priests and their kinsmen in the days of Jeshua (Neh. 12:1-7).

Now notice that 15 of the family names listed in vs. 1-7 are all repeated in vs. 12-21. The following verses contain the same list at a later time, with a few surnames dropped, only this time a personal name is connected to the surname for each family during the priesthood of Joiakim.

And Jeshua became the father of Joiakim, and Joiakim became the father of Eliashib, and Eliashib became the father of Joiada, and Joiada became the father of Jonathan [Johanan], and Jonathan [Johanan] became the father of Jaddua. Now in the days of Joiakim the priests, the heads of fathers' households were: **of Seraiah, Meraiah**; of Jeremiah, Hananiah; of Ezra, Meshullam; of Amariah, Jehohanan; of Malluchi, Jonathan; of Shebaniah, Joseph; of Harim, Adna; of Meraioth, Helkai; of Iddo, Zechariah; of Ginnethon, Meshullam; of Abijah, Zichri; of Miniamin, of Moadiah, Piltai; of Bilgah, Shammua; of Shemaiah, Jehonathan; of Joiarib, Mattenai; of Jedaiah, Uzzi; of Sallai, Kallai; of Amok, Eber; of Hilkiah, Hashabiah; of Jedaiah, Nethanel (Neh. 12:10-20).

The Hebrew text: לְעֶזְרָא מְשֻׁלָּם = *of Ezra, Meshullam*. There is no possibility of confusing the family name with the personal name here, because each surname is preceded by a lamed (ל). The priestly surnames correspond to the priestly courses or rotations as named at the time. We see that "Abijah" is mentioned above, and that Zichri was serving for that family then. "Abijah" was the eighth lot (1Chron. 24:10). We later learn that Zechariah, the father of John the Baptist, was from the "division of Abijah" (Luke 1:5). Evidently then, there was one Meshullam, surnamed "Ezra," a surname separate from the surname "Seraiah" in the return under Zerubbabel. And this Meshullam personally represented the Ezra family when Joiakim was the high priest, in the time before Nehemiah. But the Ezra family was not the Seraiah family. And our reformer belongs to the latter.

Also it is problematic for 458 b.c. advocates that we have the head of the Seraiah family in the days of Joiakim as one "Meraiah." If

Ezra the reformer came before Nehemiah, it is amazing that his name is not linked with Seraiah and with the high priest just before Nehemiah's contemporary high priest "Eliashib." It seems that Ezra son of Seraiah is no where in sight in the days of Joiakim. And it seems that way because Ezra the Scribe was not the head of Seraiah at the time, but likely still a student of Torah in 458 B.C., and not the active leader.

So then, when Nehemiah 8:1 refers to "Ezra the scribe," this is to say a scribe from the priestly family surnamed "Seraiah" (whom the reformer gives as his family name in Ezra 7:1). There is no need for "Ezra the scribe" and reformer to appear as a leader in history before Nehemiah 8:1. This is one man personally named "Ezra" that is evidently not from the family surnamed Ezra, but from the family surnamed Seraiah.

Later "Ezra the scribe" in Ezra 7 was given the executive power after Nehemiah by Artaxerxes II. Neh. 12:26 also gives the order of their governance, first Nehemiah, and then Ezra: "These served in the days of Joiakim...and in the days of Nehemiah the governor and of Ezra the Priest, the scribe." The order is given Joiakim, Nehemiah, Ezra, or three Jewish administrations falling into the reign of Artaxerxes I and II. The phrase "in the days of" is used to indicate whose administration it was. Sometimes the administrator was the high priest, and sometimes not.

It was under the administration of Joiakim that the building of the city was stopped by enemies and the wall broken down just before Nehemiah was appointed to restore them. The importance of Neh. 12:26 is that the three administrations were successive. Clearly the mentioned Joiakim's "days" were not contemporary with Nehemiah's "days." So also for Ezra's days of administration. This is not to say that the two were not personal contemporaries in Neh. 8 during Nehemiah's administration. It is only giving the succession of their administrations which were not contemporary.

Those who would not regard "Ezra," (prior to "Ezra the scribe") or the other names as surnames are left with a massive contradiction. The time between the same names that went up in the first year of Cyrus and the 7th year of Artaxerxes I is at least 70 years. A person could not even be mentioned in the list of leaders returning without being an adult. This puts at least 90 years between the same names. And if they are personal names, then this is like claiming that they were all in office for 70 years! So Ezra, prior to Neh. 8, must be a surname. We know that this Ezra family had a Meshullam Ezra heading it up in the days before Nehemiah, during the days of Joiakim, who was Nehemiah's predecessor.

Now to answer the previous question. What makes Ezra the reformer in Neh. 8:1 and Ezra 7:1 one person is not the use of the surname "Ezra," which belongs to another family; it is rather that this Ezra is consistently identified as "the scribe" in such a way that it parsimoniously appears that he is the same person in Nehemiah and Ezra. And his name "Ezra" is just a personal name, and not the family name that came up from Babylon. He read the Torah at the feast of Tabernacles starting the seventh year (445 B.C.). Could it be that he returned to Persia? Yes. Nehemiah himself, in fact, returned to Persia. So then, is it possible that Ezra the scribe was about 30 in Neh. 8:1, and then 79 when he returned to Jerusalem in 398 BC? Ezra appears as a skilled Torah reader and expositor in 445 B.C., and as an aged and wizened spiritual leader to complete his reform in 397 B.C., the 49th year.

The time span of 49 years is quite reasonable, and Nehemiah tells us that the city was not properly inhabited in his time (Neh. 7:4-5; 11:1-2). So it was that Ezra wished to go to Babylon to gather more returnees after the dedication of the wall in 431 B.C., and that this turned out to be hard spiritual work, as not many were, in fact, willing to return to Judea. For the whole time of Nehemiah and Ezra was beset by political and spiritual problems. Ezra 10:1 might directly imply that Jerusalem was well inhabited later in Ezra's time, but the real evidence of the difference is Nehemiah's pointed statement that in his time it was sparsely populated:

> Now the city *was* large and great: but the people *were* few therein, and the houses *were* not builded (Neh. 7:4). ... Now the leaders of the people lived in Jerusalem, but the rest of the people cast lots to bring one out of ten to live in Jerusalem, the holy city, while nine-tenths *remained* in the *other* cities. And the people blessed all the men, that willingly offered themselves to dwell at Jerusalem

(Neh. 11:1-2).

Nehemiah's notice of the population problem, and steps to solve it, and the corresponding absence of such problem at Ezra's return, and lack of notice of it argue loudly that Nehemiah came first, and then Ezra afterward. The gathering in Nehemiah 8 is one summoned to a feast from afar. The gathering in Ezra 10 is spontaneous, as out of the local population, and while the text does not say none came from elsewhere, it is parsimonious to assume a city is inhabited. What Nehemiah pointed out was the exception. Therefore, we should assume that Jerusalem had sufficient population in the time of Ezra.

So then, we have to take the priestly synchronism with Johanan, the grandson of Eliashib as conclusive that Ezra 7 speaks of the reign of Artaxerxes II. This, (being in the 49 years from the building of the walls), explains the "seven sevens" in Daniel's prophecy. Here is the succession of High Priests:

Table 13: Priestly Succession and Approx years

High Priest	Approx. Yrs	Yrs rules	Executive
1. Yeshua	529 – 479[352]	49 years	Zerubbabel
2. Joiakim	479 – 451	28 years	Joiakim
3. Eliashib	451 – 430	21 years	Nehemiah
4. Joiada[353]	433 – 430	4 years	Neh to 424
5. Jonathan[354]	430 – 360	70 years	Ezra in 397
6. Jaddua	360 – 318	42 years	

We know that in the "days of Joiakim" (Neh. 12:12) the head of the Ezras was named "Meshullam." This covered the period of 458 B.C.; another person named Ezra of the family "Seraiah" read the Torah in 445 B.C., when Nehemiah was governor, who is identified by

[352] Except for the 529 B.C. date, all these office terms for the high priests are estimates to show the reasonableness of the arrangement.
[353] Joiada was dismissed by Nehemiah for intermarrying his son (Neh. 13:28).
[354] Named in the Elephantine Papyri and dated to 407 B.C. (ANET, pg. 492). Josephus (Ant. 11.7.1 [297]) relates how Jonathan was forced to put his brother to death for conspiring with the Persian governor to seize the priesthood.

being called “the scribe” (הַסֹּפֵר), and then saw the need to go to Persia, or to return there in order to teach about the work of restoration, and recruit more volunteers to return to Judea. Then as an aged man, on hearing reports of problems from Jerusalem, he resolves to transfer his efforts there as soon as the Persian monarch decides to support him. He recruits as many as he can, and returns himself with an edict from the king to right the wrongs.

In order to understand the work of Ezra in 398-397 B.C. we must reconstruct what happened prior to his arrival in Jerusalem. Nehemiah returned to Persia at the end of his term (Nisan 1, 433 B.C., anno 3707). In his absence Eliashib compromised the temple (Neh. 13:4, 7) after Nisan, 433 B.C., and when Nehemiah returned, a year later,[355] evidently with authority, he corrected the problem. Eliashib had given Tobiah an office in the Temple, and then it appears, had died, shortly after this sin leaving his son Joiada as the new high priest. But then Joiada entered into an alliance with Sanballat by marrying his son to Sanballat’s daughter. That is the situation as Nehemiah found it on his return from Persia. First, he dealt with Tobiah, and then he dealt with Joiada.

When Nehemiah found out that Joiada had given a son in marriage to Sanballat, Nehemiah banished him (Neh. 13:28):

> And one of the sons of Joiada son of Eliashib, the high priest, was son in law to Sanballat the Horonite; therefore I chased him from me.

Joiada son of Eliashib (יוֹיָדָע בֶּן־אֶלְיָשִׁיב) had given a son in marriage to a daughter of Sanballat. This was a political-religious alliance with the arch-enemy of Nehemiah. To Nehemiah, this was treasonous. It had to have Joiada’s approval, for the High Priest would have never considered it for the sake of a common marriage. And,

[355] Nehemiah says he left Susa to return to Jerusalem “after the limit of days” (לְקֵץ יָמִים) Neh. 13:6. That is, he had asked for a second term (נִשְׁאַלְתִּי) then, and departed again for Judea. The limit of days is the spring equinox, which in 432 BC happened on March 25 (Nisan 5 in Judea or 5 Addaru II in Babylon). So Nehemiah departed from Jerusalem in 433 BC, on or after Nisan 1 (the 32nd year of Artaxerxes), and at the end of the 32nd year, after the spring equinox in what was Addaru II in Babylon, he asked for a second term. Sometime around Tishri 432 he is back as provincial governor in Jerusalem.

evidently Joiada was taking Torah lightly on this matter, or he was ignorant of it and only interested in the priestly office for its monetary value. It was political intrigue of the highest order, and personal disloyalty to the wall builder, not to mention Torah. Therefore, the person that Nehemiah banished was Joiada, the high priest at the time. Banishment of only Joiada's offending son would be to punish the least guilty person, and to let the most guilty go free. That's not what happened here. Joiada himself was dismissed from his position. Then Joiada's other son Johanan was made the high priest. Thus the reign of Joiada was short, and ended in disgrace during Nehemiah's second term. For this reason, Ezra names Jehohanan as "son of Eliashib" (Ezra 10:6), because of the the disgraceful disloyalty of Joiada to Judea's enemy Sanballat. Ezra omitted the offending generation in good Jewish style as the names of several wicked kings are omitted in Matthew's genealogy of Yeshua (cf. Ezra 10:6). This banishment happened sometime between 433 and 424 B.C., during Nehemiah's second term in office. It was likely in 431 B.C. just after the walls were dedicated. Shortly after it, Nehemiah's memoirs come to a close, and he either died soon after, or retired when the new king of Persia received the throne.

The dedication of the walls was most likely in 431 B.C., in the sabbatical year. It is dated by Nehemiah's remark in 13:4-6 to after 433 B.C., wherein he says "prior to this" (לִפְנֵי מִזֶּה), which "this" refers to the dedication passage (12:27-13:3). So prior to the dedication, but after the end of Nehemiah's first term, Eliashib had compromised the temple. The discovery in the Torah made in Neh. 13:1-3 dates the passage to Tabernacles in the Sabbatical year or 431/430 B.C., when the Torah would have been read to the people. And, as noted before, Nehemiah was only gone for one year. Willis Judson Beecher explains the dedication thus:

> It seems that the dedication did not take place at the gathering in the seventh month, soon after the wall was completed, for it is not mentioned in the very full account we have of that gathering, Neh. 8-10. It was held at some later time, and was made a special occasion for perfecting certain arrangements for the support of the priests, Levites, and other temple attendants, 12:44, 45… it is quite likely to

have been some years afterward, when experience had proved that the arrangements made at the gathering of the seventh month (Neh. 10:32 seq.) were inadequate. When Nehemiah left Jerusalem and went to the king, about eleven years after the wall was finished, there was a falling off of the income of the temple ministers, and after his return to Jerusalem he made strenuous efforts for restoring this income, Neh. 13:6, 10-14. It is clearly supposable, and in accord with the methods in which he and Ezra had previously operated, that they should arrange for a public gathering in the interest of this reform, and they might naturally, to this end, arrange for a public dedication of the hitherto undedicated wall.

This view thus supposed is the one actually justified by the narrative. This is proved by the double fact that the account in Neh. 12:27-13:3 is continuous with the matter that follows it, and is not continuous with that which precedes it. "Before this," 13:4, in its most natural meaning, is an expression of time, relating to the statements made in the preceding verses. The casting of Tobiah's stuff out of the temple, 13:8, seems to be mentioned as an incident of the separation from the mixed multitude, 13:1, 3. The section 13:9-14 reads like a statement of additional details connected with 12:44. That is to say, the continuity between these events and the dedication of the wall is very distinctly marked...It follows that the account of the second administration of Nehemiah begins with 12:27, while the narrative of his first administration, supplemented by certain additional materials [added by Ezra], closes with 12:26.[356]

We should note that Ezra "the scribe" was present at this dedication in 431 B.C. leading one of the processions. Sometime after this date, he returns to the exile; also Nehemiah's second term either ends, he retires, or dies leaving the government of Jerusalem and Judea without a personal connection to the king of Persia, and in the hands of the local secular Persian government.

Darius II Nothus became king of Persia in 424 B.C. And a "lord

[356] *The Old & New Testament Student*, Vol. 9, pg. 291-292, "The Postexilic History of Israel," Willis J. Beecher.

Bagoses" was made "governor of Judah"[357] Johanan son of Eliashib, had become the high priest before 407 B.C.[358] Then Josephus fills in the plot between Nehemiah and Ezra:

> (297) "When Eliashib the high priest was dead, his son Joiada[359] succeeded in the high priesthood: and when he was dead [banished,][360] his son Johanan[361] took that dignity; on whose account it was also that Bagoses,[362] the general[363] of the other Artaxerxes,[364] polluted the temple, and imposed tributes on the Jews, that out of the public stock, before they offered daily sacrifices, they should pay for every lamb fifty drachmas.[365] (298) Now Jeshua was the brother of Johanan, and was a friend of Bagoses, who had promised to procure him the high priesthood. (299) In confidence of whose support, Jeshua quarreled with Johanan in the temple, and so provoked his brother, that in his anger his brother slew him."[366]

This slaying was justified because it was "an act of self-defense against an attack by a godless would-be usurper."[367] The

---

357 ANET, pg. 492.
358 ANET (ibid.). That is, the Elephantine Papyri say that he was at least high priest by this year. Actually, he succeeded Joiada before the second term of Nehemiah ended.
359 The son of Eliashib. Josephus uses the word 'Ιώδας, which corresponds to "Joiada" in English and יוֹיָדָע in Hebrew. The same word is spelled variantly in Greek: Ιοϊδα, Ιωδαε, Ἰωαδα.
360 Josephus, or his source, has misinterpreted Neh. 13:28. The succession had to automatically happen when Joiada was dismissed, not when he died.
361 'Ιωάννης = יְהוֹחָנָן or יוֹחָנָן.
362 The Elephantine papyri makes him the "governor of Judah" (ANET, ibid.) His name is Persian, a certain "Bagohi."
363 This term does not mean that the new governor was a general. It had broader usage in the LXX and Josephus. The term simply means "governor."
364 The Elephantine papyri make it clear that Bagoses was governor of Judah in 407 B.C. during the 17th year of Darius II Nothus. But Bagoses may have remained governor until the 7th year of Artaxerxes II, so that the Elephantine Papyri refer to Bagoses earlier in time than Josephus. Josephus' source had "[ἄλλου] Ἀρταξέρξου" (Ant. 11:297), which is to say Artaxerxes II.
365 About 500 grams of Silver (*New Bible Dictionary*).
366 Ant. 11.7.1.
367 *Ezra and Nehemiah*, Hugh G. M. Williamson, pg. 57. Williamson tries to re-date Josephus episode to a later time. Nevertheless, this point of view

Persian governor was unable to unseat Johanan from the high priesthood, but he mistreated the Jews for seven years.[368] In particular the 50 *drachma* tax on the temple offerings made operation of the temple difficult, if not impossible:

> If the fine that Josephus names ("fifty drachmae for every lamb" [§297]) was in fact imposed, it would have had the effect of virtually eliminating offerings of this kind at the temple for the seven years. The Jerusalem temple may for a time, then, have joined the one in Elephantine—if it was ever reconstructed—as a place where only non-animal sacrifices were offered.[369]

So now we know what Ezra was up against—a confiscatory tax on the daily offering of the temple service. This then explains the decree of Artaxerxes II. One of the particulars in Artaxerxes II decree was that this tax be rescinded with a very severe penalty for violators:

> KJV Ezra 7:24, "Also we certify you, that touching any of the priests and Levites, singers, porters, Nethinims, or ministers of this house of Gõd, it shall not be lawful to impose **toll**, **tribute**, or **custom**, upon them. … 7:26 And whosoever will not do the law of thy Gõd, and the law of the king, let judgment be executed speedily upon him, whether *it be* unto death, or to banishment, or to confiscation of goods, or to imprisonment."

Therefore, it was 7 sevens from the building of the walls till the time that the Jews were again allowed to freely practice the Torah, and Ezra came in the 7th of Artaxerxes II to complete the reforms. Nothing, therefore, happened in 458 B.C.

In 398 B.C., Ezra came armed with the right to compel Jews in Judea to observe Torah at a national level:

> And whosoever will not do the law of thy Gõd, and the law of the king, let judgment be executed speedily upon him, whether *it be* unto death, or to banishment, or to confiscation of goods, or to

---

absolves Ezra of associating with the High Priest Johanan as a murderer. Williamson's later date shown to be unparsimonious by VanderKam.

[368] Perhaps the first seven years of Artaxerxes II (405-398), which would well explain the severity of Artaxerxes' decree to Ezra.

[369] Note **343** on page **327**, VanderKam, pg. 63.

imprisonment.

Before this, such authority had not not been given. Up to this time a Jewish Persian citizen could be a Jew in Judea and be completely secular if they so wished, as it is in Israel this day, and the consequent disaster of this choice is going to become evident soon enough. It is thus quite clear why the Jews were ignorant of their own law in 445 B.C. There was no judicial authority in place for Torah, but only a decree to have the temple rebuilt and a decree to have the walls rebuilt. It is also clear that only the decree granted to Ezra could put an end to the people's ignorance of Torah on a national scale, and ignorance which is clearly manifest in 445 B.C. at the feast of Tabernacles. Therefore, Ezra's administration and decree to cause all of Judea to follow the Torah come "seven sevens" after Nehemiah's reconstruction of the walls.

We may consider the question how and why Christian chronologers and scholars have fallen into their unparsimonious traps. One such trap is thinking that Artaxerxes'decree to Ezra qualified as a decree to rebuild Jerusalem. It is a decree, all right, but nothing is said about rebuilding the city. Daniel 9:24 clearly matches with Nehemiah's work as the inception point. What then has pushed Christianity into the unparsimonious corner of multiplying assumings, and trying to re-explain plain indications in the text like the fact that Ezra's final work was contemporary with Johanan as High Priest?

The answer is sin, and the general tendency of the house of Israel to avoid conclusions from the Torah that they do not want to believe! They are not sensitive to the difference the judicial authority in the decree to Ezra makes. What if the Scripture had, in scholarly legalese, qualified and explained every remark to the nth degree so that no misunderstanding would be possible. What if no loopholes had been left for unparsimonious minds to fall into? What would have happened, is that instead of conjuring up a complex an unreasonable explanation of Scripture, that the lawless would have rejected the Scripture all together. The enemies of the truth prefer to reinterpret rather than oppose. Because if they oppose, then they are exposed. But reinterpretation is by stealth, which is Satan's way of operating. If unparsimonious interpretation is made impossible, then enemies simply destroy the text. So requiring the reader to pay attention to context and logic is God's way of weeding out the wheat from the weeds without endangering the whole crop. And this is the reason for a sealing up of the words of Daniel 9, and that things were left a little more obscure than the demanding standards of a modern historian.

Further, the Almighty has set up the Scriptural accounts so that the reader must compare and seek to fully understand the truth. This would normally lead the seeker to the truth from the contexts of the matter. That is why everything is not spelled out in black and white. Some interpretations have been left more open to unparsimonious interpretations than others, but the reason that Israel has fallen into these byways is that they have rejected the original truth that their forefathers knew. The Jews do not want Yeshua to be the Messiah, and Christians do not what to follow the Torah, especially in any outwardly obvious way that sets them apart from the nations.

The Almighty knew exactly where Israel would backslide, and so he constructed and built all of biblical chronology to use the set times of Torah to fulfill His plan of redemption. Repentance must go with the good news. So to understand the plan of redemption requires at the same time to understand the Torah.

The reason for going through these exercises is to show that the incorrect years utterly fall apart in attempting to match them with the literal and normative chronological facts. A lot of trouble could have been saved by accepting "three days and three nights," and that "first of the Sabbaths" means the first Sabbath after Passover. A lot of trouble could have been saved by knowing that a Wednesday crucifixion was required, and that only one date in A.D. 34 satisfies this within straightforward astronomical parameters for Nisan 14, and prophetical patterns for Daniel 9.

All the trouble would be spared if Israel would seek Messiah and obey His Torah. All problems can be traced to those two points, to rejection of Messiah or rejection of the teaching of Torah, or to both at the same time.

Ezra's Self Placement in History

Also to be considered is the fact that Ezra places himself correctly in the historical context, despite the fact that his book comes before Nehemiah in the canon. To see this, we have to list the Persian Kings in Table 14: Persian King List below.

Ezra 1:1 begins with #2, Cyrus, called Cambyses by standard chronology (refer to Table 14: Persian King List). This is because "Cyrus" is the throne name, and not a personal name (cf. Isaiah 45:4: *I have surnamed thee*)[370]. This must be the case because of Jeremiah 29:10 specifying 70 years for the time that the exiles with Jehoiachin would be in Babylon. These 70 years did not come to an end until Cambyses. So this is the Cyrus meant by the Scripture in Ezra 1:1.

Table 14: Persian King List

Secular Designation	Biblical Title	Years
1. Cyrus	Darius the Mede	538-529
2. Cambyses	Cyrus[371]	529-521
3. Darius I	Darius	521-485
4. Xerxes	Ahasuerus	485-464
5. Artaxerxes I	Artaxerxes (Cyrus[372])	464-423
6. Darius II		423-404
7. Artaxerxes II	Artaxerxes	404-358
8. Artaxerxes III		358-337
9. Arses		337-335
10. Darius III	Darius the Persian	335-330

Ezra 4:5 says that Judah's enemies hired counselors against them "until the reign of Darius king of Persia. This identifies with #3 in the list. Building the Temple would be renewed under Darius.

Before, returning to the renewal of the building under Darius, Ezra details opposition to building the city under subsequent kings: Ezra 4:6 specifies "Ahasuerus," which corresponds to Xerxes, #4 in the list. Ezra 4:7 moves on to Artaxerxes I, #5 in the list. Then Ezra 4:24 returns to the reign of Darius to fill in the details.

Ezra 5:1-6:14 detail the history of the renewal of the building of

[370] Baumgartner's Lexicon defines it as an "Elamitic throne-name."
[371] So called by Isaiah and Ezra.
[372] So called by Josephus and Isaiah.

the Temple, and says that the Temple was built by the command of "Cyrus, Darius, and Artaxerxes king of Persia." Since the Temple was completed in the reign of Darius, it raises the question what Ezra means by mentioning Artaxerxes? He at least skips over Xerxes. This leaves open the possibility that he skipped Artaxerxes I and Darius II also. For if he skips one king, he can skip three.

The Temple was indeed finished in the sixth year of Darius, but it took the decree of Artaxerxes II to revoke the taxes put in place by the governor Bagoses to put it into proper operation. For when Judah's enemies had the upper hand, they could interrupt the sacrificial service by one means or another. The service was interrupted the year before Nehemiah when the wall of Jerusalem was broken down:

> And he spake before his brethren and the army of Samaria, and said, What do these feeble Jews? will they fortify themselves? <u>will they sacrifice</u>? will they make an end in a day? will they revive the stones out of the heaps of the rubbish which are burned? (Neh. 4:2).

It is quite plain here that the Temple was not in proper operation when Nehemiah came to Jerusalem. Even though the building was built, evidently political pressure from Judea's enemies, or whatever administration was running it, could put a stop to the Temple services. Likely, this was only from 446 B.C. to 445 B.C. But the remark in Nehemiah shows that by taxation of offerings, or taxation of Levites or singers, or by other interferences that the Levitical Service could be made poor and deprived of its glory and witness to the nations.

Before Nehemiah's appointment, Joiakim was the administrator, but his administration came to an end when the higher Persian administration intervened (Ezra 4:7-23). Yes, he remained the high priest, but Joiakim's administration of the work of the city was ended, and the wall burned, and the people dispersed from the city. It follows that the temple was not put back into service until Nehemiah finished the walls. It is also possible that Joiakim died around 446 B.C. and left the high priesthood to his son Eliashib.

Apparently, the Temple was a huge political issue even when Nehemiah had a decree to rebuild the city. For his enemies tempted Nehemiah to go into the Temple to save his life:

Afterward I came unto the house of Shemaiah the son of Delaiah the son of Mehetabeel, who *was* shut up; and he said, Let us meet together in the house of God, within the temple, and let us shut the doors of the temple: for they will come to slay thee; yea, in the night will they come to slay thee. [11] And I said, Should such a man as I flee? and who *is there*, that, *being* as I *am*, would go into the temple to save his life? I will not go in. [12] And, lo, I perceived that God had not sent him; but that he pronounced this prophecy against me: for Tobiah and Sanballat had hired him. [13] Therefore *was* he hired, that I should be afraid, and do so, and sin, and *that* they might have *matter* for an evil report, that they might reproach me. [14] My God, think thou upon Tobiah and Sanballat according to these their works, and on the prophetess Noadiah, and the rest of the prophets, that would have put me in fear. [15] So the wall was finished in the twenty and fifth *day* of *the month* Elul, in fifty and two days (Neh. 6:10-15).

The Temple was the only building in Jerusalem that qualified as a fortification before the walls were finished. When the walls were finished, Nehemiah was able to put the temple back into operation, which was neglected due to the politics of the enemies, and the lack of desire on the part of the Jews to support it, so that Nehemiah had the people make a covenant:

We also placed ourselves under obligation to contribute yearly one third of a shekel‡ for the service of the house of our Almighty: [33] for the show-bread, for the continual grain offering, for the continual burnt offering, the Sabbaths, the new moon, for the appointed times, for the holy things and for the sin offerings to make atonement for Israel, and all the work of the house of our Almighty. [34] Likewise we cast lots for the supply of wood *among* the priests, the Levites, and the people in order that they might bring it to the house of our Almighty, according to our fathers' households, at fixed times annually, to burn on the altar of Yahweh our Almighty as it is written in the law; [35] and in order that they might bring the first fruits of our ground and the first fruits of all the fruit of every tree to the house of Yahweh annually, [36] and bring to the house of our Almighty the first-born of our sons and of our cattle, and the first-born of our herds and

‡ This is the origin of the 1/2 shekel tax collected annually later. It began as 1/3 shekel, but was raised to 1/2 shekel to conflate it with the census tax so as to justify it perpetually. The only tax imposed by Torah was 1/2 shekel for the occasional census.

> our flocks as it is written in the law, for the priests who are
> ministering in the house of our Almighty. [37] We will also bring the
> first of our dough, our contributions, the fruit of every tree, the new
> wine and the oil to the priests at the chambers of the house of our
> Almighty, and the tithe of our ground to the Levites, for the Levites
> are they who receive the tithes in all the rural towns. [38] And the
> priest, the son of Aaron, shall be with the Levites when the Levites
> receive tithes, and the Levites shall bring up the tenth of the tithes to
> the house of our Almighty, to the chambers of the storehouse. [39] For
> the sons of Israel and the sons of Levi shall bring the contribution of
> the grain, the new wine and the oil, to the chambers; there are the
> utensils of the sanctuary, the priests who are ministering, the
> gatekeepers, and the singers. Thus we will not neglect the house of
> our Almighty (Neh 10:32-39).

But in Nehemiah's absence, the enemies gained an office in the Temple. This only makes sense on two points. The office had a monetary value. Just as the money changers in Yeshua's time were able to fleece the people by requiring one kind of money to be used to purchase offerings, so it is possible that there was a kind of tax that was levied by the priesthood, or on the priesthood, other than the usual tithe that could be diverted to the officeholder. When Nehemiah's term ended, the governing authority transferred to the greater Persian government, where the enemies had more influence. The most likely form of attack was the very one implied in the letters of the enemies, to impose a sales tax on the Temple service lest the king should suffer a loss of revenue (cf. Ezra 4:13). The purpose of the "office" or "chamber" in the Temple was to collect the tax. Of course, Tobiah had a house in Jerusalem, but he did bring some of his household stuff to the Temple office. His reason to be there was not the sanctity of the Temple, but to collect the tax levied by the default government in Nehemiah's absence. It is no doubt that Tobiah had the support of secularized Jews, who were interested in money, and not Torah. Indeed, one of the first things that happened to the high priestly families was they they became secular and liberal, and held their positions only because the office was inherited.

Instead of appealing their decisions, Eliashib compromised with them. But Nehemiah was appointed to a second term, and found the compromise out. Since Nehemiah has direct authority from the king, his first act is to cancel the sales tax and dismiss the tax collector without permitting him back in his office. Then Nehemiah has his stuff thrown out. If taxes are due to the Persian government, then Nehemiah will get them from elsewhere, and not by burdening the Temple Service.

After the end of Nehemiah's term, and after Ezra went to Persia to seek greater judicial authority for Torah in Judea, one Jeshua, who was brother to the High Priest Johanan, plotted with the Persian governor Bagoses to steal the Priesthood. This would mean power and prestige for Jeshua, and money in the pockets or coffers of Bagohi. Jeshua was supposed to slay Johanan by stealth, and then with the backing of the governor would gain the priestly office. But Johanan found out about the plot and in self-defense killed his brother Jeshua. The enraged Persian governor then took matters into his own hands, as I recounted from Josephus earlier.

The enemies gained an office again at this time, which was likely used to collect the tax. This tax was 50 drachmas for every lamb for the daily sacrifices (*Jos. Ant.* 11:297). A drachma was about a days' wages. So the amount was the same as fifty days wages for a skilled worker, perhaps $10,000 in 2011. Smart enemies. They could not undo the law of the Medes and Persians,[373] but they could impose a tax that made it impossible. They had learned a thing or two from Xerxes' Prime Minister Mordecai.

If the tax had been banned at any time prior to Bagoses administration, then the law of the Medes and Persians would have prosecuted him. Therefore, Ezra is referring to Artaxerxes II, who put an end to the confiscatory tax, and for the first time established the judicial authority of Torah in all Judea. For Josephus informs us that this tax was not ended until after Eliashib, Nehemiah's contemporary, was dead.

Another difficulty with placing Ezra in 458 B.C. is that Egypt was in revolt, backed by a "powerful Athenian fleet:"[374]

---

[373] See Dan. 6:8; 6:12; 6:15; Esther 8:1-17.

[374] Joseph Blenkinsopp, Ezra-Nehemiah: A Commentary, pg. 142.

> Artaxerxes [I] would have been too busy to bother about Judah and the journey of some eight hundred miles from Babylon far too dangerous to contemplate. By 398, on the other hand, Egypt had already won its independence and the rebellion of Cyrus the Younger had been crushed (ibid.).

Between 459-448 B.C. Egypt was under revolt against Persia, led by Megabyzos. The Persians would have been worried about revolt in Judea at this time too, that is,that the Judeans might join with Egypt, or simply use the chaos to declare their own independence. This is just what Judah's enemies accused in Ezra 4:7-23.†

It would appear that traditionalist advocates of 458 B.C. think that their position is secure by default. While they come up with *ad hoc* explanations that the reverse order is not compelling against the specific points made, they fail to *prove* their own position. What do they have on their side of the question? It seems that the only thing they have is some untrustworthy assumptions. The first of these is that Ezra 7:1 means Artaxerxes I and not Artaxerxes II. That is a fairly hazardous assumption given that only 49 years separates 445 B.C. in the 20th year of Artaxerxes I from the end of Ezra's reform in 397 B.C. during the reign of Artaxerxes II. The other assumption is that since Ezra read the Torah in Nehemiah 8 that he must have accomplished his reforms earlier than that.‡ There is no reason that his final reforms could not have been 49 years later during his old and wizened age. And there is no reason that Ezra could not have found his first opportunities to present Torah on a national scale under Nehemiah's administration.

The 458 B.C. advocates would assume that the reverse view is refuted by the contemporaneity of Nehemiah and Ezra. This is easily countered by positing a young Ezra in 445 B.C. vs. an older one in 397 B.C. The order of the books of Ezra and Nehemiah also are not compelling to the traditional err. Ezra moves from Cyrus to Darius, and then from Xerxes to Artaxerxes without ever including himself, until chapter 7. Tellingly, he skips at least Xerxes in his final statement of chapter 6:14, and it is obvious that the mention of "Artaxerxes" passes beyond any obvious rebuilding commandment. There is therefore no proof that he means Artaxerxes I over

---

† The revolt also explains why Artaxerxes put the city building on delay until he made a decree. ‡ This would make Ezra the Great Reformer a total failure then.

Artaxerxes II. Also the edict by Artaxerxes I to stop building the city "until a decree is made by me" is related by Ezra as past history before his coming in Ezra 7 is detailed.

Also devastating to putting Ezra's administration before Nehemiah's is the fact that Nehemiah does not mention the exiles who returned under Ezra. The only list Nehemiah has is the list of returnees under Zerubbabel! (cf. Neh. 7:5-73 and Ezra 8:1-14). If Ezra had come earlier, then the complete omission of those who returned with him is inexplicable. It would seem that a return 13 years before would be worthy of mention if one was going to go to the trouble to mention the returnees all the way back to Zerubbabel.

The reverse order of Ezra and Nehemiah was proposed long before Van Hoonacker in 1890:

> This was suggested as long ago as 1699 by Aegidius Strauch[ius] in *Breviarium chronologicum: being a Treatise describing...the periods, and epoch's used in chronology...Now done into English by R. Sault* (London, 1699) 360. He mentions Joseph Scaliger as a supporter for this date. It was also advocated by S. Patrick, *A Critical Commentary and Paraphrase on the Old and New Testament* (London, 1727) 1.674 (cf. 2.687 in 1822 ed.), and by W. H. Mill, *The Evangelical Account of the Descent and Parentage of the Saviour Vindicated* (Cambridge: University Press, 1842) 153, but given a new lease of life by Maurice Vernes in 1889 in his *Précis d'histoire juive depuis les origines jusqu'à l'époque persane* (Paris: Hachette, 1889) and A. van Hoonacker, "Néhémie et Esdras. Une nouvelle hypothése sur la chronologie de l'époque de la Restauration," *Le Muséon* 9 (1890) 151-84, 317-51, 389-401.[375]

---

[375] *Was Nehemiah Contemporary with Ezra in 458 BC?* Leslie McFall, note 7. McFall also details some other notable supporters: Others who championed this view were W. F. Albright, From the Stone Age to Christianity (repr. New York: Doubleday, 1957), who later abandoned this date in favour of 428 in The Biblical Period from Abraham to Ezra (New York & Evanston: Harper & Row, 1963) 93, 111, and in "Brief History,"13; cf. also Batten, Ezra, 28, 47; R. A. Bowman in The Interpreter's Bible (New York & Nashville, 1954), 3.551-68; L. H. Brockington, Ezra, Nehemiah, and Esther (Century Bible; London: Nelson, 1969) 21; H. Cazelles, "La mission

From all these scholars, and many more could be listed, it appears that the 458 B.C. advocates have been unable to vanquish the scholarly advocates of the reverse view. This is because they have no magic argument, and no final proof of their own position. The very existence of the alternative, without compelling eschatological reasons for holding to the alternative, argues eloquently for its independent truth. And now I have given most excellent eschatological and prophetic reasons for seeing why the order Nehemiah first, and then Ezra is correct. Ezra fulfills the "seven sevens" after 49 years. If this consideration is not the spiritual prize to be won after all the academic drudgery, then nothing else will be.

It may simply be noted that the real reasons that the traditional view endures are 1) it is traditional. 2) It is foundational to the most plausible errant view of Daniel 9 and Passion Chronology. That is, it discards the minimum number of facts necessary to construct a chronology that arrives at a Friday crucifixion and yet gives a sell-able explanation of Daniel 9. It would not be enough to err by equating 458 B.C. with the 7th year of Artaxerxes in Ezra 7. A corresponding err has to be accepted in ignoring the 15th year of Tiberius, so that the beginning of Messiah's ministry can be moved back from A.D. 30 or 31.

The only nagging question is not why the view I have presented in this book is better, but why the incorrect view seems to "correlate" to when Tiberius was given charge of the provinces in A.D. 11 or 12. If there must be a reason, then sometimes it is better to give people something to "believe in" rather than to insist they be perfect. This is the parable principle. Let sinners find what they will in the symbolism so that they do not find what they do not want to find. I think the principle extends to the way the Almighty arranged history. So there are 3 Artaxerxes, 3 Darius, and Cyrus turns out to be a throne name, and two Friday's in A.D. 30 and 33 to compete with the real deal in

---

d'Esdras," VT IV (1954) 113-40; J. Finegan, Light from the Ancient Past (Princeton: Princeton University, 1949) 200; Saley, "Date of Nehemiah," 151-65; de Saulcy, Chronologique, 46; N. H. Smith, "Ezra's Arrival," 53-66; Torrey, Ezra Studies 38 n. 1, 170, 239, 260 n. 11; G. Widengren, "The Persian Period," in Israelite and Judean History (ed. J. H. Hayes & J. M. Miller; London: SCM, 1977) 503-09.

A.D. 34. If these byways were not there, then there would be nothing to think about, and no parable principle.

That the one is golden truth for the seeker, and the other only a bone thrown to the dogs to keep them from rending the truth completely seems to be clear enough. The real question is what prodigal Ephraim will decide to do, to keep chewing the same bone with the dogs or to come to his senses and return to his Father's house? The reality is that the meat on the bone is only a mist and the "correlations" are an illusory comedy of errs.

The Argument for Ezra coming first

I have touched on this before briefly at several points. The advocates of the 458 or 457 B.C. date assume that they do not have to defend it. They spend their time explaining away the arguments put for the reverse order in ad hoc and non-parsimonious ways. What then do they offer as an argument that Ezra came first, other than the fact that there is a tradition that he did? Is tradition the truth by default? Many "traditions" have been proved false after being "tradition" for the longest periods of times. So tradition itself is not an argument for the priority of Ezra.

We may ask what arguments the traditionalist puts forth that we who hold that Nehemiah's administration comes first have to answer? When the traditionalist says that Ezra came in the seventh year of Artaxerxes I, he is assuming that is what Ezra meant. Is there anything unparsimonious to assuming that he meant Artaxerxes II instead? No, of course not. So the first pillar of the traditionalist against the reverse order has nothing to recommend it as better. The second argument that we may have to explain is that Nehemiah and Ezra are obviously together at the reading of the Torah in 445 B.C. and the dedication of the walls in 431 B.C.† The answer to this is that they were together, but it was Nehemiah's administration. Nehemiah went back to Persia, and was appointed to a second administration. Later, apparently Ezra went to Babylon, and came to the notice of Artaxerxes II who appointed him to a new administration in 398 B.C. This was nearly 49 years, so it is not impossible that Ezra was almost 49 years

† Nehemiah's two administrations were 445-433 and 432-424. The end of his second term is estimated to be when Darius II came to the throne. According to the Elephantine Papyri TAD A4.1 Possibly Nehemiah's brother sent a letter in the 5th year of Darius II (419/418 BC) to Yeb.

younger when he read the Torah and still living to be appointed to a new administration by Artaxerxes II. Tradition does assign Ezra a rather long life.

How then is it better to have Ezra's administration before Nehemiah as the explanation of their association in 445 B.C. and 431 B.C. ? Is a 12 or 13 year difference any better than a 49 year one? As long as a person can live to 90 or 95 years, there is no problem. Ezra could easily have been 40 years old in 445 B.C. and lived to complete an administration starting in 398 B.C. This is a lot more sensible then the constant "explaining away" that traditionalists have to provide against the arguments of putting Nehemiah's administration first. In fact, explaining away is all they do, and they are reluctant to admit that their view depends on only one and a half assumptions.

To say that the lack of population in Nehemiah's time is not an indicator of his priority is simply a special pleading. To say that Ezra 10:6 refers to some other Eliashib and Johanan, or that Johanan was not the High Priest in Ezra 10:6 is another special pleading. To explain away the fact that the people had not before heard the Torah in Nehemiah 8, and that they were weeping is yet another special pleading. To ignore the story in Josephus about the provocative tax placed on the daily offering during the high priesthood of Johanan, and that Artaxerxes II's decree is a direct answer to this is another *ad hoc* argument.

Those are just some of the arguments I have gone through. The truth is that those who want Ezra's administration first only spend time explaining away the opposition arguments because they have no secure arguments of their own to prove that Ezra's administration came first. When one reads the book of Ezra, in 6:14 Ezra mentions the kings in order, skipping at least Xerxes forward to an Artaxerxes. Ezra never comes into the story until this Artaxerxes. There is no mention of any other king in the rest of the book, and no mention of Nehemiah. There are two Artaxerxes after the Darius of 6:14. In Ezra's day, and for several generations afterward, there was no doubt that he meant Artaxerxes II.

On the other hand, in the book of Nehemiah, there is no mention of Ezra before chapter 8, and no mention after until 12:26, which gives the order of administrations. Then the next mention is 12:36 in the narrative of the wall dedication, which had to happen in 431 B.C. Nehemiah 12:1 and 12:33 have nothing to do with "Ezra the Scribe," and it may be justly assumed that Ezra himself put the book of Ezra first with Nehemiah as the appendix and some of his own editings of things that happened after the wall builder died. For sure Nehemiah 12:26 is one of Ezra's additions. In Nehemiah, Ezra is no more than an accomplished and respected scribe recognized as a leader.

The phrase "in the days of" (בִּימֵי) applies distributively in a list, which give the religious administrations of the high priestly office:

> As for the Levites, the heads of fathers' *households* were registered in the days of Eliashib, Joiada, and Johanan, and Jaddua; so *were* the priests in the reign of Darius the Persian.

One can justly supply "in the days of" before each name in the list, and take the high priestly administrations sequentially. Likewise with Neh. 12:26, which details the administrations of the civil authority:

> These *served* in the days of Joiakim the son of Jeshua, the son of Jozadak, and in the days of Nehemiah the governor and [*in the days*] of Ezra the priest *and* scribe.

Because "in the days of" is used distributively, we can supply those words for Ezra's administration after Nehemiah's. It is plainly obvious that the norm is to list administrations in order. It is special pleading to say otherwise. The parsimonious principle (Occam's Razor) indicates that we should take these statements under their normal assumptions. Even more unparsimonious is to ignore the contextual clues that Nehemiah's administration was first, and then try to explain them away.

The way then to argue with traditionalists is to point out that Nehemiah 12:26 has the order of administrations, and that this statement has the normal default sequence unless proved otherwise. This will keep the 458 or 457 B.C. advocates from getting away with assuming their position is correct and then proceeding to explain away the positive arguments for Nehemiah first while failing to provide any proof that Ezra came first. They hope that everyone gets lost in their ad hoc attacks against the pro-arguments for Nehemiah first, and that they fail to notice that they have no pro-arguments of their own.

Why does the book of Ezra come first? The answer is fairly simple. Ezra begins at a point in history earlier than Nehemiah. Nehemiah is confined purely to events of his administrations plus some additions by the Chronicler (who would be Ezra). Nehemiah covers the years 445 B.C. to no later than 424 B.C. Ezra starts in 529 B.C. and ends in 397 B.C. So Ezra covers 133 years while Nehemiah only about 21. And of Ezra's years, 84 are before Nehemiah, and only 27 or so truly come after. So it is plain, from the historical point of view why Ezra was put first, and Nehemiah is an addendum to fill in some events that Ezra did not want to duplicate or extensively rewrite.

The last person of the high priestly line mentioned by Ezra is "Jaddua." Ezra could well have included him in his editorial lists if we suppose that Jaddua was heir to the priesthood, but not yet high priest when he was included, or a close disciple could have included him before the writings were closed.

So we see that the assumption that Ezra's administration comes before Nehemiah's administration is not justified by the fact that the book of Ezra comes first in Ezra-Nehemiah. The order is justified because everything before Ezra 7 in fact comes before Nehemiah, which is an extensive scope of history. Only Ezra 7-10, which describe events of only one year actually come after Nehemiah! There is no need for thinking that the Temple is described first because it is more important. It may be more important in the spiritual scheme of things, but it is not necessary to invoke this point to justify the order of the books. The following chart sums it up:

No. 1: Rev. J. Stafford Wright tries, (in his writing that begins, "In recent years a number of commentators...,") to cast advocates for putting Nehemiah's administration first as higher critics. But scholars with both low and high views of Scripture have taken both sides. **No. 2:** Wright is compelled to suppose that Ezra 4:6-23 is out of chronological order with respect to Ezra. Not I. Ezra comes with decree to make sure the Temple runs properly, and then Wright is compelled to suppose that the king reversed his decree, because we find the Temple not functioning when Nehemiah arrives at the city (Neh. 4:2). That is to say that Ezra 4:7-23 is put by Wright after Ezra's successful reforms based on an irrevocable law to make sure the Temple does continue to function. Judah then faces the wrath that they were trying to avoid (cf. Ezra 10:14) from the same king. **No. 3:** Wright furthers the straw man picture of his opposition, supposing they all say Zerubbabel was not in the initial return of the exiles. **No. 4:** Wright paints his opposition as saying the name 'Artaxerxes' in Ezra 7 is a mistake. But we say it is only a case of assuming a I goes behind his name rather than a II. **No. 5:** Wright rightly refutes the alleged mistake view of Artaxerxes' name by pointing out that the correct history would be remembered when the books were compiled. He believes this refutes Nehemiah having the first administration. But it does not. It only refutes those critics who assume the name was a mistake. So Wright is guilty of circular reasoning using an incorrect view of some member of his opposition. **No. 6:** Again Wright paints his opposition as proposing the priority of Nehemiah because they want to show that the Scripture is 'inaccurate in many particulars.' But this is untrue. Wright is simply guilty of using a high view of Scripture

Figure 77: Why *the* Book of is Ezra first, but Ezra last

Why the book of Ezra Comes before Nehemiah And Esther in the Canon

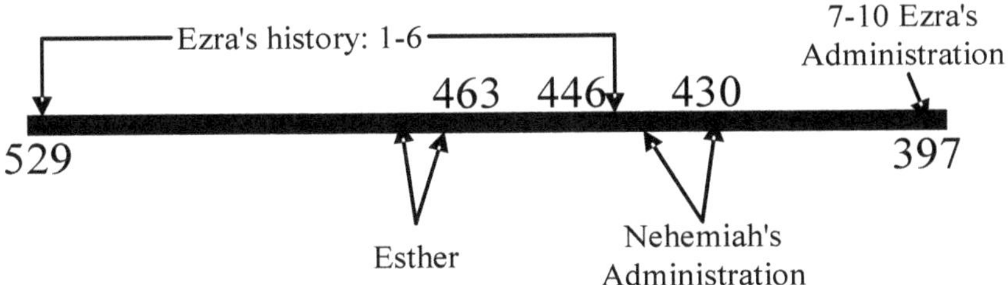

Ezra placed Nehemiah after the book of Ezra in the Canon because most of the history covered in Ezra really did happen before Nehemiah. The book of Nehemiah fills in details that happened over a relatively short period of time compared to the scope of history covered by the book of Ezra.

The Rev. J. Stafford Wright is said to have "demonstrated beyond reasonable doubt that the Artaxerxes of Ezra 7:7 must be Artaxerxes I and that Ezra came to Jerusalem in the year 458 B.C."[376] But an examination of Wright's discussion shows that he makes the whole issue depend on the mere fact that Ezra's book comes before Nehemiah in the Canon.[377] The assumption that because the book of Ezra comes first, that therefore Ezra himself comes before Nehemiah, is believed in so strongly that traditionalists suggest reversing the order posits that the Chronicler made a mistake. The only mistake is theirs.

---

[376] *Ezra and Nehemiah*, J. Carl Laney, pg. 52.

[377] J. Stafford Wright, *The Date of Ezra's Coming to Jerusalem* (London: Tyndale, 1946). Review begins on page 384 footnote.

as a cloak for continuing the ill founded dogmatism of traditional interpretation! And this kind of narrative is all too common. **No. 7:** Wright claims that the 'chamber of Jehohanan' was not that of the High Priest, but only the "High Priest elect (i.e. eldest son of the eldest son of Eliashib)." But this does not fit the context. First Ezra extracts an oath from the leaders of the priests (שָׂרֵי הַכֹּהֲנִים), because even though he is armed with a decree and the governorship, he needs the support of the people. With their backing he takes over the office of the High Priest because the High Priest *is* the problem (cf. Ezra 9:2; 10:18). The High Priest has permitted intermarriage and has not turned the people from it. His family is up to their necks in it. He was responsible because he did not address the problem. So, it is his office that Ezra takes over (cf. Ezra 10:4), and from his office Ezra will now do what the High Priest should have done. Wright's narrative makes "chamber of Jehohanan" so insignificant that it begs the question why his Ezra included it at all. **No. 8:** Wright waves away Neh. 12:26 which gives the order of administrations. **No. 9:** Wright observes that Dr. Robinson noted that none of the returnees in Ezra 7-8 are mentioned in the days of Nehemiah. If they had come to Jerusalem just 13 years before Nehemiah, surely some of them should have been mentioned among the many names contemporary with Nehemiah. Wright throws up straw men to disprove this by mentioning two names not found in Ezra 7-8. The only name in Ezra 7-8 that appears the same as a wall builder is Hattush, but in Nehemiah he is a priest or Levite. In Ezra 8:2 he is a descendant of David. So the men are not the same. **No. 10:** Wright makes no mention that with his view the 'seven sevens' are meaningless.

... continued from page 324:

a pedantic illustration for a speaker of Hebrew. We may also dispense with all the versions labeled "wooden," 5, 6, 13, and 14. Even when a construct phrase is definite, Hebrew almost never goes out of its way to use a periphrastic lamed to make it definite. This is because Hebrew relies on the context or the rule that if a nomen rectum is definite then so is the nomen regens. There are exceptions to this rule that make some usages ambiguous. See below.

We can dispense with numbers 3, 4, and 9-12 because the Greek text clearly reproduces a Hebrew idiom based on the Hebrew word for "one," with the meaning of "first." The corresponding Hebrew, therefore, should not use the word for "first."

This leaves us with the forms labeled ambiguous, 1-2 and 7-8. Forms 1-2 are more likely to appear with a definite plural nomen rectum. And forms 7-8 really accomplish nothing different with the periphrastic lamed than 1-2. While both these forms are possible, there are some very good extended reasons for preferring 1-2. Before going into those reasons we have to decide between 1 and 2. I prefer 1 because it seems more straightforward in Hebrew. The feminine numeral one agrees with the feminine word Sabbaths. But a good argument may be made for 2.

Like the Greek, the use of אֶחָד in no. 2 (בְּאַחַד הַשַּׁבָּתוֹת) implies a reference to "days." no. 2 expands to: בְּאַחַד יְמֵי הַשַּׁבָּתוֹת, 'on #one of the *days* of the Sabbaths.'

"One of the Sabbaths" and "one of the days of the Sabbaths" is however, ambiguous. For it might mean either an indefinite one among many Sabbaths or (number) one of the Sabbaths. Clearly in the context, a definite day is being described. So it means number one of the Sabbaths.

For example, we could say 'one of the month' (אֶחָד לַחֹדֶשׁ), and it is always a definite day, "the first of the month." But what about a plural: אֶחָד לֶחֳדָשִׁים? This means either *number* one of the months or some indefinite month among months. To avoid the ambiguity Hebrew resorted to רִאשׁוֹן לֶחֳדָשִׁים, "first of the months." See Exodus 12:2.

If we put the numbering of the seven Sabbaths into a counting to Shavuot context, then the context removes the ambiguity. Thus:

בְּאַחַת הַשַּׁבָּתוֹת	on one of the Sabbaths
בִּשֵׁנִית הַשַּׁבָּתוֹת	on second of the Sabbaths
בִּשְׁלִישִׁית הַשַּׁבָּתוֹת	on third of the Sabbaths

continued page 402

Abraham's Three Day Test

ON MT. MORIAH

YHWH decided he would test Abraham's faithfulness[1] to know what was in his heart, whether he would keep His commandments or not.[2] YHWH said, "Take now your only *kindred* son."[3] YHWH said, "your only *kindred*" (יְחִידְךָ) son. For Abraham had another son Ishmael.† Likewise, Yeshua is YHWH's only *kindred* Son[4], YHWH the son of YHWH[5]. "Go to the land of Moriah, and offer him there as a ascending offering on one of the mountains of which I will tell you."[6] Now on the first day Abraham proceeded to obey YHWH. He "rose early in the daybreak."[7] He kept silent suffering. So also Yeshua suffered in the morning[8] keeping his silence.[9] Abraham "bound his donkey" וַיַּחֲבֹשׁ .[10] So also Yeshua was bound on the first day.[11] He "took two of his young men" "with his son."[12] So also the son of YHWH was crucified with two men, one on the right and one on the left.[13] "And he split trees (logs) of the ascending offering" (וַיְבַקַּע עֲצֵי עֹלָה).[14] So Yeshua was hanged on a tree,[15] and upon a beam of cut wood. "And the Messenger of YHWH ascended in the flame of the altar" (Judges 13:20), "We shall surely die, because we have seen the Almighty" (vs. 22). Then Abraham "went to the place" (הַמָּקוֹם). "But at the place (הַמָּקוֹם) which YHWH your Almighty shall choose to place his name in, there you shall sacrifice the passover" (Deut. 16:6).

"Then on the third day Abraham lifted his eyes, and saw the place afar off" (בַּיּוֹם הַשְּׁלִישִׁי). So on the third day Yeshua lifted his eyes and looked toward the Temple again. (cf. 2Kings 20:8 and Jonah 2:4). In the types Yeshua was crucified on the "third day" and in the types he rose on the "third day" (cf. Matthew 26:2; Mark 14:1; Gen. 40:13, 19).

הַבֵּן הַמִּשְׁפַּחְתִּי הַיָּחִיד

1. Gen 22:1. 2. Deut. 8:2. 3. Gen 22:2. 4. John 3:16. 5. Gen. 19:24. 6. Gen. 22:2. 7. Gen. 22:3. 8. Mat. 27:1; Mark 15:1; 9. Isa. 53:7. 10. Gen. 22:3 11. Mat. 27:2; John 18:12, 24. 12. Gen. 22:3. 13. Mat. 27:38; Mark 15:27. 14. Gen. 22:3. 15. Luke 23:31; Acts 5:30; 10:31; 13:29; Gal. 3:13; 1Pe 2:24; cf. Rev. 2:7 (KJV);

† The Hebrew text just says 'only son.' The context explains this as "your only son, whom you have loved." 1: Ishmael had proved himself unworthy (Gen 21:9), and was not loved in that respect. 2: Isaac was the only son because Ishmael was sent away. 3: Isaac was the only kindred son because he was born from Sarah of Abraham's kindred (Gen. 12:1; 24:4, 7; 24:38, 40). Ishmael was half Egyptian. Abraham is set on getting a kindred wife for his only kindred son. Likewise the Almighty is set on getting the remnant of Israel as the bride of his only kindred Son.

Abraham trusted that YHWH would raise his son (Gen. 22:5) “on the third day.” For he says, “and we will worship; we will return to you” (וְנָשׁוּבָה אֲלֵיכֶם). Abraham carried a fire pot. For it says “he took the fire.” So the fire for the altar burned continuously. “And they went both of them together.” So the Father and Son walked in fellowship. Abraham “took the trees (logs) of the burnt offering and laid it on Isaac his son.” So also the beam was laid on Yeshua.

Isaac asked “Where is the lamb”? Abraham replied, “The Almighty will be seen for Himself the Lamb” (יֵרָאֶה). For Abraham prophesied that YHWH would not ask him to do what He Himself would not do. “The two of them walked together.” The Father and Son were in fellowship. Isaac would soon understand. But he would remember Abraham’s words, “and . . . we will return to you,” and “He will see for Himself the Lamb.” So the Son trusted the Father, and walked in fellowship with Him.

As Abraham was about to slay his Son, YHWH said from heaven, “Do not stretch out your hand against the lad, and do nothing to him; for now I know that you fear the Almĩghty, since you have not withheld your son, your only son, from Me.” (Gen 22:12). Now on the third day Abraham “lifted up his eyes” (Gen. 22:13). So also the Son lifted his eyes up to new life on the third day. A ram was caught in the thicket, so also Yeshua was provided for the third day, and they put a crown of thorns on his head. For the Evangelists say that the passover was “after two days” (Mat. 26:2; Mark 14:1). Abraham offered the ram “in the place of his son” (תַּחַת בְּנוֹ). So also Yeshua is offered in our stead. He has received the blow† from our transgressions, so that we might live. He shows us the ransom price our sin makes him pay.

“And Abraham called the name of that place Yãhweh will appear, as it is said to this day, “In the mount Yãhweh will appear.” (Gen. 22:14). So YHWH will be seen (יֵרָאֶה). So Yeshua was seen on the mountains of Moriah. Upon one hill was the holy Temple, and on the other hill called the Mt. of Olives, Yeshua was slain because of our sins.

YHWH OUR JUSTICE

merciful

With the death of Messiah, Yeshua is YHWH our Justice. “And this is His name by which He will be called, YHWH our Justice” Jer.

our benevolent justice

---

† Isa. 53:8. The sacrifice is a demonstration of the cost of sin, an indication of the suffering the Almighty endures in heaven while he waits for us to repent. In conjunction with forgiveness, he requires the offering to instruct us on the cost of our ransom, the cost of our sin, the price of destruction and corruption he endured upon his creation in the hope that he could deliver shalom to us (cf. Isa. 53:5) if we repented. The offering is our required instruction given us in the day of his granting merciful justice. Never does the offering compensate the Almighty for the damages of sin or remove the divine loss. God is not a creditor to be paid off.

23:6; Spanish: "Justicia Nuestra"; French "notre justice"; Latin: "iustus noster." The divine ransom cost is indicated by Messiah's suffering. For this is what YHWH requires of the repentant—to consider the cost of our sin when he declares the penalty is wiped out. "Atonement" means God is declaring our forgiveness, when he gives us his merciful justice. Atonement is not a satisfaction of divine loss, nor compensating appeasement. It is the demonstration of loss when God forgives.†

Many suppose that atonement pays a penalty that compensates YHWH for sin. If the point were to pay a penalty, then sin could be fully indulged in, since all its effects could be paid off, which means reversed or undone, because it could always be compensated for. But neither the death of Messiah nor the death of the sinner compensates the Almighty for sin. Our sin has the potential to cause others to die. If our personal sin is forgiven, it does not bring back to life those who were lost, or would be lost, due to its effects. Messiah's sacrifice does not undo all the effects of sin. Our forgiveness is declared through it, but YHWH is not compensated for his loss. The purpose of the offering is to show the cost.

Christianity has often considered human demerit to be paid for by Christ's merit so that God has nothing but merit to consider. This isn't forgiveness. Nor does it fully comprehend the destructiveness of sin. Similarly, Judaism often regards good deeds as merits which cancel demerits, or if in excess that can be passed on to their descendants to cancel their demerits.

YHWH OUR RIGHTEOUSNESS AND SHAVUOT

The same Hebrew word that means "justice" in relation to Messiah's death means "righteousness" is respect to His resurrection life. The resurrection is the beginning of our righteousness, yet we have to wait for our resurrection for that righteousness to be complete. Paul explains, "because we through the Spirit, by faithfulness eagerly await the hope of righteousness" (Gal. 5:5, GNM). See we must "wait" for the "hope of righteousness." Even though we are in the covenant, YHWH still sees the sinfulness in us. It is not necessary for him to see us as righteous to forgive this sin. Indeed, He does not see us a righteous until we obey his commandments from the heart.

Now Yeshua was raised on the first of the Sabbaths to impart to

† Even the final death of an unredeemed person does not compensate the Almighty for the loss caused by that person's sin. Not even an eternity of punitive justice can restore the plan that God intended for that person. God wanted faithfulness and not sacrifice. Atonement (kippur, כִּפֵּר) is a declarative Pi·el, meaning "to declare wiped." It is equivalent to forgiveness of divine retribution. The offering is not in satisfaction of divine wrath, because then all could be saved. It is a sign of benevolent justice and the cost of it.

us his resurrection life, which he writes on our hearts in part, now, and in completion when he returns as taught by Jeremiah 31:31-34. His resurrection is the first of *seven Sabbaths* leading to Mt. Sinai, which are contained in the *seven Shavuot* (weeks) counted to the feast. So 49 days are counted after Passover containing seven Sabbaths. The 50th day is the feast of these Shavuot. As Passover teaches us the story of redemption, so Shavuot teaches us the story of sanctification. Seven times seven is equal to forty-nine, which is perfection multiplied by seven. When these seven Sabbaths, and seven weeks are complete, then comes the 50th day.

So 50 days after the Exodus (which took place on the first of the Sabbaths at night[378]) Israel heard the Torah announced by YHWH himself from Mt. Sinai as night fell beginning the Sabbath[379]. Thus from redemption to sanctification is the *sefirah*, which is to say the *counting*. By counting we realize that we have to wait for our sanctification. We have to wait a period of time between our redemption and forgiveness of sins unto the learning of the Torah, whereby we receive the righteousness of Messiah.

The teaching that we have to wait is reinforced by Messiah. He told the disciples that they had to wait until they were given power by the Ruakh. The Ruakh (Spirit) is given on the day of Shavuot in Acts 2, and it is the Spirit that writes the Torah on our hearts (Jer. 31:31-34; Deut. 30:6). Shavuot is a prophetic foretaste of the final sanctification of Israel in the end of days, which will happen after Israel returns

---

[378] I explained Deut. 16:1 earlier. The Exodus began at daybreak on the 15th of Aviv when Israel departed from their homes, but was finished the following night. As the sun set when they were going out of Egypt the first of the Sabbaths began. The 16th day of Nisan, thus marked their passing out of Egypt and encampment at Succoth. The Shavuot counting thus brings us to Mt. Sinai when Israel received the commandments on the Sabbath at nightfall.

[379] This was the eighth Sabbath since the Exodus. But it is not counted in the 49 days, which are "seven sevens." The commandment is to count "seven sevens," which amounts to 49 days. In reality, the 50th day is the day of the feast that marks the end of the counting. Lev. 23:16 does not say "fifty days" (plural). It refers to the 50th day (singular). The seven Sabbaths, therefore, are only counted in the seven sevens. The 50th day after this count can come on any day of the week. However, in the year of the Exodus it came on the weekly Sabbath. Also, on the 50th day an eighth heptad (seven day period) is not counted, nor is the first day of it counted.

from exile according to Deuteronomy 30.

Now the reason that Christians do not recognize the Torah, or this connection between Passover and Shavuot, is that they think they are already righteous in the sight of God. They see no need to wait for the hope of righteousness. They see no need for learning YHWH's commandments. For they claim that God counts them as righteous and that they need nothing more to enter the kingdom of heaven. But they are all of them deceived who think this.

For James says:

> "Was not Abraham our father *counted* righteous by works, when he offered up Isaac his son on the altar? You see that faithfulness was working with his works, and as a result of the works, faithfulness is completed, and the Scripture is fulfilled which says, "And Abraham held faithful in Yahweh and it was counted to him as righteousness, and he was called beloved of the Almighty" (James 2:21-23).

So we see that long after Genesis 15:6, Abraham was *counted* righteous by works at the binding of Isaac when he obeyed YHWH's command to go to the land of Moriah. The Psalms explain that good works are counted as righteousness:

> Then Phinehas stood up and interposed; and so the plague was stayed. And it was reckoned to him for† righteousness, to all generations onward of time immemorial (Psalm 106:30-31).

What about Paul? Didn't he say that the gospel means that God counts the believer perfectly righteous in his sight? Didn't Paul say that Christians are forgiven because God transfers His righteousness to their account? Can you say the word "compensation"? Well, that is what the Christians who argue this way are thinking. They are thinking that Christ's righteousness compensates their legal account for all their sins, past, present, and for any they have not committed yet. Didn't Paul say that God legally sees us as perfectly righteous at the moment we believe? No Paul does not say that. Now this book is not the place to correct all the mistranslations in Paul, and indeed, the phrase "first day of the week" is only the beginning of the mistranslation work of the false Church. However, I will quote one

† More properly, 'justice,' (See GNM pp. 349-352, **Endnote No. 3.**) Messiah's covenant of peace counted to Phinehas as an administration of justice to all generations. He was to teach the people how the justice of forgiveness is administered in Messiah's covenant of peace.

passage to explain what Paul really is saying:

> Now with respect to the working the reward is not accounted as a favor, but according to what is due, but with respect to not working, yet being a person who HOLDS FAITHFUL UPON THE ONE administering justice to the guilty, HIS FAITHFULNESS IS RECKONED AS AN ADMINISTRATION OF JUSTICE, just as David also speaks about the blessing of the man to whom the Almighty is ACCOUNTING AN ADMINISTRATION OF JUSTICE apart from works (Rom. 4:4-6).

Paul is not considering two different people here, one who is being saved by works and another who is not. Rather, he is considering one person who is not perfectly righteous. When this person works and does what is right, then he is counted righteous. On the other hand, the same person does not do compensatory works, i.e. zechut, to cancel demerit, but rather holds faithful to Messiah, trusting his administration of justice. So the faithful one works to continue in life, but he does not work to reckon merit to cancel demerit.

At the beginning of our repentance we are only babes in Messiah. We are forgiven our sins, but we are not counted as perfectly righteous. When Paul says "His faithfulness is being considered as justice" at the beginning of salvation, he does not mean the believers faith is reckoned as perfect righteousness! Rather, he means that Messiah's faithfulness administers benevolent justice to us, to declare retribution wiped out, to forgive, to ransom us from the enemy called sin. This is what "His faithfulness" means. And this faithfulness is not counted as personal righteousness to the faithful one. It is only counted as God's benevolent justice to forgive us.

This is exactly what the GNM translation shows. Justice is counted to the faithful one without works. This is a gracious justice demanding no merits for the demerits. It isn't zechut of Messiah being inherited by the faithful one to pay for his demerits, so that God allegedly forgives him on that basis. Such a view assumed that God can be compensated for sin. And the very idea that God can be fully compensated for sin should be regarded with horror and approbation. Messiah shows us the ransom exacted from the Almighty by sin. This is not a legal cost, but his resultant cost of enduring with our sins, and taken from him by our sins, while he awaits our repentance.

This was explained on the previous pages, but it is more completely explained in the notes of *The Good News of Messiah*. Theologians John Miley and Albert Barnes were trying to say the same thing.

Hezekiah's Sickness

In those days Hezekiah became mortally ill. And Isaiah the prophet the son of Amoz came to him and said to him, "Thus says Yãhweh, 'Set your house in order, for you are dying and you will not live.†'" Then he turned his face to the wall, and prayed to Yãhweh, saying, "Remember now, Yãhweh, I beseech you, how I have walked before you in truth and with a whole heart, and have done what is good in your sight." And Hezekiah wept bitterly. And it came about before Isaiah had gone out of the middle court, that the word of Yãhweh came to him, saying, "Return and say to Hezekiah the leader of my people, 'Thus says Yãhweh, the Almĩghty of your father David, "I have heard your prayer, I have seen your tears; behold, I will heal you. On the third day you shall go up to the house of Yãhweh. "And I will add fifteen years to your life, and I will deliver you and this city from the hand of the king of Assyria; and I will defend this city for my own sake and for my servant David's sake."'" Then Isaiah said, "Take a cake of figs." And they took and laid it on the boil, and he recovered. And Hezekiah had said to Isaiah, "What will be the sign that Yãhweh will heal me, and that I shall go up to the house of Yãhweh the third day?" And Isaiah said, "This shall be the sign to you from Yãhweh, that Yãhweh will do the thing that He has spoken: shall the shadow go forward ten steps or go back ten steps?" So Hezekiah answered, "It is easy for the shadow to decline ten steps; no, but let the shadow turn backward ten steps." And Isaiah the prophet cried to Yãhweh, and He brought the shadow on the stairway back ten steps by which it had gone down on the stairway of Ahaz. (2Kings 20:1-11).

Hezekiah is the Anointed Son of David. So also Yeshua is the anointed Son of David. Hezekiah became sick (חָלָה). So also Yeshua was "put to grief" (Is. 53:10, הֶחֱלִי). YHWH told him "put your house in order" (צַו לְבֵיתֶךָ). So also Yeshua ordered his own house (John 13-17). The Messiah will die (כִּי מֵת אַתָּה). And for a time he

† Isa. 38:1. The statement does not express divine will or causation. It is simply an observation of what is going to happen based on untimely natural processes already occurring. The Almighty is simply calculating from what he knows nature will do.

will not live (וְלֹא תִחְיֶה). Then he turned his face and prayed. So also Yeshua prayed that the Father would deliver him, and Yeshua wept with tears as Hezekiah did. And Yeshua walked before the Father "in truth and with a whole heart" and did only what was good in His sight (2Kings 20:3).

Isaiah does not get very far before YHWH answers. "Return and say to Hezekiah Prince of My people." So the king is called "prince" (נְגִיד). So also Yeshua is called Messiah Prince: מָשִׁיחַ נָגִיד (Dan. 9:25). The promise is that "On the third day you shall go up to the house of YHWH" (בַּיּוֹם הַשְּׁלִישִׁי תַּעֲלֶה). So on the third day Yeshua ascended before heaven's Temple as the last fire of the wave offering burned. A promise was given to Hezekiah to deliver Jerusalem (vs. 6). So also a promise was given to Yeshua to deliver Jerusalem at the end of "seventy sevens":

> Sevens Seventy are decreed over your people and over your holy city, to end the transgression, even to seal up Sin, and to wipe out iniquity, and to bring in everlasting righteousness, and to seal the vision and the prophet, and to anoint the holy of holies (Daniel 9:24).[380]

Hezekiah asked what the "sign" (אוֹת) would be that he should "ascend . . . on the third day" (וְעָלִיתִי בַּיּוֹם הַשְּׁלִישִׁי). So also Yeshua was given all these signs that he should ascend on the third day. And by these signs we know that he is the Messiah.

Hezekiah asked that the shadow "return ten steps." Less than ten years before, the shadow of Assyria had covered the northern kingdom, and had swallowed it up. So also Yeshua will make the shadow of Assyria go back until all ten tribes of Israel are reunited with the their brothers in Judah.

THE PLAINNESS OF SCRIPTURE

An absolute rule for interpretation of Scripture is that the sense that is the plainest is the correct interpretation. This principle is based on the assumption that Scripture was not given to confuse, but to explain. The Holy Spirit reveals the word to make things plain and

[380] He who has received his witness has sealed that the Almighty is true. Whoever holds faithful to Messiah Yeshua has sealed he who is the Prophet like Moses, but the vision is for many days has been sealed up. He who is holy will reveal the vision at the end of a day, days, and half a day, and Israel will know that the Almighty is true.

clear. An interpretation that leaves ambiguities or loose ends behind it is not plain. Everything that is necessary to interpret the Scripture is given in the Scripture.

The aforementioned principle is a fundamental aspect of trust in the Almighty. It is a core component of faith. We have to trust him to mean what he says and say what he means. The word of the Almighty must be approached like that of a child. A child takes things plainly and literally. If the message is confusion, then the child is confused and seeks a clear answer. So if men do not become like children and seek the clear answer they will never enter the kingdom of heaven. For they will be satisfied with confusion.

What passes for Scripture, however, is often not scripture. Anyone with eyes to see can see that various translations are contradictory and that various interpretations are opposed. Also it is well known that even the Greek or Hebrew texts we have contain variations, and sometimes these variations change the meaning of the text. The principle of clarity is the only principle by which we can sort out the confusion that has been introduced into the text by rebels or careless mistakes. A child will apply the principle of clarity. A skeptic or rebel will refuse to apply it.

The corruption of Scripture, or mistranslation of it, comes about because the translators accept a tradition whose validity cannot be verified. But it is not necessary to disprove a false tradition directly. It is only necessary to show that the tradition comes out of a black hole, or black box[381], and that there is no evidence of the tradition before the information blackout surrounding its beginning. A lie that is in the past that has gotten into history is a lie that comes out of a black box.

An assertion that cannot be directly tested must be tested by its effects in the present. What particularly needs to be tested is the effect of an assertion on the state and interpretation of scripture. If an

[381] A black box is a scientific concept that refers to the fact that one can obtain data only on what comes out of the black box. But one cannot see into the black box itself to explain the origin of what is seen coming out of it. The truth or falsity of information coming out of a black box cannot be verified. For to do that one has to enter the black box to test the information. Much of recorded history is like a black box. The recorded history is what comes out of the black box. That is to say, we cannot go back into the history to verify the information.

assertion leaves the interpretation of Scripture in an ambiguous and confusing state, then the assertion must be false. For the Holy Spirit reveals the word to make things plain and clear. A false assertion is thus exposed when it fails to make things plain and clear. If two possible interpretations or translations are given, then one is bound to make things plain and the other is not. It may take a bit of logic and thinking things through to see which assertion is incorrect.

The validity of an assertion must be tested by the scientific method. That is the consistency of scripture must be tested assuming two cases. In the first case the assertion is held to be a valid truth available for the original reader. Is the resulting interpretation ambiguous or confusing? In the second case the assertion is held to be in invalid falsehood introduced later. The consistency of the scripture must be tested as if the original reader had no knowledge of the assertion, and was unable to bring it to the context. If the scripture becomes consistent and plain in absence of the assertion, then the assertion is proved to be false. Thus we see that a control method is necessary. It is necessary to test for the plainness of the scripture as if the assertion never existed.

The most serious deceptions or false assertions are based on a set of lies that mutually support each other. For instance, when false witnesses all agree to tell the same set of lies in a murder case then the judge could be deceived if he is not diligent. Hence we have another principle that is important to cracking any case of colluding falsehoods. And that is there seems to be something odd about each piece. It is this oddness, or feeling that something that does not fit which tells us what needs to be tested. This oddness is really the taking note of the trace of confusion or inconsistency in the interpretation of events. It is the clue of what to test. If things turn out consistent on doubting the assertion of certain witnesses then they are proved false.

The denial that the resurrection day was on the Sabbath is a case of colluding false witnesses. To show this, first the false assertion is shown to lack clarity. Then second, it is shown that without the false assertion, clarity returns. A lack of clarity is defined as ambiguity—a situation where two or more interpretations are possible. I will start with Matthew 12:40 "three days and three nights" as a test case.

With the Sabbath resurrection only one interpretation can be put on Matthew 12:40, and the possibility of a shorter period is denied as a possible meaning of the phrase. Under this assertion, Matthew 12:40 is unambiguous. It is plain and clear. Under a Friday-Sunday scenario, Mathew 12:40 is interpreted to be shorter, but it is still admitted by proponents that the phrase itself applied elsewhere *could* mean three literal nights. That is, they have not proved that it only means three days and two nights in all situations. Thus in the Friday-Sunday view, Matthew 12:40 lacks clarity, and this would contradict the principle that Scripture is clear.

Let us move to the next test case. It is evident that the literal texts say "one of the Sabbaths," which according to the Sabbath resurrection only means the number one sabbath in counting seven sabbaths after Passover, i.e. the "first of the Sabbaths"[382]. Using Lev. 23:15 it is clear what this means. Also it is denied that Sabbath means week. Thus, the Sabbath resurrection has full clarity.

The Friday-Sunday view introduces the black box tradition that Sabbath means week. However, it is admitted that the word Sabbath still means Sabbath in other contexts. Thus the Friday-Sunday view lacks clarity. It is proposing additional ambiguity to the word "sabbath" that does not exist with the Sabbath resurrection. Furthermore, even Sunday Christians have argued that Sunday is the Sabbath based on the use of the word Sabbath in the key phrase: μιᾷ τῶν σαββάτων. That means that in the Friday-Sunday view, it is as clear as mud which day is meant. The view lacks clarity, and thus contradicts the principle that the purpose of the Scripture is to clarify.

Let us take "on the third day" as another example. In this case the Sabbath resurrection comes on the third calendar day using a daybreak to daybreak day. The Friday-Sunday view can use the same type of day or a sunset to sunset calendar day,† or a daylight day (dawn to dusk). However, all definitions of day are admitted by both sides, so neither view is more clear or less clear than the other on this point.

When we come to "after three days" (Mark 8:31) the situation is

---

[382] For the purpose of analyzing the assertions, this is the same as "one day of the sabbaths" or "first day of the sabbaths."

† As the new notes in this fourth edition will reflect, this definition of a "calendar day" did not exist in the pre-exilic period. And it generally came about in Judaism after the fall of the Temple in AD 70. Sabbaths, strictly speaking, should be explained as beginning in the evening of the sixth calendar day before the seventh day. Even where the seven days of unleavened bread have a Sabbath on the first day and on the last, these are explained as beginning the evening before. The only indisputable Scripture occurrences of including night first in a period called "day" are to be found in Matthew 26:17, Mark 14:12, and Luke 22:7. This usage reflects Galilean time reckoning. Galilee was not resettled immediately after the Babylonian exile. In

different. The Resurrection Sabbath simply explains "day" here to refer to a daylight day, i.e. dawn to dusk (or‡twenty-four hour sunset to sunset day ending with the daylight part), and denies that "after" ever means "on." The Friday-Sunday view asserts that "after" means "on" in order to explain the text, but at the same time, advocates admit elsewhere that "after *N* days" could be after the *N*th day is ended. Therefore, in the Friday-Sunday view, the phrase "after three days" lacks clarity, where as with the Sabbath resurrection it is plain. And what is plain agrees with the principle that the word is given to make plain, and not to confuse.

When people truly appreciate the evidence and are exposed to all the facts, they often say, you have your view, and I have mine. That is they admit to the possibility of the other view, but choose to follow their own. This is a position that is based on a lack of clarity. But if we truly understand that the Scripture comes to clarify then such a position is not sensible. The proper thing for said person is to continue to seek until it is understood which view is clear and which view is ambiguous.

One of the reasons that the principle of Scriptural clarity works is that it is easier to introduce a false assumption than to completely eliminate the original truth. The original truth therefore continues to be evidenced in other contexts to even the holders of the false view. The false view can be recognized as such because it is ambiguous. It cannot demonstrate that the false view is the only absolute.

This is a key point in recognizing that while Friday-Sunday can introduce interpretations to Matthew 12:40, Mark 8:31, and the "first of the Sabbaths" passages to allow their view, they cannot disprove or eliminate the opposing view. They have only increased the entropy (disorder) in the system by increasing the ambiguities. The entropy is eliminated on the correct view because the traditional assertions supporting Friday-Sunday that come out of the "black box" are denied to be valid. While in this book, I have offered an explanation of the contents of the "black box" in the second century, the real proof of nefarious corruption in that time period is based on the principle that the Scripture is plain and clear and not confused.

fact, it was resettled by Jews around 100 BC amid a Hasmonean policy of forced conversion and integration of the existing non-Jewish population into Judaism. In Judea, they were able to maintain the dawn to dawn calendar day used before the exile, but in Galilee the civil administrations adopted the dusk to dusk usage that was most impressed upon Jews from the Babylonian civil calendar. When Judea was resettled in 529 BC, the priests saw to it that the pre-exilic reckoning of a day was imposed in Judea. But when Judea was devastated in the two Jewish revolts (AD 70 and 135), Galilee was relatively unscathed. Then Galilee became the center of post Temple Jewish culture, including the Messianic Faith. Yeshua's Galilean disciples were certaintly aware of the Judean usage and its proper biblical place, but they resorted to their civil reckoning in Galilee

‡ Posssibly by Galilean reckoning. See previous note.

Another term for what I am describing here is *parsimony* or the principle of *Occam's Razor*. This is to say that assumptions should not be needlessly multiplied. Now many have offered a Thursday-Sunday chronology as the solution to Matthew 12:40. This view requires the annual Sabbath, Nisan 15, to go together with the weekly sabbath:

	Annual Sabbath	Weekly Sabbath	
Thu	Fri	Sat	Sun
market hours	e.g. Apr 23, AD 34 Second Passover.		market hours

But, Mark 16:1 says, "And passing the Sabbath, Miraim Magdalene and Miriam of Ya'akov and Shalome bought spices." It is obvious that there are no market hours (in this view) to buy any spices after the Sabbath but before the alleged Sunday resurrection. The Thursday view is forced to say that the spices were bought Saturday night.[383] In those days the plain sense reader would assume that such things were bought during regular market hours, which were not held at night.

Further, the plain sense reader would conclude that "the Sabbath" mentioned in Mark 16:1 is the same sabbath referred to in Mark 15:42, "because it was the preparation day, that is, the day before a Sabbath." Now in the Thursday view and our view this was Nisan 15. The plain sense, then is that Mark 16:1 is also referring to Nisan 15, and that the day after must not be a Sabbath, since they bought spices then. If the Thursday view were correct, then the scripture would have to say, "and passing the sabbaths" in Mark 16:1. A reader would expect the plural of "sabbaths," and the Greek phrase would have to be "διαγενομένων τῶν σαββάτων" rather than the singular phrase "διαγενομένου τοῦ σαββάτου." So inserting Mark 16:1 into a Thursday view causes the Scripture to lack clarity.

Of course the same objection to the Friday-Sunday tradition applies to the Thursday tradition, namely that the resurrection was on

[383] This is true of the Friday-Sunday view also.

because they wanted to explain matters in terms their constituenets were used to just as I employ the Roman civil day in this book. The Galileans appended the headmost day of the feast, Nisan 14 to the other seven days of it, calling it a feast of eight days (cf. Josephus Ant. 2.15.1 [317]). Josephus also tells of, as Luke 22:7, "the day of unleavened bread" in reference to Nisan 14 (War V.99, καὶ τῆς τῶν ἀζύμων ἐνστάσης ἡμέρας τεσσαρεσκαιδεκάτῃ Ξανθικοῦ μηνός), equiv. to τῆς [ἡμέρας] τῶν ἀζύμων.) See Hoenig, Sidney B. "The Duration of the Festival of Matzot." The Jewish Quarterly Review, vol. 49, no. 4, 1959, pp. 271–277. The terminology of the Galilean passages, therefore, was plainly 14 Nisan starting at dusk on Nisan 13 in the Galilean reckoning, but later we find John having to explain this as "before the Passover" (John 13:1) because he was a Judean correcting a false doctrine that evolved from a misunderstanding of the Galilean reckoning.

"the first of the Sabbaths." Introducing the possibility of "week" as a translation of "Sabbaths" only increases the entropy and lack of clarity.

Additional difficulties for the Thursday crucifixion are revealed by astronomy in A.D. 34. In order to obtain a Thursday crucifixion, it is necessary to postpone the new moon beyond the time of its appearance by invoking clouds on the 29th day so that the moon could not be seen. But the month of Adar in A.D. 34 was already 30 days, and the next day *automatically* became the first day of the month of Nisan regardless of the weather. So to obtain a Thursday date actually requires failing to see the moon at its proper time two months in a row due to weather. The odds are exceedingly low.[384] And these months would both have to be 30 days long. But the halakhic rule is that if the moon is not seen due to weather after a preceding month fixed without seeing the moon due to weather, then one of the months must be 29 days and the other 30 days. The rule is to alternate 29 and 30 days months until the moon is really seen. Therefore two 30 day back to back months due to lack of observation are impossible, and therefore, a Thursday crucifixion in A.D. 34 is impossible.[385]

---

[384] The new moon was observed all over Israel. Just for an example in one city, Jerusalem, the sun shines 250 hours/month out of a possible 360 hours/month. That means it shines 70% of the time, and is only obscured 30% of the time. The probability that the sky is obscured on two days 30 days apart is 30% x 30 % = .3 x .3 = .09 or less than 10%. So there are 9 chances of 10 that the new moon was seen on Wednesday, March 10. And that is just for Jerusalem. When the exclusive OR probabilities are added for the rest of Israel the probability will increase drastically, but I leave that work for future statisticians.

[385] Some may propose intercalating the year a month later, in which case the 14th of that month would be Thursday. But this too was shown to be impossible earlier in this book. The barley traditions lack clarity, and are another black box tradition. What the Talmud says of them is to mislead people on the true nature of the calendar, which is to use the *tequfah*. When it comes to Yeshua's resurrection, nothing is more important than certainty. The sign of Jonah is provided to provide certainty. The Rabbis knew this, but they also know that the *tequfah* is correct, and agrees with the plain sense of Genesis 1:14. Whether the tradition was motivated by the Rabbis or by their father below is beside the point. The fact is that it brings confusion to the scripture. Meanwhile, any honest interpreter has to admit that "observe the month of the Aviv" does not need to mean watch for barley. Clarity therefore demands that it be omitted. Also, some wanting to eliminate AD 34 (or postpone a month in AD 34) wish to do so by invoking the mistaken rule from the ecclesiastical calendar that the pascha follows a full moon that follows the spring equinox. Therefore as in AD 34 and 2 BC the full moon occured before the tequfah, they would eliminate both the proper time for the birth of Messiah and also that of his ransom for Israel. This is the reason that Smith B. Goodenow, *Bible Chronology*, 1896, fails to put down the proper date as a choice in AD 34. But Scripture says nothing about the moon needing to be full by sunset on Nisan 14.

Moreover a fatal point for the Thursday view is that its existence is not justified. If the tradition started out that the crucifixion was on Thursday, then why is the tradition changed to Friday? For if the true crucifixion had ever been Thursday, then everyone would have remembered that Matthew 12:40 was the reason why. The Gnostics would have been happy with the resulting Sunday resurrection, and thus no one would have been motivated to change things around, and Matthew 12:40 or Mark 8:31 would never have been an issue.

The Wednesday crucifixion and Resurrection Sabbath are justified by the very fact that the Church rejected the Sabbath and accepted Sunday in its place. It is also justified by the fact that only the Sabbath resurrection can lay claim to a plain and clear sense of the Scripture. If the Holy Spirit had ever meant any other conclusion to be drawn, then He would not have aimed all the evidence and supporting facts in that direction. Nor would He have allowed said facts to work out parsimoniously for a view that is incorrect.

.... continued from page 386:

בִּרְבִיעִית הַשַּׁבָּתוֹת	on fourth of the Sabbaths
בַּחֲמִישִׁית הַשַּׁבָּתוֹת	on fifth of the Sabbaths
בְּשִׁישִׁית הַשַּׁבָּתוֹת	on sixth of the Sabbaths
בִּשְׁבִיעִית הַשַּׁבָּתוֹת	on seventh of the Sabbaths

The Greek text also excludes the possibility of "one of the Sabbaths" meaning an indefinite Sabbath among many because it includes the definite article, "the one" (Τῇ δὲ μιᾷ) of the Sabbaths. This usage answers to the Hebrew usage: שֵׁם הָאַחַת עָדָה וְשֵׁם הַשֵּׁנִית צִלָּה, "The name of <u>the one</u> was Adah and the name of <u>the second</u> was Tsillah" (Gen. 4:19). We see here that "the one" is coordinated with "the second." The definite article can remove ambiguity, and so may the context.

In Hebrew we may say, "One day I was walking on the road, and I saw a snake:" יוֹם אֶחָד הָלַכְתִּי בַּדֶּרֶךְ וְרָאִיתִי נָחָשׁ. But in Genesis 1:5 we have: יוֹם אֶחָד. And the sense is not indefinite as in the above example. So we see that the context makes a big difference. The Scripture is not telling us that some indefinite day in the past he made light. With this in mind let us visit an example that translators almost always misunder-

continued page 481

More Third Day Parables

The Almighty weaves his parable of the "third day" into just about every passage that mentions the "third day," "three days" or "three days." Paul says that Yeshua, "rose again the third day according to the Scriptures" (καὶ ὅτι ἐγήγερται τῇ ἡμέρᾳ τῇ τρίτῃ κατὰ τὰς γραφὰς) 1 Cor. 15:4. When one sees enough of these passages and considers all of them together, it becomes clear that the Holy Spirit means to teach about Messiah in them. A parable is a literary method of double meaning. There are hints in the texts, or in other texts which allow us to decode the parable.

There are 110 times that "three days" or "third day" occurs in the Scriptures:

		Does Passage Have Messianic Significance?		
Texts	Total	Yes	Possible	Unlikely
Torah and Prophets	77x	62x	2x	13x
The Four Evangelists	25x	25x		
Acts of the Apostles	7x	2x	4x	1x
Pauline Letters	1x	1x		
Revelation	2x	2x		

The same search with "two days" or "second day" obtains 26 hits in the NASB. Subtract three "after two days" passages which are Messianic, and five more which are part of a "third day" Messianic passage. So 26–8=18, which is comparable to the 20 passages that may not be Messianic in the "third day" category. There are 12 passages with four days. Better than 80% of third day passages are Messianic. Here is the drash[386] on the passages not discussed yet.

Gen 1:13 Omit.
Gen 22:4 Binding of Isaac. Discussed before.
Gen 30:36 possible category
Gen 31:19 Laban goes to shear sheep on the first day. Yeshua is the lamb. Rachel stole the idols. Yeshua died for such transgressions so

[386] A drash is a homilectical method of interpretation that relates passages to another situation. It is not expected to be the literal primary sense of a text. It is rather the parabolic sense of the text. The third day drash is above a normal drash however, because we are certain of the Holy Spirit's intent that it should be related to Messiah.

that Israel could outwit the power of the Assyrian (devil) and flee. Israel passed over the river of exile and out of death. The destination was the mountain of YHWH.[387] Laban learned of his loss on the third day. Yeshua rose on the third day gaining the victory and Satan learned of his loss. Laban pursued seven days, and finds Jacob on the seventh. So also the resurrection of Yeshua was on the seventh day. Israel is now under the covenant of YHWH and YHWH denies Laban (the devil) permission to attack. Jacob takes up his defense in the mountain of God. The devil complains of losing his slaves. He complains of such deliverance that he did not expect. The devil looks for cause to accuse Israel . . . he is looking for his idols, but YHWH causes it to be overlooked because the idols have been properly defiled by the maidservant that is no longer Laban's property. When the devil is done looking, Israel announces that he is innocent from transgression. For Israel is repentant. The devil contends that all belongs to him, but in fear of Israel now causes a covenant of protection to be made for him, but it will only last until the Syrian breaks that covenant and tries to subdue Israel.

Gen 34:1 A daughter of Israel suffers loss. So Yeshua suffered loss on the first day. Satan says, I have defiled you, now make a covenant with me. For you are in my power. The sons of Jacob tell the Devil he must first become an Israelite. But on the third day Dinah is delivered. So on the third day Yeshua rose.

Gen 40:12ff This was interpreted earlier in the book.

Gen 42:17 Israel is put in prison for three days. Joseph says to send one representative to the Father. On the third day he says to let only one of them be bound. So Yeshua is the one of Israel that is bound for us so that the children of Israel may not die of starvation during the famine. Israel admits guilt (Gen. 42:21), which is why one of them had to be in prison. So on the third day one was bound before their eyes. So also Messiah represents Israel.

Ex 3:18 Also, 5:3; 8:27. This is the three day journey to Mt. Sinai to meet YHWH. Now on the first day they entered the wilderness, so also Yeshua entered the wilderness of death on the first day. Then Moses met him on the third day to receive instructions. So Yeshua rose on the third day, and gave instruction to his disciples about all the scriptures concerning himself.

Ex 10:22 For three days there is darkness over Egypt. So also Messiah spent three days and three nights in the grave on behalf of Israel. During the grave experience Israel had light in their houses because

[387] Possibly this is why the text omits "of Gilead" with respect to Jacob and includes it with respect to Laban.

Israel is to know the truth of why Messiah was in darkness for three days. Then Satan (Pharaoh) relents and admits defeat and says go serve YHWH.

Ex 15:22 Israel goes three days in the wilderness. Again Messiah was three days in the wilderness of sheol suffering and dying for our sin. Messiah was thirsty, but the water of life was not found for three days. A tree was cast into the bitter waters poisoned by sin. That tree is Yeshua, and in Yeshua's resurrection the waters are made pure again. He admonishes them to purify themselves by keeping his commandments. And this is to be done by taking the life of Messiah into one's heart. See also Num. 33:8.

Ex 19:11 The Shavuot text. This passage was discussed before. Also 19:15-16.

Lev 7:17 The commandments for eating peace offerings and volunteer offerings were explained before, and how they relate to Messiah. What is needed is the reason for not eating a volunteer offering on the third day. If the volunteer offering could be eaten on the third day, then it would have to be burned on the fourth. But, this will corrupt the type of Messiah's ascension to life. Therefore, the final smoke of the volunteer offering must ascend on the third day. Also is the fact that after the second day the meat of the offering is not perfect. It is only perfect for burning but not eating. Only Yeshua's raised life is perfect for consumption. And to eat imperfect meat would detract from it and the teaching that life to be consumed must be perfect life. Thus the third day is reserved for receiving Messiah's resurrection life at the beginning of salvation, and in the eschatological third day. Also Lev. 7:18, 19:7.

Num 7:24 Omit.

Num 10:33 The ark is Yeshua. Yeshua went three days' journey in the wilderness of Sinai. The wilderness is sheol, and then a resting place was found at the resurrection on the third day. And this resting place is the resurrection on the day of rest.

Num 19:12 Being touched by death requires a two step purification, one on the third day, and a final one on the seventh day. So by immersion we are immersed into Yeshua's death so that it is accounted to us as if we had died, and this was "on the third day." For the Evangelists and types say that "after two days was the passover," which is the third day. The ram was slain on the third day and Isaac received back to life on the third day. So also Yeshua was raised on the "third day" which is the seventh day. For on the seventh day he was raised to sanctify us with new life. See also Num. 19:19. Also Num. 31:19.

Num 29:20 Omit.

Jos 1:11 They crossed the Jordan on a Wednesday,[388] which was the "third day." So also in the types Yeshua was crucified on the third day (Matt 26:2; Mark 14:1; Gen. 22:4; 40:20). Starting on the first day they prepared food. So also Yeshua was crucified on the day of preparation. They passed over the Jordan "on the third day." So also Yeshua returned to the land of life "on the third day." Also see Josh 3:2.

Jos 2:16 Rahab urged the spies to hide toward the mountain for three days. So also Yeshua was hidden in the cave for three days and three nights. On the first day she left the scarlet sign of her redemption in the window. So also Yeshua left the signs of our redemption on the first day, the blood and water. They sent pursuers after the spies, so also they set a guard on Yeshua. On the third day the spies were free. On the third day Yeshua rose. The spies business was not revealed to the enemy and so Rahab's redemption was secured because she was faithful in the covenant.

Jos 9:16 What this teaches is that YHWH will not break His covenant with us. Because Israel has become like the nations and broken the covenant. Therefore, to preserve the covenant Messiah died and rose on the "third day" according to the Scriptures.

Jud 14:14 Out of death comes life. Out of the eater sweetness. This is YHWH's riddle of three days.

Jud 19:4 Possible, but I have not figured this one out.

Jud 20:30 Israel got the victory on the third day, so Yeshua gives us the victory on the third day.

1Sam 9:20 That which was lost was recovered on the third day. So Yeshua recovered life.

Since compiling the above list, I have discovered with the help of the writings of another brother that I have fallen far short of the true number of three related and third day parables. But that would fill another volume.

---

[388] Nisan 10, 1592 B.C.

† The natural year dates from the moment of the spring equinox at dawn on the first day of creation, but the agricultural year ends with the day before the first day of the seventh month. So the first year of the first Sabbath year cycle was a part year, lasting exactly six months. The garden was planted in maturity, and the rest of the earth sowed such that growth would make up for the missing first half of the Sabbath year. For this reason, the calculation of the Sabbath year cycle is based on the spring and summer seasons of the natural year, because this is where the two year types overlap and are synchronous. The proper calculation takes the natural creation era year of the world in the first half of the year. An even division by seven will indicate that the spring and summer seasons are included in a Sabbath year that began the previous seventh month.

Scripture Chronology Determined

The following Tables lay out the essential structure of *year by year* Scripture chronology, which is explained in comprehensive detail in my other book, The *Scroll of Biblical Chronology and Prophecy*.* The truth we have discovered about the death and resurrection of Messiah enable us to discover and solve mysterious sticking points of overall scripture chronology. The inclusion of the sabbatical year institution in the Daniel 9 prophecy leads the chronologist to obvious solutions that have eluded the Church since it put the Torah and Prophets on the back shelf. Also the fruit of our research has enabled us to correct the careless errs of generations of past chronologists working without the benefit of a correct understanding of the Passion or Daniel 9.

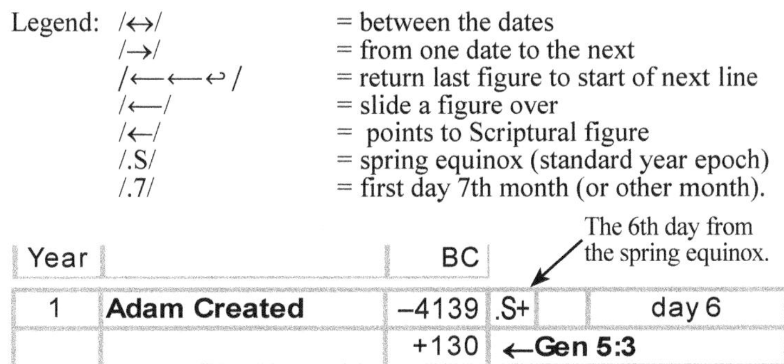

Legend:

/↔/	= between the dates
/→/	= from one date to the next
/←←↩/	= return last figure to start of next line
/⟵/	= slide a figure over
/←/	= points to Scriptural figure
/.S/	= spring equinox (standard year epoch)
/.7/	= first day 7th month (or other month).

The 6th day from the spring equinox.

Year		BC			
1	**Adam Created**	−4139	.S+		day 6
		+130	←**Gen 5:3**		

The miscalculation of just one year has cost chronologists the chance to synchronize the sabbatical and Jubilee institution with creation. Suspecting that it should synchronize enables us to catch the error before it happens. It is incorrect to say that Adam's year of age 1 is the 1st year of the world. Age refers to completed years, and indicates how many years of life have been completed in the year after they are completed. *Proof:* Adding 1 year to −4139.S+ makes the start of the first year of age −4138.S for Adam. From −4139.S+→ −4138.S is the 0th year of his age before being a whole year old. But this 0th year of Adam's age is the first year of the world. The first year of the world begins at creation: −4139.S. The first year of Adam is counted starting in −4138.S.‡ Some chronologists add in a 0th year of the world, but this does not fix the problem. Creation starts the first year of the world, and a year later starts Adam's first year of age. Age means "years completed." Counting the year of the world starts with 1, and the counting must show which year the counting is currently on. If the year from −4139.S→ −4138.S is not year one, then the counting of the seven year Sabbatical cycle and forty-nine year Jubilee will not be correct.† Other chronologists equate year one of the world with age one of Adam. This too is incorrect because it counts a full year of age before the full year is completed. The reader should observe that the 130th year of Adam is the 131st year of the world (see below). This is an easy way to detect the error in the work of others. If year 131 of the world is not the 130th year of Adam's age in the chronology, then the chronology is flawed at the very start. We have avoided this error because understanding Daniel 9

* Since renamed to *The Scroll of Biblical Chronology and Ancient Near Eastern History*, Vol. I and Vol. II. † See page 406 note †.

‡ Please note that −4139.S is not astronomers notation, and does not refer to 4138 BC. It refers to 4139 BC.

and Yeshua's death and resurrection has made us sensitive to the precision required by the sabbatical year.

Year		BC					
131	**Seth born**	−4009	.S		↔	−4008	.S
		+105	**←Gen 5:6**				

Seth was born between the limits. Scripture does not give his actual month and day of birth. The Scriptural chronology implicitly normalizes the birth year to the current standard year when it means to build on it further. This means that the standardized age will increment with the next spring equinox and not the birth day. Stating that Seth "lived 105 years" means there were 105 spring equinoxes between Seth's birth and Enosh's birth. Thus, if Seth was born just a few days before −4008.S, he will "lived" one year in these standardized years at the spring equinox of −4008.S. What the Scripture is really saying when Adam "lived 130 years" is that 130 spring equinoxes passed since his creation (not counting the spring equinox five days before his creation), and what Seth "lived 105 years" means is that there were just 105 spring equinoxes in his life.† Thus these standardized years should not be confused with birthday years of completed age. For the two to be equal Seth would have had to been born moments after the spring equinox of −4009.S. Only by understanding the chronology this way can it be unambiguously built without the need to know the month and day of each person's birth. Again, paying attention to the literal precision of Passion Chronology, e.g. "three days and three nights," "after three days," and "first of the Sabbaths," makes us sensitive to these other chronology problems and enables us to solve them.

236	**Enosh born**	−3904	.S		↔	−3903	.S
		+90	**←Gen 5:9**				
326	**Kenan born**	−3814	.S		↔	−3813	.S
		+70	**←Gen 5:12**				
396	**Mahalalel born**	−3744	.S		↔	−3743	.S
		+65	**←Gen 5:15**				
461	**Jared born**	−3679	.S		↔	−3678	.S
		+162	**←Gen 5:18**				
623	**Enoch born**	−3517	.S		↔	−3516	.S
		+65	**←Gen 5:21**				
688	**Methuselah born**	−3452	.S		↔	−3451	.S
		+187	**←Gen 5:25**				
875	**Lamech born**	−3265	.S		↔	−3264	.S
		+182	**←Gen 5:28**				
1057	**Noah born**	−3083	.S		↔	−3082	.S
	born after II.17	−3083	II	18	↔	−3082	II.17
		+599	**←Gen 7:11**				

The deluge began in the 600th year of the life of Noah. As explained, the 1st year of Adam he was age 0. In his 600th year Noah was 599 years old just as Adam was 1 year old in his 2nd year of life. Per Gen. 7:11 we have to add 599 to obtain the correct figure. In the 599th year of age, Noah was "in the 600th year." Gen. 7:6 does refer to the 600th year of age, but this is after the commencement of the deluge leading to the conclusion that his birth date was sometime between the 17th day of month 2

† i.e. so far as his son was born.

and the end of the 40 days deluge.† "And Noah is a son of six hundred years when the deluge had been waters upon the earth" (Gen. 7:6). Whereas as the start of the deluge was "in the 600th year of the life of Noah," which is to say he was age 599 (Gen. 7:11). The Genesis chronicler was counting a new year of age at each spring equinox, but as it turns out the ark log stated that Noah was 600 years old after the start of the deluge and before the end of it, according to his actual birth date. The chronicler therefore decided to state that the deluge began in the 600th year of the life of Noah (agreeing with his spring equinox method), knowing that he would reach a full 600 years sometime from the 2nd to 40th day of the deluge. By stating it the way he did, the chronicler avoided having to explain all the details I have explained here about the ark log basing Gen. 7:6 on the actual birth date of Noah rather than on the standardized year.

1656	**Noah's 600th Year**	−2484	.3		↔	−2483	.3
1657	Flood II.17, 600th Yr	−2483	.2	17			
		+150d	←**Gen 7:24**				
1657	**Ark Rests on Ararat**	**−2483**	**.7**	**17**			
	1st Year after Flood	−2483	.3	27	→	−2482	.26
1658	2nd Year after Flood	−2482	.3	27	→	−2481	.26

3rd mon

The first year after the flood is reckoned to begin with 41st day when the rain was quit. In modern times the first anniversary of an event is enumerated one year after the memorialized event. However, in good Semitic style, the counting of anniversaries is inclusive. Thus one year after −2483.III.27 marks the second anniversary. That this assumption is the norm is proved from the fact that the second anniversary after the Exodus is enumerated one full year after the Exodus, (Exo. 40:17; Num 1:1; 9:1; 10:11). Thus "two years after the flood" enumerates the actual ending of it with the first anniversary, and one year later with the "second anniversary." This sort of counting also lends itself to the start of a new era. Naturally one wants to count the first year with 1 and not with 0. Noah and his Sons were smart enough to know this, and this era continued as long as he lived for 350 years (Gen. 9:28). Thus the 602nd year of Noah's life synchronized with the 2nd year after the flood, and the limits of it are −2482.III.27 to −2481.III. 26. Now we have to decide which side of the spring equinox of −2481.S Arphaxad was born as this second year covers parts of two standard years. Being sensitive to the sabbatical periods helps to solve this problem. Knowing that the seven years of plenty, and the seven years of famine synchronize with the seven year cycles during Joseph's rule over Egypt solves this ambiguity. Arphaxad was necessarily born before −2481.S. Also, starting with Arphaxad, the method must return to standardized years. Also to be observed is that even though Noah's 600th-601st factual years are offset to the standardized year, there is still a one to one correspondence between elapsed standardized years and his age. To maintain this 1:1 correspondence Arphaxad's standardized birth year must correspond to −2482.S→ −2481.S.

1658	**Arphaxad born**	−2482	.3	27	↔	−2481	.S
		+35	←**Gen 11:12**				
1693	**Salah born**	−2447	.S		↔	−2446	.S
		+30	←**Gen 11:14**				
1723	**Eber born**	−2417	.S		↔	−2416	.S
		+34	←**Gen 11:16**				

† The deluge chronology is complicated by the frequent use of dischronological features (such as waw remote) wherein the timeline is reset. In English we would use a pluperfect, e.g. "he had..." to show a statement further back in the timeline. In Hebrew only the context remains to show this. Originally there was likely a now lost variation in pronunciation of waw consecutive (וַ, *wa* = THEN) to show a timeline reset, e.g. וָו = וָ,

continued on page 412

1757	**Peleg born**	−2383	.S		↔	−2382	.S
		+30	**←Gen 11:18**				
1787	**Reu born**	−2353	.S		↔	−2352	.S
		+32	**←Gen 11:20**				
1819	**Serug born**	−2321	.S		↔	−2320	.S
		+30	**←Gen 11:22**				
1849	**Nahor born**	−2291	.S		↔	−2290	.S
		+29	**←Gen 11:24**				
1878	**Terah born**	−2262	.S		↔	−2261	.S
		+205	**←Gen 11:32**				
2083	**205th Year of Terah**	−2057	.S		→	−2056	.S
		−75	**←Gen 12:4**				

The book of Acts clarifies that Abraham left Haran after his father died. Again, we are using standardized years, and it must be realized that there is some offset with the factual years of age. However, there is a 1:1 correspondence between the factual years and the standardized years. For without this assumption, the scriptural chronology would not be computable. It is evident that it was made to be computable, so the assumption is proved valid. Further Abraham's 75th year = Terah's 205th year. For it is not reasonable to assume that Abraham had a birthday between his father's death and his departure. To keep the chronology computable always requires all the facts and the most probable assumption to go with it.

2008	**Abram born**	−2132	.S		↔	−2131	.S
		+100	**←Gen 21:5**				
2108	**Isaac born**	−2032	.S				
		+60	**←Gen 25:26**				
2168	**Jacob & Esau born**	−1972	.S		↔	−1971	.S
		+130	**←Gen 47:9**				
2298	**Jacob to Egypt**	−1842	.S		↔	−1842	.7
		+5	**←Gen 45:6**				
2303	**Famine Ends**	−1837	.7				
		−14	**←Gen 41:29-30**				
2289	**Abundance Begins**	−1851	.7				
		−30	**←Gen 41:46**				
2259	**Joseph born**	−1881	.S		↔	−1880	.S
		+110	**←Gen 50:26**				
2369	**Joseph died**	−1771	.S		↔	−1770	.S
2108	**Isaac born**	**−2032**	**.S**	**See Above**			
		+400	**←Gen 15:13**				

The dating of the 400 years from Isaac's birth is proved by the fact that four generations spanned the time in Egypt, 1. Jacob, 2. Levi, 3. Jocabed, 4. Moses. The 400 years includes the time that Abraham's "seed," Isaac, sojourned in

Canaan before Jacob went to Egypt. Israel was only in Egypt 210 years. The dating of 430 years in Exodus is from 30 years before Isaac was born, from the time that Abraham left Ur of the Chaldees, and adds the number of years that Abraham sojourned before Isaac was born. Other chronologers have assumed that the 400 years begins with the "weaning" of Isaac at age 5. This *ad hoc* assumption substitutes a questionable legal definition of "seed" for a factual and legal definition fulfilled at the birth of Isaac, and corrupts the Sabbatical alignment. The five year difference is to be located between Abraham's sojourn out of Ur of the Chaldees and Terah's becoming too old to travel so that they had to stop in Haran for those five years.

2508	Exodus	-1632	.N.15	↔	-1591	.N
		+40	Exodus 16:35			
2548	Entry into Canaan	-1592	.N.10	↔	-1591	.N
		+6	See Scroll Books			
2554	End of War & Land divided	-1586	.N	↔	-1585	.N
		+20	See Scroll Books			
2574	Mesopotamian Oppression	-1566	.N	↔	-1565	.N
		+8	←Judges 3:8			
2582	Othniel	-1558	.N	↔	-1557	.N
		+40	Judges 3:11			
2622	Eglon of Moab	-1518	.N	↔	-1517	.N
		+18	Judges 3:14			
2640	Ehud & Shamgar	-1500	.N	↔	-1499	.N
		+80	Judges 3:30b			
2720	Jabin of Hazor	-1420	.N	↔	-1419	.N
		+20	Judges 4:3			
2740	Deborah	-1400	.N	↔	-1399	.N
		+40	Judges 5:31			
2780	Midian	-1360	.N	↔	-1359	.N
		+7	Judges 6:1			
2787	Gideon	-1353	.N	↔	-1352	.N
		+40	Judges 8:28			
2827	Abimelech	-1313	.N	↔	-1312	.N
		+3	Judges 9:22			
2830	Tola	-1310	.N	↔	-1309	.N
		+23	Judges 10:2			
2853	Jair	-1287	.N	↔	-1286	.N
		+22	Judges 10:3			
2875	Ammon	-1265	.N	↔	-1264	.N
		+18	Judges 10:6-8			
2893	Jepthah	-1247	.N	↔	-1246	.N
		+6	Judges 12:7			
2899	Ibzan	-1241	.N	↔	-1240	.N
		+7	Judges 12:8			
2906	Elon	-1234	.N	↔	-1233	.N
		+10	Judges 12:11			

The chronology between the Exodus and the building of the first Temple contains two unknown periods. The first is the number of years after the settlement of the land up to the first oppression. The second is the number of Samuel's years as a Judge. The time periods from the first oppression to the the accession of Samuel add up to 450 years, a figure convieniently confirmed in Acts 13:20.

During this period all of the oppressions occurred, which add up to 134 years. Many sum this up to 114 years or 111 years, but they failed to count the 3 years of Abimelech or the 20 years of the second Philistine oppression. A full count of 134 years combined with the Judgeships is necessary to arrive at 450 years.

As explained on pages 415 and following there were 480 non-oppression years from the Exodus to the 4th year of Solomon. Before the first oppression 40 years are accounted for in the wilderness and 6 years for the conquest. The latter figure can be derived from details about Caleb's life. After Samuel we have 40 years for Saul, 40 for David, and 4 for Solomon. The sum of the known non-oppression years is 46 + 84 or 130 years. During the 450 year period there are 316 additonal non-oppression years (450 - 134 = 316). Putting these two figures together accounts for 446 non-oppression years, which is 34 years short of 480. We may conclude that the years from the settlement of the land to the first oppression combined with those of Samuel's Judgeship make 34 years total. The problem is how to divide them up.

The full answer to this question is given in *The Scroll of Biblical Chronology and Ancient Near Eastern History,* Vol. II. Here a summary will suffice. Israel failed to observe 70 land Sabbaths during the periods when she was out of fellowship with the Almighty. The calculation of this number of Sabbath years changes with different permutations splitting up the 34 years between Samuel and the Elders period. What must also be factored in is a demographic and population study of Israel. When all the factors are put together a unique solution is obtained: 20 of the years go to the Elders period before the first oppression, and 14 go to Samuel. The *Scroll* book also deals with the 300 years of Judges 11:26.

From page 409: *uwá* = AND HAD < *wəhawáh* וְהָוָה. The two ה 's are dropped as is commonly done in Hebrew, and the first is dropped with its vowel also, as is commonly done, e.g. Ye<u>ho</u>shua reduced to Y'eshua, leaving: וָו. This then becomes: וָּו = וָ. So *wə<u>ha</u>wáh > wəwá > uwá.* A waw conjunctive *u* compounded with 'waw consecutive' signals that the *wá* is a pluperfect (i.e. past perfect) contraction of the helping verb הָוָה. Since the consonant text does not add vowels or write out double letters, this feature is indistinguishable from waw consecutive in the consonant text. It differs from the regular perfect in that (1) it cannot be present or future perfect or gnomic, (2) it is only a helping tense modifier imparting no person or number, (3) it imparts an imperfective aspect 'had been' congruent to the imperfect. This is a variation of J.D. Michaelis' theory (1745) so as to distinguish between *wá* remote and *wa+ć* consecutive, signaling this by a waw conjunctive: *uwá.* Examples of waw remote: (1) Gen. 25:34, "SO Esau HAD BEEN despising the birthright" (וַיִּבֶז). (2) Gen. 29:18, "AND Jacob HAD BEEN loving Rachel" (וַיֶּאֱהַב). (3) Gen 29:24, "AND Laban HAD BEEN giving Zilpah his maidservant to her" (וַיִּתֵּן). (4) Gen. 37:6, "AND he HAD BEEN saying to them...." (וַיֹּאמֶר). (5) Gen. 48:13, "AND Joseph HAD BEEN taking the two of them...." (וַיִּקַּח). (6) Josh. 4:12, "AND the sons of Reuben and the sons of Gad and the half tribe of Manasseh HAD BEEN crossing over" (וַיַּעַבְרוּ). (7) Gen. 7:7, "AND Noah HAD BEEN going...into the Ark from the face of the waters of the deluge" (וַיָּבֹא). (8) Gen. 7:15, 17 (וַיִּרְבּוּ), 20 (וַיְכֻסּוּ HAD BEEN GETTING COVERED), 23, 24; 8:2 (HAD BEEN GETTING STOPPED), 3b (AND HAD BEEN SLACKING), etc. Note: that even without J.D. Michaelis' theory or my variation of it, we would have to translate these passages dischronologically to make sense in the context. I do believe the complex calculus required of the contextual backup system strongly suggests the existence of an original (and primarty) disambiguation feature that did not require such close analysis of context to acheive clear communication.

2916	**Abdon**	−1224	.N				
		+8	**←Judges 12:14**				
2924	**Philistines**	−1216	.N				
		+40	**←Judges 13:1**				
2964	**Eli**	−1176	.N				
		+40	**←1Sam 4:18**				
3003	**Philistines**	−1137	.7				
		+20	**←1Sam 7:2**				
3023	**Samuel**	−1117	.7				
		+14	**←See Scroll**				
3037	**Saul**	−1103	.7				
		+40	**←Acts 13:21**				
3077	**David**	−1063	.7				
		+40	**←1Chron. 29:27**				
3117	**Solomon**	−1023	.7				
		+40	**←2Chron. 9:30**				
3157	**Rehoboam**	−983	.7				
		+17	**←1Kings 14:21**				
3174	**Abijah**	−966	.7				
		+3	**←1Kings 15:2**				
3177	**Asa**	−963	.7				
		+41	**←1Kings 15:10**				
3217	**Jehoshaphat**	−922	.7				
		+18	**←2Kings 3:1**				
3236	**Jehoram**	−904	.S		↔	−903	.S
		+12	**←2Kings 3:1**				
		−1	**overlap with next**				
3247	**Jehu**	−893	.S		↔	−892	.S
		+28	**←2Kings 10:36**				
3275	**Jehoahaz**	−865	.S				
		+17	**←2Kings 13:1**				
		−1	**overlap with next**				
3291	**Jehoash**	−849	.S				
		+16	**←2Kings 13:10**				
3307	**Jeroboam II**	−833	.S				
		+27	**←2Kings 15:1**				
		−1	**overlap with next**				
3333	**Uzziah (1 of 52)**	−807	.S		↔	−807	.7
	(2-52 of 52)	**2Kings 15:2**				+51	

3384	**Jotham**	−756	.7	←←		−756	.7
		+16	**←2Kings 15:33**				
3400	**Ahaz**	−740	.7				
		+16	**←2Kings 16:2**				
		−1	**overlap with next**				
3415	**Hezekiah**	−725	.7				
		+29	**←2Kings 18:2**				
		−1	**overlap with next**				
3443	**Manasseh**	−697	.7				
		+55	**←2Kings 21:1**				
3498	**Amon**	−642	.7				
		+2	**←2Kings 21:19**				
3500	**Josiah**	−640	.7				
	(1-30 of 31)	+30	**←2Kings 22:1**				
	(31 of 31)	−610	.7		→	−609	.5
3531	**Jehoahaz**	−609	.5	←←		↩	
		+0.25	**←2Kings 23:31**				
3531	**Jehoiakm (acc)**	−609	.8		→	-608	.7
3532	**Jehoiakim**	-608	.7	←←		↩	
	(1-10 of 11)	+10	**←2Kings 23:36**				
	(11 of 11)	−598	.7			−597	.11
3542	**Jehoiachin**	−597	.11	←←		↩	
		+0.25	**←2Kings 24:8**				
3543	**Exile (1 of 70)**	−597	.S			−597	.7
	(2 of 70)	−597	.7			↩	
	(3 of 70)	−596	.7				
	(4 of 70)	−595	.7				
	(5 of 70)	−594	.7		→	−593	.7
3547	**Ezekiel 1:1**	−593	.4	5			

Ezekiel gives the figure of 390 years for the sin of Israel. This spans the time between Jeroboam's rebellion and the date of the prophecy. |−983.7−593.7| = 390 years. (Jeroboam was made king of the Northern Kingdom shortly after Rehoboam became king of Judah). I do not explain all the details in the intervening chronology here because the long number of 390 years verifies that it is correct. The Ezekiel 1:1 date is anchored in the astronomically verified Neo-Babylonian chronology. Since the Scripture uses dates from the reign of Nebuchadnezzar, we may assume that the astronomical foundation thereof is completely sound. Otherwise, the scripture would not use the dates. For that would be to introduce err into the Scripture.

We have secured this chronology as a result of correcting the death and resurrection of Messiah and discovering how Daniel 9 works with it. We may also show that the Jubilee cycle is correctly synchronized (see Appendix VII, page 477) .

The following chart accounts for the 480 years of 1 Kings 6:1 They key to this passage is that "going out of Egypt" refers to the Passover memorial, which Israel did not observe nationally when YHWH allowed them to be oppressed by foreign nations. The 480 years does not count 134 years of foreign oppression when Israel did not observe the passover as a nation.

Era		Yrs	Ref	
Kadesh		2	Numbers	10:11
Wand.	+	38	Deut.	2:14
Conquest	+	6	Joshua	14:10
Elders	+	20	Judges	11:26
Othniel	+	40	Judges	3:11
Ehud	+	80	Judges	3:30
Deborah	+	40	Judges	5:31
Gideon	+	40	Judges	8:28
Tola	+	23	Judges	10:2
Jair	+	22	Judges	10:3
Jephthah	+	6	Judges	12:7
Ibzan	+	7	Judges	12:8
Elon	+	10	Judges	12:11
Abdon	+	8	Judges	12:13-14
Eli	+	40	1st Sam	4:18
Samuel	+	14	Computed	
Saul	+	40	Acts	13:21
David	+	40	1st Chron	29:27
Solomon	+	4	1st Kings	6:1
Total =		480	1st Kings	6:1

The Hebrew text of 1Kings 6:1 translates literally, "Then it is in eighty year and four hundreds year of going-out of sons of Israel from land of Egypt ..." The key phrase is "going out" (לְצֵאת) *le-tsayt.* This word became a technical phrase for the 15th of Nisan in every year. That is, when the 15th of Nisan was celebrated by Israel, it was called the "going out." Thus 480 years of the "going out" counts the number of times the nation celebrated Passover. That the 480 years do not count the times of oppression was noted by earlier chronologers who realized that scriptural chronology would be contradictory without omitting 134 years of oppression.*

Conclusion of the Matter

We have come to the realization that the Passion is not to be explained by Easter Sunday, but by the Passover and the first of the Sabbaths after it. Several chronologists did figure out that the 480 years did not count the oppressions. But they did not know why. It was essentially a gestalt factor to make the numbers work right. The numbers did work right. Now we can appreciate why the numbers work correctly when the oppressions are omitted. It is because someone in Israel was counting the number of national Passovers. This factor cannot be discovered unless one is first made sensitive to the importance of the Passover to Israel.

Pagan influences in Easter make people insensitive to the truth. Some points in scripture are obscure because they are liable to other interpretations less parsimonious when all the facts are considered. Idolatry, even dabbling in it, is motivated by a less then zealous appreciation for the exact truth of things. It would be plain that to have 480 years between the Exodus and Solomon's 4th year requires the ignoring certain biblical long eras. Those so dulled by idolatry are happy with this situation because idolatry tolerates falsehood alongside truth. Dismissing a few biblical numbers is essentially the same thing.

YHWH has obscured a few things to encourage us to seek out the exact truth of the matter, and to keep those who disagree with it from demolishing it by providing them with a possible (but less parsimonious) interpretation. It is the one who seeks to remove the contradictions and prays for the solutions that gets the prize and the blessing. False traditions are a huge hindrance. Christmas and Easter

* This point has become more obvious since the first edition of this book. It so happens that Egypt is called "the house of bondage" multiple times in the Torah. This makes the term Egypt a synonym for "the house of bondage." To break the cipher only requires us to substitute "house of bondage" in 1 Kings 6:1 to obtain the deciphered sense: "In the 480th year...of the going out from the house of bondage...." The going out of Egypt

tolerate the inconsistency and blind the eyes of those honoring these days to the real truth of matters.

Likewise, the honoring of Sunday blinds one to the Sabbatical institutions of Scripture. We should not so blind ourselves. The Sabbath is a blessing, and so also the sabbatical and Jubilee years. For these reinforce and support our faith in Messiah. Honoring Sunday is a curse. For it is based on a lie, and we have seen that things based on lies have no foundations, and that they do not hold up under examination. A faith without a foundation is bound to fail. Messiah has ransomed us from vain religion.

---

thus is the theme of the Passover, going out of the house of bondage. Israel went out of bondage and then back into bondage when they served other gods. The 480 years omit the time for going into bondage because they are years for going out of bondage. Josephus is in close agreement with this result:

"The entire *fifth* period in Josephus, from the Exodus out of Egypt to the building of the temple, [was] 592 [years] at first, and as corrected at last by Josephus himself, [was] 612 years" (William Whiston, Dissertation 5, *The Works of Josephus*). This last figure is exactly one year short of the correct 613 years (cf. Josephus' *Antiquities*, Book 20.230 and Book 8.61. The difference between the two figures is exactly 20 years (612–592 = 20). The 612 figure is repeated in *Against Apion*, book 2.19.

Era	Josephus	Correcting Josephus	Actual	Diff
Wilderness	40		40	
Joshua+Elders	25 (5.117)	Gain 1 from Deficit A	26	−1
Anarchy	18 (6.84)	Lose 18 to Saul	0	18
Cushan	8		8	
Othniel	40		40	
Moab	18		18	
Ehud	80		80	
Shamgar	0 (5.197)		0	
Jabin	20		20	
Deborah	40		40	
Midian	7		7	
Gideon	40		40	
Abimelech	3		3	
Tola	[23] (Jud. 10:2)			23
Jair	22		22	
Ammonites	18		18	
Jephthah	6		6	
Ibzan	7		7	
Elon	10		10	
Abdon	[8] (Jud. 12:14)		8	
Philistines I	40		40	
Samson	0 (5.316)		0	
Eli	40 (5.359)	Lose 0.5 to Samuel	39.5	0.5
Philistines II	0 (6.18)	Gain 20 from Deficit B	20	−20
Samuel	12 (6.294)	Gain 1 from Deficit C Gain 0.5 from Solomon Gain 0.5 from Eli	14	−2

Era	Josephus	Correcting Josephus	Actual	Diff
Saul	20 (6.378)	Gain 18 from Anarchy Gain 2 from Deficit A	40	−20
David	40		40	
Solomon	4	Lose 0.5 to Joshua	3.5	0.5
Total of Figures	**589**		**613**	**−24**
Deficit A	3	Add 2 to Saul Add 1 to Joshua		2 1
Jos. 1st Total	**592**			
Deficit B	20	Add 20 to Philistines II		20
Jos. 2nd Total	**612**			
Deficit C	1	Add 1 to Samuel		1
Totals	**613**		**613**	**0**

Figures in [ ] are omitted due to copiest mistakes and are restored using Judges (cf. Whiston). References are given to *Antiquities* where there is some difference to be noted. The critical parts, where the Scripture does not itself give a sum of years, are shaded grey, where there might be some disagreements about the computation thereof. The Anarchy period in Josephus' chronology was motivated by the assumption that 25 years (26) was not long enough for the time leading up to the first oppression. This period contains the appendix in the book of Judges. These 18 years had to be robbed from Saul, whose reign is put at 40 years by Paul, and also by "a son of 40 years" in cipher for his son, Ishbosheth. They have to be restored to Saul.

We have to revise Whiston's interpretations of Josephus' figures, (1) that Josephus meant to give Samson as a period to be added after the Philistines. He does not say so or give a table showing so. Everyone knew that Samson judged "in the days of the Philistines" (Judges 15:20). Accordingly, there is 100% overlap, and 0 contribution to the overall time period. (2) That Samuel judged 32.5 years. Josephus says 12 years independently, and 18 years overlap with Saul (6.294). So only 12 years count. (3) that Eli judged 20 years. Josephus says 40 (5.359). (4) That Solomon reigned 3.5. Jospehus only states the 4th year. (5) Whiston's total 610 is found nowhere in Josephus, but it does add up Whiston's figures correctly.

Josephus' actual figures add up to 589 (nowhere stated), but Josephus gives 592 as the total (8.61). In book 7.68 Josephus gives 515 years from Joshua's commencement of the wars of Canaan to David's conquest of Jerusalem. This figure also completes to 592 years (i.e. 40+515+33+4). Thus it is clear that the total 592 is given by Josephus for the first version of his chronology. Between 589 and 592 three years are missing. That is, Josephus' subtotals add up to three less than his total. These three years are restored under "**Deficit A**."

The final version of Josephus' chronology has 612 years. This clearly stems from the inclusion of 20 years following the Philistine victory during which they captured the Ark (Philistines II). Adding 20 to 592 is 612. And this is noted by Whiston himself, "As to the former number, 20 years , from the death of Eli to the victory of Samuel, it seems not to have been attended to by Josephus, when he stated Samuel's government, before the anointing of Saul, as 12 years. They were only implied in the ark's being 20 years at Kirjathjearim after the death of Eli, before the Israelites brought it to Mispeh, just before Samuel's victory at Eben-ezer. Which though it certainly implies that Samuel's government, or the interregnum before it, must then have been full 20 years, and this some considerable time before Saul was anointed king; yet were not those 20 years expressed either in the catalogue of the judges, or under the servitudes; and so might at first be easily overlooked by Josephus. Though perhaps it was the later observation of these 20 years, which he had formerly omitted, that obliged him at last to increase his number for this entire period from 592 to 612 years." These 20 years are restored under **"Deficit B."**

There is no evidence that Josephus tried to account for the 480 the non-servitude years of 1 Kings 6:1. But we may do so two ways and find him lacking one more year: (1) In the final version of his chronology, there are 134 years in the house of bondage. Adding these to 479 comes to 613. The reason to add 479 instead of 480 is because the Temple project was begun at the beginning of the 480th year. (2) We may add the non-servitude years directly, i.e. 475. Restore 3 years (Deficit A), i.e. 478, and we see we are still one year short of 479. So 612 + 1 = 613. The one year is restored with "**Deficit C.**"

Josephus' <u>net errors</u> are accounted as follows. Deficit A: Three years lacking from the actual sum 589. These are paid back, one for Joshua, and two for the anarchy. Deficit B: Twenty years Philistines II, corrected by Josephus himself. Deficit C: One year due to failure to check the 480 years, paid back to Samuel. Josephus' <u>distribution errors</u> (zero net after deficit corrections are applied) are (1) shifting 20 years from Saul to make the Anarchy, which should be transferred back to Saul. (2) shifting one more year from Samuel, one half of it each given to Eli and Solomon, which should be paid back.

It should be noted that the Acts 13:20 subchronology in Josephus' first version adds to 430 years, and in his final version to 450. The actual sum is 449.5. On this interval are 134 oppression years and a net of 315.5 non-oppression years. Joshua-Elders = x; Samuel = y. Thus 479 = 40 + x + 315.5 + y + 40 + 40 + 3.5,

Appendix I: Roman Consul List

The Roman Consul List starts in 509 B.C., but here are listed those from B.C. 100, century by century, to A.D. 541. The Roman use of lists to date events is more accurate than the use of numbers because the historians had to write out the consular names from written master lists. This eliminated the chance of simple digit mistakes. Further, the consular list could not be committed to memory. Try remembering the last 10 presidents of the United States in order, which cover 51 years. Then consider that in the Roman Consular lists, 10 names take at most 5 years. This means that the Roman method only worked with well kept written records.

Besides dating accessions and deaths of Emperors in terms of consuls, Roman historians kept track of the number of years each reigned.

First Century B.C.

AUC	**BC**	**First consul**	**Second consul**
654	100	C. Marius VI	L. Valerius Flaccus
655	99	M. Antonius	A. Postumius Albinus
656	98	Q. Caecilius Metellus Nepos	T. Didius
657	97	Cn. Cornelius Lentulus	P. Licinius Crassus
658	96	Cn. Domitius Ahenobarbus	C. Cassius Longinus
659	95	L. Licinius Crassus	Q. Mucius Scaevola
660	94	C. Coelius Caldus	L. Domitius Ahenobarbus
661	93	C. Valerius Flaccus	M. Herennius
662	92	C. Claudius Pulcher	M. Perperna
663	91	L. Marcius Philippus	Sex. Iulius Caesar
664	90	L. Iulius Caesar	P. Rutilius Lupus
665	89	Cn. Pompeius Strabo	L. Porcius Cato
666	88	L. Cornelius Sulla Felix	Quintus Pompeius Rufus
667	87	Cn. Octavius	L. Cornelius Cinna
	suff.		L. Cornelius Merula
668	86	L. Cornelius Cinna II	C. Marius VII
	suff.		L. Valerius Flaccus
669	85	L. Cornelius Cinna III	Cn. Papirius Carbo
670	84	Cn. Papirius Carbo II	L. Cornelius Cinna IV
671	83	L. Cornelius Scipio Asiaticus	C. Norbanus
672	82	C. Marius	Cn. Papirius Carbo III
673	81	M. Tullius Decula	Cn. Cornelius Dolabella
674	80	L. Cornelius Sulla Felix II	Q. Caecilius Metellus Pius
675	79	P. Servilius Vatia Isauricus	Ap. Claudius Pulcher

and 479 = x + y + 439, and x + y = 40, i.e. 26 + 14 = 40. Possible origin of Deficit C: The year of the Exodus was 2508+n, and the 479th year out of bondage 3120+n, where n is an unknown offset between Josephus chronology and the actual (where n=0). Thus to compute the duration 3120+n–(2508+n) = 3120+n–n–2508 = 3120 – 2508 = 612. Thus Josephus' source may have had had the right relative chronology, but the duration was wrongly calculated. It is necessary to add +1 to obtain an inclusive count: 3120–2508+1=613, from the start of the Exodus year to the end of the 479th year.

676	78	M. Aemilius Lepidus	Q. Lutatius Catulus
677	77	D. Iunius Brutus	Mam. Aemilius Lepidus Livianus
678	76	Cn. Octavius	C. Scribonius Curio
679	75	L. Octavius	C. Aurelius Cotta
680	74	L. Licinius Lucullus	M. Aurelius Cotta
681	73	M. Terentius Varro Lucullus	C. Cassius Longinus
682	72	L. Gellius Publicola	Cn. Cornelius Lentulus Clodianus
683	71	P. Cornelius Lentulus Sura	Cn. Aufidius Orestes
684	70	Cn. Pompeius Magnus	M. Licinius Crassus Dives
685	69	Q. Hortensius Hortalus	Q. Caecilius Metellus Creticus
686	68	L. Caecilius Metellus	Q. Marcius Rex
	suff.	Servilius Vatia (only designation)	
687	67	C. Calpurnius Piso	M'. Acilius Glabrio
688	66	M'. Aemilius Lepidus	L. Volcacius Tullus
689	65	L. Aurelius Cotta	L. Manlius Torquatus
690	64	L. Iulius Caesar	C. Marcius Figulus
691	63	M. Tullius Cicero	C. Antonius Hibrida
692	62	D. Iunius Silanus	L. Licinius Murena
693	61	M. Pupius Piso Frugi Calpurnianus	M. Valerius Messalla Niger
694	60	Q. Caecilius Metellus Celer	L. Afranius
695	59	C. Iulius Caesar	M. Calpurnius Bibulus
696	58	L. Calpurnius Piso Caesoninus	A. Gabinius
697	57	P. Cornelius Lentulus Spinther	Q. Caecilius Metellus Nepos
698	56	Cn. Cornelius Lentulus Marcellinus	L. Marcius Philippus
699	55	Cn. Pompeius Magnus II	M. Licinius Crassus Dives II
700	54	L. Domitius Ahenobarbus	Ap. Claudius Pulcher
701	53	Cn. Domitius Calvinus	M. Valerius Messalla Rufus
702	52	Cn. Pompeius Magnus III	Q. Caecilius Metellus Pius Scipio
703	51	Ser. Sulpicius Rufus	M. Claudius Marcellus
704	50	L. Aemilius Lepidus Paullus	C. Claudius Marcellus Minor
705	49	C. Claudius Marcellus Maior	L. Cornelius Lentulus Crus
706	48	C. Iulius Caesar II	P. Servilius Isauricus
707	47	Q. Fufius Calenus	P. Vatinius
708	46	C. Iulius Caesar III	M. Aemilius Lepidus
709	45	C. Iulius Caesar IV	*without colleague*
	suff.	Q. Fabius Maximus	C. Trebonius
	suff.	C. Caninius Rebilus	
710	44	C. Iulius Caesar V	M. Antonius
	suff.	P. Cornelius Dolabella	
711	43	C. Vibius Pansa Caetronianus	A. Hirtius
	suff.	C. Iulius Caesar (Octavianus)	Q. Pedius
	suff.	C. Carrinas	P. Ventidius Bassus
712	42	M. Aemilius Lepidus II	L. Munatius Plancus
713	41	L. Antonius Pietas	P. Servilius Isauricus II
714	40	Cn. Domitius Calvinus II	C. Asinius Pollio

	suff.	L. Cornelius Balbus	P. Canidius Crassus
715	39	L. Marcius Censorinus	C. Calvisius Sabinus
	suff.	C. Cocceius Balbus	P. Alfenus Varus
716	**38**	**Ap. Claudius Pulcher**	**C. Norbanus Flaccus**
	suff.	L. Cornelius Lentulus	L. Marcius Philippus
717	37	M. Vipsanius Agrippa	L. Caninius Gallus
	suff.		T. Statilius Taurus
718	36	L. Gellius Publicola	M. Cocceius Nerva
	suff.	L. Nonius Asprenas	Q. Marcius
719	35	Sex. Pompeius	L. Cornificius
	suff.	P. Cornelius Dolabella	T. Peducaeus
720	34	M. Antonius II	L. Scribonius Libo
	suff.	L. Sempronius Atratinus	
	suff.	Paullus Aemilius Lepidus	L. Decidius Saxa
	suff.		M. Herennius Picens
721	33	Imp. Caesar Divi f. II	L. Volcacius Tullus
	suff.	L. Autronius Paetus	
	suff.	L. Flavius	C. Fonteius Capito
	suff.	M. Acilius Glabrio	
	suff.	L. Vinicius	Q. Laronius
722	32	Cn. Domitius Ahenobarbus	C. Sosius
	suff.	L. Cornelius Cinna	M. Valerius Messalla
723	31	M. Antonius III (only in the east)	Imp. Caesar Divi f. III
	suff.	M. Valerius Messalla Corvinus	
	suff.	M. Titius	
	suff.	Cn. Pompeius	
724	30	Imp. Caesar Divi f. IV	M. Licinius Crassus
	suff.		C. Antistius Vetus
	suff.		M. Tullius Cicero
	suff.		L. Saenius
725	29	Imp. Caesar Divi f. V	Sex. Appuleius
	suff.		Potitus Valerius Messalla
726	28	Imp. Caesar Divi f. VI	M. Vipsanius Agrippa II
727	27	Imp. Caesar Divi f. Augustus VII	M. Vipsanius Agrippa III
728	26	Imp. Caesar Divi f. Augustus VIII	T. Statilius Taurus II
729	25	Imp. Caesar Divi f. Augustus IX	M. Iunius Silanus
730	24	Imp. Caesar Divi f. Augustus X	C. Norbanus Flaccus
731	23	Imp. Caesar Divi f. Augustus XI	A. Terentius Varro Murena
	suff.	L. Sestius Albanianus Quirinalis	Cn. Calpurnius Piso
732	22	M. Claudius Marcellus Aeserninus	L. Arruntius
733	21	M. Lollius	Q. Aemilius Lepidus
734	20	M. Appuleius	P. Silius Nerva
735	19	C. Sentius Saturninus	Q. Lucretius Vespillo

	suff.	M. Vinicius	
736	18	P. Cornelius Lentulus Marcellinus	Cn. Cornelius Lentulus
737	17	C. Furnius	C. Iunius Silanus
738	16	L. Domitius Ahenobarbus	P. Cornelius Scipio
	suff.		L. Tarius Rufus
739	15	M. Livius Drusus Libo	L. Calpurnius Piso
740	14	M. Licinius Crassus Frugi	Cn. Cornelius Lentulus Augur
741	13	Ti. Claudius Nero I	P. Quinctilius Varus
742	12	M. Valerius Messalla Appianus	P. Sulpicius Quirinius
	suff.	C. Valgius Rufus	L. Volusius Saturninus
	suff.	C. Caninius Rebilus	
743	11	Q. Aelius Tubero	Paullus Fabius Maximus
744	10	Africanus Fabius Maximus	Iullus Antonius
745	9	Nero Claudius Drusus	T. Quinctius Crispinus Sulpicianus
746	8	C. Marcius Censorinus	C. Asinius Gallus
747	7	Ti. Claudius Nero II	Cn. Calpurnius Piso
748	6	D. Laelius Balbus	C. Antistius Vetus
749	5	Imp. Caesar Divi f. Augustus XII	L. Cornelius Sulla
	suff.	L. Vinicius	Q. Haterius
	suff.	C. Sulpicius Galba	
750	4	C. Calvisius Sabinus	L. Passienus Rufus
	suff.	C. Caelius (Rufus?)	Galus Sulpicius
751	3	L. Cornelius Lentulus	M. Valerius Messalla Messallinus
752	2	Imp. Caesar Divi f. Augustus XIII	M. Plautius Silvanus
	suff.	C. Fufius Geminus	L. Caninius Gallus
	suff.	Q. Fabricius	
753	1	Cossus Cornelius Lentulus	L. Calpurnius Piso
	suff.	A. Plautius	A. Caecina Severus

First Century A.D.

AUC	AD	First consul	Second consul
754	1	C. Iulius Caesar	L. Aemilius Paullus
	suff.		M. Herennius Picens
755	2	P. Vinicius	P. Alfenus Varus
	suff.	P. Cornelius Lentulus Scipio	T. Quinctius Crispinus Valerianus
756	3	L. Aelius Lamia	M. Servilius
	suff.	P. Silius	L. Volusius Saturninus
757	4	Sex. Aelius Catus	C. Sentius Saturninus
	suff.	C. Clodius Licinus	Cn. Sentius Saturninus
758	5	L. Valerius Messalla Volesus	Cn. Cornelius Cinna Magnus
	suff.	C. Vibius Postumus	C. Ateius Capito
759	6	M. Aemilius Lepidus	L. Arruntius
	suff.		L. Nonius Asprenas
760	7	Q. Caecilius Metellus Creticus Silanus	A. Licinius Nerva Silianus

	suff.	Faustus (II) Cornelius Sulla	Lucilius Longus
761	8	M. Furius Camillus	Sex. Nonius Quinctilianus
	suff.	L. Apronius	A. Vibius Habitus
762	9	C. Poppaeus Sabinus	Q. Sulpicius Camerinus
	suff.	Q. Poppaeus Secundus	M. Papius Mutilus
763	10	P. Cornelius Dolabella	C. Iunius Silanus
	suff.	Ser. Cornelius Lentulus Maluginensis	Q. Iunius Blaesus
764	11	M'. Aemilius Lepidus	T. Statilius Taurus
	suff.	L. Cassius Longinus	
765	12	Germanicus Iulius Caesar	C. Fonteius Capito
	suff.		C. Visellius Varro
766	13	C. Silius[3]	L. Munatius Plancus
	suff.	A. Caecina Largus[3]	
767	**14**	**Sex. Pompeius**	**Sex. Appuleius**
768	15	Drusus Iulius Caesar (Jan.-Dec.)	C. Norbanus Flaccus (Jan.-June)
	suff.		M. Iunius Silanus (July-Dec.)
769	16	Sisenna Statilius Taurus	L. Scribonius Libo
	suff.	P. Pomponius Graecinus	C. Vibius Rufus
770	17	L. Pomponius Flaccus	C. Caelius Rufus
	suff.	C. Vibius Marsus	L. Voluseius Proculus
771	18	Ti. Caesar Augustus III (Jan.)	Germanicus Iulius Caesar II (Jan.-Apr.)
	suff.	L. Seius Tubero *(Feb.-July)*	Livineius Regulus *(May–July)*
	suff.	C. Rubellius Blandus (Aug.-Dec.)	M. Vipstanus Gallus (Aug.-Dec.)
772	19	M. Iunius Silanus Torquatus (Jan.-Dec.)	L. Norbanus Balbus *(Jan.-Apr.)*
	suff.		P. Petronius *(May-Dec.)*
773	20	M. Valerius Messala Barbatus Messalinus	M. Aurelius Cotta Maximus Messalinus
774	21	Ti. Caesar Augustus IV	Drusus Iulius Caesar II
775	22	D. Haterius Agrippa	C. Sulpicius Galba
776	23	C. Asinius Pollio	C. Antistius Vetus
	suff.		C. Stertinius Maximus
777	24	Ser. Cornelius Cethegus *(Jan.-June)*	L. Visellius Varro *(Jan.-June)*
	suff.	C. Calpurnius Aviola *(July-Dec.)*	P. Cornelius Lentulus Scipio *(July-Dec.)*
778	25	Cossus Cornelius Lentulus *(Jan.-Aug.)*	M. Asinius Agrippa (Jan.-Dec.)
	suff.	C. Petronius (Sept.-Dec.)	
779	26	Cn. Cornelius Lentulus Gaetulicus	C. Calvisius Sabinus
	suff.	L. Iunius Silanus	C. Vellaeus Tutor
780	27	L. Calpurnius Piso	M. Licinius Crassus Frugi
	suff.	P. Cornelius Lentulus	C. Sallustius Crispus Passienus
781	28	Ap. Iunius Silanus	P. Silius Nerva
	suff.	L. Antistius Vetus	Q. Iunius Blaesus
782	29	C. Fufius Geminus *(Jan.-June)*	L. Rubellius Geminus *(Jan.-June)*

	suff.	A. Plautius *(July-Dec.)*	L. Nonius Asprenas *(July-Dec.)*
783	30	M. Vinicius (Jan.-June)	L. Cassius Longinus *(Jan.-June)*
	suff.	L. Naevius Surdinus *(July-Dec.)*	C. Cassius Longinus (July-Dec.)
784	31	Ti. Caesar Augustus V (Jan.-May 9)	L. Aelius Seianus (Jan.-May 9)
	suff.	Faustus Cornelius Sulla *(May 10-Sept.)*	Sex. Tedius (*or* Teidius) Valerius Catullus *(May 10-June)*
	suff.		L. Fulcinius Trio *(July-Dec.)*
	suff.	P. Memmius Regulus *(Oct.-Dec.)*	
785	32	Cn. Domitius Ahenobarbus (Jan.-Dec.)	L. Arruntius Camillus Scribonianus (Jan.-June)
	suff.		A. Vitellius *(July-Dec.)*
786	33	L. Livius Ocella Ser. Sulpicius Galba (Jan.-June)	L. Cornelius Sulla Felix *(Jan.-June)*
	suff.	L. Salvius Otho *(July-Dec.)*	N.N. *(July-Dec.)*
787	34	Paullus Fabius Persicus (Jan.-June)	L. Vitellius (Jan.-June)
	suff.	Q. Marcius Barea Soranus *(July-Dec.)*	T. Rustius Nummius Gallus *(July-Dec.)*
788	35	C. Cestius Gallus (Jan.-June)	M. Servilius Nonianus (Jan.-June)
	suff.	D. Valerius Asiaticus (July-Dec.)	A. Gabinius Secundus *(July-Dec.)*
789	36	Sex. Papinius Allenius *(Jan.-June)*	Q. Plautius *(Jan.-June)*
	suff.	C. Vettius Rufus *(July-Dec.)*	M. Porcius Cato *(July-Dec.)*
790	37	Cn. Acerronius Proculus (Jan.-June)	C. Petronius Pontius Nigrinus *(Jan.-June)*
	suff.	C. Caesar Augustus Germanicus (July-Aug.)	Ti. Claudius Nero Germanicus (July-Aug.)
	suff.	A. Caecina Paetus *(Sept.–Dec.)*	C. Caninius Rebilus *(Sept.–Dec.)*
791	38	M. Aquila Iulianus *(Jan.-June)*	P. Nonius Asprenas *(Jan.-June)*
	suff.	Ser. Asinius Celer *(July-Dec.)*	Julius Africanus (July-Dec.)
792	39	C. Caesar Augustus Germanicus II (only Jan.)	Cn. Domitius Corbulo (Jan.-June)
	suff.	A. Didius Gallus (Feb.-Dec.)	Cn. Domitius Afer (July-Dec.)
793	40	C. Caesar Augustus Germanicus III	*without colleague*
	suff.	C. Laecanius Bassus	Q. Terentius Culleo
794	41	C. Caesar Augustus Germanicus IV (1.–13. Jan.)	Cn. Sentius Saturninus
	suff.	Q. Pomponius Secundus *(for Caligula)*	
	suff.	Q. Futius Lusius Saturninus *(in office on 17 July 41)*	M. Seius Varanus *(in office on 17 July 41)*
795	42	Ti. Claudius Caesar Augustus Germanicus II	C. Calpurnius Piso
796	43	Ti. Claudius Caesar Augustus Germanicus III (Jan.–Feb.)	L. Vitellius II (Jan.–Feb.)
	suff.	Sex. Palpellius Hister *(Mar.–July)*	L. Pedanius Secundus *(Mar.–July)*
	suff.	A. Gabinius Secundus *(Aug.–Sept.)*	N.N. *(Aug.–Sept.)*
	suff.	Q. Curtius Rufus (Oct.–Dec.)	Sp. Oppius *(Oct.–Dec.)*
797	44	C. Sallustius Crispus Passienus II (Jan.–Feb.)	T. Statilius Taurus (Jan.–June)

	suff.	P. Calvisius Sabinus Pomponius Secundus *(Mar.–June)*	
798	45	M. Vinicius II (Jan.–Feb.)	T. Flavius Sabinus (Jan.–June)
	suff.	Ti. Plautius Silvanus Aelianus (Mar.–Dec.)	T. Statilius Taurus Corvinus *(July-Dec.)*
799	46	D. Valerius Asiaticus II (Jan.–Feb.)	M. Iunius Silanus (Jan.–Dec.)
	suff.	Camerinus Antistius Vetus *(Mar.)*	
	suff.	Q. Sulpicius Camerinus *(Mar.–June)*	
	suff.	D. Laelius Balbus *(July–Aug.)*	
	suff.	C. Terentius Tullius Geminus *(Sept.–Dec.)*	
800	47	Ti. Claudius Caesar Augustus Germanicus IV	L. Vitellius III
	suff.	C. Calpetanus Rantius Sedatus *(Mar.–Apr.)*	M. Hordeonius Flaccus *(Mar.–Apr.)*
	suff.	Cn. Hosidius Geta *(July–Dec.)*	T. Flavius Sabinus (July–Aug.)
	suff.		L. Vagellius *(Sept.–Oct.)*
	suff.		C. Volasenna Severus *(Nov.–Dec.)*
801	48	A. Vitellius (Jan.–June)	L. Vipstanus Poplicola (Jan.–June)
	suff.	L. Vitellius (July–Dec.)	G. Vipstanus Messalla Gallus (July–Dec.)
802	49	C. Pompeius Longus Gallus	Q. Veranius
	suff.	L. Mammius Pollio *(Mar.–June)*	Q. Allius Maximus *(Mar.–June)*
803	50	C. Antistius Vetus	M. Suillius Nerullinus
804	51	Ti. Claudius Caesar Augustus Germanicus V	Ser. Cornelius Scipio Salvidienus Orfitus
	suff.		L. Calventius Vetus C. Carminius *(Sept.–Oct.)*
	suff.		T. Flavius Vespasianus (Nov.–Dec.)
805	52	Faustus Cornelius Sulla Felix	L. Salvius Otho Titianus
	suff.		Q. Marcius Barea Soranus (June–Aug.)
	suff.		N.N. *(Sept.–Oct.)*
	suff.		L. Salvidienus Rufus Salvianus *(Nov.–Dec.)*
806	53	D. Iunius Silanus Torquatus (Jan.–June)	Q. Haterius Antoninus (Jan.–June)
	suff.	N.N. *(July–Aug.)*	N.N. *(July–Aug.)*
	suff.	Q. Caecina Primus *(Sept–Oct.)*	P. Trebonius *(Sept.–Dec.)*
	suff.	P. Calvisius Ruso *(Oct.–Dec.)*	
807	54	Cossos Cornelius Lentulus	M. Asinius Marcellus
808	55	Nero Claudius Caesar Augustus Germanicus (Jan.–Feb.)	L. Antistius Vetus *(Jan.–Apr.)*
	suff.	N. Cestius *(Mar.–Apr.)*	
	suff.	L. Annaeus Seneca (May–Oct.)	P. Cornelius Dolabella *(May)*

	suff.		M. Trebellius Maximus *(Aug.)*
	suff.		P.(?) Palfurius *(Sept./Oct.)*
	suff.	Cn. Cornelius Lentulus Gaetulicus *(Nov./Dec.)*	T. Curtilius Mancia *(Nov./Dec)*
809	56	Q. Volusius Saturninus	P. Cornelius Scipio
	suff.	L. Iunius Gallio Annaeanus *(July/Aug.)*	T. Cutius Ciltus *(July/Aug.)*
	suff.	NN. *(Sept./Okt.)*	NN. *(Sept./Okt.)*
	suff.	L. Duvius Avitus *(Nov./Dez.)*	P. Clodius Thrasea Paetus *(Nov./Dez.)*
810	57	Nero Claudius Caesar Augustus Germanicus II (whole year?)	L. Calpurnius Piso *(Jan.–June)*
	suff.		L. Caesius Martialis *(July–Dec.)*
811	58	Nero Claudius Caesar Augustus Germanicus III (Jan–Apr.)	M. Valerius Messalla Corvinus (Jan.–June)
	suff.	C. Fonteius Agrippa (May/June)	
	suff.	A. Petronius Lurco *(July–Dec.)*	A. Paconius Sabinus *(July–Dec.)*
812	59	C. Vipstanus Apronianus *(Jan.–June)*	C. Fonteius Capito (Jan.–June)
	suff.	T. Sextius Africanus *(July–Dec.)*	M. Ostorius Scapula *(July–Dec.)*
813	60	Nero Claudius Caesar Augustus Germanicus IV	Cn. Domitius Afer II
814	61	P. Petronius Turpilianus (Jan.–June?)	L. Iunius Caesennius Paetus (Jan.–June?)
	suff.	Cn. Pedanius Fuscus Salinator *(July/Aug.)*	L. Velleius Paterculus *(July/Aug.)*
815	62	P. Marius *(Jan.–Apr.?)*	L. Afinius (Asinius) Gallus *(Jan.–June)*
	suff.	P. Petronius Niger *(Juli/Aug.)*	Q. Manlius Ancharius Tarquitius Saturninus *(July/Aug.)*
	suff.	Q. Iunius Marullus *(Sept.–Dec.)*	N.N. *(Sept.–Nov.)*
	suff.		T. Clodius Eprius Marcellus (Nov.–Dec.)
816	63	C. Memmius Regulus *(Jan.–June)*	L. Verginius Rufus (Jan.–June)
817	64	C. Laecanius Bassus *(Jan.–June)*	M. Licinius Crassus Frugi *(Jan.–June)*
	suff.	C. Licinius Mucianus? *(July–Oct.)*	Q. Fabius Barbarus Antonius Macer? *(July–Oct.)*
	suff.	N.N. *(Nov./Dec.)*	N.N. *(Nov./Dec.)*
818	65	A. Licinius Nerva Silianus *(Jan.–June)*	M. Iulius Vestinus Atticus *(Jan.–Apr.)*
	suff.		P. Pasidienus Firmus *(May–June)*
	suff.	C. Pomponius Pius *(July/Aug.)*	C. Anicius Cerialis *(July/Aug.)*
	suff.	N.N. *(Sept.–Dec.)*	N.N. *(Sept.–Dec.)*
819	66	C. Luccius Telesinus *(Jan.–June?)*	C. Suetonius Paullinus (Jan.–June?)
	suff.	M. Annius Afrinus *(July/Aug.)*	C. Paccius Africanus *(July/Aug.)*
	suff.	M. Arruntius Aquila *(Sept.–Dec.)*	M. Vettius Bolanus *(Sept.–Dec.)*
820	67	L. Iulius Rufus	Fonteius Capito

	suff.	L. Aurelius Priscus *(Mar./Apr.?)*	Ap. Annius Gallus *(Mar./Apr.?)*
821	68	Ti. Catius Asconius Silius Italicus	P. Galerius Trachalus
	suff.	Imp. Nero Claudius Caesar Augustus Germanicus V (Apr.?–June)	*without colleague*
	suff.	N.N. *(July/Aug.)*	N.N. *(July/Aug.)*
	suff.	C. Bellicus Natalis *(Sept.–Dec.)*	P. Cornelius Scipio Asiaticus *(Sept.–Dec.)*
		Cingonius Varro *(designated)*	
822	69	Ser. Galba Imp. Caesar Augustus II (Jan.)	T. Vinius (Rufinus?) (Jan.)
	suff.	M. Otho Caesar Augustus (Jan. 22-Feb. 28)	L. Salvius Otho Titianus II *(Jan. 22-Feb. 28)*
	suff.	L. Verginius Rufus II (Mar-Apr. 22)	T. Flavius Sabinus (Mar.-Apr. 22)
	suff.	A. Marius Celsus *(May-Aug.)*	Cn. Arrius Antoninus (May-Aug.)
	suff.	Fabius Valens (Sept.-Oct.)	A. Caecina Alienus (Sept.-Oct. 30)
	suff.		
	suff.	C. Quintius Atticus *(Nov.-Dec.)*	Cn. Caecilius Simplex *(Nov.-Dec.)*
823	70	Imp. Caesar Vespasianus Augustus II	T. Caesar Vespasianus
824	71	Imp. Caesar Vespasianus Augustus III	M. Cocceius Nerva
	suff.	Caesar Domitianus	Cn. Pedius Cascus
825	72	Imp. Caesar Vespasianus Augustus IV	T. Caesar Vespasianus II
826	73	Caesar Domitianus II	L. Valerius Catullus Messallinus
827	74	Imp. Caesar Vespasianus Augustus V	T. Caesar Vespasianus III
	suff.	Ti. Plautius Silvanus Aelianus II	L. Iunius Vibius Crispus II
	suff.	Q. Petillius Cerialis Caesius Rufus II	T. Clodius Eprius Marcellus II
828	75	Imp. Caesar Vespasianus Augustus VI	T. Caesar Vespasianus IV
	suff.	Caesar Domitianus III	L. Pasidienus Firmus
829	76	Imp. Caesar Vespasianus Augustus VII	T. Caesar Vespasianus V
	suff.	Caesar Domitianus IV	
830	77	Imp. Caesar Vespasianus Augustus VIII	T. Caesar Vespasianus VI
	suff.	Caesar Domitianus V	Cn. Iulius Agricola
831	78	D. Iunius Novius Priscus	L. Ceionius Commodus
832	79	Imp. Caesar Vespasianus Augustus IX	T. Caesar Vespasianus VII
	suff.	Caesar Domitianus VI	
833	80	Imp. T. Caesar Vespasianus Augustus VIII (Jan. 1-14)	Caesar Domitianus VII (Jan. 1-14)
	suff.	L. Aelius Lamia Plautius Aelianus (Jan. 14 until June)	A. Didius Gallus Fabricius Veiento II *(Jan. 14-Feb. 11)*
	suff.	Q. Aurelius Pactumeius Fronto *(Mar.-May)*	

	suff.	C. Marius Marcellus Cluvius Rufus *(June-?)*	
	suff.	M. Tittius Frugi *(?-Dec.)*	T. Vinucius Iulianus *(?-Dec.)*
834	81	L. Flavius Silva Nonius Bassus (Jan.-Feb.)	L. Asinius Pollio Verrucosus *(Jan.-Feb.)*
	suff.	C. Iulius Iuvenalis *(Mar.-Apr.)*	M. Roscius Coelius *(Mar.-Apr.)*
	suff.	L. Vettius Paullus *(May–June)*	T. Iunius Montanus *(May–June)*
	suff.	N.N. *(July-Aug.)*	N.N. *(July-Aug.)*
	suff.	L. Carminius Lusitanicus *(Sept.-Oct.)*	M. Petronius Umbrinus *(Sept.-Oct.)*
835	82	Imp. Caesar Domitianus Augustus VIII	T. Flavius Sabinus
	suff.	N.N.	Servaeus Innocens
	suff.	N.N.	L. Salvius Otho Cocceianus
	suff.	N.N.	(? C. Arinius) Modestus
	suff.	L. Antonius Saturinus *(July-?)*	P. Valerius Patriunus *(July-?)*
836	83	Imp. Caesar Domitianus Augustus IX	Q. Petillius Rufus II
	suff.	L. Tettius Iulianus	Terentius Strabo Erucius Homullus
837	84	Imp. Caesar Domitianus Augustus X	C. Oppius Sabinus
	suff.	L. Iulius Ursus	
	suff.	C. Cornelius Gallicanus *(Sept.-?)*	C. Tullius Capito Pomponians Plotius Firmus *(Sept.-?)*
838	85	Imp. Caesar Domitianus Augustus XI (Jan.-Feb.)	T. Aurelius Fulvus II (Jan.-Feb.)
	suff.	Q. Gavius Atticus	L. Aelius Oculatus
	suff.	M. Annius Herrenius Pollio (July-Aug.)	P. Herrenius Pollio *(July.-Aug.)*
	suff.	D. Aburius Bassus *(Sept.-Oct.)*	Q. Iulius Balbus *(Sept.-Oct.)*
	suff.	C. Salvius Liberalis Nonius Bassus *(Nov.-Dec.)*	... Orestes *(Nov.-Dec.)*
839	86	Imp. Caesar Domitianus Augustus XII (Jan.)	Ser. Cornelius Dolabella Petronianus *(Jan.-Apr.)*
	suff.	C. Secius Campanus *(Jan.-Feb.)*	
	suff.	N.N.	Q. Vibius Secundus *(Mar.-Apr.)*
	suff.	Sex. Octavius Fronto *(May-?)*	Ti. Iulius Candidus Marius Celsus *(May-?)*
	suff.	A. Bucius Lappius Maximus *(Sept.-?)*	C. Octavius Tidius Tossianus L. Iavolenus Priscus *(Sept.-?)*
840	87	Imp. Caesar Domitianus Augustus XIII (Jan.)	L. Volusius Saturninus *(Jan.-Apr.)*
	suff.	Calpurnius Piso Crassus Frugi Licinianus *(Feb.-Apr.)*	
	suff.	C. Bellicus Natalis Trebanianus *(May-Aug.)*	C. Ducenius Proculus *(May-Aug.)*
	suff.	C. Cilnius Proculus *(Sept.-Dec.)*	L. Neratius Priscus *(Sept.-Dec.)*
841	88	Imp. Caesar Domitianus Augustus XIV (Jan.)	L. Minicius Rufus *(Jan.-Apr.)*
	suff.	D. Plotius Grypus *(Jan-Apr.)*	

	suff.	Q. Ninnius Hasta *(May-Aug.)*	L. Scribonius Libo Rupilius Frugi Bonus (May-Aug.)
	suff.	M'. Otacilius Catulus *(Sept.-Dec.)*	Sex. Iulius Sparsus *(Sept.-Dec.)*
842	89	T. Aurelius Fulvus (Jan.-Apr.)	M. Asinius Atratinus *(Jan.-Apr.)*
	suff.	P. Sallustius Blaesus *(May-Aug.)*	M. Peducaeus Saenianus *(May-Aug.)*
	suff.	A. Vicirius Proculus *(Sept.-Dec.)*	M'. Laberius Maximus (Sept.-Dec.)
843	90	Imp. Caesar Domitianus Augustus XV	M. Cocceius Nerva II
	suff.	L. Cornelius Pusio Annius Messala (replaced Domitian)	
	suff.	L. Antistius Rusticus	Ser. Iulius Servianus
	suff.	Q. Accaeus Rufus	C. Caristanius Fronto
	suff.	P. Baebius Italicus	C. Aquillius Proculus
	suff.	L. Albius Pullaienus Pollio	Cn. Pinarius Aemilius Cicatricula Pompeius Longinus
	suff.	M. Tullius Cerialis	Cn. Pompeius Catullinus
844	91	M'. Acilius Glabrio	M. Ulpius Traianus
	suff.	Cn. Minicius Faustinus	P. Valerius Marinus
	suff.	Q. Valerius Vegetus	P. Metilius Sabinus Nepos
845	92	Imp. Caesar Domitianus Augustus XVI	Q. Volusius Saturninus
	suff.	L. Venuleius Montanus Apronianus	
	suff.	L. Stertinius Avitus	Ti. Iulius Celsus Polemaeanus
	suff.	C. Iulius Silanus	Q. Iunius Arulenus Rusticus
846	93	Sex. Pompeius Collega	Q. Peducaeus Priscinus
	suff.	T. Avidius Quietus	Sex. Lusianus Proculus
	suff.	C. Cornelius Rarus	Tuccius Cerialis
847	94	L. Nonius Calpurnius Torquatus Asprenas *(Jan.-Apr.)*	T. Sextius Magius Lateranus *(Jan.-Apr.)*
	suff.	M. Lollius Paullinus D. Valerius Asiaticus Saturninus	C. Antius A. Iulius Quadratus
	suff.	L. Silius Decianus	T. Pomponius Bassus
848	95	Imp. Caesar Domitianus Augustus XVII (Jan.)	T. Flavius Clemens (Jan.-Apr.)
	suff.	L. Neratius Marcellus *(Jan.-Apr.)*	
	suff.	A. Bucius Lappius Maximus II *(May-Aug.)*	P. Ducenius Verus *(May-Aug.)*
	suff.	Q. Pomponius Rufus *(Sept.-Dec.)*	L. Baebius Tullus *(Sept.-Dec.)*
849	96	C. Manlius Valens *(Jan.-Apr.)*	C. Antistius Vetus *(Jan.-Apr.)*
	suff.	Q. Fabius Postuminus *(May-Aug.)*	T. Prifernius Paetus *(May-Aug.)*
	suff.	Ti. Catius Caesius Fronto *(Sept.-Dec.)*	M. Calpurnius [...]icus *(Sept.-Dec.)*
850	97	Imp. Nerva Caesar Augustus III (Jan.-Feb.)	L. Verginius Rufus III (Jan.-Feb.)
	suff.	Cn. Arrius Antoninus II (Mar.-Apr.)	L. Calpurnius Piso *(Mar.-Apr.)*
	suff.	M. Annius Verus (May–June)	L. Neratius Priscus *(May–June)*

	suff.	L. Domitius Apollinaris *(July-Aug.)*	Sex. Hermentidius Campanus *(July-Aug.)*
	suff.	Q. Glitius Atilius Agricola *(Sept.-Oct.)*	L. Pomponius Maternus *(Sept.-Oct.)*
	suff.	P. Cornelius Tacitus (Nov.-Dec.)	M. Ostorius Scapula *(Nov.-Dec.)*
851	98	Imp. Nerva Caesar Augustus IV (to Jan. 12)	Imp. Caesar Nerva Traianus II (Jan.-June)
	suff.	Cn. Domitius Tullus II *(Jan. 13-Jan. 31)*	
	suff.	Sex. Iulius Frontinus II (Feb.)	
	suff.	L. Iulius Ursus II *(Mar.)*	
	suff.	T. Vestricius Spurinna II *(Apr.)*	
	suff.	C. Pomponius Rufus Priscus Coelius Sparsus *(May–June)*	
	suff.	A. Vicirius Martialis *(July-Aug.)*	L. Maecius Postumus *(July-Aug.)*
	suff.	C. Pomponius Rufus Acilius (Tu?)scus Coelius Sparsus *(Sept.-Oct.)*	Cn. Pompeius Ferox Licinianus *(Sept.-Oct.)*
	suff.	P. Iulius Lupus *(Nov.-Dec.)*	N.N.
852	99	A. Cornelius Palma Frontonianus	Q. Sosius Senecio
	suff.	Sulpicius Lucretius Barba	Senecio Memmius Afer
	suff.	Q. Fabius Barbarus Valerius Magnus Iulianus	A. Caecilius Faustinus
	suff.	Q. Fulvius Gillo Bittius Proculus	M. Ostorius Scapula
	suff.	Ti. Iulius Ferox	N.N.
853	100	Imp. Caesar Nerva Traianus Augustus III (Jan.)	Sex. Iulius Frontinus III *(Jan.-Feb.)*
	suff.		L. Iulius Ursus III *(Jan.-Feb.)*
	suff.	M. Marcius Macer *(Mar.-Apr.)*	C. Cilnius Proculus *(Mar.-Apr.)*
	suff.	L. Herennius Saturninus *(May–June)*	T. Pomponius Mamilianus *(May–June)*
	suff.	Q. Acutius Nerva *(July-Aug.)*	L. Fabius Tuscus *(July-Aug.)*
	suff.	C. Iulius Cornutus Tertullus *(Sept.-Oct.)*	C. Plinius Caecilius Secundus (Sept.-Oct.)
	suff.	L. Roscius Aelianus Maecius Celer *(Nov.-Dec.)*	Ti. Claudius Sacerdos Iulianus *(Nov.-Dec.)*

Second Century

AUC	AD	First consul	Second consul
854	101	Imp. Caesar Nerva Traianus Augustus IV (Jan.)	Q. Articuleius Paetus (Jan.-Mar.)
	suff.	Sex. Attius Suburanus Aemilianus (Feb.-Mar.)	
	suff.	C. Sertorius Brocchus Q. Servaeus Innocens (Apr.-?)	M. Maecius Celer (Apr.-?)
	suff.	[...]us Proculus	NN.

855	102	L. Iulius Ursus Servianus II	L. Licinius Sura II
	suff.		L. Fabius Iustus (Mar.-Apr.)
	suff.	NN. (May-?)	L. Publilius Celsus (May-?)
	suff.	L. Antonius Albus (Sept.-?)	M. Iunius Homullus (Sept.-?)
856	103	Imp. Caesar Nerva Traianus Augustus V (Jan.)	M'. Laberius Maximus II
	suff.	Q. Glitius Atilius Agricola II (Jan.-?)	
	suff.	P. Metilius Nepos	Q. Baebius Macer
	suff.	M. Flavius Aper	C. Trebonius Proculus Mettius Modestus
	suff.	(A?)nnius Mela	P. Calpurnius Macer Caulius Rufus
857	104	Sex. Attius Suburanus Aemilianus II	M. Asinius Marcellus
858	105	Ti. Iulius Candidus Marius Celsus II	C. Antius A. Iulius Quadratus II
	suff.	C. Iulius Quadratus Bassus (BIRLEY) (May–June)	Cn. Afranius Dexter (PROSOP) (May–June)
	suff.		Q. Caelius Honotatus (July-Aug.)
	suff.	M. Vitorius Marcellus (Sept.-Dec.)	C. Caecilius Strabo (Sept.-Dec.)
859	106	L. Ceionius Commodus	Sex. Vettulenus Civica Cerialis
	suff.	L. Minicius Natalis	Q. Licinius Silvanus Granianus Quadronius Proculus
860	107	L. Licinius Sura III	Q. Sosius Senecio II
	suff.	L. Acilius Rufus (Mar.-May)	
	suff.	C. Minicius Fundanus (May-Aug.)	T. Vettennius Severus (May-Aug.)
	suff.	C. Iulius Longinus (Sept.–Dec.)	Q. Valerius Paullinus (Sept.-Dec.)
861	108	Ap. Annius Trebonius Gallus (Jan.-Apr.)	M. Appius Bradua (Jan.-Apr.)
	suff.	P. Aelius Hadrianus (May-Aug.)	M. Trebatius Priscus (May-Aug.)
	suff.	Q. Pompeius Falco (Sept.-Dec.)	Lustricus Bruttianus (Sept.-Dec.)
862	109	A. Cornelius Palma Frontonianus (Jan.-Feb.)	P. Calvisius Tullus Ruso (Jan.-Apr.)
	suff.	L. Annius Largus (Mar.-Apr.)	
	suff.	Cn. Antonius Fuscus (May-Aug.)	C. Iulius Antiochus Epiphanes Philopappus (May-Aug.)
	suff.	C. Alburnius Valens (Sept.-Dec.)	C. Iulius Proculus (Sept.-Dec.)
863	110	M. Peducaeus Priscinus	Ser. Cornelius Scipio Salvidienus Orfitus
	suff.	C. Avidius Nigrinus	Ti. Iulius Aquila Polemaeanus
	suff.	L. Catilius Severus Iulianus Claudius Reginus (I)	C. Erucianus Silo
	suff.	A. Larcius Priscus	Sex. Marcius Honoratus
864	111	C. Calpurnius Piso	M. Vettius Bolanus
	suff.	T. Avidius Quietus (May-Aug.)	L. Eggius Marullus (May-Aug.)
	suff.	L. Octavius Crassus (Sept.-Dec.)	P. Coelius Apollinaris (Sept.-Dec.)
865	112	Imp. Caesar Nerva Traianus Augustus VI (Jan.)	T. Sextius Cornelius Africanus (Jan.-?)
	suff.	M.(?) Licinius Ruso (Jan.-?)	

	suff.	Cn. Pinarius Cornelius Severus	L. Mummius Niger Q. Valerius Vegetus
	suff.	P. Stertinius Quartus	T. Iulius Maximus Manlianus Brocchus Servilianus
	suff.	C. Claudius Severus	T. Settidius Firmus
866	113	L. Publilius Celsus II (Jan.-Mar.)	C. Clodius Crispinus (Jan.-Apr.)
	suff.	Ser. Cornelius Dolabella Metilianus Pompeius Marcellus (Apr.)	
	suff.	L. Stertinius Noricus (May-Aug.)	L. Fadius Rufinus (May-Aug.)
	suff.	Cn. Cornelius Urbicus (Sept.-Dec.)	T. Sempronius Rufus (Sept.-Dec.)
867	114	Q. Ninnius Hasta	P. Manilius Vopiscus Vicinillianus
	suff.	C. Clodius Nummus	L. Caesennius Sospes
	suff.	L. Hedius Rufus Lollianus Atitus (Sept.-?)	L. Messius Rusticus (Sept.-?)
868	115	L. Vipstanus Messalla	M. Pedo Vergilianus
	suff.	L. Iulius Frugi	P. Iuventius Celsus T. Aufidius Hoenius Severianus
	suff.	M. Pompeius Macrinus Neos Theophanes	NN.
869	116	L. Fundanius Lamia Aelianus	Sex. Carminius Vetus
	suff.	Ti. Iulius Secundus	M. Egnatius Marcellinus
	suff.	D. Terentius Gentianus	L. Cossonius Gallus
	suff.	L. Statius Aquila	C. Julius Alexander Berenicianus
870	117	Q. Aquilius Niger	M. Rebilus Apronianus
	suff.	Cn. Minicius Faustinus	NN.
	suff.	M. Erucius Clarus	Ti. Julius Alexander Julianus
871	118	Imp. Caesar Traianus Hadrianus Augustus II (Jan.-June)	Cn. Pedanius Fuscus Salinator (Jan.-Feb.)
	suff.		Bellicius Tebanianus (replaced Salinator)[mar]
	suff.		C. Ummidius Quadratus (replaced Tebanianus) (attested May)
	suff.	L. Pompeius Bassus (attested July/Aug.)	T. Sabinius Barbarus (attested July/Aug.)
872	119	Imp. Caesar Traianus Hadrianus Augustus III	P. Dasumius Rusticus
	suff.		A. Platorius Nepos (replaced Rusticus)
	suff.	M. Paccius Silvanus Q. Goredius Gallus Gargilius Antiquus	Q. Vibius Gallus
	suff.	C. Herennius Capella (Nov.-Dec.)	L. Coelius Rufus (Nov.-Dec.)
873	120	L. Catilius Severus Iulianus Claudius Reginus II	T. Aurelius Fulvus Boionius Arrius Antoninus
	suff.	C. Quinctius Certus Poblicius Marcellus (May–June)	T. Rutilius Propinquus (May–June)
	suff.	C. Carminius Gallus (July-?)	C. Atilius Serranus (July-?)
874	121	M. Annius Verus II	Cn. Arrius Augur
	suff.	M. Herennnius Faustus (Mar.-Apr.)	Q. Pomponius Marcellus (Mar.-Apr.)

	suff.	T. Pomponius Antistianus Funisulanus Vettonianus (May-?)	L. Pomponius Silvanus (May-?)
	suff.	M. Statorius Secundus	L. Sempronius Merula Auspicatus
875	122	M'. Acilius Aviola	L. Corellius Neratius Pansa
	suff.	Ti. Iulius Candidus Capito (July-Oct.)	L. Vitrasius Flamininus (July–Oct.)
	suff.	C. Trebius Maximus (Nov.-Dec.)	T. Calestrius Tiro Orbius Speratus (Nov.-Dec.)
876	123	Q. Articuleius Paetinus	L. Venuleius Apronianus Octavius Priscus
	suff.	T. Salvius Rufinus Minicius Opimianus	Cn. Sentius Aburnianus
877	124	M'. Acilius Glabrio	C. Bellicius Flaccus Torquatus Tebanianus
	suff.	A. Larcius Macedo	P. Ducenius Verres
	suff.	C. Iulius Gallus (Sept.-?)	C. Valerius Severus (Sept.-?)
878	125	M. Lollius Paullinus D. Valerius Asiaticus Saturninus II	L. Epidius Titius Aquilinus
	suff.	(M.?) Accenna Verus	P. Lucius Cosconianus
879	126	M. Annius Verus III (Jan.-Feb.)	C. Eggius Ambibulus
	suff.	... Propinquus (replaced Verus) (Mar.-?)	
	suff.	L. Cuspius Camerinus	C. Saenius Severus
880	127	T. Atilius Rufus Titianus (Jan.-Mar.)	M. Gavius Squilla Gallicanus (Jan.-Mar.)
	suff.	P. Tullius Varro (Apr.)	(D.?) Iunius Paetus (Apr.)
	suff.	Q. Tineius Rufus (May-Sept.)	M. Licinius Celer Nepos (May-Sept.)
	suff.	L. Aemilius Iuncus (Oct.-Dec.)	Cn. Minicius Faustinus Sex. Iulius Severus (Oct.-Dec.)
881	128	L. Nonius Calpurnius Torquatus Asprenas II (Jan.)	M. Annius Libo (Jan.-Mar.)
	suff.	L. Caesennius Antoninus (Feb.-Mar.)	
	suff.	M. Iunius Mettius Rufus (May–June)	Q. Pomponius Maternus (May–June)
	suff.	L. Valerius Flaccus (July-Sept.)	M. [Iunius Homullus ?] (July-Sept.)
	suff.	A. Egrilius Plarianus (Oct.-Dec.)	Q. Planius Sardus L. Varius Ambibulus (Oct.-Dec.)
882	129	P. Iuventius Celsus T. Aufidius Hoenius Severianus II	L. Neratius Marcellus II
	suff.		Q. Iulius Balbus (Feb.-Mar.)
	suff.	Ti. Iulius Iulianus	Castus
	suff.	L. Flavius Arrianus Xenophon (? ann. incert.)	
883	130	Q. Fabius Catullinus	M. Flavius Aper
	suff.	Cassius Agrippa (or perhaps "Agrippinus"?)	Ti. Claudius Quartinus
884	131	Sergius Octavius Laenas Pontianus	M. Antonius Rufinus
	suff.	L. Fabius Gallus	Q. Fvabius Iulianus

885	132	C. Iulius Serius Augurinus	C. Trebius Sergianus
	suff.	P. Sufenas Verus	Ti. Claudius Atticus Herodes
886	133	M. Antonius Hiberus	P. Mummius Sisenna
	suff.	Q. Flavius Tertullus (July-?)	Q. Iunius Rusticus (July-?)
887	134	L. Iulius Ursus Servianus III	T. Vibius Varus
	suff.	T. Haterus Nepos (in place of Servianus)	
	suff.	P. Licinius Pansa (Sept.-Oct.)	L. Attius Macro (Sept.-Oct.)
888	135	T. Tutilius Lupercus Pontianus	P. Calpurnius Atilianus (Atticus Rufus ?)
	suff.	M. Aemilius Papus	L. Burbuleius Optatus Ligarianus
	suff.	Q. Lollius Urbicus	NN.
	suff.	P. Rutilius Fabianus	Cn. Papirius Aelianus Aemilius Tuscillus
889	136	L. Ceionius Commodus	Sex. Vettulenus Civica Pompeianus
890	137	L. Aelius Caesar II	P. Coelius Balbinus Vibullius Pius
891	138	Kanus Iunius Niger	C. Pomponius Camerinus
	suff.	M. Vindius Verus (June-?)	P. Pactumeius Clemens (June-?)
	suff.	P. Cassius Secudus (Oct.-Dec.)	M. Nonius Mucianus (Oct.-Dec.)
892	139	Imp. Caesar T. Aelius Hvadrianus Antoninus Augustus Pius II	C. Bruttius Praesens L. Fulvius Rusticus II
	suff.	NN.	... Scapula
	suff.	M. Ceccius Justinus (Nov.-Dec.)	C. Iulius Bassus (Nov.-Dec.)
893	140	Imp. Caesar T. Aelius Hadrianus Antoninus Augustus Pius III (Jan.-June)	M. Aurelius Caesar (Jan.-June)
	suff.	N.N. (July-Aug.)	N.N. (July-Aug.)
	suff.	N.N. (Sept.-Oct.)	N.N. (Sept.-Oct.)
	suff.	M. Barbius Aemilianus (Nov.-Dec.)	T. Flavius Iulianus (Nov.-Dec.)
894	141	T. Hoenius Severus	M. Peducaeus Stloga Priscinus
	suff.	NN.	T. Caesernius Statius Quinctius Statianus Memmius Macrinus
	suff.	L. Annius Fabianus	NN.
895	142	L. Cuspius Pactumeius Rufinus	L. Statius Quadratus
	suff.	Castus	NN.
	suff.	M. Cornelius Fronto	L. Laberius Priscus
	suff.	L. Tusidius Campester	Q. Cornelius (Senecio Annianus ?)
	suff.	Iulianus	NN.
896	143	C. Bellicius Torquatus	L. Vibullius Hipparchus Ti. Claudius Atticus Herodes
	suff.	Q. Iunius Calamus	M. Valerius Iunianus
897	144	L. Hedius Rufus Lollianus Avitus	T. Statilius Maximus
	suff.	NN.	Q. Laberius Licinianus
	suff.	M. Calpurnius Longus	D. Velius Fidus
898	145	Imp. Caesar T. Aelius Hadrianus Antoninus Augustus Pius IV	M. Aurelius Caesar II
	suff.	L. Lamia Silvanus	L. Poblicola Priscus

	suff.	Cn. Arrius Cornelius Proculus (May–June)	D. Iunius Paetus (May–June)
	suff.	Q. Mustius Priscus	M. Pontius Laelianus Larcius Sabinus
	suff.	L. Petronius Sabinus (Sept.-Oct.)	C. Vicrius Rufus (Sept.-Oct.)
	suff.	C. Fadius Rufus (Nov.-Dec.)	P. Vicrius (Nov.-Dec.)
899	146	Sex. Erucius Clarus II	Cn. Claudius Severus Arabianus
	suff.	Q. Licinius Modestinus Sex. Attius Labeo (Mar.-May)	
	suff.	P. Mummius Sisenna Rutilianus (June)	T. Prifernius Paetus (June)
	suff.	L. Aurelius Gallus (July-?)	Cn. L. Terentius Homullus Iunior (July-?)
	suff.	Q. Voconius Saxa Fidus	C. Annianus Verus
	suff.	L. Aemilius Longus	Q. Cornelius Proculus
900	147	C. Prastina Messalinus	L. Annius Largus
	suff.	A. Claudius Charax	Q. Fuficius Cornutus
	suff.	Cupressenus Gallus	Q. Cornelius Quadratus
	suff.	Sex. Cocceius Severianus Honorinus	Ti. Licinius Cassius Cassianus
	suff.		C. Popilius Carus Pedo (In place of Cassianus)
901	148	L. Octavius Cornelius P. Salvius Iulianus Aemilianus	C. Bellicius Calpurnius Torquatus
	suff.	Saturius Firmus	C. Salvius Capito
	suff.	L. Coelius Festus	P. Orfidius Senecio
	suff.	C. Fabius Agrippinus	M. Antonius Zeno
902	149	Ser. Cornelius Scipio Salvidienus Orfitus	Q. Pompeius Sosius Priscus
	suff.	Q. Passienus Licinus	C. Iulius Avitus
	suff.	T. Flavius Longinus Quintus Marcius Turbo	NN.
903	150	M. Gavius Squilla Gallicanus	Sex. Carminius Vetus
	suff.	M. Cassius Apollinaris (Aug.-?)	M. Petonius Mamertinus (Aug.-?)
904	151	Sex. Quintilius Condianus	Sex. Quintilius Valerius Maximus
	suff.	L. Attidius Cornelianus	M. Cominius Secundus
905	152	M'. Acilius Glabrio Cn. Cornelius Severus	M. Valerius Homullus
	suff.	L. Claudius Modestus (Aug.)	L. Dasumius Tuscus (Aug.)
	suff.	C. Novius Priscus (Sept.)	L. Iulius Romulus (Sept.)
	suff.	P. Cluvius Maximus	M. Servilius Silanus
906	153	L. Fulvius Rusticus C. Bruttius Praesens	A. Iunius Rufinus
	suff.	Sex. Caecilius? Max[imus] (?-June)	M. Pontius Sabin[us] (?-June)
	suff.	P. Septimius Aper (July-?)	M. Sedatius Severianus (July-?)
	suff.	Q. Petiedius Gallus (?-Dec.)	C. Catius Marcellus (?-Dec.)
907	154	L. Aelius Aurelius Commodus	T. Sextius Lateranus
	suff.	Prifernius Paetus	M. Nonius Macrinus

	suff.	M. Valerius Etruscus	L.[Aemilius Juncus]
	suff.	Cn. Julius Verus	L . .
	suff.	Tib. Claudius Julianus	Sex. [Calpurnius Agricola]
	suff.	C. Iulius Statius Severus (Nov.-Dec.)	T. Iunius Severus (Nov.-Dec.)
908	155	C. Iulius Severus	M. Iunius Rufinus Sabinianus
	suff.	C. Aufidius Victorinus (May-?)	M. Gavius (May-?)
	suff.	... Antius Pollio (Nov.)	... Minicius Opimianus (Nov.)
	suff.	(? D. Rupilius) Severus (Dec.)	L. Iulius Severus (Dec.)
909	156	M. Ceionius Silvanus	C. Serius Augurinus
	suff.	A. Avillius Urinatius Quadratus (Mar.)	Strabo Aemilianus (Mar.)
	suff.	Q. Canusius Praenestinus (Dec.)	C. Lusius Sparsus (Dec.)
910	157	M. Vettulenus Civica Barbarus	M. Metilius Aquillius Regulus Nepos Volusius Torquatus Fronto
	suff.	C. Caelius Secundus	C. Iulius Commodus Orfitianus
	suff.	L. Roscius Aelianus	Cn. Papirius Aelianus
911	158	Sex. Sulpicius Tertullus	Q. Tineius Sacerdos Clemens
	suff.	M. Servilius Fabianus Maximus (July)	Q. Iallius Bassius (July)
912	159	Plautius Quintillus	M. Statius Priscus Licinius Italicus
	suff.	M. Pisibanius Lepidus	L. Matuccius Fuscinus
	suff.	Cornelius Dexter	NN.
	suff.	A. Curtius Crispinus	NN.
913	160	Ap. Annius Atilius Bradua	T. Clodius Vibius Varus
	suff.	A. Platorius Nepos Calpurnianus (Marcellus?)	M. Postumius Festus
	suff.		(? C. Septimius) Severus
	suff.	N.N.	(?Cae)sorius Paulus
	suff.	Ti. Oclatius Severus	... Ninnius Hastianus
	suff.	N.N.	... Novius Sabinianus
914	161	M. Aurelius Caesar III	L. Aelius Aurelius Commodus II
	suff.	M. Annius Libo	Q. Camurius Numisius Iunior
915	162	Q. Iunius Rusticus II	L. Titius Plautius Aquilinus
	suff.	Ti. Claudius Paullinus	Ti. Claudius Pompeianus
	suff.	M. Insteius Bithynicus	NN.
916	163	M. Pontius Laelianus	A. Iunius Pastor L. Caesennius Sospes
917	164	M. Pompeius Macrinus	P. Iuventius Celsus
	suff.	Ti. Haterius Saturninus	Q. Caecilius Avitus
918	165	M. Gavius Orfitus	L. Arrius Pudens
919	166	Q. Servilius Pudens	L. Fufidius Pollio
	suff.	M. Vibius Liberalis (Mar.-?)	P. Martius Verus (Mar.-?)
920	167	Imp. Caesar L. Aurelius Verus Augustus III	M. Ummidius Quadratus
	suff.	Q. Caecilius Dentilianus (May-?)	M. Antonius Pallas (May-?)
	suff.	(L.?) Sempronius Gracchus	NN.

	suff.	Q. Antistius Adventus Postumius (?)	N.N.
	suff.	Ti. Claudius Pompeianus I	
921	168	L. Venuleius Apronianus Octavius Priscus II	L. Sergius Paullus II
922	169	Q. Pompeius Senecio Roscius Murena Coelius Sex. Iulius Frontinus Silius Decianus C. Iulius Eurycles Herculaneus L. Vibullius Pius Augustanus Alpinus Bellicus Sollers Iulius Aper Ducenius Proculus Rutilianus Rufinus Silius Valens Valerius Niger Claudius Fuscus Saxa Amyntianus Sosius Priscus[4]	P. Coelius Apollinaris
923	170	C. Erucius Clarus	M. Gavius Cornelius Cethegus
	suff.	T. Hoenius Severus	NN.
924	171	T. Statilius Severus	L. Alfidius Herennianus
925	172	Ser. Calpurnius Scipio Orfitus	Sex. Quintilius Maximus
926	173	Cn. Claudius Severus II	Ti. Claudius Pompeianus II
	suff.	M'. Acilius Glabrio	NN.
927	174	L. Aurelius Gallus	Q. Volusius Flaccus Cornelianus
928	175	L. Calpurnius Piso	P. Salvius Iulianus
	suff.	P. Helvius Pertinax	M. Didius Severus Iulianus
929	176	T. Pomponius Proculus Vitrasius Pollio II	M. Flavius Aper II
930	177	L. Aurelius Commodus Caesar	M. Peducaeus Plautius Quintillus
931	178	Ser. Cornelius Scipio Salvidienus Orfitus	D. Velius Rufus (Iulianus?)
932	179	Imp. Caesar L. Aurelius Commodus Augustus II	P. Martius Veru II
	suff.	T. Flavius Claudianus	L. Aemilius Iuncus
	suff.	M'. Acilius Faustinus	L. Iulius Proculianus
933	180	L. Fulvius Rusticus C. Bruttius Praesens II	Sex. Quintilius Condianus
934	181	Imp. Caesar L. Aurelius Commodus Augustus III	L. Antistius Burrus
935	182	M. Petronius Sura Mamertinus	Q. Tineius Rufus
936	183	Imp. Caesar M. Aurelius Commodus Antoninus Augustus IV	C. Aufidius Victorinus II
	suff.	L. Tutilius Pontianus Gentianus	
	suff.	M. Herennius Secundus	M. Egnatius Postumus
	suff.	T. Pactumeius Magnus	L. Septimius Flaccus
937	184	L. Cossonius Eggius Marullus	Cn. Papirius Aelianus
	suff.	C. Octavius Vindex	NN.
938	185	Triarius Maternus Lascivius	Ti. Claudius M. Ap. Atilius Bradua Regillus Atticus
	suff.	M. Umbrius Primus	NN.

939	186	Imp. Caesar M. Aurelius Commodus Antoninus Augustus V	M' Acilius Glabrio II
	suff.	L. Novius Rufus	L. Annius ...vus
	suff.	C. Sabucius Maior Caecilianus	Valerius Senecio
940	187	L. Bruttius Quintius Crispinus	L. Roscius Aelianus Paculus
941	188	L. Seius Fuscianus II	M. Servilius Silanus II
942	189	Dulius Silanus	Q. Servilius Silanus
943	190	Imp. Caesar M. Aurelius Commodus Antoninus Augustus VI	M. Petronius Sura Septimianus
	suff.	L. Septimius Severus (future emperor) (May-?)	Apuleius (Atulenus?) Rufinus (May-?)
944	191	Popilius Pedo Apronianus	M. Valerius Bradua Mauricus
945	192	Imp. Caesar L. Aelius Aurelius Commodus Augustus VII	P. Helvius Pertinax II
	suff.	Q. Tineius Sacerdos (March-?)	P. Iulius Scapula Priscus (March-?)
	suff.	L. Iulius Messala Rutilianus	C. Aemilius Severus Cantabrinus
946	193	Q. Pompeius Sosius Falco	C. Iulius Erucius Clarus Vibianus
	suff.	L. Fabius Cilo Septiminus Catinius Acilianus Lepidus Fulcinianus	NN.
	suff.	M. Silius Messala (May–June)	NN.
947	194	Imp. Caesar L. Septimius Severus Pertinax Augustus II	D. Clodius Septimius Albinus Caesar II
948	195	P. Iulius Scapula Tertullus Priscus	Q. Tineius Clemens
949	196	C. Domitius Dexter II	L. Valerius Messalla Thrasea Priscus
950	197	T. Sextius Magius Lateranus	L./C. Cuspius Rufinus
951	198	P. Martius Sergius Saturninus	L. Aurelius Gallus
952	199	P. Cornelius Anullinus II	M. Aufidius Fronto
953	200	Ti. Claudius Severus Proculus	C. Aufidius Victorinus

Third Century

AUC	AD	First consul	Second consul
954	201	L. Annius Fabianus	M. Nonius Arrius Mucianus
955	202	Imp. Caesar L. Septimius Severus Pertinax Augustus III	Imp. Caesar M. Aurelius Antoninus Augustus
	suff.	T. Murrenius Severus	C. Cassius Regallianus
956	203	C. Fulvius Plautianus II	P. Septimius Geta II
957	204	L. Fabius Cilo Septiminus Catinius Acilianus Lepidus Fulcinianus II	M. Annius Flavius Libo
958	205	Imp. Caesar M. Aurelius Antoninus Augustus II	P. Septimius Geta Caesar
959	206	M. Nummius Umbrius Primus Senecio Albinus	L. Fulvius Gavius Numisius Petronius Aemilianus
	suff.	P. Tullius Marsus	M. Caelius Faustinus
960	207	L. Annius Maximus	L. Septimius Severus Aper
961	208	Imp. Caesar M. Aurelius Antoninus Augustus III	P. Septimius Geta Caesar II
962	209	L. Aurelius Commodus Pompeianus	Q. Hedius Lollianus Plautius Avitus

963	210	M'. Acilius Faustinus	A. Triarius Rufinus
964	211	Hedius Lollianus Terentius Gentianus	Pomponius Bassus
965	212	C. Iulius Asper II	C. Iulius Camilius Asper
	suff.	Ti. Claudius Pompeianus Quintianus	NN
966	213	Imp. Caesar M. Aurelius Severus Antoninus Augustus IV	D. Caelius Calvinus Balbinus II
967	214 suff.	L. Valerius Messalla Apollinaris	C. Octavius Ap. Suetrius Sabinus Aemilianus
968	215	Q. Maecius Laetus II	M. Munatius Sulla Cerialis
969	216	P. Catius Sabinus II	P. Cornelius Anullinus
970	217	C. Bruttius Praesens	T. Messius Extricatus II
971	218	Imp. Caesar M. Opellius Severus Macrinus Augustus II	M. Oclatinius Adventus II
	suff.	Imp. Caesar M. Aurelius Antoninus Augustus	
972	219	Imp. Caesar M. Aurelius Antoninus Augustus II	Q. Tineius Sacerdos II
973	220	Imp. Caesar M. Aurelius Antoninus Augustus III	P. Valerius Comazon Eutychianus II
974	221	C. Vettius Gratus Sabinianus	M. Flavius Vitellius Seleucus
975	222	Imp. Caesar M. Aurelius Antoninus Augustus IV	M. Aurelius Severus Alexander Caesar
976	223	L. Marius Maximus Perpetuus Aurelianus II	L. Roscius Aelianus Paculus Salvius Iulianus
977	224	Ap. Claudius Iulianus II	C. Bruttius Crispinus
978	225	Ti. Manilius Fuscus II	Ser. Calpurnius Domitius Dexter
979	226	Imp. Caesar M. Aurelius Severus Alexander Augustus II	C. Aufidius Marcellus II
980	227	M. Nummius Senecio Albinus	M. Laelius Fulvius Maximus Aemilianus
981	228	Q. Aiacius Modestus Crescentianus II	M. Pomponius Maecius Probus
982	229	Imp. Caesar M. Aurelius Severus Alexander Augustus III	L. Claudius Cassius Dio Cocceianus II
983	230	L. Virius Agricola	Sex. Catius Clementinus Priscillianus
984	231	L. Ti. Claudius Pompeianus	T. Flavius Sallustius Paelignianus
985	232	L. Virius Lupus Iulianus	L. Marius Maximus
986	233	L. Valerius Claudius Acilius Priscillianus Maximus	Cn. Cornelius Paternus
987	234	M. Clodius Pupienus Maximus II	M. Munatius Sulla Urbanus
988	235	Cn. Claudius Severus	Ti. Claudius Quintianus
989	236	Imp. Caesar C. Iulius Verus Maximinus Augustus	M. Pupienus Africanus Maximus
990	237	L. Marius Perpetuus	L. Mummius Felix Cornelianus
991	238	Fulvius Pius	Pontius Proculus Pontianus
992	239	Imp. Caesar M. Antonius Gordianus Augustus	M'. Acilius Aviola

993	240	C. Octavius Ap. Suetrius Sabinus II	Ragonius Venustus
994	241	Imp. Caesar M. Antonius Gordianus Augustus II	Clodius Pompeianus
995	242	C. Vettius Gratus Atticus Sabinianus	C. Asinius Lepidus Praetextatus
996	243	L. Annius Arrianus	C. Cervonius Papus
997	244	Ti. Pollenius Armenius Peregrinus	Fulvius Aemilianus
998	245	Imp. Caesar M. Iulius Philippus Augustus	C. Maesius Titianus
999	246	C. Bruttius Praesens	C. Allius Albinus
1000	247	Imp. Caesar M. Iulius Philippus Augustus II	M. Iulius Severus Philippus Caesar
1001	248	Imp. Caesar M. Iulius Philippus Augustus III	Imp. Caesar M. Iulius Severus Philippus Augustus II
1002	249	L. Fulvius Gavius Numisius Aemilianus II	L. Naevius Aquilinus
1003	250	Imp. Caesar C. Messius Quintus Traianus Decius Augustus II	Vettius Gratus
1004	251	Imp. Caesar C. Messius Quintus Traianus Decius Augustus III	Q. Herennius Etruscus Messius Decius Caesar
1005	252	Imp. Caesar C. Vibius Trebonianus Gallus Augustus II	Imp. Caesar C. Vibius Volusianus Augustus
1006	253	Imp. Caesar C. Vibius Volusianus Augustus II	L. Valerius Claudius Poplicola Balbinus Maximus
1007	254	Imp. Caesar P. Licinius Valerianus Augustus II	Imp. Caesar P. Licinius Gallienus Augustus
1008	255	Imp. Caesar P. Licinius Valerianus Augustus III	Imp. Caesar P. Licinius Gallienus Augustus II
1009	256	L. Valerius Claudius Acilius Priscillianus Maximus II	M. Acilius Glabrio
1010	257	Imp. Caesar P. Licinius Valerianus Augustus IV	Imp. Caesar P. Licinius Gallienus Augustus III
1011	258	M. Nummius Tuscus	Mummius Bassus
1012	259	Aemilianus	Pomponius Bassus
1013	260	P. Cornelius Saecularis II	C. Iunius Donatus II
		Imp. Caesar M. Cassianius Latinius Postumus Augustus II (Gaul)	Honoratianus? *(Gaul)*
1014	261	Imp. Caesar P. Licinius Gallienus Augustus IV	L. Petronius Taurus Volusianus
		Imp. Caesar M. Cassianius Latinius Postumus Augustus III (Gaul)	
		Imp. Caesar Fulvius Macrianus Augustus II (East)	Imp. Caesar Fulvius Quietus Augustus (East)
1015	262	Imp. Caesar P. Licinius Gallienus Augustus V	L. Mummius Faustianus[5]
1016	263	Nummius Albinus II	Dexter
1017	264	Imp. Caesar P. Licinius Gallienus Augustus VI	Saturninus
1018	265	P. Licinius Valerianus II	Lucillus
1019	266	Imp. Caesar P. Licinius Gallienus	Sabinillus

		Augustus VII	
1020	267	Paternus	Arcesilaus
		Imp. Caesar M. Cassianius Latinius Postumus Augustus IV (Gaul)	M. Piavonius Victorinus I (Gaul)
1021	268	Paternus II	Publius Licinius Egnatius Marinianus
		Imp. Caesar M. Cassianius Latinius Postumus Augustus V (Gaul)	
1022	269	Imp. Caesar M. Aurelius Claudius Augustus	Paternus
		Imp. Caesar M. Piavonius Victorinus II (Gaul)	Sanctus *(Gaul)*
1023	270	Flavius Antiochianus II	Virius Orfitus
		Imp. Caesar M. Piavonius Victorinus II (Gaul)	
1024	271	Imp. Caesar L. Domitius Aurelianus Augustus I	Pomponius Bassus II
		Imp. Caesar C. Pius Esuvius Tetricus Augustus I (Gaul)	
1025	272	T. Flavius Postumius Quietus	Iunius Veldumnianus
		Imp. Caesar C. Pius Esuvius Tetricus Augustus II (Gaul)	
1026	273	M. Claudius Tacitus	Iulius Placidianus
		Imp. Caesar C. Pius Esuvius Tetricus Augustus III (Gaul)	
1027	274	Imp. Caesar L. Domitius Aurelianus Augustus II	Capitolinus
1028	275	Imp. Caesar L. Domitius Aurelianus Augustus III	Marcellinus
1029	276	Imp. Caesar M. Claudius Tacitus Augustus II	(Fulvius?) Aemilianus II
1030	277	Imp. Caesar M. Aurelius Probus Augustus I	Paulinus
1031	278	Imp. Caesar M. Aurelius Probus Augustus II	Virius Lupus II
1032	279	Imp. Caesar M. Aurelius Probus Augustus III	Nonius Paternus II
1033	280	Lucius Valerius Messalla	(Vettius?) Gratus
1034	281	Imp. Caesar M. Aurelius Probus Augustus IV	C. Iunius Tiberianus
1035	282	Imp. Caesar M. Aurelius Probus Augustus V	Victorinus
1036	283	Imp. Caesar M. Aurelius Carus Augustus II	Imp. Caesar M. Aurelius Carinus Augustus I
1037	284	Imp. Caesar M. Aurelius Carinus Augustus II	Imp. Caesar M. Aurelius Numerianus Augustus
DIO	suff.	Imp. Caesar C. Aurelius Valerius Diocletianus Augustus	Bassus
1	285	Imp. Caesar M. Aurelius Carinus	T. Claudius Aurelius Aristobulus

		Augustus III	
2	286	M. Iunius Maximus II	Vettius Aquilinus
3	287	Imp. Caesar C. Aurelius Valerius Diocletianus Augustus III	Imp. Caesar M. Aurelius Valerius Maximianus Augustus I
4	288	Imp. Caesar M. Aurelius Valerius Maximianus Augustus II	Pomponius Ianuarianus
	suff.	... ivianus	
5	289	M. Magrius Bassus	L. Ragonius Quintianus
	suff.	M. Umbrius Primus (*Feb.*)	T. Flavius Coelianus (*Feb.*)
		Ceionius Proculus (*Mar.*)	
		Helvius Clemens (*Apr.*)	
		Flavius Decimus (*May*)	
		... ninius Maximus (*Jun?*)	
6	290	Imp. Caesar C. Aurelius Valerius Diocletianus Augustus IV	Imp. Caesar M. Aurelius Valerius Maximianus Augustus III
7	291	C. Iunius Tiberianus II	Cassius Dio
8	292	Afranius Hannibalianus	Iulius Asclepiodotus
9	293	Imp. Caesar C. Aurelius Valerius Diocletianus Augustus V	Imp. Caesar M. Aurelius Valerius Maximianus Augustus IV
10	294	Flavius Valerius Constantius Caesar I	C. Galerius Valerius Maximianus Caesar I
11	295	Nummius Tuscus	Annius Anullinus
12	296	Imp. Caesar C. Aurelius Valerius Diocletianus Augustus VI	Flavius Valerius Constantius Caesar II
13	297	Imp. Caesar M. Aurelius Valerius Maximianus Augustus V	C. Galerius Valerius Maximianus Caesar II
14	298	Anicius Faustus II	Virius Gallus
15	299	Imp. Caesar C. Aurelius Valerius Diocletianus Augustus VII	Imp. Caesar M. Aurelius Valerius Maximianus Augustus VI
16	300	Flavius Valerius Constantius Caesar III	C. Galerius Valerius Maximianus Caesar III

Sixth Century (IVth-Vth century omitted to save space)

DIO	AD	East	West
217	501	Flavius Avienus iunior	Flavius Pompeius
218	502	Rufius Magnus Faustus Avienus iunior	Flavius Probus
219	503	Flavius Volusianus	Flavius Dexicrates
220	504	Rufius Petronius Nicomachus Cethegus	*without colleague*
221	505	Flavius Theodorus	Flavius Sabinianus
222	506	Flavius Ennodius Messala	Flavius Areobindus Dagalaiphus Areobindus
223	507	Flavius Anastasius Augustus III	Venantius iunior
224	508	Basilius Venantius iunior	Flavius Celer
225	509	Flavius Inportunus iunior	*without colleague*

226	510	Anicius Manlius Severinus Boethius iunior	*without colleague*
227	511	Felix	Flavius Secundinus
228	512	Flavius Paulus	Flavius Moschianus
229	513	Flavius Probus	Flavius Taurus Clementinus Armonius Clementinus
230	514	Magnus Aurelius Cassiodorus Senator	*without colleague*
231	515	Flavius Florentius	Procopius Anthemius
232	516	Flavius Petrus	*without colleague*
233	517	Flavius Agapitus	Flavius Anastasius Paulus Probus Sabinianus Pompeius Anastasius
234	518	Flavius Anastasius Paulus Probus Moschianus Probus Magnus	*Post consulatum Agapiti* (West)
235	519	Flavius Iustinus Augustus	Eutharicus Cillica
236	520	Flavius Rusticius	Flavius Vitalianus
237	521	Flavius Petrus Sabbatius Iustinianus	Flavius Valerius
238	522	Flavius Symmachus (West)	Flavius Boethius (West)
239	523	Flavius Anicius Maximus	*without colleague*
240	524	Flavius Iustinus Augustus II	Venantius Opilio
241	525	Flavius Anicius Probus iunior	Flavius Theodorus Philoxenus Soterichus Philoxenus
242	526	Flavius Anicius Olybrius Iunior	*without colleague*
243	527	*without colleague*	Vettius Agorius Basilius Mavortius
244	528	Flavius Petrus Sabbatius Iustinianus Augustus II	*Post consulatum Mavortii* (West)
245	529	Flavius Decius Iunior	*II post consulatum Mavortii* (Gaul)
246	530	Flavius Lampadius	Rufius Gennadius Probus Orestes
247	531	*Post consulatum Lampadii et Orestis*	
	532	*II post consulatum Lampadii et Orestis*	
	533	Flavius Petrus Sabbatius Iustinianus Augustus III	*III post consulatum Lampadii et Orestis* (West)
	534	Flavius Petrus Sabbatius Iustinianus Augustus IV	Flavius Decius Paulinus iunior
	535	Flavius Belisarius	*Post consulatum Paulini* (West)
	536	*Post consulatum Belisarii*	*II post consulatum Paulini* (West)
	537	*II post consulatum Belisarii*	*III post consulatum Paulini* (West)
	538	Flavius Iohannes Orientalis	*IV post consulatum Paulini* (West)
	539	Flavius Strategius Apion Strategius Apion	*Post consulatum Iohannis* (West) *V post consulatum Paulini* (West)
	540	Flavius Mar(ianus?) Petrus Theodorus Valentinus Rusticius Boraides Germanus Iustinus	*II post consulatum Iohannis* (West) *VI post consulatum Paulini* (West)
	541	Anicius Faustus Albinus Basilius iunior	*Post consulatum Iustini* (West)

Consular Office lapsed and merged with imperial titles

Appendix II: Ancient Lunar Visibility

Introduction

Lunar visibility depends on several factors, which can be simulated with astronomical software. I use my own program called "Calendar of Israel" and the program called "Cartes du Ciel"* to double check it, which is a free desktop planetarium, and is better than most software you can buy for this purpose. The program uses the plan404 ephemeris, which is good from –3000 b.c. to 3000 a.d. and allows the user to set delta T. I have successfully pushed the limits of my own program to 4139 BC.

The first section assumes that the user has correctly set the time and place of observation, and it shows how to calculate if the new moon is visible. The second section shows how to set the time and location. The information is necessarily brief, and its purpose is to allow experienced astronomers confirm my calculations with independent third party sources.

Visibility Given Time and Place

Once the program is set to the right time and place. You need to obtain the following information:

AZ_s = Azimuth of the sun in degrees
AZ_m = Azimuth of the moon in degrees
AL_s = Altitude of the sun in degrees
AL_m = Altitude of the moon in degrees
D = Diameter of Moon in arc minutes

With these figures I calculate if the moon is visible using Maunder, Yallop, Bruin, and Indian criteria. Here are the mathematics needed for the four tests. Comments follow the //.

$S_D = \frac{1}{2} D$ // $14 < S_D < 16$ [390]
Arc of Vision = $\alpha = | AL_m - AL_s |$ // $3° < \alpha < 35°$ [391]

---

[390] The apparent diameter of the moon varies. The moon measures about ½ degree or 30 arc-minutes from edge to edge. Values around 15 are typical for the calculated semi-diameter (radius) of the moon.

[391] The range given are typical values. Always check to see if computations produce typical values. This is a check against arithmetical err. The arc of

* Now superceded by Stellarium, where ΔT can be better customized. Bradley Shaeffer provides a more refined method: Schaefer, Bradley E. "An Algorithm for Predicting the Visibility of the Lunar Crescent." Proceedings of the IIIT Lunar Calendar Conference, 1998, pp. 10-1-10-10. JSTOR, www.jstor.org/stable/j.ctvkc683s.16. See also Roy Hoffman, Israeli New Moon Society.

Azimuth Difference = $\delta = | AZ_s - AZ_m |$ // $0° < < 35°$ [392]
Arc of Light = $\lambda = \cos^{-1}[\cos \alpha \cos \delta]$ // $3° < \lambda < 35°$
If $\lambda \le 22°$, then solve the easier equation // $\lambda^2 = \alpha^2 + \delta^2$ [393]
Crescent width = $\omega = S_D (1 - \cos \lambda)$ // $0' < \omega < 32'$ [394]

Figure 78: Geometry of New Moon

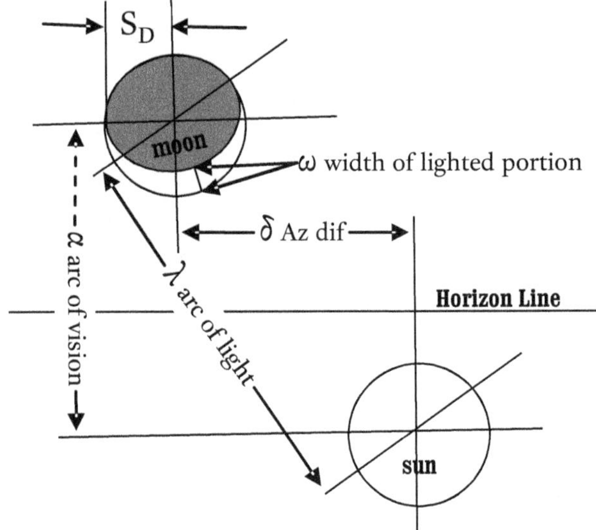

The best test is the Yallop "*q*" test. Calculate "*q*" as follows:

$q = (\alpha - (11.8371 - 6.3226\ \omega + 0.7319\ \omega^2 - 0.1018\ \omega^3))/10$

(A) $q > +0.216$ Easily Visible ($\lambda \ge 12°$)
(B) $+0.216 \ge q > -0.014$ Visible under perfect conditions

---

vision measures the sum of the height of the moon above the horizon and the depth of the sun below the horizon at the time of the observation.

[392] Typical values are between zero and twenty-degrees.

[393] Normally calculations are done using spherical trigonometry. This equation is a plane geometry substitution that works when the portion of the sphere is small enough to approximate a plane. The value to be solved for is λ, the arc of light. This value measures the distance in degrees between the center of the sun and the center of the moon.

[394] The crescent width measures the width of the lighted portion of the moon that can be visible from the center of the lighted edge toward the center of the moon. The width of a quarter moon crescent is 15 arc-minutes, and the width of a full moon lighted portion is 30 arc-minutes. Typical values for new crescent visibility tests are when: $0' < \omega < 3'$. Values of 0.2' to 0.7' are typical for very young crescents that may be visible. "The Calendar of Israel" Program uses a more complicated method of measuring crescent width based on Roy Hoffman's Paper.

(C) $-0.014 \geq q > -0.160$	May need optical aid to find moon
(D) $-0.160 \geq q > -0.232$	Will need optical aid to find moon
(E) $-0.232 \geq q > -0.293$	Not visible with a telescope ($\lambda \leq 8.5°$)
(F) $-0.293 \geq q$	Not visible, below Danjon limit ($\lambda \leq 8°$)

The next best test is the Indian test. The moon is visible if:

$$\alpha > 11.8371 - 6.3226\,\omega + 0.7319\,\omega^2 - 0.1018\,\omega^3$$

You will see that the Yallop test is simply a way of evaluating the results of the Indian test by observing that the equation used in the Yallop test is exactly the same as the Indian test. The use of the width of the crescent was developed by Bruin. Here is his test:

$$\alpha > 12.4023 - 9.4878\,\omega + 3.9512\,\omega^2 - 0.5632\,\omega^3$$

Here is the most primitive test by Maunder expressed in the form of the width of the lighted portion:

$$\alpha > 13.1783 - 9.0812\,\omega + 2.0709\,\omega^2 - 0.3360\,\omega^3$$

Yallop's "*q*" test is based on fitting the Indian curve to 295 eyewitness observations of the moon such that the test gives a maximum of correct results according to whether the eyewitnesses saw the moon or did not see the moon.†

Setting Location And Time

To properly calculate lunar visibility for ancient dates requires astronomical software that allows the user to set the value of ΔT. There is a program in the public domain called "Cartes du Ciel"[395] which allows this to be done under menu item "Setup"→ "Date/Time" → "More options" → "Use another DT–UT value". This parameter measures the deviation between the earth's longitude and uniformitarian ephemeris time (or dynamical time). There are several known factors that have caused calculated orbital time to deviate from the actual times kept by sunrise and sunset. The first is well known as due to tidal effects. The correction factor for this is derived from historical eclipse records. But these records have to be interpreted, and so there are several equations for ΔT to express various fits of the eclipse data with

[395] http://www.ap-i.net/skychart/en/download.

† The best free program is now Stellarium (latest 0.19.2). Use the ∠ tool to estimate the values used in the calculation. The program also allows the user to adjust ΔT (Configuration-->Time). I use Espenak and Meeus (2006) after the long day. The time format may be adjusted to show the weekday also. Location may be set to any ancient city whose location is known.

various interpretations of the eclipses:

(1) **$\Delta T = 32.5\ T^2$** $= 32.5(33.92)^2 = 37393$ seconds = 10.4 hrs. Stephenson & Yau (1992, 32.5). Morrison and Stephenson (1982, 32.5±2).
(2) **$\Delta T = 30\ T^2$** $= 30(33.92)^2 = 34517$ seconds = 9.59 hrs. Rén Wáng, Keiiti Aki [1995, 30±2.5].
(3) **$\Delta T = 30\ T^2$** Liu and Yau (1990, 30±5).
4) ΔT = 30.5 T2 Pang (1988, ±1.5)

T is the number of centuries before A.D. 1800. And the result ΔT is in seconds. Thus, for 1592 B.C., there are 18 centuries + 15.92 centuries, which is 33.92 centuries, and for the fourth equation, ΔT = 35,454 seconds (9.8 hours). This is to say that the earth's longitude relative to the celestial sphere, the sun, and the moon, must be corrected by 9.8 hours or 156°. The expected err for 1600 B.C. is 38 minutes or 9.5° longitude. From about the 13th century B.C. and backward the curve is extrapolated without any historical data points. For my calculations, I use **$\Delta T = 30.5\ T^2$**.†

The second factor to be corrected for is Joshua's long day. The Scripture says, "Then the sun was standing in the middle of the heavens, and hasteneth not to go according to a perfect day" (Jos. 10:13). Thus the sun stood at zenith (called "in transit") along the north-south meridian for twelve-hours. The moon also stood *up* over the western end of the valley of Aijalon (Joshua 10:12).

Figure 79: The Battle For Gibeon, July 26, 1592 B.C.

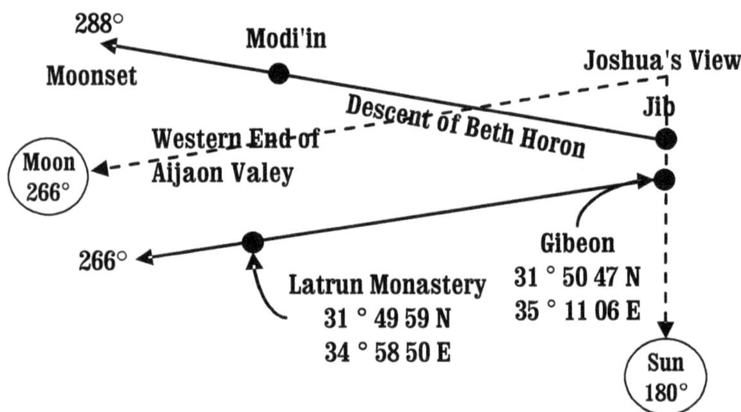

The locations can be reproduced on Google Earth, and using the

† I now use Espenak and Meeus (2006) in Stellarium after July 26, 1592 BC. Before this date $\Delta T = \Delta T_{Espenak} - 43200$. This is achieved by using Stellarium's "Custom equation for ΔT." Set a= −43200; b=0; c=32; y =1820; n= –26. Rather obscure, to enter these values, you must click on the three dots to the right of the equation dropdown menu to edit the "Custom equation for ΔT," and clicking there does nothing unless you have the custom equation selected. It takes some experience using known values to be sure of results. In fact, the date of the first and third month in 1632 BC is not changed even if the long day ΔT correction is neglected. But the second month is changed by one day.

line measuring tool, the compass headings can be read off. The time the sun was stopped amounts to exactly 12 hours, "the sun hasteneth not to go according to a perfect day" (כְּיוֹם תָּמִים), Jos. 10:13. A perfect day is a mean solar day or 12 hours.

Figure 80:Celestial Mechanics of Joshua's Long Day†

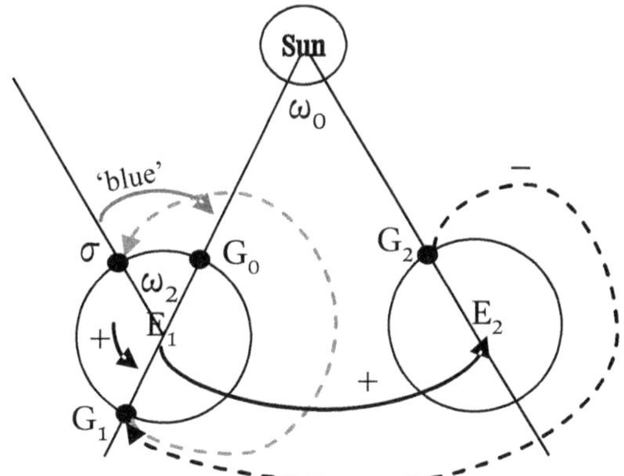

This is a simplified orbital diagram. Looking down at the north pole of the **Sun**, the earth, **E,** orbits counterclockwise in forward time (from $\mathbf{E}_1$ to $\mathbf{E}_2$), and rotates counterclockwise in forward time.[396] The rotation arrow is a small one just to the left of $\mathbf{E}_1$ with the + sign. We are looking down at the north pole of the earth. $\mathbf{E}_1$ is the earth at time 1, and $\mathbf{E}_2$ is the earth +12 hours later. The earth moves from $\mathbf{E}_1$ to $\mathbf{E}_2$ through angle $\boldsymbol{\omega}_0$ along the long solid arrow with the + sign. The measure of angle $\boldsymbol{\omega}_2 = \boldsymbol{\omega}_0$ because line $\mathbf{G}_2\,\mathbf{E}_2$ is parallel to line $\boldsymbol{\sigma}\,\mathbf{E}_1$, and cut by transversal $\mathbf{E}_1\,\mathbf{G}_0$, and alternate interior angles are equal.

$\mathbf{G}_2$ marks the longitude of Gibeon[398] at the end of Joshua's long day. When time is reversed along the long dashed black line for 12 hours, then Gibeon would be at $\mathbf{G}_1$, which is $180°+\boldsymbol{\omega}_2°$ rotation. This is where we would expect Gibeon to be if Joshua's long day never happened. For the situation at $\mathbf{E}_2$ the conversion from TDT (dynamic Time) to UT is: $\mathbf{TDT_2 = -20+30.5\,T^2 - UT_2}$; $\mathbf{\Delta T = -20+30.5\,T^2}$. The purpose of the equation is to correct the Universal Time **UT** for the slowing of the earth's rotation. To model Joshua's long day, the first step is to stop earth's rotation for –12 hours going from $\mathbf{E}_2$ to $\mathbf{E}_1$. This

[396] Make a fist with the thumb pointing up with the right hand. The thumb is the north pole and the fingers point the way the earth rotates.

† During the long day, the earth swings like a pendulum ball from the fulcrum of the sun without rotating. If anyone wishes to derive the whole from the fundamentals, the concept is simple: allow the sun to grab 'hold' of Gibeon at the end of the long day, and drag the whole geography of earth backward for 12 hours and release it. To get close to the right answer is sufficient for lunar calculation. To get it exact is harder. Using the standard model and geographic relocation is sounder.

gives us **TDT**$_1$ = **–20+30.5 T**^{2} **– 43,200 –UT**$_1$. –12 hours is converted to **43200** seconds. Calculating **TDT**$_2$ at time **E**$_2$ and **TDT**$_1$ at time **E**$_1$ is the same as saying earth's rotation stopped for 12 hours. There is a hitch however, and that is the fixed relation between hours and degrees of rotation with respect to the stars. Stopping the earth for 12 hours causes G_2 to end up at σ, or put another way corrects the location of G_1 to σ along the dashed red line. We need G_2 to end up at G_0, and thus it is clear that the earth's rotation cannot completely stop with respect to the stars. In the 12 hours G_0 must move through angle ω_2 against the blue arrow toward σ (when at Time **TDT**$_2$, G_0 arrives at G_2). So while **TDT**$_1$ = **–20+30.5 T**^{2} **– 43,200 –UT**$_1$ is correct for a stopped rotation through an orbital distance of 12 hours (ω_0), it cannot be further modified because the proportion between time and degrees rotated is fixed. Therefore, since G_1 is moved to σ, we have to rotate G_1 through the blue angle, ω_2, to G_0. This is done by deducting angle ω_2 from the longitude of G_2 when it is at σ, so that it is now correctly at G_0. This is done in place so that the dynamical time stays fixed.

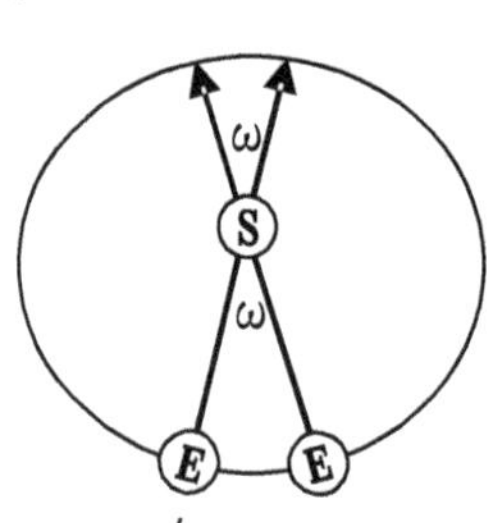

What remains is the value of ω to be computed. Cartes Du Ciel shows that the hour angle of σ is 2 min 5 sec. The hour angle of G_0 is equal to 0.

$$\omega = \left(2\text{ min} + 5\text{ sec} * \frac{\text{min}}{60\text{ sec}}\right) * \frac{\text{hr}}{60\text{ min}} * \frac{15\text{ deg}}{\text{hr}}$$

ω = **0.520833°**. This is the correction we apply to the longitude, and represents the exact amount of turning from G_0 to G_2 that is necessary to keep the longitude of Gibeon under the sun for 12 hours. It is the same turning as if the earth were a giant pendulum with the cable connected at Gibeon. Thus the sun "stood" over Gibeon a perfect day.

To calculate back to the end of Joshua's long day, I simply calculate when the sun is in transit (high noon) on July 26, 1592 b.c. for the longitude of Gibeon[397] without the 12 hour correction. So I use the

[397] Gibeon at end of long day, Lat: **31° 50' 46" N**, Long: **35° 11' 07"**. Corrected Longitude for beginning of long day = **–0.520833°** = **–(31' 15")** = **34° 39' 52"**. The latitude is unchanged.

shorter equation **ΔT = -20+30.5 T², T=34.104 centuries**. This comes to **ΔT = 35,454 sec** to set in the "more options"→ "Use another DT-UT value" (DT means "Dynamical Time" and UT "Universal Time"). The time is set at **9h 39m 10s** (GMT), **July 26, 1592 B.C**, and location set to the coordinates of Gibeon, as specified in the figure. This will represent the situation at the end of the long day with the hour angle at 0. The positions of the sun and moon are:

	Azimuth	Altitude	Time
Sun	**+180° 00' 10"**	**80° 46' 20"**	**9h 39m 10s**
Moon	**+265° 59' 59"**	**40° 32' 17"**	**9h 39m 10s**

Now to calculate for the start of Joshua's Long day we need to transpose Gibeon's location by **ω = 0.520833°**.[398]

So now at the start of Joshua's long day, the positions are as follows. The **UT** being the same (noon) means that:

$$\mathbf{TDT_1 = -20+30.5\,T^2 - 43{,}200 - UT_1}$$
$$\underline{\mathbf{TDT_2 = -20+30.5\,T^2 \qquad\qquad - UT_2}}$$
$$\mathbf{TDT_1 - TDT_2 = 0 - 43{,}200,\ i.e.\ TDT_2 = TDT_1 + 12\ hours.}$$

	Azimuth	Altitude	Time
Sun	**+180° 00' 28"**	**80° 50' 16"**	**9h 39m 10s**
Moon	**+267° 11' 43"**	**34° 10' 45"**	**9h 39m 10s**

The azimuth figures for the sun represent the closest Cartes du Ciel will calculate to the nearest second (for noon transit). To target the value of 180° 0' 0" for the sun exactly would require fractions of a second, and the program does not allow entering fractions of a second. However, the sun's location has changed by 4' arc in altitude. This is because the daily motion of the sun was arrested on the meridian, but not the yearly motion.[398]

The moon has moved by 6°21'32" (6.4°) in altitude and 1° 11' 44" in Azimuth, i.e. 6.47° total (using Pythagorus). From Joshua's

---

[398] In its yearly motion the sun moves north 23.5° and then south by the same amount. Since it is after the summer solstice, the sun continuously moves south in latitude. From the start of Joshua's long day to the end, it moves 4' lower in altitude. This movement is only 4'/31.8's of the sun's size, i.e. 1/8th.

vantage point it appears to rise in the sky by 6.4°. The scripture thus reads:

> Then was still the sun, and the moon stood up until the nation avenged themselves of their enemies" (Josh. 10:13).

Two different verbs are used in this text, one for the sun, and another for the moon. The sun was "silenced," or "stilled" (יִדֹּם), and the moon "stood up" (עָמָד). It also says the sun "stood in the middle of the heavens" (וַיַּעֲמֹד הַשֶּׁמֶשׁ בַּחֲצִי הַשָּׁמַיִם), but this is qualified "in the middle of the heavens," whereas of the moon it simply says, "it standeth." The sun did not move from the meridian. The moon stood up 6.4° degrees in altitude.

Figure 81: The moon standeth; the sun stands

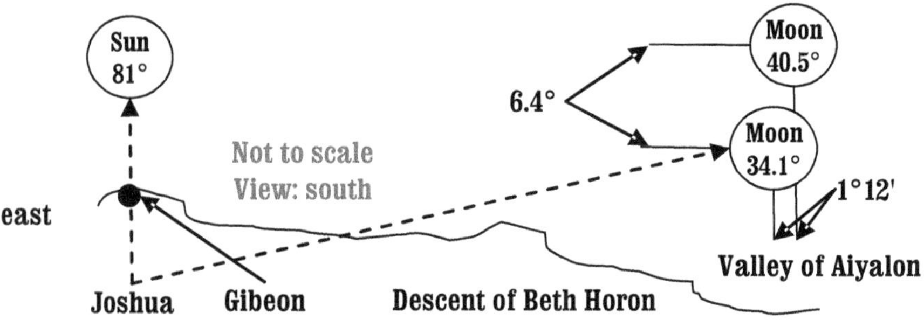

It is a necessary consequence that if the sun is standing still on the meridian line that the moon stands up (עָמָד) in altitude. This is because only the motion of the sun relative to the earth stopped. All other celestial motions continued. From a heliocentric point of view the earth's rotation stopped with the sun over Gibeon. However, the moon continued in its celestial motion, which in this case was mostly up and hardly a noticeable change in azimuth.†

Now how did they know that the time the sun stopped was a perfect day? Because with a simple sextant, the moon's rise could be measured to 6.5° ±30'. Modern sextants are capable of measuring 1' arc minute (1/60°). A simple 14 inch sextant would gradate a half degree every 1/8 inch. Outfitted with a string and plumb weight, an Israelite astronomer could determine that the moon rose 6.5° ±15'. The sidereal period of the moon was known to be 27.3 days by watching the moon return to the same star in 27.3 days. This means

† When a person stands up, they do not typically make a perfectly vertical ascent, but their head ends up offset somewhat from purely straight up.

that the moon must average 360°/27.3 = 13.19°/day, or in 12 hours 13.19°/2 = 6.6°. Thus a 6.5° ±30' measurement of the moon would show that the sun had stopped for twelve hours.

Figure 82: Simple Sextant

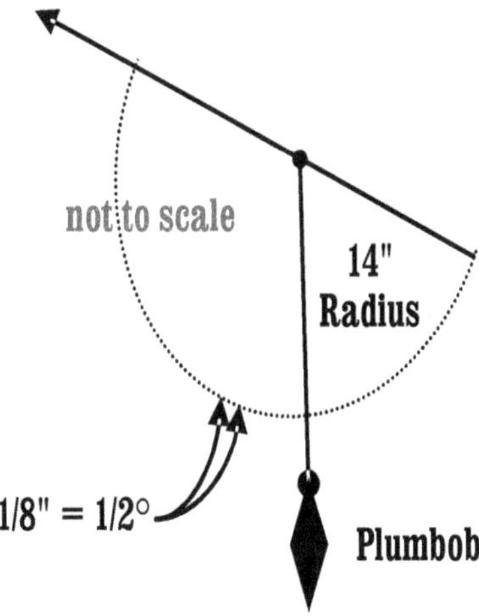

To interpret Joshua's long day we say the sun stood at zenith over Gibeon for twelve hours. In celestial mechanics point of view is relative. One can choose any observation point and come up with a system of mathematics to describe motion from that point of view. In fact, most planetarium software simulates everything with the earth as a stationary point. It is easier to compute Kepler's equations from the solar point of view, but the fact that a coordinate transformation can be performed shows that it is just a matter of pure mathematics to change the point of view. It is thus equally correct to say the sun stood over Gibeon as to say that the earth stopped rotating for twelve hours (with respect to the sun). It all depends where one is fixing their observation point.

These results are confirmed in the chronology of Mesopotamia and Egypt prior to 1592 BC. Without these results, historians, who have adopted the Middle Chronology, e.g. fall of Amorite Babylon in 1587 BC to the Hititte king, and those astronomical scholars trying to place Akkadian, Uruk, Ur, and Assyrian astronomical records onto the timeline have been at loggerheads. The astronomers propose radical chronologies to align the astronomy that the historians will not accept. The long day correction moves the eclipse maps one solar day and resolves the dispute.‡

‡ See page 481, note no. 4.

Figure 83: Joshua's Long Day and New Moons

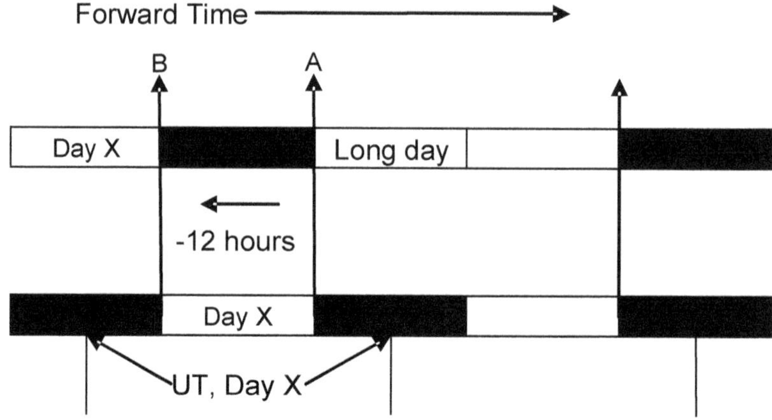

If the long day did not exist then one would calculate for new moon visibility at point "A" according to the astronomical model in the bottom row. However, the long day moves the preceding sunset back 12 hours to point "B." Before July 26th, 1592 b.c., the proper way to calculate is to correct the longitude via delta T, and then correct the longitude again, without changing the time, by half the difference between a solar day and sidereal day.

No correction is considered for the sun-dial of Ahaz because the scripture says that only, "He returned the shadow by the steps it had gone down in the steps of Ahaz backward ten steps" (2 Kings 20:11).

The correction for Joshua's long day does not make a difference in the date of the Exodus Passover or the date of Shavuot that year. However, it does cause the new moon of the second month to be one day later, which agrees with the story of the manna in Exodus 16, whereas the date without the correction does not agree so well. The other new moon is that for Nisan 1 upon the entry into the land of Israel in 1592 B.C., with which we are most concerned in this book. This falls one day later after the correction is made, according to the following calendar:

---

‡ The texts say: וַיָּשֶׁב אֶת־הַצֵּל בַּֽמַּעֲלוֹת אֲשֶׁר יָרְדָה בְּמַעֲלוֹת אָחָז אֲחֹרַנִּית עֶשֶׂר מַעֲלוֹת, "Then he returned the shadow on the stairs, which had gone down on the stairs of Aħaz, backward ten steps," and Isa. 38:8: הִנְנִי מֵשִׁיב אֶת־צֵל הַמַּעֲלוֹת אֲשֶׁר יָרְדָה בְמַעֲלוֹת אָחָז בַּשֶּׁמֶשׁ אֲחֹרַנִּית עֶשֶׂר מַעֲלוֹת וַתָּשָׁב הַשֶּׁמֶשׁ עֶשֶׂר מַעֲלוֹת בַּמַּעֲלוֹת אֲשֶׁר יָרָדָה, "Behold I will make the shadow on the stairs, which has gone down on the stairs of Aħaz with the sun (rise), return backwards ten steps. Then he returned (set) the sun ten steps on the stairs, which it had descended." This happened in the morning. The shadow went down the steps as the sun rose, and then the sun appeared to reverse direction with the shadow going back up the steps. The apparent location of the sun rose and then set in the morning. This was a miracle of refraction and not rotation, because further decrease in $\Delta T \approx \Delta T - 4000$ sec would put eclipses before 1592 BC too far west.

```
Month: I AVIV, 1592 BC 2548 A.M. Sab. Cyc: 7. Jub. Cyc: 49 Cycle No: 52
              Sabbatical Year in Progress until Trumpets.
Q1: 1.355 A Q2: -0.276 E LG:  95m W: 1.019' AL: 21.2 AV: 19.6
New Moon calculated for longitude: 35.20 and latitude 31.77
Location of calculations: Mt. Nebo, Jordan
   Designed and Programmed By Daniel Gregg
```

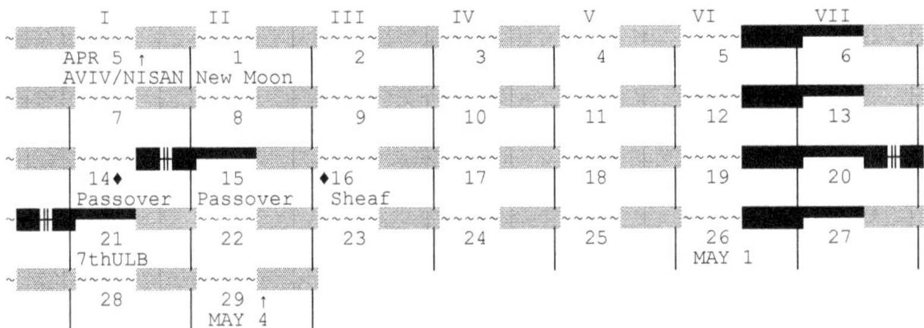

I
II
III
IV
V
VI
VII
APR 5 ↑
AVIV/NISAN
1
New Moon
2
3
4
5
6
7
8
9
10
11
12
13
14♦
Passover
15
Passover
♦16
Sheaf
17
18
19
20
21
7thULB
22
23
24
25
26
MAY 1
27
28
29 ↑
MAY 4

The new moon therefore was first seen on April 5th in this year a bit after sunset. Details of the calculation are:

Observation Point: Mt. Nebo: 31° 46' 4' N, 35° 43' 31" E. Transpose longitude –31'15" to 35° 12' 16.7' since this is before Joshua's long day.

Seconds Delta T (extrapolated): -7739.64s, +/- 2196 sec sigma err
DT Equation: [-20+30.5T^2-43200, T=(Y-1819)/100
---corrected for Joshua's long day-----]

$\Delta T = -20+30.5\ T^2 - 43200 = -7739.64$ seconds

sunset = $T_s = 15^h\ 47^m$ moonset = $T_m = 17^h\ 19^m$

$T_b = (5\ T_s + 4\ T_m) / 9$

[Yallop, Eq. 4.1][399]

$\mathbf{T_s}$ = Time of sunset on the day for which we are testing if the new moon will be visible. $\mathbf{T_m}$ = Time of moonset on the day for which we are testing if the new moon will be visible. T_b = Best time. The time for which the calculation should be made, i.e. at which is the best chance to see the new moon. This calculation simply finds the best time to calculate visibility. T_b is some time after sunset but some time before moon set. <u>Reset the astronomy software for time:</u>

[399] The Yallop method is considered best, and is taken from, "A Method for Predicting the First Sighting of the New Crescent Moon" by BD Yallop. However, Yallop first reviews older methods, which are simpler to calculate.

$T_b = (5\ T_s + 4\ T_m\ ) / 9 = (5\ (15^h47^m) + 4\ (17^h19^m)\ ) / 9$
$T_b = 16^h30^m11^s$; best time to observe, reset software:

AZ_s = Azimuth of the sun = 276.50°
AZ_m = Azimuth of the moon = 268.48°
AL_s = Altitude of the sun = –9.72°
AL_m = Altitude of the moon = 9.89°
D = Diameter of Moon = 30.8'
Semi-diameter = SD = ½D
Arc of Vision = $\alpha = |\ AL_m - AL_s\ |$ = 19.61
Azimuth Difference = $\delta = |\ AZ_s - AZ_m\ |$ = 8.02

α = arc of vision; this is the difference between the altitude of the sun and the altitude of the moon at the best time around sunset.

δ = difference in the azimuth of the sun and moon
Solve λ for the Arc of Light in degrees:
$\lambda = \cos^{-1}(\cos\alpha\cos\delta) = 21.17$
$\omega = SD\ (1 - \cos\lambda)$ = Width of Crescent in degrees = 1.039.
$q = (\alpha - (11.8371 - 6.3226\ \omega + 0.7319\ \omega^2 - 0.1018\ \omega^3))/10 = 1.366$
$q = 1.366$

Criteria Code & Range	Remarks
(A) $q > +0.216$	Easily Visible ($\lambda \geq 12°$)
(B) $+0.216 \geq q > -0.014$	Visible under perfect conditions
(C) $-0.014 \geq q > -0.160$	May need optical aid to find moon
(D) $-0.160 \geq q > -0.232$	Will need optical aid to find moon
(E) $-0.232 \geq q > -0.293$	Not visible with a telescope ($\lambda \leq 8.5°$)
(F) $-0.293 \geq q$	Not visible, below Danjon limit ($\lambda \leq 8°$)

Since q > + 0.216, criteria "A" applies. The moon will be easily seen.
And on the preceding day April 4 at Mt. Nebo.
Longitude: 35° 12' 16.70" E
Latitude: 31° 46' 3.63" N

$T_s = 15^h\ 47^m$; $T_m = 16^h\ 23^m$
$T_b = 16^h\ 3^m\ 0^s$

$AZ_s = +272°27' 50''$
$AZ_m = 266° 11' 32''$
$AL_s = -04°03' 27''$
$AL_m = 3° 38' 36''$
$D = 30.4'$
$\alpha = | AL_m - AL_s | \quad = 7.7$
$\delta = | AZ_s - AZ_m | = 6.27$
$\lambda = \cos^{-1}(\cos \alpha \cos \delta) = 9.92$
$\omega = SD (1 - \cos \lambda) = 0.227$
$q = (\alpha -(11.8371-6.3226\omega+0.7319 \omega^2-0.1018\omega^3))/10 = -.274$
(Note: Calendar of Israel returns q = -0.276 E.)

q = –0.274, hence criteria "E" applies: **Not visible with a telescope**. Therefore, the calendar above is correct, the new moon for Nisan 1 was seen in the evening of April 5, and the new moon day was Monday, April 6.

The key dates that I have been using in this section are fully explained in the Scroll of Biblical Chronology. In regard to ancient calculation of the new moon, two more may be added. The date of the flood is 2483 BC, and the date of Creation in 4139 BC. The Calendar of Israel places the first day of the first month on the fourth day of the week in 4139 B.C. and also places the 10th and 17th of the 2nd month in 2483 BC on the Sabbath. The 17th day of the 2nd month is day 50 of the year, and the 17th day of the 7th month is day 199 of the year. Inclusively counted, they are 150 days. In the year of the flood, the 11th, 18th, and 25th days of the 11th month are on Sunday. This is when Noah sent the birds out, and then waited seven days before trying again. Neither Dodwell's research on the change in the obliquity of the ecliptic from ancient value of 26.5° nor a difference in the axial precession rate would upset these calculations.

Walt Brown assumes there is a biblical basis for a 360 day year. This assumption is mistaken. The earth did lose mass during the flood, but this does not change rotational velocity. When a man on a merry-go-round jumps off at a right angle, it does not speed up. But redistribution of mass does affect rotational velocity. Some mass went down. Some mass came up. It appears that net velocity change was 0.

Large Military Numbers

Many reject the large numbers given in Scripture because they do not think they are reasonable. Here I will inventory solutions for the skeptics. Biblical figures are usually given as the sum of a professional army plus reserves. Counted in the reserves was every man between 20 and 50 who could use some sort of weapon. In ancient times, foreign wars, especially the defensive kind, were won when the professional army had the support of the reserves called up right behind them.

The critics almost always begin their arguments with a discrepancy, such as 22,000 Levites vs. 22,300 Levites (Num. 3:39 and the sum from 3:22, 28, and 34). Then with the straightest face they can muster they dogmatically say it is an error of some sort. (Errors do occur in copying sometimes, but far, far less frequently than the critics claim.) Then they use the instances of errors they cite as levers to get itching ears to disbelieve the rest of the numbers, "because they appear unreasonable." The 22,300 Levites counts all a month old and over. 22,000 Levites omits 300 first born Levites who were born in the year between the Exodus and the first census a year later.

David's census reports the reserve forces of Israel as 800,000 and Judah as 500,000 in 2 Sam. 24:9. The figures are given as 1,100,000 and 470,000 in 1 Chron. 21:5. It is easy to see that military figures in Scripture were customarily rounded off to one or two significant digits. Thus 470,000 is rounded to 500,000. The explanation of the 1,100,000 vs. 800,000 number is that David had ordered the counting of the reserve forces. The number of the standing army was already known to be 288,000, taken from all 12 tribes and thus 'called the army of Israel.' The Chronicler wanted to include the numbers of the standing army in Israel's numbers because he wanted to underline Israel's birthright and support for king David. This he rounded off to 300,000 and added to the 800,000 reserve number for 1,100,000. This was a tribal rivalry which amounts to "Israel contributed more than Judah did."

In some few cases the word for a 'division', אֲלֻף has been mistaken for 1000: אֶלֶף. II Sam. 10:18 has 700 chariots and 1 Chron 17:18: 7000, but the latter text should say "7 divisions of chariots," and there are 100 chariots per division. In like manner 1 Kings 4:26 should be "40 divisions of stalls of horses for chariots" to agree with 2 Chron. 9:25: "4000 stalls of horses and chariots." *Aluf* means a division of 100 chariots.

In 2 Sam. 23:8 (800) vs. 1 Chron. 11:11 (300) the critics have confused a son who succeeded in his father's position with the father.

In 2 Sam. 10:18, 40,000 horsemen is thought to contradict 1 Chron. 19:18, 40,000 footmen. But this is based on a modern misconception of cavalry. In ancient times is was common for horse infantry to manuever into battle position on horse, but to dismount to fight.

In 2 Sam. 10:6, "20,000 foot soldiers," "[from] the king of Maacah, 1000 men, and 12,000 men from Tov" is thought to contradict "32,000 רכב and the king of Maacah" (1 Chron. 19:7). In this case רכב does not mean "chariot." רֶכֶב Rather it means rider: רֹכֵב. This word is collectively used to mean 'riders.' As in the case above, they rode to manuever, but dismounted to fight.

In 2 Sam. 8:4, "David seized from him a division (אֲלֻף), and 700 horsemen, and 20,000 footmen. David hamstrung all the chariot [horses], but he left a hundred chariots." That is, he kept one division of chariots and horses for himself. Compare, 1 Chron. 18:4, "And David seized from him a division of chariots, and seven divisions (אֲלָפִים) of horsemen, and 20,000 footmen."

In 1 Sam. 6:19 Josephus and three Hebrew texts support omitting '50,000' men (cf. BHS) leaving '70.' But the latter number seems too small for a 'great slaughter.' Of all the suggestions it seems to me easier to suppose that the 50,000 was the number of Philistines struck (10,000 each for the five cities), "He struck among the people 70 men; 50,000 men. And then the people mourned, because Yahweh had struck the people with a great slaughter." In some sense 'the people' of that town who sinned were identified with the Philistine people because of their impiety, and joined them in mourning the great slaughter. Indeed, they were without a doubt struck with the very same plague uniting them with the Philistines.

The numbers in Ezra 2 and Nehemiah 7 do not add up to the total 42,360. These lists are very obviously incomplete, giving only a sample listing of the returnees' census along with the total. There are some differences in the sample numbers, and this may be attributed to Nehemiah's less accurate copy, which Ezra presents, but then corrects. (Ezra-Nehemiah were originally one book.) Nehemiah is thus canonical with Ezra's corrections (cf. BASOR No. 136, H.L. Allrick).

1 Kings 7:26 says that the sea holds "2000 baths," and 2 Chron. 4:5 says it is "strong enough to hold 3000 baths." The explanation is that which it is usually filled with vs. what its design maximum will hold.

1 Sam. 13:5, "thirty divisions (אֲלֻף) of chariots, and six thousand mounted troops, and people as the sand of the sea." אֲלֻף = chiefs, chariot division commanders, with each division being 100 chariots. Syriac and Arabic versions have 3000 chariots.

As I said, the errors are far, far fewer than the critics claim. One of these places is probably 1 Chron. 22:14, where the numbers become reasonable when we put for gold "hundred hundred (מֵאָה מאות) talents" and silver "hundred thousands" (מֵאָה אֲלָפִים), which is a 20 year output of mines at 500 talents/year of gold (19 tons/year or 36 cu feet). These figures agree with Josephus. Much of this gold probably came from the mines of Ophir, probably Mahd adh Dhahab in Saudi Arabia.

Appendix III: Noah's Flood Year

Here are the key calendar months for Noah's Flood year:

```
Month: II ZIV, 2483 BC 1657 A.M. Sab. Cyc: 5. Jub. Cyc: 40 Cycle No: 33
Q1: 0.090 B Q2: -1.176 F LG:  55m W: 0.284' AL: 11.5 AV: 11.0
New Moon calculated for longitude: 34.65 and latitude 31.77
Location of calculations: Jerusalem
   Designed and Programmed By Daniel Gregg
```

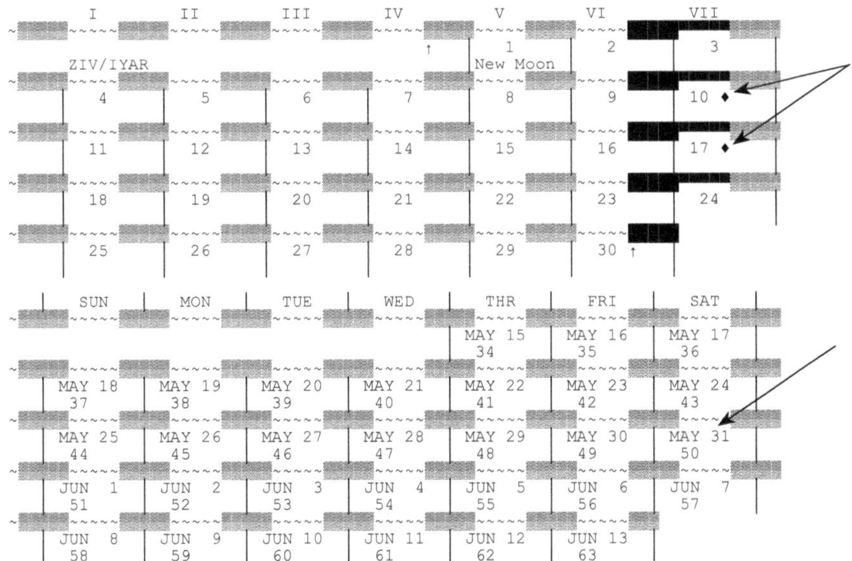

I II III IV V VI VII
1 New Moon 2 3
ZIV/IYAR
4 5 6 7 8 9 10 ♦
11 12 13 14 15 16 17 ♦
18 19 20 21 22 23 24
25 26 27 28 29 30
SUN MON TUE WED THR FRI SAT
MAY 15 34 MAY 16 35 MAY 17 36
MAY 18 37 MAY 19 38 MAY 20 39 MAY 21 40 MAY 22 41 MAY 23 42 MAY 24 43
MAY 25 44 MAY 26 45 MAY 27 46 MAY 28 47 MAY 29 48 MAY 30 49 MAY 31 50
JUN 1 51 JUN 2 52 JUN 3 53 JUN 4 54 JUN 5 55 JUN 6 56 JUN 7 57
JUN 8 58 JUN 9 59 JUN 10 60 JUN 11 61 JUN 12 62 JUN 13 63

Note the diamonds on II.10 and II.17. The flood began on II.17, then skip down to the parallel calendar, and note the Julian date is May 31, and that it is the 50th day of the year.

The next chart is for month VII. Notice that VII.17 corresponds to the 199th day of the year in the parallel Julian calendar, i.e. October 27th. The inclusive count from II.17 to VII.17 is 150 days (199 - 50 + 1 = 150) .

```
Month: VII ETHANIM, 2483 BC
```

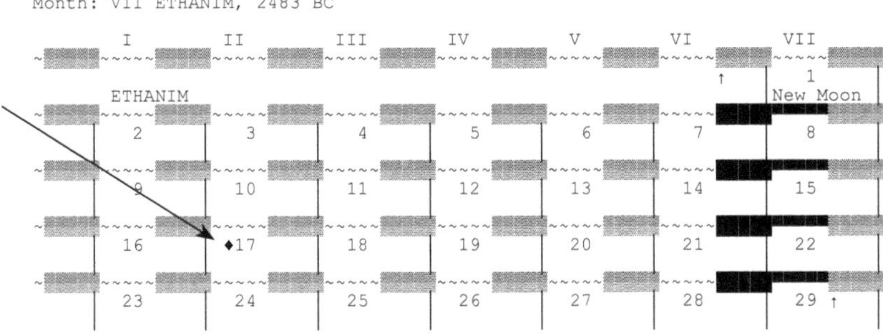

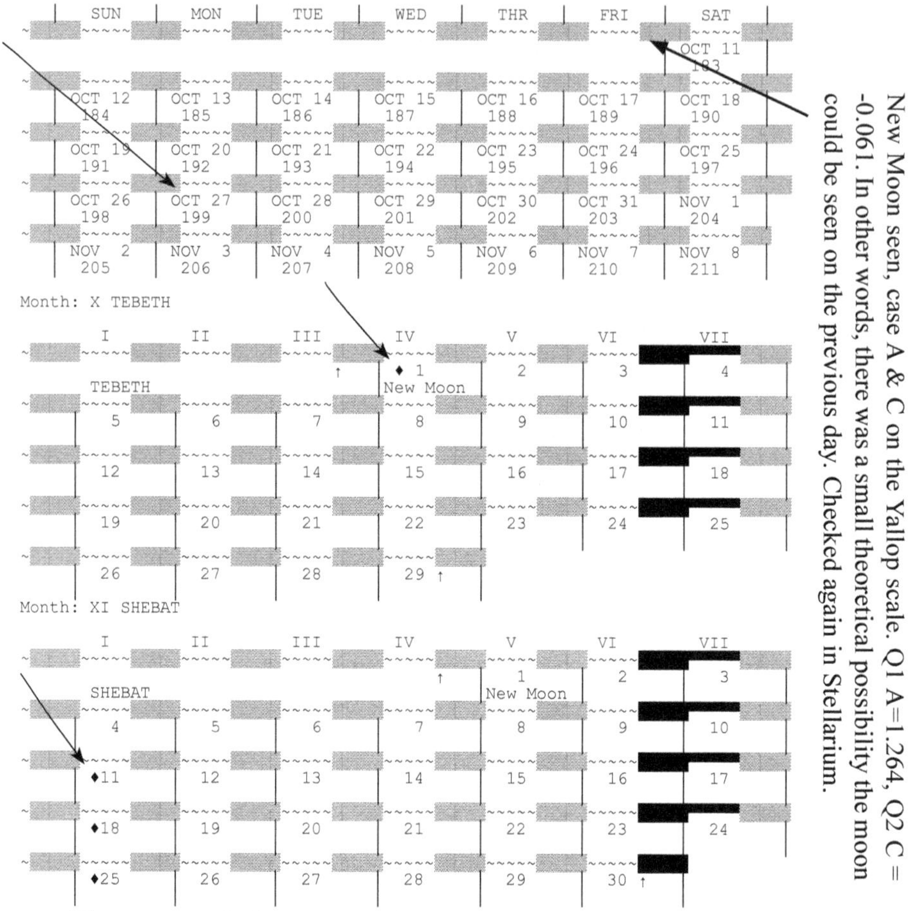

SUN	MON	TUE	WED	THR	FRI	SAT
						OCT 11 183
OCT 12 184	OCT 13 185	OCT 14 186	OCT 15 187	OCT 16 188	OCT 17 189	OCT 18 190
OCT 19 191	OCT 20 192	OCT 21 193	OCT 22 194	OCT 23 195	OCT 24 196	OCT 25 197
OCT 26 198	OCT 27 199	OCT 28 200	OCT 29 201	OCT 30 202	OCT 31 203	NOV 1 204
NOV 2 205	NOV 3 206	NOV 4 207	NOV 5 208	NOV 6 209	NOV 7 210	NOV 8 211

Month: X TEBETH

I	II	III	IV	V	VI	VII
		↑	♦ 1 New Moon	2	3	4
TEBETH 5	6	7	8	9	10	11
12	13	14	15	16	17	18
19	20	21	22	23	24	25
26	27	28	29 ↑			

Month: XI SHEBAT

I	II	III	IV	V	VI	VII
			↑	1 New Moon	2	3
SHEBAT 4	5	6	7	8	9	10
♦11	12	13	14	15	16	17
♦18	19	20	21	22	23	24
♦25	26	27	28	29	30 ↑	

New Moon seen, case A & C on the Yallop scale. Q1 A=1.264, Q2 C = -0.061. In other words, there was a small theoretical possibility the moon could be seen on the previous day. Checked again in Stellarium.

The tops of the mountains are seen on X.1, marked by the diamond on the new moon day, then 40 days later was XI.11, the first day of the week,when Noah sent out a dove. A week later on XI.18 he sends the dove again. A week later on XI.25 he sends the dove out, and it does not return. The nearest other year after 2483 that matches the weekdays and the 150 days and the Jubilee cycle is 2385 BC, almost 100 years later. There are no matches of this sort before 2483 all the way back to 3000 BC. The Scriptural chronological data are not so open to interpretation as to allow a 500 year shift in the flood date, or even a 100 year shift. Consider the following:

Ezek 1:1	Ezekiel's Vision IV.5 Sabbath July 1,		593.T	
Ezek 4:5	Era of the division of the kingdom	+	390	
1 Ki 12:20	Division of the Kingdom	=	983.T	
1 Ki 11:42	Solomon's reign	+	40	
1 Chr 29:27	David's reign	+	40	
Acts 13:31	Saul's reign	+	40	

Subtotal	Saul made first king		=	1103.T
variable	Samuel		+	x
1 Sam 7:2	Philistines		+	20
1 Sam 4:18	Eli		+	39.5
Jud 13:1	Philistines		+	40
Subtotal			=	1202.S + x
Jud 12:13	Abdon		+	8
Jud 12:11	Elon		+	10
Jud 12:8	Ibzan		+	7
Jud 12:7	Jephthah		+	6
Jud 10:8	Ammon		+	18
Jud 10:3	Jair		+	22
Jud 10:1-2	Tola		+	23
Jud 9:22	Abimelech		+	3
Jud 8:28	Gideon		+	40
Jud 6:1	Midian		+	7
Jud 5:31	Deborah		+	40
Jud 4:3	Jabin of Hazor		+	20
Jud 3:30	Ehud/Shamgar		+	80
Jud 3:14	Eglon of Moab		+	18
Jud 3:11	Othniel		+	40
Jud 3:8	Cushan-rishathaim		+	8
	Elders		+	y
Josh 14:10	Conquest		+	6
Exo 16:35	Wilderness		+	40
Subtotal	Exodus		=	1598.S + x + y
Gen 15:13	Sojourn of Abraham's seed		+	400
Gen 12:4	Abram departs from Haran		+	25
Gen 11:32	Life of Terah		+	205
Gen 11:24	Nahor's life before Terah		+	29
Gen 11:22	Serug's life before Nahor		+	30
Gen 11:20	Reu's life before Serug		+	32
Gen 11:18	Peleg's life before Reu		+	30
Gen 11:16	Eber's life before Peleg		+	34
Gen 11:14	Salah's life before Eber		+	30

[400] Nebuchadnezzar took Jerusalem in 597 B.C. BM 21946 dates this to March 16, 597. The 70 years exile are counted on a fall epoch, so counting inclusively makes the 5th year of the exile Tishri 594-Tishri 593. Ezekiel's vision was in the 4th month, 5th day, which is during this 5th year of exile. Astronomical calculation via VAT 4956 fixes Nebuchadnezzar's 37th year to 568/567 B.C.

Gen 11:12	Arphaxad's life before Salah	+	35	
subtotal	start of birth year of Arphaxad	=	2448.S + x + y	
Gen 11:10	add one for year of the deluge	+	1	
Total	Standardized year of deluge	=	2449.S + x + y	
Weekday/Jubilee match to deluge start:		2483.S	=2449.S + x + y	
	Solution to equation:	x + y	=34	

Year = -2960 ----MATCH----111
Year = -2943 ----MATCH----111
Year = -2889 ----MATCH----111
Year = -2862 ----MATCH----111
Year = -2791 ----MATCH----111
Year = -2740 ----MATCH----111
Year = -2642 ----MATCH----111
Year = -2615 ----MATCH----111
Year = -2571 ----MATCH----111
Year = -2544 ----MATCH----111
Year = -2543 *****FAILS******000
Year = -2542 *****FAILS******000
Year = -2541 *****FAILS******000
Year = -2540 *****FAILS******101
Year = -2539 *****FAILS******000
Year = -2538 *****FAILS******000
Year = -2537 *****FAILS******011
Year = -2536 *****FAILS******000
Year = -2535 *****FAILS******000
Year = -2534 *****FAILS******000
Year = -2533 *****FAILS******000
Year = -2532 *****FAILS******000
Year = -2531 *****FAILS******000
Year = -2530 *****FAILS******011
Year = -2529 *****FAILS******000
Year = -2528 *****FAILS******000
Year = -2527 *****FAILS******000
Year = -2526 *****FAILS******000
Year = -2525 *****FAILS******000
Year = -2524 *****FAILS******000
Year = -2523 *****FAILS******000
Year = -2522 *****FAILS******000
Year = -2521 *****FAILS******000
Year = -2520 *****FAILS******100
Year = -2519 *****FAILS******000
Year = -2518 *****FAILS******000
Year = -2517 *****FAILS******110

Year = -2516 *****FAILS******001
Year = -2515 *****FAILS******000
Year = -2514 *****FAILS******010
Year = -2513 *****FAILS******101
Year = -2512 *****FAILS******000
Year = -2511 *****FAILS******000
Year = -2510 *****FAILS******011
Year = -2509 *****FAILS******000
Year = -2508 *****FAILS******000
Year = -2507 *****FAILS******010
Year = -2506 *****FAILS******000
Year = -2505 *****FAILS******000
Year = -2504 *****FAILS******010
Year = -2503 *****FAILS******001
Year = -2502 *****FAILS******000
Year = -2501 *****FAILS******000
Year = -2500 *****FAILS******000
Year = -2499 *****FAILS******000
Year = -2498 *****FAILS******000
Year = -2497 *****FAILS******000
Year = -2496 *****FAILS******100
Year = -2495 *****FAILS******000
Year = -2494 *****FAILS******000
Year = -2493 *****FAILS******000
Year = -2492 *****FAILS******000
Year = -2491 *****FAILS******000
Year = -2490 *****FAILS******010
Year = -2489 *****FAILS******001
Year = -2488 *****FAILS******000
Year = -2487 *****FAILS******010
Year = -2486 *****FAILS******001
Year = -2485 *****FAILS******000
Year = -2484 *****FAILS******000
Year = -2483 ----MATCH----111
-----Jubilee Cycle Match-----
Year = -2482 *****FAILS******000
Year = -2481 *****FAILS******000

Year = -2480 *****FAILS******010
Year = -2479 *****FAILS******000
Year = -2478 *****FAILS******000
Year = -2477 *****FAILS******000
Year = -2476 *****FAILS******000
Year = -2475 *****FAILS******000
Year = -2474 *****FAILS******000
Year = -2473 *****FAILS******000
Year = -2472 *****FAILS******000
Year = -2471 *****FAILS******000
Year = -2470 *****FAILS******010
Year = -2469 *****FAILS******000
Year = -2468 *****FAILS******000
Year = -2467 *****FAILS******000
Year = -2466 *****FAILS******100
Year = -2465 *****FAILS******000
Year = -2464 *****FAILS******000
Year = -2463 *****FAILS******110
Year = -2462 *****FAILS******000
Year = -2461 *****FAILS******000
Year = -2460 *****FAILS******010
Year = -2459 *****FAILS******100
Year = -2458 *****FAILS******000
Year = -2457 *****FAILS******000
~~Year = -2456 ----MATCH----111~~

The chronology is charted from the astronomically verified dates connected to Nebuchadnezzar's reign back to the deluge date with only two unknowns, x for Samuel's Judgeship and y for the Elder's period. These figures are known from non astronomical data to sum up to x + y = 34. Each year is tested to see if the correct week day sequence is obtained in month II, VII, and XI. This is considered three independent tests based on the new moons of month II, VII, and X. The two Sabbaths in month II are dependent (1 or 0). Month VII is tested for the 150th day (1 or 0). And month XI for the three dependent Sabbaths therein linked to the new moon of month X (1 or 0). A 1 means a pass, and 0 means a fail. The three tests are composited in the triples figure and 000 is the usual result. Matches are listed first with the years 2960 BC to 2544 omitting the fail cases, then in 2543 BC every year is listed thereafter down to 2456 where a second match occurs after 2483 BC.

The match in 2456 must be rejected because it implies that x + y = 7 which is too small by all accounts for Samuel's judgeship and the Elder's period. This match is also contradicted by the Lagash and Umma chronologies linked to the Akkadian chronology. This match also fails to synchronize the Jubilee to creation or the seven years of plenty, famine, and return of the land in a Jubilee to the Egyptians under tenancy. Since it implies a post Exodus sum for x and y, the actually implemented Jubilee cycle also fails to match and not just the proleptically reckoned Jubilee back to creation.

Thus the Match 111 and the Jubilee Cycle Match only work in the year 2483 BC for 8 Jubilees (see Appendix VII, page 477). This exercise is just one more method of confirming the accuracy of the Calendar of Israel for the flood year. It also shows that the long advocated 360 day pre-flood year is not necessary to explain the data we are given in Genesis, namely that of the 17th day of the 2nd month to the 17th day of the 7th month spanning 150 days. It can be done with the current 29 and 30 day months. In this case, there are four 30 day months and one 29 day month. The inclusive counting provides 150 days.

As explained on page 412, the 34 years of x + y are divided up as 20 years for the Elders period and 14 years for Samuel. This allotment is determined by a unique solution for counting 70 Sabbath years and allowing enough time for the Elders, for the demographics of the generation that died out before the first oppression, and also for matters in the appendix to the book of Judges, to take place.

Discussion of The End Times Chart

See chart of page 476.

That chart is framed around the 2084 Jubilee. When the third ediition was put out, I thought this one very likely, but a reconsideration of the technology used in Ezek. 38-39 and the promises to Israel have led me to reconsider this for the Jubilee of 2133. At a later date I hope to publish this scenario. Still, the 2084 chart is indicative of the context for the prophetical times in Daniel and Revelation. And so it remains an instructive study. Only some details differ from 2133.

Concerning the day or hour no one knows. But Matthew 24:36 does not say none will ever know. The faithful must still keep watch, because it may still happen at an hour when they do not expect (Matt. 24:44). I don't count myself as knowing, except perhaps I see the paramaters and know where they might fit. But even if most of the faithful are surprised, there may be some who make a good guess when, and there will at the end certainly be some who expect it and then will turn out to be correct! But the prize is not to be won in guessing correctly. It is to be won in doing the will of Adonai and keeping his commandments before that day. Understanding the appointed times is necessary to being ready for the King. Keeping a watch on the appointed times is necessary.

He who keeps a watch on the appointed times merely to guess when the end is, and who does not himself guard them, is like a man who is eager to know when the banquet begins, but who has no intention of acquiring proper clothes for the wedding and coronation of the king. Be assured that such a man will either be beaten with many stripes or worse, thrown out of the feast altogether into the outer darkness.

If my end times 'predictions' are attractive, then let the reader be attracted to a correct understanding and observance of the seasons. Because I make every claim that these are the Law of the Almighty, but absolutely no claim that things will come about as I have forecast. I only hope they do. I hope it might be sooner, but I do not see how it can be sooner than I have placed it. I hope it might be later because I will see evil if it is sooner, but I hope it will be sooner because less evil will be allowed if it is.

One thing is for sure, those who preach and teach against the appoint-

continued on page 470

Appendix IV: New Moons

Starting with AD 2012, the date on which the new moon may first be visible is stated. The next day will be the first day of the month. For example, shortly after sunset on March 23, Friday, the new moon will be first visible. The Sabbath, will be the first day of the month.

6151

2012	3/23	FRI	AVIV/NISAN	30
2012	4/22	SUN	ZIV/IYAR	30
2012	5/22	TUE	SIVAN	30
2012	6/21	THR	SHOSHANNIM	29
2012	7/20	FRI	AV	30
2012	8/19	SUN	ELUL	29
2012	9/17	MON	ETHANIM	30
2012	10/17	WED	BUL	29
2012	11/15	THR	KISLEV	29
2012	12/14	FRI	TEBETH	29
2013	1/12	SAT	SHEBAT	30
2013	2/11	MON	ADAR	30

6152

2013	3/13	WED	AVIV/NISAN	29
2013	4/11	THR	ZIV/IYAR	30
2013	5/11	SAT	SIVAN	30
2013	6/10	MON	SHOSHANNIM	30
2013	7/10	WED	AV	29
2013	8/ 8	THR	ELUL	30
2013	9/ 7	SAT	ETHANIM	29
2013	10/ 6	SUN	BUL	29
2013	11/ 4	MON	KISLEV	30
2013	12/ 4	WED	TEBETH	29
2014	1/ 2	THR	SHEBAT	29
2014	1/31	FRI	ADAR	30
2014	3/ 2	SUN	ADAR II	29

6153

2014	3/31	MON	AVIV/NISAN	30
2014	4/30	WED	ZIV/IYAR	30
2014	5/30	FRI	SIVAN	30
2014	6/29	SUN	SHOSHANNIM	29
2014	7/28	MON	AV	30
2014	8/27	WED	ELUL	30
2014	9/26	FRI	ETHANIM	29
2014	10/25	SAT	BUL	29
2014	11/23	SUN	KISLEV	30
2014	12/23	TUE	TEBETH	29
2015	1/21	WED	SHEBAT	30
2015	2/20	FRI	ADAR	29

6154

2015	3/21	SAT	AVIV/NISAN	29
2015	4/19	SUN	ZIV/IYAR	30
2015	5/19	TUE	SIVAN	30
2015	6/18	THR	SHOSHANNIM	29
2015	7/17	FRI	AV	30
2015	8/16	SUN	ELUL	30
2015	9/15	TUE	ETHANIM	29
2015	10/14	WED	BUL	30
2015	11/13	FRI	KISLEV	29
2015	12/12	SAT	TEBETH	30
2016	1/11	MON	SHEBAT	29
2016	2/ 9	TUE	ADAR	30

6155

2016	3/10	THR	AVIV/NISAN	29
2016	4/ 8	FRI	ZIV/IYAR	30
2016	5/ 8	SUN	SIVAN	29
2016	6/ 6	MON	SHOSHANNIM	29
2016	7/ 5	TUE	AV	30
2016	8/ 4	THR	ELUL	30
2016	9/ 3	SAT	ETHANIM	29
2016	10/ 2	SUN	BUL	30
2016	11/ 1	TUE	KISLEV	29
2016	11/30	WED	TEBETH	30
2016	12/30	FRI	SHEBAT	30
2017	1/29	SUN	ADAR	29
2017	2/27	MON	ADAR II	30

6156

2017	3/29	WED	AVIV/NISAN	29
2017	4/27	THR	ZIV/IYAR	30
2017	5/27	SAT	SIVAN	29
2017	6/25	SUN	SHOSHANNIM	29
2017	7/24	MON	AV	30
2017	8/23	WED	ELUL	29
2017	9/21	THR	ETHANIM	30
2017	10/21	SAT	BUL	29
2017	11/19	SUN	KISLEV	30
2017	12/19	TUE	TEBETH	30
2018	1/18	THR	SHEBAT	30
2018	2/17	SAT	ADAR	29

6157

2018	3/18	SUN	AVIV/NISAN	30
2018	4/17	TUE	ZIV/IYAR	29
2018	5/16	WED	SIVAN	30
2018	6/15	FRI	SHOSHANNIM	29
2018	7/14	SAT	AV	29
2018	8/12	SUN	ELUL	29
2018	9/10	MON	ETHANIM	30
2018	10/10	WED	BUL	29
2018	11/ 8	THR	KISLEV	30
2018	12/ 8	SAT	TEBETH	30
2019	1/ 7	MON	SHEBAT	30
2019	2/ 6	WED	ADAR	30

6158

2019	3/ 8	FRI	AVIV/NISAN	29
2019	4/ 6	SAT	ZIV/IYAR	30
2019	5/ 6	MON	SIVAN	29
2019	6/ 4	TUE	SHOSHANNIM	30
2019	7/ 4	THR	AV	29
2019	8/ 2	FRI	ELUL	29
2019	8/31	SAT	ETHANIM	29
2019	9/29	SUN	BUL	30
2019	10/29	TUE	KISLEV	29
2019	11/27	WED	TEBETH	30
2019	12/27	FRI	SHEBAT	30

Bernard Yallop Grades: A: Easily Visible, B: Visible under perfect conditions, C: Unlikely without optical aid, D: Will need optical aid, E: not visible with a telescope, F: Not visible q < −0.293, G: AL <= 8, AL<Danjon limit 7 deg + 1 deg parallax, Z: moon set before sunset.

(grade of previous day)

Grade	Year	Date	Day	Month	Days
	2020	1/26	SUN	ADAR	30
	2020	2/25	TUE	ADAR II	29
			6159		
A G	2020	3/25	WED	AVIV/NISAN	30
	2020	4/24	FRI	ZIV/IYAR	30
	2020	5/24	SUN	SIVAN	29
	2020	6/22	MON	SHOSHANNIM	29
	2020	7/21	TUE	AV	30
	2020	8/20	THR	ELUL	29
A G	2020	9/18	FRI	ETHANIM	30
	2020	10/18	SUN	BUL	29
	2020	11/16	MON	KISLEV	30
	2020	12/16	WED	TEBETH	29
	2021	1/14	THR	SHEBAT	30
	2021	2/13	SAT	ADAR	29
			6160		
A G	2021	3/14	SUN	AVIV/NISAN	30
	2021	4/13	TUE	ZIV/IYAR	30
	2021	5/13	THR	SIVAN	29
	2021	6/11	FRI	SHOSHANNIM	30
	2021	7/11	SUN	AV	29
	2021	8/ 9	MON	ELUL	30
A F	2021	9/ 8	WED	ETHANIM	29
	2021	10/ 7	THR	BUL	30
	2021	11/ 6	SAT	KISLEV	29
	2021	12/ 5	SUN	TEBETH	30
	2022	1/ 4	TUE	SHEBAT	29
	2022	2/ 2	WED	ADAR	29
	2022	3/ 3	THR	ADAR II	30
			6161		
A G	2022	4/ 2	SAT	AVIV/NISAN	30
	2022	5/ 2	MON	ZIV/IYAR	29
	2022	5/31	TUE	SIVAN	30
	2022	6/30	THR	SHOSHANNIM	30
	2022	7/30	SAT	AV	29
	2022	8/28	SUN	ELUL	30
A F	2022	9/27	TUE	ETHANIM	30
	2022	10/27	THR	BUL	29
	2022	11/25	FRI	KISLEV	29
	2022	12/24	SAT	TEBETH	30
	2023	1/23	MON	SHEBAT	29
	2023	2/21	TUE	ADAR	29
			6162		
B Z	2023	3/22	WED	AVIV/NISAN	30
	2023	4/21	FRI	ZIV/IYAR	29
	2023	5/20	SAT	SIVAN	30
	2023	6/19	MON	SHOSHANNIM	30
	2023	7/19	WED	AV	29
	2023	8/17	THR	ELUL	30
A G	2023	9/16	SAT	ETHANIM	30
	2023	10/16	MON	BUL	30
	2023	11/15	WED	KISLEV	29
	2023	12/14	THR	TEBETH	29
	2024	1/12	FRI	SHEBAT	30
	2024	2/11	SUN	ADAR	29
			6163		
A G	2024	3/11	MON	AVIV/NISAN	29
	2024	4/ 9	TUE	ZIV/IYAR	30
	2024	5/ 9	THR	SIVAN	29
	2024	6/ 7	FRI	SHOSHANNIM	30
	2024	7/ 7	SUN	AV	29
	2024	8/ 5	MON	ELUL	30
B G	2024	9/ 4	WED	ETHANIM	30
	2024	10/ 4	FRI	BUL	30

Year	Date	Day	Month	Days	Grade
2024	11/ 3	SUN	KISLEV	30	
2024	12/ 3	TUE	TEBETH	29	
2025	1/ 1	WED	SHEBAT	29	
2025	1/30	THR	ADAR	30	
2025	3/ 1	SAT	ADAR II	29	
		6164			
2025	3/30	SUN	AVIV/NISAN	29	A G
2025	4/28	MON	ZIV/IYAR	30	
2025	5/28	WED	SIVAN	29	
2025	6/26	THR	SHOSHANNIM	30	
2025	7/26	SAT	AV	29	
2025	8/24	SUN	ELUL	30	
2025	9/23	TUE	ETHANIM	30	B F
2025	10/23	THR	BUL	30	
2025	11/22	SAT	KISLEV	29	
2025	12/21	SUN	TEBETH	30	
2026	1/20	TUE	SHEBAT	29	
2026	2/18	WED	ADAR	30	
		6165			
2026	3/20	FRI	AVIV/NISAN	29	A G
2026	4/18	SAT	ZIV/IYAR	29	
2026	5/17	SUN	SIVAN	30	
2026	6/16	TUE	SHOSHANNIM	29	
2026	7/15	WED	AV	30	
2026	8/14	FRI	ELUL	29	B G
2026	9/12	SAT	ETHANIM	30	
2026	10/12	MON	BUL	30	
2026	11/11	WED	KISLEV	29	
2026	12/10	THR	TEBETH	30	
2027	1/ 9	SAT	SHEBAT	30	
2027	2/ 8	MON	ADAR	29	
		6166			
2027	3/ 9	TUE	AVIV/NISAN	30	A G
2027	4/ 8	THR	ZIV/IYAR	29	
2027	5/ 7	FRI	SIVAN	29	
2027	6/ 5	SAT	SHOSHANNIM	30	
2027	7/ 5	MON	AV	29	
2027	8/ 3	TUE	ELUL	30	
2027	9/ 2	THR	ETHANIM	29	A F
2027	10/ 1	FRI	BUL	30	
2027	10/31	SUN	KISLEV	29	
2027	11/29	MON	TEBETH	30	
2027	12/29	WED	SHEBAT	30	
2028	1/28	FRI	ADAR	29	
2028	2/26	SAT	ADAR II	30	
		6167			
2028	3/27	MON	AVIV/NISAN	30	A G
2028	4/26	WED	ZIV/IYAR	29	
2028	5/25	THR	SIVAN	30	
2028	6/24	SAT	SHOSHANNIM	29	
2028	7/23	SUN	AV	30	
2028	8/22	TUE	ELUL	29	
2028	9/20	WED	ETHANIM	29	A F
2028	10/19	THR	BUL	30	
2028	11/18	SAT	KISLEV	29	
2028	12/17	SUN	TEBETH	30	
2029	1/16	TUE	SHEBAT	29	
2029	2/14	WED	ADAR	30	
		6168			
2029	3/16	FRI	AVIV/NISAN	30	A G
2029	4/15	SUN	ZIV/IYAR	29	
2029	5/14	MON	SIVAN	30	
2029	6/13	WED	SHOSHANNIM	30	
2029	7/13	FRI	AV	29	

```
      2029  8/11 SAT    ELUL     30
  A F 2029  9/10 MON   ETHANIM   29
      2029 10/ 9 TUE     BUL     29
      2029 11/ 7 WED   KISLEV    29
      2029 12/ 6 THR   TEBETH    30
      2030  1/ 5 SAT   SHEBAT    29
      2030  2/ 3 SUN    ADAR     30
    ------------6169-------------
  A G 2030  3/ 5 TUE AVIV/NISAN 30
      2030  4/ 4 THR  ZIV/IYAR   29
      2030  5/ 3 FRI    SIVAN    30
      2030  6/ 2 SUN SHOSHANNIM 30
      2030  7/ 2 TUE     AV      30
      2030  8/ 1 THR    ELUL     29
  B F 2030  8/30 FRI   ETHANIM   30
      2030  9/29 SUN     BUL     29
      2030 10/28 MON   KISLEV    29
      2030 11/26 TUE   TEBETH    29
      2030 12/25 WED   SHEBAT    30
      2031  1/24 FRI    ADAR     29
      2031  2/22 SAT   ADAR II   30
    ------------6170-------------
etc.. 2031  3/24 MON AVIV/NISAN 29
      2031  4/22 TUE  ZIV/IYAR   30
      2031  5/22 THR    SIVAN    30
      2031  6/21 SAT SHOSHANNIM 30
      2031  7/21 MON     AV      30
      2031  8/20 WED    ELUL     29
      2031  9/18 THR   ETHANIM   30
      2031 10/18 SAT     BUL     29
      2031 11/16 SUN   KISLEV    29
      2031 12/15 MON   TEBETH    29
      2032  1/13 TUE   SHEBAT    30
      2032  2/12 THR    ADAR     29
    ------------6171-------------
      2032  3/12 FRI AVIV/NISAN 30
      2032  4/11 SUN  ZIV/IYAR   29
      2032  5/10 MON    SIVAN    30
      2032  6/ 9 WED SHOSHANNIM 30
      2032  7/ 9 FRI     AV      30
      2032  8/ 8 SUN    ELUL     29
      2032  9/ 6 MON   ETHANIM   30
      2032 10/ 6 WED     BUL     29
      2032 11/ 4 THR   KISLEV    30
      2032 12/ 4 SAT   TEBETH    29
      2033  1/ 2 SUN   SHEBAT    30
      2033  2/ 1 TUE    ADAR     29
      2033  3/ 2 WED   ADAR II   29
    ------------6172-------------
      2033  3/31 THR AVIV/NISAN 30
      2033  4/30 SAT  ZIV/IYAR   29
      2033  5/29 SUN    SIVAN    30
      2033  6/28 TUE SHOSHANNIM 30
      2033  7/28 THR     AV      29
      2033  8/26 FRI    ELUL     30
      2033  9/25 SUN   ETHANIM   29
      2033 10/24 MON     BUL     30
      2033 11/23 WED   KISLEV    30
      2033 12/23 FRI   TEBETH    29
      2034  1/21 SAT   SHEBAT    30
      2034  2/20 MON    ADAR     29
    ------------6173-------------
      2034  3/21 TUE AVIV/NISAN 29
      2034  4/19 WED  ZIV/IYAR   30

      2034  5/19 FRI    SIVAN    29
      2034  6/17 SAT SHOSHANNIM 30
      2034  7/17 MON     AV      29
      2034  8/15 TUE    ELUL     30
      2034  9/14 THR   ETHANIM   29
      2034 10/13 FRI     BUL     30
      2034 11/12 SUN   KISLEV    30
      2034 12/12 TUE   TEBETH    29
      2035  1/10 WED   SHEBAT    30
      2035  2/ 9 FRI    ADAR     30
    ------------6174-------------
      2035  3/11 SUN AVIV/NISAN 29
      2035  4/ 9 MON  ZIV/IYAR   30
      2035  5/ 9 WED    SIVAN    29
      2035  6/ 7 THR SHOSHANNIM 29
      2035  7/ 6 FRI     AV      30
      2035  8/ 5 SUN    ELUL     29
      2035  9/ 3 MON   ETHANIM   29
      2035 10/ 2 TUE     BUL     30
      2035 11/ 1 THR   KISLEV    30
      2035 12/ 1 SAT   TEBETH    29
      2035 12/30 SUN   SHEBAT    30
      2036  1/29 TUE    ADAR     30
      2036  2/28 THR   ADAR II   30
    ------------6175-------------
      2036  3/29 SAT AVIV/NISAN 29
      2036  4/27 SUN  ZIV/IYAR   30
      2036  5/27 TUE    SIVAN    29
      2036  6/25 WED SHOSHANNIM 29
      2036  7/24 THR     AV      30
      2036  8/23 SAT    ELUL     29
      2036  9/21 SUN   ETHANIM   29
      2036 10/20 MON     BUL     30
      2036 11/19 WED   KISLEV    30
      2036 12/19 FRI   TEBETH    29
      2037  1/17 SAT   SHEBAT    30
      2037  2/16 MON    ADAR     30
    ------------6176-------------
      2037  3/18 WED AVIV/NISAN 30
      2037  4/17 FRI  ZIV/IYAR   29
      2037  5/16 SAT    SIVAN    30
      2037  6/15 MON SHOSHANNIM 29
      2037  7/14 TUE     AV      29
      2037  8/12 WED    ELUL     29
      2037  9/10 THR   ETHANIM   30
      2037 10/10 SAT     BUL     29
      2037 11/ 8 SUN   KISLEV    30
      2037 12/ 8 TUE   TEBETH    29
      2038  1/ 6 WED   SHEBAT    30
      2038  2/ 5 FRI    ADAR     30
    ------------6177-------------
      2038  3/ 7 SUN AVIV/NISAN 30
      2038  4/ 6 TUE  ZIV/IYAR   29
      2038  5/ 5 WED    SIVAN    30
      2038  6/ 4 FRI SHOSHANNIM 29
      2038  7/ 3 SAT     AV      30
      2038  8/ 2 MON    ELUL     29
      2038  8/31 TUE   ETHANIM   29
      2038  9/29 WED     BUL     30
      2038 10/29 FRI   KISLEV    29
      2038 11/27 SAT   TEBETH    30
      2038 12/27 MON   SHEBAT    29
      2039  1/25 TUE    ADAR     30
      2039  2/24 THR   ADAR II   30
```

------------6178------------				
2039	3/26	SAT	AVIV/NISAN	29
2039	4/24	SUN	ZIV/IYAR	30
2039	5/24	TUE	SIVAN	30
2039	6/23	THR	SHOSHANNIM	29
2039	7/22	FRI	AV	30
2039	8/21	SUN	ELUL	29
2039	9/19	MON	ETHANIM	30
2039	10/19	WED	BUL	29
2039	11/17	THR	KISLEV	30
2039	12/17	SAT	TEBETH	29
2040	1/15	SUN	SHEBAT	29
2040	2/13	MON	ADAR	30
------------6179------------				
2040	3/14	WED	AVIV/NISAN	29
2040	4/12	THR	ZIV/IYAR	30
2040	5/12	SAT	SIVAN	30
2040	6/11	MON	SHOSHANNIM	29
2040	7/10	TUE	AV	30
2040	8/ 9	THR	ELUL	30
2040	9/ 8	SAT	ETHANIM	29
2040	10/ 7	SUN	BUL	30
2040	11/ 6	TUE	KISLEV	29
2040	12/ 5	WED	TEBETH	30
2041	1/ 4	FRI	SHEBAT	29
2041	2/ 2	SAT	ADAR	29
2041	3/ 3	SUN	ADAR II	30
------------6180------------				
2041	4/ 2	TUE	AVIV/NISAN	29
2041	5/ 1	WED	ZIV/IYAR	30
2041	5/31	FRI	SIVAN	29
2041	6/29	SAT	SHOSHANNIM	30
2041	7/29	MON	AV	30
2041	8/28	WED	ELUL	30
2041	9/27	FRI	ETHANIM	29
2041	10/26	SAT	BUL	30
2041	11/25	MON	KISLEV	29
2041	12/24	TUE	TEBETH	30
2042	1/23	THR	SHEBAT	29
2042	2/21	FRI	ADAR	29
------------6181------------				
2042	3/22	SAT	AVIV/NISAN	30
2042	4/21	MON	ZIV/IYAR	29
2042	5/20	TUE	SIVAN	29
2042	6/18	WED	SHOSHANNIM	30
2042	7/18	FRI	AV	30
2042	8/17	SUN	ELUL	30
2042	9/16	TUE	ETHANIM	30
2042	10/16	THR	BUL	29
2042	11/14	FRI	KISLEV	30
2042	12/14	SUN	TEBETH	29
2043	1/12	MON	SHEBAT	30
2043	2/11	WED	ADAR	29
------------6182------------				
2043	3/12	THR	AVIV/NISAN	29
2043	4/10	FRI	ZIV/IYAR	30
2043	5/10	SUN	SIVAN	29
2043	6/ 8	MON	SHOSHANNIM	29
2043	7/ 7	TUE	AV	30
2043	8/ 6	THR	ELUL	30
2043	9/ 5	SAT	ETHANIM	30
2043	10/ 5	MON	BUL	29
2043	11/ 3	TUE	KISLEV	30
2043	12/ 3	THR	TEBETH	30
2044	1/ 2	SAT	SHEBAT	29
2044	1/31	SUN	ADAR	30
2044	3/ 1	TUE	ADAR II	29
------------6183------------				
2044	3/30	WED	AVIV/NISAN	29
2044	4/28	THR	ZIV/IYAR	30
2044	5/28	SAT	SIVAN	29
2044	6/26	SUN	SHOSHANNIM	29
2044	7/25	MON	AV	30
2044	8/24	WED	ELUL	30
2044	9/23	FRI	ETHANIM	29
2044	10/22	SAT	BUL	30
2044	11/21	MON	KISLEV	30
2044	12/21	WED	TEBETH	29
2045	1/19	THR	SHEBAT	30
2045	2/18	SAT	ADAR	29
------------6184------------				
2045	3/19	SUN	AVIV/NISAN	30
2045	4/18	TUE	ZIV/IYAR	29
2045	5/17	WED	SIVAN	30
2045	6/16	FRI	SHOSHANNIM	29
2045	7/15	SAT	AV	30
2045	8/14	MON	ELUL	29
2045	9/12	TUE	ETHANIM	30
2045	10/12	THR	BUL	29
2045	11/10	FRI	KISLEV	30
2045	12/10	SUN	TEBETH	29
2046	1/ 8	MON	SHEBAT	30
2046	2/ 7	WED	ADAR	30
------------6185------------				
2046	3/ 9	FRI	AVIV/NISAN	29
2046	4/ 7	SAT	ZIV/IYAR	30
2046	5/ 7	MON	SIVAN	29
2046	6/ 5	TUE	SHOSHANNIM	30
2046	7/ 5	THR	AV	29
2046	8/ 3	FRI	ELUL	30
2046	9/ 2	SUN	ETHANIM	29
2046	10/ 1	MON	BUL	30
2046	10/31	WED	KISLEV	29
2046	11/29	THR	TEBETH	29
2046	12/28	FRI	SHEBAT	30
2047	1/27	SUN	ADAR	30
2047	2/26	TUE	ADAR II	29
------------6186------------				
2047	3/27	WED	AVIV/NISAN	30
2047	4/26	FRI	ZIV/IYAR	30
2047	5/26	SUN	SIVAN	29
2047	6/24	MON	SHOSHANNIM	30
2047	7/24	WED	AV	30
2047	8/23	FRI	ELUL	29
2047	9/21	SAT	ETHANIM	29
2047	10/20	SUN	BUL	30
2047	11/19	TUE	KISLEV	29
2047	12/18	WED	TEBETH	29
2048	1/16	THR	SHEBAT	30
2048	2/15	SAT	ADAR	29
------------6187------------				
2048	3/15	SUN	AVIV/NISAN	30
2048	4/14	TUE	ZIV/IYAR	30
2048	5/14	THR	SIVAN	30
2048	6/13	SAT	SHOSHANNIM	29
2048	7/12	SUN	AV	30
2048	8/11	TUE	ELUL	30
2048	9/10	THR	ETHANIM	29

2048	10/ 9	FRI	BUL	29
2048	11/ 7	SAT	KISLEV	29
2048	12/ 6	SUN	TEBETH	30
2049	1/ 5	TUE	SHEBAT	29
2049	2/ 3	WED	ADAR	30

------------6188-------------

2049	3/ 5	FRI	AVIV/NISAN	29
2049	4/ 3	SAT	ZIV/IYAR	30
2049	5/ 3	MON	SIVAN	30
2049	6/ 2	WED	SHOSHANNIM	29
2049	7/ 1	THR	AV	30
2049	7/31	SAT	ELUL	30
2049	8/30	MON	ETHANIM	30
2049	9/29	WED	BUL	29
2049	10/28	THR	KISLEV	29
2049	11/26	FRI	TEBETH	29
2049	12/25	SAT	SHEBAT	30
2050	1/24	MON	ADAR	29
2050	2/22	TUE	ADAR II	30

------------6189-------------

2050	3/24	THR	AVIV/NISAN	29
2050	4/22	FRI	ZIV/IYAR	30
2050	5/22	SUN	SIVAN	29
2050	6/20	MON	SHOSHANNIM	30
2050	7/20	WED	AV	30
2050	8/19	FRI	ELUL	30
2050	9/18	SUN	ETHANIM	29
2050	10/17	MON	BUL	30
2050	11/16	WED	KISLEV	29
2050	12/15	THR	TEBETH	29
2051	1/13	FRI	SHEBAT	30
2051	2/12	SUN	ADAR	29

------------6190-------------

2051	3/13	MON	AVIV/NISAN	30
2051	4/12	WED	ZIV/IYAR	29
2051	5/11	THR	SIVAN	30
2051	6/10	SAT	SHOSHANNIM	29
2051	7/ 9	SUN	AV	30
2051	8/ 8	TUE	ELUL	30
2051	9/ 7	THR	ETHANIM	29
2051	10/ 6	FRI	BUL	30
2051	11/ 5	SUN	KISLEV	29
2051	12/ 4	MON	TEBETH	30
2052	1/ 3	WED	SHEBAT	29
2052	2/ 1	THR	ADAR	30
2052	3/ 2	SAT	ADAR II	29

------------6191-------------

2052	3/31	SUN	AVIV/NISAN	30
2052	4/30	TUE	ZIV/IYAR	29
2052	5/29	WED	SIVAN	30
2052	6/28	FRI	SHOSHANNIM	29
2052	7/27	SAT	AV	30
2052	8/26	MON	ELUL	29
2052	9/24	TUE	ETHANIM	30
2052	10/24	THR	BUL	29
2052	11/22	FRI	KISLEV	30
2052	12/22	SUN	TEBETH	30
2053	1/21	TUE	SHEBAT	29
2053	2/19	WED	ADAR	30

------------6192-------------

2053	3/21	FRI	AVIV/NISAN	29
2053	4/19	SAT	ZIV/IYAR	30
2053	5/19	MON	SIVAN	29
2053	6/17	TUE	SHOSHANNIM	30
2053	7/17	THR	AV	29
2053	8/15	FRI	ELUL	29
2053	9/13	SAT	ETHANIM	30
2053	10/13	MON	BUL	29
2053	11/11	TUE	KISLEV	30
2053	12/11	THR	TEBETH	30
2054	1/10	SAT	SHEBAT	30
2054	2/ 9	MON	ADAR	29

------------6193-------------

2054	3/10	TUE	AVIV/NISAN	30
2054	4/ 9	THR	ZIV/IYAR	30
2054	5/ 9	SAT	SIVAN	29
2054	6/ 7	SUN	SHOSHANNIM	29
2054	7/ 6	MON	AV	30
2054	8/ 5	WED	ELUL	29
2054	9/ 3	THR	ETHANIM	29
2054	10/ 2	FRI	BUL	30
2054	11/ 1	SUN	KISLEV	29
2054	11/30	MON	TEBETH	30
2054	12/30	WED	SHEBAT	30
2055	1/29	FRI	ADAR	29
2055	2/27	SAT	ADAR II	30

------------6194-------------

2055	3/29	MON	AVIV/NISAN	30
2055	4/28	WED	ZIV/IYAR	29
2055	5/27	THR	SIVAN	30
2055	6/26	SAT	SHOSHANNIM	29
2055	7/25	SUN	AV	30
2055	8/24	TUE	ELUL	29
2055	9/22	WED	ETHANIM	29
2055	10/21	THR	BUL	30
2055	11/20	SAT	KISLEV	29
2055	12/19	SUN	TEBETH	30
2056	1/18	TUE	SHEBAT	29
2056	2/16	WED	ADAR	30

------------6195-------------

2056	3/17	FRI	AVIV/NISAN	30
2056	4/16	SUN	ZIV/IYAR	30
2056	5/16	TUE	SIVAN	29
2056	6/14	WED	SHOSHANNIM	30
2056	7/14	FRI	AV	29
2056	8/12	SAT	ELUL	29
2056	9/10	SUN	ETHANIM	30
2056	10/10	TUE	BUL	29
2056	11/ 8	WED	KISLEV	30
2056	12/ 8	FRI	TEBETH	29
2057	1/ 6	SAT	SHEBAT	30
2057	2/ 5	MON	ADAR	29

------------6196-------------

2057	3/ 6	TUE	AVIV/NISAN	30
2057	4/ 5	THR	ZIV/IYAR	30
2057	5/ 5	SAT	SIVAN	29
2057	6/ 3	SUN	SHOSHANNIM	30
2057	7/ 3	TUE	AV	29
2057	8/ 1	WED	ELUL	30
2057	8/31	FRI	ETHANIM	29
2057	9/29	SAT	BUL	30
2057	10/29	MON	KISLEV	29
2057	11/27	TUE	TEBETH	30
2057	12/27	THU	SHEBAT	29
2057	1/25	FRI	ADAR	30
2057	2/24	SUN	ADAR II	29

from page 464
ed times have zero chance of being right in the end. So with this said and will the warnings noted, let me outline the reasons behind the chart. The kingdom comes at the end of Daniel 9:24-27. The final seven is an actual Sabbath year period. Furthermore, since cleansing from all sin is on the day of Atonement, then the second coming will also be then, which will be announced with a great Trumpet. If I am correct, this is the Jubilee trumpet, the last Trumpet at the end of seven Sabbath years.

For this reason, the 'last seven' is framed with an actual Jubilee year at the end of it. And, of course, there would be no way of knowing it except for the death and resurrection of Messiah according to the appointed times! Now, in the middle of the "last seven," "the Anti-messiah" will cause the daily offering to cease. And thereupon there are 1290 days until the end, which as noted before is on the eve of the day of Atonement.

Upon inspection, we find that there are exactly 1260 days before the 1290 days going back to Tishri 1 in the first year of the Sabbath year cycle. This is when the two witnesses prophesy for 180 weeks. They begin on the first day and pass through 180 Sabbaths until finishing on the last Sabbath.† If you have read this book, you will have no doubt that the two witnesses are using the Temple offerings to announce the good news of Messiah. Therefore, the Beast wishes to get rid of what honors Messiah. I really cannot come by a better place to fit their testimony than at the start of the 70th seven. We shall see. The 1260 days I have specified is the only non-arbitrary choice one can make. So it seems best.

Now, in the same context as the 1290 days, 1335 days are mentioned, and a blessing for reaching the end thereof. The text specifies no beginning point for the 1335 days. But the character of the endpoint yielding a blessing suggests that it ends on the same day as the 1290 days, on eve of the day of atonement. For there is no greater blessing than to be made pure from all sin. Now we can go back to find that it begins in the month of Shevat one month before the two witnesses finish their testimony, and one month before the 1290 days begin. Something bad happens in Shevat, something that must be waited out till the day of redemption.

---

†The 2133 Jubilee does not have this feature, but there is a compensating feature that 2084 does not have that 2133 does. In 2133 their testimony would end on Wednesday, the same day as the crucifixion.

Appendix V: Yeshua's Ministry

Month: I AVIV, AD 30   1657 A.M. Sab. Cyc: 4. Jub. Cyc: 4 Cycle No: 85
Q1: 1.352 A Q2: -0.154 C LG: 95m W: 0.958' AL: 20.9 AV: 19.9
New Moon calculated for longitude: 35.17 and latitude 31.77
Location of calculations: Jerusalem
Designed and Programmed By Daniel Gregg Passover **John 2:13**.

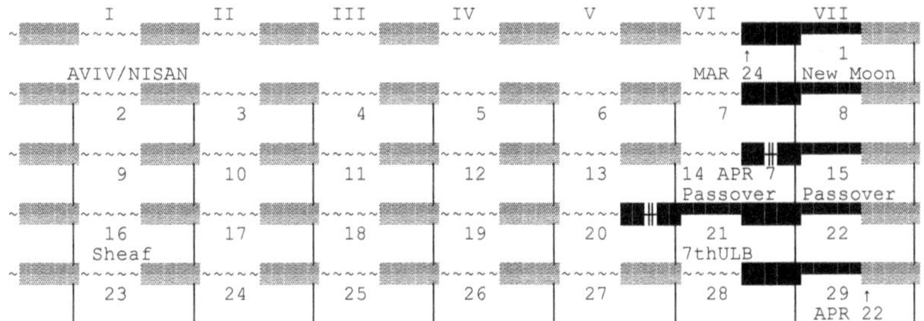

I	II	III	IV	V	VI	VII
AVIV/NISAN					↑ MAR 24	1 New Moon
2	3	4	5	6	7	8
9	10	11	12	13	14 APR 7 Passover	15 Passover
16 Sheaf	17	18	19	20	21 7thULB	22
23	24	25	26	27	28	29 ↑ APR 22

Month: I AVIV, AD 31   4170 A.M. Sab. Cyc: 5. Jub. Cyc: 5 Cycle No: 85
Q1: 1.299 A Q2: -0.340 F LG: 94m W: 0.931' AL: 20.3 AV: 19.5
New Moon calculated for longitude: 35.17 and latitude 31.77
Location of calculations: Jerusalem
Designed and Programmed By Daniel Gregg, **Luke 6:1**, Shavuot Counting Enabled.
18-1-3 = Nisan 18, First of Sabbaths, or "Second First Sabbath", and Day 3 on the 50 day count to Shavuot. Format: [Day of Month]-[Shabbat Count]-[Day Count]

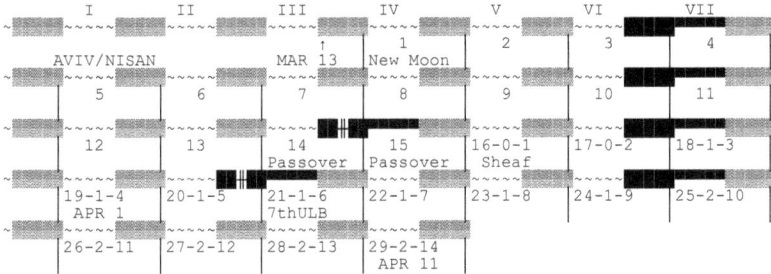

I	II	III	IV	V	VI	VII
AVIV/NISAN		↑ MAR 13	1 New Moon	2	3	4
5	6	7	8	9	10	11
12	13	14 Passover	15 Passover	16-0-1 Sheaf	17-0-2	18-1-3
19-1-4 APR 1	20-1-5	21-1-6 7thULB	22-1-7	23-1-8	24-1-9	25-2-10
26-2-11	27-2-12	28-2-13	29-2-14 APR 11			

Month: I AVIV, AD 32   4171 A.M. Sab. Cyc: 6. Jub. Cyc: 6 Cycle No: 85
Q1: 1.715 A Q2: -0.084 C LG: 111m W: 1.182' AL: 22.6 AV: 22.4
New Moon calculated for longitude: 35.17 and latitude 31.77
Location of calculations: Jerusalem
Designed and Programmed By Daniel Gregg, **John 6:4**

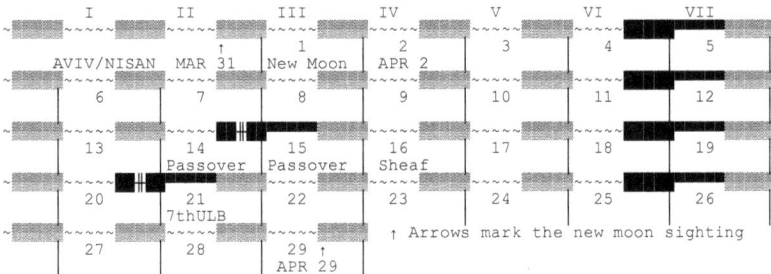

I	II	III	IV	V	VI	VII
AVIV/NISAN	↑ MAR 31	1 New Moon	2 APR 2	3	4	5
6	7	8	9	10	11	12
13	14 Passover	15 Passover	16 Sheaf	17	18	19
20	21 7thULB	22	23	24	25	26
27	28	29 ↑ APR 29				

↑ Arrows mark the new moon sighting

Beginning Year 7 of the Sabbatical Cycle, Year 7 of the Jubilee Cycle
Month: VII TISHRI, AD 32 4171 A.M. Sab. Cyc: 7. Jub. Cyc: 7 Cycle No: 85
Q1: 0.934 A Q2: -0.191 D LG: 63m W: 1.500' AL: 25.8 AV: 13.0
New Moon calculated for longitude: 35.17 and latitude 31.77
Location of calculations: Jerusalem
Designed and Programmed By Daniel Gregg, **John 7:2**

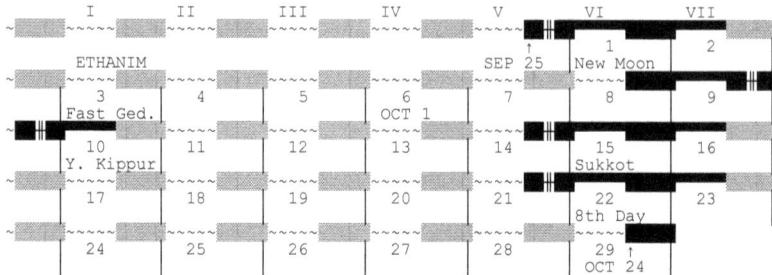

I	II	III	IV	V	VI	VII
ETHANIM				↑ SEP 25	1 New Moon	2
3 Fast Ged.	4	5	6 OCT 1	7	8	9
10 Y. Kippur	11	12	13	14	15 Sukkot	16
17	18	19	20	21	22 8th Day	23
24	25	26	27	28	29 ↑ OCT 24	

Month: IX KISLEV, AD 32 4171 A.M. Sab. Cyc: 7. Jub. Cyc: 7 Cycle No: 85
Q1: 1.068 A Q2: -0.527 F LG: 81m W: 1.525' AL: 25.3 AV: 14.2
New Moon calculated for longitude: 35.17 and latitude 31.77
Location of calculations: Jerusalem
Designed and Programmed By Daniel Gregg, **John 10:22-38**, Hanukah

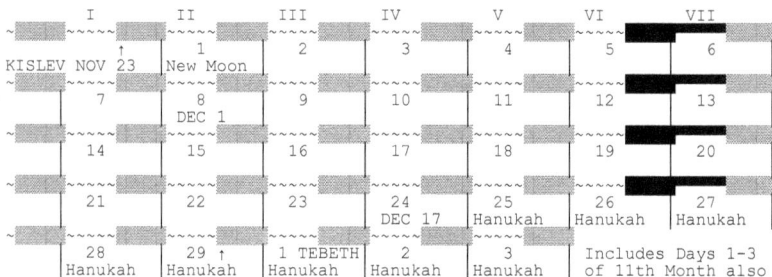

I	II	III	IV	V	VI	VII
↑ KISLEV NOV 23	1 New Moon	2	3	4	5	6
7	8 DEC 1	9	10	11	12	13
14	15	16	17	18	19	20
21	22	23	24 DEC 17	25 Hanukah	26 Hanukah	27 Hanukah
28 Hanukah	29 ↑ Hanukah	1 TEBETH Hanukah	2 Hanukah	3 Hanukah	Includes Days 1-3 of 11th Month also	

Month: XII ADAR, AD 33 4171 A.M. Sab. Cyc: 7. Jub. Cyc: 7 Cycle No: 85
Q1: 1.591 A Q2: -0.435 F LG: 105m W: 1.168' AL: 21.8 AV: 21.2
New Moon calculated for longitude: 35.17 and latitude 31.77
Location of calculations: Jerusalem
Designed and Programmed By Daniel Gregg, **Matthew 17:24**, temple tax

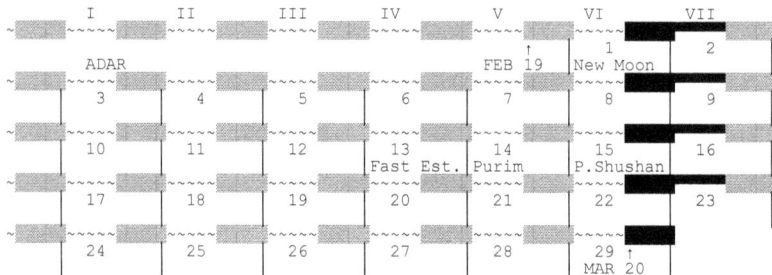

I	II	III	IV	V	VI	VII
ADAR				↑ FEB 19	1 New Moon	2
3	4	5	6	7	8	9
10	11	12	13 Fast Est.	14 Purim	15 P.Shushan	16
17	18	19	20	21	22	23
24	25	26	27	28	29 ↑ MAR 20	

Beginning Year 1 of the Sabbatical Cycle, Year 8 of the Jubilee Cycle
Month: VII ETHANIM, AD 33 4172 A.M. Sab. Cyc: 1. Jub. Cyc: 8 Cycle No: 85
Q1: 0.677 A Q2: -0.322 F LG: 56m W: 1.272' AL: 24.1 AV: 11.5
New Moon calculated for longitude: 35.17 and latitude 31.77
Location of calculations: Jerusalem
Designed and Programmed By Daniel Gregg, **Luke 13:1-8**.

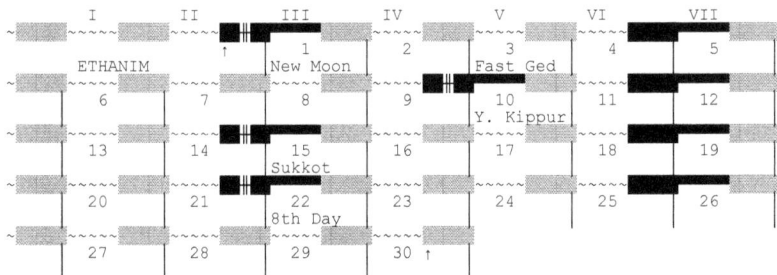

I	II	III	IV	V	VI	VII
ETHANIM	↑	1 New Moon	2	3 Fast Ged	4	5
6	7	8	9	10 Y. Kippur	11	12
13	14	15 Sukkot	16	17	18	19
20	21	22 8th Day	23	24	25	26
27	28	29	30 ↑			

Month: I AVIV, AD 34 4173 A.M. Sab. Cyc: 1. Jub. Cyc: 8 Cycle No: 85
Q1: 1.501 A Q2: -0.493 F LG: 102m W: 1.068' AL: 20.8 AV: 20.8
New Moon calculated for longitude: 35.17 and latitude 31.77
Location of calculations: Jerusalem
Designed and Programmed By Daniel Gregg, **John 11:55**,

I	II	III	IV	V	VI	VII
AVIV/NISAN			↑ MAR 10	1 New Moon	2	3
4	5	6	7	8	9	10
11	12	13 MAR 23	14♦ Passover	15 Passover	16 Sheaf	♦ 17
18	19	20 MAR 30	21 7thULB	22 APR 1	23	24
25	26	27	28	29 ↑ APR 8		

14♦ = Crucifixion
♦ = Resurrection

Month: I AVIV, AD 34 4173 A.M. Sab. Cyc: 1. Jub. Cyc: 8 Cycle No: 85
Q1: 1.501 A Q2: -0.493 F LG: 102m W: 1.068' AL: 20.8 AV: 20.8
New Moon calculated for longitude: 35.17 and latitude 31.77
Location of calculations: Jerusalem
Designed and Programmed By Daniel Gregg, Shavuot Counting Enabled. Format: [Day of Month]-[Sabbath Count]-[Day Count], so 17-1-2 = 17th Nisan, First Sabbath, second day. John 11:55, Matthew 28:1, Mark 16:1-2, Luke 23-24, John 20:1.

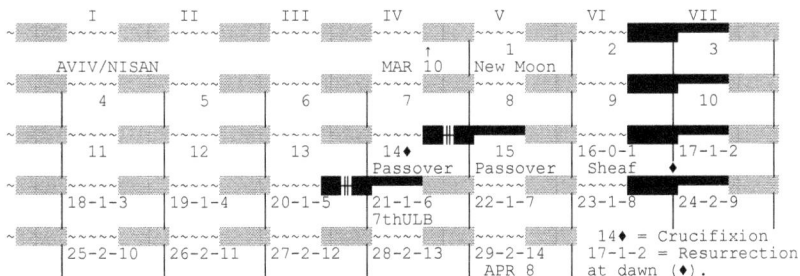

I	II	III	IV	V	VI	VII
AVIV/NISAN			↑ MAR 10	1 New Moon	2	3
4	5	6	7	8	9	10
11	12	13	14♦ Passover	15 Passover	16-0-1 Sheaf	17-1-2 ♦
18-1-3	19-1-4	20-1-5	21-1-6 7thULB	22-1-7	23-1-8	24-2-9
25-2-10	26-2-11	27-2-12	28-2-13	29-2-14 APR 8		

14♦ = Crucifixion
17-1-2 = Resurrection at dawn (♦).

Month: II ZIV, AD 34 4173 A.M. Sab. Cyc: 1. Jub. Cyc: 8 Cycle No: 85
Q1: 0.866 A Q2: -0.975 F LG: 84m W: 0.673' AL: 16.6 AV: 16.5
New Moon calculated for longitude: 35.17 and latitude 31.77
Location of calculations: Jerusalem
Designed and Programmed By Daniel Gregg, Shavuot Counting Enabled, **Acts 1:3**

I	II	III	IV	V	VI	VII
ZIV/IYAR				↑ APR 8	1-2-15 New Moon	2-3-16
3-3-17	4-3-18	5-3-19	6-3-20	7-3-21	8-3-22	9-4-23
10-4-24	11-4-25	12-4-26	13-4-27	14-4-28 2nd Pass.	15-4-29	16-5-30
17-5-31	18-5-32	19-5-33	20-5-34	21-5-35	22-5-36	23-6-37 MAY 1
24-6-38	25-6-39	26-6-40	27-6-41 ASCENSION	28-6-42	29-6-43 MAY 7	

The 40th day inclusive from the resurrection is day 41 of the Shavuot Count. 41 - 2 + 1 = 40. Yeshua was lifted up to heaven on day IV.

Month: III SIVAN, AD 34 4173 A.M. Sa . Cyc: 1. Jub. Cyc: 8 Cycle No: 85
Q1: 0.319 A Q2: -9.000 Z LG: 69m W: 0.389' AL: 12.7 AV: 12.7
New Moon calculated for longitude: 35.17 and latitude 31.77
Location of calculations: Jerusalem
Designed and Programmed By Daniel Gregg, **Acts 2**.

I	II	III	IV	V	VI	VII
SIVAN					↑ MAY 7	1-7-44 New Moon
2-7-45	3-7-46	4-7-47	5-7-48	6-7-49	7-50th Shavuot	8
9	10	11	12	13	14	15
16	17	18	19	20	21	22
23	24	25	26	27	28	29
30 ↑ JUN 6						

Seven Sabbaths are completed on May 8, (the new moon day) on day 44. The 50 days continue to be counted in the time after this seventh sabbath until FRI, Sivan 7 (May 14).

Appendix VI: Exodus-Torah

Month: I AVIV, 1632 BC 2508 A.M. Sab. Cyc: 2. Jub. Cyc: 9 Cycle No: 51
Q1: 0.454 A Q2: -1.164 F LG: 65m W: 0.484' AL: 14.3 AV: 13.5
New Moon calculated for longitude: 31.30 and latitude 30.79
Location of calculations: Tell ed-Dab'a, Egypt (Goshen)
Designed and Programmed By Daniel Gregg, Exodus 12-15

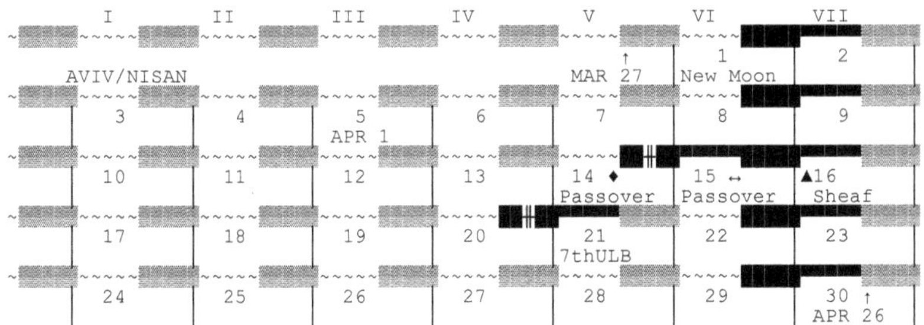

I II III IV V VI VII
MAR 27 ↑
1 New Moon
2
AVIV/NISAN
3 4 5 APR 1 6 7 8 9
10 11 12 13
14 ♦ Passover
15 ↔ Passover
▲16 Sheaf
17 18 19 20
21 7thULB
22 23
24 25 26 27 28 29
30 ↑ APR 26

The Passover was killed at the ♦ on the 14th of Aviv. The Exodus began at daybreak on the 15th of Aviv and lasted till daybreak on the 16th of Aviv, when they were allowed to eat and rest on the Sabbath, marked by ▲.

Month: II ZIV, 1632 BC 2508 A.M. Sab. Cyc: 2. Jub. Cyc: 9 Cycle No: 51
Q1: 1.419 A Q2: -0.291 E LG: 95m W: 1.071' AL: 21.6 AV: 20.0
New Moon calculated for longitude: 34.59 and latitude 28.68
Location of calculations: Near Rephidim
Designed and Programmed By Daniel Gregg, Manna and Sabbath, Exodus 16.

I	II	III	IV	V	VI	VII
↑ 1 New Moon	2 APR 28	3	4	5 MAY 1	6	7
8	9	10	11	12	13	14
♦15	16	17	18	19	20	♦21
22	23	24	25	26	27	28
29 ↑ MAY 25						

Israel camps on the 15th in the wilderness of Sin, where they are sent quail at setting time, and manna at daybreak on the 16th. The quail came "between the settings" on the 15th (between noon and sunset). On the sixth day, the 20th of Ziv, there was twice as much manna. And on the Sabbath ♦21, there was none.

Month: III SIVAN, 1632 BC 2508 A.M. Sab. Cyc: 2. Jub. Cyc: 9 Cycle No: 51
Q1: 0.417 A Q2: -1.001 F LG: 63m W: 0.555' AL: 15.7 AV: 12.7
New Moon calculated for longitude: 34.72 and latitude 28.72
Location of calculations: N. of Rephidim
Designed and Programmed By Daniel Gregg, The Torah, Exodus 19-24.

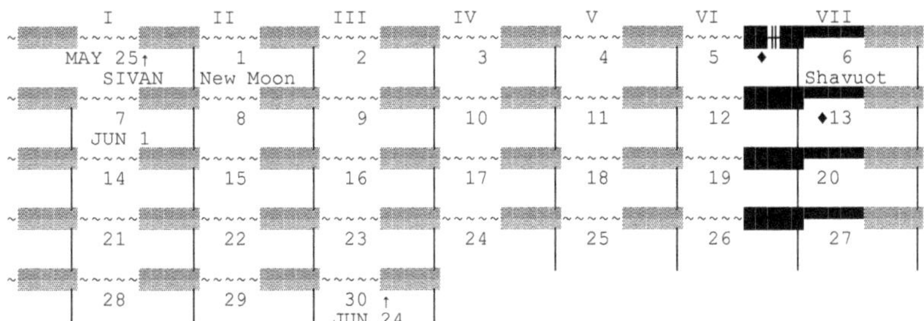

I II III IV V VI VII
MAY 25↑ SIVAN
1 New Moon
2 3 4 5 ♦
6 Shavuot
7 JUN 1
8 9 10 11 12 ♦13
14 15 16 17 18 19 20
21 22 23 24 25 26 27
28 29
30 ↑ JUN 24

The first diamond ♦ marks when YHWH spoke the Torah to Israel. Then on the day part of the Sabbath the 70 elders of Israel ascended the mountain and they saw YHWH (Exodus 24). After Shavuot, on Sivan 6 (the Sabbath), the cloud covered Mt. Sinai 6 days (Sivan 7 to Sivan 12) and then YHWH spoke to Moses on the 7th day (Sivan 13).

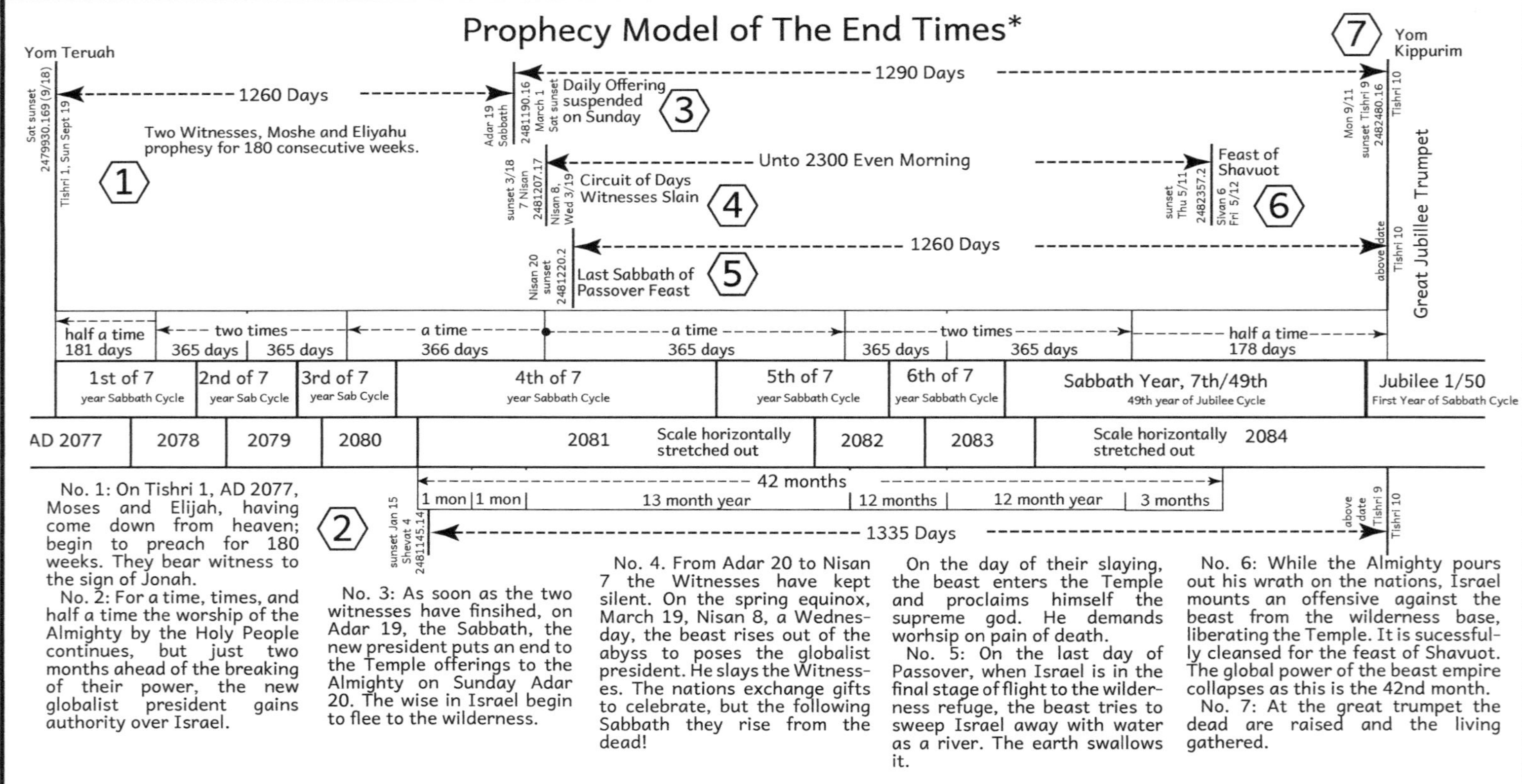

No. 1: On Tishri 1, AD 2077, Moses and Elijah, having come down from heaven; begin to preach for 180 weeks. They bear witness to the sign of Jonah.

No. 2: For a time, times, and half a time the worship of the Almighty by the Holy People continues, but just two months ahead of the breaking of their power, the new globalist president gains authority over Israel.

No. 3: As soon as the two witnesses have finsihed, on Adar 19, the Sabbath, the new president puts an end to the Temple offerings to the Almighty on Sunday Adar 20. The wise in Israel begin to flee to the wilderness.

No. 4. From Adar 20 to Nisan 7 the Witnesses have kept silent. On the spring equinox, March 19, Nisan 8, a Wednesday, the beast rises out of the abyss to poses the globalist president. He slays the Witnesses. The nations exchange gifts to celebrate, but the following Sabbath they rise from the dead!

On the day of their slaying, the beast enters the Temple and proclaims himself the supreme god. He demands worhsip on pain of death.

No. 5: On the last day of Passover, when Israel is in the final stage of flight to the wilderness refuge, the beast tries to sweep Israel away with water as a river. The earth swallows it.

No. 6: While the Almighty pours out his wrath on the nations, Israel mounts an offensive against the beast from the wilderness base, liberating the Temple. It is sucessfully cleansed for the feast of Shavuot. The global power of the beast empire collapses as this is the 42nd month.

No. 7: At the great trumpet the dead are raised and the living gathered.

* This model is an exercise in what is possible. It is not a commitment to what "will happen" beyond what the Scripture says. It must be understood that all hypotheses are interpretations that could well be incorrect. It's value lies in its illustration of biblical calendar principles, its ability to get the Almighty's appointed times the attention they deserve, and to spark interest in educating the faithful about the historical chronology of Israel. At this time this scenario appears to be just perfect.

Appendix VII: The Jubilee Year

Knowing the year of the crucifixion and resurrection to be A.D. 34 and the date of Nehemiah's wall building to be 445 B.C. enables us to pin down Daniel 9:24-26 with precision, and consequently the Sabbatical year also. We have discovered that the only legal way to determine a month is with the first appearance of the new moon, and that scripture never departs from this method. Also discovered is that the year is intercalated such that the 15th of Nisan falls on or after the equinox, but never so much after that Adar 15 should fall on or after the equinox. According to scriptural commandments it would be illegal to declare the first month any other way. Further known is the fact that no month can have more than 30 days, and that Adar had 30 days in A.D. 34. Thus the legal time of the Passover sacrifice in that year was Wednesday, March 24, the 14th of Nisan, between 1 and 5 p.m. This is all according to the rules of Torah, which in this matter cannot be changed or altered. Further, three days and three nights limits the resurrection so that it must occur before sunrise on the Sabbath day, and the scripture declares plainly that the resurrection was on the "first of the Sabbaths."

Knowing the truth about this leads us to more truth. Since Daniel 9:24-26 fits precisely between A.D. 34 and 445 B.C. we know when the Sabbatical year occurs. Legally the Jubilee year can only occur after a Sabbatical year. It will be expected then that if two Jubilees are known, then the Scriptural chronology will confirm it by setting forth a number of years between them that are divisible by 49, and further that the known Jubilees will fall after the known Sabbatical years of Daniel 9.

The first year upon which sowing and reaping was possible after the entry into Canaan in 1592.S was 1592.T/1591.T, because they entered when the harvest was ripe after 1592.S. This year (1592.T/1591.T) counts as the first year of the cycle. The agricultural cycle runs from the fall to the spring, with sowing for the grain crop in the fall and the reaping of it after the spring equinox. This covers two Julian years with a Jan. 1 epoch, and two Creation years with a spring equinox epoch. Therefore, when stating the Jubilee cycle in terms of either the Julian system or the Creation year system, I will by convention refer to the year in which the harvesting phase takes place. This is analogous to stating calendar day numbers according to the daylight portion of a day, it being understood that for Sabbaths the night before goes with the day, and for all other calendar days, it is the night after. Likewise, for the Sabbath year the sowing season before the harvest is reckoned with the year. Note the harvest season in the creation year did not have a corresponding sowing season because the Almighty planted it mature. When Israel came into Canaan in Nisan, the crop they found was not sown by them. For this reason the counting begins after Tishri 1, because with this year they could sow and reap. They were commanded to count sowing and reaping years and not any years wherein they did not sow. For it says, "Six years you shall sow" (Lev. 25:3). Another way to look at this is that the first Edenic crop was holy, and therefore counted, but the Canaanite crop they found was profane, and treated as the spoil of war.

A.M.	First Years of Jubilee Cycle	B.C.	
1	Creation	4139	
2304	Joseph returns the land to Egypt		Gen 47:43
2549	First sowed harvest after coming into Canaan.	1591	Lev 25:3
3039	The second year of Saul	1101	1 Sam 13:1-3
3088	David's 4th year over all Israel	1052	2 Sam 6:15
3431	The 16th year of Hezekiah	709	Isa 37:30
3529	The fall of Nineveh	611	Isa 27:13
3578	The 43rd year of Nebuchadnezzar	562	Dan 4:34ff

Thus 2304 – 1 = 2303, and 2303/49 = 47. Or 2549 – 1 = 2548. And 2548/49 = 52. Even division by 49 means the year is a Jubilee. The 50th year is also the first year of the next cycle. So any year from Creation that is a Jubilee may be checked by reducing its number by 1 to the previous 7th year, and then dividing by 49 to show that 7th year to be the seventh 7th year.

We expect the Jubilee to synchronize with Creation, and we expect the seven years of plenty and famine to synchronize with the sabbatical cycle. We expect crossing the Jordan to start a cycle, and thus to synchronize. The other events are more obscure. However, Saul blew the Jubilee trumpet in his 2nd year (1Sam. 13:1-3; Lev. 25:9). The ark was brought to Jerusalem in David's 11th year with the trumpet of the Jubilee (2Sam. 6:15). I have worked out the details to this, but have not published it yet. Hezekiah's Jubilee is most well known from Isa. 37:30, wherein his 15th year was a Sabbatical year and his 16th a Jubilee. More obscure is the fall of Nineveh in 612 B.C. announced prophetically with the Jubilee trumpet (Isa. 27:13).

Finally, we have the completion of Nebuchadnezzar's madness in 563/62 B.C., since we expect his seven years to synchronize with the Sabbatical cycle.† The king says that he lifts up his eyes "at the end of days" (Dan. 4:34), which points prophetically to the Jubilee of Messiah's return.

Now the Sabbatical year ends where the Jubilee begins, so according to Daniel 9 and Messiah's resurrection, the end points of the Sabbatical year are:

Sabbatical Year ends:	444 BC
Sabbatical Year ends:	AD 33

And 1592 - 444 = 1148. 1148 / 7 = 164. Thus the division is even. There is a mathematical shorthand for this operation, called *modulo* division. The operator is the "%" sign, read *modulo*. Thus 14 % 7 = 0 because the division of 14 by 7 has 0 remainder. This is another way of saying the division is even. Thus 1148 % 7 = 0. Now to compute across the BC/AD divide we have to convert our BC date to an astronomical year. Thus 1592 BC = –1591 BC. The rule is: change BC dates to a negative number and add 1. Now |–1591–33| % 7 = 0.

I'll do that again in slow motion. The absolute value of –1591–33 = 1624. 1624 / 7 = 232 remainder 0.

Probability Test: Given that the chronology is derived without using the Jubilee, and that the Jubilee lines up with the expected points, what is the probability of an incorrect chronology synchronizing the eight Jubilees by accident? Compute P = (1/49)^8.

$$\frac{1}{49} * \frac{1}{49} * \frac{1}{49} * \frac{1}{49} * \frac{1}{49} * \frac{1}{49} * \frac{1}{49} * \frac{1}{49} = \frac{1}{33\,232\,930\,569\,601}$$

What is the probability the Almighty would put all the numbers He did into Scripture and then arrange things so that a false chronology would work out anywhere near as perfectly as the true one?

And supposing all of this to be by pure chance, where is the scholar or prophet who can do better with a different chronology, demonstrating it to be true and in agreement with all the facts? Whether this chronology is maligned or ignored, they will have no truth to replace it with. They only have destruction! If anyone has an ear, let him show that he also can hear what the Spirit says.

† Updated edition: since the first edition I have more carefully deciphered the meaning of the phrase "the end of days," and "seven times." A 'time' is the Hebrew and

Some of these Jubilee texts are plainly more obvious than others. The obvious texts are:

No. 1: The 50th year after entering the land.
No. 2: The 2nd year of king Saul.
No. 3: The 16th year of king Hezekiah.

Matches I would categorize as very good are:

No. 4: 50th year after creation.
No. 5: 50th year at end of Egypt famine.

Matches that I would categorize as fair are:

No. 6: 11th year of king David.

Matches that are obscure, but probably are intended to indicate the Jubilee:

No. 7: The downfall of Nineveh.
No. 8: The 43rd year of Nebuchadnezzar.

Aramaic designation for a solar year. It is specifically 365 or 366 days from one spring equinox to the next. And the 'end of days' is technically the day upon which the old year ends and the new begins, i.e. the spring equinox. I have therefore adjusted the king's madness by six months downward. These times still translate accross the harvest season of the Sabbath year cyle, and the king still returns in the Jubilee.

Like Ezekiel's 390 years, the most reasonable explanation that the "seven sevens" for Nebuchadnezzar's madness is not exactly synchronized to the Sabbath year system is a dual purpose. The 390 years in their strict application count up all the individual segments of time during which Israel sinned, but they also count up the time of the divided kingdom. This second use does not match all the details of the text, but it is clearly intended as the results show. It is likewise for the Jubilee interpretation of "end of days" in the 43rd year of Nebuchadnezzar. This interpretation is clearly secondary, but it also appears to be clearly intended to work out. But one may ask why the prophecy is in terms of the standard solar year in the first place? I think the reason might be because in Daniel's 70th 7, the regular Sabbath year cycle is matched up with solar years, "a time, times, and half a time." The parallelism suggests that the Sabbath year cycle is being put up next to solar years in the end of days.

...continued from page 402

stand: וְהִנֵּה מִיכָאֵל אַחַד הַשָּׂרִים הָרִאשֹׁנִים בָּא לְעָזְרֵנִי (Dan. 10:13). "And behold, Michael one of the princes, the firstmost, had come to help me." Now it may seem that Michael is just one among many to someone who does not know Hebrew. But the case is that Michael is *numero uno* of the princes, that is, he is number one over the princes of heaven. Thus, "And there will have been war in heaven, Miḵa'el and his messengers waged war with the dragon. And the dragon and his messengers waged war" (GNM Rev. 12:7). John Gill noted this:

> But, lo, Michael one of the chief Princes, came to help me; called in the New Testament an Archangel, the Prince of angels, the Head of all principality and power; and is no other than Christ the Son of God, an uncreated Angel; who is "one", or "the first of the chief Princes" (John Gill, Daniel 10:13).

I may likewise cite Young's Literal Translation:

> And lo, Michael, first of the chief heads, hath come in to help me (YLT, Daniel 10:13).

I point out that Miḵa'el means, 'Who is like God.' He is also the prince who stands up for Israel (Dan. 12:1). And it is Messiah that calls out with the voice of the Chief Messenger (cf. 1 Thess. 4:16). See *The Good News of Messiah* for further notes on this. cont. pg. 483

End Notes

No. 1: A corral-cipher is a text engineered to lead those with no ears to hear into a predictable error rather than a purely random one. A corral is an enclosure meant to steer animals in a certain direction or keep them within a pen until such time as the sheep can be separated from the goats. Since a corral-cipher pens up false teachers in a certain way the answers may be pre-prepared in Scripture. That is their solutions may be designed and put into the context ahead of time. Then when the gates of the kingdom are opened and the mysteries of it understood, then the sheep will go the right way, and the goats—those who did not listen well enough to set themselves apart from rebels—will go left and be destroyed.

No. 2: On one occasion I entered into personal discussion with Dr. Bacchiocchi on this topic, and at least one other time participated in a discussion forum. Toward the end of his life Dr. Bacchiocchi showed great interest and favor toward the other feast days in Scripture besides the Sabbath.

No. 3: Codex Bezae moves Luke 6:5 right after Luke 6:10. And then where Luke 6:5 is in current texts, it is replaced with, "On the same day, seeing one working on the Sabbath day, he said to him, 'Man, if you know what your are doing, you are blessed; but if you do not know, you are accursed and a transgressor of the law.'" The reasoning behind this is that work on the Sabbath has to be justified by knowing that it falls into one of the exceptions such as a redemptive work to relieve man or beast of pain and suffering.

No. 4: From an earth centered point of view, the sun moves east to west across the map. Now imagine the sun grabbing ahold of a city and dragging the map along westward to keep the city under the sun. This happens in forward time. The calculated paths of eclipses, however, will not be dragged, so that the city will be dragged westward underneath an eclipse that is west of the city. But modern astronomy is good only back to the end of the long day. Now at the end of the long day, we have to reverse this motion. Going in reverse time the city is dragged to the east where it ends up under an eclipse eastward of the city. Now if we regard the eclipse track as moving instead of the city, then the eclipse track is regarded as moving westward until it ends up over the city. So a proper map transform for an eclipse before the long day is to move its track as calcualted by NASA westward. This is accomplished by an increasingly negative ΔT until $\Delta T = \Delta T - 43200$. This means that some eclipse tracks will be completely transposed westward to the other side of the international date line into the next day. Some eclipses that did not before straddle the date line will now do so after being moved west. There is indeed a missing 12 hours in standard eclipse calcuations. But you will not find it in a computer glitch. You will find it where historians say an eclipse record goes in history vs. astronomers who are trying to calculate it without taking the long day into account. This has caused the historians to consider the eclipse record corrupt and the astronomers to consider the historians in error.

...cont. from 481

Conclusion. I have therefore settled on אחת השבתות as the probable original Hebrew used in the counting of the first of the Sabbaths. In literal English, "(the) one of the Sabbaths," meaning the number one in a series. This differs from the translation given in the previous edition which more slavishly imitated the Greek. The justification for not slavishly following the Greek is as follows. (1) We are dealing with a Hebraism, wherein the Hebrew is the source, and not Greek. (2) The original Greek translation for Sabbath was taken from Aramaic and not Hebrew, viz. σαββατα from Aramaic שבתא. The form of the Aramaic definite article was taken over into Greek, and the form misconstrued as a plural neuter gender. This was inadequate by the time of NT Greek, so the ending was changed to distinguish plural and singular and case. Therefore the plural became σαββατων, but the neuter gender still stuck. Because the Aramaic ending was taken to be an accusative, the genitive use in the LXX of Exodus 20:8 was reduced to a proper genitive plural. So we see that the resulting Greek idiom is not a slavishly literal translation of the Hebrew source texts. The feminine word שבת has been reduced to a neuter in Greek, and the plural σαββατων employed when the idiom uses a singular in Hebrew.

The Evangelists, therefore, making their Greek versions, were faced with a given situation in Greek which did not perfectly match their Hebrew usage in gender or number. Therefore, it is justified in supplying a Hebrew translation that agrees more with the Hebrew, and is a natural idiom for counting Sabbaths.

The Evangelists did not seek to correct the Greek idiom to more reflect the Hebrew. Rather they made use of the differing features of the Greek idiom and the unleavened bread passages to encode the Greek idioms in such a manner that it would be impossible for anyone knowing Greek and honestly applying it to reinterpret the sense to refer to anything except the first of the Sabbaths. This of course did not stop the dishonest from changing the meaning of Sabbath to week, or explaining it as such.

By this sin of reinterpretation, assisted by Jewish *agents provocateurs*, Gnostic Christianity participates in the original sin of Adam, partaking of the forbidden tree to reinterpret divine truth. And the results of a small lie grow to enormous proportions.

Daniel's Prediction of Messiah's Coming

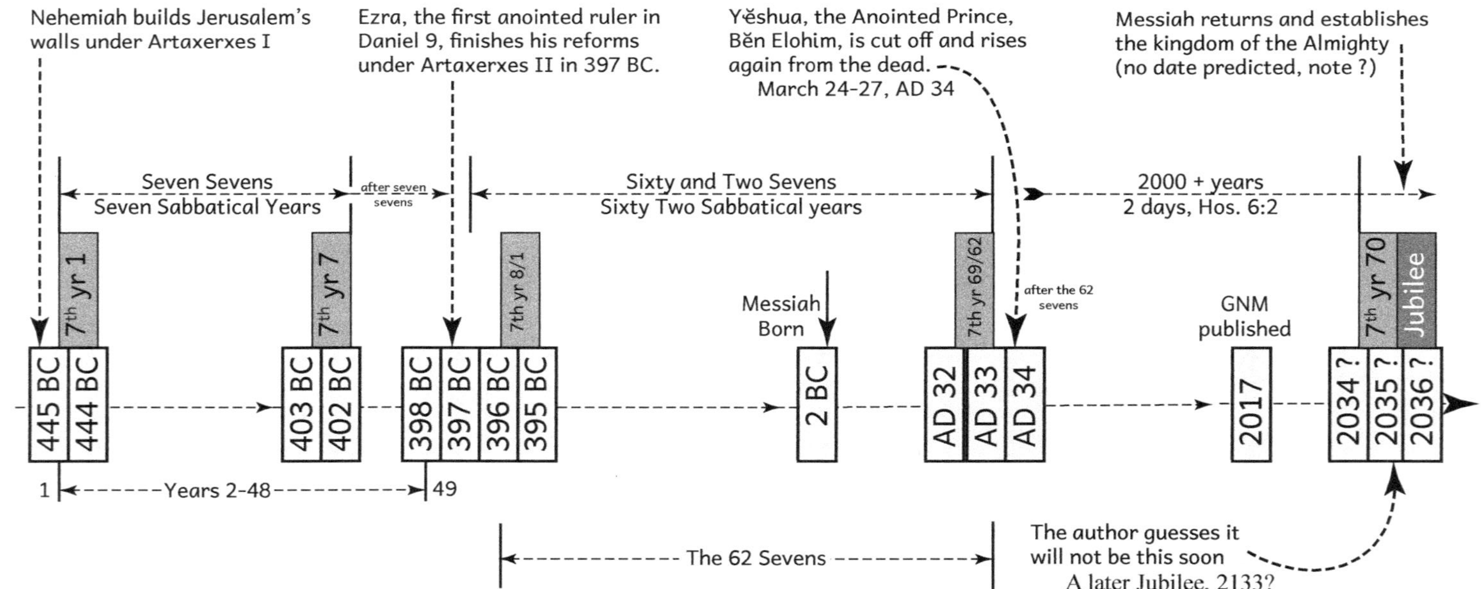

Seventy sevens have been cut out for your people, and for your holy city, to make to be finished the transgression, to seal up sin, to make to be wiped away iniquity, and to bring everlasting righteousness, and to make sealed the vision, and the Prophet, and to anoint the holy of holies. Dan. 9:24

Three Days and Three Nights and Resurrection Ṣabbaŧh

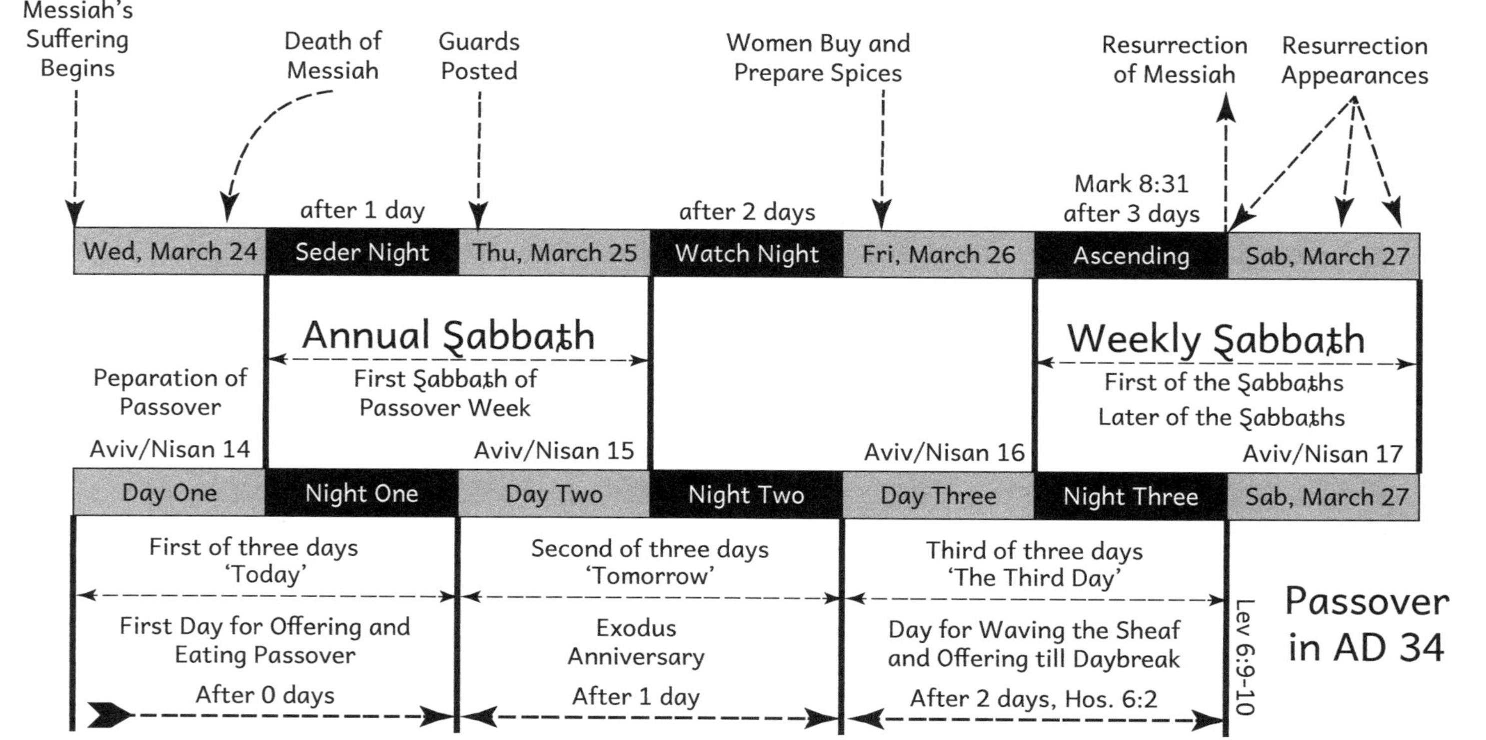

Messiah's Suffering Begins
Death of Messiah
Guards Posted
Women Buy and Prepare Spices
Resurrection of Messiah
Resurrection Appearances
after 1 day
after 2 days
Mark 8:31
after 3 days
Wed, March 24
Seder Night
Thu, March 25
Watch Night
Fri, March 26
Ascending
Sab, March 27
Annual Ṣabbaŧh
First Ṣabbaŧh of Passover Week
Weekly Ṣabbaŧh
First of the Ṣabbaŧhs
Later of the Ṣabbaŧhs
Peparation of Passover
Aviv/Nisan 14
Aviv/Nisan 15
Aviv/Nisan 16
Aviv/Nisan 17
Day One
Night One
Day Two
Night Two
Day Three
Night Three
Sab, March 27
First of three days
'Today'
First Day for Offering and Eating Passover
After 0 days
Second of three days
'Tomorrow'
Exodus Anniversary
After 1 day
Third of three days
'The Third Day'
Day for Waving the Sheaf and Offering till Daybreak
After 2 days, Hos. 6:2
Lev 6:9-10
Passover in AD 34

The Ministry of Mĕssiah Yĕshua

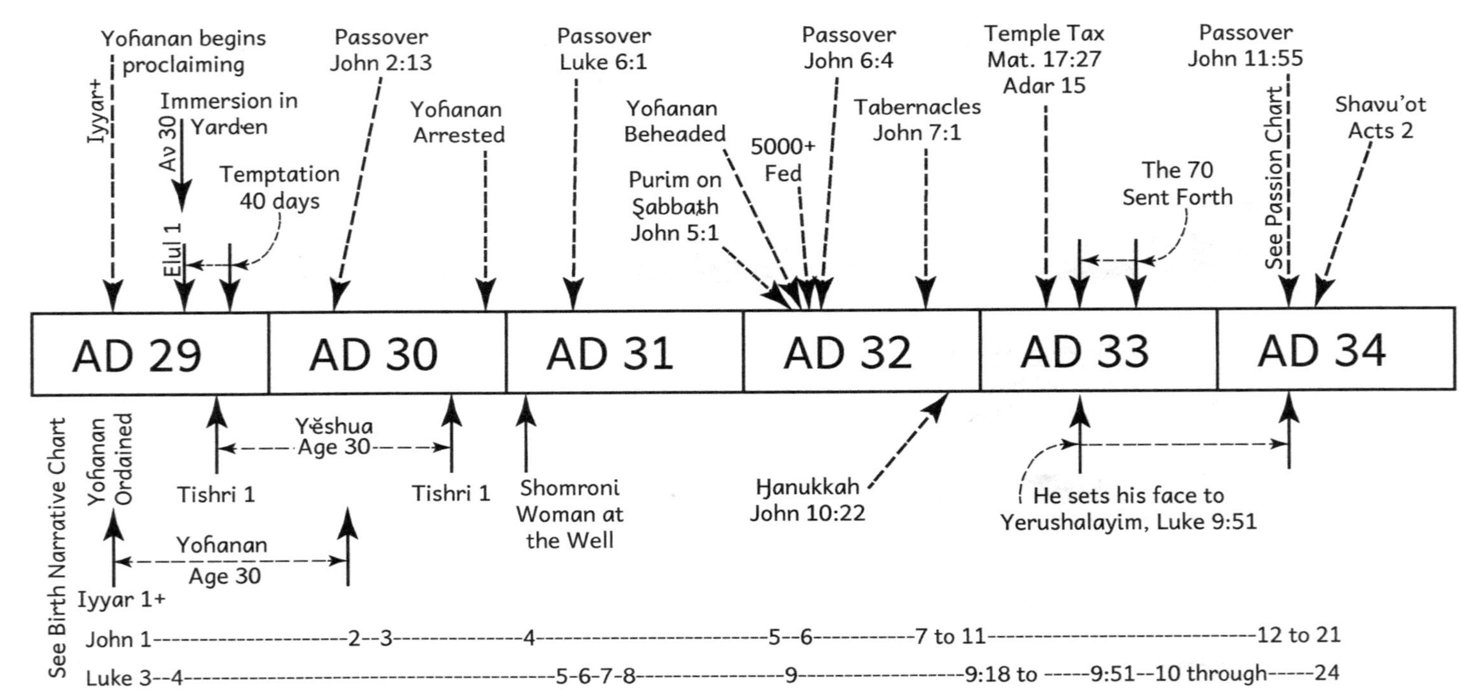

Yoḥanan begins proclaiming
Iyyar+
Immersion in Yardĕn
Av 30
Elul 1
Temptation 40 days
Passover John 2:13
Yoḥanan Arrested
Passover Luke 6:1
Yoḥanan Beheaded
Purim on Ṣabbaṯh John 5:1
5000+ Fed
Passover John 6:4
Tabernacles John 7:1
Temple Tax Mat. 17:27 Adar 15
The 70 Sent Forth
Passover John 11:55
See Passion Chart
Shavu'ot Acts 2
AD 29
AD 30
AD 31
AD 32
AD 33
AD 34
See Birth Narrative Chart
Yoḥanan Ordained
Tishri 1
Yĕshua Age 30
Tishri 1
Shomroni Woman at the Well
Ḥanukkah John 10:22
He sets his face to Yerushalayim, Luke 9:51
Yoḥanan Age 30
Iyyar 1+
John 1--------------------2--3-------------4------------------------5--6-----------7 to 11---------------------------12 to 21
Luke 3--4--------------------------------------5-6-7-8----------------9-----------------9:18 to -----9:51--10 through-----24

The Births of Yoȟanan the Immerser and Mĕssiah Yĕshua

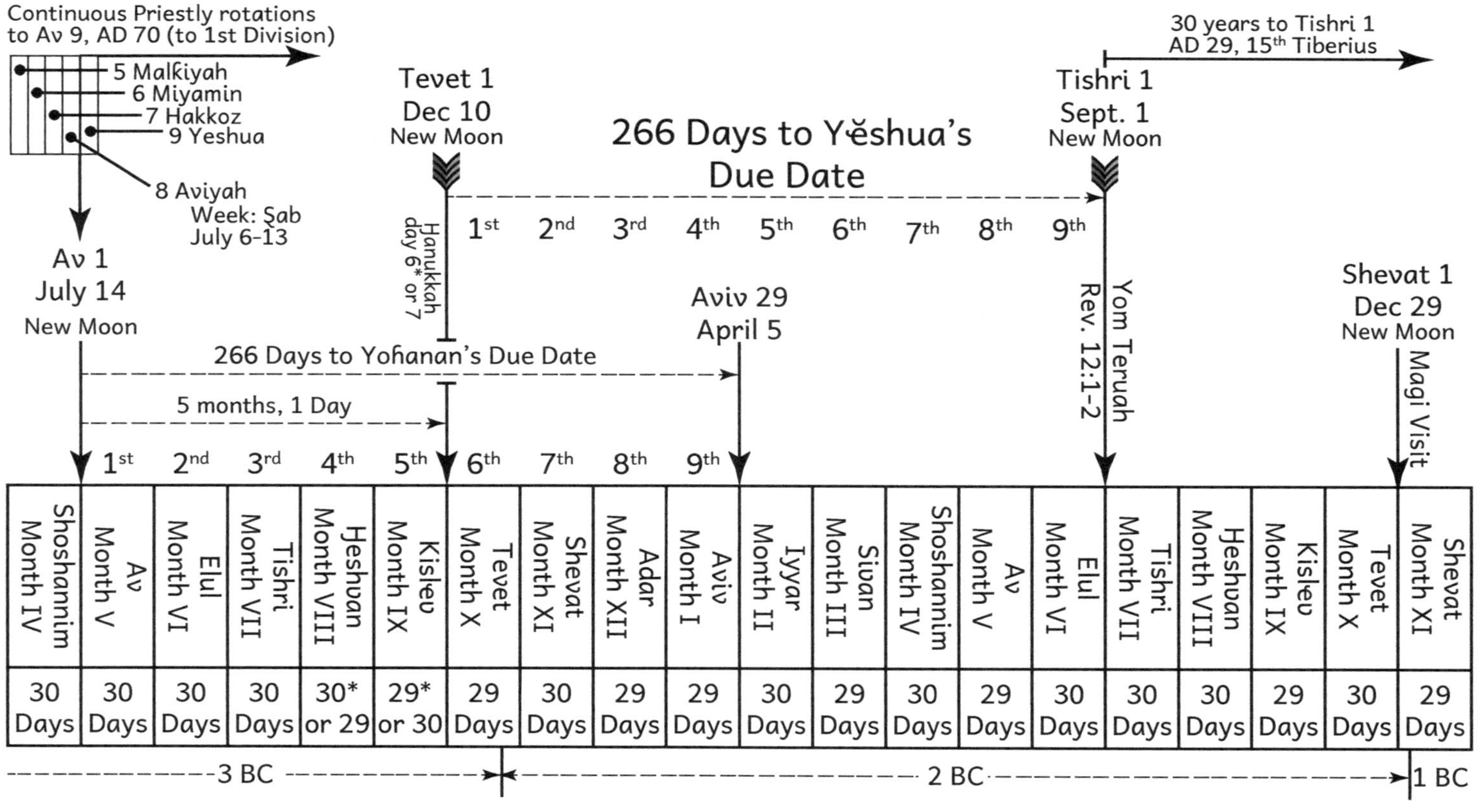

Continuous Priestly rotations
to Aυ 9, AD 70 (to 1st Division)

5 Malk̄iyah
6 Miyamin
7 Hakkoz
9 Yeshua
8 Aviyah
Week: Ṣab
July 6-13

Aυ 1
July 14
New Moon

Tevet 1
Dec 10
New Moon

Ḥanukkah
day 6* or 7

266 Days to Yĕshua's
Due Date

1st 2nd 3rd 4th 5th 6th 7th 8th 9th

Tishri 1
Sept. 1
New Moon

Yom Teruah
Rev. 12:1-2

30 years to Tishri 1
AD 29, 15th Tiberius

Aviυ 29
April 5

Shevat 1
Dec 29
New Moon

Magi Visit

266 Days to Yoȟanan's Due Date

5 months, 1 Day

1st 2nd 3rd 4th 5th 6th 7th 8th 9th

Month	Days
Shoshannim Month IV	30 Days
Aυ Month V	30 Days
Elul Month VI	30 Days
Tishri Month VII	30 Days
Ḥeshυan Month VIII	30* or 29
Kisleυ Month IX	29* or 30
Tevet Month X	29 Days
Shevat Month XI	30 Days
Adar Month XII	29 Days
Aviυ Month I	29 Days
Iyyar Month II	30 Days
Siυan Month III	29 Days
Shoshannim Month IV	30 Days
Aυ Month V	29 Days
Elul Month VI	30 Days
Tishri Month VII	30 Days
Ḥeshυan Month VIII	30 Days
Kisleυ Month IX	29 Days
Tevet Month X	30 Days
Shevat Month XI	29 Days

3 BC — 2 BC — 1 BC

(continued from end of Preface)

Slanderer), who replaces his caricature of "harsh" God with a "loving" Father who neither believes in repentance or forgiveness, but only in getting paid off and compensated by what proves to be a legal gimmick. Even if fakely so, it serves to do away with real forgiveness. And this was the real Mr. Hyde's goal (aka Satan).

Some theologians have come real close to exposing this error. Presbyterian Albert Barnes was tried for heresy several times by his Church for pointing it out. His commentaries were edited to disagree with him later. Methodist Theologian John Miley rightly refuted the compensation theory of atonement. But while they understood the illogic of Mr. Hyde's pseudo-forgiveness, they did not grasp the degree of misinterpretation and mistranslation that Paul's letters were subjected to. These errors in mistranslation are just beginning to surface in the 21st century with the "faithfulness of Messiah" controversy.*

The saga of what Paul really said is much like the saga of the resurrection day told here. It is a story of passages mistranslated and misinterpreted in Satan's campaign to get what happened on one Passover eve in AD 34 re-explained. It is not about the justification† of the sinner, because Yahweh, since he is willing to forgive sin, is not willing to acquit the sinner of sin (cf. Exodus 34:7).

The Jews misunderstood Gen. 15:6b and twisted it all around to teach the merit of the ancestors as the means of solving the demerit problem. The Jews likewise twisted the Phinehas' texts around (Psalm 106:31; Num. 25). Paul does not say which text he is explaining in Romans 4 (Both read the same way in the LXX). Paul is really explaining the Phinehas' passages and refuting the doctrine of imputed merits, but over the next centuries, agents of Satan in the Church managed to get enough of the key terms redefined so that the subtleties of Paul's argument would be misunderstood, and Judaisms' teaching of merit could be continued in the Church, namely that God would look upon imputed merits when deciding for a sinner rather than simply forgiving those who are repentant.

In some sense the Almighty allowed this to happen, knowing the col-

---

* See N.T. Wright, Richard B. Hays, and Daniel B. Wallace.

† As in this book I expose the corruption of the "first day of the week" translation, so in the Good News of Messiah I expose the corruption of the "justified by faith" error, and show how it is opposed to forgiveness of sins by a loving Yahweh Almighty.

lective evil of humanity, by their reinterpretations of his words, knowing that much of his word would reach repentant ears despite the corruptions believed by most of those spreading the word, so that in the last days he could reveal the corrections, to the end that those who are truly listening might return to his Law, so that he may call his bride out of exile into the brightness of the truth in his kingdom, not according to the purpose and intent of the majority, but for the sake of the redeemed, and for a demonstration that the Almighty of Old keeps his covenant promises in the sight of all nations.

To be sure, this is my opinion, since it regards the future: The beast that was, the prince of Babylon, ascends from the Abyss, to deceive the whole world, so that he can prevent the Almighty from restoring Zion. This is the globalist cancel culture at work. The same is the mystery of iniquity. But he rises from slumber too soon, and will be dealt a fatal wound. It will become the beast that "is not." But before he goes, secular Israel will receive his dying blow, allowed by the Almighty, to restore righteousness in Israel, after which the Almighty will call forth the return of his children from all nations. After this the whole world will suffer a disaster so great as to wipe out the common use of modern technology. Imagine life without electricity or long distance communication. That's what it will be like. It will be their collective judgment for insulting Zion. They roar like the sea, but they will be chased far away from Israel. The world will enter a dark age. When it recovers, the righteous in Israel will shine as the stars of heaven, and they will see it. Some will repent and be joined to Israel. The rest will be jealous and will hate Israel's prosperity. They will revive the beast, who will be healed, and will be released from the Abyss, to test the new generation, to destroy all other religion except his own. But Israel will be delivered from him, those who obey the Almighty and keep his commandments, and the faithful witness of Messiah Yeshua. This is because the Almighty loves his people, and will not bear to see his faithful ones harmed. They will be kept from the hour of tribulation for 1260 days. But the offspring of those who do not listen, the rest of the seed of Israel among the nations, that does not wake up soon enough from their spiritual slumber, these will find themselves in the path of the beast's final cancellation. But he who endures to the end will be saved. Fear not the one who can destroy the body. Fear the one who can destroy both. Perhaps he will be merciful and grant a few more generations the chance to seek him out. The beast is wounded while you decide.

www.ingramcontent.com/pod-product-compliance
Lightning Source LLC
Chambersburg PA
CBHW070642150426
42811CB00050B/504
9780979190759